T0185817

Kubernetes Microservices with Docker

Deepak Vohra

Apress®

Kubernetes Microservices with Docker

Deepak Vohra
White Rock, British Columbia
Canada

ISBN-13 (pbk): 978-1-4842-1906-5 ISBN-13 (electronic): 978-1-4842-1907-2
DOI 10.1007/978-1-4842-1907-2

Library of Congress Control Number: 2016937418

Managing Director: Welmoed Spahr
Lead Editor: Michelle Lowman
Technical Reviewer: Massimo Nardone
Editorial Board: Steve Anglin, Pramila Balan, Louise Corrigan, Jonathan Gennick, Robert Hutchinson, Celstin Suresh John, Michelle Lowman, James Markham, Susan McDermott, Matthew Moodie, Jeffrey Pepper, Douglas Pundick, Ben Renow-Clarke, Gwenan Spearing
Coordinating Editor: Mark Powers
Compositor: SPi Global
Indexer: SPi Global
Artist: SPi Global

Distributed to the book trade worldwide by Springer Science+Business Media New York, 233 Spring Street, 6th Floor, New York, NY 10013. Phone 1-800-SPRINGER, fax (201) 348-4505, e-mail `orders-ny@springer-sbm.com`, or visit `www.springeronline.com`. Apress Media, LLC is a California LLC and the sole member (owner) is Springer Science + Business Media Finance Inc (SSBM Finance Inc). SSBM Finance Inc is a Delaware corporation.

For information on translations, please e-mail `rights@apress.com`, or visit `www.apress.com`.

Apress and friends of ED books may be purchased in bulk for academic, corporate, or promotional use. eBook versions and licenses are also available for most titles. For more information, reference our Special Bulk Sales–eBook Licensing web page at `www.apress.com/bulk-sales`.

Any source code or other supplementary material referenced by the author in this text is available to readers at `www.apress.com/9781484219065`. For additional information about how to locate and download your book's source code, go to `www.apress.com/source-code/`. Readers can also access source code at `SpringerLink` in the Supplementary Material section for each chapter.

Printed on acid-free paper

Contents at a Glance

Contents

About the Author

Deepak Vohra is a consultant and a principal member of the NuBean.com software company. Deepak is a Sun-certified Java programmer and Web component developer. He has worked in the fields of XML, Java programming, and Java EE for over seven years. Deepak is the coauthor of *Pro XML Development with Java Technology* (Apress, 2006). Deepak is also the author of the *JDBC 4.0* and *Oracle JDeveloper for J2EE Development, Processing XML Documents with Oracle JDeveloper 11g, EJB 3.0 Database Persistence with Oracle Fusion Middleware 11g,* and *Java EE Development in Eclipse IDE* (Packt Publishing). He also served as the technical reviewer on *WebLogic: The Definitive Guide (O'Reilly Media, 2004)* and *Ruby Programming for the Absolute Beginner* (Cengage Learning PTR, 2007). Deepak is the author of *Pro Couchbase Development, Pro MongoDB Development,* and *Pro Docker,* all published by Apress in 2015.

About the Technical Reviewer

Massimo Nardone holds a Master of Science degree in Computing Science from the University of Salerno, Italy. He has worked as a Project Manager, Software Engineer, Research Engineer, Chief Security Architect, Information Security Manager, PCI/SCADA Auditor, and Senior Lead IT Security/Cloud/SCADA Architect for many years. He currently works as Chief Information Security Office (CISO) for Cargotec Oyj. He has more than 22 years of work experience in IT including Security, SCADA, Cloud Computing, IT Infrastructure, Mobile, Security, and WWW technology areas for both national and international projects. He worked as a visiting lecturer and supervisor for exercises at the Networking Laboratory of the Helsinki University of Technology (Aalto University). He has been programming and teaching how to program with Android, Perl, PHP, Java, VB, Python, C/C++, and MySQL for more than 20 years. He holds four international patents (PKI, SIP, SAML, and Proxy areas).

He is the coauthor of *Pro Android Games* (Apress, 2015).

Massimo dedicates his work on this book to his loving brothers Mario Nardone and Roberto Nardone, who are always there when he needs them.

Foreword

It is a great pleasure to provide the Foreword for this book, as I've been reading and following Deepak Vohra's work for some time. Deepak has been developing Web components and Java applications for many years, and the scope of his expertise is reflected in the books he has written - as is his passion to share that knowledge with others.

About a year ago, I was given the opportunity to perform a technical review on his Pro Couchbase Development book, and we formed an immediate connection. Since then, I've served as technical reviewer on several more of his books, including this one. The reason I keep coming back is simple - I always come away knowing more than I did before.

Docker is a new container technology that has become very popular because it is great for building and sharing disk images and enables users to run different operating systems such as Ubuntu, Fedora, and Centos. Docker is often used when a version control framework is required for an application's operating system, to distribute applications on different machines, or to run code on laptop in the same environment as on the server. In general, Docker will always run the same, regardless of the environment in which it will be running.

Kubernetes is an open source container cluster manager that complements and extends Docker's software encapsulation power and makes it easier to organize and schedule applications across a fleet of machines. It's a lightweight, portable (suited for the cloud architecture) and modular tool that can be run on almost any platform with different local machine solutions. Kubernetes offers a number of distinct advantages, first and foremost being that it combines all necessary tools - orchestration, service discovery, and load balancing - together in one nice package for you. Kubernetes also boasts heavy involvement from the developer community.

Kubernetes Microservices with Docker will show you how to use these two powerful tools in unison to manage complex big data and enterprise applications. Installing Kubernetes on single nodes and multi-node clusters, creating multi-container pods, using Kubernetes with the Apache Hadoop Ecosystem and NoSQL Databases - it's all here, and more. So sit back, and let Deepak be your guide.

—Massimo Nardone

Chief Security Information Officer (CISO), Cargotec Oyj

PART I

Getting Started

CHAPTER 1

Installing Kubernetes Using Docker

Kubernetes is software for managing a cluster of Docker containers. Kubernetes orchestration includes scheduling, distributing workload, and scaling. Kubernetes takes the software encapsulation provided by Docker further by introducing Pods. A Pod is a collection of one or more Docker containers with single interface features such as providing networking and filesystem at the Pod level rather than at the container level. Kubernetes also introduces "labels" using which services and replication controllers (replication controller is used to scale a cluster) identify or select the containers or pods they manage. Kubernetes is lightweight, portable (suited for the cloud architecture), and modular.

Kubernetes may be run on almost any platform. Local machine solutions include local Docker based, Vagrant, and no-VM local cluster. Hosted solutions include Google Container Engine. Some of the other platforms supported by Kubernetes are Fedora (Ansible and Manual), Amazon Web Services, Mesos, vSphere, and CoreOS. Kubernetes is an orchestration software for Docker containers; the recommended solution for installation is to use the Docker Engine. In this chapter we shall install Kubernetes on Docker, which runs on Ubuntu. We shall use an Amazon EC2 instance hosting Ubuntu as the operating system. In this chapter, a single node installation of Kubernetes is discussed. Multi-node installation of Kubernetes is discussed in chapter 14. This chapter has the following sections.

Setting the Environment

Installing Docker

Installing Kubernetes

Starting etcd

Starting Kubernetes Master

Starting Service Proxy

Listing the Kubernetes Docker Containers

Installing kubectl

Listing Services

Listing Nodes

Testing the Kubernetes Installation

D. Vohra, *Kubernetes Microservices with Docker*, DOI 10.1007/978-1-4842-1907-2_1

Setting the Environment

The following software is required for this chapter.

- Docker Engine (latest version)
- Kubernetes (version 1.01)

Linux is required to support 64-bit software. We have used an Amazon EC2 instance created from AMI Ubuntu Server 14.04 LTS (HVM), SSD Volume Type - ami-d05e75b8. An Amazon EC2 instance based on the Ubuntu AMI is shown in Figure 1-1.

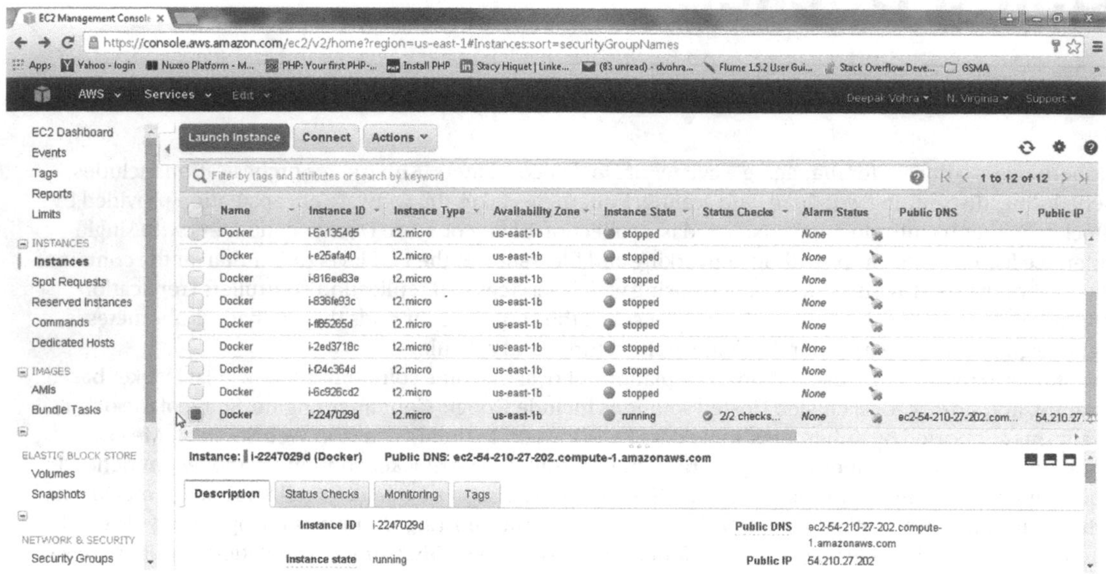

Figure 1-1. *Amazon EC2 Instance Based on Ubuntu AMI*

A different Ubuntu version may be used if the requirement of a 64-bit architecture is met. The minimum kernel version requirement is 3.10. The kernel version may be verified with the following command.

```
uname -r
```

The Public IP would be different for different users. Multiple Amazon EC2 instances and therefore multiple Public IP addresses have been used in the book as a different Public IP is assigned each time an Amazon EC2 instance is started. The Private IP Address of an Amazon EC2 instance is the same across restarts. SSH into an Ubuntu instance on Amazon EC2 (Public IP is 52.91.80.173 in following command).

```
ssh -i "docker.pem" ubuntu@52.91.80.173
```

The Amazon EC2 instance gets logged in as shown in Figure 1-2. The command prompt becomes "ubuntu@ip-172-30-1-190" instead of root@localhost. Ip 172.30.1.190 is the Private IP of the Amazon EC2 instance and would also be different for different users.

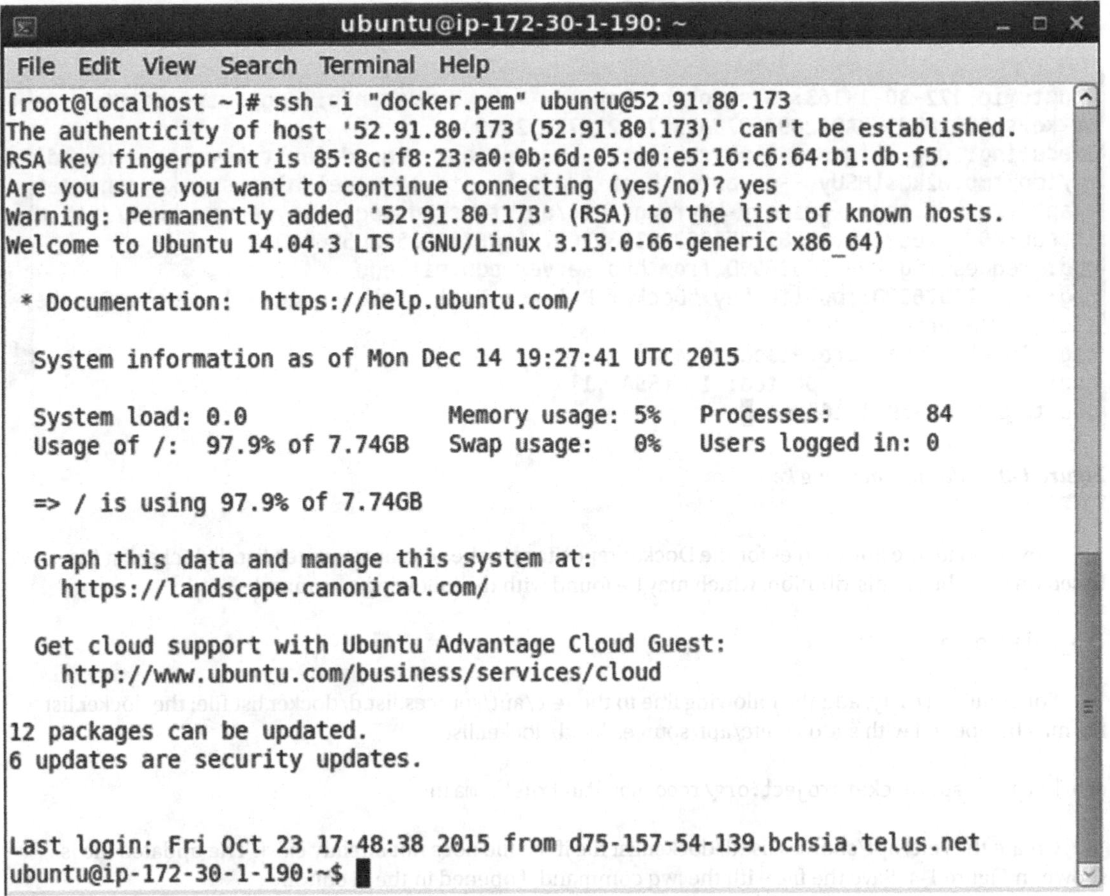

ubuntu@ip-172-30-1-190: ~
File Edit View Search Terminal Help
[root@localhost ~]# ssh -i "docker.pem" ubuntu@52.91.80.173
The authenticity of host '52.91.80.173 (52.91.80.173)' can't be established.
RSA key fingerprint is 85:8c:f8:23:a0:0b:6d:05:d0:e5:16:c6:64:b1:db:f5.
Are you sure you want to continue connecting (yes/no)? yes
Warning: Permanently added '52.91.80.173' (RSA) to the list of known hosts.
Welcome to Ubuntu 14.04.3 LTS (GNU/Linux 3.13.0-66-generic x86_64)
* Documentation: https://help.ubuntu.com/
System information as of Mon Dec 14 19:27:41 UTC 2015
System load: 0.0 Memory usage: 5% Processes: 84
Usage of /: 97.9% of 7.74GB Swap usage: 0% Users logged in: 0
=> / is using 97.9% of 7.74GB
Graph this data and manage this system at:
https://landscape.canonical.com/
Get cloud support with Ubuntu Advantage Cloud Guest:
http://www.ubuntu.com/business/services/cloud
12 packages can be updated.
6 updates are security updates.
Last login: Fri Oct 23 17:48:38 2015 from d75-157-54-139.bchsia.telus.net
ubuntu@ip-172-30-1-190:~$

***Figure 1-2.** Loging into an Amazon EC2 instance*

In the next section we shall install Docker on Ubuntu hosted on an Amazon EC2 instance.

Installing Docker

Ubuntu uses apt for package management; apt stores a list of repositories in the /etc/apt/sources.list list. Docker's apt repository is kept in the /etc/apt/sources.list.d/docker.list file. First, add the new repository key (gpg key) for the Docker repository with the following command.

```
sudo apt-key adv --keyserver hkp://pgp.mit.edu:80 --recv-keys
58118E89F3A912897C070ADBF76221572C52609D
```

The new gpg key gets added as shown in Figure 1-3.

```
ubuntu@ip-172-30-1-163:~$ sudo apt-key adv --keyserver hkp://pgp.mit.edu:80 --re
cv-keys 58118E89F3A912897C070ADBF76221572C52609D
Executing: gpg --ignore-time-conflict --no-options --no-default-keyring --homedi
r /tmp/tmp.w2kdslHSUy --no-auto-check-trustdb --trust-model always --keyring /et
c/apt/trusted.gpg --primary-keyring /etc/apt/trusted.gpg --keyserver hkp://pgp.m
it.edu:80 --recv-keys 58118E89F3A912897C070ADBF76221572C52609D
gpg: requesting key 2C52609D from hkp server pgp.mit.edu
gpg: key 2C52609D: public key "Docker Release Tool (releasedocker) <docker@docke
r.com>" imported
gpg: Total number processed: 1
gpg:               imported: 1  (RSA: 1)
ubuntu@ip-172-30-1-163:~$ █
```

Figure 1-3. *Adding a new gpg key*

Next, update the apt sources for the Docker repository in the /etc/apt/sources.list.d/docker.list file based on the Ubuntu distribution, which may be found with the following command.

```
lsb_release -a
```

For Ubuntu Trusty, add the following line to the /etc/apt/sources.list.d/docker.list file; the docker.list file may be opened with sudo vi /etc/apt/sources.list.d/docker.list.

```
deb https://apt.dockerproject.org/repo ubuntu-trusty main
```

Create the /etc/apt/sources.list.d/docker.list file if the file does not already exist. The updated file is shown in Figure 1-4. Save the file with the :wq command if opened in the vi editor.

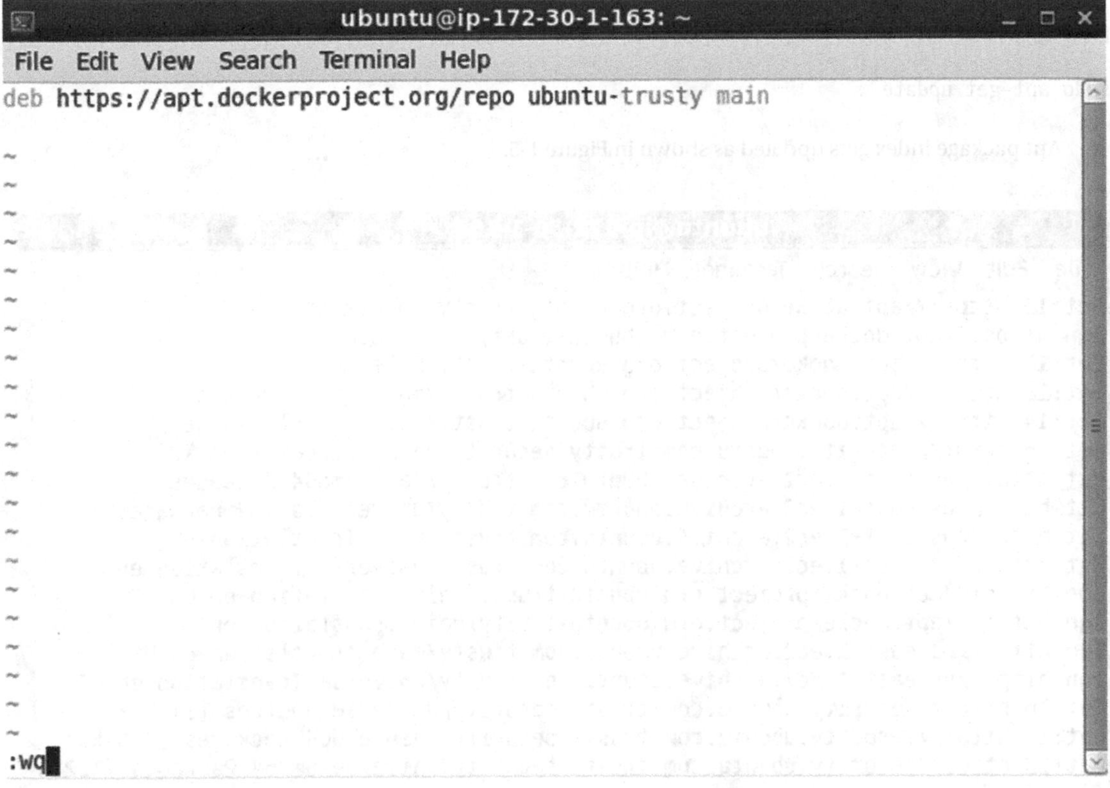

Figure 1-4. Creating the docker.list file

The entry to be added would be different for different Ubuntu distributions as listed in Table 1-1.

Table 1-1. *The docker.list file Entry Based on Ubuntu Distribution*

Ubuntu Distribution	Entry
Ubuntu Precise 12.04 (LTS)	deb `https://apt.dockerproject.org/repo` ubuntu-precise main
Ubuntu Trusty 14.04 (LTS)	deb `https://apt.dockerproject.org/repo` ubuntu-trusty main
Ubuntu Vivid 15.04	deb `https://apt.dockerproject.org/repo` ubuntu-vivid main

Run the following commands after updating the /etc/apt/sources.list.d/docker.list file to update the apt package index.

```
sudo apt-get update
```

Apt package index gets updated as shown in Figure 1-5.

Figure 1-5. *Updating Ubuntu Package List*

Purge the old repository if it exists with the following command.

```
sudo apt-get purge lxc-docker*
```

The output in Figure 1-6 indicates that the old packages lxc-docker and lxc-docker-virtual-package are not installed and therefore not removed.

```
ubuntu@ip-172-30-1-163:~$ sudo  apt-get purge lxc-docker*
Reading package lists... Done
Building dependency tree
Reading state information... Done
Note, selecting 'lxc-docker' for regex 'lxc-docker*'
Note, selecting 'lxc-docker-virtual-package' for regex 'lxc-docker*'
Package 'lxc-docker' is not installed, so not removed
Package 'lxc-docker-virtual-package' is not installed, so not removed
0 upgraded, 0 newly installed, 0 to remove and 139 not upgraded.
ubuntu@ip-172-30-1-163:~$
```

Figure 1-6. *Purging the Old Repository*

Run the following command to verify that apt is pulling from the updated repository for Docker.

```
sudo apt-cache policy docker-engine
```

The output in Figure 1-7 indicates that the new repository ubuntu-trusty as specified in the /etc/apt/sources.list.d/docker.list is being used.

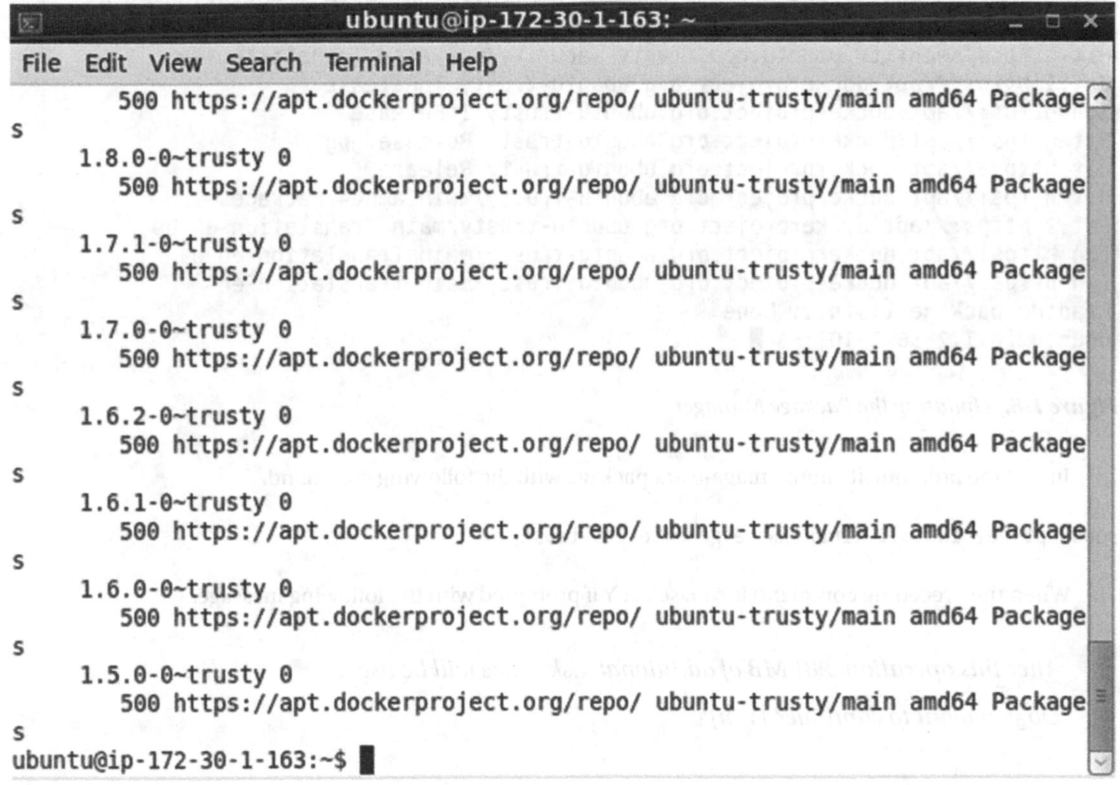

Figure 1-7. *Using the Updated Repository verification*

Next, install the prerequisites for Ubuntu, but first update the package manager with the following command.

```
sudo apt-get update
```

The package manager gets updated as shown in Figure 1-8.

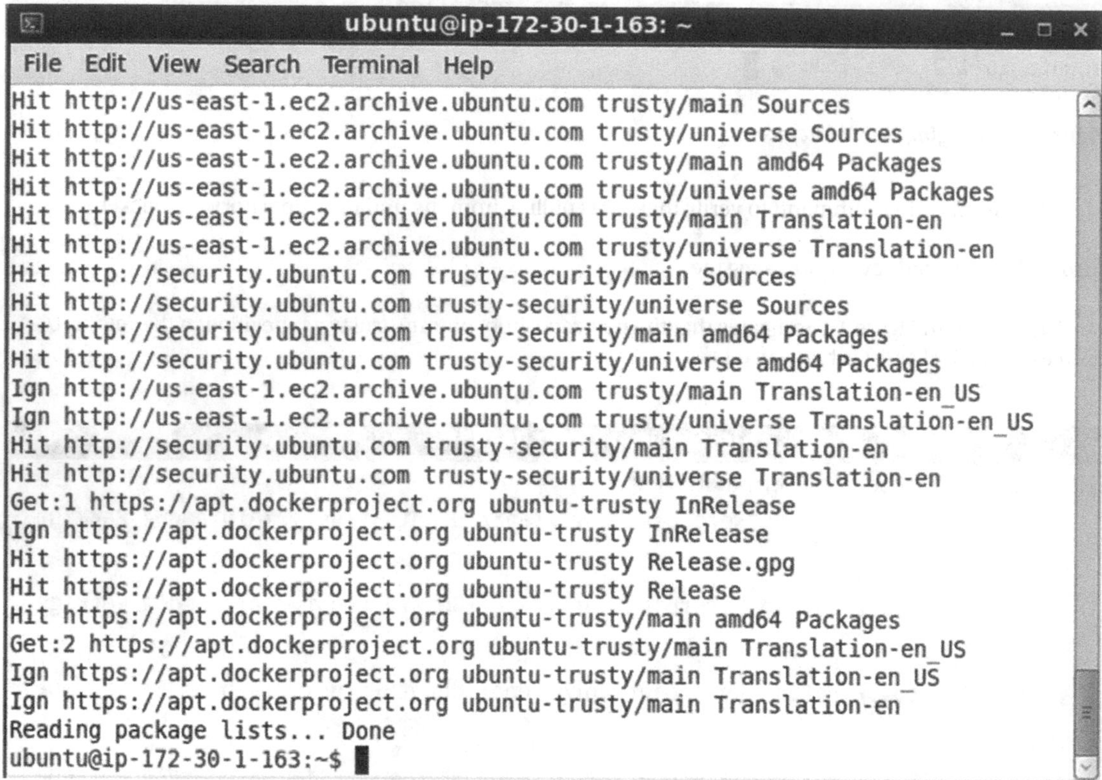

Figure 1-8. *Updating the Package Manager*

Install the prerequisite linux-image-extra package with the following command.

```
sudo apt-get install linux-image-generic-lts-trusty
```

When the preceding command is run, select Y if prompted with the following message.

After this operation, 281 MB of additional disk space will be used.

Do you want to continue? [Y/n]

The message prompt is shown in Figure 1-9.

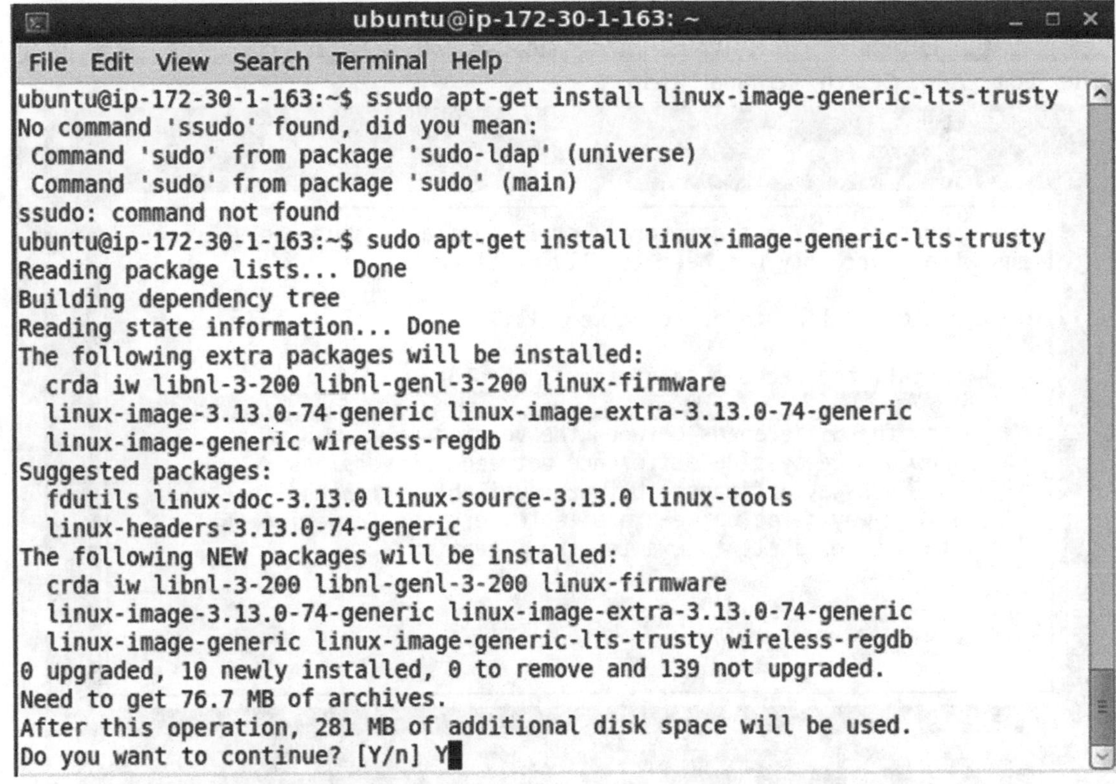

Figure 1-9. *Message Prompt to Continue*

Subsequently, before the command completes, a Package Configuration dialog might prompt with the following message:

> *A new version of /boot/grub/menu.lst is available, but the version installed currently has been locally modified. What would you like to do about menu.lst?*

Select the default selection, which is "keep the local version currently installed" and click on Enter as shown in Figure 1-10.

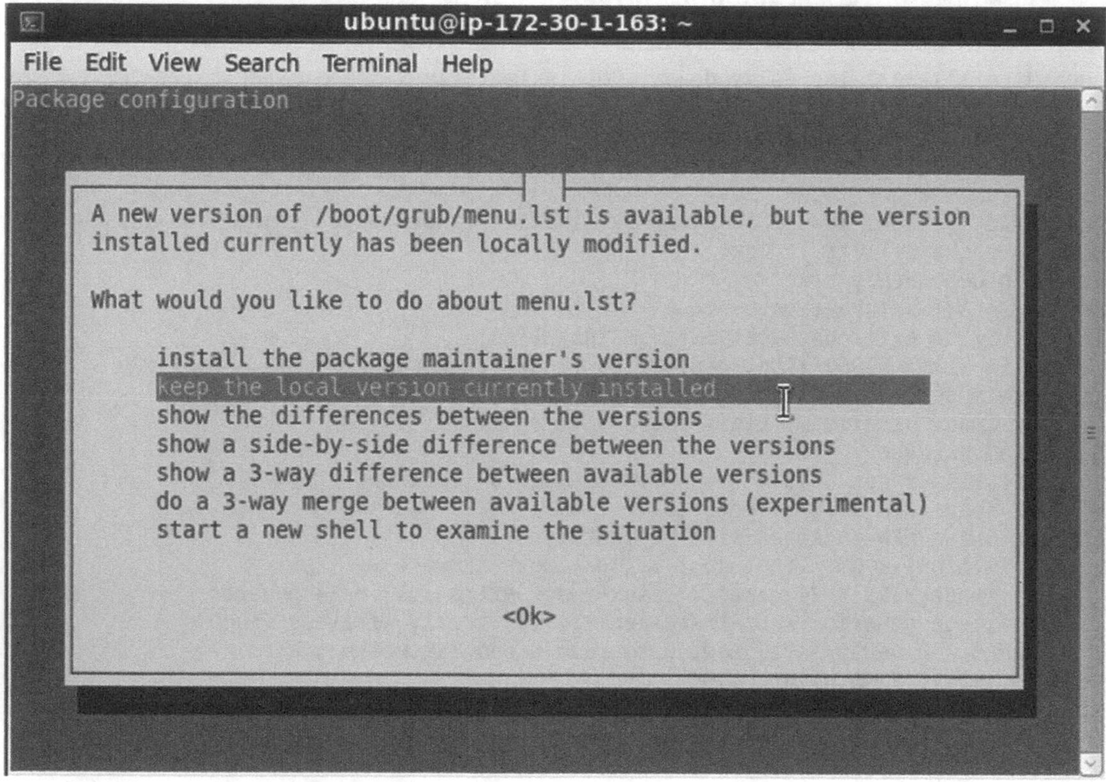

Figure 1-10. *Selecting the Default Package Configuration*

Reboot the system with the following command.

```
sudo reboot
```

When the sudo reboot command is run the AmazonEC2 instance is exited. Reconnect with the Amazon EC2 Ubuntu instance with the same ssh command as before.

```
ssh -i "docker.pem" ubuntu@52.91.80.173
```

After the host system reboots, update the package manager again with the following command.

```
sudo apt-get update
```

Package manager gets updated as shown in Figure 1-11.

```
ubuntu@ip-172-30-1-163: ~
File Edit View Search Terminal Help
en
Hit http://us-east-1.ec2.archive.ubuntu.com trusty/main Sources
Hit http://us-east-1.ec2.archive.ubuntu.com trusty/universe Sources
Hit http://us-east-1.ec2.archive.ubuntu.com trusty/main amd64 Packages
Hit http://us-east-1.ec2.archive.ubuntu.com trusty/universe amd64 Packages
Hit http://us-east-1.ec2.archive.ubuntu.com trusty/main Translation-en
Hit http://us-east-1.ec2.archive.ubuntu.com trusty/universe Translation-en
Hit http://security.ubuntu.com trusty-security/main Sources
Hit http://security.ubuntu.com trusty-security/universe Sources
Ign http://us-east-1.ec2.archive.ubuntu.com trusty/main Translation-en_US
Hit http://security.ubuntu.com trusty-security/main amd64 Packages
Ign http://us-east-1.ec2.archive.ubuntu.com trusty/universe Translation-en_US
Hit http://security.ubuntu.com trusty-security/universe amd64 Packages
Hit http://security.ubuntu.com trusty-security/main Translation-en
Hit http://security.ubuntu.com trusty-security/universe Translation-en
Get:1 https://apt.dockerproject.org ubuntu-trusty InRelease
Ign https://apt.dockerproject.org ubuntu-trusty InRelease
Hit https://apt.dockerproject.org ubuntu-trusty Release.gpg
Hit https://apt.dockerproject.org ubuntu-trusty Release
Hit https://apt.dockerproject.org ubuntu-trusty/main amd64 Packages
Ign https://apt.dockerproject.org ubuntu-trusty/main Translation-en_US
Ign https://apt.dockerproject.org ubuntu-trusty/main Translation-en
Reading package lists... Done
ubuntu@ip-172-30-1-163:~$
```

Figure 1-11. *Updating Package Manager List after Reboot*

Install Docker with the following command.

```
sudo apt-get install docker-engine
```

Select Y at the following prompt, if displayed, as shown in Figure 1-12.

After this operation, 60.3 MB of additional disk space will be used.

Do you want to continue? [Y/n]

```
ubuntu@ip-172-30-1-163:~$ sudo apt-get install docker-engine
Reading package lists... Done
Building dependency tree
Reading state information... Done
The following extra packages will be installed:
  aufs-tools cgroup-lite git git-man liberror-perl
Suggested packages:
  git-daemon-run git-daemon-sysvinit git-doc git-el git-email git-gui gitk
  gitweb git-arch git-bzr git-cvs git-mediawiki git-svn
The following NEW packages will be installed:
  aufs-tools cgroup-lite docker-engine git git-man liberror-perl
0 upgraded, 6 newly installed, 0 to remove and 139 not upgraded.
Need to get 11.0 MB of archives.
After this operation, 60.3 MB of additional disk space will be used.
Do you want to continue? [Y/n] Y
```

Figure 1-12. *Message Prompt about the additional disk space being added*

The Docker engine gets installed as shown in Figure 1-13.

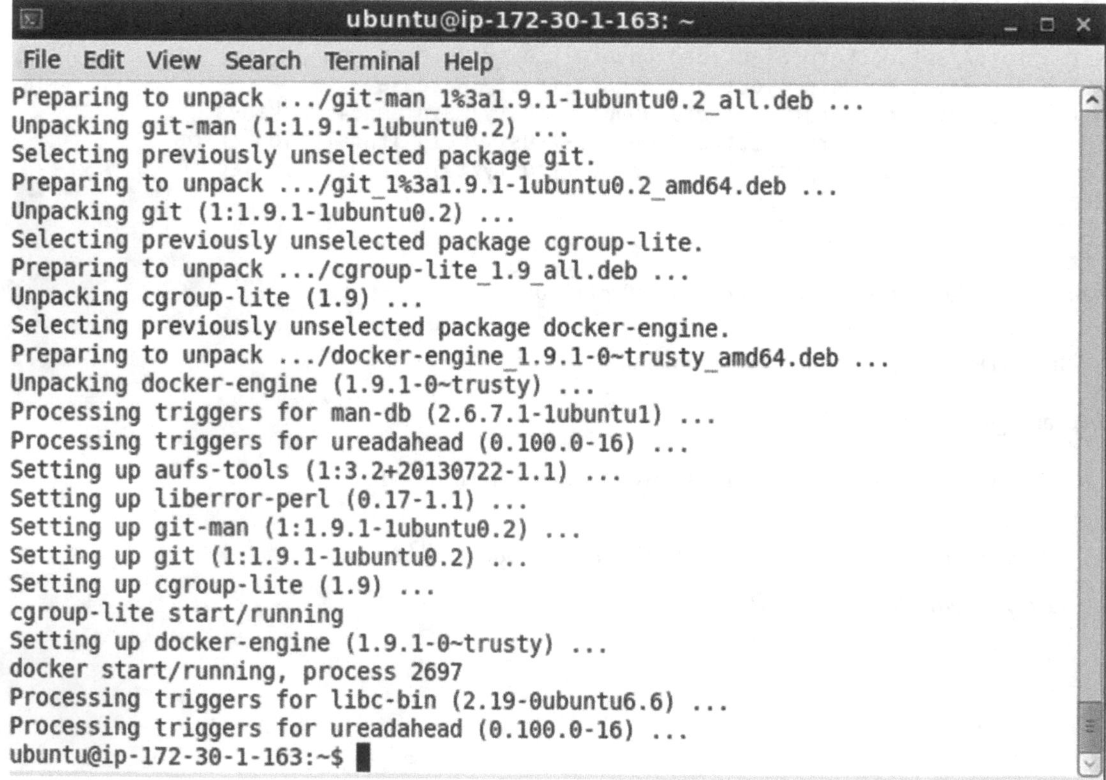

Figure 1-13. *Installing the Docker Engine*

Start the Docker service with the following command.

```
sudo service docker start
```

To verify the status of the Docker service, run the following command.

```
sudo service docker status
```

The output from the preceding commands is shown in Figure 1-14. The docker engine is indicated as running as process 2697.

```
ubuntu@ip-172-30-1-163:~$ sudo service docker start
start: Job is already running: docker
ubuntu@ip-172-30-1-163:~$ sudo service docker status
docker start/running, process 2697
ubuntu@ip-172-30-1-163:~$
```

Figure 1-14. *Starting Docker and verifying its Status*

Having installed Docker, next we shall install Kubernetes.

Installing Kubernetes

Kubernetes is an open source container cluster manager. The main components of Kubernetes are the following:

1. etcd
2. Kubernetes master
3. Service proxy
4. kubelet

etcd is a simple, secure, fast and reliable distributed key-value store.

Kubernetes master exposes the Kubernetes API using which containers are run on nodes to handle tasks.

kubelet is an agent that runs on each node to monitor the containers running on the node, restarting them if required to keep the replication level.

A service proxy runs on each node to provide the Kubernetes service interface for clients. A service is an abstraction for the logical set of pods represented by the service, and a service selector is used to select the pods represented by the service. The service proxy routes the client traffic to a matching pod. Labels are used to match a service with a pod.

Optionally create a directory (/kubernetes) to install Kubernetes and set its permissions to global (777).

```
sudo mkdir /kubernetes
sudo chmod -R 777 /kubernetes
```

The output from the preceding commands is shown in Figure 1-15.

```
ubuntu@ip-172-30-1-190:~$ sudo mkdir /kubernetes
ubuntu@ip-172-30-1-190:~$ sudo chmod -R 777 /kubernetes
```

Figure 1-15. *Creating a Directory to install Kubernetes*

Change directory to the /kubernetes directory and start the Docker engine.

```
cd /kubernetes
sudo service docker start
```

If the Docker Engine is not running, it gets started. The Docker Engine is shown as already running in Figure 1-16.

```
ubuntu@ip-172-30-1-190:~$  cd /kubernetes
ubuntu@ip-172-30-1-190:/kubernetes$ sudo service docker start
start: Job is already running: docker
ubuntu@ip-172-30-1-190:/kubernetes$
```

Figure 1-16. *Starting Docker if not already running*

As a prerequisite we need to set some Linux kernel parameters if not already set. Add support for memory and swap accounting. The following configs should be turned on in the kernel.

```
CONFIG_RESOURCE_COUNTERS=y
CONFIG_MEMCG=y
CONFIG_MEMCG_SWAP=y
CONFIG_MEMCG_SWAP_ENABLED=y
CONFIG_MEMCG_KMEM=y
```

The kernel configs are enabled when the Ubuntu system boots and the kernel configuration file is in the /boot directory. Change directory (cd) to the /boot directory and list the files/directories.

```
cd /boot
ls -l
```

The files in the /boot directory get listed as shown in Figure 1-17. The kernel configs are configured in the config-3.13.0-48-generic file. The kernel version could be different for different users; for example, the kernel config file could /boot/config-3.13.0-66-generic.

```
ubuntu@ip-172-30-1-10:/$ cd /boot
ubuntu@ip-172-30-1-10:/boot$ ls -l
total 51924
-rw-r--r-- 1 root root  1164723 Mar 12  2015 abi-3.13.0-48-generic
-rw-r--r-- 1 root root  1165334 Dec 18 00:42 abi-3.13.0-74-generic
-rw-r--r-- 1 root root   165773 Mar 12  2015 config-3.13.0-48-generic
-rw-r--r-- 1 root root   165763 Dec 18 00:42 config-3.13.0-74-generic
drwxr-xr-x 5 root root     4096 Jan  2 18:42 grub
-rw-r--r-- 1 root root  7266051 Mar 25  2015 initrd.img-3.13.0-48-generic
-rw-r--r-- 1 root root 24794508 Jan  1 04:10 initrd.img-3.13.0-74-generic
-rw------- 1 root root  3389235 Mar 12  2015 System.map-3.13.0-48-generic
-rw------- 1 root root  3392888 Dec 18 00:42 System.map-3.13.0-74-generic
-rw------- 1 root root  5815680 Mar 12  2015 vmlinuz-3.13.0-48-generic
-rw------- 1 root root  5825376 Dec 18 00:42 vmlinuz-3.13.0-74-generic
ubuntu@ip-172-30-1-10:/boot$
```

Figure 1-17. *Listing the Files in the /boot Directory*

Open the config-3.13.0-48-generic file in a vi editor.

```
sudo vi /boot/config-3.13.0-48-generic
```

The kernel configuration parameters get listed as shown in Figure 1-18.

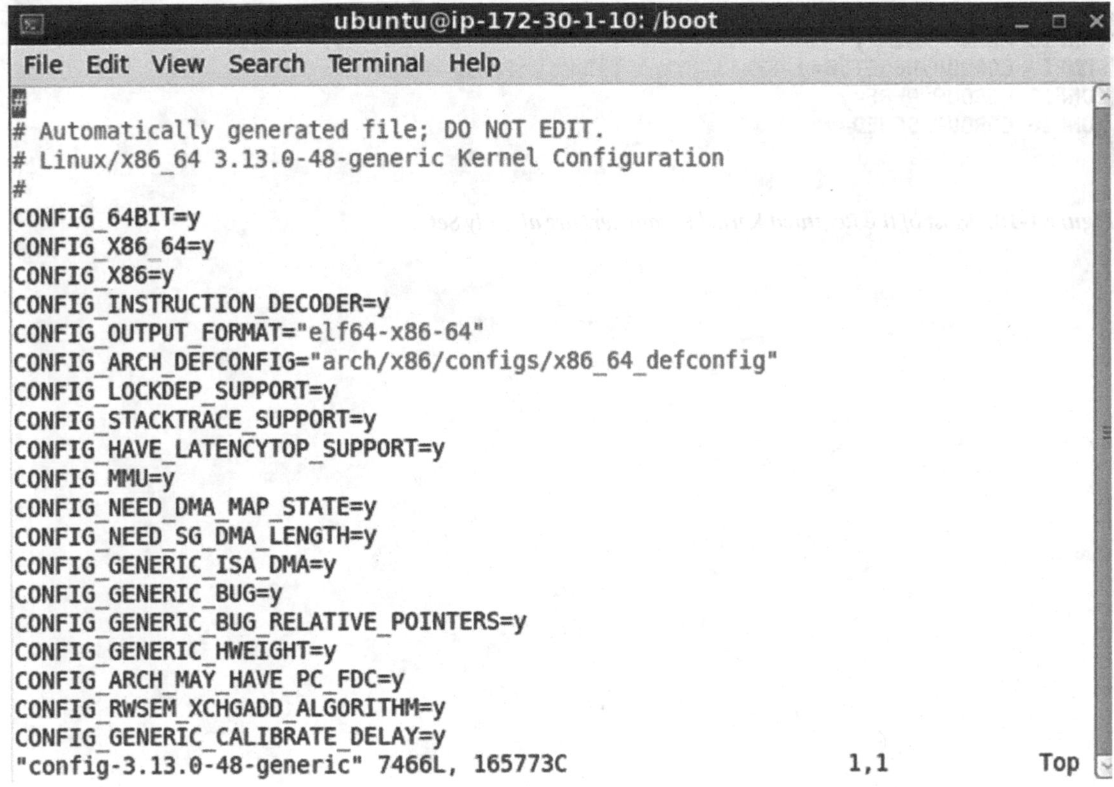

Figure 1-18. *Kernel Configuration Parameter*

Most of the configs listed earlier are already turned on as shown in Figure 1-19. The CONFIG_MEMCG_SWAP_ENABLED config is not set.

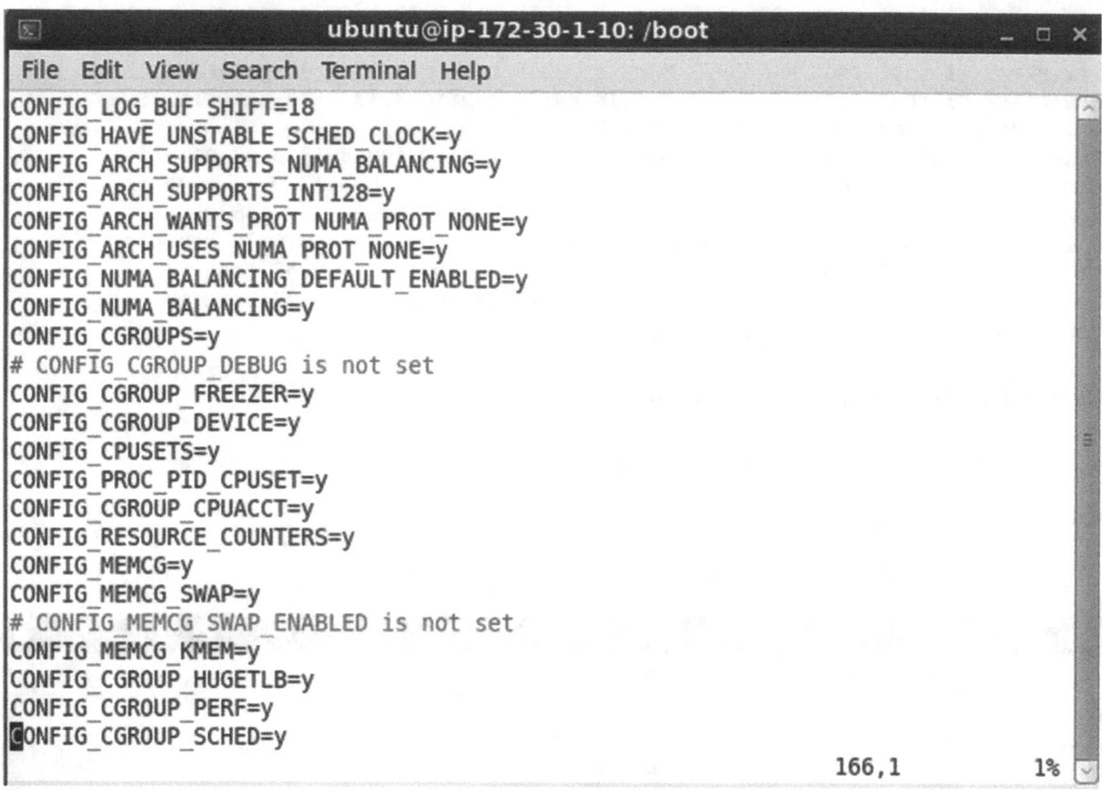

Figure 1-19. *Most of the Required Kernel Parameters are already Set*

Set CONFIG_MEMCG_SWAP_ENABLED = y and save the kernel configuration file as shown in Figure 1-20.

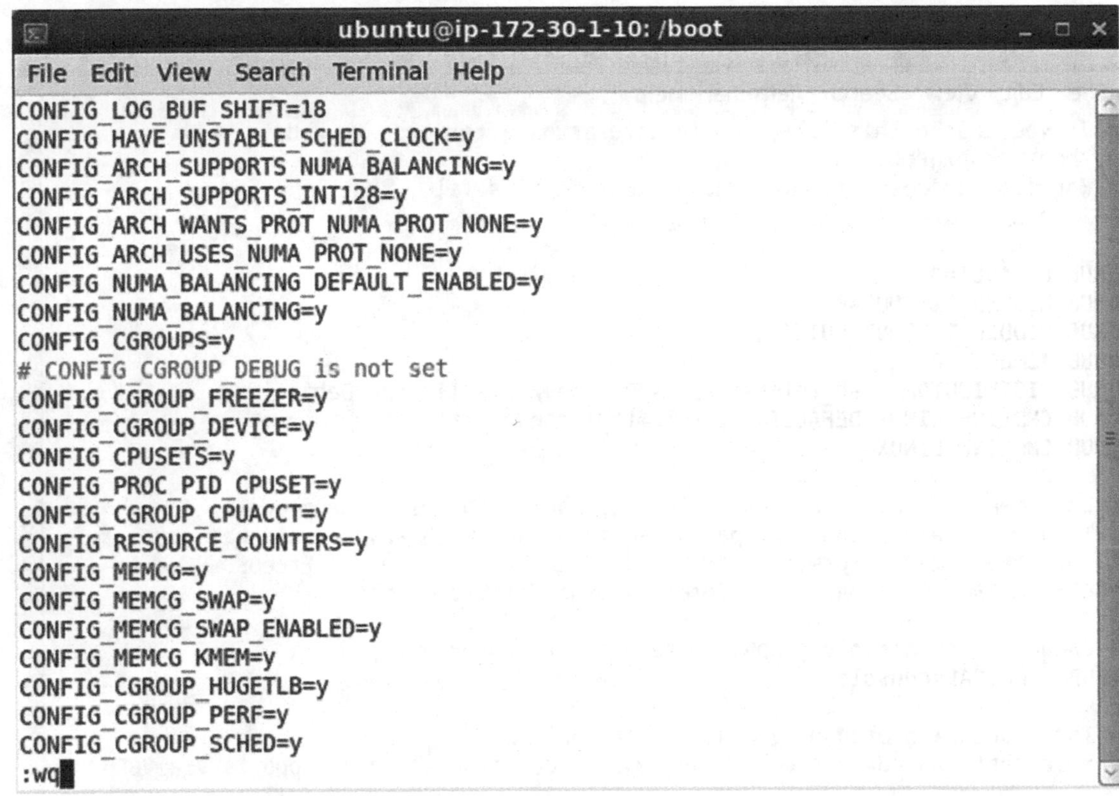

Figure 1-20. *Setting the CONFIG_MEMCG_SWAP_ENABLED Kernel Parameter*

Next, we need to add support for memory and swap accounting to the kernel. The command-line parameters provided to the kernel may be listed with the following command.

```
cat /proc/cmdline
```

As shown in Figure 1-21 memory and swap accounting are not turned on.

```
ubuntu@ip-172-30-1-10:~$ cat /proc/cmdline
BOOT_IMAGE=/boot/vmlinuz-3.13.0-74-generic root=UUID=d4f2aafc-946a-4514-930d-4c4
5e676f198 ro console=tty1 console=ttyS0
ubuntu@ip-172-30-1-10:~$
```

Figure 1-21. *Listing the Command-Line Parameters*

Grub 2 is the default boot loader for Ubuntu. To turn on memory and swap accounting, open the /etc/default/grub file in the vi editor. The GRUB_CMDLINE_LINUX is set to an empty string as shown in Figure 1-22.

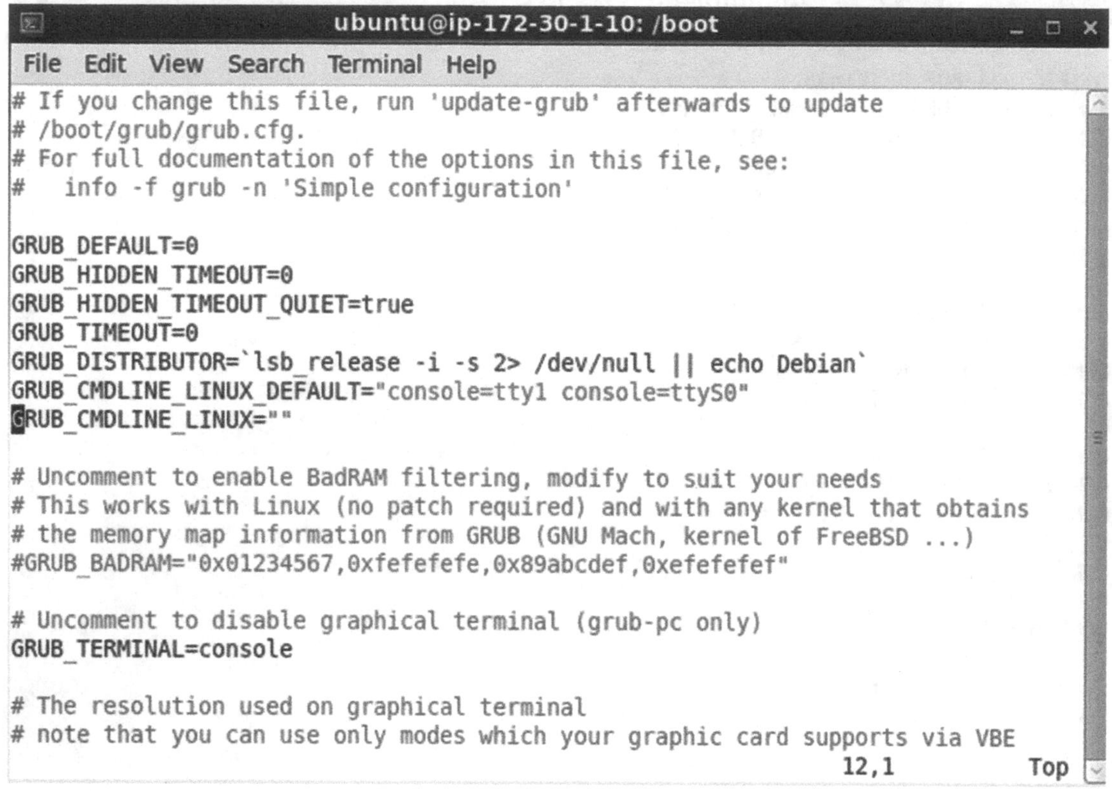

Figure 1-22. *The /etc/default/grub file*

Set the GRUB_CMDLINE_LINU as follows, which enables memory and swap accounting in the kernel at boot.

```
GRUB_CMDLINE_LINUX="cgroup_enable=memory swapaccount=1"
```

The modified /etc/default/grub file is shown in Figure 1-23. Save the file with the :wq command.

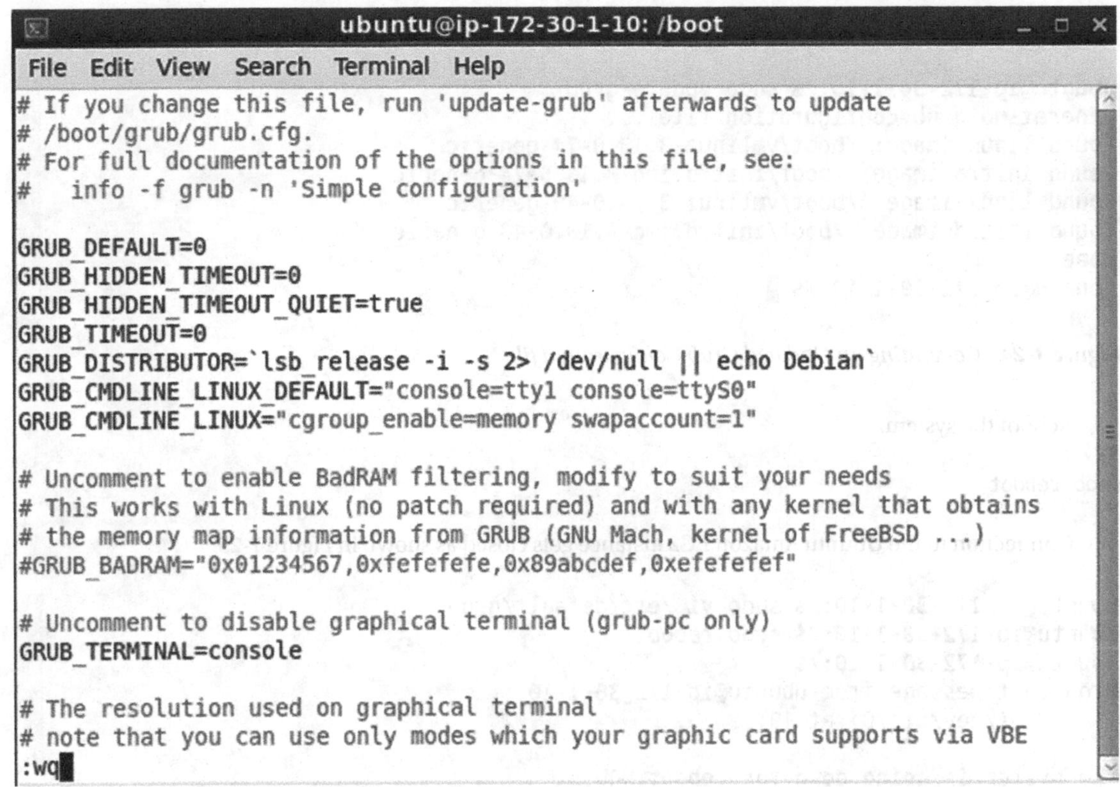

Figure 1-23. *Modified /etc/default/grub file*

Update the grub.cfg file with the following command.

```
sudo update-grub
```

The grub configuration file gets generated as shown in Figure 1-24.

```
ubuntu@ip-172-30-1-10:/$ sudo update-grub
Generating grub configuration file ...
Found linux image: /boot/vmlinuz-3.13.0-74-generic
Found initrd image: /boot/initrd.img-3.13.0-74-generic
Found linux image: /boot/vmlinuz-3.13.0-48-generic
Found initrd image: /boot/initrd.img-3.13.0-48-generic
done
ubuntu@ip-172-30-1-10:/$
```

Figure 1-24. *Generating an Updated Grub Configuration file*

Reboot the system.

```
sudo reboot
```

Connection to the Ubuntu Amazon EC2 instance gets closed as shown in Figure 1-25.

```
ubuntu@ip-172-30-1-10:/$ sudo vi /etc/default/grub
ubuntu@ip-172-30-1-10:/$ sudo reboot
ubuntu@ip-172-30-1-10:/$
Broadcast message from ubuntu@ip-172-30-1-10
        (/dev/pts/0) at 19:29 ...

The system is going down for reboot NOW!
Connection to 52.91.212.17 closed by remote host.
Connection to 52.91.212.17 closed.
[root@localhost ~]#
```

Figure 1-25. *Rebooting Ubuntu Instance*

SSH log in back into the Ubuntu instance. Rerun the command to list the command-line kernel parameters.

```
cat /proc/cmdline
```

The cgroup_enable = memory swapaccount = 1 settings get output as shown in Figure 1-26.

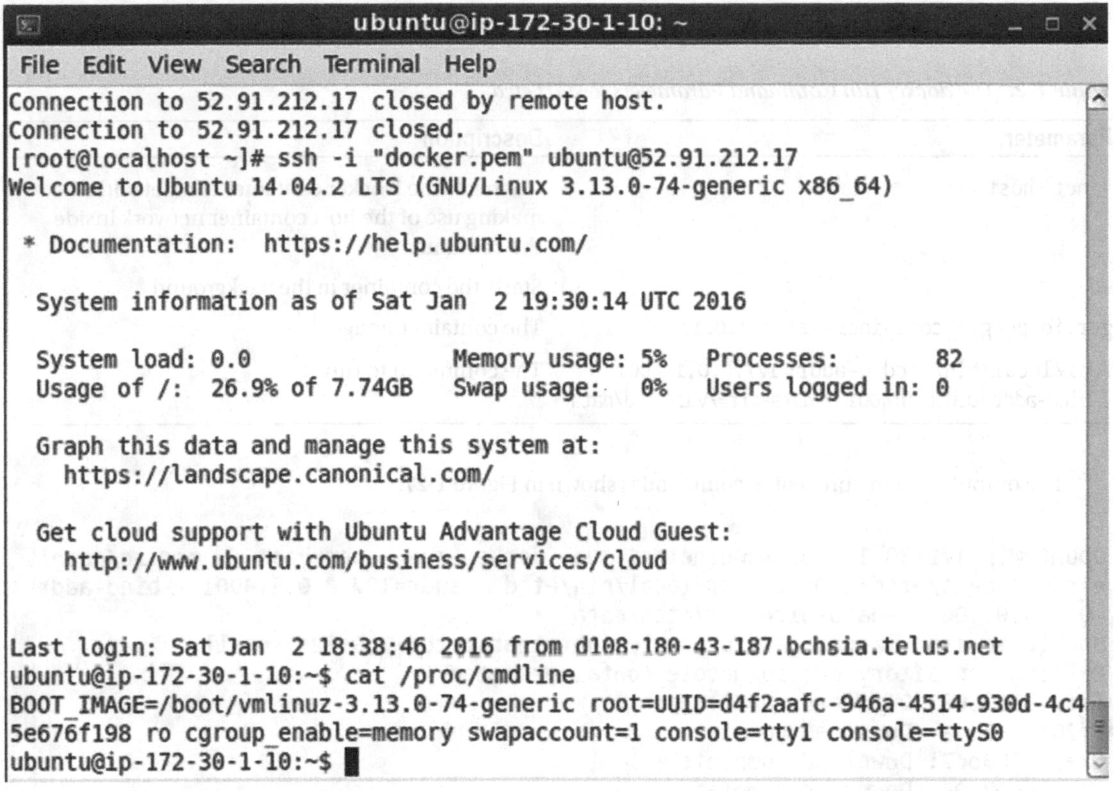

Figure 1-26. *Updated Settings*

Having set the prerequisite kernel parameters, next we shall start the Kubernetes components etcd, master, and service proxy.

Starting etcd

Run etcd with the following docker run command.

```
sudo docker run --net=host -d gcr.io/google_containers/etcd:2.0.12 /usr/local/bin/etcd
--addr=127.0.0.1:4001 --bind-addr=0.0.0.0:4001 --data-dir=/var/etcd/data
```

The docker run command parameters are as follows (Table 1-2).

Table 1-2. *The docker run Command Parameters to start etcd*

Parameter	Description
--net=host	Connects the Docker container to a network making use of the host container network inside the container
-d	Starts the container in the background
gcr.io/google_containers/etcd:2.0.12	The container image
/usr/local/bin/etcd --addr=127.0.0.1:4001 --bind-addr=0.0.0.0:4001 --data-dir=/var/etcd/data	The command to run

The output from the preceding command is shown in Figure 1-27.

```
ubuntu@ip-172-30-1-190:/kubernetes$ sudo docker run --net=host -d gcr.io/googl
e_containers/etcd:2.0.12 /usr/local/bin/etcd --addr=127.0.0.1:4001 --bind-addr
=0.0.0.0:4001 --data-dir=/var/etcd/data
Unable to find image 'gcr.io/google_containers/etcd:2.0.12' locally
Pulling repository gcr.io/google_containers/etcd
fafe47352699: Download complete
cf2616975b4a: Download complete
6ce2e90b0bc7: Download complete
8c2e06607696: Download complete
25b7f6392583: Download complete
b4b56c254ad5: Download complete
Status: Downloaded newer image for gcr.io/google_containers/etcd:2.0.12
gcr.io/google_containers/etcd: this image was pulled from a legacy registry.
Important: This registry version will not be supported in future versions of d
ocker.
71f375db4ea024bb81b02e13b903b431fa933e0e567324f21b26328a3bdc7d30
ubuntu@ip-172-30-1-190:/kubernetes$
```

Figure 1-27. *Starting etcd*

The docker run command to start etcd is required to be run each time the Kubernetes cluster manager is to be started. Subsequent starts of etcd do not need to download the container image as shown in Figure 1-28.

```
ubuntu@ip-172-30-1-190:~$ sudo docker run --net=host -d gcr.io/google_containe
rs/etcd:2.0.12 /usr/local/bin/etcd --addr=127.0.0.1:4001 --bind-addr=0.0.0.0:4
001 --data-dir=/var/etcd/data
59d9f36f35e2a09e787f876c2df4e66e71ac168fa60923324f104e6bdf296a23
```

Figure 1-28. *Subsequent Start of etcd does not need to download the container Image again*

Starting Kubernetes Master

The Kubernetes master is started using the kubelet, which also starts the other Master components apiserver, scheduler, controller, and pause, which are discussed in Table 1-3.

Table 1-3. *The docker run Command Parameters to start etcd*

Master Component	Description
Apiserver	The apiserver takes API requests, processes them, and stores the result in etcd if required and returns the result.
Scheduler	The scheduler monitors the API for unscheduled pods and schedules them on a node to run and also notifies the about the same to the API.
Controller	The controller manages the replication level of the pods, starting new pods in a scale up event and stopping some of the pods in a scale down.
Pause	The pause keeps the port mappings of all the containers in the pod or the network endpoint of the pod.

Run the Kubernetes master with the following command.

```
sudo docker run \
    --volume=/:/rootfs:ro \
    --volume=/sys:/sys:ro \
    --volume=/dev:/dev \
    --volume=/var/lib/docker/:/var/lib/docker:ro \
    --volume=/var/lib/kubelet/:/var/lib/kubelet:rw \
    --volume=/var/run:/var/run:rw \
    --net=host \
    --pid=host \
    --privileged=true \
    -d \
    gcr.io/google_containers/hyperkube:v1.0.1 \
    /hyperkube kubelet --containerized --hostname-override="127.0.0.1"
    --address="0.0.0.0" --api-
servers=http://localhost:8080 --config=/etc/kubernetes/manifests
```

The docker run command parameters are discussed in Table 1-4.

Table 1-4. *The docker run Command Parameters to start etcd*

Parameter	Description

`--volume=/:/rootfs:ro \`
`--volume=/sys:/sys:ro \`
`--volume=/dev:/dev \`
`--volume=/var/lib/docker/:/var/lib/docker:ro \`
`--volume=/var/lib/kubelet/:/var/lib/kubelet:rw \`
`--volume=/var/run:/var/run:rw \`
	The Docker volumes to use

`--net=host`	Connects the Docker container to a network making use of the host container network inside the container
`--pid=host`	Sets the pid namespace
`--privileged=true`	Provides access to most of the capabilities of the host machine in terms of kernel features and host access
`-d`	Starts the container in the background
`gcr.io/google_containers/hyperkube:v1.0.1`	The container image

`hyperkube kubelet`
`--containerized`
`--hostname-override="127.0.0.1"`
`--address="0.0.0.0"`
`--api-`
`servers=http://localhost:8080`
`--config=/etc/kubernetes/manifests`
	The command run

The output from the docker run command to start the master is shown in Figure 1-29.

```
ubuntu@ip-172-30-1-190: /kubernetes
File  Edit  View  Search  Terminal  Help
ubuntu@ip-172-30-1-190:/kubernetes$ sudo docker run \
>     --volume=/:/rootfs:ro \
>     --volume=/sys:/sys:ro \
>     --volume=/dev:/dev \
>     --volume=/var/lib/docker/:/var/lib/docker:ro \
>     --volume=/var/lib/kubelet/:/var/lib/kubelet:rw \
>     --volume=/var/run:/var/run:rw \
>     --net=host \
>     --pid=host \
>     --privileged=true \
>     -d \
>     gcr.io/google_containers/hyperkube:v1.0.1 \
>     /hyperkube kubelet --containerized --hostname-override="127.0.0.1" --add
ress="0.0.0.0" --api-servers=http://localhost:8080 --config=/etc/kubernetes/ma
nifests
Unable to find image 'gcr.io/google_containers/hyperkube:v1.0.1' locally
Pulling repository gcr.io/google_containers/hyperkube
1ec3ce7c7eb4: Download complete
511136ea3c5a: Download complete
541923dd11eb: Download complete
11971b6377ef: Download complete
0fb4e3175771: Download complete
6a2d29983094: Download complete
cb486f5a5698: Download complete
b40f9401b132: Download complete
2891dee46d2f: Download complete
dd4e74f5fbe5: Download complete
97210d4778a8: Download complete
Status: Downloaded newer image for gcr.io/google_containers/hyperkube:v1.0.1
gcr.io/google_containers/hyperkube: this image was pulled from a legacy regist
ry.  Important: This registry version will not be supported in future versions
 of docker.
```

Figure 1-29. *The docker run Command to start Kubernetes Master*

The Master is required to be started each time the Kubernetes cluster manager is to be started. The container image is downloaded only the first time the command is run, and on subsequent runs the image is not downloaded as shown in Figure 1-30.

```
ubuntu@ip-172-30-1-190:~$ sudo docker run --net=host -d gcr.io/google_containe
rs/etcd:2.0.12 /usr/local/bin/etcd --addr=127.0.0.1:4001 --bind-addr=0.0.0.0:4
001 --data-dir=/var/etcd/data
59d9f36f35e2a09e787f876c2df4e66e71ac168fa60923324f104e6bdf296a23
ubuntu@ip-172-30-1-190:~$
ubuntu@ip-172-30-1-190:~$ sudo docker run \
>     --volume=/:/rootfs:ro \
>     --volume=/sys:/sys:ro \
>     --volume=/dev:/dev \
>     --volume=/var/lib/docker/:/var/lib/docker:ro \
>     --volume=/var/lib/kubelet/:/var/lib/kubelet:rw \
>     --volume=/var/run:/var/run:rw \
>     --net=host \
>     --pid=host \
>     --privileged=true \
>     -d \
>     gcr.io/google_containers/hyperkube:v1.0.1 \
>     /hyperkube kubelet --containerized --hostname-override="127.0.0.1" --add
ress="0.0.0.0" --api-servers=http://localhost:8080 --config=/etc/kubernetes/ma
nifests
9f030558236112fedb6a463b1c4d69dee34bec953a7b6edd935b06ddd4602e86
ubuntu@ip-172-30-1-190:~$
```

Figure 1-30. *Subsequent starts of Kubernetes Master do not need to download Container image again*

Starting Service Proxy

To start the service proxy, which is a proxy for the Kubernetes service providing a pod/s interface using a service selector with labels, start the service proxy by running the following docker run command.

```
sudo docker run -d --net=host --privileged gcr.io/google_containers/hyperkube:v1.0.1
/hyperkube proxy -- master=http://127.0.0.1:8080 --v=2
```

The command parameters for the preceding command are discussed in Table 1-5.

Table 1-5. The docker run Command Parameters to start service proxy

Parameter	Description
`-d`	Runs the container in the background
`--net=host`	Sets the network for the container to the host's network
`--privileged`	Provides access to most of the capabilities of the host machine in terms of kernel features and host access
`gcr.io/google_containers/hyperkube:v1.0.1`	The container image
`hyperkube proxy -- master= http://127.0.0.1:8080 --v=2`	The command to run. The master url is set to `http://127.0.0.1:8080`.

The output from the preceding docker run command is shown in Figure 1-31.

```
ubuntu@ip-172-30-1-190:/kubernetes$ sudo docker run -d --net=host --privileged
 gcr.io/google_containers/hyperkube:v1.0.1 /hyperkube proxy --master=http://12
7.0.0.1:8080 --v=2
ce152e8ae0ac60766381ee4a7925e82e4ebfee48bdf7bae81d7b71e24c1edb60
ubuntu@ip-172-30-1-190:/kubernetes$
```

Figure 1-31. Starting the Service proxy

Listing the Kubernetes Docker Containers

The Docker containers started for a Kubernetes cluster manager may be listed with the following command.

```
sudo docker ps
```

The Docker containers listed include a container for the service proxy; a container for the kubelet; a container for etcd; and containers each for the master scheduler, controller, and apiserver, and pause as shown in Figure 1-32.

```
ubuntu@ip-172-30-1-190:~$ sudo docker ps
CONTAINER ID        IMAGE                                       COMMAND
           CREATED             STATUS              PORTS               NAMES
0b850f877d8b        gcr.io/google_containers/hyperkube:v1.0.1   "/hyperkube pr
oxy --m"   20 seconds ago      Up 19 seconds                           sad_le
akey
92d7e1a1aa57        gcr.io/google_containers/hyperkube:v1.0.1   "/hyperkube sc
heduler"   49 seconds ago      Up 48 seconds                           k8s_sc
heduler.2744e742_k8s-master-127.0.0.1_default_f3ccbffbd75e3c5d2fb4ba69c8856c4a
_7cf13aaf
9b8a8b75a22f        gcr.io/google_containers/hyperkube:v1.0.1   "/hyperkube ap
iserver"   49 seconds ago      Up 49 seconds                           k8s_ap
iserver.cfb70250_k8s-master-127.0.0.1_default_f3ccbffbd75e3c5d2fb4ba69c8856c4a
_645c4127
37971b53f2c1        gcr.io/google_containers/hyperkube:v1.0.1   "/hyperkube co
ntrolle"   50 seconds ago      Up 49 seconds                           k8s_co
ntroller-manager.1598ee5c_k8s-master-127.0.0.1_default_f3ccbffbd75e3c5d2fb4ba6
9c8856c4a_1b4e0ed5
f6c8f7f8ea70        gcr.io/google_containers/pause:0.8.0        "/pause"
           About a minute ago   Up 59 seconds                          k8s_PO
D.e4cc795_k8s-master-127.0.0.1_default_f3ccbffbd75e3c5d2fb4ba69c8856c4a_055f4a
5a
9f0305582361        gcr.io/google_containers/hyperkube:v1.0.1   "/hyperkube ku
belet -"   About a minute ago   Up About a minute                      sleepy
_cori
59d9f36f35e2        gcr.io/google_containers/etcd:2.0.12        "/usr/local/bi
n/etcd "   About a minute ago   Up About a minute                      tender
_ptolemy
ubuntu@ip-172-30-1-190:~$
```

Figure 1-32. *Listing the Docker Containers*

The Docker container info may be found using the Docker container id. For example, obtain the container id for the Docker container running the controller as shown in Figure 1-33.

```
ubuntu@ip-172-30-1-190:~$ sudo docker ps
CONTAINER ID        IMAGE                                        COMMAND
        CREATED             STATUS              PORTS               NAMES
0b850f877d8b        gcr.io/google_containers/hyperkube:v1.0.1   "/hyperkube pr
oxy --m"   37 minutes ago      Up 37 minutes                           sad_lea
key
92d7e1a1aa57        gcr.io/google_containers/hyperkube:v1.0.1   "/hyperkube sc
heduler"   38 minutes ago      Up 38 minutes                           k8s_sch
eduler.2744e742_k8s-master-127.0.0.1_default_f3ccbffbd75e3c5d2fb4ba69c8856c4a_
7cf13aaf
9b8a8b75a22f        gcr.io/google_containers/hyperkube:v1.0.1   "/hyperkube ap
iserver"   38 minutes ago      Up 38 minutes                           k8s_api
server.cfb70250_k8s-master-127.0.0.1_default_f3ccbffbd75e3c5d2fb4ba69c8856c4a_
645c4127
37971b53f2c1        gcr.io/google_containers/hyperkube:v1.0.1   "/hyperkube co
ntrolle"   38 minutes ago      Up 38 minutes                           k8s_con
troller-manager.1598ee5c_k8s-master-127.0.0.1_default_f3ccbffbd75e3c5d2fb4ba69
c8856c4a_1b4e0ed5
f6c8f7f8ea70        gcr.io/google_containers/pause:0.8.0        "/pause"
        38 minutes ago      Up 38 minutes                           k8s_POD
.e4cc795_k8s-master-127.0.0.1_default_f3ccbffbd75e3c5d2fb4ba69c8856c4a_055f4a5
a
9f0305582361        gcr.io/google_containers/hyperkube:v1.0.1   "/hyperkube ku
belet -"   38 minutes ago      Up 38 minutes                           sleepy_
cori
59d9f36f35e2        gcr.io/google_containers/etcd:2.0.12        "/usr/local/bi
n/etcd "   38 minutes ago      Up 38 minutes                           tender_
ptolemy
ubuntu@ip-172-30-1-190:~$
```

Figure 1-33. *Obtaining the Docker Container Id*

Run the following command to find the detail about the Docker container.

```
sudo docker inspect 37971b53f2c1
```

The detail such as the master ip and about the Docker container running the controller manager gets output as shown in Figure 1-34.

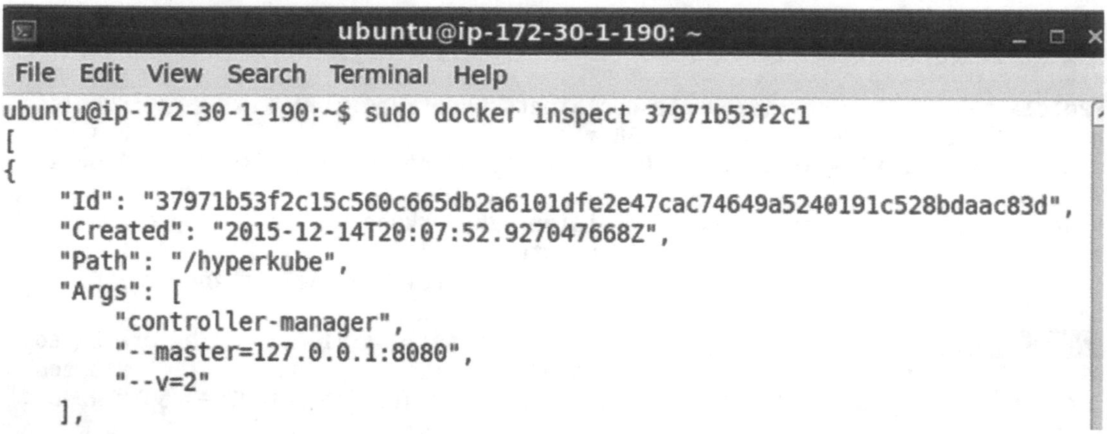

```
ubuntu@ip-172-30-1-190: ~
File Edit View Search Terminal Help
ubuntu@ip-172-30-1-190:~$ sudo docker inspect 37971b53f2c1
[
{
    "Id": "37971b53f2c15c560c665db2a6101dfe2e47cac74649a5240191c528bdaac83d",
    "Created": "2015-12-14T20:07:52.927047668Z",
    "Path": "/hyperkube",
    "Args": [
        "controller-manager",
        "--master=127.0.0.1:8080",
        "--v=2"
    ],
```

Figure 1-34. *Listing Docker Container Information*

Installing kubectl

The kubectl is used to control the Kubernetes cluster manager including running an image, getting the pods, getting the replication controller, making an application available as a service exposed at a specified port, and scaling the cluster. Download Kubectl binaries with the following command.

```
sudo wget https://storage.googleapis.com/kubernetes-release/release/v1.0.1/bin/linux/amd64/kubectl
```

The kubectl binaries get downloaded as shown in Figure 1-35.

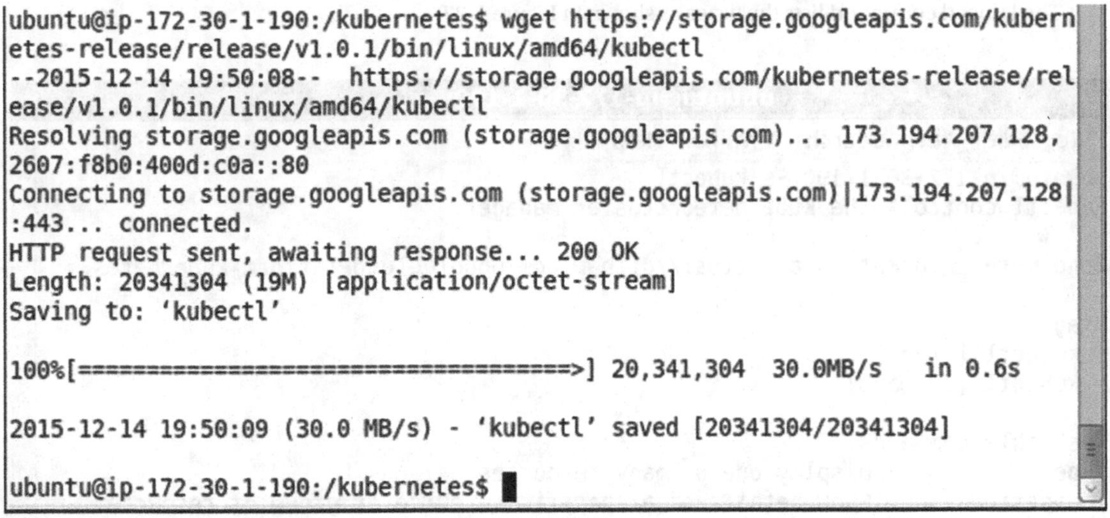

```
ubuntu@ip-172-30-1-190:/kubernetes$ wget https://storage.googleapis.com/kubern
etes-release/release/v1.0.1/bin/linux/amd64/kubectl
--2015-12-14 19:50:08--  https://storage.googleapis.com/kubernetes-release/rel
ease/v1.0.1/bin/linux/amd64/kubectl
Resolving storage.googleapis.com (storage.googleapis.com)... 173.194.207.128,
2607:f8b0:400d:c0a::80
Connecting to storage.googleapis.com (storage.googleapis.com)|173.194.207.128|
:443... connected.
HTTP request sent, awaiting response... 200 OK
Length: 20341304 (19M) [application/octet-stream]
Saving to: 'kubectl'

100%[=====================================>] 20,341,304  30.0MB/s   in 0.6s

2015-12-14 19:50:09 (30.0 MB/s) - 'kubectl' saved [20341304/20341304]

ubuntu@ip-172-30-1-190:/kubernetes$
```

Figure 1-35. *Installing Kubectl*

Make the kubectl application executable by applying the + x permissions.

```
sudo chmod +x kubectl
```

Move the kubectl binaries to the /usr/local/bin/ directory.
sudo mv kubectl /usr/local/bin/
The output from the preceding commands is shown in Figure 1-36.

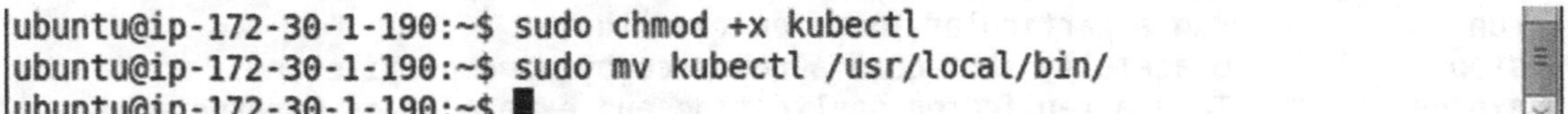

```
ubuntu@ip-172-30-1-190:~$ sudo chmod +x kubectl
ubuntu@ip-172-30-1-190:~$ sudo mv kubectl /usr/local/bin/
ubuntu@ip-172-30-1-190:~$
```

Figure 1-36. *Moving and making kubectl Binaries executable*

The kubectl command lists the usage as shown in Figure 1-37.

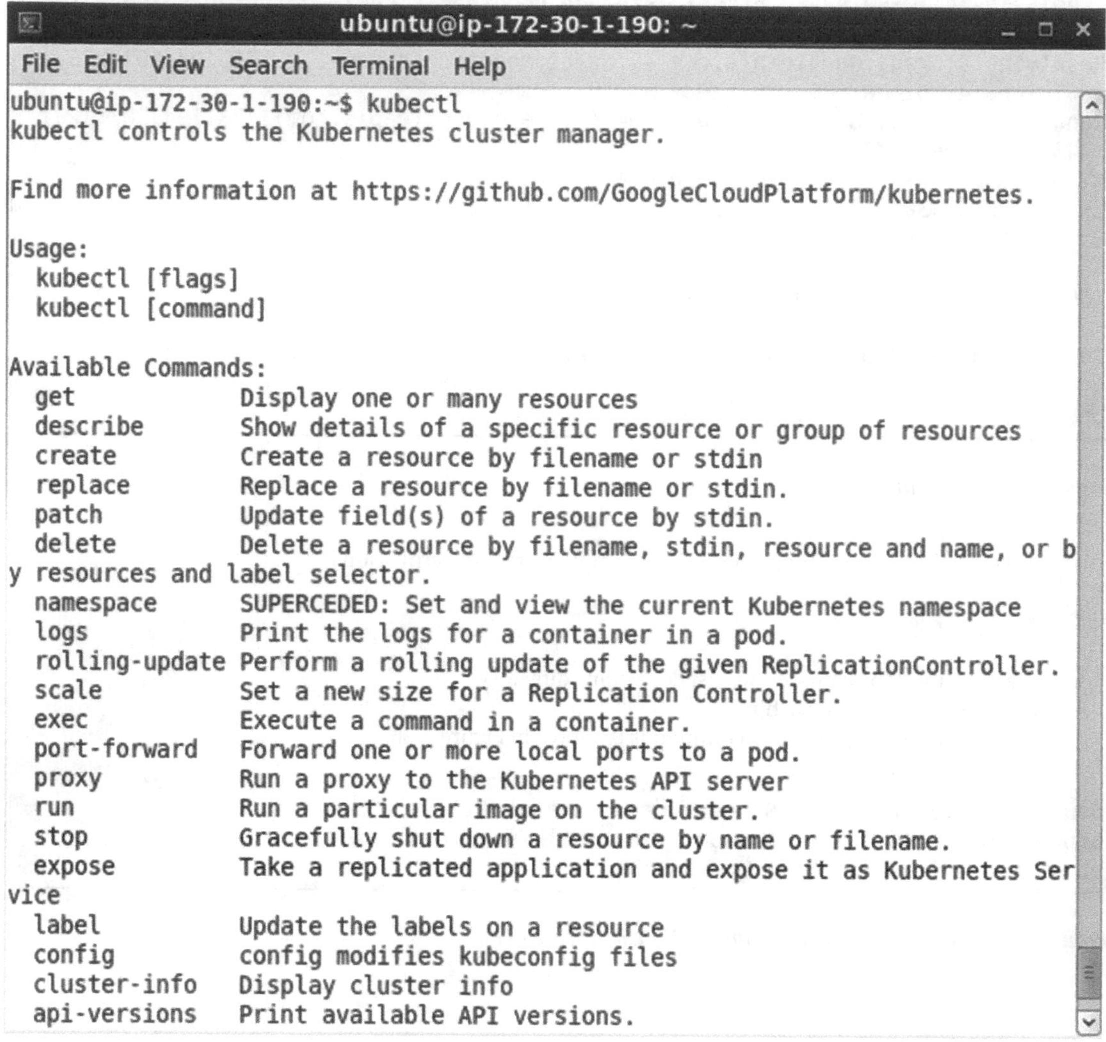

Figure 1-37. *Kubectl Command Usage*

The command parameters also get listed as shown in Figure 1-38.

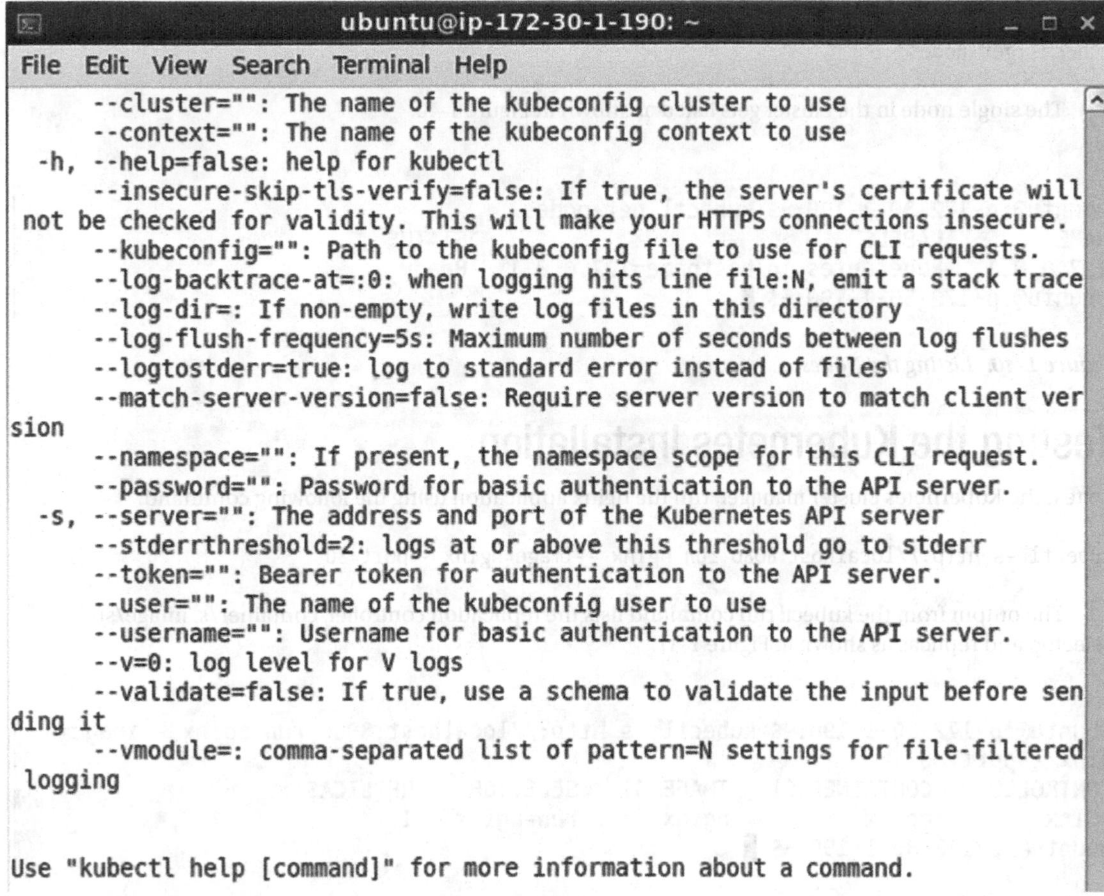

Figure 1-38. Command Parameters for Kubectl

Listing Services

The following command should list the Kubernetes service.

```
kubectl get services
```

The kubernetes service gets listed as shown in Figure 1-39.

```
ubuntu@ip-10-16-236-144:~$ kubectl get services
NAME         LABELS                                    SELECTOR   IP(S)      POR
T(S)
kubernetes   component=apiserver,provider=kubernetes   <none>     10.0.0.1   443
/TCP
```

Figure 1-39. Listing the Kubernetes Service

Listing Nodes

The following command should list the Kubernetes node.

```
kubectl get nodes
```

The single node in the cluster gets listed as shown in Figure 1-40.

```
ubuntu@ip-172-30-1-190:~$ kubectl get nodes
NAME        LABELS                              STATUS
127.0.0.1   kubernetes.io/hostname=127.0.0.1    Ready
ubuntu@ip-172-30-1-190:~$ ▌
```

Figure 1-40. *Listing the Nodes*

Testing the Kubernetes Installation

To test the Kubernetes cluster manager, run the nginx application using the following command.

```
kubectl -s http://localhost:8080 run nginx --image=nginx --port=80
```

The output from the kubectl run command lists the replication controller, container/s, image/sm selector, and replicas as shown in Figure 1-41.

```
ubuntu@ip-172-30-1-190:~$ kubectl -s http://localhost:8080 run nginx --image=n
ginx --port=80
CONTROLLER   CONTAINER(S)   IMAGE(S)   SELECTOR    REPLICAS
nginx        nginx          nginx      run=nginx   1
ubuntu@ip-172-30-1-190:~$ ▌
```

Figure 1-41. *Running he nginx Application on Kubernetes Cluster*

Expose the nginx application replication controller as a service with the kubectl expose command.

```
kubectl expose rc nginx --port=80
```

The nginx Kubernetes service gets created running on port 80 as shown in Figure 1-42.

```
ubuntu@ip-172-30-1-190:~$ kubectl expose rc nginx --port=80
NAME     LABELS      SELECTOR    IP(S)     PORT(S)
nginx    run=nginx   run=nginx             80/TCP
ubuntu@ip-172-30-1-190:~$ ▌
```

Figure 1-42. *Creating a Kubernetes Service for nginx Application*

List the detail about the nginx service with the kubectl get svc command.

```
kubectl get svc nginx
```

The nginx service detail gets listed as shown in Figure 1-43.

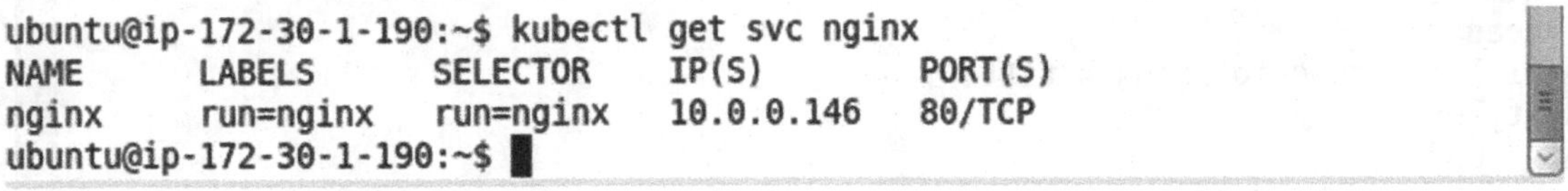

```
ubuntu@ip-172-30-1-190:~$ kubectl get svc nginx
NAME      LABELS      SELECTOR    IP(S)        PORT(S)
nginx     run=nginx   run=nginx   10.0.0.146   80/TCP
ubuntu@ip-172-30-1-190:~$
```

Figure 1-43. Listing the Kubernetes Service nginx

The cluster IP may be obtained with the following command.

```
kubectl get svc nginx --template={{.spec.clusterIP}}
```

The cluster ip is listed as 10.0.0.146 as shown in Figure 1-44.

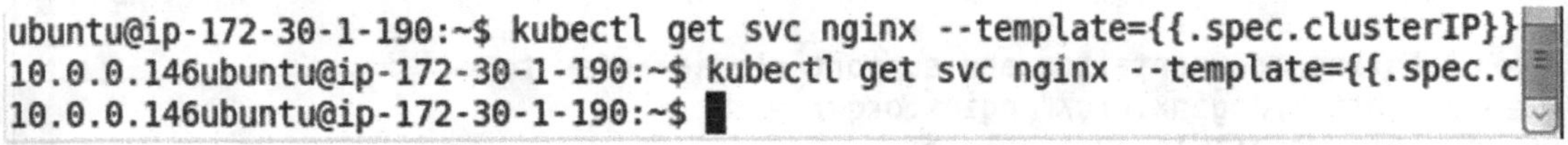

```
ubuntu@ip-172-30-1-190:~$ kubectl get svc nginx --template={{.spec.clusterIP}}
10.0.0.146ubuntu@ip-172-30-1-190:~$ kubectl get svc nginx --template={{.spec.c
10.0.0.146ubuntu@ip-172-30-1-190:~$
```

Figure 1-44. Listing the Cluster IP

The web server may be called making use of the cluster ip with the following command.

```
curl 10.0.0.146
```

The html output as text gets output as shown in Figure 1-45.

```
10.0.0.146ubuntu@ip-172-30-1-190:~$ kubectl get svc nginx --template={{.spec.c
10.0.0.146ubuntu@ip-172-30-1-190:~$ curl 10.0.0.146
<!DOCTYPE html>
<html>
<head>
<title>Welcome to nginx!</title>
<style>
    body {
        width: 35em;
        margin: 0 auto;
        font-family: Tahoma, Verdana, Arial, sans-serif;
    }
</style>
</head>
<body>
<h1>Welcome to nginx!</h1>
<p>If you see this page, the nginx web server is successfully installed and
working. Further configuration is required.</p>

<p>For online documentation and support please refer to
<a href="http://nginx.org/">nginx.org</a>.<br/>
Commercial support is available at
<a href="http://nginx.com/">nginx.com</a>.</p>

<p><em>Thank you for using nginx.</em></p>
</body>
</html>
ubuntu@ip-172-30-1-190:~$
```

Figure 1-45. *Using curl to invoke Application*

Summary

In this chapter we installed Kubernetes using Docker. An Amazon EC2 instance running Ubuntu is used to install Docker and Kubernetes. The nginx application is run only to test the installation of the Kubernetes cluster manager. The kubectl commands to create an application, replication controller, and service are discussed in more detail in the next chapter.

CHAPTER 2

Hello Kubernetes

Kubernetes is a cluster manager for Linux containers. While Kubernetes supports other types of containers such as Rocket, and support for more types is to be added, we shall discuss Kubernetes in the context of Docker containers only. Docker is an open source container virtualization platform to build, package, and run distributed applications in containers that are lightweight snapshots of the underlying OS. A Docker image, which is application specific, encapsulates all the required software including dependencies for an application and is used to create Docker containers to run applications in the containers. The Docker containers are isolated from each other and have their own networking and filesystem and provide Container as a Service (CaaS). Docker is similar to virtual machines based on virtualization platforms such as Oracle VirtualBox and VMWare Player in that it is a virtualization over the underlying OS, but is different in that while a virtual machine makes use of an entire operating system, multiple Docker containers share the kernel and run in isolation on the host OS. Docker containers run on the Docker Engine, which runs on the underlying OS kernel.

In this chapter we shall introduce Kubernetes concepts using a Hello-World application. This chapter has the following sections.

Overview

Why Kubernetes

Setting the Environment

Creating an Application Imperatively

Creating an Application Declaratively

Using JSON for the Resource Definitions

Overview

Kubernetes concepts include Pod, Service, and Replication controller and are defined in the following subsections.

What Is a Node?

A *node* is a machine (physical or virtual) running Kubernetes onto which Pods may be scheduled. The node could be the *master node* or one of the *worker nodes*. In the preceding chapter on installing Kubernetes only a single node was used. In a later chapter, Chapter 14, we shall discuss creating a multi-node cluster with a master and worker node/s.

D. Vohra, *Kubernetes Microservices with Docker*, DOI 10.1007/978-1-4842-1907-2_2

What Is a Cluster?

A *cluster* is a collection of nodes including other resources such as storage to run Kubernetes applications. A cluster has a single Kubernetes master node and zero or more worker nodes. A highly available cluster consists of multiple masters or master nodes.

What Is a Pod?

A *Pod* is a collection of containers that are collocated and form an atomic unit. Multiple applications may be run within a Pod and though the different containers within a Pod could be for the same application, typically the different containers are for different applications. A Pod is a higher level abstraction for managing a group of containers with shared volumes and network namespace. All the applications (containers) in a Pod share the same filesystem and IP address with the port on which each application is exposed being different. Applications running in a Pod may access each other at "localhost". Scheduling and replication are performed at the Pod level rather than at the individual container level. For example if a Pod defines two containers for different applications and replication level is set at 1, a single replica of the Pod consists of two containers, one each for the two applications. Pods facilitate resource sharing and communication what would otherwise be implemented using --link in individually running Docker containers. A Pod consisting of multiple containers would typically be used for tightly coupled applications. For example, if an `nginx` application makes use of MySQL database, the two applications are able to interact by Kubernetes running containers for each in the same Pod.

What Is a Service?

A *Service* is the external interface for one or more Pods providing endpoint/s at which the application/s represented by the Service may be invoked. A Service is hosted at a single IP address but provides zero or more endpoints depending on the application/s interfaced by the Service. Services are connected to Pods using label selectors. Pods have label/s on them and a Service with a selector expression the same as a Pod label represents the Pod to an external client. An external client does not know or need to know about the Pods represented by a Service. An external client only needs to know the name of the Service and the port at which a particular application is exposed. The Service routes requests for an application based on a round-robin manner to one of the Pods selected using a label selector/. Thus, a Service is a high level abstraction for a collection of applications leaving the detail of which Pod to route a request to up to the Service. A Service could also be used for load balancing.

What Is a Replication Controller?

A *Replication Controller* manages the replication level of Pods as specified by the "replicas" setting in a Replication Controller definition or on the command line with the `-replicas` parameter. A Replication Controller ensures that the configured level of Pod replicas are running at any given time. If a replica fails or is stopped deliberately a new replica is started automatically. A Replication Controller is used for scaling the Pods within a cluster. A replica is defined at the Pod level implying that if a Pod consists of two containers a group of the two configured containers constitute a replica.

What Is a Label?

A *Label* is a key-value pair identifying a resource such as a Pod, Service, or Replication Controller: most commonly a Pod. Labels are used to identify a group or subset of resources for tasks such as assigning them to a Service. Services use label selectors to select the Pods they manage. For example, if a Pod is labeled “app = helloApp” and a Service “selector” is set as “app = helloApp” the Pod is represented by the Service. Service selectors are based on labels and not on the type of application they manage. For example, a Service could be representing a Pod running a hello-world application container with a specific label. Another Pod also running a hello-world container but with a label different than the Service selector expression would not be represented by the Service. And a third Pod running an application that is not a hello-world application but has the same label as the Service selector would also be represented by the same Service.

What Is a Selector?

A *selector* is a key-value expression to identify resources using matching labels. As discussed in the preceding subsection a Service selector expression “app = helloApp” would select all Pods with the label “app = helloApp”. While typically a Service defines a selector to select Pods a Service could be defined to not include a selector and be defined to abstract other kinds of back ends. Two kinds of selectors are supported: equality-based and set-based. A selector could be made of multiple requirements implying that multiple expressions (equality-based or set-based) separated by ',' could be specified. All of the requirements must be met by a matching resource such as a Pod for the resource to be selected. A resource such as a Pod could have additional labels, but the ones in the selector must be specified for the resource to be selected. The equality-based selector, which is more commonly used and also the one used in the book, supports =,!=,== operators, the = being synonymous to ==.

What Is a Name?

A *name* is identifies a resource. A name is not the same as a label. For matching resources with a Service a label is used and not a name.

What Is a Namespace?

A *namespace* is a level above the name to demarcate a group of resources for a project or team to prevent name collisions. Resources within different namespaces could have the same name, but resources within a namespace have different names.

What Is a Volume?

A *volume* is a directory within the filesystem of a container. A volume could be used to store data. Kubernetes volumes evolve from Docker volumes.

Why Kubernetes?

Docker containers introduced a new level of modularity and fluidity for applications with the provision to package applications including dependencies, and transfer and run the applications across different environments. But with the use of Docker containers in production, practical problems became apparent such as which container to run on which node (scheduling), how to increase/decrease the number of running containers for an application (scaling), and how to communicate within containers. Kubernetes was designed to overcome all these and other practical issues of container cluster management. Kubernetes provides dynamic container cluster orchestration in real time. Kubernetes as a cluster manager provides the following benefits.

-Microservices by breaking an application into smaller, manageable, scalable components that could be used by groups with different requirements.

-Fault-tolerant cluster in which if a single Pod replica fails (due to node failure, for example), another is started automatically.

-Horizontal scaling in which additional or fewer replicas of a Pod could be run by just modifying the "replicas" setting in the Replication Controller or using the `-replicas` parameter in the `kubectl scale` command.

-Higher resource utilization and efficiency.

-Separation of concerns. The Service development team does not need to interface with the cluster infrastructure team.

Setting the Environment

The following software is required for this chapter.

-Docker Engine (latest version)

-Kubernetes (version 1.01)

-Kubectl (version 1.01)

We have used an Amazon EC2 Linux instance created from AMI Ubuntu Server 14.04 LTS (HVM), SSD Volume Type - ami-d05e75b8.

SSH Login to the Ubuntu interface (Public IP address would be different for different users and multiple IP Addresses may have been used in this chapter).

```
ssh -i "docker.pem" ubuntu@54.152.82.142
```

Install Docker as discussed in Chapter 1 and start the Docker Engine and verify its status using the following commands.

```
sudo service docker start
sudo service docker status
```

Install kubectl and start the Kubernetes cluster manager as discussed in Chapter 1. Output the Kubernetes cluster information using the following command.

```
kubectl cluster-info
```

The Kubernetes Master is shown running on `http://localhost:8080` in Figure 2-1.

```
ubuntu@ip-172-30-1-235:~$ kubectl cluster-info
Kubernetes master is running at http://localhost:8080
```

Figure 2-1. Getting Cluster Info

In the following sections we shall run a hello-world application using the Kubernetes cluster manager. An application may be run imperatively using the kubectl tool on the command line or declaratively using definition files for a Pod, Replication Controller, and Service. We shall discuss each of these methods. The kubectl tool is used throughout this chapter and in subsequent chapters and a complete command reference is available at https://cloud.google.com/container-engine/docs/kubectl/.

Creating an Application Imperatively

With the Kubernetes master running on http://localhost:8080, as obtained in the preceding section, run the following kubectl run command to run a hello-world application using the image tutum/hello-world. The -s option specifies the Kubernetes API server host and port. The -image command parameter specifies the Docker image to run as tutum/hello-world. The -replicas parameter specifies the number of replicas to create as 1. A Replication Controller is created even if the -replicas parameter is not specified. The default number of replicas is 1. The -port parameter specifies the container port the application is hosted at as 80.

```
kubectl -s http://localhost:8080 run hello-world --image=tutum/hello-world --replicas=1 --port=80
```

A new application container called hello-world gets created as shown in Figure 2-2. A Replication Controller called "hello-world" also gets created. The Pod is created implicitly and label "run = hello-world" is added to the Pod. The number of replicas created is 1. The Replication Controller's selector field is also set to "run=hello-world". The Pods managed by a Replication Controller must specify a label that is the same as the selector specified at the Replication Controller level. By default a Replication Controller selector is set to the same expression as the Pod label.

```
ubuntu@ip-172-30-1-235:~$ kubectl -s http://localhost:8080 run hello-world --ima
ge=tutum/hello-world --replicas=1 --port=80
CONTROLLER     CONTAINER(S)   IMAGE(S)            SELECTOR          REPLICAS
hello-world    hello-world    tutum/hello-world   run=hello-world   1
```

Figure 2-2. *Creating an Application including a Replication Controller and Pod Replica/s*

The Replication Controller created may be listed with the following command.

```
kubectl get rc
```

The hello-world Replication Controller gets listed as shown in Figure 2-3.

```
ubuntu@ip-172-30-1-235:~$ kubectl get rc
CONTROLLER     CONTAINER(S)   IMAGE(S)            SELECTOR          REPLICAS
hello-world    hello-world    tutum/hello-world   run=hello-world   1
```

Figure 2-3. *Listing the Replication Controllers*

The Pods created and started are listed with the following command.

```
kubectl get pods
```

The single Pod created gets listed as shown in Figure 2-4. A Pod name is assigned automatically. A Pod STATUS "Running" is listed, but the Pod may still not be ready and available. The READY column value of 0/1 indicates that 0 of 1 containers in the Pod are ready, which implies that the Pod has been created and is running but not yet ready. It could take a few seconds for a Pod to become Ready.

```
ubuntu@ip-172-30-1-235:~$ kubectl get pods
NAME                   READY     STATUS    RESTARTS   AGE
hello-world-syrqz      0/1       Running   0          12s
k8s-master-127.0.0.1   3/3       Running   0          2m
```

Figure 2-4. *Listing the Pods*

Run the same command again after a few seconds or a minute.

```
kubectl get pods
```

The Pod gets listed as ready as indicated by 1/1 in the READY column in Figure 2-5. A value of 1/1 in the READY column indicates that 1 of 1 containers in the Pod are ready. The syntax for the READY column value is `nReady/nTotal`, which implies that `nReady` of the total `nTotal` containers in the Pod are ready. The Kubernetes Pod `k8s-master-127.0.0.1`, for example, has a READY column value of 3/3, which implies that 3 of 3 containers in the Kubernetes Pod are ready.

```
ubuntu@ip-172-30-1-235:~$ kubectl get pods
NAME                   READY     STATUS    RESTARTS   AGE
hello-world-syrqz      1/1       Running   0          43s
k8s-master-127.0.0.1   3/3       Running   0          3m
ubuntu@ip-172-30-1-235:~$ 
```

Figure 2-5. *Listing a Pod as ready with all containers in the Pod as ready*

Running a Pod and a Replication Controller does not implicitly create a Service. In the next subsection we shall create a Service for the `hello-world` application.

Creating a Service

Create a Kubernetes Service using the `kubectl expose` command, which creates a Service from a Pod, Replication Controller, or another Service. As we created a Replication Controller called `hello-world`, create a Service using the following command in which the port to expose the Service is set to 8080 and the Service type is `LoadBalancer`.

```
kubectl expose rc hello-world --port=8080 --type=LoadBalancer
```

A Kubernetes Service called hello-world gets created as shown in Figure 2-6. The Service labels and selector also get set. The Service selector, listed in Figure 2-6, is set to the same expression run=hello-world as the Replication Controller selector, which is shown in Figure 2-3, which implies that the Service manages the Pods in the Replication Controller hello-world.

```
ubuntu@ip-172-30-1-235:~$ kubectl expose rc hello-world --port=8080 --type=LoadB
alancer
NAME          LABELS            SELECTOR          IP(S)        PORT(S)
hello-world   run=hello-world   run=hello-world                8080/TCP
```

Figure 2-6. Creating a Kubernetes Service

The different types of Services are ClusterIp, NodePort, and LoadBalancer with the default being ClusterIP, as discussed in Table 2-1.

Table 2-1. Types of Services

Service Type	Description
ClusterIp	Uses a cluster-internal IP only.
NodePort	In addition to a cluster IP exposes the Service on each node of the cluster.
LoadBalancer	In addition to exposing the Service on a cluster internal Ip and a port on each node on the cluster, requests the cloud provider to provide a load balancer for the Service. The load balancer balances the load between the Pods in the Service.

List all the Kubernetes Services with the following command.

```
kubectl get services
```

In addition to the "kubernetes" Service for the Kubernetes cluster manager a "hello-world" Service gets created as shown in Figure 2-7.

```
ubuntu@ip-172-30-1-235:~$ kubectl get services
NAME          LABELS                                    SELECTOR          IP(S)
      PORT(S)
hello-world   run=hello-world                           run=hello-world   10.0.0
.57   8080/TCP
kubernetes    component=apiserver,provider=kubernetes   <none>            10.0.0
.1    443/TCP
```

Figure 2-7. Listing the Services

Describing a Pod

Using the Pod name `hello-world-syrqz` obtained from the NAME column in the result for the `kubectl get pods` command use the `kubectl describe pod` command to list detailed information about the Pod.

```
kubectl describe pod hello-world-syrqz
```

Detailed information about the Pod including the IP address gets listed as shown in Figure 2-8. The Pod has a Label run=hello-world, which is the same as the replication controller `selector` and also same as the service `selector`, which implies that the replication controller manages the Pod when scaling the cluster of Pods for example, and the service represents the Pod to external clients.

Figure 2-8. Describing a Pod

Next, we shall invoke the application using the IP Address 172.0.17.2 listed in the IP field.

Invoking the Hello-World Application

The hello-world application may be invoked using the IP for the application as listed in Figure 2-8 with the following curl command.

```
curl 172.17.0.2
```

The HTML output from the application is shown in Figure 2-9.

```
ubuntu@ip-172-30-1-235:~$ curl 172.17.0.2
<html>
<head>
        <title>Hello world!</title>
        <link href='http://fonts.googleapis.com/css?family=Open+Sans:400,700' re
l='stylesheet' type='text/css'>
        <style>
        body {
                background-color: white;
                text-align: center;
                padding: 50px;
                font-family: "Open Sans","Helvetica Neue",Helvetica,Arial,sans-s
erif;
        }

        #logo {
                margin-bottom: 40px;
        }
        </style>
</head>
<body>
        <img id="logo" src="logo.png" />
        <h1>Hello world!</h1>
        <h3>My hostname is hello-world-syrqz</h3>                       <h3>Link
s found</h3>
                                        <b>KUBERNETES</b> listening in 443 avail
able at tcp://10.0.0.1:443<br />
                                </body>
</html>
ubuntu@ip-172-30-1-235:~$
```

Figure 2-9. *Invoking a Application using Pod IP with curl*

To display the HTML output in a browser we need to invoke the application from a browser using URL `172.17.0.2:80`. If a browser is not available on the Amazon EC2 Ubuntu instance, as it is not by default, we need to set up a SSH tunnel to the IP Address of the application using local port forwarding. Obtain the Public DNS for the Amazon EC2 instance (`ec2-52-91-200-41.compute-1.amazonaws.com` in the example) and run the following command to set up a SSH tunnel to the `172.17.0.2:80 host:port` from a local machine. The `-L` indicates that local port forwarding is used to forward local port 80 to `172.17.0.2:80`.

```
ssh -i "docker.pem" -f -nNT -L 80:172.17.0.2:80 ubuntu@ec2-52-91-200-41.compute-1.amazonaws.com
```

Invoke the URL `http://localhost` in a browser on the local machine. The HTML output from the `hello-world` application gets displayed as shown in Figure 2-10. The hostname is listed the same as the Pod name in Figure 2-5.

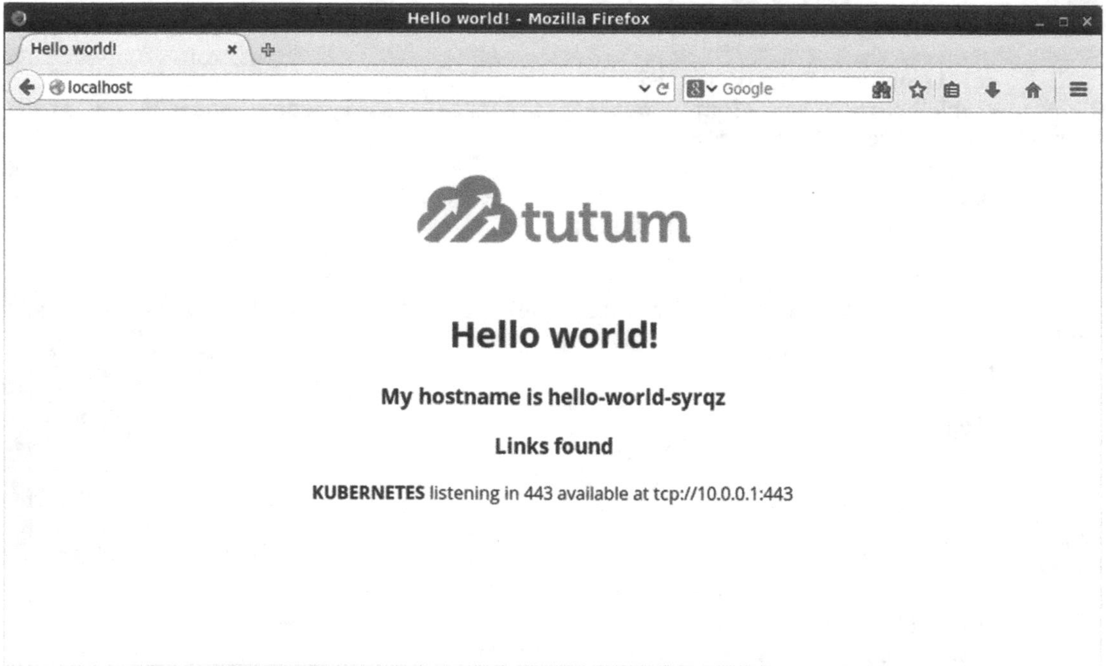
Hello world! - Mozilla Firefox
Hello world!
localhost
Google
tutum
Hello world!
My hostname is hello-world-syrqz
Links found
KUBERNETES listening in 443 available at tcp://10.0.0.1:443

Figure 2-10. *Invoking the Hello-World Application in a Browser*

Scaling the Application

A Replication Controller was created by default when we created the `hello-world` application with replicas set as 1. Next, we shall scale up the number of Pods to 4. The `kubectl scale` command is used to scale a Replication Controller. Run the following command to scale up the Replication Controller `hello-world` to 4.

```
kubectl scale rc hello-world --replicas=4
```

Subsequently, list the Pods using the following command.

```
kubectl get pods
```

The additional Pods get listed but some of the new Pods could be listed in various states such as running but not ready, or image ready and container creating as shown in Figure 2-11.

```
ubuntu@ip-172-30-1-235:~$ kubectl scale rc hello-world --replicas=4
scaled
ubuntu@ip-172-30-1-235:~$ kubectl get pods
NAME                    READY     STATUS
          RESTARTS      AGE
hello-world-53evr       0/1       Running
          0             10s
hello-world-ju6d7       0/1       Image: tutum/hello-world is ready, container is
 creating   0           10s
hello-world-syrqz       1/1       Running
          0             1h
hello-world-yyjme       0/1       Running
          0             10s
k8s-master-127.0.0.1    3/3       Running
          0             1h
ubuntu@ip-172-30-1-235:~$
```

Figure 2-11. *Scaling the Cluster of Pods with the Replication Controller*

After a few seconds run the same command again to list the Pods.

```
kubectl get pods
```

If the Pods have started all the Pods are listed with STATUS- > Running and READY state 1/1 as shown in Figure 2-12. Scaling to 4 replicas does not create 4 new Pods, but the total number of Pods is scaled to 4 and the single Pod created initially is included in the new scaled replicas of 4.

```
ubuntu@ip-172-30-1-235:~$ kubectl get pods
NAME                    READY     STATUS    RESTARTS   AGE
hello-world-53evr       1/1       Running   0          35s
hello-world-ju6d7       1/1       Running   0          35s
hello-world-syrqz       1/1       Running   0          1h
hello-world-yyjme       1/1       Running   0          35s
k8s-master-127.0.0.1    3/3       Running   0          1h
ubuntu@ip-172-30-1-235:~$
```

Figure 2-12. *Listing all the Pods as Running and Ready*

Describe the hello-world Service using the following command.

```
kubectl describe svc hello-world
```

The Service name, label/s, selector, type, IP, and Endpoints get listed as shown in Figure 2-13. The Service may be invoked using the Endpoints for the various Pod replicas.

```
ubuntu@ip-172-30-1-235:~$ kubectl describe svc hello-world
Name:                   hello-world
Namespace:              default
Labels:                 run=hello-world
Selector:               run=hello-world
Type:                   LoadBalancer
IP:                     10.0.0.57
Port:                   <unnamed>       8080/TCP
NodePort:               <unnamed>       31236/TCP
Endpoints:              172.17.0.2:8080,172.17.0.3:8080,172.17.0.4:8080 + 1 more
...
Session Affinity:       None
No events.

ubuntu@ip-172-30-1-235:~$ 
```

Figure 2-13. *Describing the Service hello-world*

As discussed previously, set up SSH tunneling with port forwarding for the newly added endpoints. The following command sets up a SSH tunnel with port forwarding from localhost port 8081 to 172.17.0.3:80 on the Amazon EC2 instance.

```
ssh -i "docker.pem" -f -nNT -L 8081:172.17.0.3:80 ubuntu@ec2-52-91-200-41.compute-1.
amazonaws.com
```

Subsequently invoke the hello-world application in a browser on a local machine with url http://localhost:8081 to display the application output as shown in Figure 2-14.

Hello world! - Mozilla Firefox
Hello world!
localhost:8081
Google

tutum
Hello world!
My hostname is hello-world-yyjme
Links found
HELLO_WORLD listening in 8080 available at tcp://10.0.0.57:8080
KUBERNETES listening in 443 available at tcp://10.0.0.1:443

Figure 2-14. *Invoking an Application in a Local Browser*

Similarly the following command from a local machine sets up a SSH tunnel with port forwarding from `localhost` port 8082 to `172.17.0.4:80` on the Amazon EC2 instance.

```
ssh -i "docker.pem" -f -nNT -L 8082:172.17.0.4:80 ubuntu@ec2-52-91-200-41.compute-1.
amazonaws.com
```

Subsequently invoke the `hello-world` application using url `http://localhost:8082` to display the application output as shown in Figure 2-15.

Hello world!

My hostname is hello-world-53evr

Links found

HELLO_WORLD listening in 8080 available at tcp://10.0.0.57:8080
KUBERNETES listening in 443 available at tcp://10.0.0.1:443

Figure 2-15. Invoking the second Service Endpoint in a Local Browser

Deleting a Replication Controller

The Replication Controller `hello-world` may be deleted with the following command.

```
kubectl delete rc hello-world
```

The Replication Controller gets deleted as shown in Figure 2-16. Subsequently invoke the following command to list the Replication Controllers.

```
ubuntu@ip-172-30-1-235:~$ kubectl delete rc hello-world
replicationcontrollers/hello-world
ubuntu@ip-172-30-1-235:~$ kubectl get rc
CONTROLLER   CONTAINER(S)   IMAGE(S)   SELECTOR   REPLICAS
```

Figure 2-16. Deleting a Replication Controller

```
kubectl get rc
```

The `hello-world` Replication Controller does not get listed as shown in Figure 2-16.

Deleting a Replication Controller deletes the Replication Controller and the Pods associated with the Replication Controller but does not delete the Service representing the Replication Controller. The `kubectl get services` command still lists the Service as shown in Figure 2-17.

```
ubuntu@ip-172-30-1-235:~$ kubectl get services
NAME          LABELS                                     SELECTOR           IP(S)
    PORT(S)
hello-world   run=hello-world                            run=hello-world    10.0.0
.57    8080/TCP
kubernetes    component=apiserver,provider=kubernetes    <none>             10.0.0
.1     443/TCP
```

Figure 2-17. *Deleting a Replication Controller does not delete the Service*

Deleting a Service

To delete the Service `hello-world` run the following command.

```
kubectl delete svc hello-world
```

Subsequently invoke the following command to list the Services.

```
kubectl get services
```

The output from the preceding two commands is shown in Figure 2-18 and does not list the `hello-world` Service.

```
ubuntu@ip-172-30-1-235:~$ kubectl delete svc hello-world
services/hello-world
ubuntu@ip-172-30-1-235:~$ kubectl get services
NAME          LABELS                                     SELECTOR   IP(S)        POR
T(S)
kubernetes    component=apiserver,provider=kubernetes    <none>     10.0.0.1     443
/TCP
ubuntu@ip-172-30-1-235:~$ █
```

Figure 2-18. *Deleting the hello-world Service*

Creating an Application Declaratively

Next, we shall create the same hello-world application declaratively using definition files for a Pod, Service, and Replication Controller. The definition files may be configured in YAML or JSON. We have used YAML initially and also discussed the JSON alternative later.

Creating a Pod Definition

Create a `hello-world.yaml` file and specify a definition for a Pod in the file. For the `hello-world` application the following definition is used in which the `apiVersion` mapping is for the API schema version (`v1`), `kind` mapping is the resource and set to `Pod`. The metadata mapping specifies the Pod's metadata and sets the name to `hello-world` (arbitrary). The `spec` mapping specifies the Pod behavior. The `spec->containers` mapping specifies a collection of images to run. The `hello-world.yaml` specifies a single container for image `tutum/hello-world`. Container name is set to `hello-world` and container `ports` mapping is a list of ports with a single `containerPort` mapping for 8080 port.

```
apiVersion: v1
kind: Pod
metadata:
name: hello-world
spec:
  containers:
    -
      image: tutum/hello-world
      name: hello-world
      ports:
        -containerPort: 8080
```

The preceding is equivalent to the following command.

```
kubectl run hello-world --image=tutum/hello-world --port=8080
```

Only a few of the schema elements have been used in the `hello-world.yaml`. For the complete Pod schema refer `http://kubernetes.io/v1.1/docs/api-reference/v1/definitions.html#_v1_pod`.

Next, create the `hello-world` application using the `hello-world.yaml` definition file with the following `kubectl create` command. The `-validate` option validates the Pod definition file. A YAML lint validator (`http://www.yamllint.com/`) may be used to validate the YAML syntax in the `hello-world.yaml` . The syntax validation does not validate if the definition file conforms to the Pod schema.

```
kubectl create -f hello-world.yaml --validate
```

A Pod called `hello-world` gets created as shown in Figure 2-19.

```
ubuntu@ip-172-30-1-235:~$ kubectl create -f hello-world.yaml  --validate
pods/hello-world
```

Figure 2-19. *Creating a Pod using a Definition File*

List the Pods with the following command, which is the same regardless of how a Pod has been created.

```
kubectl get pods
```

The `hello-world` Pod gets listed as shown in Figure 2-20. Initially, the Pod may not be READY->1/1. A READY column value of "0/1" implies that 0 of 1 containers in the Pod are ready.

```
ubuntu@ip-172-30-1-235:~$ kubectl get pods
NAME                     READY     STATUS    RESTARTS   AGE
hello-world              0/1       Running   0          11s
k8s-master-127.0.0.1     3/3       Running   0          1h
ubuntu@ip-172-30-1-235:~$ kubectl get pods
NAME                     READY     STATUS    RESTARTS   AGE
hello-world              0/1       Running   0          18s
k8s-master-127.0.0.1     3/3       Running   0          1h
ubuntu@ip-172-30-1-235:~$
```

Figure 2-20. *Listing the Pods soon after creating the Pods*

Run the same command again after a few more seconds.

```
kubectl get pods
```

The `hello-world` Pod gets listed with STATUS as "Running" and READY state as "1/1," which implies that 1 of 1 containers in the Pod are ready, as shown in Figure 2-21.

```
ubuntu@ip-172-30-1-235:~$ kubectl create -f hello-world.yaml  --validate
pods/hello-world
ubuntu@ip-172-30-1-235:~$ kubectl get pods
NAME                     READY     STATUS    RESTARTS   AGE
hello-world              0/1       Running   0          11s
k8s-master-127.0.0.1     3/3       Running   0          1h
ubuntu@ip-172-30-1-235:~$ kubectl get pods
NAME                     READY     STATUS    RESTARTS   AGE
hello-world              0/1       Running   0          18s
k8s-master-127.0.0.1     3/3       Running   0          1h
ubuntu@ip-172-30-1-235:~$ kubectl get pods
NAME                     READY     STATUS    RESTARTS   AGE
hello-world              1/1       Running   0          43s
k8s-master-127.0.0.1     3/3       Running   0          1h
ubuntu@ip-172-30-1-235:~$
```

Figure 2-21. *Listing the Pod as Ready and Running*

Describe the `hello-world` Pod with the following command.

```
kubectl describe pod hello-world
```

The output from the preceding command is shown in Figure 2-22.

***Figure 2-22.** Describing the hello-world Pod*

Invoke the `hello-world` Pod application using the IP `172.17.0.2`.

```
curl 172.17.0.2
```

The HTML output from the `hello-world` application gets listed as shown in Figure 2-23.

```
ubuntu@ip-172-30-1-235: ~
File  Edit  View  Search  Terminal  Help
ubuntu@ip-172-30-1-235:~$ curl 172.17.0.2
<html>
<head>
        <title>Hello world!</title>
        <link href='http://fonts.googleapis.com/css?family=Open+Sans:400,700' re
l='stylesheet' type='text/css'>
        <style>
        body {
                background-color: white;
                text-align: center;
                padding: 50px;
                font-family: "Open Sans","Helvetica Neue",Helvetica,Arial,sans-s
erif;
        }

        #logo {
                margin-bottom: 40px;
        }
        </style>
</head>
<body>
        <img id="logo" src="logo.png" />
        <h1>Hello world!</h1>
        <h3>My hostname is hello-world</h3>                     <h3>Links found<
/h3>
                                        <b>HELLO_WORLD</b> listening in 8080 ava
ilable at tcp://10.0.0.57:8080<br />
                                                <b>KUBERNETES</b> listening in 4
43 available at tcp://10.0.0.1:443<br />
                                        </body>
</html>
ubuntu@ip-172-30-1-235:~$ █
```

Figure 2-23. *Invoking the hello-world Application with curl*

Set up port forwarding from a local machine to the IP address of the `hello-world` Pod.

```
ssh -i "docker.pem" -f -nNT -L 80:172.17.0.2:80 ubuntu@ec2-52-91-200-41.compute-1.amazonaws.com
```

Subsequently invoke the url `http://localhost:80` in a browser on a local machine to display the HTML output from the application as shown in Figure 2-24. The default Hypertext transfer protocol port being 80, has been be omitted from the URL, as shown in Figure 2-24.

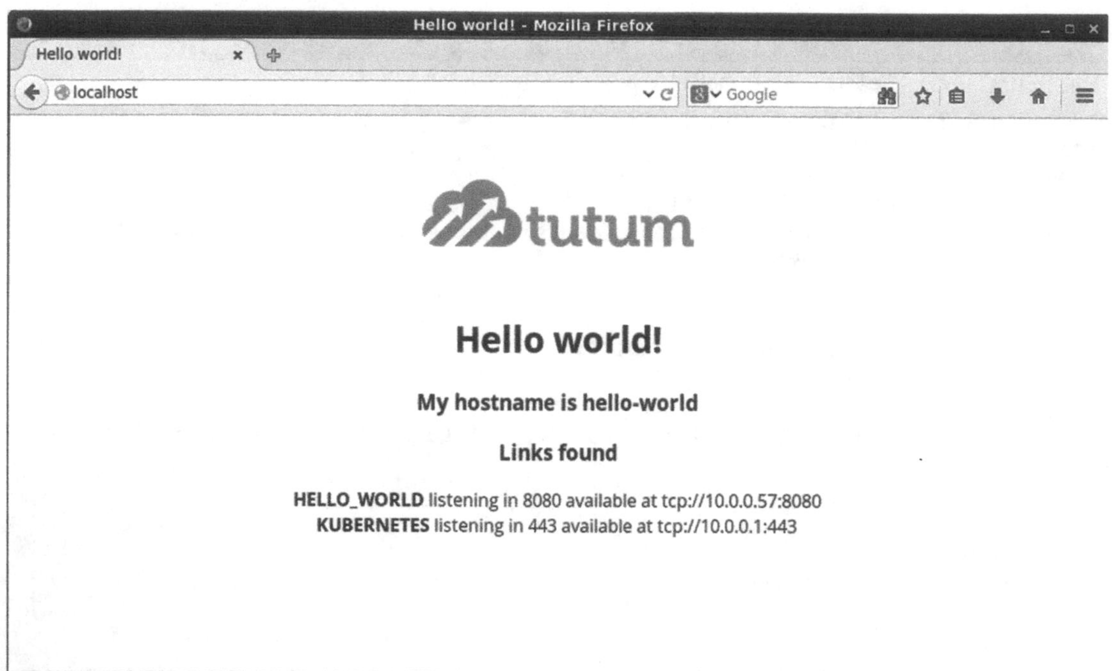
Hello world! - Mozilla Firefox
Hello world!
localhost
Google
tutum
Hello world!
My hostname is hello-world
Links found
HELLO_WORLD listening in 8080 available at tcp://10.0.0.57:8080
KUBERNETES listening in 443 available at tcp://10.0.0.1:443

Figure 2-24. *Invoking the hello-world Application in a Browser on a local machine*

Creating a Service Definition

We created a Pod definition file and started a single Pod, but the Pod is not associated with any Service or Replication Controller. External clients have to access the Pod directly and are not able to scale the application with just a single unassociated Pod. Create a Service definition file `hello-world-service.yaml` as listed below. If copying and pasting YAML files listed in this chapter and other chapters it is recommended to use the YAML Lint (`http://www.yamllint.com/`) to format the files before using in an application.

```
apiVersion: v1
kind: Service
metadata:
  labels:
    app: hello-world
  name: hello-world
spec:
  ports:
    -
      name: http
      port: 80
      targetPort: http
  selector:
    app: hello-world
  type: LoadBalancer
```

The main mappings of the Service definition file are `kind`, `metadata`, and `spec`. The `kind` is set to `Service` to indicate a Kubernetes Service. The label app and the `name` constitute the metadata. The `spec` mapping includes a `ports` mapping for port 80 with name `http`. Optionally a `targetPort` may be set, which defaults to the same value as port. The `selector` is the main mapping in the spec and specifies a mapping to be used for selecting the Pods to expose via the Service. The `app:hello-world` selector implies that all Pods with label app=`hello-world` are selected. The definition file may be created in the vi editor and saved with the `:wq` command as shown in Figure 2-25.

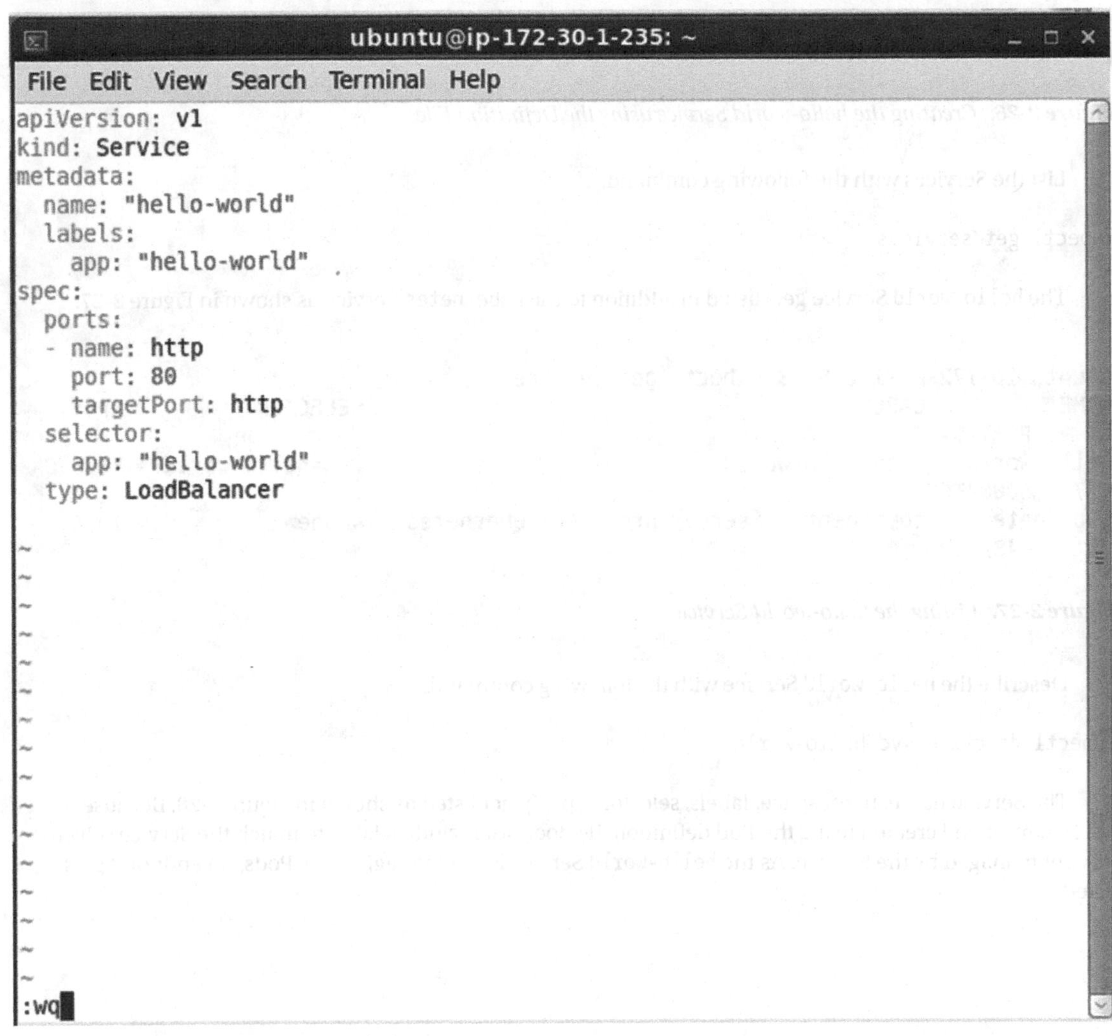

Figure 2-25. *Service Definition File hello-world-service.yaml*

A complete reference to the Kubernetes Service schema is available at http://kubernetes.io/v1.1/docs/api-reference/v1/definitions.html#_v1_service.

Create a Service using the definition file with the kubectl create command.

```
kubectl create -f hello-world-service.yaml
```

The hello-world Service gets created as shown in Figure 2-26.

```
ubuntu@ip-172-30-1-235:~$ kubectl create -f hello-world-service.yaml
services/hello-world
```

***Figure 2-26.** Creating the hello-world Service using the Definition File*

List the Services with the following command.

```
kubectl get services
```

The hello-world Service gets listed in addition to the kubernetes Service as shown in Figure 2-27.

```
ubuntu@ip-172-30-1-235:~$ kubectl get services
NAME           LABELS                                    SELECTOR            IP(S)
      PORT(S)
hello-world    run=hello-world                           run=hello-world     10.0.0
.57    8080/TCP
kubernetes     component=apiserver,provider=kubernetes   <none>              10.0.0
.1     443/TCP
```

***Figure 2-27.** Listing the hello-world Service*

Describe the hello-world Service with the following command.

```
kubectl describe svc hello-world
```

The Service name, namespace, labels, selector, type, Ip get listed as shown in Figure 2-28. Because the hello-world Pod created using the Pod definition file does not include a label to match the Service selector, it is not managed by the Service. As the hello-world Service is not managing any Pods, no endpoint gets listed.

```
ubuntu@ip-172-30-1-235:~$ kubectl create -f hello-world-service.yaml
services/hello-world
ubuntu@ip-172-30-1-235:~$ kubectl get services
NAME          LABELS                                    SELECTOR          IP(S)
      PORT(S)
hello-world   app=hello-world                           app=hello-world   10.0.0
.206   80/TCP
kubernetes    component=apiserver,provider=kubernetes   <none>            10.0.0
.1     443/TCP
ubuntu@ip-172-30-1-235:~$ kubectl describe service hello-world
Name:                   hello-world
Namespace:              default
Labels:                 app=hello-world
Selector:               app=hello-world
Type:                   LoadBalancer
IP:                     10.0.0.206
Port:                   http    80/TCP
NodePort:               http    32600/TCP
Endpoints:              <none>
Session Affinity:       None
No events.

ubuntu@ip-172-30-1-235:~$
```

Figure 2-28. *Describing the hello-world Service*

Creating a Replication Controller Definition

Next, we shall create a Replication Controller and label the Replication Controller to match the selector of the Service created previously. Create a Service definition file `hello-rc.yaml`. The kind mapping of a Replication Controller is `ReplicationController`. The `replicas`' sub-mapping in the `spec` mapping is set to 2 to create two replicas from the Pod also specified in the `spec`. At least one of the labels in the template- > metadata- > labels must match the Service selector in the Service definition file for the Pod to be exposed by the Service. As the Service selector in the `hello-world` Service is `app:hello-world` add the `app:hello-world` label to the Replication Controller template. The app:hello-world setting in YAML translates to app=hello-world. The template may define one or more containers to be included in the Pod created from the Replication Controller. We have included container definition for only one container for image `tutum/hello-world`. The `hello-rc.yaml` is listed below. A YAML lint (`http://www.yamllint.com/`) may be used to validate the YAML syntax.

```
apiVersion: v1
kind: ReplicationController
metadata:
  name: hello-world
spec:
  replicas: 2
  template:
    metadata:
      labels:
        app: hello-world
```

```
spec:
  containers:
    -
      image: tutum/hello-world
      name: hello-world
      ports:
        -
          containerPort: 8080
          name: http
```

A complete schema for the Replication Controller is available at `http://kubernetes.io/v1.1/docs/api-reference/v1/definitions.html#_v1_replicationcontroller`.

Create the Replication Controller using the definition file with the `kubectl create` command, the same command that was used to create a Pod and a Service.

```
kubectl create -f hello-rc.yaml
```

Subsequently run the following command to list the Replication Controllers.

```
kubectl get rc
```

A `hello-world` Replication Controller gets created and gets listed as shown in Figure 2-29. The number of replicas are listed as 2 as specified in the definition file.

```
ubuntu@ip-172-30-1-235:~$ kubectl create -f hello-rc.yaml
replicationcontrollers/hello-world
ubuntu@ip-172-30-1-235:~$ kubectl get rc
CONTROLLER    CONTAINER(S)   IMAGE(S)            SELECTOR          REPLICAS
hello-world   hello-world    tutum/hello-world   app=hello-world   2
```

***Figure 2-29.** Creating a Replication Controller*

List the Pods created with the Replication Controller with the following command.

```
kubectl get pods
```

The two Pods created from the definition file get listed as shown in Figure 2-30. The Pod created the Pod definition file also gets listed but is not associated with the Replication Controller. Initially some or all of the new Pods may be listed as not ready as indicated by the 0/1 value in the READY column for one of the Pods in Figure 2-30.

```
ubuntu@ip-172-30-1-235:~$ kubectl get pods
NAME                    READY     STATUS    RESTARTS   AGE
hello-world             1/1       Running   0          7m
hello-world-7p6mf       1/1       Running   0          10s
hello-world-husbv       0/1       Running   0          10s
k8s-master-127.0.0.1    3/3       Running   0          1h
ubuntu@ip-172-30-1-235:~$
```

***Figure 2-30.** Listing the Pods soon after creating a Replication Controller*

Invoke the same command again to list the Pods after a few more seconds.

```
kubectl get pods
```

All the Pods get listed as READY- > 1/1 and Running as shown in Figure 2-31.

```
ubuntu@ip-172-30-1-235:~$ kubectl get pods
NAME                     READY     STATUS    RESTARTS   AGE
hello-world              1/1       Running   0          7m
hello-world-7p6mf        1/1       Running   0          34s
hello-world-husbv        1/1       Running   0          34s
k8s-master-127.0.0.1     3/3       Running   0          1h
ubuntu@ip-172-30-1-235:~$
```

Figure 2-31. *Listing all the Pods as Running and Ready*

To describe the hello-world Service run the following command.

```
kubectl describe service hello-world
```

The Service detail including the Endpoints get listed as shown in Figure 2-32. The service selector is app = hello-world and the service endpoints are 172.17.0.3:8080 and 172.17.0.4:8080.

```
ubuntu@ip-172-30-1-235:~$ kubectl describe service hello-world
Name:                   hello-world
Namespace:              default
Labels:                 app=hello-world
Selector:               app=hello-world
Type:                   LoadBalancer
IP:                     10.0.0.206
Port:                   http    80/TCP
NodePort:               http    32600/TCP
Endpoints:              172.17.0.3:8080,172.17.0.4:8080
Session Affinity:       None
No events.

ubuntu@ip-172-30-1-235:~$
```

Figure 2-32. *Describing the Service hello-world*

All the preceding commands to create the hello-world Replication Controller, list its Pods and endpoints association with the hello-world Service shown in Figure 2-33.

```
ubuntu@ip-172-30-1-235: ~
File  Edit  View  Search  Terminal  Help

ubuntu@ip-172-30-1-235:~$ kubectl create -f hello-rc.yaml
replicationcontrollers/hello-world
ubuntu@ip-172-30-1-235:~$ kubectl get rc
CONTROLLER    CONTAINER(S)   IMAGE(S)             SELECTOR          REPLICAS
hello-world   hello-world    tutum/hello-world    app=hello-world   2
ubuntu@ip-172-30-1-235:~$ kubectl get pods
NAME                    READY     STATUS     RESTARTS    AGE
hello-world             1/1       Running    0           7m
hello-world-7p6mf       1/1       Running    0           10s
hello-world-husbv       0/1       Running    0           10s
k8s-master-127.0.0.1    3/3       Running    0           1h
ubuntu@ip-172-30-1-235:~$ kubectl get pods
NAME                    READY     STATUS     RESTARTS    AGE
hello-world             1/1       Running    0           7m
hello-world-7p6mf       1/1       Running    0           34s
hello-world-husbv       1/1       Running    0           34s
k8s-master-127.0.0.1    3/3       Running    0           1h
ubuntu@ip-172-30-1-235:~$ kubectl describe service hello-world
Name:                   hello-world
Namespace:              default
Labels:                 app=hello-world
Selector:               app=hello-world
Type:                   LoadBalancer
IP:                     10.0.0.206
Port:                   http    80/TCP
NodePort:               http    32600/TCP
Endpoints:              172.17.0.3:8080,172.17.0.4:8080
Session Affinity:       None
No events.

ubuntu@ip-172-30-1-235:~$
```

Figure 2-33. *Summary of Commands to create a Replication Controller*

Invoking the Hello-World Application

The Pods associated with the hello-world Replication Controller and Service by the same name may be invoked using the Service endpoints as listed in the Service description in Figure 2-33. For example, invoke the `172.17.0.3` endpoint with the following `curl` command.

```
curl 172.17.0.3
```

The HTML output from the Pod gets output as shown in Figure 2-34.

```
ubuntu@ip-172-30-1-235: ~
File  Edit  View  Search  Terminal  Help
ubuntu@ip-172-30-1-235:~$ curl 172.17.0.3
<html>
<head>
        <title>Hello world!</title>
        <link href='http://fonts.googleapis.com/css?family=Open+Sans:400,700' re
l='stylesheet' type='text/css'>
        <style>
        body {
                background-color: white;
                text-align: center;
                padding: 50px;
                font-family: "Open Sans","Helvetica Neue",Helvetica,Arial,sans-s
erif;
        }

        #logo {
                margin-bottom: 40px;
        }
        </style>
</head>
<body>
        <img id="logo" src="logo.png" />
        <h1>Hello world!</h1>
        <h3>My hostname is hello-world-7p6mf</h3>                       <h3>Link
s found</h3>
                                                <b>KUBERNETES</b> listening in 443 avail
able at tcp://10.0.0.1:443<br />
                                                        <b>HELLO_WORLD</b> listening in
80 available at tcp://10.0.0.206:80<br />
                                        </body>
</html>
ubuntu@ip-172-30-1-235:~$
```

Figure 2-34. *HTML Output from invoking the hello-world Application with curl*

Similarly, invoke the 172.17.0.4 endpoint with the following curl command.

```
curl 172.17.0.4
```

The HTML output from the other Pod gets output as shown in Figure 2-35.

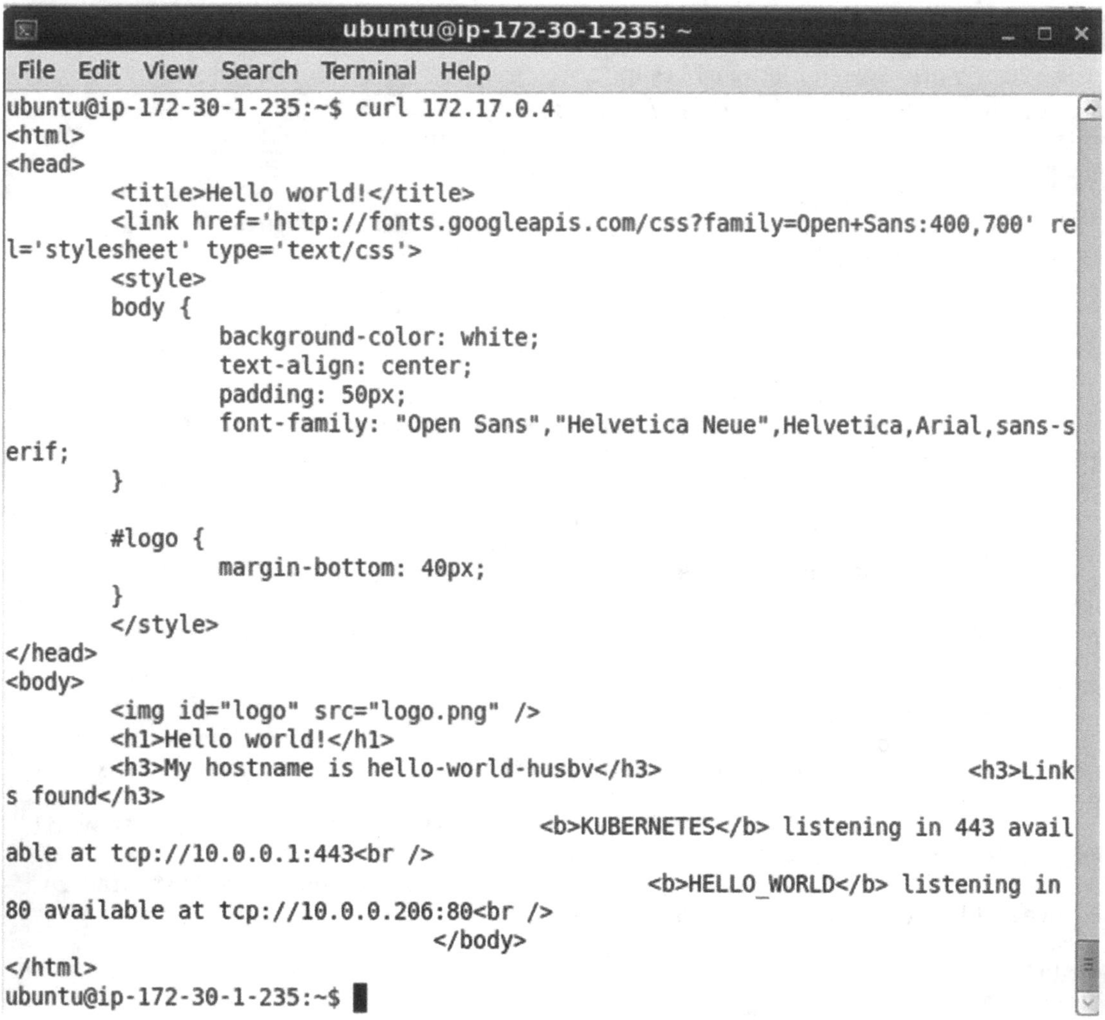

```
ubuntu@ip-172-30-1-235: ~
File  Edit  View  Search  Terminal  Help
ubuntu@ip-172-30-1-235:~$ curl 172.17.0.4
<html>
<head>
        <title>Hello world!</title>
        <link href='http://fonts.googleapis.com/css?family=Open+Sans:400,700' re
l='stylesheet' type='text/css'>
        <style>
        body {
                background-color: white;
                text-align: center;
                padding: 50px;
                font-family: "Open Sans","Helvetica Neue",Helvetica,Arial,sans-s
erif;
        }

        #logo {
                margin-bottom: 40px;
        }
        </style>
</head>
<body>
        <img id="logo" src="logo.png" />
        <h1>Hello world!</h1>
        <h3>My hostname is hello-world-husbv</h3>                        <h3>Link
s found</h3>
                                            <b>KUBERNETES</b> listening in 443 avail
able at tcp://10.0.0.1:443<br />
                                                    <b>HELLO_WORLD</b> listening in
80 available at tcp://10.0.0.206:80<br />
                                    </body>
</html>
ubuntu@ip-172-30-1-235:~$ █
```

Figure 2-35. *Invoking another Service Endpoint with curl*

To invoke the Service endpoints in a browser on a local machine configure local port forwarding for the Service endpoints.

```
ssh -i "docker.pem" -f -nNT -L 8081:172.17.0.3:8080 ubuntu@ec2-52-91-200-41.compute-1.
amazonaws.com
ssh -i "docker.pem" -f -nNT -L 8082:172.17.0.4:8080 ubuntu@ec2-52-91-200-41.compute-1.
amazonaws.com
```

Subsequently invoke the `localhost:8081` URL in a browser on a local machine as shown in Figure 2-36 to display the HTML output from the Pod at endpoint `172.17.0.3:8080`.

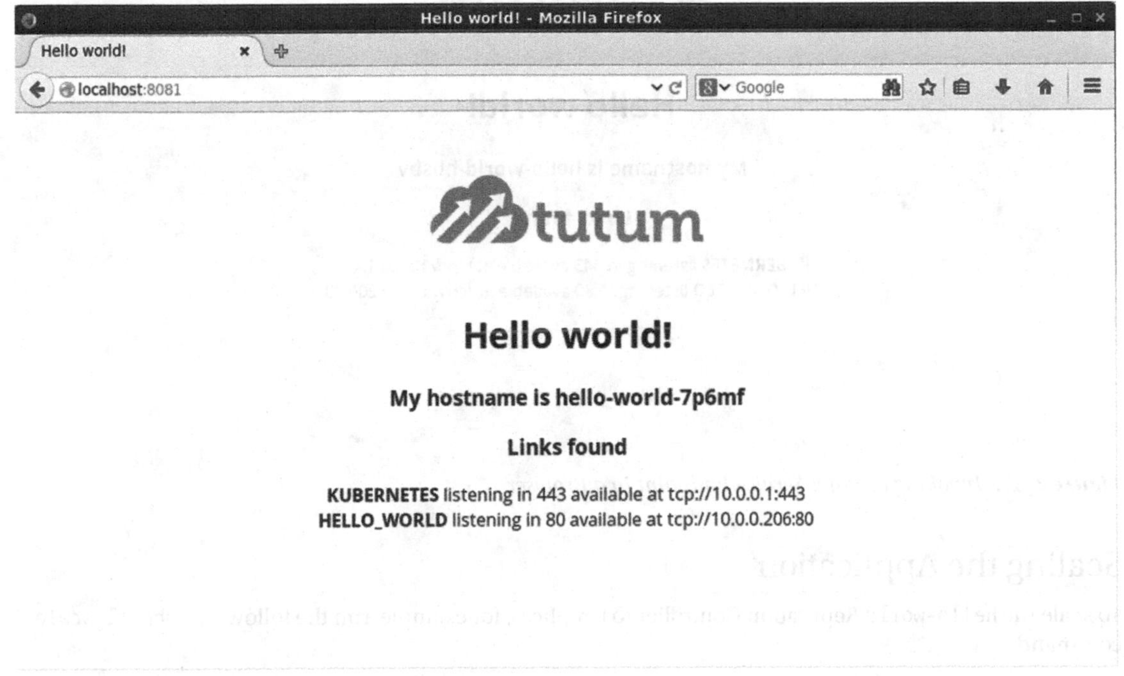
Hello world! - Mozilla Firefox
Hello world!
localhost:8081
Google
tutum
Hello world!
My hostname is hello-world-7p6mf
Links found
KUBERNETES listening in 443 available at tcp://10.0.0.1:443
HELLO_WORLD listening in 80 available at tcp://10.0.0.206:80

***Figure 2-36.** Invoking the hello-world Application in a Local machine Browser with its Service Endpoint*

Similarly invoke the `localhost:8082` URL in a browser on a local machine as shown in Figure 2-37 to display the HTML output from the Pod at endpoint `172.17.0.4:8080`.

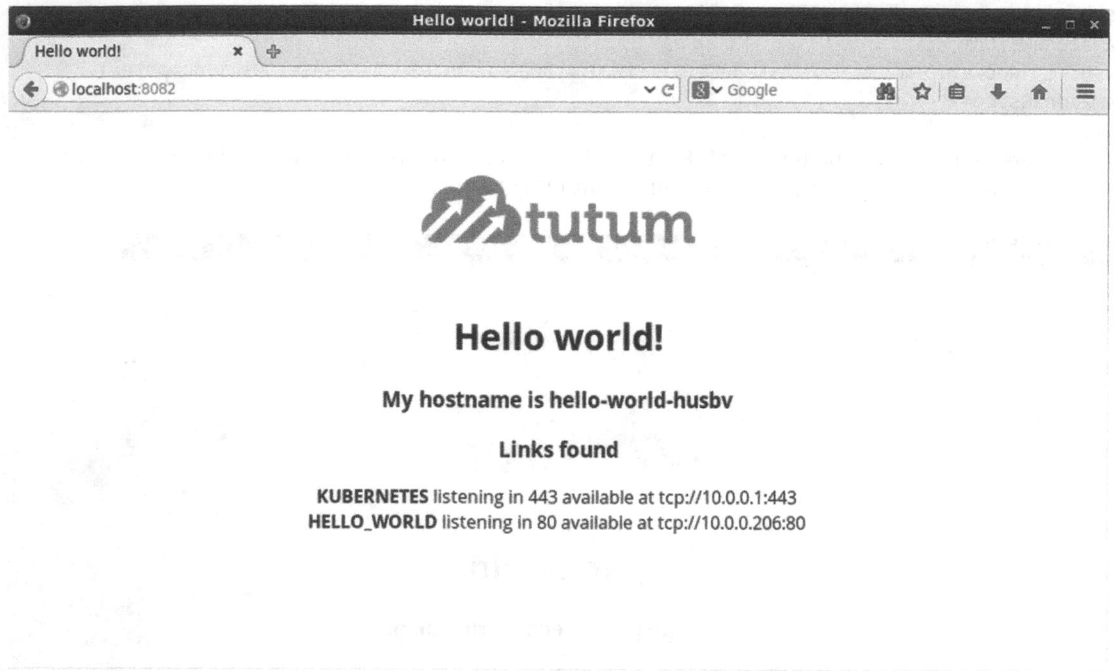
Hello world! - Mozilla Firefox
Hello world!
localhost:8082
Google
tutum
Hello world!
My hostname is hello-world-husbv
Links found
KUBERNETES listening in 443 available at tcp://10.0.0.1:443
HELLO_WORLD listening in 80 available at tcp://10.0.0.206:80

Figure 2-37. *Invoking another Service Endpoint in a Browser*

Scaling the Application

To scale the `hello-world` Replication Controller to 6 replicas, for example, run the following `kubectl scale` command.

```
kubectl scale rc hello-world --replicas=6
```

An output of "scaled" as shown in Figure 2-38 indicates the Replication Controller has been scaled.

```
ubuntu@ip-172-30-1-235:~$ kubectl scale rc hello-world --replicas=6
scaled
```

Figure 2-38. *Scaling an Application*

The number of Pods for the hello-world Replication Controller increases when the Replication Controller is scaled up to 6. To list the Pods run the following command.

```
kubectl get pods
```

Six Pods get listed in addition to the hello-world Pod created initially using a Pod definition file as shown in Figure 2-39. The preceding command may have to be run more than once to list all the Pods with STATUS as Running and READY state as 1/1. The hello-world Pod is not associated with the hello-world Replication Controller as it does not include a label that matches the selector label (same as template label) in the Replication Controller.

```
ubuntu@ip-172-30-1-235:~$ kubectl get pods
NAME                    READY     STATUS    RESTARTS   AGE
hello-world             1/1       Running   0          14m
hello-world-3ad39       1/1       Running   0          21s
hello-world-7p6mf       1/1       Running   0          7m
hello-world-gpoy5       1/1       Running   0          21s
hello-world-gr8j8       0/1       Running   0          21s
hello-world-hujw9       1/1       Running   0          21s
hello-world-husbv       1/1       Running   0          7m
k8s-master-127.0.0.1    3/3       Running   0          2h
ubuntu@ip-172-30-1-235:~$ kubectl get pods
NAME                    READY     STATUS    RESTARTS   AGE
hello-world             1/1       Running   0          14m
hello-world-3ad39       1/1       Running   0          30s
hello-world-7p6mf       1/1       Running   0          7m
hello-world-gpoy5       1/1       Running   0          30s
hello-world-gr8j8       1/1       Running   0          30s
hello-world-hujw9       1/1       Running   0          30s
hello-world-husbv       1/1       Running   0          7m
k8s-master-127.0.0.1    3/3       Running   0          2h
ubuntu@ip-172-30-1-235:~$
```

Figure 2-39. *Listing Pods after Scaling*

In the preceding example we scaled *up* the Replication Controller, but the kubectl scale command may also be used to scale *down* the Replication Controller. As an example, scale down the hello-world Replication Controller to 2 replicas.

```
kubectl scale rc hello-world --replicas=2
```

Subsequently list the Pods.

```
kubectl get pods
```

The number of replicas gets listed as 2 in addition to the hello-world Pod as shown in Figure 2-40.

```
ubuntu@ip-172-30-1-235:~$ kubectl scale rc hello-world --replicas=2
scaled
ubuntu@ip-172-30-1-235:~$ kubectl get pods
NAME                    READY     STATUS    RESTARTS   AGE
hello-world             1/1       Running   0          15m
hello-world-3ad39       1/1       Running   0          1m
hello-world-gr8j8       1/1       Running   0          1m
k8s-master-127.0.0.1    3/3       Running   0          2h
ubuntu@ip-172-30-1-235:~$
```

Figure 2-40. *Scaling Down to 2 Replicas*

Using JSON for the Resource Definitions

In the preceding section we used the YAML format to create the Pod, Service, and Replication Controller definition files. The definition files may be developed in JSON format instead. The YAMLToJSON utility (`http://yamltojson.com/`) may be used to convert from YAML to JSON and the JSON lint (`http://jsonlint.com/`) may be used to validate the JSON. A JSON to YAML utility is also available at `http://jsontoyaml.com/`. The JSON definition file `hello-world-service.json` for the `hello-world` Service is listed:

```
{
  "apiVersion": "v1",
  "kind": "Service",
  "metadata": {
    "name": "hello-world",
    "labels": {
      "app": "hello-world"
    }
  },
  "spec": {
    "ports": [
      {
        "name": "http",
        "port": 80,
        "targetPort": "http"
      }
    ],
    "selector": {
      "app": "hello-world"
    },
    "type": "LoadBalancer"
  }
}
```

Create a `hello-world-service.json` file using a vi editor and copy and paste the preceding listing to the file. Save the file using :wq as shown in Figure 2-41.

```
ubuntu@ip-172-30-1-163: ~
File  Edit  View  Search  Terminal  Help
{
  "apiVersion": "v1",
  "kind": "Service",
  "metadata": {
    "name": "hello-world",
    "labels": {
      "app": "hello-world"
    }
  },
  "spec": {
    "ports": [
      {
        "name": "http",
        "port": 80,
        "targetPort": "http"
      }
    ],
    "selector": {
      "app": "hello-world"
    },
    "type": "LoadBalancer"
  }
}
~
~
~
~
~
:wq
```

Figure 2-41. *Service Definition File in JSON Format*

Delete the hello-world Service and hello-world Replication Controller created previously. Run the following command to create a Service from the JSON format definition file.

```
kubectl create -f hello-world-service.json
```

The hello-world Service gets created as shown in Figure 2-42.

```
ubuntu@ip-172-30-1-163:~$ kubectl create -f hello-world-service.json
services/hello-world
```

Figure 2-42. *Creating a Service from the JSON Definition File*

Subsequently list all the Kubernetes Services.

```
kubectl get services
```

The hello-world Service gets listed as shown in Figure 2-43.

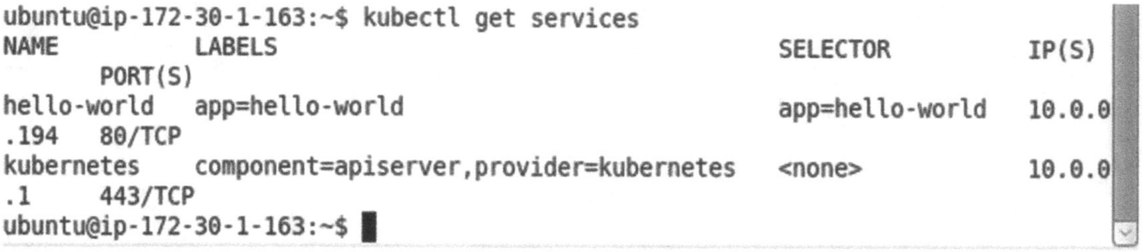

```
ubuntu@ip-172-30-1-163:~$ kubectl get services
NAME           LABELS                                    SELECTOR          IP(S)
        PORT(S)
hello-world    app=hello-world                           app=hello-world   10.0.0
.194    80/TCP
kubernetes     component=apiserver,provider=kubernetes   <none>            10.0.0
.1      443/TCP
ubuntu@ip-172-30-1-163:~$
```

Figure 2-43. *Listing the Services*

The JSON format version of the Replication Controller definition file, hello-rc.json, is as follows.

```
{
  "apiVersion": "v1",
  "kind": "ReplicationController",
  "metadata": {
    "name": "hello-world"
  },
  "spec": {
    "replicas": 2,
    "template": {
      "metadata": {
        "labels": {
          "app": "hello-world"
        }
      },
      "spec": {
        "containers": [
          {
            "image": "tutum/hello-world",
            "name": "hello-world",
            "ports": [
              {
                "containerPort": 8080,
                "name": "http"
              }
            ]
          }
        ]
      }
    }
  }
}
```

Create the hello-rc.json file in a vi editor and save the file with :wq as shown in Figure 2-44.

```
ubuntu@ip-172-30-1-163: ~
File Edit View Search Terminal Help
{
  "apiVersion": "v1",
  "kind": "ReplicationController",
  "metadata": {
    "name": "hello-world"
  },
  "spec": {
    "replicas": 2,
    "template": {
      "metadata": {
        "labels": {
          "app": "hello-world"
        }
      },
      "spec": {
        "containers": [
          {
            "image": "tutum/hello-world",
            "name": "hello-world",
            "ports": [
              {
                "containerPort": 8080,
                "name": "http"
              }
            ]
          }
        ]
      }
    }
  }
:wq
```

Figure 2-44. *Creating the hello-rc.json File in vi Editor*

Delete all previously created Pods and Replication Controllers. Run the following command to create the hello-world Replication Controller.

```
kubectl create -f hello-rc.json
```

The hello-world Replication Controller gets created as shown in Figure 2-45. Subsequently run the following command to list the Replication Controllers.

```
kubectl get rc
```

The hello-world Replication Controller gets listed as shown in Figure 2-45. List the Pods created by the Replication Controller using the following command.

```
kubectl get pods
```

Because replicas is set as 2 two Pods get listed as shown in Figure 2-45.

```
ubuntu@ip-172-30-1-163:~$ kubectl create -f hello-rc.json
replicationcontrollers/hello-world
ubuntu@ip-172-30-1-163:~$ kubectl get rc
CONTROLLER    CONTAINER(S)   IMAGE(S)             SELECTOR            REPLICAS
hello-world   hello-world    tutum/hello-world    app=hello-world     2
ubuntu@ip-172-30-1-163:~$ kubectl get pods
NAME                     READY     STATUS    RESTARTS   AGE
hello-world-hg7zs        1/1       Running   0          26s
hello-world-m7exj        1/1       Running   0          26s
k8s-master-127.0.0.1     3/3       Running   0          1h
ubuntu@ip-172-30-1-163:~$
```

***Figure 2-45.** Creating a Replication Controller from the JSON format Definition File*

Describe the hello-world Service with the following command.

```
kubectl describe svc hello-world
```

Because the label on the hello-world Replication Controller matches the Service selector, the two Pods created using the Replication Controller are represented by the Service and have endpoints in the Service as shown in Figure 2-46.

```
ubuntu@ip-172-30-1-163:~$ kubectl describe svc hello-world
Name:                   hello-world
Namespace:              default
Labels:                 app=hello-world
Selector:               app=hello-world
Type:                   LoadBalancer
IP:                     10.0.0.194
Port:                   http    80/TCP
NodePort:               http    32469/TCP
Endpoints:              172.17.0.2:8080,172.17.0.3:8080
Session Affinity:       None
No events.

ubuntu@ip-172-30-1-163:~$
```

***Figure 2-46.** Describing the hello-world Service*

Invoke a Service endpoint using a curl command as follows.

```
curl 172.17.0.2
```

The HTML output from the curl command gets output as shown in Figure 2-47.

```
ubuntu@ip-172-30-1-163: ~
File Edit View Search Terminal Help
ubuntu@ip-172-30-1-163:~$ curl 172.17.0.2
<html>
<head>
        <title>Hello world!</title>
        <link href='http://fonts.googleapis.com/css?family=Open+Sans:400,700' re
l='stylesheet' type='text/css'>
        <style>
        body {
                background-color: white;
                text-align: center;
                padding: 50px;
                font-family: "Open Sans","Helvetica Neue",Helvetica,Arial,sans-s
erif;
        }

        #logo {
                margin-bottom: 40px;
        }
        </style>
</head>
<body>
        <img id="logo" src="logo.png" />
        <h1>Hello world!</h1>
        <h3>My hostname is hello-world-hg7zs</h3>                        <h3>Link
s found</h3>
                                        <b>HELLO_WORLD</b> listening in 80 avail
able at tcp://10.0.0.194:80<br />
                                               <b>KUBERNETES</b> listening in 4
43 available at tcp://10.0.0.1:443<br />
                                  </body>
</html>
ubuntu@ip-172-30-1-163:~$
```

Figure 2-47. Invoking the hello-world Application with curl

Set up local port forwarding to a Service endpoint.

```
ssh -i "docker.pem" -f -nNT -L 80:172.17.0.2:8080 ubuntu@ec2-52-91-200-41.compute-1.
amazonaws.com
```

Subsequently invoke the Service endpoint in a browser in a local machine to display the HTML output as shown in Figure 2-48.

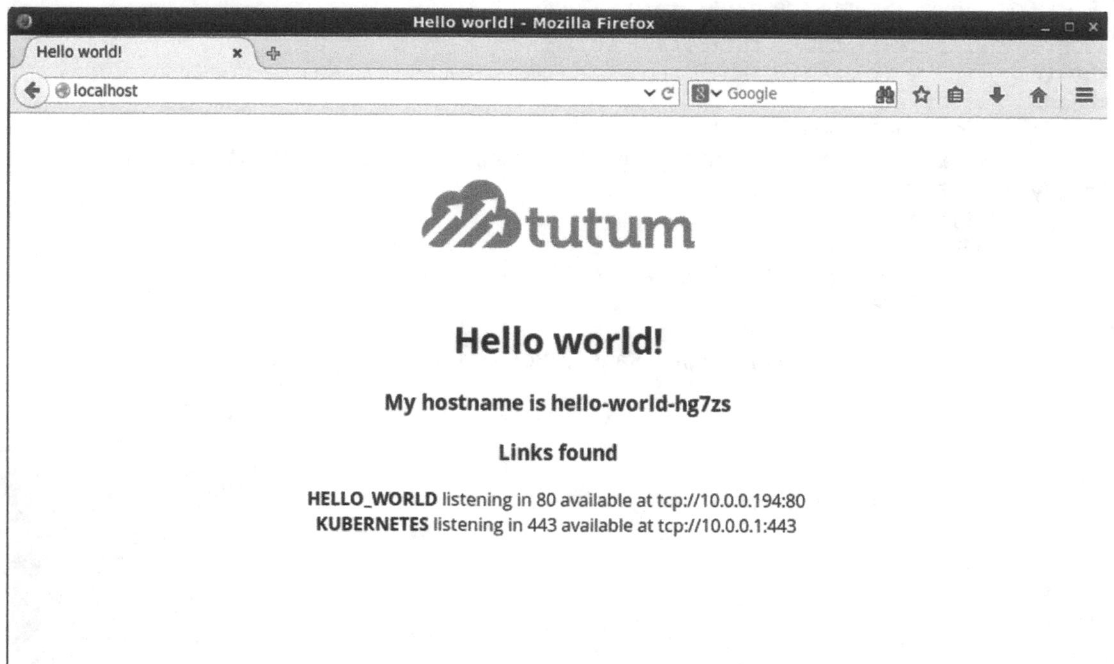
Hello world! - Mozilla Firefox
Hello world!
localhost
Google
tutum
Hello world!
My hostname is hello-world-hg7zs
Links found
HELLO_WORLD listening in 80 available at tcp://10.0.0.194:80
KUBERNETES listening in 443 available at tcp://10.0.0.1:443

Figure 2-48. *Displaying hello-world Application HTML in a Browser*

Summary

In this chapter we introduced the Kubernetes concepts such as Pod, Service, Replication Controller, Labels, and Selector. We also developed a hello-world application both imperatively on the command line, and declaratively using definition files. We discussed two different supported formats for the definition files: YAML and JSON. In the next chapter we shall discuss using environment variables in Pod definitions.

CHAPTER 3

Using Custom Commands and Environment Variables

Kubernetes orchestrates Docker containers, and the instructions to run for a Docker image are specified in the Dockerfile. The ENTRYPOINT instruction specifies the command to run, and the CMD instruction specifies the default arguments for the ENTRYPOINT command. Kubernetes provides two fields, "Command" and "Args", to be specified for a container image in a Pod definition to override the default settings of ENTRYPOINT and CMD. We shall discuss these fields in this chapter. We shall also discuss using environment variables in a Pod definition's container mapping with the "env" field mapping.

This chapter has the following sections.

Setting the Environment

The ENTRYPOINT and CMD Instructions

The Command and Args Fields in a Pod Definition

Environment Variables

Using the default ENTRYPOINT and CMD from a Docker Image

Overriding Both the ENTRYPOINT and CMD in a Docker Image

Specifying both the Executable and the Parameters in the Command Mapping

Specifying both the Executable and the Parameters in the Args Mapping

Setting the Environment

The following software is used in this chapter.

-Docker Engine (latest version)

-Kubernetes (version 1.01)

-Kubectl (version 1.01)

Install Docker engine, Kubernetes, and Kubectl as discussed in chapter 1. Start Docker Engine and verify its status with the following commands.

```
sudo service docker start
sudo service docker status
```


D. Vohra, *Kubernetes Microservices with Docker*, DOI 10.1007/978-1-4842-1907-2_3

The output shown in Figure 3-1 indicates that Docker is running.

```
ubuntu@ip-172-30-1-41:~$ sudo service docker start
start: Job is already running: docker
ubuntu@ip-172-30-1-41:~$ sudo service docker status
docker start/running, process 2699
ubuntu@ip-172-30-1-41:~$
```

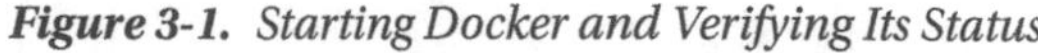

Figure 3-1. *Starting Docker and Verifying Its Status*

The ENTRYPOINT and CMD Instructions

The `ENTRYPOINT` in a Docker image's `Dockerfile` specifies the command to run when the image is run. The `ENTRYPOINT` has two forms discussed in Table 3-1. A `Dockerfile` may have only one `ENTRYPOINT`. If multiple `ENTRYPOINT`s are specified, the last `ENTRYPOINT` entry is run.

Table 3-1. *ENTRYPOINT Forms*

Form	Description	Format
Exec form	Runs an executable using the specified parameters. The exec form is the preferred form if environment variable substitution is not used. But if environment variable substitution is used the shell form must be used. The exec form does not perform any environment variable substitution.	ENTRYPOINT [“executable“", “param1”, “param2”]
Shell form	Runs the command in a shell and prevents any CMD or run command-line arguments to be used in conjunction with ENTRYPOINT. The shell form starts a shell with /bin/sh -c even though a shell is not invoked explicitly.	ENTRYPOINT command param1 param2

The `CMD` instruction specifies the args for the `ENTRYPOINT` command in exec form. The `CMD` has three forms as discussed in Table 3-2. A Dockerfile may have only one `CMD` entry. If multiple `CMD`s are specified the last `CMD` entry is run. The `CMD` instruction may include an executable.

Table 3-2. *CMD Forms*

Form	Description	Format
Exec form	The exec form specifies the command to invoke and the command parameters in JSON array format. The exec form does not perform environment variable substitution. If environment variable substitution is to be performed, use the shell form or invoke the shell explicitly in the exec form. In JSONs array format, double quotes "" must be used around names.	CMD ["executable", "param1", "param2"]
Default parameters to ENTRYPOINT	Specifies the default args to the ENTRYPOINT command. Both the ENTRYPOINT and CMD must be specified. Both the ENTRYPOINT and CMD must be specified using JSON array formats. In JSONs array format, double quotes "" must be used around names.	CMD ["param1", "param2"]
Shell form	Invokes a shell to invoke the specified command using the parameters. The command is invoked as a sub-command of /bin/sh -c.	CMD command param1 param2

If command-line args are provided to the `docker run` command those override the default args in `CMD` instruction. The `ENTRYPOINT` instruction could also be used in combination with a helper script. Next, we shall discuss the two fields, "command" and "args" that could be used to override the `ENTRYPOINT` and `CMD` instructions in a `Dockerfile` respectively.

The Command and Args Fields in a Pod Definition

Kubernetes has the provision to override the `ENTRYPOINT` (command) and `CMD` (args) instructions specified in the Dockerfile. Two field mappings in a Pod's definition file could be used to override the `ENTRYPOINT` and `CMD` instructions. These fields are "Command" and "Args," and they override the Dockerfile "ENTRYPOINT "and "CMD" instructions respectively. The overriding applies based on which of these instructions and fields are specified. Some examples of overriding are discussed in Table 3-3.

Table 3-3. Examples of Overriding ENTRYPOINT and CMD with Command and Args

	ENTRYPOINT	CMD	Command	Args	Used
Example 1	yes	yes	yes	yes	The Command and Args field mappings in the Pod definition file override the ENTRYPOINT and CMD instructions in Dockerfile.
Example 2	yes	yes	no	no	The Dockerfile ENTRYPOINT command and CMD args are used.
Example 3	yes	yes	yes	no	Only the command in the Command is used and Dockerfile ENTRYPOINT and CMD instructions are ignored.
Example 4	yes	yes	no	yes	The Docker image's command as specified in the ENTRYPOINT is used with the args specified in the Pod definition's Args. The args from the Dockerfile's CMD are ignored.
Example 5	no	yes	no	no	The command and parameters from the CMD instruction are run.
Example 6	no	yes	yes	yes	The Command and Args field mappings in the Pod definition file are used. The CMD instruction in Dockerfile is overridden.
Example 7	no	yes	no	yes	The Args field mapping in the Pod definition file is used. The CMD instruction in Dockerfile is overridden.
Example 8	no	yes	yes	no	The command in the Command mapping is used, and Dockerfile CMD instruction is ignored.

Environment Variables

A Pod's schema has the provision to specify environment variables. The environment variables are specified as "name" and "value" field mappings as a collection within a container definition's "env" mapping. The format for specifying environment variables is as follows.

```
spec:
  containers:
    -
    image: "image name"
    name: "container name "
    env:
      -
        name: "env variable 1"
        value: " env variable 1 value"
      -
        name: "env variable 2"
        value: " env variable 2 value"
```

The environment variables are added to the docker run command using -e when the Docker image is run by Kubernetes. The environment variables may also be used in "command" and "args" mappings using the environment variable substitution if a shell is used to run the Docker image command. A shell is invoked if one or more of the following is used:

-The shell form of the ENTRYPOINT or CMD is used

-The shell is invoked explicitly in the ENTRYPOINT or CMD instruction

In the following sections we shall use the "ubuntu" Docker image to demonstrate overriding the default ENTRYPOINT command and the default CMD args. We shall start with using the default ENTRYPOINT and CMD instructions.

Using the Default ENTRYPOINT and CMD from a Docker Image

The Dockerfile for the Ubuntu image does not provide an ENTRYPOINT instruction but the CMD instruction is set to CMD ["/bin/bash"]. In the example in this section we shall create a Pod definition that does not override the ENTRYPOINT or CMD instruction from the Docker image. Create a Pod definition file as follows with the image as "ubuntu" and some environment variables set.

```
apiVersion: v1
kind: Pod
metadata:
  name: "hello-world"
  labels:
    app: "helloApp"
spec:
  restartPolicy: Never
  containers:
    -
      image: "ubuntu"
      name: "hello"
      ports:

  containerPort: 8020
      env:
        -
          name: "MESSAGE1"
          value: "hello"
        -
          name: "MESSAGE2"
          value: "kubernetes"
```

The env.yaml file may be created in a vi editor and saved with the :wq command as shown in Figure 3-2.

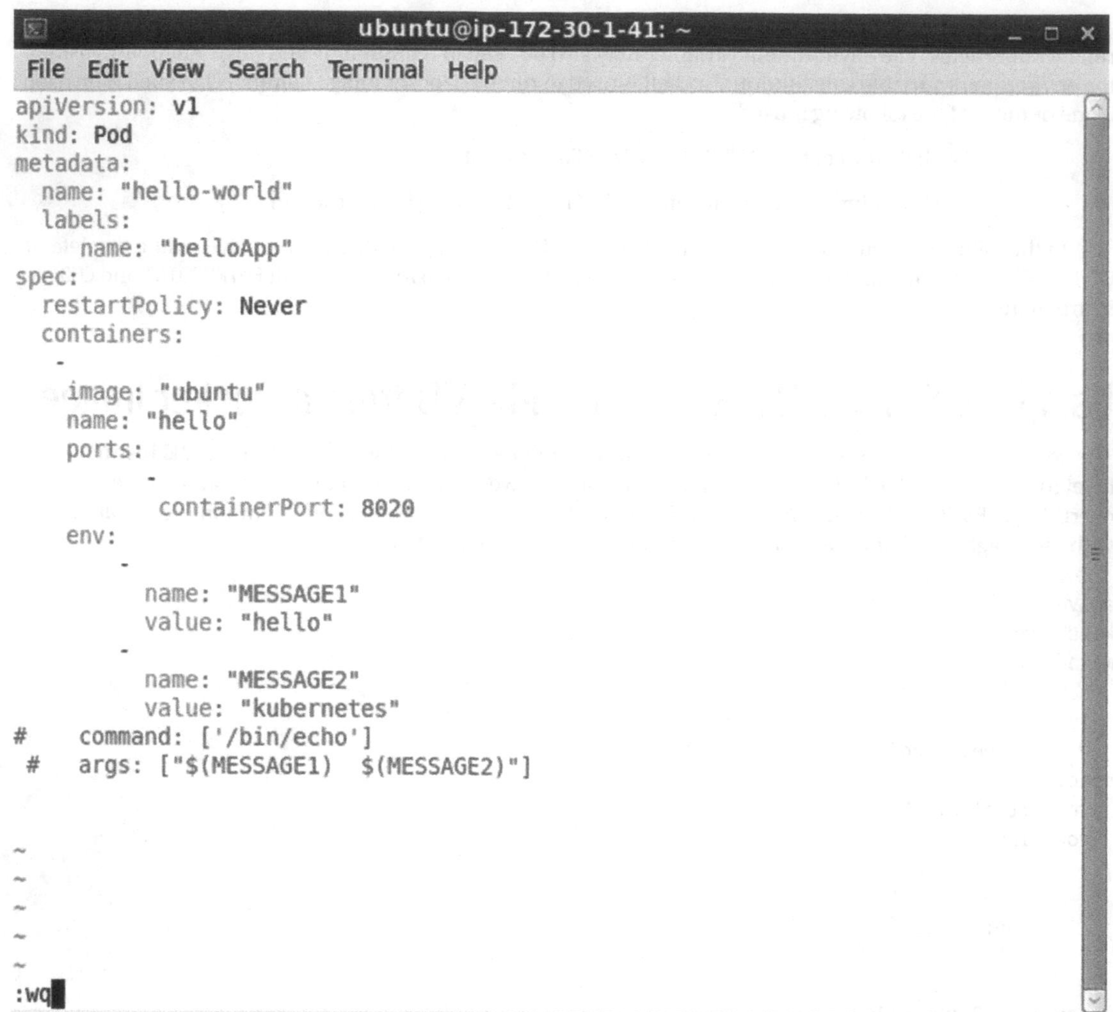
ubuntu@ip-172-30-1-41: ~
File Edit View Search Terminal Help
apiVersion: v1
kind: Pod
metadata:
  name: "hello-world"
  labels:
    name: "helloApp"
spec:
  restartPolicy: Never
  containers:
   -
    image: "ubuntu"
    name: "hello"
    ports:
          -
           containerPort: 8020
    env:
        -
          name: "MESSAGE1"
          value: "hello"
        -
          name: "MESSAGE2"
          value: "kubernetes"
command: ['/bin/echo']
 #   args: ["$(MESSAGE1) $(MESSAGE2)"]
~
~
~
~
~
:wq

Figure 3-2. *A Pod definition file env.yaml to demonstrate Environment Variables*

Run the following command to create a Pod from the definition file `env.yaml`.

```
kubectl create -f env.yaml
```

The `hello-world` pod gets created as shown in Figure 3-3. Run the following command to list the pods.

```
ubuntu@ip-172-30-1-41:~$ kubectl create -f  env.yaml
pods/hello-world
ubuntu@ip-172-30-1-41:~$ kubectl get pods
NAME                      READY     STATUS
 RESTARTS   AGE
hello-world               0/1       Image: ubuntu is ready, container is creating
 0          8s
k8s-master-127.0.0.1      3/3       Running
```

Figure 3-3. Creating and listing a Pod

```
kubectl get pods
```

The hello-world pod gets created but the Docker container created is listed as "creating" as shown in Figure 3-3.

When the Docker container gets created the STATUS column value transitions to "Running" and the READY column value becomes 1/1, which indicates that 1 of 1 containers in the Pod are ready and which is not shown in Figure 3-4 because the READY state transitions to 0/1 quickly thereafter. After the Pod command/args have run the Pod terminates and STATUS becomes ExitCode:0 as shown in Figure 3-4.

```
ubuntu@ip-172-30-1-41:~$ kubectl get pods
NAME                      READY     STATUS    RESTARTS   AGE
hello-world               0/1       Running   0          11s
k8s-master-127.0.0.1      3/3       Running   0          2h
ubuntu@ip-172-30-1-41:~$ kubectl get pods
NAME                      READY     STATUS    RESTARTS   AGE
hello-world               0/1       Running   0          13s
k8s-master-127.0.0.1      3/3       Running   0          2h
ubuntu@ip-172-30-1-41:~$ kubectl get pods
NAME                      READY     STATUS    RESTARTS   AGE
hello-world               0/1       Running   0          16s
k8s-master-127.0.0.1      3/3       Running   0          2h
ubuntu@ip-172-30-1-41:~$ kubectl get pods
NAME                      READY     STATUS       RESTARTS   AGE
hello-world               0/1       ExitCode:0   0          22s
k8s-master-127.0.0.1      3/3       Running      0          2h
ubuntu@ip-172-30-1-41:~$
```

Figure 3-4. After the Command/Args have run, a Pod terminates and the Pod's Status becomes ExitCode:0

Run the following command to list the output from the Pod.

```
kubectl logs hello-world
```

As the default CMD ["/bin/bash"] in the "Ubuntu" Docker image is just the invocation of the bash shell using /bin/bash, no output is generated as shown in Figure 3-5.

```
ubuntu@ip-172-30-1-41:~$ kubectl logs hello-world
ubuntu@ip-172-30-1-41:~$ ▌
```

Figure 3-5. *No output generated with Default CMD ["/bin/bash"] in "ubuntu" Docker Image*

Overriding Both the ENTRYPOINT and CMD

In the second example we shall override both the `ENTRYPOINT` and `CMD` in a `Dockerfile` using `Command` and `Args` mappings in the Pod definition file. Using in combination `ENTRYPOINT` and CMD will help us to specify the default executable for the image and also it will provide the default arguments to that executable. Environment variable substitution is used for the `MESSAGE1` and `MESSAGE2` environment variables with the `$(VARIABLE_NAME)` syntax.

```
command: ["/bin/echo"]
args: [" $(MESSAGE1)", " $(MESSAGE2)"]
```

The `env.yaml` Pod definition file is listed:

```
apiVersion: v1
kind: Pod
metadata:
  name: "hello-world"
  labels:
    app: "helloApp"
spec:
  restartPolicy: Never
  containers:
    -
      image: "ubuntu"
      name: "hello"
      ports:
          -
          containerPort: 8020
      env:
        -
          name: "MESSAGE1"
          value: "hello"
        -
          name: "MESSAGE2"
          value: "kubernetes"
      command: ["/bin/echo"]
      args: [" $(MESSAGE1)", " $(MESSAGE2)"]
```

The `env.yaml` file may be opened and modified in the vi editor and saved using the :wq command as shown in Figure 3-6.

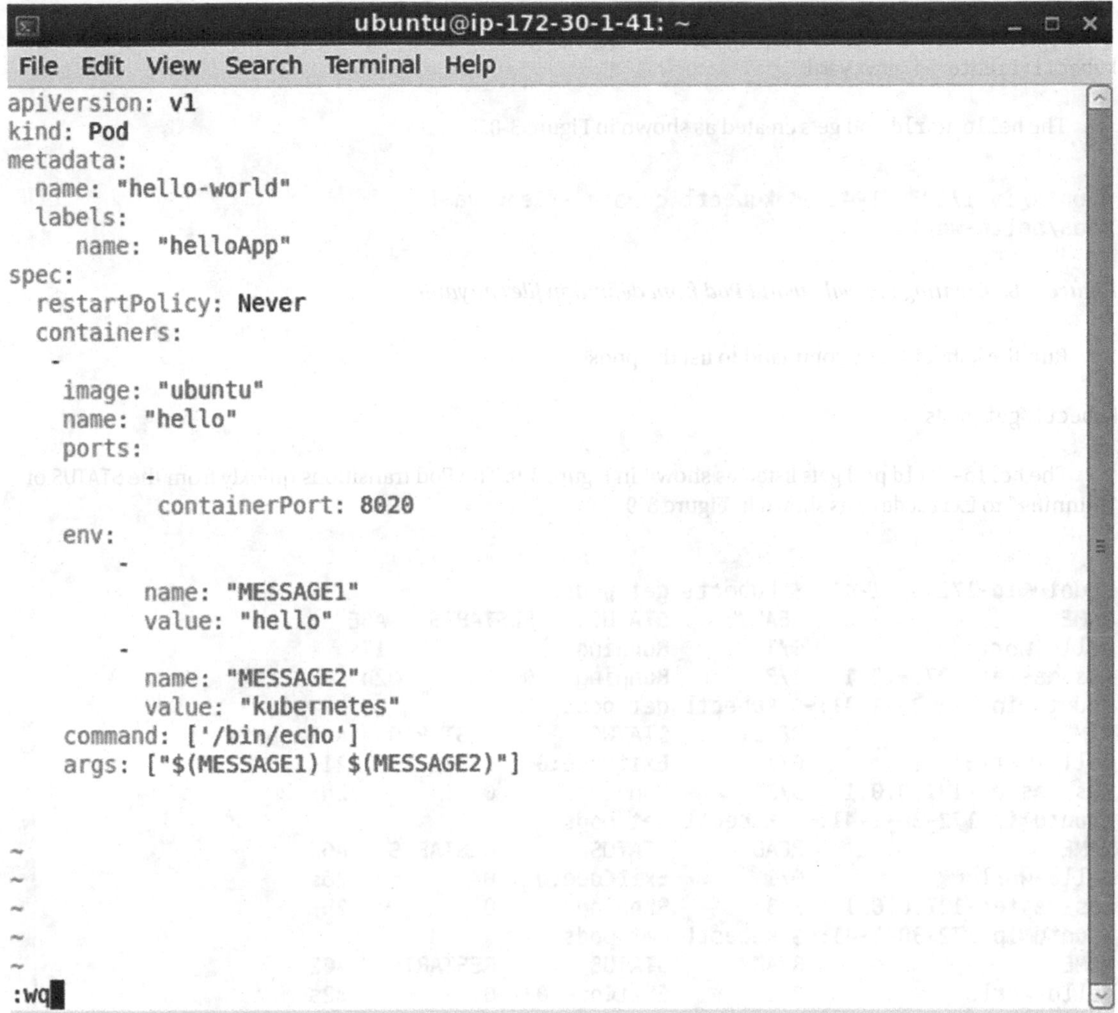
ubuntu@ip-172-30-1-41: ~
File Edit View Search Terminal Help
apiVersion: v1
kind: Pod
metadata:
  name: "hello-world"
  labels:
    name: "helloApp"
spec:
  restartPolicy: Never
  containers:
    -
     image: "ubuntu"
     name: "hello"
     ports:
       -
           containerPort: 8020
     env:
       -
         name: "MESSAGE1"
         value: "hello"
       -
         name: "MESSAGE2"
         value: "kubernetes"
     command: ['/bin/echo']
     args: ["$(MESSAGE1) $(MESSAGE2)"]
:wq

***Figure 3-6.** Modifying env.yaml in a vi Editor*

First, we need to delete the `hello-world` pod created in the first example with the following command.

```
kubectl delete pod hello-world
```

The `hello-world` pod gets deleted as shown in Figure 3-7.

```
ubuntu@ip-172-30-1-41:~$ kubectl delete pod hello-world
pods/hello-world
```

***Figure 3-7.** Deleting the hello-world Pod*

Run the kubectl create command to create a Pod from the definition file env.yaml.

```
kubectl create -f env.yaml
```

The hello-world Pod gets created as shown in Figure 3-8.

```
ubuntu@ip-172-30-1-41:~$ kubectl create -f env.yaml
pods/hello-world
```

Figure 3-8. *Creating the hello-world Pod from definition file env.yaml*

Run the kubectl get command to list the pods.

```
kubectl get pods
```

The hello-world pod gets listed as shown in Figure 3-9. The Pod transitions quickly from the STATUS of "Running" to ExitCode:0 as shown in Figure 3-9.

```
ubuntu@ip-172-30-1-41:~$ kubectl get pods
NAME                   READY     STATUS     RESTARTS   AGE
hello-world            0/1       Running    0          17s
k8s-master-127.0.0.1   3/3       Running    0          2h
ubuntu@ip-172-30-1-41:~$ kubectl get pods
NAME                   READY     STATUS        RESTARTS   AGE
hello-world            0/1       ExitCode:0    0          21s
k8s-master-127.0.0.1   3/3       Running       0          2h
ubuntu@ip-172-30-1-41:~$ kubectl get pods
NAME                   READY     STATUS        RESTARTS   AGE
hello-world            0/1       ExitCode:0    0          26s
k8s-master-127.0.0.1   3/3       Running       0          2h
ubuntu@ip-172-30-1-41:~$ kubectl get pods
NAME                   READY     STATUS        RESTARTS   AGE
hello-world            0/1       ExitCode:0    0          32s
```

Figure 3-9. *Listing the Pods with transitioning STATUS value*

Run the following command to list the output from the Pod.

```
kubectl logs hello-world
```

The message created from environment variables MESSAGE1 and MESSAGE2 using substitution gets listed as shown in Figure 3-10.

```
ubuntu@ip-172-30-1-41:~$ kubectl logs hello-world
hello  kubernetes
ubuntu@ip-172-30-1-41:~$ ▌
```

Figure 3-10. *Outputting Message Generated from Environment Variables using Value Substitution*

Specifying both the Executable and the Parameters in the Command Mapping

In the third example, specify that both the executable and the parameters are specified in the Command mapping in the Pod definition file. Environment variable substitution is used for the `MESSAGE1` and `MESSAGE2` environment variables. The shell is not required to be invoked/started explicitly if the environment variable syntax `$(VARIABLE_NAME)` is used, which is what we have used.

```
command: ["/bin/echo", " $(MESSAGE1)", " $(MESSAGE2)"]
```

The `env.yaml` Pod definition file is listed:

```
apiVersion: v1
kind: Pod
metadata:
  name: "hello-world"
  labels:
    app: "helloApp"
spec:
  restartPolicy: Never
  containers:
    -
      image: "ubuntu"
      name: "hello"
      ports:
          -
          containerPort: 8020
      env:
        -
          name: "MESSAGE1"
          value: "hello"
        -
          name: "MESSAGE2"
          value: "kubernetes"
      command: ["/bin/echo", " $(MESSAGE1)", " $(MESSAGE2)"]
```

The `env.yaml` file may be opened and modified in the vi editor and saved using the :wq command as shown in Figure 3-11.

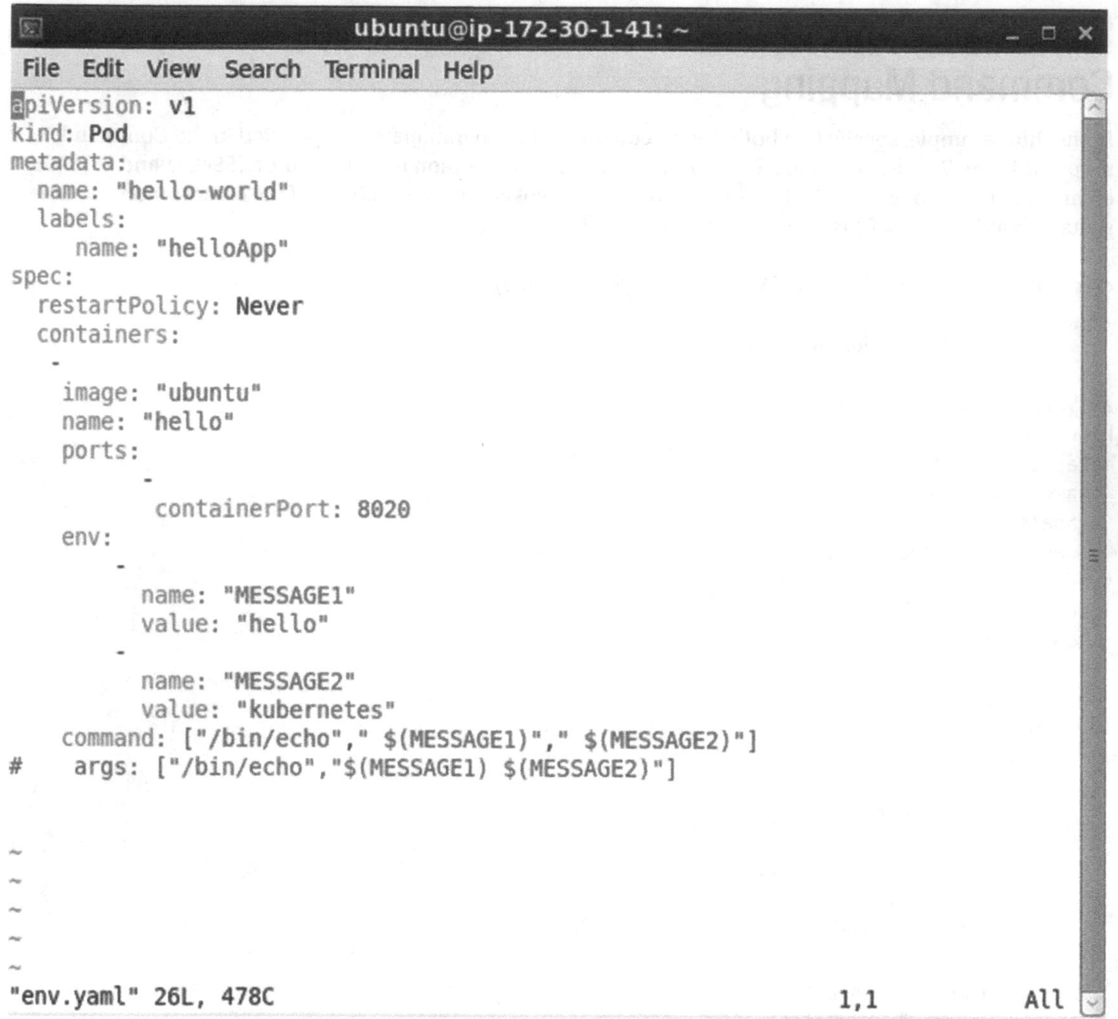
ubuntu@ip-172-30-1-41: ~
File Edit View Search Terminal Help
apiVersion: v1
kind: Pod
metadata:
name: "hello-world"
labels:
name: "helloApp"
spec:
restartPolicy: Never
containers:
-
image: "ubuntu"
name: "hello"
ports:
-
containerPort: 8020
env:
-
name: "MESSAGE1"
value: "hello"
-
name: "MESSAGE2"
value: "kubernetes"
command: ["/bin/echo"," $(MESSAGE1)"," $(MESSAGE2)"]
args: ["/bin/echo","$(MESSAGE1) $(MESSAGE2)"]
"env.yaml" 26L, 478C
1,1
All

Figure 3-11. *The Command mapping with both the Command Executable and the Parameters*

Run the `kubectl create` command to create a Pod from the definition file `env.yaml`.

```
kubectl create -f env.yaml
```

The `hello-world` pod gets created as shown in Figure 3-12. Run the `kubectl get` command to list the pods.

```
ubuntu@ip-172-30-1-41: ~
File  Edit  View  Search  Terminal  Help
ubuntu@ip-172-30-1-41:~$ sudo vi env.yaml
ubuntu@ip-172-30-1-41:~$ kubectl create -f env.yaml
pods/hello-world
ubuntu@ip-172-30-1-41:~$ kubectl get pods
NAME                      READY     STATUS
 RESTARTS   AGE
hello-world               0/1       Image: ubuntu is ready, container is creating
 0          4s
k8s-master-127.0.0.1      3/3       Running
 0          3h
ubuntu@ip-172-30-1-41:~$ kubectl get pods
NAME                      READY     STATUS
 RESTARTS   AGE
hello-world               0/1       Image: ubuntu is ready, container is creating
 0          9s
k8s-master-127.0.0.1      3/3       Running
 0          3h
ubuntu@ip-172-30-1-41:~$ kubectl get pods
NAME                      READY     STATUS     RESTARTS   AGE
hello-world               0/1       Running    0          12s
k8s-master-127.0.0.1      3/3       Running    0          3h
ubuntu@ip-172-30-1-41:~$ kubectl get pods
NAME                      READY     STATUS     RESTARTS   AGE
hello-world               0/1       Running    0          16s
k8s-master-127.0.0.1      3/3       Running    0          3h
ubuntu@ip-172-30-1-41:~$ kubectl get pods
NAME                      READY     STATUS       RESTARTS   AGE
hello-world               0/1       ExitCode:0   0          21s
k8s-master-127.0.0.1      3/3       Running      0          3h
```

Figure 3-12. *Creating and Listing the Pod with Definition file from Figure 3-11*

```
kubectl get pods
```

The `hello-world` pod gets listed though initially the Pod `STATUS` is not listed as "Running" as shown in Figure 3-12. The Pod transitions quickly to the `READY` value of 1/1 and subsequently 0/1. The 1/1 READY value is not shown in Figure 3-12 as it transitions quickly to 0/1. After the command has run the Pod terminates and the `STATUS` becomes `ExitCode:0` as shown in Figure 3-12.

Subsequently invoke the following command to list the output generated by the Pod.

```
kubectl get logs
```

The message created from environment variables `MESSAGE1` and `MESSAGE2` gets listed as shown in Figure 3-13.

```
ubuntu@ip-172-30-1-41:~$ kubectl logs hello-world
 hello  kubernetes
ubuntu@ip-172-30-1-41:~$ █
```

Figure 3-13. *Message output by Pod created in Figure 3-12*

Specifying Both the Executable and the Parameters in the Args Mapping

In the fourth example, specify both the executable and the parameters in the Args mapping in the Pod definition file as a result overriding the CMD instruction in the Dockerfile. Environment variable substitution is used for the MESSAGE1 and MESSAGE2 environment variables with the environment variable syntax $(VARIABLE_NAME).

```
args: ["/bin/echo", " $(MESSAGE1)", " $(MESSAGE2)"]
```

The env.yaml Pod definition file is listed:

```
apiVersion: v1
kind: Pod
metadata:
  name: "hello-world"
  labels:
    app: "helloApp"
spec:
  restartPolicy: Never
  containers:
    -
      image: "ubuntu"
      name: "hello"
      ports:
          -
          containerPort: 8020
      env:
        -
          name: "MESSAGE1"
          value: "hello"
        -
          name: "MESSAGE2"
          value: "kubernetes"
      args: ["/bin/echo", " $(MESSAGE1)", " $(MESSAGE2)"]
```

The env.yaml file may be opened and modified in the vi editor and saved using the :wq command as shown in Figure 3-14.

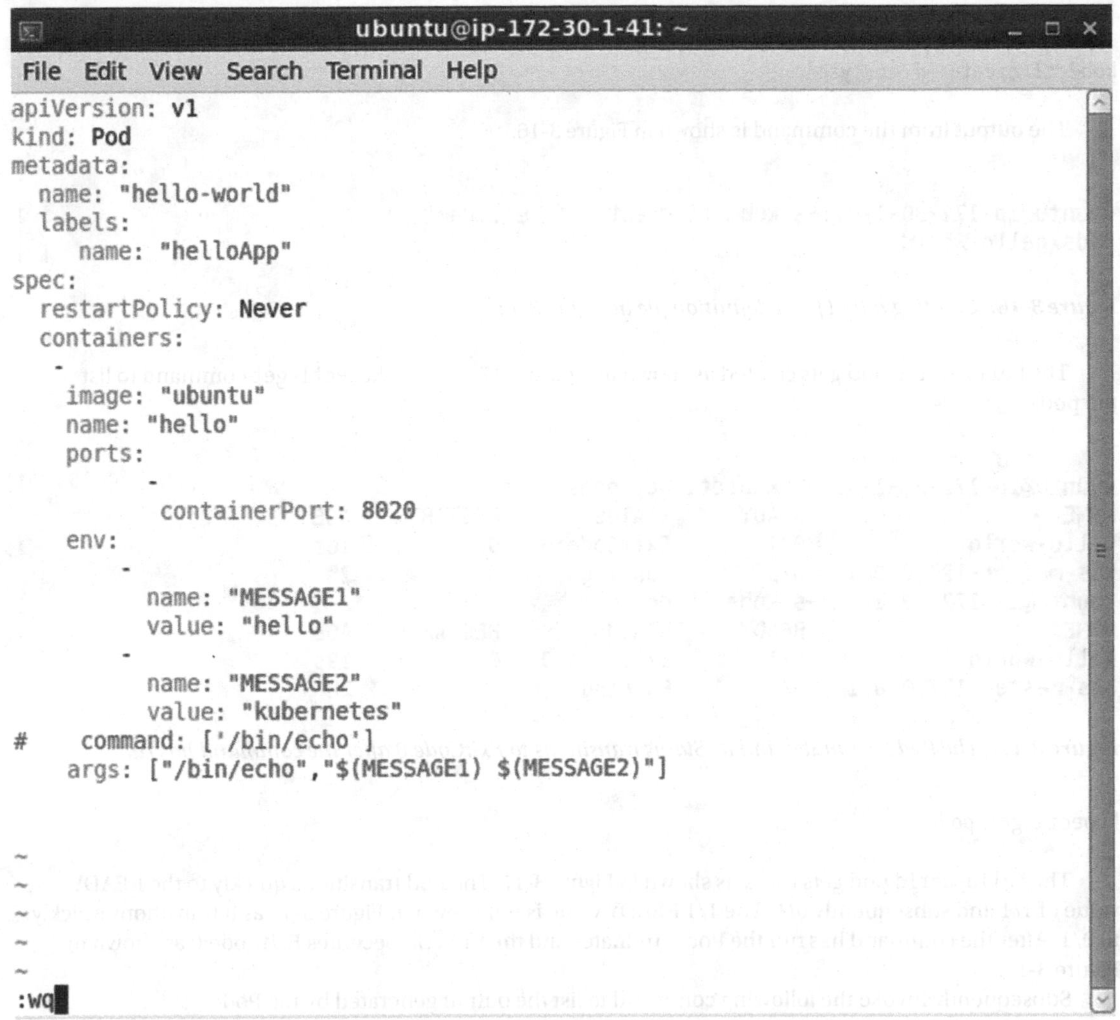
ubuntu@ip-172-30-1-41: ~
File Edit View Search Terminal Help
apiVersion: v1
kind: Pod
metadata:
name: "hello-world"
labels:
name: "helloApp"
spec:
restartPolicy: Never
containers:
-
image: "ubuntu"
name: "hello"
ports:
-
containerPort: 8020
env:
-
name: "MESSAGE1"
value: "hello"
-
name: "MESSAGE2"
value: "kubernetes"
command: ['/bin/echo']
args: ["/bin/echo","$(MESSAGE1) $(MESSAGE2)"]
:wq

Figure 3-14. The args Mapping in the Pod definition file specifies both the Command Executable and the Parameters

The hello-world Pod created from the previous example must be deleted as otherwise the error shown in Figure 3-15 gets generated when the kubectl create command is run.

```
ubuntu@ip-172-30-1-41:~$ kubectl create -f  env.yaml
Error from server: error when creating "env.yaml": pods "hello-world" already ex
ists
ubuntu@ip-172-30-1-41:~$ kubectl delete pod hello-world
pods/hello-world
```

Figure 3-15. Error Generated if hello-world Pod already exists

Run the kubectl create command to create a Pod from the definition file env.yaml.

```
kubectl create -f env.yaml
```

The output from the command is shown in Figure 3-16.

```
ubuntu@ip-172-30-1-41:~$ kubectl create -f  env.yaml
pods/hello-world
```

Figure 3-16. *Creating a Pod from definition file in Figure 3-14*

The hello-world pod gets created as shown in Figure 3-17. Run the kubectl get command to list the pods.

```
ubuntu@ip-172-30-1-41:~$ kubectl get pods
NAME                   READY     STATUS        RESTARTS    AGE
hello-world            0/1       ExitCode:0    0           16s
k8s-master-127.0.0.1   3/3       Running       0           2h
ubuntu@ip-172-30-1-41:~$ kubectl get pods
NAME                   READY     STATUS        RESTARTS    AGE
hello-world            0/1       ExitCode:0    0           19s
k8s-master-127.0.0.1   3/3       Running       0           2h
```

Figure 3-17. *The Pod terminates and its Status transitions to ExitCode:0 after the command has run*

```
kubectl get pods
```

The hello-world pod gets listed as shown in Figure 3-17. The Pod transitions quickly to the READY value of 1/1 and subsequently 0/1. The 1/1 READY value is not shown in Figure 3-17 as it transitions quickly to 0/1. After the command has run the Pod terminates and the STATUS becomes ExitCode:0 as shown in Figure 3-17.

Subsequently invoke the following command to list the output generated by the Pod.

```
kubectl get logs
```

The message created with environment variables substitution from MESSAGE1 and MESSAGE2 gets listed as shown in Figure 3-18.

```
ubuntu@ip-172-30-1-41:~$ kubectl logs hello-world
hello kubernetes
ubuntu@ip-172-30-1-41:~$ ▌
```

Figure 3-18. *Outputting the Message Generated by Pod*

Summary

In this chapter we discussed the `ENTRYPOINT` and `CMD` instructions in a Docker image `Dockerfile`: instructions used to run the default command with the default parameters when the image is run in a Kubernetes Pod. We also discussed the `Command` and `Args` mappings in a Pod definition file that could be used to override the `ENTRYPOINT` and `CMD` instructions. We discussed various examples of overriding the default instructions for the "ubuntu" Docker image with "command" and "args" field mappings in a Pod definition file. We also demonstrated the use of environment variables in a Pod definition file. In the next chapter we shall discuss using MySQL Database with Kubernetes.

PART II

Relational Databases

CHAPTER 4

Using MySQL Database

MySQL database is the most commonly used open source database. The Docker image "mysql" could be used to create a Docker container running a MySQL database instance. Running Docker separately for a single MySQL instance or multiple instances lacks the features of scheduling multiple instances, scaling, and providing a service for external clients. In this chapter we shall discuss how the Kubernetes container cluster manager could be used to overcome all of those deficiencies.

Setting the Environment

Creating a Service

Creating a Replication Controller

Listing the Pods

Listing Logs

Describing the Service

Starting an Interactive Shell

Starting the MySQL CLI

Creating a Database Table

Exiting the MySQL CLI and Interactive Shell

Scaling the Replicas

Deleting the Replication Controller

Setting the Environment

The following software is required for this chapter.

-Docker Engine (latest version)

-Kubernetes Cluster Manager (version 1.01)

-Kubectl (version 1.01)

-Docker image "mysql" (latest version)

D. Vohra, *Kubernetes Microservices with Docker*, DOI 10.1007/978-1-4842-1907-2_4

We have used an Amazon EC2 instance created from AMI Ubuntu Server 14-04 LTS (HVM), SSD Volume Type - ami-d05e75b8 to install the required software. The procedure to install Docker, Kubernetes, and Kubectl is discussed in chapter 1. Obtain the Public IP address of the Amazon EC2 instance as shown in Figure 4-1.

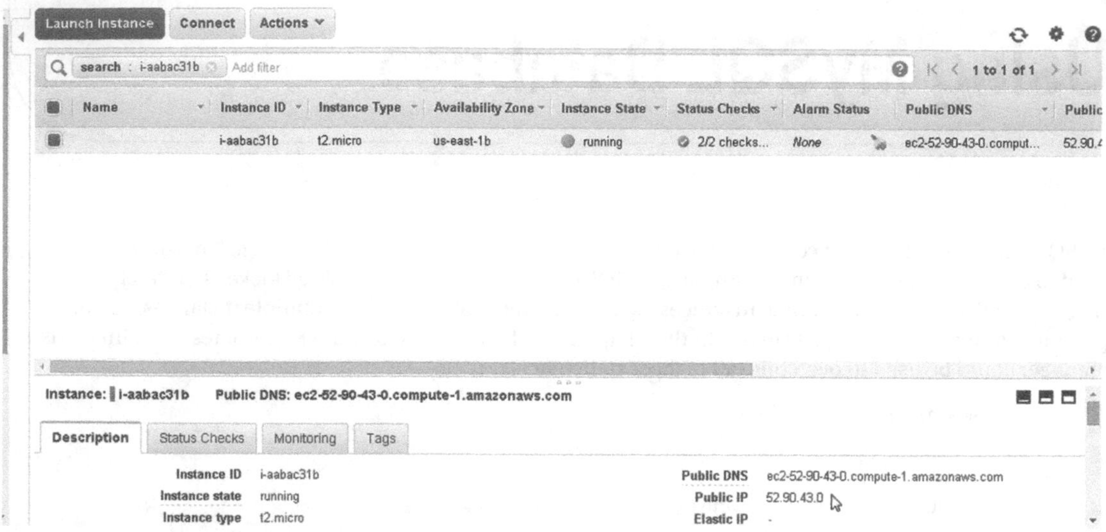

Figure 4-1. *Obtaining the Public IP Address*

SSH log in to the Ubuntu instance using the Public IP Address, which would be different for different users.

```
sh -i "docker.pem" ubuntu@52.90.43.0
```

Start the Docker engine and verify its status.

```
sudo service docker start
sudo service docker status
```

The Docker Engine should be listed as "running" as shown in Figure 4-2.

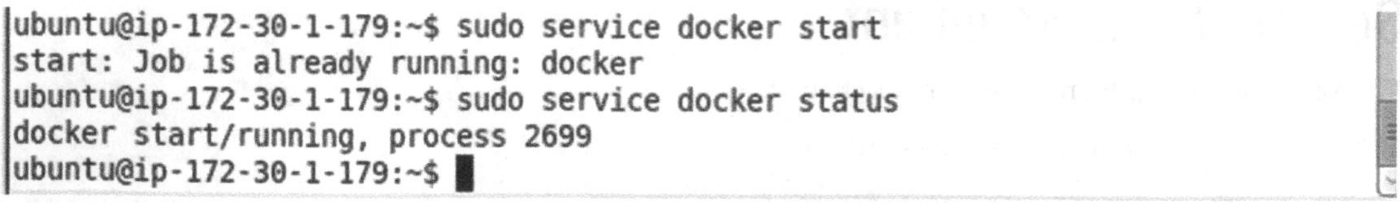

```
ubuntu@ip-172-30-1-179:~$ sudo service docker start
start: Job is already running: docker
ubuntu@ip-172-30-1-179:~$ sudo service docker status
docker start/running, process 2699
ubuntu@ip-172-30-1-179:~$
```

Figure 4-2. *Starting Docker and Verifying Its Status*

Creating a Service

In this section we shall create a Kubernetes service using a definition file. We have used the YAML format for definition files, but JSON could be used just as well. Create a service definition file called `mysql-service.yaml` and copy the following listing to the file. Within the spec field mapping for the service the "selector" expression is set to `app: "mysql-app,"` which translates to service selector app=mysql-app and which implies that the service routes traffic to Pods with the label `app=mysql-app`. If the `selector` expression is empty all Pods are selected. The port to expose the service is set to 3306 within the ports listing. And the service has a label `app: "mysql-app"`. The `kind field` mapping must have value "Service."

```
apiVersion: v1
kind: Service
metadata:
 name: "mysql"
 labels:
  app: "mysql-app"
spec:
 ports:
  # the port that this service should serve on
  - port: 3306
 # label keys and values that must match in order to receive traffic for this service
 selector:
  app: "mysql-app"
```

The service schema is available at `http://kubernetes.io/v1.1/docs/api-reference/v1/definitions.html#_v1_service`. Setting the `selector` field in the YAML definition file to `app: "mysql-app"` implies that all Pods with the YAML definition file label setting `app: "mysql-app"` are managed by the service. Create the service using the definition file with the `kubectl create` command.

```
kubectl create -f mysql-service.yaml
```

The `mysql` service gets created and the output is "services/mysql" as shown in Figure 4-3.

```
ubuntu@ip-172-30-1-179:~$ kubectl create -f mysql-service.yaml
services/mysql
```

Figure 4-3. *Creating a Service for MySQL Database*

List the service using the following command.

```
kubectl get services
```

The mysql service gets listed as shown in Figure 4-4.

```
ubuntu@ip-172-30-1-179:~$ kubectl get services
NAME          LABELS                                        SELECTOR          IP(S)
   PORT(S)
kubernetes    component=apiserver,provider=kubernetes      <none>            10.0.0.1
   443/TCP
mysql         app=mysql-app                                 app=mysql-app     10.0.0.14
3   3306/TCP
ubuntu@ip-172-30-1-179:~$
```

Figure 4-4. *Listing the mysql Service*

Creating a Replication Controller

In this section we shall create a replication controller managed by the service created in the previous section. Create a replication controller definition file called `mysql-rc.yaml` and copy the following/next listing to the file. The `kind` field mapping must have value "ReplicationController." The replication controller has a label `app: "mysql-app"` in the `metadata` field mapping. If the labels are empty they are defaulted to the labels of the Pods the replication controller manages. The `"spec"` field mapping defines the replication controller and includes the `"replicas"` field mapping for the number of replicas to create. The `replicas` is set to 1 in the following/next listing. The default number of replicas is also 1. The `spec` includes a `selector field` mapping called `app: "mysql-app,"` which selects all Pods with label `app: "mysql-app"` for the replication controller to manage and count toward the "replicas" setting. A Pod could have other labels in addition to the selector, but must include the selector expression/s of a replication controller to be managed by the replication controller. Similarly, a replication controller could be managing Pods not started with the replication controller definition file.

Labels and selector expression settings in YAML definition files are not used as such, but are translated to a label/selector by replacing the ':' with the '='. For example, service/replication controller selector setting app: "mysql-app" becomes selector app = mysql-app selector and label setting app: "mysql-app" becomes label app = mysql-app.

If a `selector` is not specified the labels on the template are used to match the Pods and count toward the "replicas" setting. The `"template"` field mapping defines a Pod managed by the replication controller. The `spec` field mapping within the `template` field specifies the behavior of the Pod. The `"containers"` field mapping within the `"spec"` field defines the collection/list of containers to create including the image, the environment variables if any, and the ports to use for each container.

We need to use an environment variable for the MySQL database replication controller. The Docker image "mysql" requires (is mandatory) the environment variable `MYSQL_ROOT_PASSWORD` to run a Docker container for MySQL database. The `MYSQL_ROOT_PASSWORD` variable sets the password for the `root` user. Environment variables are set with the `"env"` mapping within a `containers` field listing. An `env` mapping consists of a `name` mapping and a `value` mapping. The `MYSQL_ROOT_PASSWORD` environment variable is set as shown in the following listing. The `"ports"` field collection includes a `containerPort` mapping for port 3306. The indentations and hyphens in a YAML file must be well formatted and the following listing should be copied and syntax validated in the YAML Lint (`http://www.yamllint.com/`). The YAML lint only validates the syntax and does not validate if the Pod definition field conforms to the schema for a pod. The Pod schema is available at `http://kubernetes.io/v1.1/docs/api-reference/v1/definitions.html#_v1_podspec`.

```
---
apiVersion: v1
kind: ReplicationController
metadata:
  labels:
    app: "mysql-app"
spec:
  replicas: 1
  selector:
    app: "mysql-app"
  template:
    metadata:
      labels:
        app: "mysql-app"
    spec:
      containers:
      -
        env:
          -
            name: "MYSQL_ROOT_PASSWORD"
            value: "mysql"
        image: "mysql"
        name: "mysql"
        ports:
          -
            containerPort: 3306
```

The `mysql-rc.yaml` definition file may be created in the vi editor and saved with the :wq command as shown in Figure 4-5.

```
ubuntu@ip-172-30-1-179: ~
File Edit View Search Terminal Help
---
apiVersion: v1
kind: ReplicationController
metadata:
  name: "mysql"
  labels:
    app: "mysql-app"
spec:
  replicas: 1
  selector:
    app: "mysql-app"
  template:
    metadata:
      labels:
        app: "mysql-app"
    spec:
      containers:
        -
          env:
            -
              name: "MYSQL_ROOT_PASSWORD"
              value: "mysql"
          image: "mysql"
          name: "mysql"
          ports:
            -
              containerPort: 3306
~
:wq
```

***Figure 4-5.** Definition File for Replication Controller*

Create a replication controller from the service definition file with the kubectl create command.

```
kubectl create -f mysql-rc.yaml
```

As the output in Figure 4-6 indicates, the mysql replication controller gets created.

```
ubuntu@ip-172-30-1-179:~$ kubectl create -f mysql-rc.yaml
replicationcontrollers/mysql
```

***Figure 4-6.** Creating a Replication Controller for MySQL Database*

List the replication with the following command.

```
kubectl get rc
```

The `mysql` replication controller including the container name, image name, selector expression (app=mysql-app), and number of replicas get listed as shown in Figure 4-7.

```
ubuntu@ip-172-30-1-179:~$ kubectl get rc
CONTROLLER   CONTAINER(S)   IMAGE(S)   SELECTOR        REPLICAS
mysql        mysql          mysql      app=mysql-app   1
```

Figure 4-7. *Listing the MySQL Replication Controller*

To describe the `mysql` replication controller run the following command.

```
kubectl describe rc mysql
```

The replication controller name, namespace, image, selector, labels, replicas, pod status, and events get listed as shown in Figure 4-8.

```
ubuntu@ip-172-30-1-179:~$ kubectl describe rc mysql
Name:           mysql
Namespace:      default
Image(s):       mysql
Selector:       app=mysql-app
Labels:         app=mysql-app
Replicas:       1 current / 1 desired
Pods Status:    1 Running / 0 Waiting / 0 Succeeded / 0 Failed
Events:
  FirstSeen                             LastSeen                        Count   F
rom                             SubobjectPath   Reason                  Message
  Fri, 01 Jan 2016 01:58:45 +0000       Fri, 01 Jan 2016 01:58:45 +0000 1       {
replication-controller }                        successfulCreate        Created
pod: mysql-wuo7x


ubuntu@ip-172-30-1-179:~$
```

Figure 4-8. *Describing the MySQL Replication Controller*

Listing the Pods

The Pods created may be listed with the following command.

```
kubectl get pods
```

As shown in Figure 4-9 the 2 replicas created by the replication controller get listed. Initially the Pods may not be listed as READY 1/1. Run the preceding command after a few seconds, multiple times if required, to list all the Pods as ready.

```
ubuntu@ip-172-30-1-179:~$ kubectl get pods
NAME                   READY     STATUS    RESTARTS   AGE
k8s-master-127.0.0.1   3/3       Running   0          48m
mysql-wuo7x            0/1       Running   0          14s
ubuntu@ip-172-30-1-179:~$ kubectl get pods
NAME                   READY     STATUS    RESTARTS   AGE
k8s-master-127.0.0.1   3/3       Running   0          48m
mysql-wuo7x            0/1       Running   0          18s
ubuntu@ip-172-30-1-179:~$ kubectl get pods
NAME                   READY     STATUS    RESTARTS   AGE
k8s-master-127.0.0.1   3/3       Running   0          48m
mysql-wuo7x            1/1       Running   0          21s
ubuntu@ip-172-30-1-179:~$
```

Figure 4-9. *Listing the Pod/s for MySQL Database*

Listing Logs

List the Pod logs for a pod: for example, the `mysql-wuo7x` pod, with the following command.

```
kubectl logs mysql-wuo7x
```

The Pod logs get listed as shown in Figure 4-10.

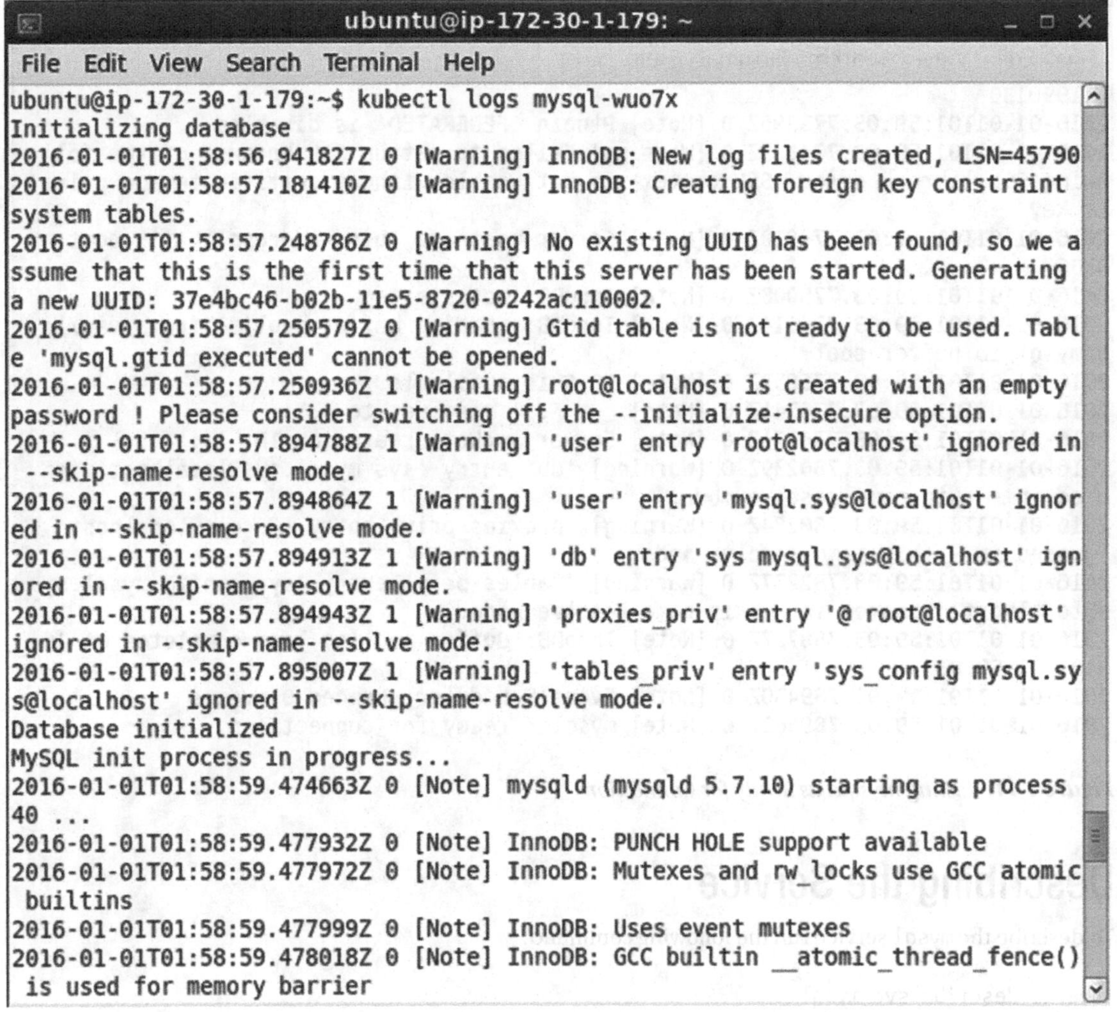

Figure 4-10. Listing the Logs generated by the Pod for MySQL Database

The MySQL Server is listed as started and "ready for connections" as shown in Figure 4-11.

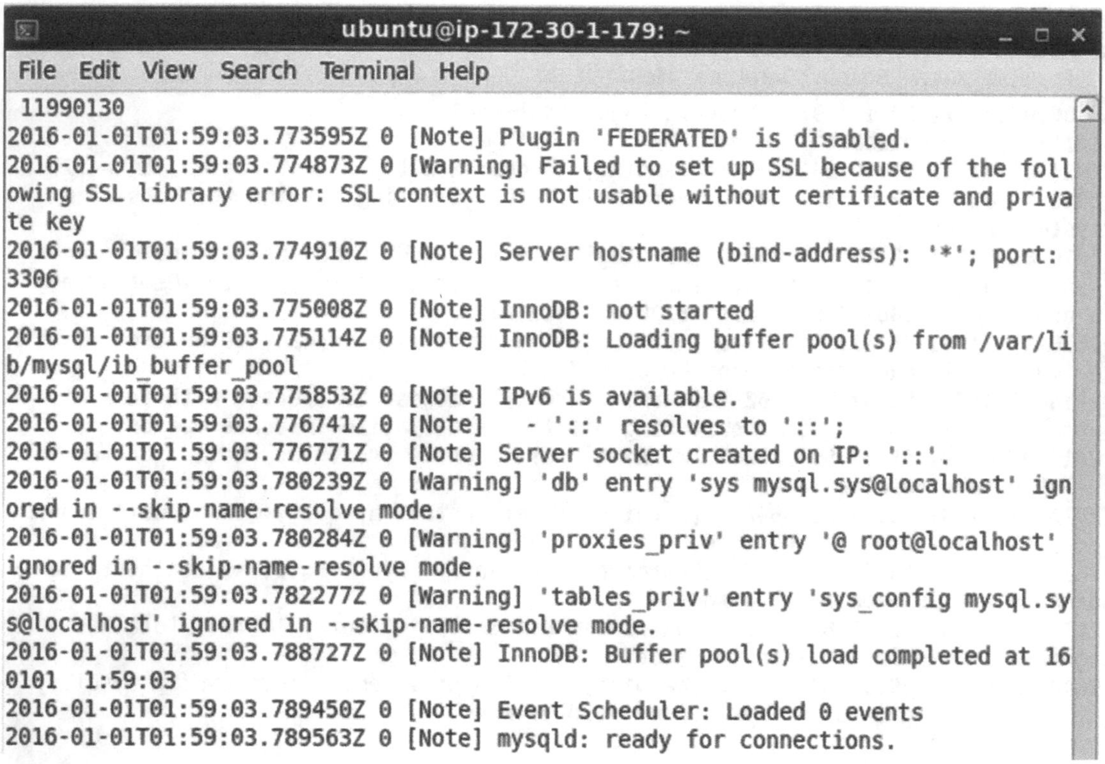

```
ubuntu@ip-172-30-1-179: ~
File Edit View Search Terminal Help
 11990130
2016-01-01T01:59:03.773595Z 0 [Note] Plugin 'FEDERATED' is disabled.
2016-01-01T01:59:03.774873Z 0 [Warning] Failed to set up SSL because of the foll
owing SSL library error: SSL context is not usable without certificate and priva
te key
2016-01-01T01:59:03.774910Z 0 [Note] Server hostname (bind-address): '*'; port:
3306
2016-01-01T01:59:03.775008Z 0 [Note] InnoDB: not started
2016-01-01T01:59:03.775114Z 0 [Note] InnoDB: Loading buffer pool(s) from /var/li
b/mysql/ib_buffer_pool
2016-01-01T01:59:03.775853Z 0 [Note] IPv6 is available.
2016-01-01T01:59:03.776741Z 0 [Note]   - '::' resolves to '::';
2016-01-01T01:59:03.776771Z 0 [Note] Server socket created on IP: '::'.
2016-01-01T01:59:03.780239Z 0 [Warning] 'db' entry 'sys mysql.sys@localhost' ign
ored in --skip-name-resolve mode.
2016-01-01T01:59:03.780284Z 0 [Warning] 'proxies_priv' entry '@ root@localhost'
ignored in --skip-name-resolve mode.
2016-01-01T01:59:03.782277Z 0 [Warning] 'tables_priv' entry 'sys_config mysql.sy
s@localhost' ignored in --skip-name-resolve mode.
2016-01-01T01:59:03.788727Z 0 [Note] InnoDB: Buffer pool(s) load completed at 16
0101  1:59:03
2016-01-01T01:59:03.789450Z 0 [Note] Event Scheduler: Loaded 0 events
2016-01-01T01:59:03.789563Z 0 [Note] mysqld: ready for connections.
```

Figure 4-11. *Listing mysqld as Ready for Connections*

Describing the Service

To describe the `mysql` service run the following command.

```
kubectl describe svc mysql
```

The service name, namespace, labels, selector, type, Ip, port and endpoints get listed. Because the number of replicas is set to 1 only one endpoint is listed as shown in Figure 4-12.

```
ubuntu@ip-172-30-1-179:~$ kubectl describe service mysql
Name:                   mysql
Namespace:              default
Labels:                 app=mysql-app
Selector:               app=mysql-app
Type:                   ClusterIP
IP:                     10.0.0.143
Port:                   <unnamed>       3306/TCP
Endpoints:              172.17.0.2:3306
Session Affinity:       None
No events.

ubuntu@ip-172-30-1-179:~$
```

Figure 4-12. *Describing the MySQL Service*

Starting an Interactive Shell

Bash is the free version of the Bourne shell distributed with Linux and GNU operating systems (OS). For Docker images that have a Linux OS image as the base image as specified in the `FROM` instruction in the `Dockerfile`, the software running in a Docker container may be accessed using the Bash shell. The `"mysql"` Docker image is based on the `"debian"` image and as a result supports access to software running in the Docker containers via a bash interactive shell.

Next, we shall start an interactive shell to start the MySQL CLI. But first we need to obtain the container id for one of the containers running MySQL. Run the following command to list the Docker containers.

```
sudo docker ps
```

The Docker container for the `mysql` image is shown listed in Figure 4-13.

```
ubuntu@ip-172-30-1-179:~$ sudo docker ps
CONTAINER ID        IMAGE                                           COMMAND
         CREATED             STATUS              PORTS               NAMES
526f5d5f6c2e        mysql                                           "/entrypoint.sh
mysql"   2 minutes ago       Up 2 minutes                            k8s_mysql.c
ee40a2a_mysql-wuo7x_default_31260fe7-b02b-11e5-b23e-12f950ce75ef_9f9a3ac1
d0cb27674b17        gcr.io/google_containers/pause:0.8.0            "/pause"
         2 minutes ago       Up 2 minutes                            k8s_POD.34b
1e8b5_mysql-wuo7x_default_31260fe7-b02b-11e5-b23e-12f950ce75ef_0626965c
e5a6aecdc22d        gcr.io/google_containers/hyperkube:v1.0.1       "/hyperkube apis
erver"   50 minutes ago      Up 50 minutes                           k8s_apiserv
er.cfb70250_k8s-master-127.0.0.1_default_f3ccbffbd75e3c5d2fb4ba69c8856c4a_e73ec6
59
b54e261a68d6        gcr.io/google_containers/hyperkube:v1.0.1       "/hyperkube cont
rolle"   50 minutes ago      Up 50 minutes                           k8s_control
ler-manager.1598ee5c_k8s-master-127.0.0.1_default_f3ccbffbd75e3c5d2fb4ba69c8856c
4a_a67e9916
2d89f7dcb6d6        gcr.io/google_containers/hyperkube:v1.0.1       "/hyperkube sche
duler"   50 minutes ago      Up 50 minutes                           k8s_schedul
er.2744e742_k8s-master-127.0.0.1_default_f3ccbffbd75e3c5d2fb4ba69c8856c4a_7bbdc5
94
fc71fab17c41        gcr.io/google_containers/hyperkube:v1.0.1       "/hyperkube prox
y --m"   51 minutes ago      Up 50 minutes                           agitated_ch
andrasekhar
11724fa32151        gcr.io/google_containers/pause:0.8.0            "/pause"
         51 minutes ago      Up 51 minutes                           k8s_POD.e4c
c795_k8s-master-127.0.0.1_default_f3ccbffbd75e3c5d2fb4ba69c8856c4a_14d01177
ae22e68886b3        gcr.io/google_containers/hyperkube:v1.0.1       "/hyperkube kube
let -"   51 minutes ago      Up 51 minutes                           admiring_be
ll
4d1be6207c1c        gcr.io/google_containers/etcd:2.0.12            "/usr/local/bin/
etcd "   51 minutes ago      Up 51 minutes                           silly_frank
```

Figure 4-13. *Listing the Docker Containers*

Using the Docker container id from the output from the preceding command, start an interactive shell.

```
sudo docker exec -it 526f5d5f6c2e bash
```

An interactive shell or tty gets started as shown in Figure 4-14.

```
ubuntu@ip-172-30-1-179:~$ sudo docker exec -it 526f5d5f6c2e bash
root@mysql-wuo7x:/#
```

Figure 4-14. *Starting the Interactive Terminal*

Starting the MySQL CLI

Within the interactive shell run the following command to start the MySQL CLI as user root.

```
mysql -u root -p
```

When prompted with Password: set the password as the value of the environment variable MYSQL_ROOT_PASSWORD, which was set as "mysql" in the mysql-rc.yaml definition file. The MySQL CLI gets started as shown in Figure 4-15.

```
root@mysql-wuo7x:/# mysql -u root -p
Enter password:
Welcome to the MySQL monitor.  Commands end with ; or \g.
Your MySQL connection id is 5
Server version: 5.7.10 MySQL Community Server (GPL)

Copyright (c) 2000, 2015, Oracle and/or its affiliates. All rights reserved.

Oracle is a registered trademark of Oracle Corporation and/or its
affiliates. Other names may be trademarks of their respective
owners.

Type 'help;' or '\h' for help. Type '\c' to clear the current input statement.

mysql>
```

Figure 4-15. Starting the MySQL CLI Shell

List the databases with the following command.

```
show databases;
```

The default databases shown in Figure 4-16 include the "mysql" database, which we shall use to create a database table. The other databases are system databases and should not be used for user tables.

```
mysql> show databases;
+--------------------+
| Database           |
+--------------------+
| information_schema |
| mysql              |
| performance_schema |
| sys                |
+--------------------+
4 rows in set (0.00 sec)

mysql>
```

Figure 4-16. Listing the Databases

Set the database "mysql" as the current database with the following command.

```
use mysql
```

The database gets set as mysql as indicated by the "Database changed" output in Figure 4-17.

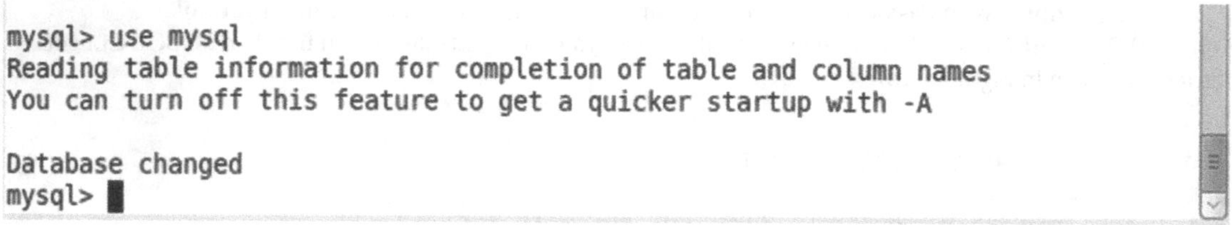

```
mysql> use mysql
Reading table information for completion of table and column names
You can turn off this feature to get a quicker startup with -A

Database changed
mysql> █
```

Figure 4-17. *Setting the Database*

Creating a Database Table

Next, create a database table called Catalog with the following SQL statement.

```
CREATE TABLE Catalog(CatalogId INTEGER PRIMARY KEY,Journal VARCHAR(25),
Publisher VARCHAR(25),Edition VARCHAR(25),Title VARCHAR(45),Author VARCHAR(25));
```

Add a row of data to the Catalog table with the following SQL statement.

```
INSERT INTO Catalog VALUES('1','Oracle Magazine','Oracle Publishing',
'November December 2013','Engineering as a Service','David A. Kelly');
```

The Catalog table gets created and a row of data gets added as shown in Figure 4-18.

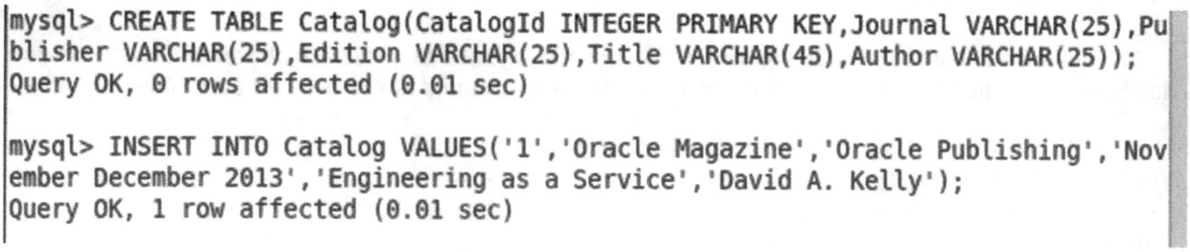

```
mysql> CREATE TABLE Catalog(CatalogId INTEGER PRIMARY KEY,Journal VARCHAR(25),Pu
blisher VARCHAR(25),Edition VARCHAR(25),Title VARCHAR(45),Author VARCHAR(25));
Query OK, 0 rows affected (0.01 sec)

mysql> INSERT INTO Catalog VALUES('1','Oracle Magazine','Oracle Publishing','Nov
ember December 2013','Engineering as a Service','David A. Kelly');
Query OK, 1 row affected (0.01 sec)
```

Figure 4-18. *Creating a MySQL Database Table*

Subsequently run the following SQL statement to query the database table Catalog.

```
SELECT * FROM Catalog;
```

The single row of data added gets listed as shown in Figure 4-19.

```
mysql> SELECT * FROM Catalog;
+-----------+----------------+--------------------+------------------------+---
----------------------+----------------+
| CatalogId | Journal        | Publisher          | Edition                | Tit
le                    | Author         |
+-----------+----------------+--------------------+------------------------+---
----------------------+----------------+
|         1 | Oracle Magazine | Oracle Publishing | November December 2013 | Eng
ineering as a Service | David A. Kelly |
+-----------+----------------+--------------------+------------------------+---
----------------------+----------------+
1 row in set (0.00 sec)

mysql> ▮
```

Figure 4-19. Querying the Database Table

Exiting the MySQL CLI and Interactive Shell

Exit the MySQL CLI with the "quit" command.

```
quit
```

Exit the interactive terminal with the "exit" command.

```
exit
```

The output from the preceding commands is shown in Figure 4-20.

```
mysql> quit
Bye
root@mysql-wuo7x:/# exit
exit
ubuntu@ip-172-30-1-179:~$ ▮
```

Figure 4-20. Exiting the MySQL CLI Shell and Docker Container Interactive Shell

Scaling the Replicas

One of the main benefits of Kubernetes is to be able to scale the number of MySQL instances in the cluster. Run the following `kubectl scale` command to scale the replicas from 1 to 4.

```
kubectl scale rc mysql --replicas=4
```

Subsequently run the following command to list the Pods.

```
kubectl get pods
```

The number of Pods for the MySQL database gets increased to 4 as shown in Figure 4-21. Some of the Pods may be listed as READY- > 0/1, which implies the Pod/s are not ready yet. When READY becomes 1/1 a Pod is ready to be accessed. The 0/1 value implies that 0 of the 1 Docker containers in the Pod are ready and similarly the 1/1 value implies that 1 of 1 containers is ready. The general syntax for the READY column value if all the n containers in the Pod are running is of the form n/n. The STATUS must be "Running" for a Pod to be considered available.

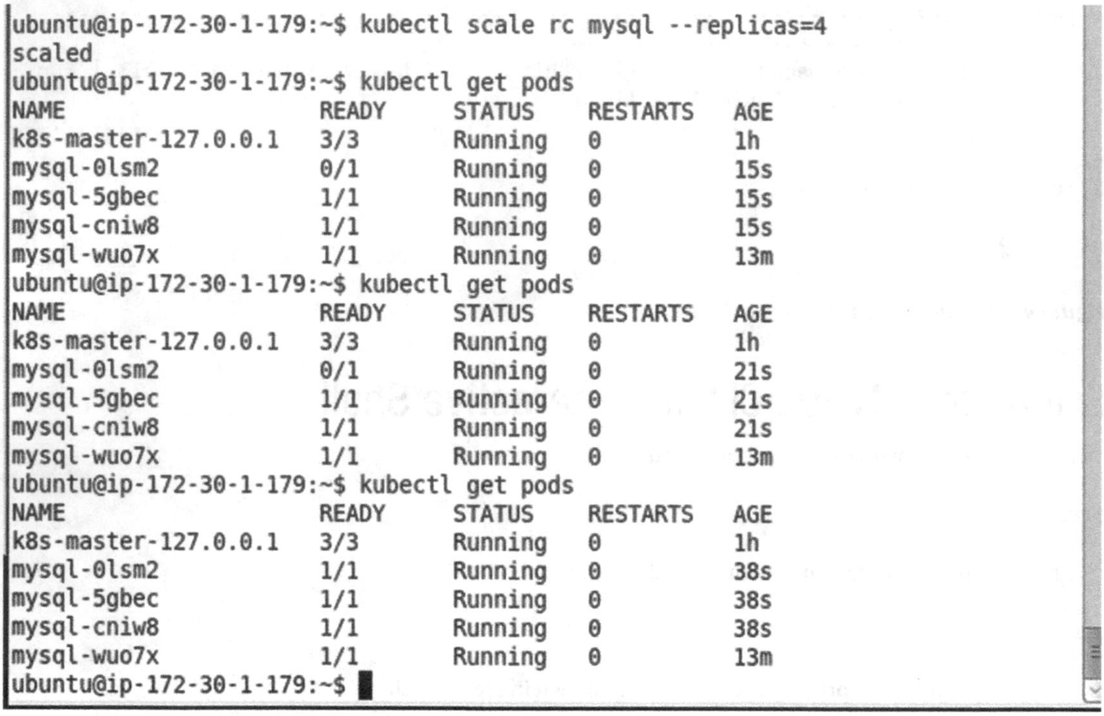

```
ubuntu@ip-172-30-1-179:~$ kubectl scale rc mysql --replicas=4
scaled
ubuntu@ip-172-30-1-179:~$ kubectl get pods
NAME                    READY     STATUS    RESTARTS   AGE
k8s-master-127.0.0.1    3/3       Running   0          1h
mysql-0lsm2             0/1       Running   0          15s
mysql-5gbec             1/1       Running   0          15s
mysql-cniw8             1/1       Running   0          15s
mysql-wuo7x             1/1       Running   0          13m
ubuntu@ip-172-30-1-179:~$ kubectl get pods
NAME                    READY     STATUS    RESTARTS   AGE
k8s-master-127.0.0.1    3/3       Running   0          1h
mysql-0lsm2             0/1       Running   0          21s
mysql-5gbec             1/1       Running   0          21s
mysql-cniw8             1/1       Running   0          21s
mysql-wuo7x             1/1       Running   0          13m
ubuntu@ip-172-30-1-179:~$ kubectl get pods
NAME                    READY     STATUS    RESTARTS   AGE
k8s-master-127.0.0.1    3/3       Running   0          1h
mysql-0lsm2             1/1       Running   0          38s
mysql-5gbec             1/1       Running   0          38s
mysql-cniw8             1/1       Running   0          38s
mysql-wuo7x             1/1       Running   0          13m
ubuntu@ip-172-30-1-179:~$
```

Figure 4-21. *Scaling the Pod Replicas to Four*

To describe the `mysql` service, run the following command.

```
kubectl describe svc mysql
```

The service description is the same as before except that the number of endpoints has increased to 4 as shown in Figure 4-22.

```
ubuntu@ip-172-30-1-179:~$ kubectl describe service mysql
Name:                   mysql
Namespace:              default
Labels:                 app=mysql-app
Selector:               app=mysql-app
Type:                   ClusterIP
IP:                     10.0.0.143
Port:                   <unnamed>       3306/TCP
Endpoints:              172.17.0.2:3306,172.17.0.3:3306,172.17.0.4:3306 + 1 more
...
Session Affinity:       None
No events.

ubuntu@ip-172-30-1-179:~$ ▌
```

Figure 4-22. *Describing the MySQL Service After Scaling the Pod Replicas*

The command "scale" will also allow us to specify one or more preconditions for the scale actions needed. The following (Table 4-1) preconditions are supported.

Table 4-1. *Preconditions for the 'kubernetes scale' command*

Precondition	Description
--current-replicas	The current number of replicas for the scale to be performed.
--resource-version	The resource version to match for the scale to be performed.

Deleting the Replication Controller

To delete the replication controller `mysql`, run the following command.

```
kubectl delete rc mysql
```

The replication controller gets deleted as shown in Figure 4-23. Whenever a `kubectl` command output to create or delete an artifact (a Pod, service or replication controller) is of the form *artifact type/artifact name*, it implies that the command has succeeded to create/delete the pod/service/replication controller.

```
ubuntu@ip-172-30-1-179:~$ kubectl delete rc mysql
replicationcontrollers/mysql
```

Figure 4-23. *Deleting the Replication Controller*

Subsequently run the following command to get the replication controllers. The `mysql` rc does not get listed as shown in Figure 4-24.

```
kubectl get rc
```

```
ubuntu@ip-172-30-1-179:~$ kubectl delete rc mysql
replicationcontrollers/mysql
ubuntu@ip-172-30-1-179:~$ kubectl get rc
CONTROLLER   CONTAINER(S)   IMAGE(S)   SELECTOR   REPLICAS
ubuntu@ip-172-30-1-179:~$ kubectl describe svc mysql
Name:                   mysql
Namespace:              default
Labels:                 app=mysql-app
Selector:               app=mysql-app
Type:                   ClusterIP
IP:                     10.0.0.143
Port:                   <unnamed>       3306/TCP
Endpoints:              <none>
Session Affinity:       None
No events.

ubuntu@ip-172-30-1-179:~$
```

Figure 4-24. *Describing the Service after Deleting the Replication Controllers*

Describe the service `mysql` again with the following command.

```
kubectl describe svc mysql
```

No “Endpoints” get listed as shown in Figure 4-24 because all the Pods get deleted when the replication controller managing them is deleted.

Summary

In this chapter we discussed orchestrating the MySQL database cluster using the Kubernetes cluster manager. We created a Kubernetes service to represent a MySQL-based Pod. The “mysql” Docker image is used to create a Pod. We used a replication controller to create replicas for MySQL base Pods. Initially the number of replicas is set to 1. We used a Docker container running a MySQL instance to start the MySQL CLI and create a database table. Subsequently, we scaled the number of replicas to 4 using the replication controller. When scaled, the number of replicas and therefore the number of MySQL instances becomes 4. The replication controller maintains the replication level through replica failure or replica shut down by a user. This chapter also demonstrates the use of environment variables. The `MYSQL_ROOT_PASSWORD` environment variable is required to run a container for the Docker image “mysql” and we set the `MYSQL_ROOT_PASSWORD` environment variable in the Pod spec in the replication controller. In the next chapter we shall discuss using another open source database, the PostgreSQL database.

CHAPTER 5

Using PostgreSQL Database

PostgreSQL is an open source object-relational database. PostgreSQL is scalable both in terms of the quantity of data and number of concurrent users. PostgreSQL is supported in several of Apache Hadoop ecosystem projects such as Apache Sqoop and may be used for Apache Hive Metastore. PostgreSQL 9.5 offers several new features such as support for `UPSERT`, `BRIN` indexing, faster sorts, and the `TABLESAMPLE` clause for getting a statistical sample of a large table. In this chapter we shall discuss creating a PostgreSQL 9.5 cluster using the Kubernetes cluster manager. We shall discuss both the imperative approach and the declarative approach for creating and scaling a PostgreSQL cluster. This chapter has the following sections.

Setting the Environment

Creating a PostgreSQL Cluster Declaratively

Creating a PostgreSQL Cluster Imperatively

Setting the Environment

We have used the same type of Amazon EC2 instance in this chapter as in other chapters, an instance based on Ubuntu Server 14.04 LTS (HVM), SSD Volume Type - ami-d05e75b8 AMI. The following software is required for this chapter.

-Docker Engine (latest version)

-Kubernetes Cluster Manager (version 1.01)

-Kubectl (version 1.01)

-Docker Image “postgres” (latest version)

The procedure to install the required software, start Docker engine and Kubernetes cluster manager, is discussed in chapter 1. To install the software first we need to log in to the Amazon EC2 instance. Obtain the Public IP Address of the Amazon EC2 instance as shown in Figure 5-1.

D. Vohra, *Kubernetes Microservices with Docker*, DOI 10.1007/978-1-4842-1907-2_5

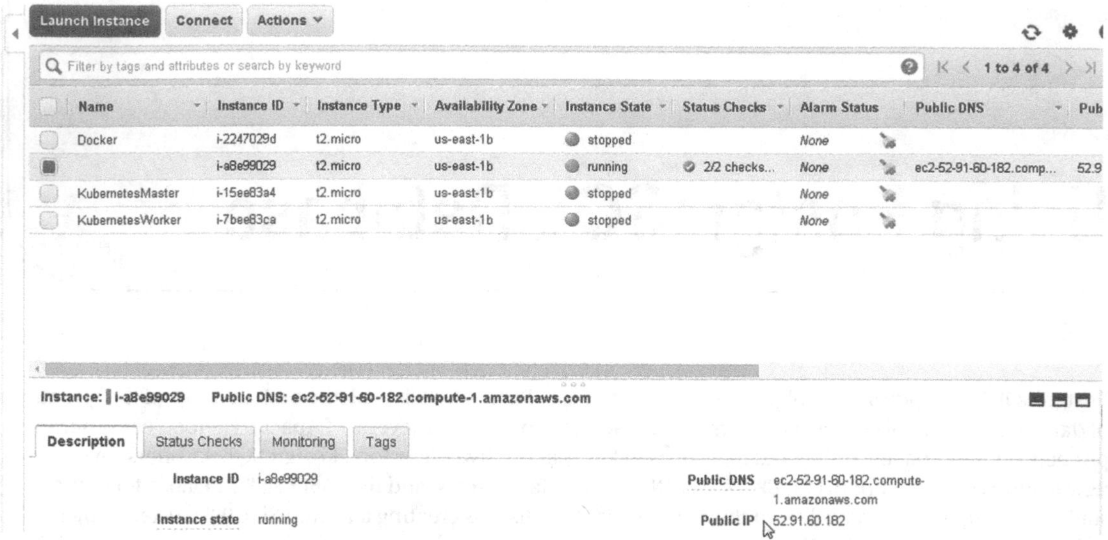

Figure 5-1. *Obtaining the Public IP Address*

SSH Login to the Ubuntu instance using the Public IP Address.

```
ssh -i "docker.pem" ubuntu@52.91.60.182
```

Start the Docker engine and verify its status.

```
sudo service docker start
sudo service docker status
```

Docker should be indicated as "running" as shown in Figure 5-2.

```
ubuntu@ip-172-30-1-13:~$ sudo service docker start
start: Job is already running: docker
ubuntu@ip-172-30-1-13:~$ sudo service docker status
docker start/running, process 2698
ubuntu@ip-172-30-1-13:~$
```

Figure 5-2. *Starting Docker*

List the services with the following command.

```
kubectl get services
```

The kubernetes service should get listed as shown in Figure 5-3.

```
ubuntu@ip-172-30-1-13:~$ kubectl get services
NAME         LABELS                                    SELECTOR   IP(S)      POR
T(S)
kubernetes   component=apiserver,provider=kubernetes   <none>     10.0.0.1   443
/TCP
ubuntu@ip-172-30-1-13:~$ 
```

Figure 5-3. *Listing the Kubernetes Services*

Creating a PostgreSQL Cluster Declaratively

In the following subsections we shall create and manage a PostgreSQL cluster declaratively, which implies we shall use definition files. The definition files could be based on the YAML format or the JSON format. We shall be using YAML format. It is recommended to create the service first so that any pods created subsequently have a service available to represent them. If the RC (replication controller) is created first, the pods are not usable until a service is created.

Creating a Service

Create a service definition file `postgres-service.yaml` and copy the following listing to the file. The `"spec"` field mapping for the service specifies the behavior of the service. The ports on which the service is exposed are defined in the `"ports"` field mapping. Only the port 5432 is exposed because PostgreSQL runs on port 5432. The `selector` expression is set to `app: "postgres"`. All Pods with the label `app=postgres` are managed by the service.

```
apiVersion: v1
kind: Service
metadata:
  name: "postgres"
  labels:
    app: "postgres"
spec:
  ports:
    - port: 5432
  selector:
    app: "postgres"
```

The `postgres-service.yaml` file may be created using the vi editor and saved with the :wq command as shown in Figure 5-4.

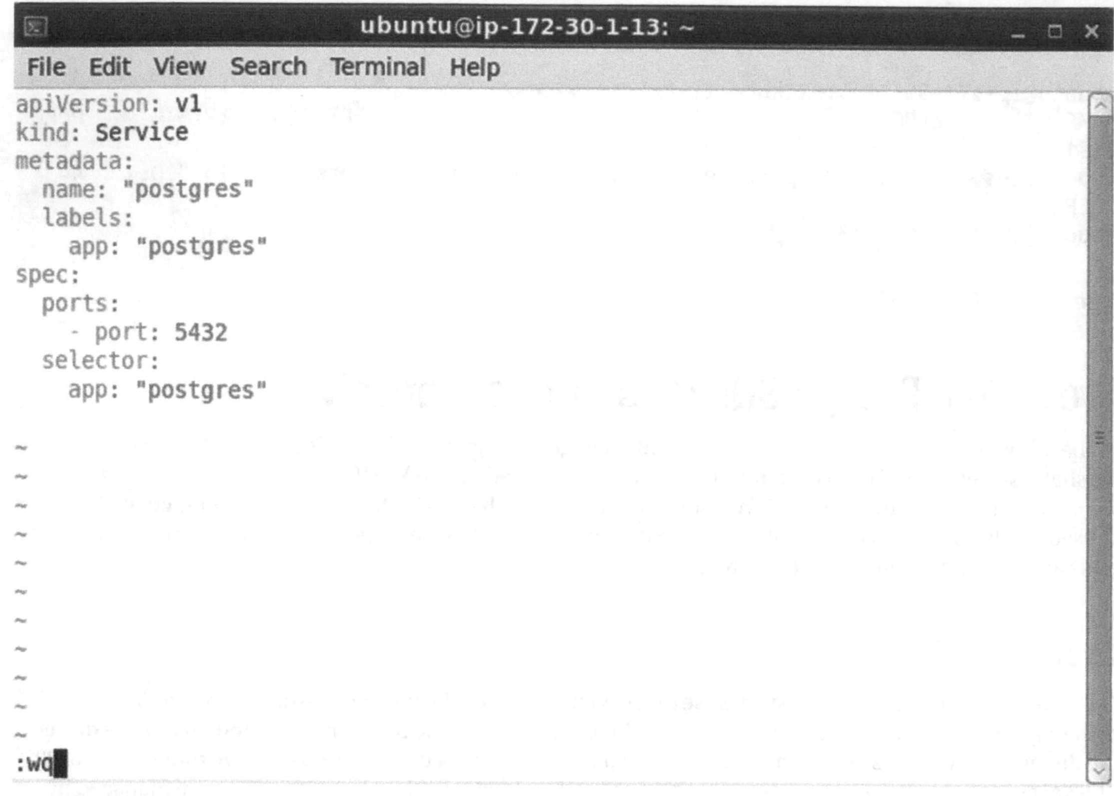

Figure 5-4. *Service Definition File postgres-service.yaml*

Create the service using the `kubectl create` command with the `postgres-service.yaml` definition file.

```
kubectl create -f postgres-service.yaml
```

Subsequently list the services.

```
kubectl get services
```

Also list the Pods.

```
kubectl get pods
```

An output of `services/postgres` from the first command indicates that the service has been created. The second command lists the `postgres` service as running at port 5432 as shown in Figure 5-5. The IP Address of the service is also listed. Creating a service by itself does not create a Pod by itself and only the Pod for the Kubernetes is listed. A service only manages or provides an interface for Pods with the label that matches the `selector` expression in the service.

```
ubuntu@ip-172-30-1-13:~$ kubectl create -f postgres-service.yaml
services/postgres
ubuntu@ip-172-30-1-13:~$ kubectl get services
NAME          LABELS                                    SELECTOR       IP(S)
  PORT(S)
kubernetes    component=apiserver,provider=kubernetes   <none>         10.0.0.1
  443/TCP
postgres      app=postgres                              app=postgres   10.0.0.46
  5432/TCP
ubuntu@ip-172-30-1-13:~$ kubectl get pods
NAME                    READY     STATUS    RESTARTS   AGE
k8s-master-127.0.0.1    3/3       Running   0          3m
ubuntu@ip-172-30-1-13:~$
```

***Figure 5-5.** Creating a Service and listing the Service*

Describe the service `postgres` with the following command.

```
kubectl describe svc postgres
```

The service name, namespace, labels, selector, type, IP address, Port exposed on, and Endpoints get listed. Because no Pods are initially associated with the service, no endpoints are listed as shown in Figure 5-6.

```
ubuntu@ip-172-30-1-13:~$ kubectl describe svc postgres
Name:                   postgres
Namespace:              default
Labels:                 app=postgres
Selector:               app=postgres
Type:                   ClusterIP
IP:                     10.0.0.46
Port:                   <unnamed>       5432/TCP
Endpoints:              <none>
Session Affinity:       None
No events.

ubuntu@ip-172-30-1-13:~$
```

***Figure 5-6.** Describing the postgres Service*

Creating a Replication Controller

In this section we shall create a definition file for a replication controller. Create a definition file called `postgres-rc.yaml`. The definition file has the field discussed in Table 5-1.

Table 5-1. Replication Controller Definition File postgres-rc.yaml

Field	Value	Description
apiVersion	v1	The API version.
kind	ReplicationController	Defines the file to be a replication controller.
metadata		Metadata for the replication controller.
metadata->name		The name of the replication controller. Either the name or the generateName field must be specified. The generateName field is the prefix to use in an automatically generated name.
spec		The specification for the replication controller.
spec->replicas	2	The number of Pod replicas to create.
template		Specifies the template for the Pod that the replication controller manages.
template->metadata		The metadata for the Pod including labels. The label is used to select the Pods managed by the replication controller and must manage the selector expression in the service definition file if the service is to represent the Pod.
template->spec		Pod specification or configuration.
template->spec->containers		The containers in a Pod. Multiple containers could be specified but in this chapter only the container for PostgreSQL is specified.
template->spec->containers->image template->spec->containers->name		The Docker image to run in the container. For PostgreSQL the image is "postgres." The name field specifies the container name.

Optionally the replication controller's `selector` field mapping may be specified. The key:value mapping in the `selector` must match a label in the template->metadata field mapping for the replication controller to manage the Pod in the template. The `selector` field mapping if not specified defaults to the template->metadata->`labels` field mapping. In the following listing the `selector` is italicized and not included in the definition file used. The Pod's template->metadata->labels field mapping specifies an expression `app: "postgres", which translates to Pod label app=postgres`. The `labels` field expression must be the same as the `"selector"` field expression in the service definition file, which was discussed in the previous section, for the service to manage the Pod.

```
apiVersion: v1
kind: ReplicationController
metadata:
  name: "postgres"
```

```
spec:
  replicas: 2
  selector:
    - app: "postgres"
  template:
    metadata:
      labels:
        app: "postgres"
    spec:
      containers:
      -
        image: "postgres"
        name: "postgres"
```

Copy the preceding listing to the postgres-rc.yaml file. The postgres-rc.yaml file may be opened in the vi editor and saved with :wq as shown in Figure 5-7.

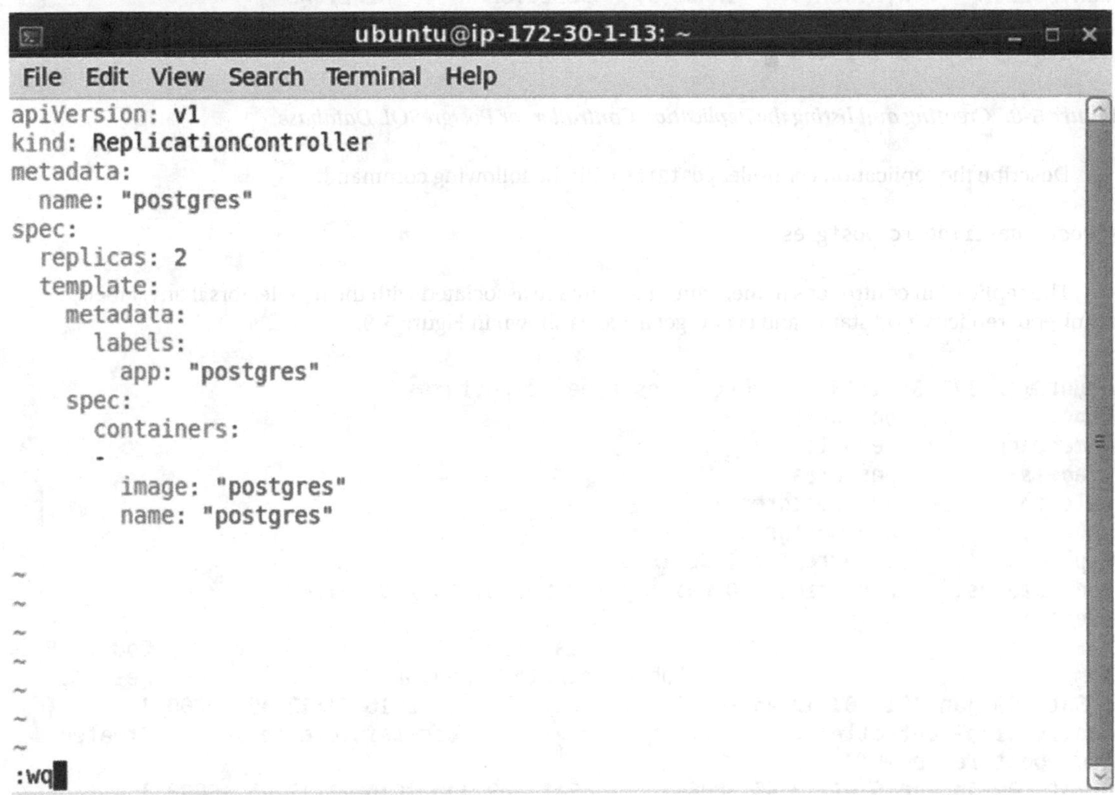

***Figure 5-7.** Replication Controller Definition File*

Create a replication controller using the definition file `postgres-rc.yaml`.

```
kubectl create -f postgres-rc.yaml
```

Subsequently list the replication controllers.

```
kubectl get rc
```

An output of `replicationcontrollers/postgres` from the first command as shown in Figure 5-8 indicates that the replication controller `postgres` has been created. The second command lists the `postgres` replication controller. As discussed before the Replication Controller SELECTOR column is set to the same value as the Pod label, app=postgres.

```
ubuntu@ip-172-30-1-13:~$ kubectl create -f  postgres-rc.yaml
replicationcontrollers/postgres
ubuntu@ip-172-30-1-13:~$ kubectl get rc
CONTROLLER   CONTAINER(S)   IMAGE(S)   SELECTOR       REPLICAS
postgres     postgres       postgres   app=postgres   2
ubuntu@ip-172-30-1-13:~$
```

***Figure 5-8.** Creating and listing the Replication Controller for PostgreSQL Database*

Describe the replication controller `postgres` with the following command.

```
kubectl describe rc postgres
```

The replication controller's name, namespace, image associated with the rc, selectors if any, labels, number of replicas, pod status, and events get listed as shown in Figure 5-9.

```
ubuntu@ip-172-30-1-13:~$ kubectl describe rc postgres
Name:           postgres
Namespace:      default
Image(s):       postgres
Selector:       app=postgres
Labels:         app=postgres
Replicas:       2 current / 2 desired
Pods Status:    2 Running / 0 Waiting / 0 Succeeded / 0 Failed
Events:
  FirstSeen                             LastSeen                        Count  F
rom                             SubobjectPath   Reason                  Message
  Sat, 09 Jan 2016 01:12:45 +0000       Sat, 09 Jan 2016 01:12:45 +0000 1      {
replication-controller }                        successfulCreate        Created
pod: postgres-bqwhe
  Sat, 09 Jan 2016 01:12:45 +0000       Sat, 09 Jan 2016 01:12:45 +0000 1      {
replication-controller }                        successfulCreate        Created
pod: postgres-lmuut


ubuntu@ip-172-30-1-13:~$
```

***Figure 5-9.** Describing the Replication Controller for PostgreSQL Database*

Getting the Pods

To get and list the Pods run the following command.

```
kubectl get pods
```

The two Pods created by the replication controller get listed as shown in Figure 5-10. The Pods should have the Running STATUS and have the READY column value as 1/1.

```
ubuntu@ip-172-30-1-13:~$ kubectl get pods
NAME                  READY     STATUS    RESTARTS   AGE
k8s-master-127.0.0.1  3/3       Running   0          5m
postgres-bqwhe        1/1       Running   0          1m
postgres-lmuut        1/1       Running   0          1m
ubuntu@ip-172-30-1-13:~$
```

Figure 5-10. *Listing the Pods for PostgreSQL Database*

Starting an Interactive Command Shell

To be able to create a PostgreSQL table we need to start an interactive bash shell to access the PostgreSQL server running in a Docker container, and start the psql SQL shell for PostgreSQL. But, first we need to find the container id for a Docker container running the PostgreSQL database. Run the following command to list the Docker containers.

```
sudo docker ps
```

Two of the Docker containers are based on the "postgres" image as shown in Figure 5-11. Copy the container id for the first Docker container for the `postgres` image from the CONTAINER ID column.

```
ubuntu@ip-172-30-1-13: ~
File  Edit  View  Search  Terminal  Help
ubuntu@ip-172-30-1-13:~$ sudo docker ps
CONTAINER ID        IMAGE                                          COMMAND
         CREATED              STATUS                   PORTS                NAMES
a786960b2cb6        postgres                                       "/docker-entrypo
int.s"   52 seconds ago       Up 51 seconds                                 k8s_postgr
es.1121cd19_postgres-v0k42_default_62b21090-b66e-11e5-b153-12bccdb330eb_1591f63a
36fdb7a33c3d        postgres                                       "/docker-entrypo
int.s"   About a minute ago   Up About a minute                             k8s_postgr
es.1121cd19_postgres-sz0ga_default_62b1e640-b66e-11e5-b153-12bccdb330eb_90a3a009
e69d0477357b        gcr.io/google_containers/pause:0.8.0           "/pause"
         About a minute ago   Up About a minute                             k8s_POD.e4
cc795_postgres-v0k42_default_62b21090-b66e-11e5-b153-12bccdb330eb_740ac2dd
273fa84cbf93        gcr.io/google_containers/pause:0.8.0           "/pause"
         About a minute ago   Up About a minute                             k8s_POD.e4
cc795_postgres-sz0ga_default_62b1e640-b66e-11e5-b153-12bccdb330eb_6ab2588a
ffa4172b379e        postgres                                       "/docker-entrypo
int.s"   2 minutes ago        Up 2 minutes                                  k8s_postgr
es.1121cd19_postgres-bqwhe_default_173efb5f-b66e-11e5-b153-12bccdb330eb_3d3ac343
b0604e0a9677        postgres                                       "/docker-entrypo
int.s"   2 minutes ago        Up 2 minutes                                  k8s_postgr
es.1121cd19_postgres-lmuut_default_173f0d4c-b66e-11e5-b153-12bccdb330eb_16a3edcb
f8a3cbd11dc2        gcr.io/google_containers/pause:0.8.0           "/pause"
         3 minutes ago        Up 3 minutes                                  k8s_POD.e4
cc795_postgres-lmuut_default_173f0d4c-b66e-11e5-b153-12bccdb330eb_5a26e3fb
9888f3829724        gcr.io/google_containers/pause:0.8.0           "/pause"
         3 minutes ago        Up 3 minutes                                  k8s_POD.e4
```

Figure 5-11. *Listing the Docker Containers*

Using the container id start the interactive shell.

```
sudo docker exec -it a786960b2cb6 bash
```

The interactive shell gets started as shown in Figure 5-12.

```
ubuntu@ip-172-30-1-13:~$ sudo docker exec -it a786960b2cb6 bash
root@postgres-v0k42:/#
```

Figure 5-12. *Starting an Interactive Shell*

Starting the PostgreSQL SQL Terminal

Next, start the psql SQL shell for PostgreSQL. Set the user as `postgres`.

```
su -l postgres
```

Start the psql command line shell with the following command.

```
psql postgres
```

The psql shall get started as shown in Figure 5-13.

```
root@postgres-v0k42:/# su -l postgres
No directory, logging in with HOME=/
$ psql postgres
psql (9.5.0)
Type "help" for help.

postgres=#
```

Figure 5-13. *Starting the psql CLI Shell*

For the general command syntax for the psql command refer `http://www.postgresql.org/docs/9.5/static/app-psql.html`.

Creating a Database Table

In the psql shell run the following SQL statements to create a database table called `wlslog` and add data to the table.

```
CREATE TABLE wlslog(time_stamp VARCHAR(255) PRIMARY KEY,category VARCHAR(255),type
VARCHAR(255),servername VARCHAR(255),code VARCHAR(255),msg VARCHAR(255));
INSERT INTO wlslog(time_stamp,category,type,servername,code,msg) VALUES('Apr-8-2014-7:
06:16-PM-PDT','Notice','WebLogicServer','AdminServer','BEA-000365','Server state changed
to STANDBY');
INSERT INTO wlslog(time_stamp,category,type,servername,code,msg) VALUES('Apr-8-2014-7:
06:17-PM-PDT','Notice','WebLogicServer','AdminServer','BEA-000365','Server state changed
to STARTING');
INSERT INTO wlslog(time_stamp,category,type,servername,code,msg) VALUES('Apr-8-2014-7:
06:18-PM-PDT','Notice','WebLogicServer','AdminServer','BEA-000360','Server started in
RUNNING mode');
```

Database table `wlslog` gets created and a row of data gets added as shown in Figure 5-14.

```
<),servername VARCHAR(255),code VARCHAR(255),msg VARCHAR(255));
CREATE TABLE
<rver','AdminServer','BEA-000365','Server state changed to STANDBY');
INSERT 0 1
<rver','AdminServer','BEA-000365','Server state changed to STARTING');
INSERT 0 1
<rver','AdminServer','BEA-000360','Server started in RUNNING mode');
INSERT 0 1
postgres=#
```

Figure 5-14. *Creating a Database Table*

Run the following SQL statement to query the database table `wlslog`.

```
SELECT * FROM wlslog;
```

The 3 rows of data added get listed as shown in Figure 5-15.

```
postgres=# SELECT * FROM wlslog;
        time_stamp          | category |      type        | servername   |    code
  |                 msg
--------------------------+----------+------------------+--------------+----------
--+----------------------------------
 Apr-8-2014-7:06:16-PM-PDT | Notice    | WebLogicServer | AdminServer | BEA-00036
5 | Server state changed to STANDBY
 Apr-8-2014-7:06:17-PM-PDT | Notice    | WebLogicServer | AdminServer | BEA-00036
5 | Server state changed to STARTING
 Apr-8-2014-7:06:18-PM-PDT | Notice    | WebLogicServer | AdminServer | BEA-00036
0 | Server started in RUNNING mode
(3 rows)

postgres=# 
```

Figure 5-15. *Querying the Database Table*

Exiting the Interactive Command Shell

To exit the psql shell run the following command.

```
\q
```

To exit the interactive terminal run the following command.

```
exit
```

The psql shell and the interactive shell get exited as shown in Figure 5-16.

```
postgres=# \q
could not save history to file "/home/postgres/.psql_history": No such file or d
irectory
$ exit
root@postgres-v0k42:/# exit
exit
ubuntu@ip-172-30-1-13:~$ 
```

Figure 5-16. *Exiting the psql Shell and Docker Container Interactive Shell*

Scaling the PostgreSQL Cluster

One of the main benefits of the Kubernetes cluster manager is to be able to scale the cluster as required. Initially we created 2 replicas. For example, to scale up the number of PostgreSQL instances to 4 run the following command.

```
kubectl scale rc postgres --replicas=4
```

An output of "scaled" from the preceding command indicates that the cluster has been scaled as shown in Figure 5-17.

```
ubuntu@ip-172-30-1-13:~$ kubectl scale rc postgres --replicas=4
scaled
```

Figure 5-17. *Scaling the number of Pod Replicas to 4*

Subsequently list the pods with the following command.

```
kubectl get pods
```

The 4 Pods get listed as shown in Figure 5-18. Initially some of the Pods could be listed as not "Running" and/or not in READY (1/1) state.

```
ubuntu@ip-172-30-1-13:~$ kubectl get pods
NAME                     READY     STATUS
   RESTARTS   AGE
k8s-master-127.0.0.1     3/3       Running
   0          5m
postgres-bqwhe           1/1       Running
   0          2m
postgres-lmuut           1/1       Running
   0          2m
postgres-sz0ga           0/1       Running
   0          8s
postgres-v0k42           0/1       Image: postgres is ready, container is creating
   0          8s
ubuntu@ip-172-30-1-13:~$
```

Figure 5-18. *Listing the Pods after Scaling*

Run the preceding command again after a few seconds.

```
kubectl get pods
```

The new Pods added to the cluster also get listed as "Running" and in READY state 1/1 as shown in Figure 5-19.

```
ubuntu@ip-172-30-1-13:~$ kubectl get pods
NAME                    READY     STATUS    RESTARTS   AGE
k8s-master-127.0.0.1    3/3       Running   0          6m
postgres-bqwhe          1/1       Running   0          2m
postgres-lmuut          1/1       Running   0          2m
postgres-sz0ga          1/1       Running   0          23s
postgres-v0k42          1/1       Running   0          23s
ubuntu@ip-172-30-1-13:~$
```

Figure 5-19. *Listing all the Pods as running and ready*

Describe the postgres service again.

```
kubectl describe svc postgres
```

Initially no Endpoint was listed as being associated with the service when the service was initially started. With 4 Pods running 4 Endpoints get listed as shown in Figure 5-20.

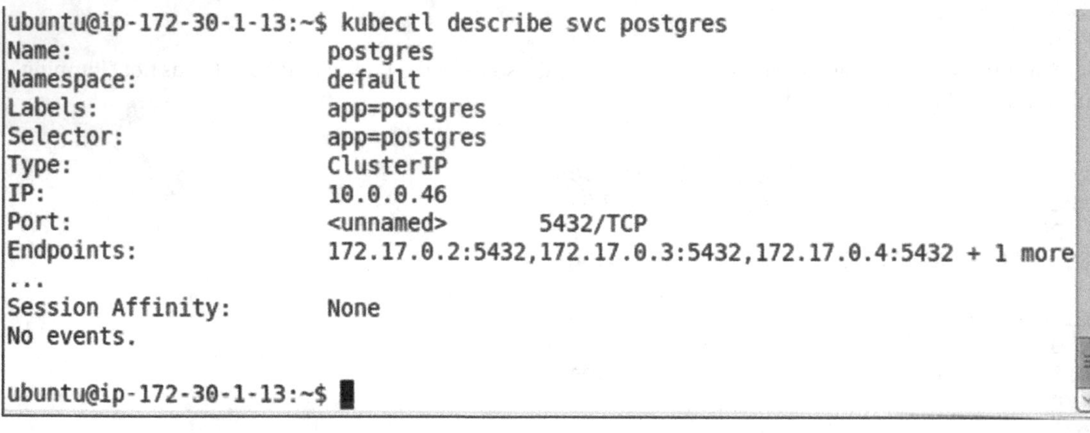

ubuntu@ip-172-30-1-13:~$ kubectl describe svc postgres
Name: postgres
Namespace: default
Labels: app=postgres
Selector: app=postgres
Type: ClusterIP
IP: 10.0.0.46
Port: <unnamed> 5432/TCP
Endpoints: 172.17.0.2:5432,172.17.0.3:5432,172.17.0.4:5432 + 1 more
...
Session Affinity: None
No events.
ubuntu@ip-172-30-1-13:~$

Figure 5-20. *Describing the postgres Service*

Listing the Logs

To list the logs data for a Pod, for example the postgres-v0k42 Pod, run the following command.

```
kubectl logs postgres-v0k42
```

The output in Figure 5-21 lists the PostgreSQL starting.

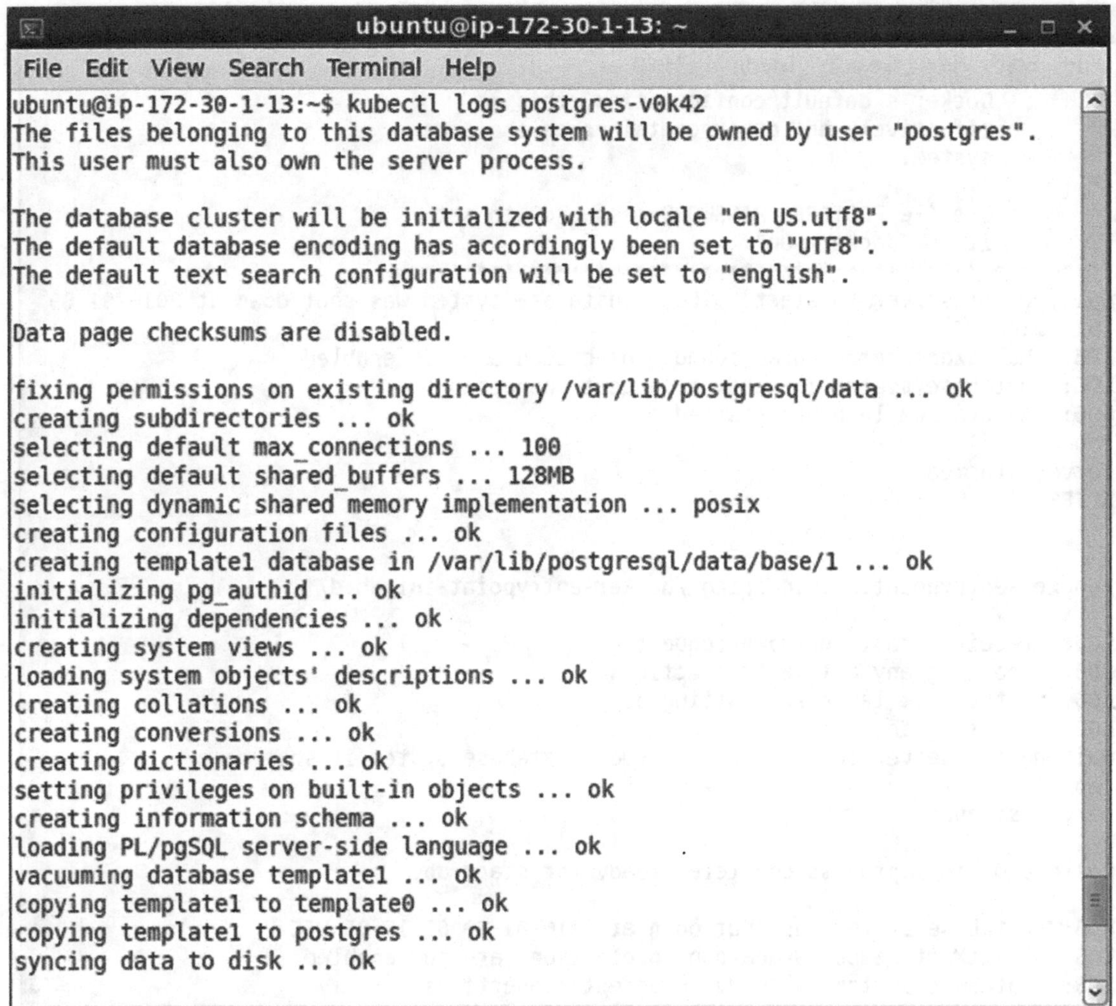

Figure 5-21. *Listing the Logs for a Pod running PostgreSQL Database*

When the PostgreSQL database gets started completely the message "database system is ready to accept connections" gets output as shown in Figure 5-22.

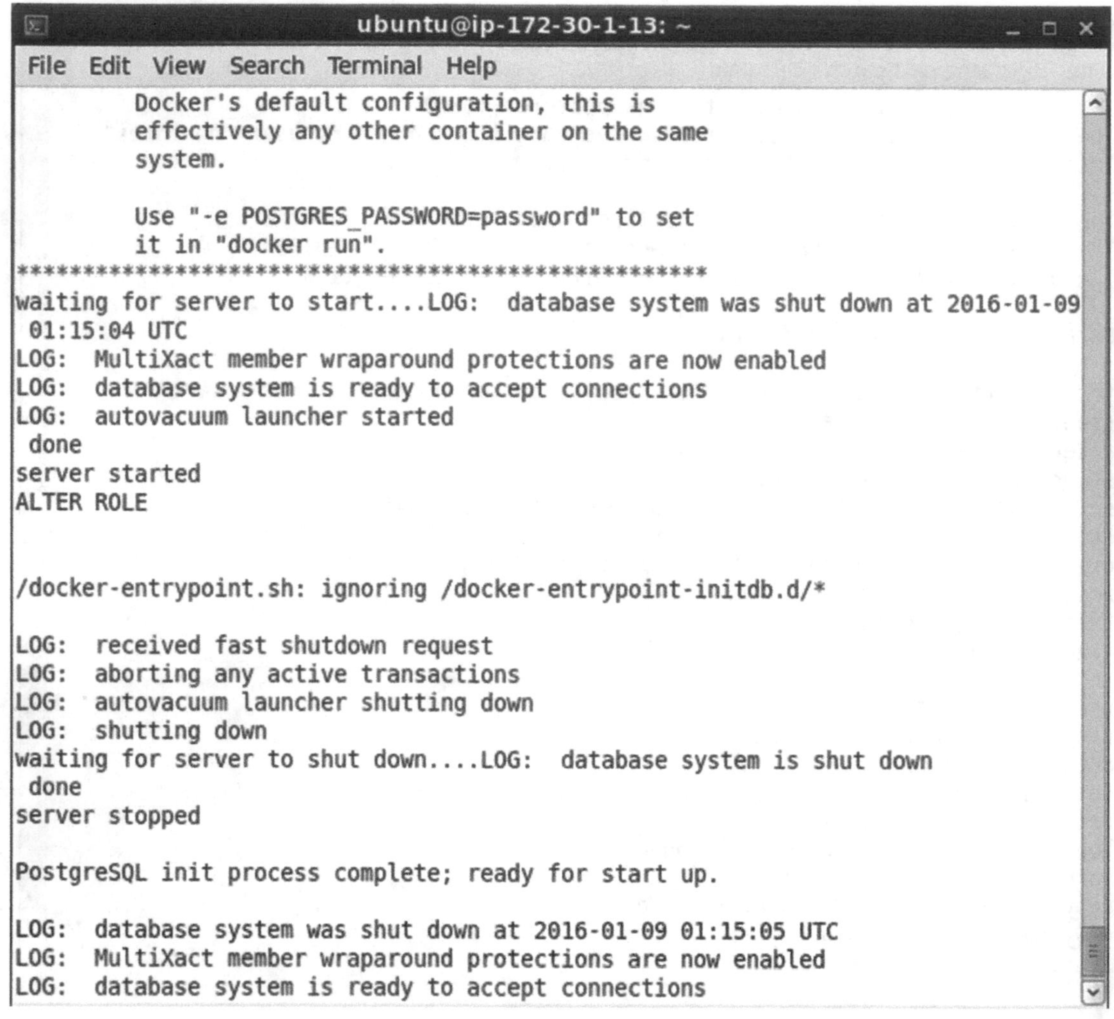

Figure 5-22. *PostgreSQL Database listed as Started and subsequently Shutdown in the Logs*

Deleting the Replication Controller

To delete the replication controller `postgres` and as a result delete all the Pods managed by the replication controller run the following command.

```
kubectl delete rc postgres
```

The `postgres` replication controller gets deleted as indicated by the `replicationcontrollers/postgres` output shown in Figure 5-23. Subsequently, run the following command to list the replication controllers.

```
kubectl get rc
```

The postgres replication controller does not get listed as shown in Figure 5-23. Deleting the replication controller does not delete the service managing the replication controller. To demonstrate list the services.

```
kubectl get services
```

The postgres service is still getting listed, as shown in Figure 5-23.

```
ubuntu@ip-172-30-1-13:~$ kubectl delete rc postgres
replicationcontrollers/postgres
ubuntu@ip-172-30-1-13:~$ kubectl get rc
CONTROLLER   CONTAINER(S)   IMAGE(S)   SELECTOR   REPLICAS
ubuntu@ip-172-30-1-13:~$ kubectl get services
NAME         LABELS                                    SELECTOR       IP(S)
  PORT(S)
kubernetes   component=apiserver,provider=kubernetes   <none>         10.0.0.1
  443/TCP
postgres     app=postgres                              app=postgres   10.0.0.46
  5432/TCP
ubuntu@ip-172-30-1-13:~$
```

Figure 5-23. *Deleting a Replication Controller*

Stopping the Service

To stop the service postgres run the following command.

```
kubectl stop service postgres
```

Subsequently run the following command again.

```
kubectl get services
```

The postgres service does not get listed as shown in Figure 5-24.

```
ubuntu@ip-172-30-1-13:~$ kubectl stop service postgres
services/postgres
ubuntu@ip-172-30-1-13:~$ kubectl get services
NAME         LABELS                                    SELECTOR   IP(S)      POR
T(S)
kubernetes   component=apiserver,provider=kubernetes   <none>     10.0.0.1   443
/TCP
ubuntu@ip-172-30-1-13:~$
```

Figure 5-24. *Stopping the postgres Service*

Creating a PostgreSQL Cluster Imperatively

Using a declarative approach with definition files offers finer control over the service and replication controller. But a replication controller and service could also be created on the command line with kubectl commands. In the following subsections we shall create a replication controller and a service.

Creating a Replication Controller

To create a replication controller called postgres for image "postgres" with number of replicas as 2 and Post as 5432 run the following command.

```
kubectl run postgres --image=postgres --replicas=2 --port=5432
```

The postgres replication controller with 2 replicas of Pod with image postgres and selector expression run=postgres gets created as shown in Figure 5-25.

```
ubuntu@ip-172-30-1-200:~$ kubectl  run postgres --image=postgres --replicas=2 --
port=5432
CONTROLLER   CONTAINER(S)   IMAGE(S)   SELECTOR       REPLICAS
postgres     postgres       postgres   run=postgres   2
```

Figure 5-25. *Creating a Replication Controller Imperatively*

List the replication controllers with the following command.

```
kubectl get rc
```

The postgres replication controller gets listed as shown in Figure 5-26.

```
ubuntu@ip-172-30-1-200:~$ kubectl get rc
CONTROLLER   CONTAINER(S)   IMAGE(S)   SELECTOR       REPLICAS
postgres     postgres       postgres   run=postgres   2
```

Figure 5-26. *Listing the Replication Controllers*

Getting the Pods

To list the Pods managed by the replication controller run the following command.

```
kubectl get pods
```

The two Pods get listed as shown in Figure 5-27. Initially some of the Pods could be listed not Ready as indicated by the 0/1 READY column value. Run the preceding command again to list the Pods as ready with READY column value as 1/1.

```
ubuntu@ip-172-30-1-200:~$ kubectl get pods
NAME                   READY     STATUS    RESTARTS   AGE
k8s-master-127.0.0.1   3/3       Running   0          1h
postgres-c7kvs         1/1       Running   0          16s
postgres-yml3b         0/1       Running   0          16s
ubuntu@ip-172-30-1-200:~$ kubectl get pods
NAME                   READY     STATUS    RESTARTS   AGE
k8s-master-127.0.0.1   3/3       Running   0          1h
postgres-c7kvs         1/1       Running   0          21s
postgres-yml3b         1/1       Running   0          21s
```

Figure 5-27. *Listing the Pods*

Creating a Service

To create a service we need to run the kubectl expose command. Initially only the kubernetes service is running. To demonstrate, run the following command.

```
kubectl get services
```

As shown in Figure 5-28 only the kubernetes service is listed.

```
ubuntu@ip-172-30-1-200:~$ kubectl get services
NAME         LABELS                                      SELECTOR    IP(S)       POR
T(S)
kubernetes   component=apiserver,provider=kubernetes     <none>      10.0.0.1    443
/TCP
ubuntu@ip-172-30-1-200:~$
```

Figure 5-28. *Listing the "kubernetes" Service*

To create a service for the replication controller "postgres" run the following command in which the -port parameter specifies the port at which the service is exposed. The service type is set as LoadBalancer.

```
kubectl expose rc postgres --port=5432 --type=LoadBalancer
```

Subsequently list the services.

```
kubectl get services
```

The postgres service gets listed as shown in Figure 5-29.

```
ubuntu@ip-172-30-1-200:~$ kubectl expose rc postgres --port=5432 --type=LoadBala
ncer
NAME       LABELS         SELECTOR       IP(S)     PORT(S)
postgres   run=postgres   run=postgres             5432/TCP
ubuntu@ip-172-30-1-200:~$ kubectl get services
NAME         LABELS                                      SELECTOR       IP(S)
   PORT(S)
kubernetes   component=apiserver,provider=kubernetes     <none>         10.0.0.1
   443/TCP
postgres     run=postgres                                run=postgres   10.0.0.191
   5432/TCP
ubuntu@ip-172-30-1-200:~$
```

Figure 5-29. *Creating a Service exposed at Port 5432*

Creating a Database Table

The procedure to create a database table is the same as discussed previously for the declarative section and is discussed only briefly in this section. List the Docker containers with the following command.

```
sudo docker ps
```

Two of the Docker containers are listed with image as `postgres` in the IMAGE column as shown in Figure 5-30. Copy the container id for one of these columns from the CONTAINER ID column.

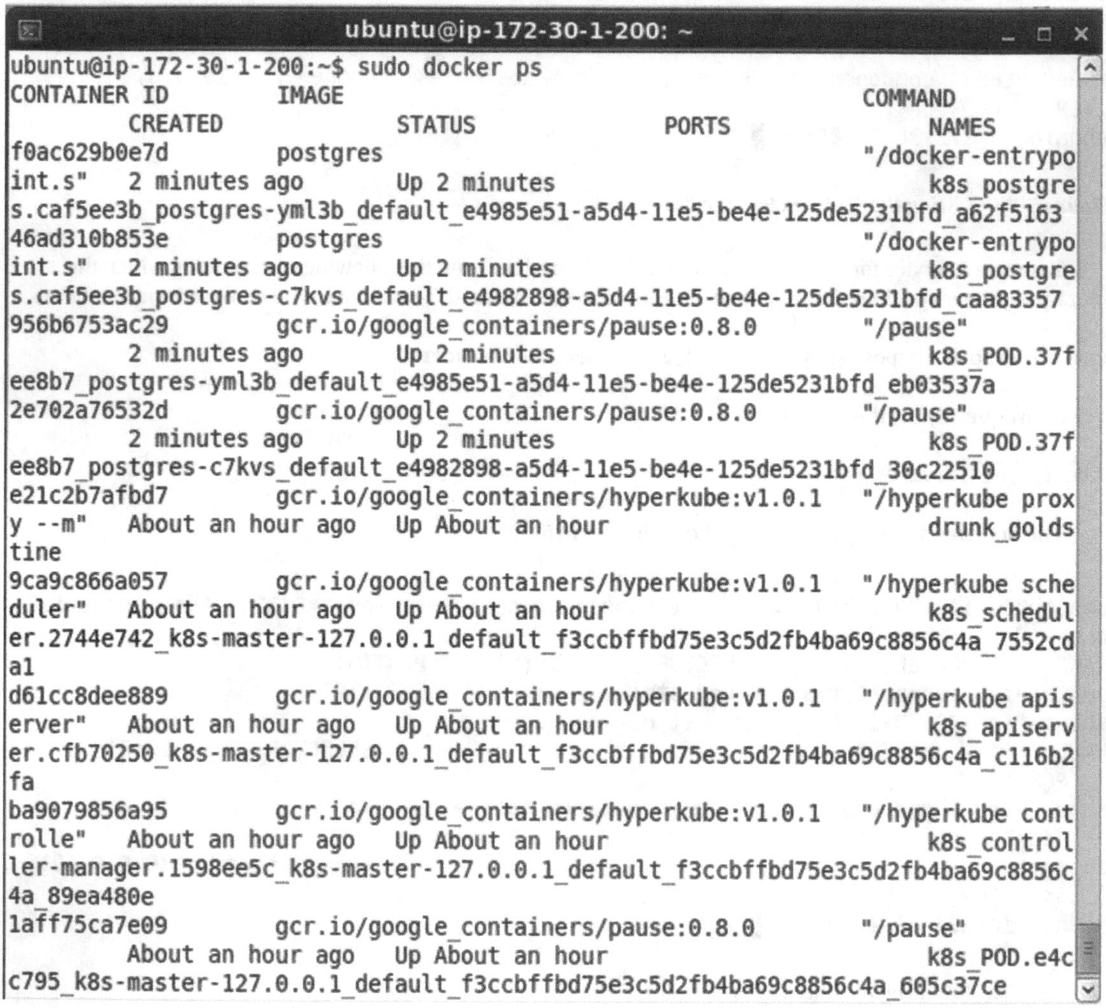

```
ubuntu@ip-172-30-1-200: ~
ubuntu@ip-172-30-1-200:~$ sudo docker ps
CONTAINER ID        IMAGE                                              COMMAND
         CREATED             STATUS              PORTS               NAMES
f0ac629b0e7d        postgres                                           "/docker-entrypo
int.s"   2 minutes ago       Up 2 minutes                            k8s_postgre
s.caf5ee3b_postgres-yml3b_default_e4985e51-a5d4-11e5-be4e-125de5231bfd_a62f5163
46ad310b853e        postgres                                           "/docker-entrypo
int.s"   2 minutes ago       Up 2 minutes                            k8s_postgre
s.caf5ee3b_postgres-c7kvs_default_e4982898-a5d4-11e5-be4e-125de5231bfd_caa83357
956b6753ac29        gcr.io/google_containers/pause:0.8.0               "/pause"
         2 minutes ago       Up 2 minutes                            k8s_POD.37f
ee8b7_postgres-yml3b_default_e4985e51-a5d4-11e5-be4e-125de5231bfd_eb03537a
2e702a76532d        gcr.io/google_containers/pause:0.8.0               "/pause"
         2 minutes ago       Up 2 minutes                            k8s_POD.37f
ee8b7_postgres-c7kvs_default_e4982898-a5d4-11e5-be4e-125de5231bfd_30c22510
e21c2b7afbd7        gcr.io/google_containers/hyperkube:v1.0.1          "/hyperkube prox
y --m"   About an hour ago   Up About an hour                        drunk_golds
tine
9ca9c866a057        gcr.io/google_containers/hyperkube:v1.0.1          "/hyperkube sche
duler"   About an hour ago   Up About an hour                        k8s_schedul
er.2744e742_k8s-master-127.0.0.1_default_f3ccbffbd75e3c5d2fb4ba69c8856c4a_7552cd
a1
d61cc8dee889        gcr.io/google_containers/hyperkube:v1.0.1          "/hyperkube apis
erver"   About an hour ago   Up About an hour                        k8s_apiserv
er.cfb70250_k8s-master-127.0.0.1_default_f3ccbffbd75e3c5d2fb4ba69c8856c4a_c116b2
fa
ba9079856a95        gcr.io/google_containers/hyperkube:v1.0.1          "/hyperkube cont
rolle"   About an hour ago   Up About an hour                        k8s_control
ler-manager.1598ee5c_k8s-master-127.0.0.1_default_f3ccbffbd75e3c5d2fb4ba69c8856c
4a_89ea480e
1aff75ca7e09        gcr.io/google_containers/pause:0.8.0               "/pause"
         About an hour ago   Up About an hour                        k8s_POD.e4c
c795_k8s-master-127.0.0.1_default_f3ccbffbd75e3c5d2fb4ba69c8856c4a_605c37ce
```

Figure 5-30. *Listing the Docker Containers*

Start the interactive shell with the following command.

```
sudo docker exec -it af0ac629b0e7d bash
```

The interactive terminal gets started as shown in Figure 5-31.

```
ubuntu@ip-172-30-1-200:~$ sudo docker exec -it f0ac629b0e7d bash
root@postgres-yml3b:/#
```

Figure 5-31. *Starting the TTY*

Set the user as postgres.

```
su -l postgres
```

Start the psql command line shell.

```
psql postgres
```

The psql shell is shown in Figure 5-32.

```
$ psql postgres
psql (9.4.5)
Type "help" for help.

postgres=#
```

Figure 5-32. *Starting the psql Shell*

Run the following SQL statements to create a database table called wlslog and add data to the table.

```
CREATE TABLE wlslog(time_stamp VARCHAR(255) PRIMARY KEY,category VARCHAR(255),type
VARCHAR(255),servername VARCHAR(255),code VARCHAR(255),msg VARCHAR(255));

INSERT INTO wlslog(time_stamp,category,type,servername,code,msg) VALUES('Apr-8-2014-7:
06:16-PM-PDT','Notice','WebLogicServer','AdminServer','BEA-000365','Server state changed
to STANDBY');
INSERT INTO wlslog(time_stamp,category,type,servername,code,msg) VALUES('Apr-8-2014-7:
06:17-PM-PDT','Notice','WebLogicServer','AdminServer','BEA-000365','Server state changed
to STARTING');
INSERT INTO wlslog(time_stamp,category,type,servername,code,msg) VALUES('Apr-8-2014-7:
06:18-PM-PDT','Notice','WebLogicServer','AdminServer','BEA-000360','Server started in
RUNNING mode');
```

The database table wlslog gets created as shown in Figure 5-33.

```
<),servername VARCHAR(255), code VARCHAR(255),msg VARCHAR(255));
CREATE TABLE
<rver','AdminServer','BEA-000365','Server state changed to STANDBY');
INSERT 0 1
<rver','AdminServer','BEA-000365','Server state changed to STARTING');
INSERT 0 1
<rver','AdminServer','BEA-000360','Server started in RUNNING mode');
INSERT 0 1
postgres=#
```

Figure 5-33. *Creating a Database Table*

Run the following SQL statement to query the wlslog table.

```
SELECT * FROM wlslog;
```

The three rows of data added get listed as shown in Figure 5-34.

```
postgres=# SELECT * FROM wlslog;
       time_stamp         | category |      type      | servername  |    code
  |             msg
--------------------------+----------+----------------+-------------+----------
--+---------------------------------
 Apr-8-2014-7:06:16-PM-PDT | Notice   | WebLogicServer | AdminServer | BEA-00036
5 | Server state changed to STANDBY
 Apr-8-2014-7:06:17-PM-PDT | Notice   | WebLogicServer | AdminServer | BEA-00036
5 | Server state changed to STARTING
 Apr-8-2014-7:06:18-PM-PDT | Notice   | WebLogicServer | AdminServer | BEA-00036
0 | Server started in RUNNING mode
(3 rows)

postgres=#
```

Figure 5-34. *Querying the wlslog Database Table*

To quit the psql shell and the interactive shell for the Docker container running PostgreSQL, run the following commands.

```
\q
exit
```

The psql shell and the tty get exited as shown in Figure 5-35.

```
postgres=# \q
could not save history to file "/home/postgres/.psql_history": No such file or d
irectory
$ exit
root@postgres-yml3b:/# exit
exit
ubuntu@ip-172-30-1-200:~$ ▌
```

Figure 5-35. *Exiting the Shells*

Scaling the PostgreSQL Cluster

When we created the cluster initially we set the replicas to 2. List the pods as follows.

```
kubectl get pods
```

Only two Pods get listed as shown in Figure 5-36.

```
ubuntu@ip-172-30-1-200:~$ kubectl get pods
NAME                     READY     STATUS    RESTARTS   AGE
k8s-master-127.0.0.1     3/3       Running   0          1h
postgres-c7kvs           1/1       Running   0          8m
postgres-yml3b           1/1       Running   0          8m
```

Figure 5-36. *Listing the Pods*

Scale the cluster to 4 replicas with the following command.

```
kubectl scale rc postgres --replicas=4
```

An output of "scaled" as shown in Figure 5-37 indicates that the cluster has been scaled.

```
ubuntu@ip-172-30-1-200:~$ kubectl scale rc postgres --replicas=4
scaled
```

Figure 5-37. *Scaling the Pod Replicas to 4*

Subsequently list the Pods.

```
kubectl get pods
```

The preceding command may have to be run multiple times to list all the Pods as "Running" and in READY state 1/1 as shown in Figure 5-38.

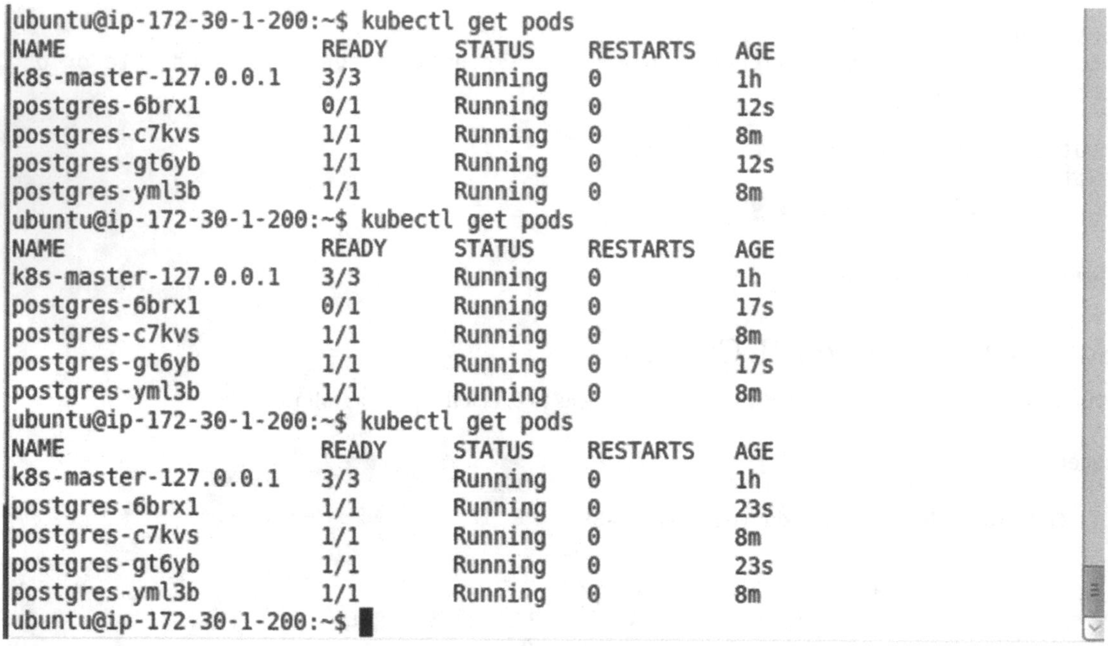

```
ubuntu@ip-172-30-1-200:~$ kubectl get pods
NAME                    READY     STATUS    RESTARTS   AGE
k8s-master-127.0.0.1    3/3       Running   0          1h
postgres-6brx1          0/1       Running   0          12s
postgres-c7kvs          1/1       Running   0          8m
postgres-gt6yb          1/1       Running   0          12s
postgres-yml3b          1/1       Running   0          8m
ubuntu@ip-172-30-1-200:~$ kubectl get pods
NAME                    READY     STATUS    RESTARTS   AGE
k8s-master-127.0.0.1    3/3       Running   0          1h
postgres-6brx1          0/1       Running   0          17s
postgres-c7kvs          1/1       Running   0          8m
postgres-gt6yb          1/1       Running   0          17s
postgres-yml3b          1/1       Running   0          8m
ubuntu@ip-172-30-1-200:~$ kubectl get pods
NAME                    READY     STATUS    RESTARTS   AGE
k8s-master-127.0.0.1    3/3       Running   0          1h
postgres-6brx1          1/1       Running   0          23s
postgres-c7kvs          1/1       Running   0          8m
postgres-gt6yb          1/1       Running   0          23s
postgres-yml3b          1/1       Running   0          8m
ubuntu@ip-172-30-1-200:~$
```

Figure 5-38. *Listing the Pods in various states of starting*

Deleting the Replication Controller

To delete the replication controller run the following command.

```
kubectl delete rc postgres
```

List the Pods subsequent to deleting the rc.

```
kubectl get pods
```

List the services.

```
kubectl get services
```

The `postgres` replication controller gets deleted and does not get listed subsequently as shown in Figure 5-39. The `postgres` service still gets listed also shown in Figure 5-39.

```
ubuntu@ip-172-30-1-200:~$ kubectl delete rc postgres
replicationcontrollers/postgres
ubuntu@ip-172-30-1-200:~$ kubectl get pods
NAME                    READY     STATUS    RESTARTS   AGE
k8s-master-127.0.0.1    3/3       Running   0          1h
ubuntu@ip-172-30-1-200:~$ kubectl get services
NAME         LABELS                                      SELECTOR       IP(S)
   PORT(S)
kubernetes   component=apiserver,provider=kubernetes    <none>         10.0.0.1
   443/TCP
postgres     run=postgres                                run=postgres   10.0.0.191
   5432/TCP
```

Figure 5-39. *Deleting the Replication Controller*

Stopping the Service

To stop the service run the following command.

```
kubectl stop service postgres
```

The `postgres` service gets stopped as shown in Figure 5-40. Subsequently run the following command.

```
kubectl get services
```

The `postgres` service does not get listed as shown in Figure 5-40 also.

```
ubuntu@ip-172-30-1-200:~$ kubectl stop service postgres
services/postgres
ubuntu@ip-172-30-1-200:~$ kubectl get services
NAME         LABELS                                      SELECTOR    IP(S)       POR
T(S)
kubernetes   component=apiserver,provider=kubernetes    <none>      10.0.0.1    443
/TCP
ubuntu@ip-172-30-1-200:~$
```

Figure 5-40. *Stopping the Service*

Summary

In this chapter we used the Kubernetes cluster manager to start and manage a PostgreSQL server cluster. We demonstrated creating a cluster both imperatively on the command line and declaratively using definition files. We scaled the cluster using a replication controller and exposed a service for the cluster using a Kubernetes service. In the next chapter we shall discuss creating and managing an Oracle Database cluster.

CHAPTER 6

Using Oracle Database

Oracle Database is the most commonly used relational database (RDBMS). Installing and configuring Oracle Database would usually involve downloading the software, setting the kernel parameters, installing and configuring the software, all of which is quite involved. Using Docker containers coordinated with Kubernetes makes the task of installing, configuring, and orchestrating a Oracle Database cluster much easier. Oracle Database cluster consisting of multiple instances could benefit from the schedulability, scalability, distributedness, and failover features of the Kubernetes container cluster manager. In this chapter we shall install Oracle Database using a Docker image for the database. We shall create multiple replicas of the database Pod using a replication controller and expose the database as a service. This chapter has the following sections.

Setting the Environment

Creating an Oracle Database Instance Imperatively

Creating an Oracle Database Instance Declaratively

Keeping the Replication Level

Scaling the Database

Starting the Interactive Shell

Connecting to Database

Creating a User

Creating a Database Table

Exiting the Interactive Shell

Setting the Environment

The following software is required for this chapter.

-Docker Engine (latest version)

-Kubernetes (version 1.01)

-Kubectl (version 1.01)

-Docker Image for Oracle Database (Oracle Database XE 11g)

D. Vohra, *Kubernetes Microservices with Docker*, DOI 10.1007/978-1-4842-1907-2_6

If not already installed, install Docker Engine, Kubernetes, and Kubectl as discussed in Chapter 1. SSH login to the Ubuntu instance on Amazon EC2 using the Public IP Address of the EC2 instance.

```
ssh -i "docker.pem" ubuntu@52.90.115.30
```

Start the Docker instance and verify its status with the following commands.

```
sudo service docker start
sudo service docker status
```

Docker is indicated as running in Figure 6-1.

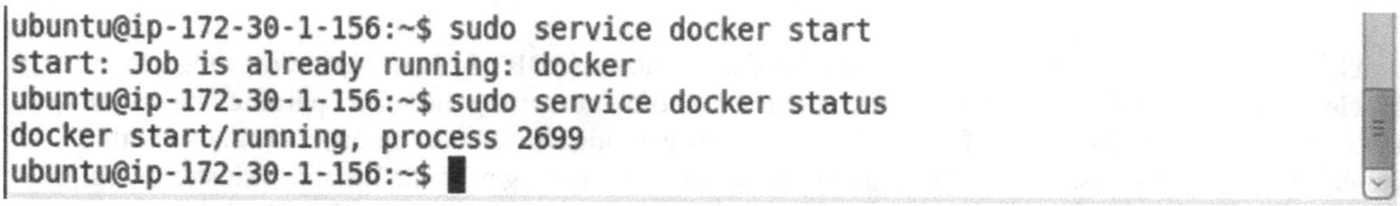

```
ubuntu@ip-172-30-1-156:~$ sudo service docker start
start: Job is already running: docker
ubuntu@ip-172-30-1-156:~$ sudo service docker status
docker start/running, process 2699
ubuntu@ip-172-30-1-156:~$
```

Figure 6-1. *Starting Docker and verifying its Status*

List the services running.

```
kubectl get services
```

Only the `kubernetes` service is listed as running in Figure 6-2.

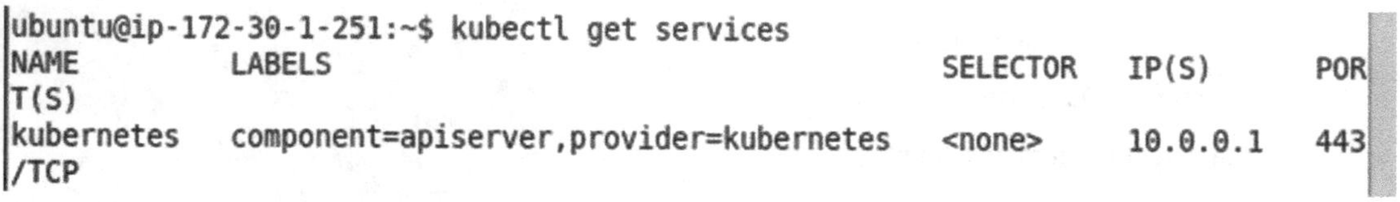

```
ubuntu@ip-172-30-1-251:~$ kubectl get services
NAME         LABELS                                      SELECTOR    IP(S)       POR
T(S)
kubernetes   component=apiserver,provider=kubernetes    <none>      10.0.0.1    443
/TCP
```

Figure 6-2. *Listing the Kubernetes Service*

Creating an Oracle Database Instance Imperatively

In this section we shall create an Oracle Database cluster using `kubectl` on the command line. Several Docker images are available for Oracle Database and we shall be using the `sath89/oracle-xe-11g` image (`https://hub.docker.com/r/sath89/oracle-xe-11g/`). Run the following `kubectl` command to create an Oracle Database cluster consisting of 2 replicas with port set as 1521.

```
kubectl run oradb --image=sath89/oracle-xe-11g --replicas=2 --port=1521
```

The output from the command in Figure 6-3 lists a replication controller called `oradb`, a Docker container called `oradb`, a selector (`run=oradb`) to select Pods that comprise the replication controller replicas, and the number of replicas (2). The Pod label is also set to `run=oradb`.

```
ubuntu@ip-172-30-1-156:~$ kubectl  run oradb --image=sath89/oracle-xe-11g --repl
icas=2 --port=1521
CONTROLLER   CONTAINER(S)   IMAGE(S)                SELECTOR    REPLICAS
oradb        oradb          sath89/oracle-xe-11g    run=oradb   2
ubuntu@ip-172-30-1-156:~$
```

Figure 6-3. *Creating a Replication Controller and Pod Replicas for Oracle Database*

List the replication controller with the following command.

```
kubectl get rc
```

The oradb replication controller shown in Figure 6-4 gets listed.

```
ubuntu@ip-172-30-1-156:~$ kubectl get rc
CONTROLLER   CONTAINER(S)   IMAGE(S)                SELECTOR    REPLICAS
oradb        oradb          sath89/oracle-xe-11g    run=oradb   2
ubuntu@ip-172-30-1-156:~$
```

Figure 6-4. *Listing the Replication Controllers*

List the Pods using the following command.

```
kubectl get pods
```

In addition to the Kubernetes Pod `k8s-master-127.0.0.1` two other pods get listed for Oracle Database as shown in Figure 6-5. Initially the Pods could be listed as "not ready" as shown in Figure 6-5 also. Run the preceding command after a duration of a few seconds, multiple times if required, to list the two Pods are Running and READY (1/1).

```
ubuntu@ip-172-30-1-156:~$ kubectl get pods
NAME                      READY     STATUS
        RESTARTS   AGE
k8s-master-127.0.0.1      3/3       Running
        0          6m
oradb-ea57r               0/1       Image: sath89/oracle-xe-11g is not ready on the
 node    0          45s
oradb-wjv2t               0/1       Image: sath89/oracle-xe-11g is not ready on the
 node    0          45s
ubuntu@ip-172-30-1-156:~$ kubectl get pods
NAME                      READY     STATUS     RESTARTS   AGE
k8s-master-127.0.0.1      3/3       Running    0          6m
oradb-ea57r               1/1       Running    0          51s
oradb-wjv2t               1/1       Running    0          51s
ubuntu@ip-172-30-1-156:~$
```

Figure 6-5. *Listing the Pods in various stages of running*

Get the nodes with the following command.

```
kubectl get nodes
```

And get the Kubernetes services with the following command.

```
kubectl get services
```

Only the `kubernetes` service gets listed as shown in Figure 6-6 because we have not yet created a service for Oracle Database.

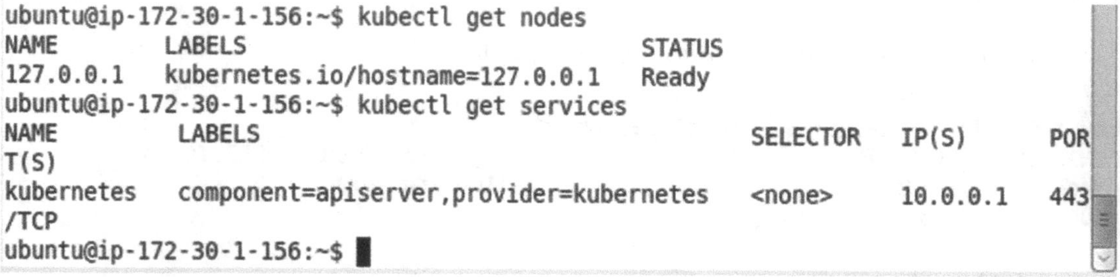

```
ubuntu@ip-172-30-1-156:~$ kubectl get nodes
NAME        LABELS                              STATUS
127.0.0.1   kubernetes.io/hostname=127.0.0.1    Ready
ubuntu@ip-172-30-1-156:~$ kubectl get services
NAME         LABELS                                     SELECTOR   IP(S)      POR
T(S)
kubernetes   component=apiserver,provider=kubernetes   <none>     10.0.0.1   443
/TCP
ubuntu@ip-172-30-1-156:~$
```

Figure 6-6. *Creating a Replication Controller does not create a Service*

Listing Logs

List the logs for one of the Pods using the following command.

```
kubectl logs oradb-ea57r
```

The logs generated by a started Oracle Database instance get output as shown in Figure 6-7. Oracle Net Listener is indicated as having been started.

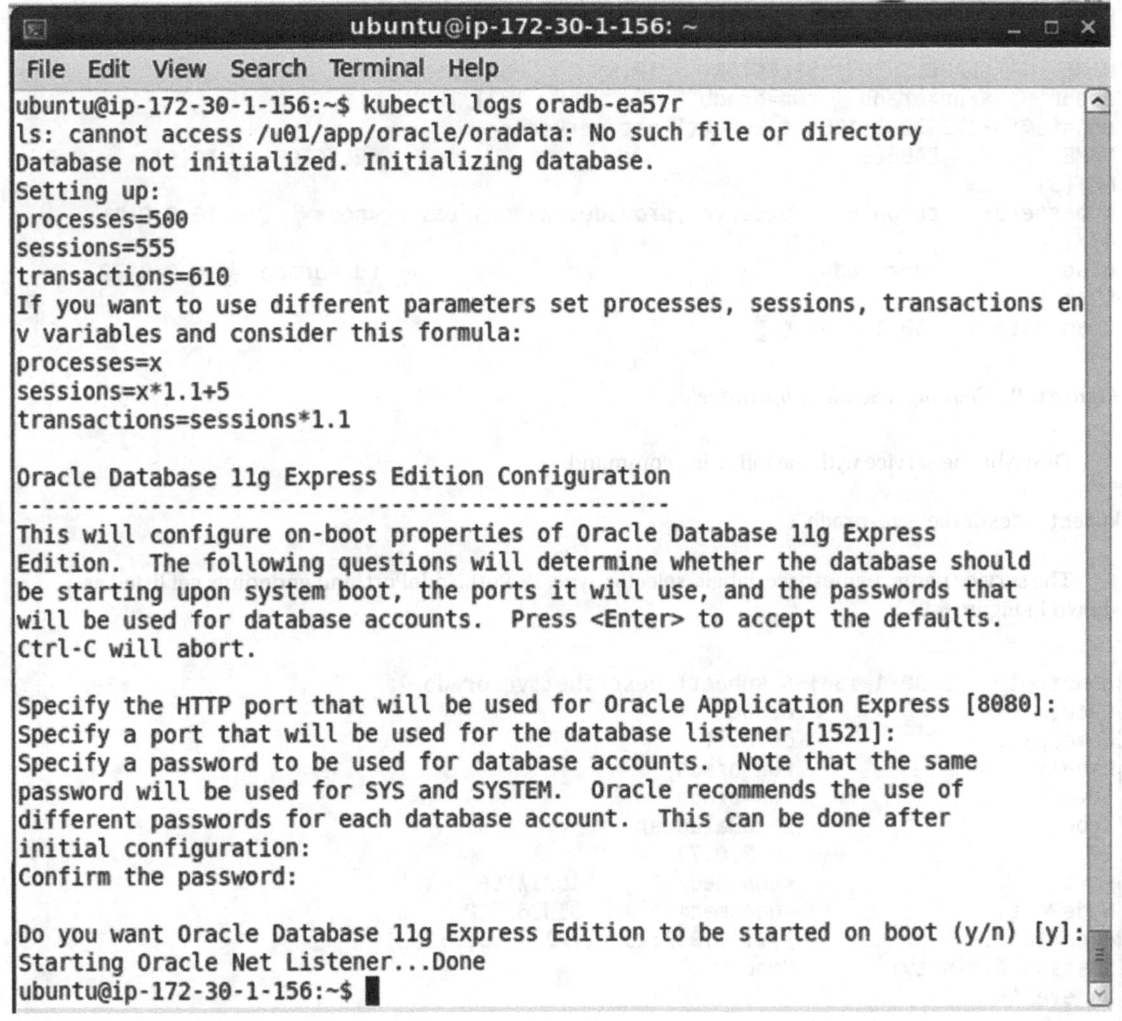

Figure 6-7. *Listing Logs for a Pod*

Creating a Service

Next, expose the replication controller oradb as a Kubernetes service on port 1521. Subsequently list the Kubernetes services.

```
kubectl expose rc oradb --port=1521 --type=LoadBalancer
kubectl get services
```

The first of the two preceding commands starts the oradb service. Subsequently the service gets listed as shown in Figure 6-8. The service selector is run=oradb, which is the same as the replication controller selector.

```
ubuntu@ip-172-30-1-156:~$ kubectl expose rc oradb --port=1521 --type=LoadBalance
r
NAME        LABELS        SELECTOR     IP(S)      PORT(S)
oradb       run=oradb     run=oradb               1521/TCP
ubuntu@ip-172-30-1-156:~$ kubectl get services
NAME           LABELS                                      SELECTOR     IP(S)         P
ORT(S)
kubernetes     component=apiserver,provider=kubernetes     <none>       10.0.0.1      4
43/TCP
oradb          run=oradb                                   run=oradb    10.0.0.72     1
521/TCP
ubuntu@ip-172-30-1-156:~$
```

Figure 6-8. *Creating a Service Imperatively*

Describe the service with the following command.

```
kubectl describe svc oradb
```

The service name, namespace, labels, selector, type, IP, Port,NodePort, and endpoints get listed as shown in Figure 6-9.

```
ubuntu@ip-172-30-1-156:~$ kubectl describe svc oradb
Name:                     oradb
Namespace:                default
Labels:                   run=oradb
Selector:                 run=oradb
Type:                     LoadBalancer
IP:                       10.0.0.72
Port:                     <unnamed>       1521/TCP
NodePort:                 <unnamed>       31626/TCP
Endpoints:                172.17.0.2:1521,172.17.0.3:1521
Session Affinity:         None
No events.

ubuntu@ip-172-30-1-156:~$
```

Figure 6-9. *Describing the oradb Service*

Scaling the Database

Run the `kubectl scale` command to scale the replicas. For example, reduce the number of replicas to 1.

```
kubectl scale rc oradb --replicas=1
```

An output of "scaled" indicates that the replicas have been scaled as shown in Figure 6-10.

```
ubuntu@ip-172-30-1-156:~$ kubectl scale rc oradb --replicas=1
scaled
ubuntu@ip-172-30-1-156:~$
```

Figure 6-10. *Scaling the Replicas to 1*

Subsequently list the running Pods.

```
kubectl get pods
```

Only one Oracle Database Pod gets listed as the other has been stopped to reduce the replication level to one as shown in Figure 6-11. Subsequently, describe the service.

```
ubuntu@ip-172-30-1-156:~$ kubectl scale rc oradb --replicas=1
scaled
ubuntu@ip-172-30-1-156:~$ kubectl get pods
NAME                   READY     STATUS    RESTARTS   AGE
k8s-master-127.0.0.1   3/3       Running   0          17m
oradb-06z2g            1/1       Running   0          6m
ubuntu@ip-172-30-1-156:~$ kubectl describe svc oradb
Name:                  oradb
Namespace:             default
Labels:                run=oradb
Selector:              run=oradb
Type:                  LoadBalancer
IP:                    10.0.0.72
Port:                  <unnamed>     1521/TCP
NodePort:              <unnamed>     31626/TCP
Endpoints:             172.17.0.5:1521
Session Affinity:      None
No events.
```

Figure 6-11. *Listing and Describing the Single Pod*

```
kubectl describe svc oradb
```

Because the cluster has been scaled down to one replica the number of endpoints also gets reduced to one as shown in Figure 6-11.

Deleting the Replication Controller and Service

In subsequent sections we shall be creating a cluster of Oracle Database instances declaratively using definition files. As we shall be using the same configuration parameters, delete the "oradb" replication controller and the "oradb" service with the following commands.

```
kubectl delete rc oradb
kubectl delete svc oradb
```

Both the replication controller and the service get deleted as shown in Figure 6-12.

```
ubuntu@ip-172-30-1-156:~$ kubectl delete  rc  oradb
replicationcontrollers/oradb
ubuntu@ip-172-30-1-156:~$ kubectl delete  service  oradb
services/oradb
ubuntu@ip-172-30-1-156:~$ ▌
```

Figure 6-12. *Deleting the Replication Controller and Service*

Creating an Oracle Database Instance Declaratively

In this section we shall create Oracle Database cluster declaratively using definition files for a Pod, replication controller, and service. We have used the YAML format in the definition files but the JSON format may be used instead.

Creating a Pod

Create a definition file for a Pod called `oradb.yaml`. Copy the following listing, which defines a Pod named "oradb" with a label setting `name: "oradb"`, which translates to Pod label name=oradb. The container image is set as "sath89/oracle-xe-11g" and the container port is set as 1521.

```
apiVersion: v1
kind: Pod
metadata:
  name: "oradb"
  labels:
    name: "oradb"
spec:
  containers:
    -
      image: "sath89/oracle-xe-11g"
      name: "oradb"
      ports:
        -
          containerPort: 1521
  restartPolicy: Always
```

The `oradb.yaml` file may be created in the vi editor and saved with the :wq command as shown in Figure 6-13.

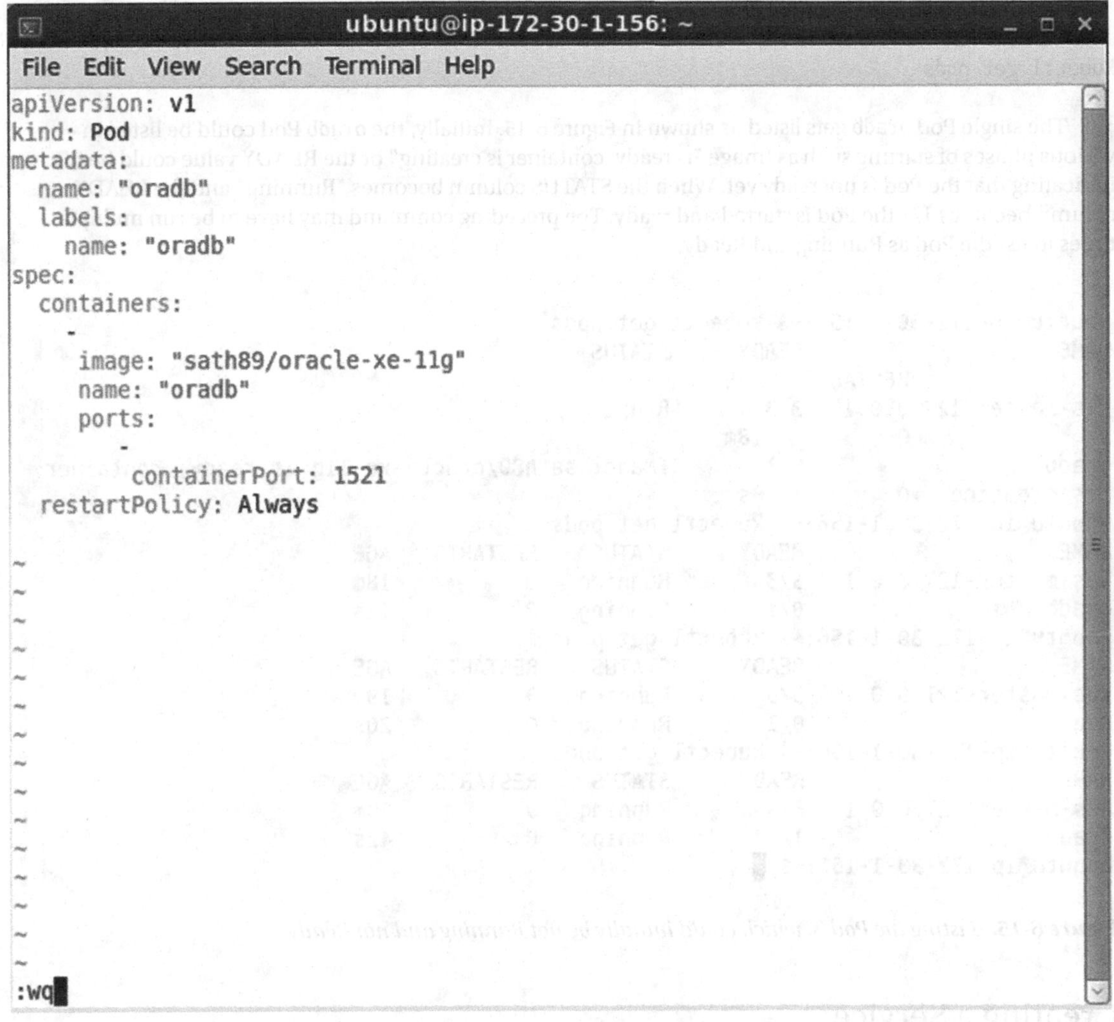

Figure 6-13. Pod Definition File

Create a Pod using the definition file `oradb.yaml` with the `kubectl create` command.

```
kubectl create -f oradb.yaml --validate
```

An output of "pods/oradb" in Figure 6-14 indicates that the oradb Pod has been created.

```
ubuntu@ip-172-30-1-156:~$ kubectl create -f oradb.yaml  --validate
pods/oradb
```

Figure 6-14. Creating a Pod from a Definition File

Subsequently list the running Pods with the following command.

```
kubectl get pods
```

The single Pod `oradb` gets listed as shown in Figure 6-15. Initially, the `oradb` Pod could be listed in various phases of starting such as Image "is ready, container is creating" or the READY value could be 0/1 indicating that the Pod is not ready yet. When the STATUS column becomes "Running" and the READY column becomes 1/1 the Pod is started and ready. The preceding command may have to be run multiple times to list the Pod as Running and Ready.

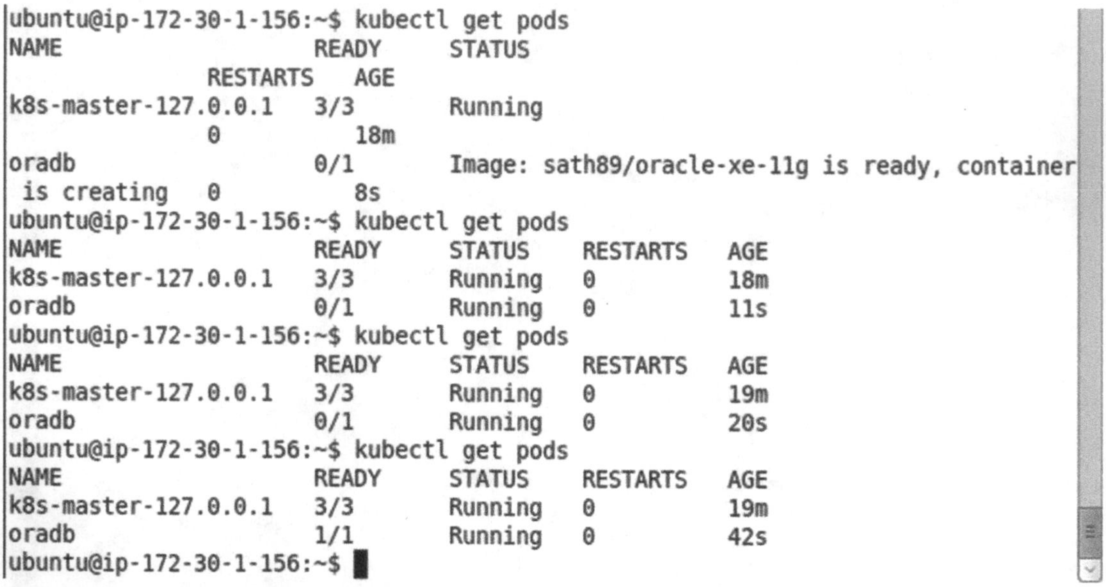

```
ubuntu@ip-172-30-1-156:~$ kubectl get pods
NAME                      READY     STATUS
               RESTARTS   AGE
k8s-master-127.0.0.1      3/3       Running
               0          18m
oradb                     0/1       Image: sath89/oracle-xe-11g is ready, container
 is creating   0          8s
ubuntu@ip-172-30-1-156:~$ kubectl get pods
NAME                      READY     STATUS    RESTARTS   AGE
k8s-master-127.0.0.1      3/3       Running   0          18m
oradb                     0/1       Running   0          11s
ubuntu@ip-172-30-1-156:~$ kubectl get pods
NAME                      READY     STATUS    RESTARTS   AGE
k8s-master-127.0.0.1      3/3       Running   0          19m
oradb                     0/1       Running   0          20s
ubuntu@ip-172-30-1-156:~$ kubectl get pods
NAME                      READY     STATUS    RESTARTS   AGE
k8s-master-127.0.0.1      3/3       Running   0          19m
oradb                     1/1       Running   0          42s
ubuntu@ip-172-30-1-156:~$
```

Figure 6-15. *Listing the Pod/s, which could initially be not Running and not Ready*

Creating a Service

Next, create a service for an Oracle Database cluster. The service does not specify how many instances (replicas) of the Oracle Database image are running or should be running. The replicas are controlled by the replication controller. The service only defines a port to expose the service at, a label for the service and a selector to match the Pods to be managed by the service. The selector setting is app: "oradb", which translates to service selector app=oradb. Create a service definition file `oradb-service.yaml` and copy the following listing to the definition file.

```
apiVersion: v1
kind: Service
metadata:
  name: "oradb"
  labels:
    app: "oradb"
```

```
spec:
  ports:
    -
      port: 1521
  selector:
    app: "oradb"
```

The oradb-service.yaml definition file may be created in the vi editor and saved with :wq as shown in Figure 6-16.

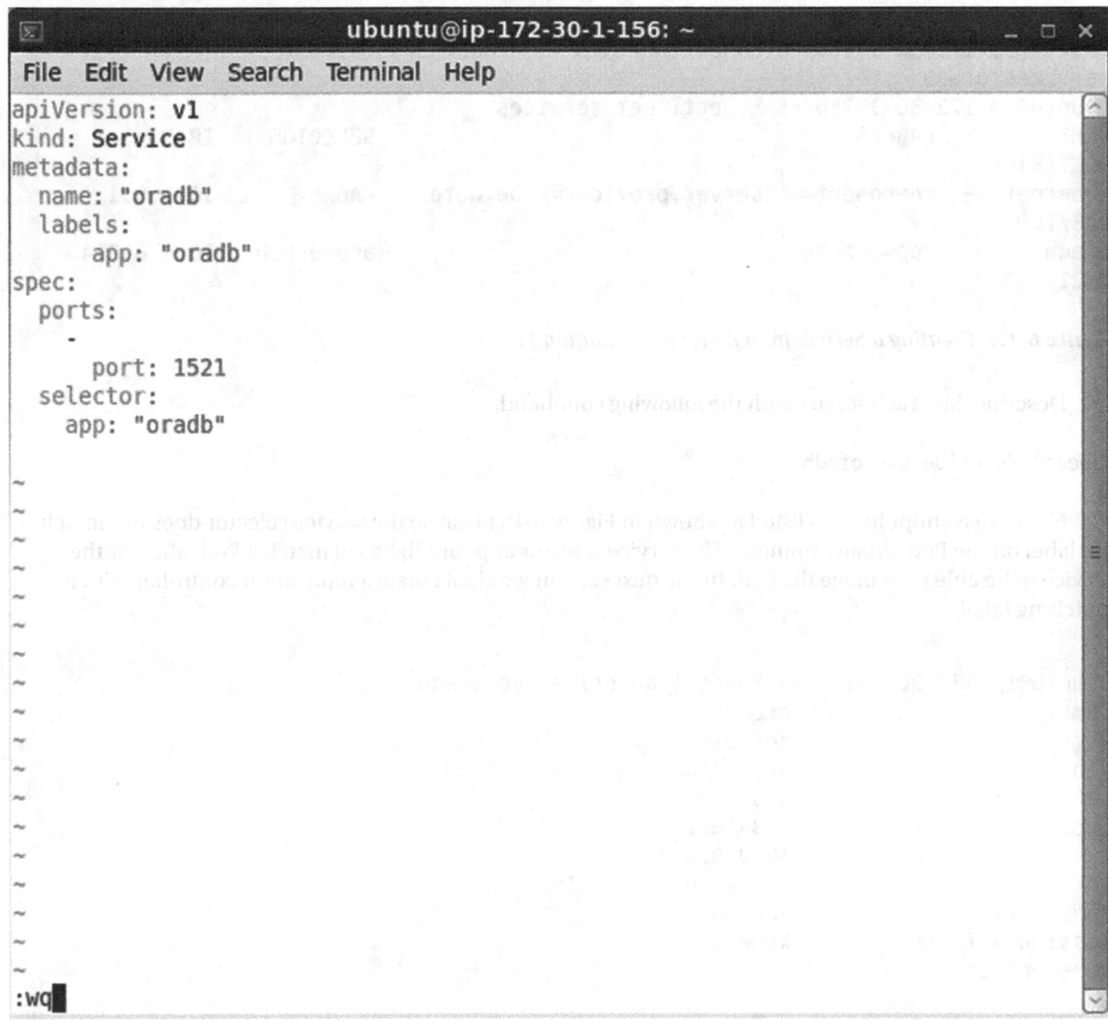

Figure 6-16. *Service Definition File*

Run the following command to create a service from the service definition file.

```
kubectl create -f oradb-service.yaml
```

The oradb service gets created as indicated by the "services/oradb" output in Figure 6-17. Subsequently list the services.

```
kubectl get services
```

The oradb service gets listed as shown in Figure 6-17.

```
ubuntu@ip-172-30-1-156:~$ kubectl create -f oradb-service.yaml
services/oradb
ubuntu@ip-172-30-1-156:~$ kubectl get services
NAME          LABELS                                      SELECTOR    IP(S)
PORT(S)
kubernetes    component=apiserver,provider=kubernetes     <none>      10.0.0.1
443/TCP
oradb         app=oradb                                   app=oradb   10.0.0.214
1521/TCP
```

Figure 6-17. *Creating a Service from a Service Definition File*

Describe the oradb service with the following command.

```
kubectl describe svc oradb
```

No service endpoint gets listed as shown in Figure 6-18 because the service selector does not match the label on the Pod already running. The service selector app=oradb has to match a Pod label for the service to be able to manage the Pod. In the next section we shall create a replication controller with a matching label.

```
ubuntu@ip-172-30-1-156:~$ kubectl describe svc oradb
Name:                   oradb
Namespace:              default
Labels:                 app=oradb
Selector:               app=oradb
Type:                   ClusterIP
IP:                     10.0.0.214
Port:                   <unnamed>       1521/TCP
Endpoints:              <none>
Session Affinity:       None
No events.

ubuntu@ip-172-30-1-156:~$
```

Figure 6-18. *Describing a Service for Oracle Database*

Creating a Replication Controller

Create a replication controller definition file called `oradb-rc.yaml` and copy the following listing, which defines a replication controller, to the definition file. For the replication controller to manage the Pods defined in the spec field the key:value expression of the selector in the replication controller has to match a label in the Pod template mapping. The `selector` is omitted in the `oradb-rc.yaml` but the spec->template->metadata->labels must be specified. The selector defaults to the same setting as the `spec->template->metadata->labels`. The template->spec->containers mapping defines the containers in the Pod. Only the Oracle Database container "sath89/oracle-xe-11g" is defined.

```
apiVersion: v1
kind: ReplicationController
metadata:
  name: "oradb"
  labels:
    app: "oradb"
spec:
  replicas: 2
  template:
    metadata:
      labels:
        app: "oradb"
    spec:
      containers:
        -
          image: "sath89/oracle-xe-11g"
          name: "oradb"
```

The `oradb-rc.yaml` file may be edited in the vi editor and saved with the :wq command as shown in Figure 6-19.

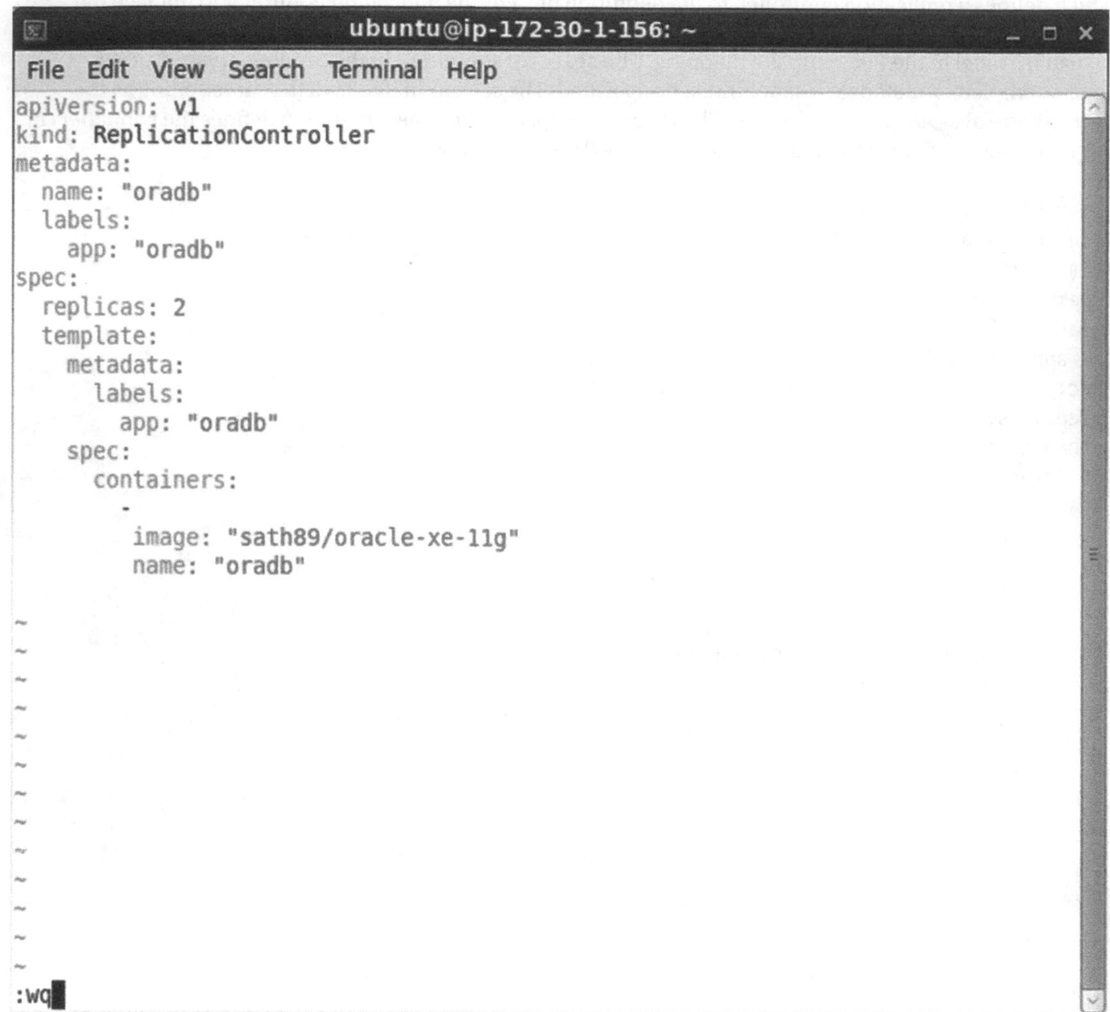

Figure 6-19. *Replication Controller Definition File*

Next, run the following command to create a replication controller from the definition file `oradb-rc.yaml`.

```
kubectl create -f oradb-rc.yaml
```

The replication controller gets created as shown in Figure 6-20. List the replication controller with the following command.

```
kubectl get rc
```

The oradb replication controller gets created as shown in Figure 6-20.

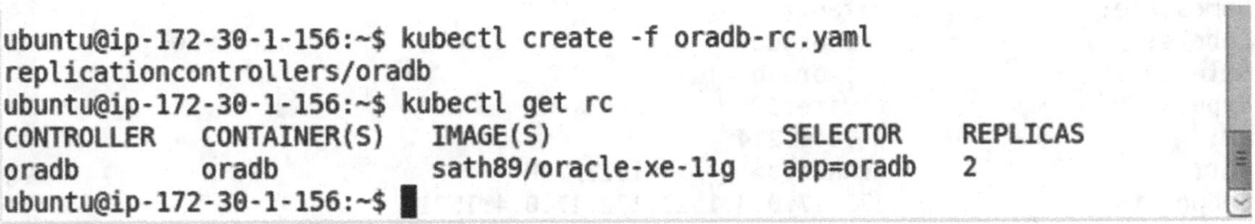

```
ubuntu@ip-172-30-1-156:~$ kubectl create -f oradb-rc.yaml
replicationcontrollers/oradb
ubuntu@ip-172-30-1-156:~$ kubectl get rc
CONTROLLER   CONTAINER(S)   IMAGE(S)                 SELECTOR    REPLICAS
oradb        oradb          sath89/oracle-xe-11g     app=oradb   2
ubuntu@ip-172-30-1-156:~$
```

Figure 6-20. *Creating and listing a Replication Controller from a Definition File*

The Pods created by the replication controller are listed with the following command.

```
kubectl get pods
```

Three Oracle Database Pods get listed as shown in Figure 6-21. Why do three Pods get listed even though the replication controller replicas are set to 2? Because the Pod started using the Pod definition file `oradb.yaml` does not include a label that matches the selector in the replication controller. The replication controller selector is `app: "oradb"` while the label on the Pod is `name: "oradb"`. Two replicas are started by the replication controller and one Pod was started earlier by the pod definition file.

```
ubuntu@ip-172-30-1-156:~$ kubectl get pods
NAME                     READY     STATUS    RESTARTS   AGE
k8s-master-127.0.0.1     3/3       Running   0          21m
oradb                    1/1       Running   0          2m
oradb-5ntnj              1/1       Running   0          44s
oradb-ulavr              1/1       Running   0          44s
ubuntu@ip-172-30-1-156:~$
```

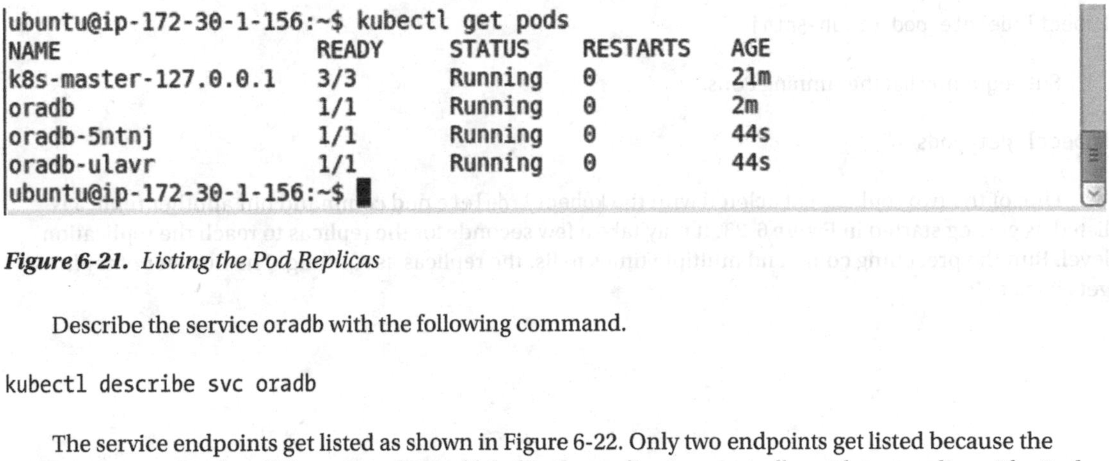

Figure 6-21. *Listing the Pod Replicas*

Describe the service oradb with the following command.

```
kubectl describe svc oradb
```

The service endpoints get listed as shown in Figure 6-22. Only two endpoints get listed because the service selector app: "oradb" matches the Pod label in the replication controller with two replicas. The Pod created earlier does not include a label that matches the selector expression.

```
ubuntu@ip-172-30-1-156:~$ kubectl describe svc oradb
Name:                   oradb
Namespace:              default
Labels:                 app=oradb
Selector:               app=oradb
Type:                   ClusterIP
IP:                     10.0.0.214
Port:                   <unnamed>       1521/TCP
Endpoints:              172.17.0.3:1521,172.17.0.4:1521
Session Affinity:       None
No events.

ubuntu@ip-172-30-1-156:~$ 
```

Figure 6-22. *Describing the Service after creating the Replication Controller*

Keeping the Replication Level

The task of the replication controller is to maintain the replication level of the Pods. Because the `replicas` field mapping in the replication controller spec is 2, two replicas of the Pod configured in the Pod spec must be running at all time while the replication controller is running. To demonstrate that the replication level is kept, delete a Pod.

```
kubectl delete pod oradb-5ntnj
```

Subsequently list the running Pods.

```
kubectl get pods
```

One of the two replicas got deleted with the `kubectl delete` pod command but another replica is listed as getting started in Figure 6-23. It may take a few seconds for the replicas to reach the replication level. Run the preceding command multiple times to list the replicas as running. The number of replicas gets back to 2.

```
ubuntu@ip-172-30-1-156:~$ kubectl delete pod oradb-5ntnj
pods/oradb-5ntnj
ubuntu@ip-172-30-1-156:~$ kubectl get pods
NAME                     READY     STATUS
            RESTARTS   AGE
k8s-master-127.0.0.1     3/3       Running
            0          22m
oradb                    1/1       Running
            0          3m
oradb-ulavr              1/1       Running
            0          1m
oradb-wh9j2              0/1       Image: sath89/oracle-xe-11g is ready, container
 is creating   0         12s
ubuntu@ip-172-30-1-156:~$ kubectl get pods
NAME                     READY     STATUS    RESTARTS   AGE
k8s-master-127.0.0.1     3/3       Running   0          22m
oradb                    1/1       Running   0          3m
oradb-ulavr              1/1       Running   0          2m
oradb-wh9j2              0/1       Running   0          34s
ubuntu@ip-172-30-1-156:~$ kubectl get pods
NAME                     READY     STATUS    RESTARTS   AGE
k8s-master-127.0.0.1     3/3       Running   0          23m
oradb                    1/1       Running   0          4m
oradb-ulavr              1/1       Running   0          2m
oradb-wh9j2              1/1       Running   0          1m
ubuntu@ip-172-30-1-156:~$
```

Figure 6-23. *Maintaining the Replication Level*

The "oradb" Pod is not associated with the replication controller and therefore it is not counted as one of the replicas managed by the replication controller. The oradb Pod is not managed by the replication controller because, as discussed earlier, the label on the oradb Pod does not match the label on the replication controller. To demonstrate that the oradb pod is not managed by the replication controller delete the Pod.

```
kubectl delete pod oradb
```

Subsequently list the running Pods.

```
kubectl get pods
```

The oradb Pod gets deleted and a replacement Pod does not get started and does not get listed in the running Pods as shown in Figure 6-24.

```
ubuntu@ip-172-30-1-156:~$ kubectl delete pod oradb
pods/oradb
ubuntu@ip-172-30-1-156:~$ kubectl get pods
NAME                    READY     STATUS    RESTARTS   AGE
k8s-master-127.0.0.1    3/3       Running   0          28m
oradb-ulavr             0/1       Running   1          8m
oradb-wh9j2             1/1       Running   0          6m
ubuntu@ip-172-30-1-156:~$ kubectl get pods
NAME                    READY     STATUS    RESTARTS   AGE
k8s-master-127.0.0.1    3/3       Running   0          28m
oradb-ulavr             1/1       Running   1          8m
oradb-wh9j2             1/1       Running   0          6m
ubuntu@ip-172-30-1-156:~$
```

Figure 6-24. *The oradb Pod is not managed by the Replication Controller*

Scaling the Database

The replication controller may be used to scale the number of Pods running for Oracle Database. As an example scale up the number of Pod replicas to 3 from 2.

```
kubectl scale rc oradb --replicas=3
```

The "scaled" output indicates that the replicas have been scaled. Subsequently run the following command, multiple times if required, to list the new Pod replica as running and ready.

```
kubectl get pods
```

Three replicas of the Pod get listed as shown in Figure 6-25.

```
ubuntu@ip-172-30-1-156:~$ kubectl scale rc oradb --replicas=3
scaled
ubuntu@ip-172-30-1-156:~$ kubectl get pods
NAME                    READY     STATUS
               RESTARTS   AGE
k8s-master-127.0.0.1    3/3       Running
               0          29m
oradb-b0lks             0/1       Image: sath89/oracle-xe-11g is ready, container
 is creating   0          10s
oradb-ulavr             1/1       Running
               1          8m
oradb-wh9j2             1/1       Running
               0          7m
ubuntu@ip-172-30-1-156:~$ kubectl get pods
NAME                    READY     STATUS    RESTARTS   AGE
k8s-master-127.0.0.1    3/3       Running   0          30m
oradb-b0lks             1/1       Running   0          50s
oradb-ulavr             1/1       Running   1          9m
oradb-wh9j2             1/1       Running   0          8m
ubuntu@ip-172-30-1-156:~$
```

Figure 6-25. *Scaling the Cluster to 3 Replicas*

Describe the service again.

```
kubectl describe svc oradb
```

Three endpoints get listed instead of two as shown in Figure 6-26. The service has a single IP address.

```
ubuntu@ip-172-30-1-156:~$ kubectl describe svc oradb
Name:                   oradb
Namespace:              default
Labels:                 app=oradb
Selector:               app=oradb
Type:                   ClusterIP
IP:                     10.0.0.214
Port:                   <unnamed>       1521/TCP
Endpoints:              172.17.0.2:1521,172.17.0.3:1521,172.17.0.4:1521
Session Affinity:       None
No events.

ubuntu@ip-172-30-1-156:~$
```

Figure 6-26. *Listing the 3 Endpoints in the Service*

Starting the Interactive Shell

In this section we shall start an interactive tty (shell) to connect to the software, which is Oracle Database, running in a Docker container started with and managed by Kubernetes. First, list the Docker containers with the following command.

```
sudo docker ps
```

Copy the container id for one of the Docker containers for the `sath89/oracle-xe-11g` image as shown in Figure 6-27.

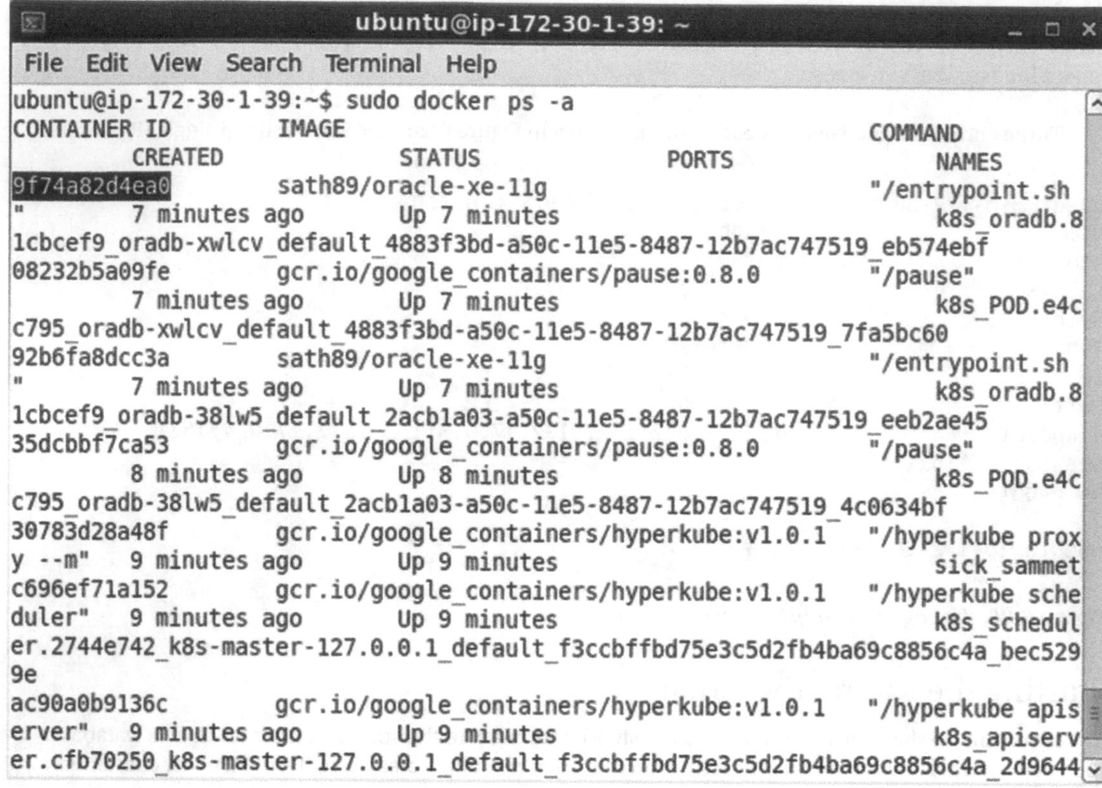

Figure 6-27. *Copying the Container Id for a Docker Container*

Using the container id start an interactive shell with the following command.

```
sudo docker exec -it 9f74a82d4ea0 bash
```

The interactive shell gets started as shown in Figure 6-28.

```
ubuntu@ip-172-30-1-39:~$ sudo docker exec -it 9f74a82d4ea0 bash
root@oradb-xwlcv:/# 
```

Figure 6-28. *Starting an Interactive Shell*

Connecting to Database

In the interactive tty change the user to "oracle."

```
su -l oracle
```

The difference between `su oracle` and `su - oracle` is that the latter logs in with the environment variables of `oracle` user and also sets the current directory to oracle home directory while the former logs in as `oracle` but the environment variables and current directory remain unchanged.

Subsequently start the SQL*Plus. Using the /nolog option does not establish an initial connection with the database.

```
sqlplus /nolog
```

Run the following command to connect SYS as SYSDBA.

```
CONNECT SYS AS SYSDBA
```

Specify the Password as "oracle" when prompted. The output from the preceding commands to start SQL*Plus and connect SYS are shown in Figure 6-29. A connection gets established.

```
root@oradb-xwlcv:/# su -l oracle
oracle@oradb-xwlcv:~$ sqlplus /nolog

SQL*Plus: Release 11.2.0.2.0 Production on Thu Dec 17 22:29:00 2015

Copyright (c) 1982, 2011, Oracle.  All rights reserved.

SQL> CONNECT SYS AS SYSDBA
Enter password:
Connected.
SQL>
```

Figure 6-29. *Starting SQL*Plus*

Creating a User

To create a user called OE and grant CONNECT and RESOURCE roles to the user, run the following commands.

```
CREATE USER OE QUOTA UNLIMITED ON SYSTEM IDENTIFIED BY OE;
GRANT CONNECT, RESOURCE TO OE;
```

The OE user gets created and the roles get granted as shown in Figure 6-30.

```
SQL> CONNECT SYS AS SYSDBA
Enter password:
Connected.
SQL> CREATE USER OE QUOTA UNLIMITED ON SYSTEM IDENTIFIED BY OE;
GRANT CONNECT, RESOURCE TO OE;

User created.

SQL>
Grant succeeded.

SQL>
```

Figure 6-30. *Connecting as SYSDBA and creating a User*

Creating a Database Table

Create a database table called `OE.Catalog` with the following SQL statement.

```
CREATE TABLE OE.Catalog(CatalogId INTEGER PRIMARY KEY,Journal VARCHAR2(25),Publisher
VARCHAR2(25),Edition VARCHAR2(25),Title VARCHAR2(45),Author VARCHAR2(25));
```

Add a row of data to the OE.Catalog table with the following SQL statement.

```
INSERT INTO OE.Catalog VALUES('1','Oracle Magazine','Oracle Publishing',
'November December 2013','Engineering as a Service','David A. Kelly');
```

The `OE.Catalog` table gets created and a row of data gets added as shown in Figure 6-31.

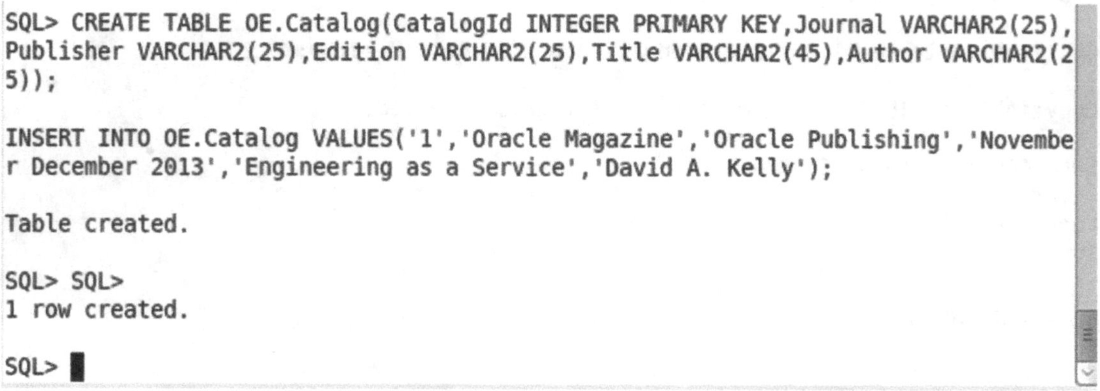

```
SQL> CREATE TABLE OE.Catalog(CatalogId INTEGER PRIMARY KEY,Journal VARCHAR2(25),
Publisher VARCHAR2(25),Edition VARCHAR2(25),Title VARCHAR2(45),Author VARCHAR2(2
5));

INSERT INTO OE.Catalog VALUES('1','Oracle Magazine','Oracle Publishing','Novembe
r December 2013','Engineering as a Service','David A. Kelly');

Table created.

SQL> SQL>
1 row created.

SQL>
```

Figure 6-31. *Creating a Database Table*

Run the following SQL statement to query the `OE.CATALOG` table.

```
SELECT * FROM OE.CATALOG;
```

The single row of data added gets listed as shown in Figure 6-32.

```
SQL> SELECT * FROM OE.CATALOG;

 CATALOGID JOURNAL                  PUBLISHER
---------- ------------------------ ------------------------
EDITION                  TITLE
------------------------ ------------------------------------------------
AUTHOR
------------------------
         1 Oracle Magazine          Oracle Publishing
November December 2013   Engineering as a Service
David A. Kelly

SQL> 
```

Figure 6-32. *Querying the Database Table*

Exiting the Interactive Shell

Logout from SQL*Plus command with the "exit" command and exit the "oracle" user with the "exit" command and exit the interactive terminal with the "exit" command also as shown in Figure 6-33.

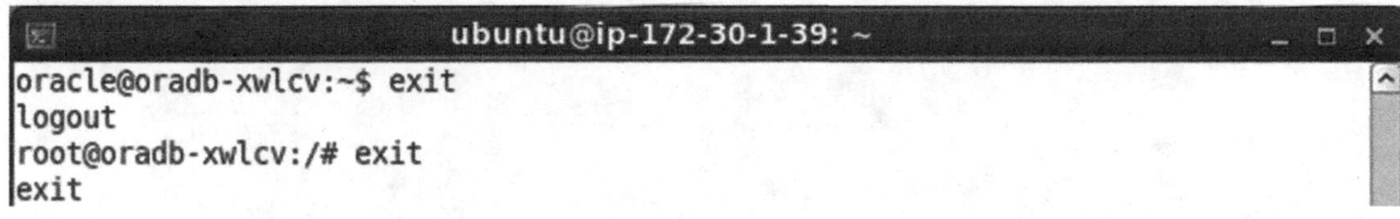
ubuntu@ip-172-30-1-39: ~
oracle@oradb-xwlcv:~$ exit
logout
root@oradb-xwlcv:/# exit
exit

Figure 6-33. *Exiting the Interactive Shell*

Summary

In this chapter we used Kubernetes to create and orchestrate an Oracle Database cluster. We discussed both the imperative and declarative approaches to creating and managing a cluster. Using the imperative method, the `kubectl` commands may be used directly without a definition file to create a replication controller and a service. With the declarative method definition files for a Pod, replication controller and service have to be used. We demonstrated scaling a cluster. We also used a Docker container to log in to SQL*Plus and create a database table. In the next chapter we shall discuss using MongoDB with Kubernetes.

PART III

NoSQL Database

CHAPTER 7

Using MongoDB Database

MongoDB is a flexible schema model NoSQL data store, the most commonly used NoSQL data store. MongoDB is based on the BSON (binary JSON) storage model. Documents are stored in collections. Being a schema-free data store, no two documents need to be alike in terms of the fields in a BSON document. In a large scale cluster several instances of MongoDB could be running and several issues could arise.

-MongoDB instances scheduling

-Scaling the MongoDB Cluster

-Load Balancing

-Providing MongoDB as a Service

While Docker has made it feasible to provide Container as a Service (CaaS) it does not provide by itself any of the features listed previously. In this chapter we discuss using Kubernetes container cluster manager to manage and orchestrate a cluster of Docker containers running MongoDB. This chapter has the following sections.

Setting the Environment

Creating a MongoDB Cluster Declaratively

Creating a MongoDB Cluster Imperatively

Setting the Environment

The following software is required for this chapter.

-Docker Engine (latest version)

-Kubernetes (version 1.01)

-Kubectl (version 1.01)

-Docker image for MongoDB (latest version)

Install the required software on an Amazon EC2 instance running Ubuntu 14; the same AMI is used as in the other chapters. SSH Login to the Ubuntu instance using the Public IP Address, which would be different for different users.

```
ssh -i "docker.pem" ubuntu@52.91.190.195
```


D. Vohra, *Kubernetes Microservices with Docker*, DOI 10.1007/978-1-4842-1907-2_7

The Ubuntu instance gets logged into as shown in Figure 7-1.

```
ubuntu@ip-172-30-1-39: ~
File  Edit  View  Search  Terminal  Help
[root@localhost ~]# ssh -i "docker.pem" ubuntu@52.91.190.195
The authenticity of host '52.91.190.195 (52.91.190.195)' can't be established.
RSA key fingerprint is 35:40:5c:41:4b:49:63:44:7e:ce:8c:7c:e7:60:0f:87.
Are you sure you want to continue connecting (yes/no)? yes
Warning: Permanently added '52.91.190.195' (RSA) to the list of known hosts.
Welcome to Ubuntu 14.04.2 LTS (GNU/Linux 3.13.0-73-generic x86_64)

 * Documentation:  https://help.ubuntu.com/

  System information as of Sat Dec 19 13:55:12 UTC 2015

  System load: 0.0               Memory usage: 5%   Processes:       81
  Usage of /:  16.6% of 7.74GB   Swap usage:   0%   Users logged in: 0

  Graph this data and manage this system at:
    https://landscape.canonical.com/

  Get cloud support with Ubuntu Advantage Cloud Guest:
    http://www.ubuntu.com/business/services/cloud


Last login: Fri Dec 18 19:51:11 2015 from d108-180-43-187.bchsia.telus.net
ubuntu@ip-172-30-1-39:~$ sudo service docker start
start: Job is already running: docker
ubuntu@ip-172-30-1-39:~$
```

Figure 7-1. *Logging into Ubuntu Instance on Amazon EC2*

The procedure to install is discussed in chapter 1. To verify that Docker is running run the following command.

```
sudo service docker start
```

Docker should be listed as running as shown in Figure 7-2.

```
ubuntu@ip-172-30-1-39:~$ sudo service docker start
start: Job is already running: docker
```

Figure 7-2. *Starting Docker*

List the Pods with the following command.

```
kubectl get pods
```

And list the nodes with the following command.

```
kubectl get nodes
```

The Kubernetes Pod gets listed and the node also gets listed as shown in Figure 7-3.

```
ubuntu@ip-172-30-1-39:~$ kubectl get pods
NAME                    READY     STATUS    RESTARTS   AGE
k8s-master-127.0.0.1    3/3       Running   0          3m
ubuntu@ip-172-30-1-39:~$ kubectl get nodes
NAME        LABELS                              STATUS
127.0.0.1   kubernetes.io/hostname=127.0.0.1    Ready
ubuntu@ip-172-30-1-39:~$ 
```

***Figure 7-3.** Listing Kubernetes Pod and the single Node*

To list the services run the following command.

```
kubectl get services
```

The “kubernetes” service gets listed as shown in Figure 7-4.

```
ubuntu@ip-172-30-1-39:~$ kubectl get services
NAME         LABELS                                      SELECTOR   IP(S)      POR
T(S)
kubernetes   component=apiserver,provider=kubernetes    <none>     10.0.0.1   443
/TCP
ubuntu@ip-172-30-1-39:~$ 
```

***Figure 7-4.** Listing the Kubernetes Service*

Creating a MongoDB Cluster Declaratively

In the following subsections we shall create a Kubernetes service and replication controller for a MongoDB cluster. We shall scale the cluster and also demonstrate features such as using a volume and a host port. We shall create a MongoDB collection and add documents to the collection in a Mongo shell running in a Docker container tty (interactive terminal or shell).

Creating a Service

Create a service definition file `mongo-service-yaml`. Add the following (Table 7-1) field mappings in the definition file.

Table 7-1. *Service Definition File mongo-service-yaml File Fields*

Field	Value	Description
apiVersion	v1	The API version.
kind	Service	Specifies the definition file to be a service.
metadata		The service metadata.
metadata->labels	name: mongo	
metadata->name	mongo	A label mapping. A label may be added multiple times and does not generate an error and has no additional significance.
spec		The service specification.
spec->ports		The port/s on which the service is exposed.
spec->ports->port	27017	The port on which the service is hosted.
spec->ports->targetPort	27017	The port that an incoming port is mapped to. The targetPort field is optional and defaults to the same value as the port field. The targetPort could be useful if the service is to evolve without breaking clients' settings. For example, the targetPort could be set to a string port name of a back-end Pod, which stays fixed. And the actual port number the back-end Pod exposes could be varied without affecting the clients' settings.
selector	name: mongo	The service selector used to select Pods. Pods with label expression the same as the selector are managed by the service.

Copy the following listing to the `mongo-service.yaml`.

```
apiVersion: v1
kind: Service
metadata:
  labels:
    name: mongo
  name: mongo
spec:
  ports:
    - port: 27017
      targetPort: 27017
  selector:
    name: mongo
```

The vi editor could be used to create the `mongo-service.yaml` file and saved using the :wq command as shown in Figure 7-5.

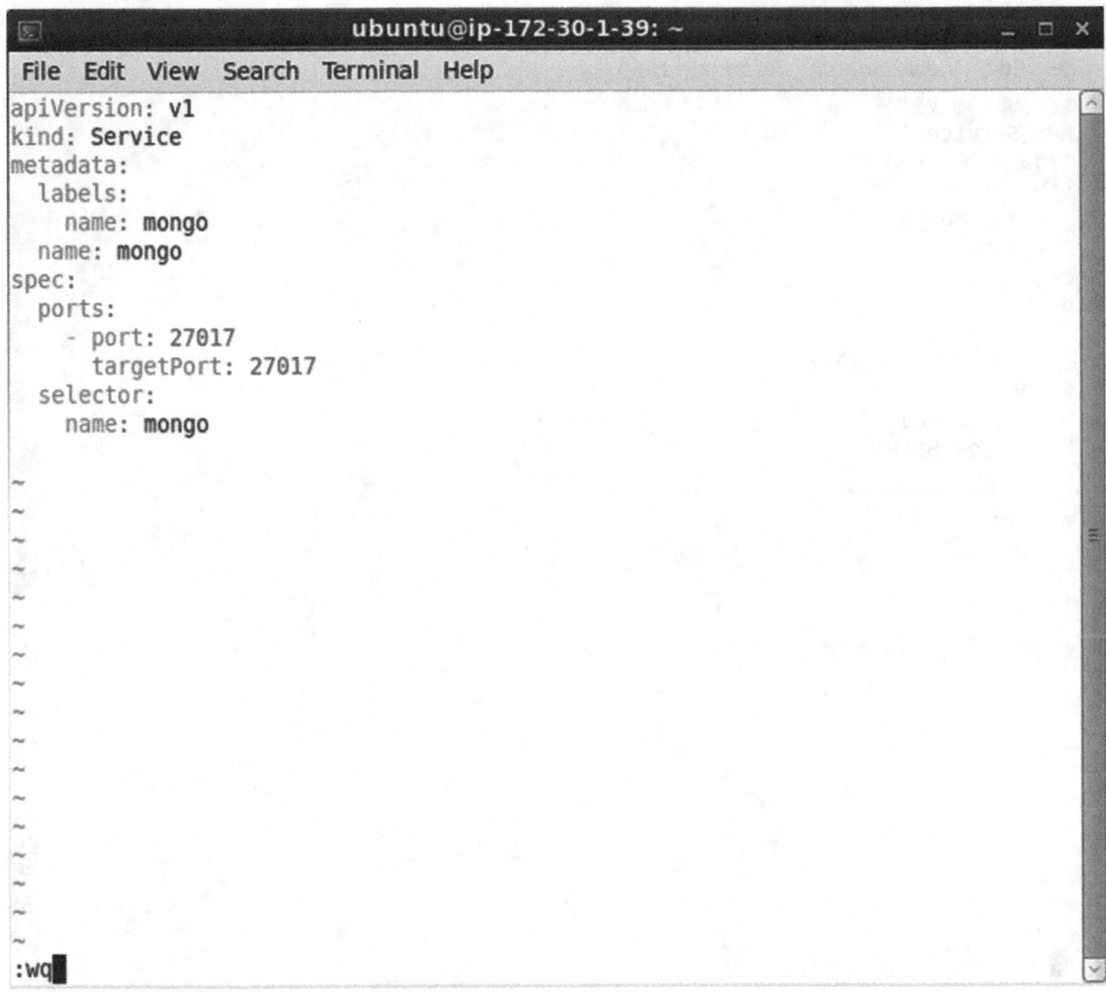

Figure 7-5. *Service Definition File in vi Editor*

The default service type is `ClusterIp`, which uses a cluster-internal IP only. The type could be set to `LoadBalancer` as shown in Figure 7-6 to also expose the service on each of the nodes in the cluster and also requests the cloud provider to provision a load balancer.

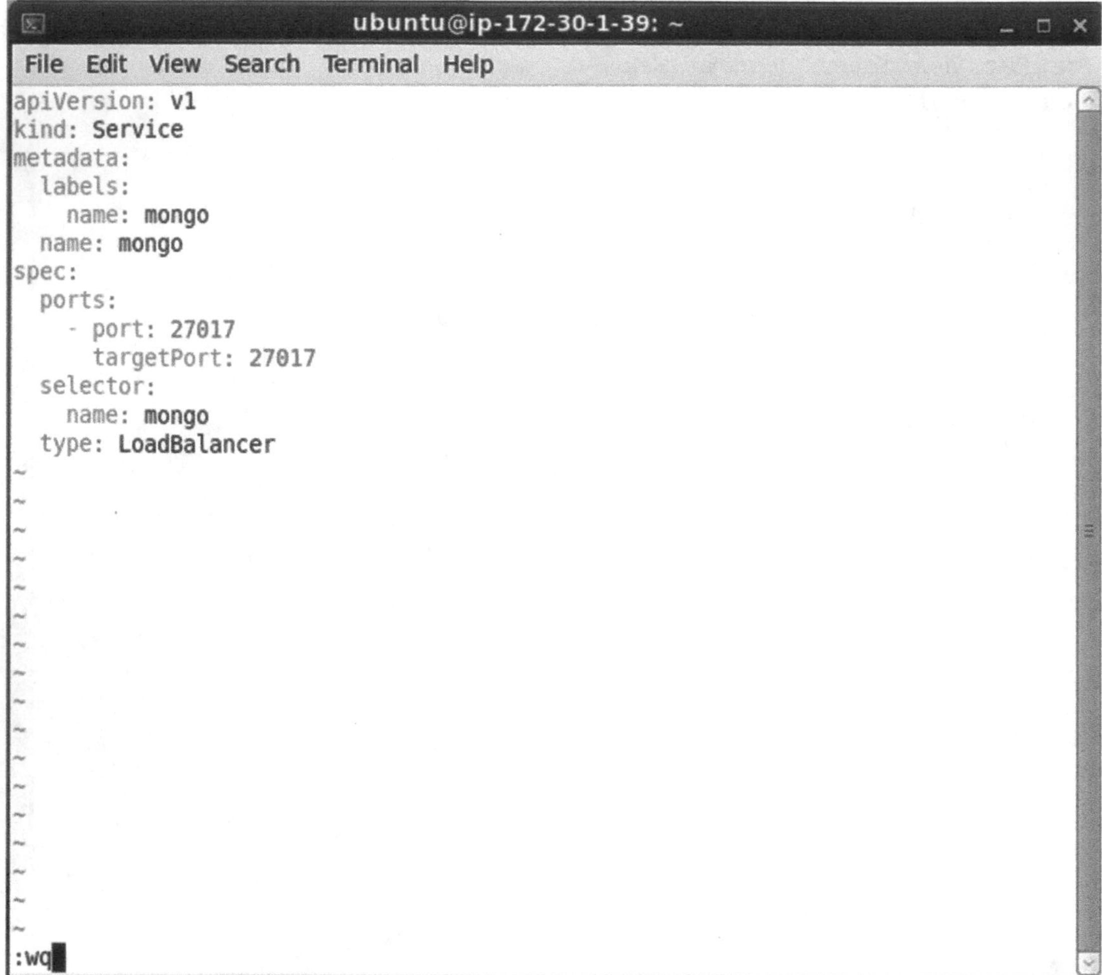

Figure 7-6. *Setting the Service Type*

To create the service from the definition file run the following command.

```
kubectl create -f mongo-service.yaml
```

List the services with the following command.

```
kubectl get services
```

The mongo service gets listed as shown in Figure 7-7.

```
ubuntu@ip-172-30-1-39:~$ kubectl create -f mongo-service.yaml
services/mongo
ubuntu@ip-172-30-1-39:~$ kubectl get services
NAME         LABELS                                    SELECTOR     IP(S)
 PORT(S)
kubernetes   component=apiserver,provider=kubernetes   <none>       10.0.0.1
 443/TCP
mongo        name=mongo                                name=mongo   10.0.0.161
 27017/TCP
```

Figure 7-7. *Creating the Service from the Definition File*

Creating a Replication Controller

In this section we shall create a replication controller. Create a definition file `mongo-rc.yaml`. Add the following (Table 7-2) field mappings to the definition file.

Table 7-2. *Replication Controller Definition File Fields*

Field	Value	Description
apiVersion	v1	The API version.
kind	ReplicationController	Specifies the definition file to be for a replication controller.
metadata		Specifies the metadata for the replication controller.
metadata - > labels	name: mongo	The labels mapping for the replication controller.
metadata - > name	mongo-rc	The replication controller name.
spec		The replication controller specification.
spec- > replicas	2	The number of replicas to keep at all times.
spec- > template		The template for a Pod.
spec- > template- > metadata		The metadata for the Pod.
spec- > template- > metadata- > labels		The Pod labels. The labels are used by the replication controller and service to select Pods to manage. The selector in a replication controller and a service must match a Pod label for the replication controller and Service to managed the Pod.
spec- > template- > metadata- > labels- > name	mongo	A Pod label.
spec- > template- > spec		The specification for the Pod.

(*continued*)

Table 7-2. (*continued*)

Field	Value	Description
spec->template->spec->containers		The containers in a Pod. Multiple containers could be specified but we have configured only one container.
spec->template->spec->containers ->image	mongo	The container for "mongo" Docker image.
spec->template->spec->containers ->name	mongo	The container name.
spec->template->spec->containers ->ports		The container ports to reserve.
spec->template->spec->containers ->ports->name	mongo	The port name.
spec->template->spec->containers ->ports ->containerPort	27017	The container port number.

Each of the Pod, Service, and Replication Controllers are defined in a separate YAML mapping file. The `mongo-rc.yaml` is listed.

```
apiVersion: v1
kind: ReplicationController
metadata:
  labels:
    name: mongo
  name: mongo-rc
spec:
  replicas: 2
  template:
    metadata:
      labels:
        name: mongo
    spec:
      containers:
        -
          image: mongo
          name: mongo
          ports:
            -
              containerPort: 27017
              name: mongo
```

The mongo-rc.yaml file may be edited in a vi editor and saved with :wq as shown in Figure 7-8.

```
File  Edit  View  Search  Terminal  Help
apiVersion: v1
kind: ReplicationController
metadata:
  labels:
    name: mongo
  name: mongo-rc
spec:
  replicas: 2
  template:
    metadata:
      labels:
        name: mongo
    spec:
      containers:
      - image: mongo
        name: mongo
        ports:
        - name: mongo
          containerPort: 27017
~
~
~
~
~
~
~
~
~
~
:wq
```

Figure 7-8. Replication Controller Definition File

To create a replication controller from the definition file, run the following command.

```
kubectl create -f mongo-rc.yaml
```

The mongo-rc replication controller gets created as shown in Figure 7-9.

```
ubuntu@ip-172-30-1-39:~$ kubectl create -f  mongo-rc.yaml
replicationcontrollers/mongo-rc
```

Figure 7-9. Creating the Replication Controller

Run the following command to list the replication containers.

```
kubectl get rc
```

The mongo-rc replication controller gets listed as shown in Figure 7-10.

```
ubuntu@ip-172-30-1-39:~$ kubectl create -f  mongo-rc.yaml
replicationcontrollers/mongo-rc
ubuntu@ip-172-30-1-39:~$ kubectl get rc
CONTROLLER   CONTAINER(S)   IMAGE(S)   SELECTOR     REPLICAS
mongo-rc     mongo          mongo      name=mongo   2
```

Figure 7-10. *Creating and isting Replication Controllers*

Creating a Volume

Kubernetes supports volumes. A *volume* is a directory in a Pod that is accessible to containers in the Pod that provide a volume mount for the volume. Volumes persist as long as the Pod containing the volumes exists. Volumes are useful for the following purposes.

-Persist data across container crash. When a container that mounts a volume crashes, the data in the volume is not deleted as the volume is not on the container but is on the Pod.

-Data in a volume may be shared by multiple containers that mount the volume.

A volume in a Pod is specified with the spec->volume field. A container mounts a volume with the spec.containers.volumeMounts field. Several types of volumes are supported, some of which are discussed in Table 7-3.

Table 7-3. *Types of Volumes*

Volume Type	Description
emptyDir	An empty directory in the Pod that could be used to keep some files used by one or more containers. An empty directory could also be used for checkpointing.
hostPath	Mounts a directory from the host node into the Pod.
gcePersistentDisk	Mounts a Google Compute Engine Persistent disk into a Pod.
awsElasticBlockStore	Mounts an Amazon Web Services EBS volume into a Pod.
gitRepo	Mounts a git repo into the pod.
flocker	Mounts a Flocker dataset into a pod.
nfs	Mounts a Network File System into a Pod.

Next, we shall add a volume of type emptyDir to the replication controller definition file mongo-rc.yaml. A modified version of mongo-rc.yaml is listed.

```
apiVersion: v1
kind: ReplicationController
metadata:
  labels:
    name: mongo
  name: mongo-rc
```

```
spec:
  replicas: 2
  template:
    metadata:
      labels:
        name: mongo
    spec:
      containers:
        -
          image: mongo
          name: mongo
          ports:
            -
              containerPort: 27017
              name: mongo
          volumeMounts:
            -
              mountPath: /mongo/data/db
              name: mongo-storage
      volumes:
        -
          emptyDir: {}
          name: mongo-storage
```

The preceding definition file includes the following volume configuration for a volume named mongo-storage of type emptyDir.

```
      volumes:
        -
          emptyDir: {}
          name: mongo-storage
```

The volume exists in the Pod and individual containers in the Pod may mount the volume using field spec->containers->volumeMounts. The modified mongo-rc.yaml includes the following volume mount for the mongo container.

```
volumeMounts:
            -
              mountPath: /mongo/data/db
              name: mongo-storage
```

The preceding configuration adds a volume mount for the mongo-storage volume at mount path or directory path /mongo/data/db in the container. Within a container the volume may be accessed at /mongo/data/db. For example, in an interactive terminal for a container change directory (cd) to the /mongo/data/db directory.

```
cd /mongo/data/db
```

List the files and directories in the in the /mongo/data/db directory.

```
ls -l
```

The directory is empty as it is supposed to be initially as shown in Figure 7-11.

```
root@mongo-rc-o3tet:/# cd /mongo/data/db
root@mongo-rc-o3tet:/mongo/data/db# ls -l
total 0
```

Figure 7-11. *Empty Directory*

The volume should not be confused with the data directory for the MongoDB server. The data directory is created at `/data/db` by default and is created in each Docker container running a MongoDB server instance. The `/mongo/data/db` is common to all Docker containers while the `/data/db` exists in each Docker container.

Listing the Logs

After having started a replication controller, list the Pods with the following command.

```
kubectl get pods
```

The two Pods get listed as shown in Figure 7-12.

```
ubuntu@ip-172-30-1-39:~$ kubectl get pods
NAME                  READY     STATUS    RESTARTS   AGE
k8s-master-127.0.0.1  3/3       Running   0          7m
mongo-rc-4t43s        1/1       Running   0          22s
mongo-rc-bio0b        1/1       Running   0          22s
```

Figure 7-12. *Listing the Pods*

The logs for a Pod, for example, the `mongo-rc-4t43s` Pod, may be listed with the following command.

```
kubectl logs mongo-rc-4t43s
```

The Pod logs show the MongoDB server starting as shown in Figure 7-13.

```
ubuntu@ip-172-30-1-39: ~
File Edit View Search Terminal Help
ubuntu@ip-172-30-1-39:~$ kubectl logs mongo-rc-4t43s
2015-12-19T20:07:48.752+0000 I CONTROL  [initandlisten] MongoDB starting : pid=1
 port=27017 dbpath=/data/db 64-bit host=mongo-rc-4t43s
2015-12-19T20:07:48.752+0000 I CONTROL  [initandlisten] db version v3.2.0
2015-12-19T20:07:48.752+0000 I CONTROL  [initandlisten] git version: 45d947729a0
315accb6d4f15a6b06be6d9c19fe7
2015-12-19T20:07:48.752+0000 I CONTROL  [initandlisten] OpenSSL version: OpenSSL
 1.0.1e 11 Feb 2013
2015-12-19T20:07:48.752+0000 I CONTROL  [initandlisten] allocator: tcmalloc
2015-12-19T20:07:48.752+0000 I CONTROL  [initandlisten] modules: none
2015-12-19T20:07:48.752+0000 I CONTROL  [initandlisten] build environment:
2015-12-19T20:07:48.752+0000 I CONTROL  [initandlisten]     distmod: debian71
2015-12-19T20:07:48.753+0000 I CONTROL  [initandlisten]     distarch: x86_64
2015-12-19T20:07:48.753+0000 I CONTROL  [initandlisten]     target_arch: x86_64
2015-12-19T20:07:48.753+0000 I CONTROL  [initandlisten] options: {}
2015-12-19T20:07:48.765+0000 I STORAGE  [initandlisten] wiredtiger_open config:
create,cache_size=1G,session_max=20000,eviction=(threads_max=4),config_base=fals
e,statistics=(fast),log=(enabled=true,archive=true,path=journal,compressor=snapp
y),file_manager=(close_idle_time=100000),checkpoint=(wait=60,log_size=2GB),stati
stics_log=(wait=0),
2015-12-19T20:07:48.829+0000 I CONTROL  [initandlisten]
2015-12-19T20:07:48.829+0000 I CONTROL  [initandlisten] ** WARNING: /sys/kernel/
mm/transparent_hugepage/enabled is 'always'.
2015-12-19T20:07:48.829+0000 I CONTROL  [initandlisten] **        We suggest set
ting it to 'never'
2015-12-19T20:07:48.829+0000 I CONTROL  [initandlisten]
2015-12-19T20:07:48.829+0000 I CONTROL  [initandlisten] ** WARNING: /sys/kernel/
mm/transparent_hugepage/defrag is 'always'.
2015-12-19T20:07:48.829+0000 I CONTROL  [initandlisten] **        We suggest set
ting it to 'never'
2015-12-19T20:07:48.829+0000 I CONTROL  [initandlisten]
```

Figure 7-13. *Listing the Pod Logs*

When the MongoDB server gets started, the message "waiting for connections on port 27017" gets output as shown in Figure 7-14.

```
ubuntu@ip-172-30-1-39: ~
File Edit View Search Terminal Help
 1.0.1e 11 Feb 2013
2015-12-19T20:07:48.752+0000 I CONTROL  [initandlisten] allocator: tcmalloc
2015-12-19T20:07:48.752+0000 I CONTROL  [initandlisten] modules: none
2015-12-19T20:07:48.752+0000 I CONTROL  [initandlisten] build environment:
2015-12-19T20:07:48.752+0000 I CONTROL  [initandlisten]     distmod: debian71
2015-12-19T20:07:48.753+0000 I CONTROL  [initandlisten]     distarch: x86_64
2015-12-19T20:07:48.753+0000 I CONTROL  [initandlisten]     target_arch: x86_64
2015-12-19T20:07:48.753+0000 I CONTROL  [initandlisten] options: {}
2015-12-19T20:07:48.765+0000 I STORAGE  [initandlisten] wiredtiger_open config:
create,cache_size=1G,session_max=20000,eviction=(threads_max=4),config_base=fals
e,statistics=(fast),log=(enabled=true,archive=true,path=journal,compressor=snapp
y),file_manager=(close_idle_time=100000),checkpoint=(wait=60,log_size=2GB),stati
stics_log=(wait=0),
2015-12-19T20:07:48.829+0000 I CONTROL  [initandlisten]
2015-12-19T20:07:48.829+0000 I CONTROL  [initandlisten] ** WARNING: /sys/kernel/
mm/transparent_hugepage/enabled is 'always'.
2015-12-19T20:07:48.829+0000 I CONTROL  [initandlisten] **        We suggest set
ting it to 'never'
2015-12-19T20:07:48.829+0000 I CONTROL  [initandlisten]
2015-12-19T20:07:48.829+0000 I CONTROL  [initandlisten] ** WARNING: /sys/kernel/
mm/transparent_hugepage/defrag is 'always'.
2015-12-19T20:07:48.829+0000 I CONTROL  [initandlisten] **        We suggest set
ting it to 'never'
2015-12-19T20:07:48.829+0000 I CONTROL  [initandlisten]
2015-12-19T20:07:48.830+0000 I FTDC     [initandlisten] Initializing full-time d
iagnostic data capture with directory '/data/db/diagnostic.data'
2015-12-19T20:07:48.830+0000 I NETWORK  [HostnameCanonicalizationWorker] Startin
g hostname canonicalization worker
2015-12-19T20:07:48.839+0000 I NETWORK  [initandlisten] waiting for connections
on port 27017
ubuntu@ip-172-30-1-39:~$
```

Figure 7-14. *MongoDB Running on Port 27017*

Starting the Interactive Shell for Docker Container

In this section we shall start an interactive terminal or bash shell for MongoDB server for which we need the container id of a Docker container running a MongoDB server. List the Docker containers.

```
sudo docker ps
```

Copy the container id for a container with image as "mongo" as shown in Figure 7-15.

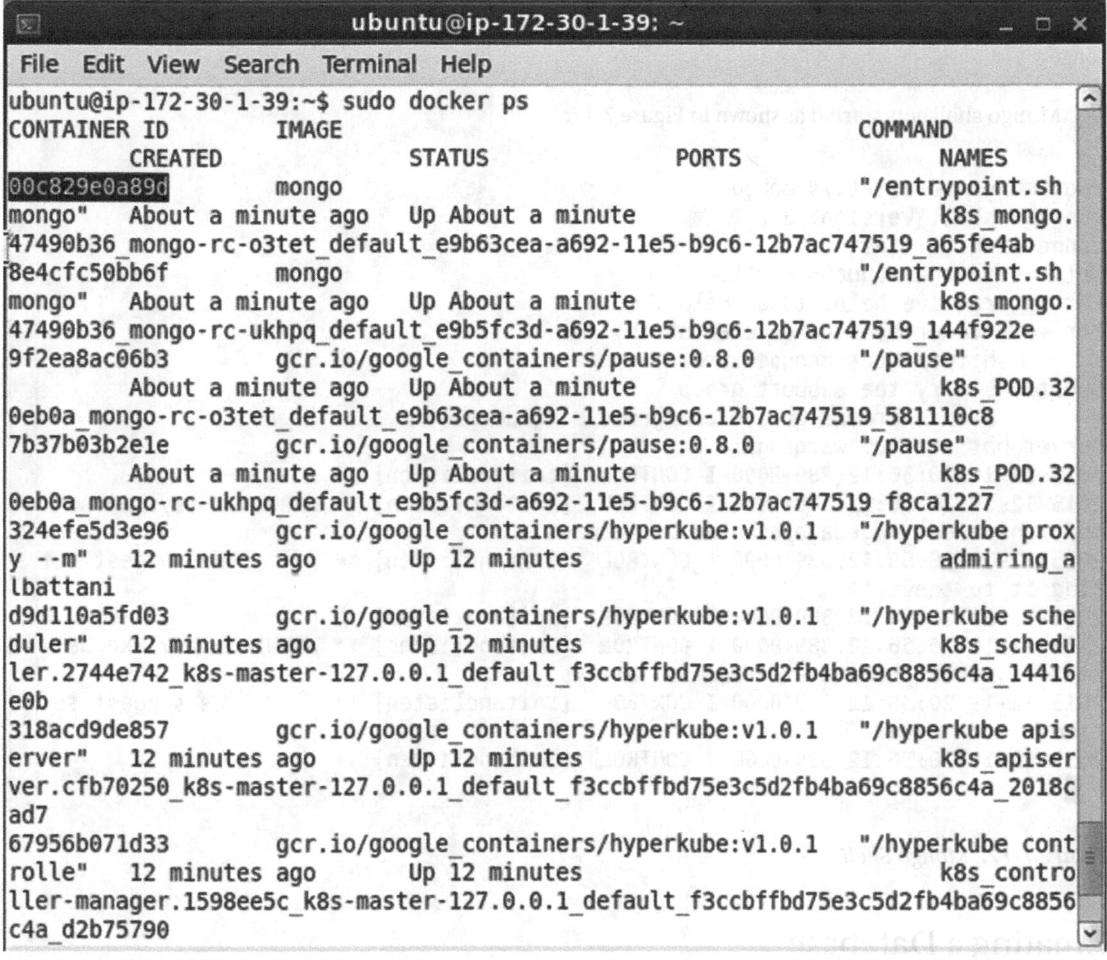

Figure 7-15. *Copying Docker Container ID*

Because the "mongo" Docker image is based on the "debian" Docker image as speciifed in the FROM instruction, we are able to start a bash shell to interact with the MongoDB server running in a Docker container based on the "mongo" image. Start an interactive bash shell using the following command.

```
sudo docker exec -it 00c829e0a89d bash
```

An interactive shell gets started as shown in Figure 7-16.

```
ubuntu@ip-172-30-1-39:~$ sudo docker exec -it 00c829e0a89d bash
root@mongo-rc-o3tet:/#
```

Figure 7-16. *Starting an Interactive Shell*

Starting a Mongo Shell

Start the Mongo shell with the following command.

```
mongo
```

Mongo shell gets started as shown in Figure 7-17.

```
root@mongo-rc-o3tet:/# mongo
MongoDB shell version: 3.2.0
connecting to: test
Welcome to the MongoDB shell.
For interactive help, type "help".
For more comprehensive documentation, see
        http://docs.mongodb.org/
Questions? Try the support group
        http://groups.google.com/group/mongodb-user
Server has startup warnings:
2015-12-19T20:56:12.389+0000 I CONTROL  [initandlisten]
2015-12-19T20:56:12.389+0000 I CONTROL  [initandlisten] ** WARNING: /sys/kernel/
mm/transparent_hugepage/enabled is 'always'.
2015-12-19T20:56:12.389+0000 I CONTROL  [initandlisten] **        We suggest set
ting it to 'never'
2015-12-19T20:56:12.389+0000 I CONTROL  [initandlisten]
2015-12-19T20:56:12.389+0000 I CONTROL  [initandlisten] ** WARNING: /sys/kernel/
mm/transparent_hugepage/defrag is 'always'.
2015-12-19T20:56:12.389+0000 I CONTROL  [initandlisten] **        We suggest set
ting it to 'never'
2015-12-19T20:56:12.389+0000 I CONTROL  [initandlisten]
>
```

Figure 7-17. *Mongo Shell*

Creating a Database

List the databases with the following command from the Mongo shell.

```
show dbs
```

A database gets created implicitly when a database is used or set. For example, set the database to use as mongodb, which is not listed with show dbs and does not exist yet.

```
use mongodb
```

But, setting the database to use as mongodb does not create the database mongodb till the database is used. Run the following command to list the databases.

```
show dbs
```

The mongodb database does not get listed as shown in Figure 7-19. To create the mongodb database, invoke some operation on the database such as create a collection called catalog with the following command.

```
db.createCollection("catalog")
```

Subsequently list the databases again.

```
show dbs
```

The mongodb database gets listed as shown in Figure 7-18. To list the collections run the following command.

```
show collections
```

The catalog collection gets listed.

```
> show dbs
local  0.000GB
> use mongodb
switched to db mongodb
> show dbs
local  0.000GB
> db.createCollection("catalog")
{ "ok" : 1 }
> show dbs
local    0.000GB
mongodb  0.000GB
> show collections
catalog
```

Figure 7-18. *Creating and Listing a MongoDB Database*

Creating a Collection

The catalog collection was created using the db.createCollection method in the previous section. As another example, create a capped collection called catalog_capped using the following command: a capped collection is a fixed size collection that supports high throughput operations to add and get documents based on insertion order.

```
db.createCollection("catalog_capped", {capped: true, autoIndexId: true, size: 64 * 1024,
max: 1000} )
```

A capped collection gets added as shown in Figure 7-19. Initially the collection is empty. Get the documents in the catalog collection with the following command.

```
db.catalog.count()
```

The document count is listed as 0 as we have not yet added any documents.

```
> db.createCollection("catalog_capped", {capped: true, autoIndexId: true, size:
64 * 1024, max: 1000} )
{
        "note" : "the autoIndexId option is deprecated and will be removed in a
future release",
        "ok" : 1
}
> db.catalog.count()
0
```

Figure 7-19. *Creating a Capped Collection*

Adding Documents

In this section we shall add documents to the catalog collection. Specify the JSON for the documents to be added. The _id field is required in each document stored in MongoDB. The _id field may be added explicitly as in the doc2 document. If not provided in the document JSON the _id is generated automatically.

```
doc1 = {"catalogId" : "catalog1", "journal" : 'Oracle Magazine', "publisher" :
'Oracle Publishing', "edition" : 'November December 2013',"title" : 'Engineering as a
Service',"author" : 'David A. Kelly'}
doc2 = {"_id": ObjectId("507f191e810c19729de860ea"), "catalogId" : "catalog1", "journal"
: 'Oracle Magazine', "publisher" : 'Oracle Publishing', "edition" : 'November December
2013',"title" : 'Engineering as a Service',"author" : 'David A. Kelly'};
```

The doc1 and doc2 are shown in Figure 7-20.

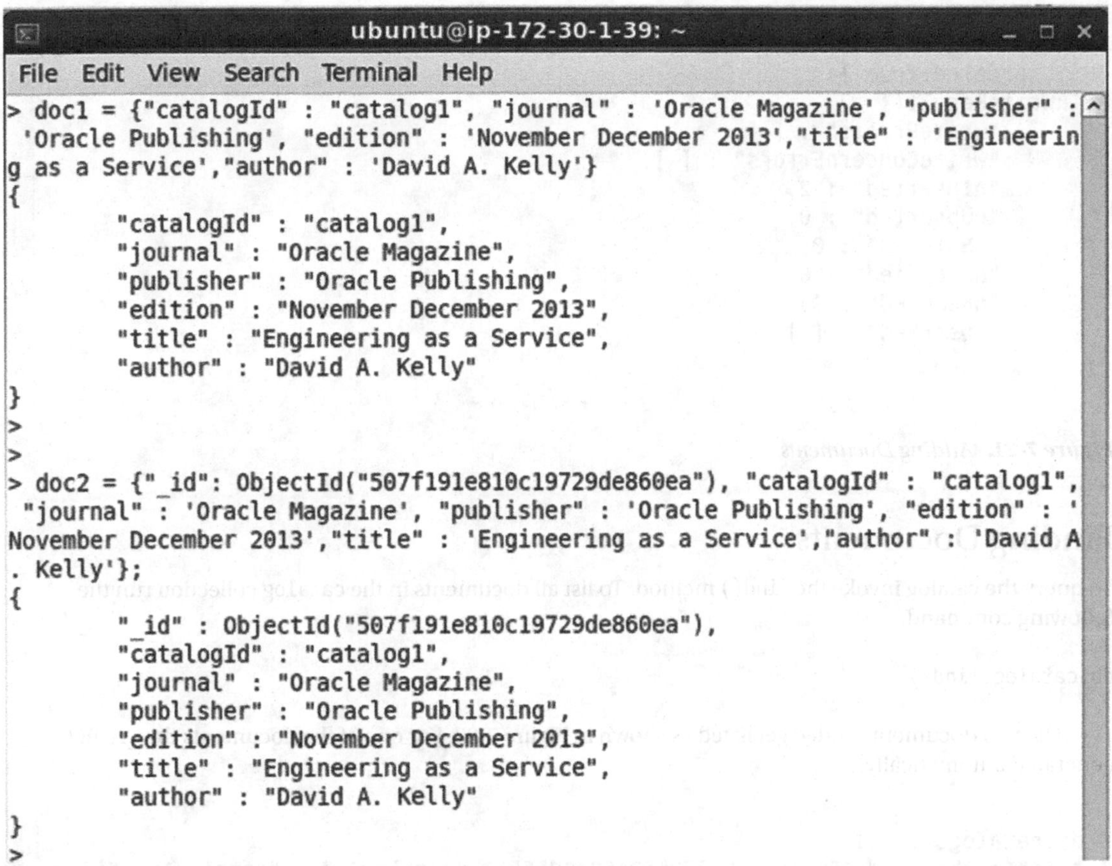
ubuntu@ip-172-30-1-39: ~
File Edit View Search Terminal Help
> doc1 = {"catalogId" : "catalog1", "journal" : 'Oracle Magazine', "publisher" : 'Oracle Publishing', "edition" : 'November December 2013',"title" : 'Engineering as a Service',"author" : 'David A. Kelly'}
{
"catalogId" : "catalog1",
"journal" : "Oracle Magazine",
"publisher" : "Oracle Publishing",
"edition" : "November December 2013",
"title" : "Engineering as a Service",
"author" : "David A. Kelly"
}
>
>
> doc2 = {"_id": ObjectId("507f191e810c19729de860ea"), "catalogId" : "catalog1", "journal" : 'Oracle Magazine', "publisher" : 'Oracle Publishing', "edition" : 'November December 2013',"title" : 'Engineering as a Service',"author" : 'David A. Kelly'};
{
"_id" : ObjectId("507f191e810c19729de860ea"),
"catalogId" : "catalog1",
"journal" : "Oracle Magazine",
"publisher" : "Oracle Publishing",
"edition" : "November December 2013",
"title" : "Engineering as a Service",
"author" : "David A. Kelly"
}
>

Figure 7-20. *Documents doc1 and doc2*

To add the documents to the catalog collection run the following command.

```
db.catalog.insert([doc1, doc2], { writeConcern: { w: "majority", wtimeout: 5000 },
ordered:true })
```

As indicated by the nInserted field in the JSON result in Figure 7-21 documents get added.

```
>
> db.catalog.insert([doc1, doc2],  { writeConcern: { w: "majority", wtimeout: 50
00 }, ordered:true })
BulkWriteResult({
        "writeErrors" : [ ],
        "writeConcernErrors" : [ ],
        "nInserted" : 2,
        "nUpserted" : 0,
        "nMatched" : 0,
        "nModified" : 0,
        "nRemoved" : 0,
        "upserted" : [ ]
})
>
```

Figure 7-21. *Adding Documents*

Finding Documents

To query the catalog invoke the `find()` method. To list all documents in the `catalog` collection run the following command.

```
db.catalog.find()
```

The two documents added get listed as shown in Figure 7-22. For one of the documents the `_id` field is generated automatically.

```
> db.catalog.find()
{ "_id" : ObjectId("5675c5db96172b52e58e08b6"), "catalogId" : "catalog1", "journ
al" : "Oracle Magazine", "publisher" : "Oracle Publishing", "edition" : "Novembe
r December 2013", "title" : "Engineering as a Service", "author" : "David A. Kel
ly" }
{ "_id" : ObjectId("507f191e810c19729de860ea"), "catalogId" : "catalog1", "journ
al" : "Oracle Magazine", "publisher" : "Oracle Publishing", "edition" : "Novembe
r December 2013", "title" : "Engineering as a Service", "author" : "David A. Kel
ly" }
> █
```

Figure 7-22. *Finding Documents*

Finding a Single Document

To find a single document from the `catalog` collection run the following command to invoke the `findOne()` method.

```
db.catalog.findOne()
```

A single document gets listed as shown in Figure 7-23.

```
> db.catalog.findOne()
{
        "_id" : ObjectId("5675c5db96172b52e58e08b6"),
        "catalogId" : "catalog1",
        "journal" : "Oracle Magazine",
        "publisher" : "Oracle Publishing",
        "edition" : "November December 2013",
        "title" : "Engineering as a Service",
        "author" : "David A. Kelly"
}
>
```

Figure 7-23. *Finding a Single Document*

Finding Specific Fields in a Single Document

To get only specific fields, edition, title, and author, for example, from a single document run the following command.

```
db.catalog.findOne(
    { },
{ edition: 1, title: 1, author: 1 }
)
```

Only the specific fields in a single document get listed as shown in Figure 7-24. The _id field always gets listed.

```
> db.catalog.findOne(
...     { },
... { edition: 1, title: 1, author: 1 }
... )
{
        "_id" : ObjectId("5675c5db96172b52e58e08b6"),
        "edition" : "November December 2013",
        "title" : "Engineering as a Service",
        "author" : "David A. Kelly"
}
>
```

Figure 7-24. *Finding Selected Fields in a Document*

Dropping a Collection

To drop the catalog collection run the following command.

```
db.catalog.drop()
```

Subsequently list the collections with the following command.

```
show collections
```

The catalog collection does not get listed and only the catalog_capped collection gets listed as shown in Figure 7-25.

```
>
> db.catalog.drop()
true
> show collections
catalog_capped
>
```

Figure 7-25. *Dropping the catalog Collection*

Exiting Mongo Shell and Interactive Shell

To exit the Mongo shell run the following command.

```
exit
```

To exit the interactive terminal run the following command.

```
exit
```

The Mongo shell and the interactive terminal get exited as shown in Figure 7-26.

```
> exit
bye
root@mongo-rc-laqpl:/# exit
exit
ubuntu@ip-172-30-1-39:~$
```

Figure 7-26. *Exiting the Shells*

Scaling the Cluster

To scale the Mongo cluster run the kubectl scale command. For example, the following command scales the cluster to 4 replicas.

```
kubectl scale rc mongo --replicas=4
```

An output of "scaled" as shown in Figure 7-27 scales the cluster to 4 replicas.

```
ubuntu@ip-172-30-1-39:~$ kubectl scale rc mongo-rc --replicas=4
scaled
```

Figure 7-27. *Scaling a Replication Controller*

List the Pods after scaling.

```
kubectl get pods
```

The four Pods get listed. Initially some of the Pods could be listed as not in READY (1/1) state. Run the preceding command multiple times to list all pods running and ready as shown in Figure 7-28.

```
ubuntu@ip-172-30-1-39:~$ kubectl get pods
NAME                    READY     STATUS    RESTARTS   AGE
k8s-master-127.0.0.1    3/3       Running   0          1h
mongo-rc-a26uq          1/1       Running   0          2m
mongo-rc-ja5t6          1/1       Running   0          11s
mongo-rc-rhf2n          0/1       Running   0          11s
mongo-rc-w7qu6          1/1       Running   0          2m
ubuntu@ip-172-30-1-39:~$ kubectl get pods
NAME                    READY     STATUS    RESTARTS   AGE
k8s-master-127.0.0.1    3/3       Running   0          1h
mongo-rc-a26uq          1/1       Running   0          2m
mongo-rc-ja5t6          1/1       Running   0          14s
mongo-rc-rhf2n          0/1       Running   0          14s
mongo-rc-w7qu6          1/1       Running   0          2m
ubuntu@ip-172-30-1-39:~$ kubectl get pods
NAME                    READY     STATUS    RESTARTS   AGE
k8s-master-127.0.0.1    3/3       Running   0          1h
mongo-rc-a26uq          1/1       Running   0          3m
mongo-rc-ja5t6          1/1       Running   0          20s
mongo-rc-rhf2n          1/1       Running   0          20s
mongo-rc-w7qu6          1/1       Running   0          3m
ubuntu@ip-172-30-1-39:~$
```

Figure 7-28. *Listing the Pods after Scaling*

Deleting the Replication Controller

To delete a replication controller mongo-rc run the following command.

```
kubectl delete replicationcontroller mongo-rc
```

All the Pods managed by the replication controller also get deleted. Subsequently run the following command to list the Pods.

```
kubectl get pods
```

The mongo Pods do not get listed as shown in Figure 7-29.

```
ubuntu@ip-172-30-1-39:~$ kubectl delete replicationcontroller mongo-rc
replicationcontrollers/mongo-rc
ubuntu@ip-172-30-1-39:~$ kubectl get pods
NAME                   READY     STATUS    RESTARTS   AGE
k8s-master-127.0.0.1   3/3       Running   0          33m
```

Figure 7-29. *Deleting a Replication Controller*

Deleting the Service

To delete the service called mongo run the following command.

```
kubectl delete service mongo
```

The mongo service does not get listed as shown in Figure 7-30.

```
ubuntu@ip-172-30-1-39:~$ kubectl delete service mongo
services/mongo
ubuntu@ip-172-30-1-39:~$ kubectl get services
NAME         LABELS                                    SELECTOR   IP(S)      POR
T(S)
kubernetes   component=apiserver,provider=kubernetes   <none>     10.0.0.1   443
/TCP
```

Figure 7-30. *Deleting the mongo Service*

Using a Host Port

The container specification within a Pod has the provision to configure a host port. A host port is a container port mapping to the host implying that the specified host port gets reserved for a single container The hostPort field should be used for a single machine container. Multiple containers of the type in which the hostPort is specified cannot be started because the host port can be reserved only by a single container. Other Pods that do not specify a hostPort field could be run, however, on the same machine on which a container with hostPort field mapping is running. As a variation of the replication controller we used earlier add a hostPort field in the spec->containers->ports field. The modified mongo-rc.yaml is listed.

```
---
apiVersion: v1
kind: ReplicationController
metadata:
  labels:
    name: mongo
  name: mongo-rc
spec:
  replicas: 2
  template:
    metadata:
```

```
    labels:
      name: mongo
  spec:
    containers:
      -
        image: mongo
        name: mongo
        ports:
          -
            containerPort: 27017
            hostPort: 27017
            name: mongo
```

Run the following command to create a replication controller.

```
kubectl create -f mongo-rc.yaml
```

List the replication controllers with the following command.

```
kubectl get rc
```

The mongo-rc replication controller gets created and listed as shown in Figure 7-31.

```
ubuntu@ip-172-30-1-39:~$ kubectl create -f  mongo-rc.yaml
replicationcontrollers/mongo-rc
ubuntu@ip-172-30-1-39:~$ kubectl get rc
CONTROLLER   CONTAINER(S)   IMAGE(S)   SELECTOR     REPLICAS
mongo-rc     mongo          mongo      name=mongo   2
ubuntu@ip-172-30-1-39:~$
```

Figure 7-31. *Creating a Replication Controller from a Definition File*

List the Pods with the following command.

```
kubectl get pods
```

Only one of the two replicas is listed as Running and READY (1/1). Even if the preceding command is run multiple times, only one replica is listed as running as shown in Figure 7-32.

```
ubuntu@ip-172-30-1-39:~$ kubectl create -f  mongo-rc.yaml
replicationcontrollers/mongo-rc
ubuntu@ip-172-30-1-39:~$ kubectl get rc
CONTROLLER   CONTAINER(S)   IMAGE(S)   SELECTOR     REPLICAS
mongo-rc     mongo          mongo      name=mongo   2
ubuntu@ip-172-30-1-39:~$ kubectl get pods
NAME                   READY     STATUS    RESTARTS   AGE
k8s-master-127.0.0.1   3/3       Running   0          7m
mongo-rc-28rwu         0/1       Pending   0          1m
mongo-rc-laqpl         1/1       Running   0          1m
ubuntu@ip-172-30-1-39:~$ kubectl get pods
NAME                   READY     STATUS    RESTARTS   AGE
k8s-master-127.0.0.1   3/3       Running   0          7m
mongo-rc-28rwu         0/1       Pending   0          1m
mongo-rc-laqpl         1/1       Running   0          1m
ubuntu@ip-172-30-1-39:~$ kubectl get pods
NAME                   READY     STATUS    RESTARTS   AGE
k8s-master-127.0.0.1   3/3       Running   0          7m
mongo-rc-28rwu         0/1       Pending   0          1m
mongo-rc-laqpl         1/1       Running   0          1m
ubuntu@ip-172-30-1-39:~$ kubectl get pods
NAME                   READY     STATUS    RESTARTS   AGE
k8s-master-127.0.0.1   3/3       Running   0          7m
mongo-rc-28rwu         0/1       Pending   0          1m
mongo-rc-laqpl         1/1       Running   0          1m
ubuntu@ip-172-30-1-39:~$
```

Figure 7-32. *Listing the Pods after creating a Replication Controller*

Scale the MongoDB cluster to 4 replicas with the following command.

```
kubectl scale rc mongo --replicas=4
```

Though the output from the command is "Scaled" and 4 Pods get created but only one Pod is in READY (1/1) state at any particular time as shown in Figure 7-33.

```
ubuntu@ip-172-30-1-39:~$ kubectl scale rc mongo-rc  --replicas=4
scaled
ubuntu@ip-172-30-1-39:~$ kubectl get pods
NAME                      READY     STATUS     RESTARTS   AGE
k8s-master-127.0.0.1      3/3       Running    0          29m
mongo-rc-1olyf            0/1       Pending    0          18s
mongo-rc-28rwu            0/1       Pending    0          24m
mongo-rc-laqpl            1/1       Running    0          24m
mongo-rc-yu720            0/1       Pending    0          18s
ubuntu@ip-172-30-1-39:~$ kubectl get pods
NAME                      READY     STATUS     RESTARTS   AGE
k8s-master-127.0.0.1      3/3       Running    0          30m
mongo-rc-1olyf            0/1       Pending    0          42s
mongo-rc-28rwu            0/1       Pending    0          24m
mongo-rc-laqpl            1/1       Running    0          24m
mongo-rc-yu720            0/1       Pending    0          42s
```

Figure 7-33. *Scaling the Replication Controller to 4 Replicas*

Even if the single running Pod is stopped only one new Pod gets started. To demonstrate, stop the single running Pod.

```
kubectl stop pod mongo-rc-laqpl
```

The Pod gets removed but a replacement Pod gets created to maintain the replication level of 1 as shown in Figure 7-34.

```
ubuntu@ip-172-30-1-39:~$ kubectl stop pod mongo-rc-laqpl
pods/mongo-rc-laqpl
ubuntu@ip-172-30-1-39:~$ kubectl get pods
NAME                      READY     STATUS     RESTARTS   AGE
k8s-master-127.0.0.1      3/3       Running    0          30m
mongo-rc-1olyf            0/1       Pending    0          1m
mongo-rc-28rwu            0/1       Pending    0          25m
mongo-rc-eih4s            0/1       Running    0          12s
mongo-rc-yu720            0/1       Pending    0          1m
ubuntu@ip-172-30-1-39:~$ █
```

Figure 7-34. *Another Pod gets created when the single running Pod is stopped*

List the Pods again after a few seconds and only one Pod gets listed as shown in Figure 7-35.

```
ubuntu@ip-172-30-1-39:~$ kubectl get pods
NAME                   READY     STATUS    RESTARTS   AGE
k8s-master-127.0.0.1   3/3       Running   0          31m
mongo-rc-1olyf         0/1       Pending   0          1m
mongo-rc-28rwu         0/1       Pending   0          25m
mongo-rc-eih4s         1/1       Running   0          51s
mongo-rc-yu720         0/1       Pending   0          1m
ubuntu@ip-172-30-1-39:~$
```

Figure 7-35. *Only a single Pod is Running and Ready*

Using the `hostPort` field is not recommended unless a single container machine is to be used or only a single container is required to be mapped to the host port.

Creating a MongoDB Cluster Imperatively

In the following subsections we shall create a Kubernetes replication controller and service for a MongoDB cluster on the command line using kubectl.

Creating a Replication Controller

To create a replication controller for the Docker image "mongo" with 2 replicas and port 27017 run the following command.

```
kubectl run mongo --image=mongo --replicas=2 --port=27017
```

The replication controller gets created as shown in Figure 7-36.

```
ubuntu@ip-172-30-1-39:~$ kubectl  run mongo --image=mongo --replicas=2 --port=27
017
CONTROLLER   CONTAINER(S)   IMAGE(S)   SELECTOR    REPLICAS
mongo        mongo          mongo      run=mongo   2
```

Figure 7-36. *Creating a Replication Controller Imperatively*

List the Pods with the following command.

```
kubectl get rc
```

The mongo-rc gets listed as shown in Figure 7-37.

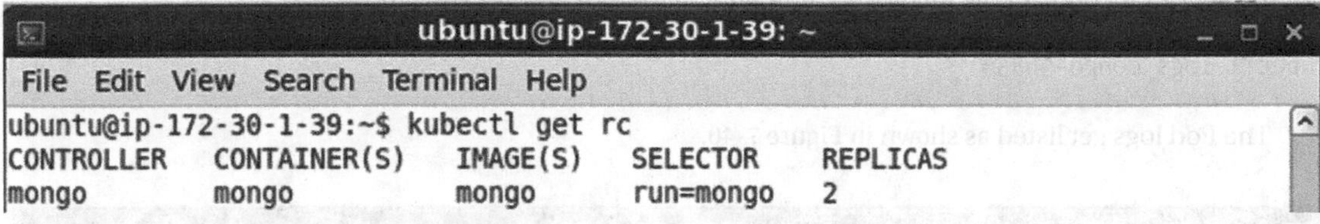
ubuntu@ip-172-30-1-39: ~
File Edit View Search Terminal Help
ubuntu@ip-172-30-1-39:~$ kubectl get rc
CONTROLLER CONTAINER(S) IMAGE(S) SELECTOR REPLICAS
mongo mongo mongo run=mongo 2

Figure 7-37. *Listing the Replication Controllers*

Listing the Pods

List the Pods with the following command.

```
kubectl get pods
```

The two Pods started for MongoDB get listed as shown in Figure 7-38. Initially the Pods could be listed as not running.

```
ubuntu@ip-172-30-1-39:~$ kubectl get pods
NAME                     READY     STATUS
RESTARTS   AGE
k8s-master-127.0.0.1     3/3       Running
0          5m
mongo-15n17              0/1       Image: mongo is ready, container is creating
0          10s
mongo-cbjct              0/1       Running
0          10s
ubuntu@ip-172-30-1-39:~$
```

Figure 7-38. *Listing the Pods with some of the pods not Running yet*

Run the following preceding multiple times if required to list the Pods as running as shown in Figure 7-39.

```
ubuntu@ip-172-30-1-39:~$ kubectl get pods
NAME                     READY     STATUS    RESTARTS   AGE
k8s-master-127.0.0.1     3/3       Running   0          5m
mongo-15n17              1/1       Running   0          29s
mongo-cbjct              1/1       Running   0          29s
ubuntu@ip-172-30-1-39:~$
```

Figure 7-39. *Listing all the Pods as Running*

Listing the Logs

List the logs for a Pod with the following command. The `mongo-56850` is the Pod name.

```
kubectl logs mongo-56850
```

The Pod logs get listed as shown in Figure 7-40.

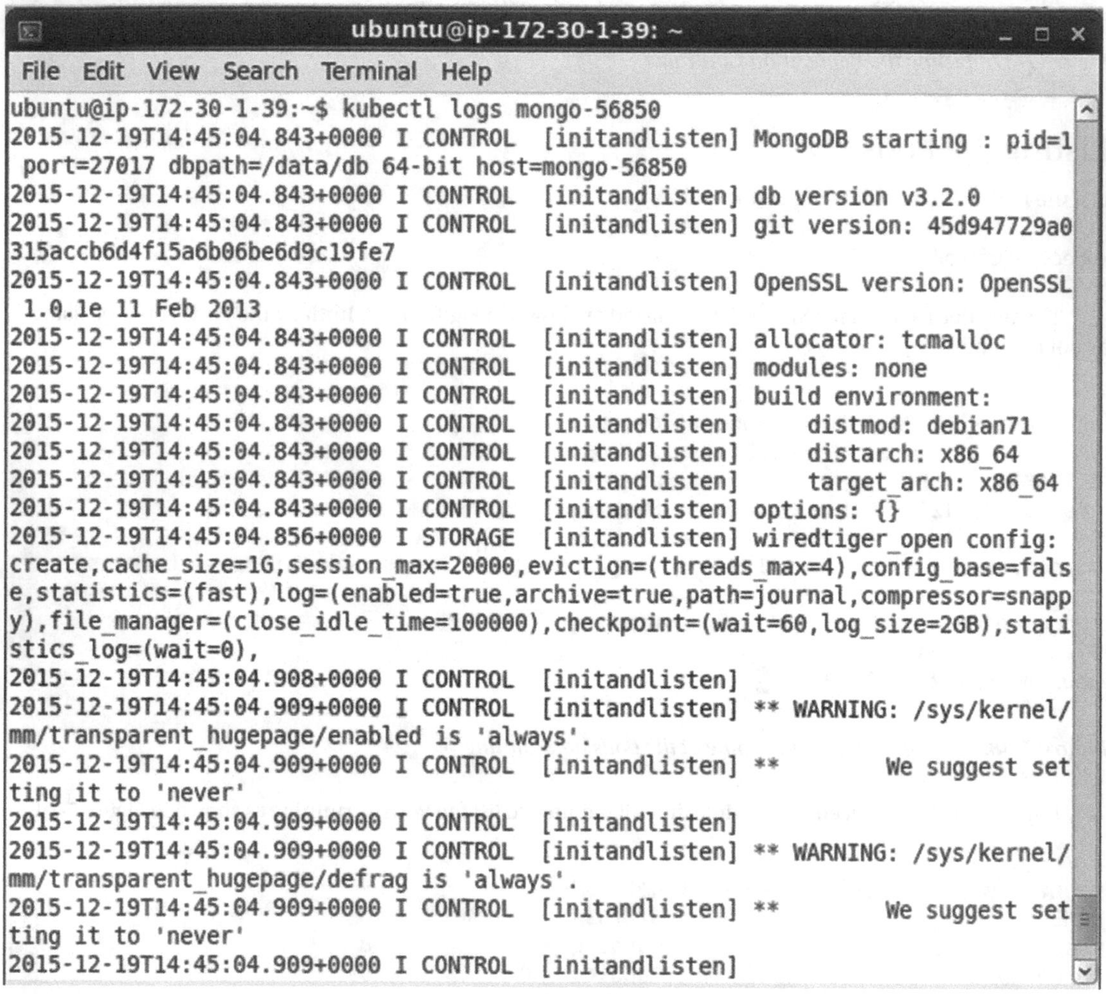

```
ubuntu@ip-172-30-1-39: ~
File Edit View Search Terminal Help
ubuntu@ip-172-30-1-39:~$ kubectl logs mongo-56850
2015-12-19T14:45:04.843+0000 I CONTROL  [initandlisten] MongoDB starting : pid=1
 port=27017 dbpath=/data/db 64-bit host=mongo-56850
2015-12-19T14:45:04.843+0000 I CONTROL  [initandlisten] db version v3.2.0
2015-12-19T14:45:04.843+0000 I CONTROL  [initandlisten] git version: 45d947729a0
315accb6d4f15a6b06be6d9c19fe7
2015-12-19T14:45:04.843+0000 I CONTROL  [initandlisten] OpenSSL version: OpenSSL
 1.0.1e 11 Feb 2013
2015-12-19T14:45:04.843+0000 I CONTROL  [initandlisten] allocator: tcmalloc
2015-12-19T14:45:04.843+0000 I CONTROL  [initandlisten] modules: none
2015-12-19T14:45:04.843+0000 I CONTROL  [initandlisten] build environment:
2015-12-19T14:45:04.843+0000 I CONTROL  [initandlisten]     distmod: debian71
2015-12-19T14:45:04.843+0000 I CONTROL  [initandlisten]     distarch: x86_64
2015-12-19T14:45:04.843+0000 I CONTROL  [initandlisten]     target_arch: x86_64
2015-12-19T14:45:04.843+0000 I CONTROL  [initandlisten] options: {}
2015-12-19T14:45:04.856+0000 I STORAGE  [initandlisten] wiredtiger_open config:
create,cache_size=1G,session_max=20000,eviction=(threads_max=4),config_base=fals
e,statistics=(fast),log=(enabled=true,archive=true,path=journal,compressor=snapp
y),file_manager=(close_idle_time=100000),checkpoint=(wait=60,log_size=2GB),stati
stics_log=(wait=0),
2015-12-19T14:45:04.908+0000 I CONTROL  [initandlisten]
2015-12-19T14:45:04.909+0000 I CONTROL  [initandlisten] ** WARNING: /sys/kernel/
mm/transparent_hugepage/enabled is 'always'.
2015-12-19T14:45:04.909+0000 I CONTROL  [initandlisten] **        We suggest set
ting it to 'never'
2015-12-19T14:45:04.909+0000 I CONTROL  [initandlisten]
2015-12-19T14:45:04.909+0000 I CONTROL  [initandlisten] ** WARNING: /sys/kernel/
mm/transparent_hugepage/defrag is 'always'.
2015-12-19T14:45:04.909+0000 I CONTROL  [initandlisten] **        We suggest set
ting it to 'never'
2015-12-19T14:45:04.909+0000 I CONTROL  [initandlisten]
```

Figure 7-40. *Listing Pod Logs*

MongoDB is listed as started as shown in Figure 7-41. Output on commands run on the server also get output.

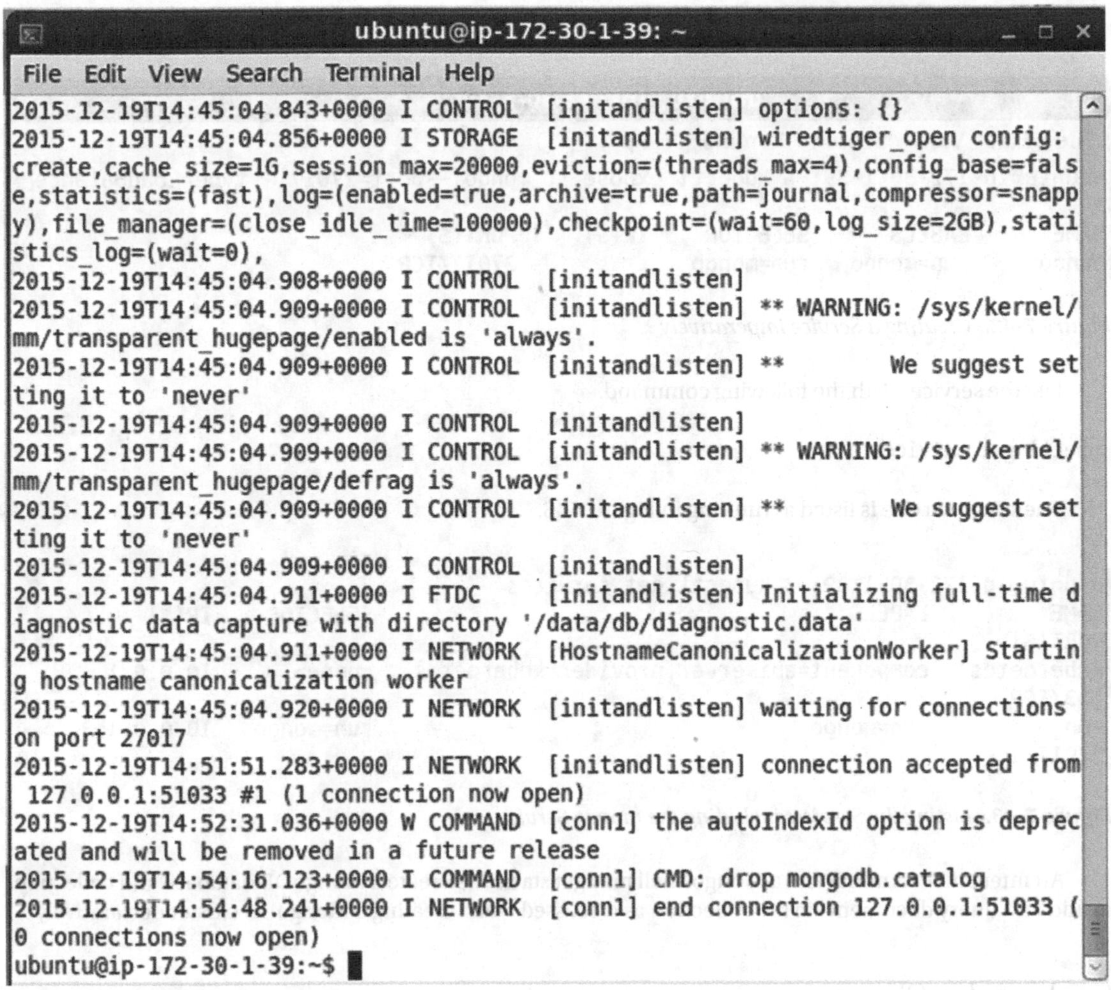

```
ubuntu@ip-172-30-1-39: ~
File  Edit  View  Search  Terminal  Help
2015-12-19T14:45:04.843+0000 I CONTROL  [initandlisten] options: {}
2015-12-19T14:45:04.856+0000 I STORAGE  [initandlisten] wiredtiger_open config:
create,cache_size=1G,session_max=20000,eviction=(threads_max=4),config_base=fals
e,statistics=(fast),log=(enabled=true,archive=true,path=journal,compressor=snapp
y),file_manager=(close_idle_time=100000),checkpoint=(wait=60,log_size=2GB),stati
stics_log=(wait=0),
2015-12-19T14:45:04.908+0000 I CONTROL  [initandlisten]
2015-12-19T14:45:04.909+0000 I CONTROL  [initandlisten] ** WARNING: /sys/kernel/
mm/transparent_hugepage/enabled is 'always'.
2015-12-19T14:45:04.909+0000 I CONTROL  [initandlisten] **        We suggest set
ting it to 'never'
2015-12-19T14:45:04.909+0000 I CONTROL  [initandlisten]
2015-12-19T14:45:04.909+0000 I CONTROL  [initandlisten] ** WARNING: /sys/kernel/
mm/transparent_hugepage/defrag is 'always'.
2015-12-19T14:45:04.909+0000 I CONTROL  [initandlisten] **        We suggest set
ting it to 'never'
2015-12-19T14:45:04.909+0000 I CONTROL  [initandlisten]
2015-12-19T14:45:04.911+0000 I FTDC     [initandlisten] Initializing full-time d
iagnostic data capture with directory '/data/db/diagnostic.data'
2015-12-19T14:45:04.911+0000 I NETWORK  [HostnameCanonicalizationWorker] Startin
g hostname canonicalization worker
2015-12-19T14:45:04.920+0000 I NETWORK  [initandlisten] waiting for connections
on port 27017
2015-12-19T14:51:51.283+0000 I NETWORK  [initandlisten] connection accepted from
 127.0.0.1:51033 #1 (1 connection now open)
2015-12-19T14:52:31.036+0000 W COMMAND  [conn1] the autoIndexId option is deprec
ated and will be removed in a future release
2015-12-19T14:54:16.123+0000 I COMMAND  [conn1] CMD: drop mongodb.catalog
2015-12-19T14:54:48.241+0000 I NETWORK  [conn1] end connection 127.0.0.1:51033 (
0 connections now open)
ubuntu@ip-172-30-1-39:~$ █
```

Figure 7-41. *Listing MongoDB Server as running and waiting for connections on port 27017*

Creating a Service

To create a service for the mongo replication controller run the following command to expose a service on port 27017 of type LoadBalancer, which was discussed earlier.

```
kubectl expose rc mongo --port=27017 --type=LoadBalancer
```

The mongo service gets created as shown in Figure 7-42.

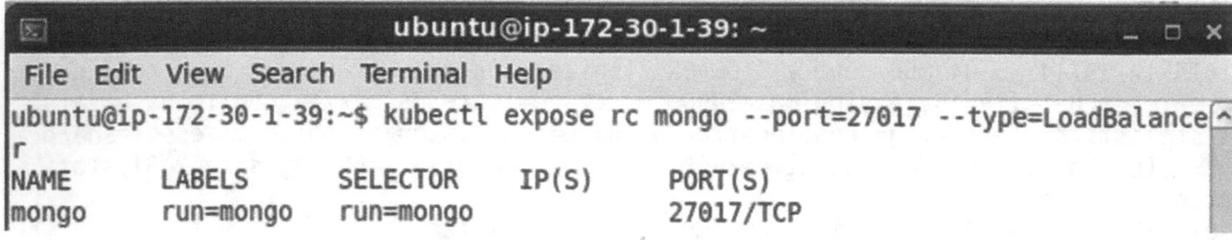
ubuntu@ip-172-30-1-39: ~
File Edit View Search Terminal Help
ubuntu@ip-172-30-1-39:~$ kubectl expose rc mongo --port=27017 --type=LoadBalance
r
NAME LABELS SELECTOR IP(S) PORT(S)
mongo run=mongo run=mongo 27017/TCP

Figure 7-42. *Creating a Service Imperatively*

List the services with the following command.

```
kubectl get services
```

The mongo service is listed as running in Figure 7-43.

```
ubuntu@ip-172-30-1-39:~$ kubectl get services
NAME          LABELS                                    SELECTOR    IP(S)
PORT(S)
kubernetes    component=apiserver,provider=kubernetes   <none>      10.0.0.1
443/TCP
mongo         run=mongo                                 run=mongo   10.0.0.153
27017/TCP
```

Figure 7-43. *Listing the Services including the mongo Service*

An interactive terminal and a Mongo shell may get started to create a MongoDB database and collection to add and query documents in the collection as discussed when creating a MongoDB cluster declaratively.

Scaling the Cluster

To scale the cluster to 4 replicas, for example, run the following command.

```
kubectl scale rc mongo --replicas=4
```

An output of "scaled" indicates that the cluster has been scaled as shown in Figure 7-44.

```
ubuntu@ip-172-30-1-39:~$ kubectl scale rc mongo  --replicas=4
scaled
```

Figure 7-44. *Scaling the Cluster created Imperatively*

Subsequently get the Pods.

```
kubectl get pods
```

Four pods get listed as shown in Figure 7-45. Initially some of the Pods could be shown as not running or ready.

```
ubuntu@ip-172-30-1-39:~$ kubectl get pods
NAME                    READY     STATUS    RESTARTS   AGE
k8s-master-127.0.0.1    3/3       Running   0          50m
mongo-56850             1/1       Running   0          10m
mongo-j5amq             1/1       Running   0          10m
mongo-kygrc             1/1       Running   0          15s
mongo-nc2dh             0/1       Running   0          15s
ubuntu@ip-172-30-1-39:~$ kubectl get pods
NAME                    READY     STATUS    RESTARTS   AGE
k8s-master-127.0.0.1    3/3       Running   0          50m
mongo-56850             1/1       Running   0          11m
mongo-j5amq             1/1       Running   0          11m
mongo-kygrc             1/1       Running   0          23s
mongo-nc2dh             1/1       Running   0          23s
ubuntu@ip-172-30-1-39:~$
```

Figure 7-45. *Listing Pods after Scaling*

To describe the mongo service run the following command.

```
kubectl describe svc mongo
```

The service description includes the service label, selector in addition to the service endpoints, one for each of the four pods as shown in Figure 7-46.

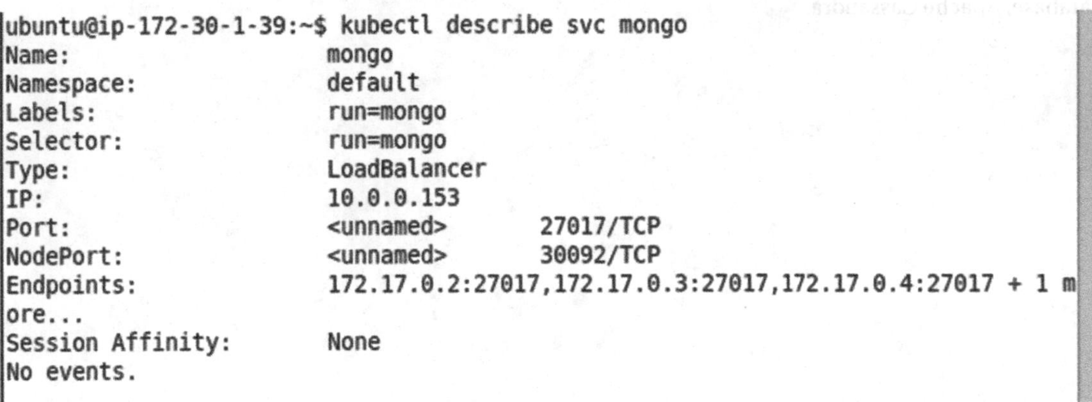

```
ubuntu@ip-172-30-1-39:~$ kubectl describe svc mongo
Name:                   mongo
Namespace:              default
Labels:                 run=mongo
Selector:               run=mongo
Type:                   LoadBalancer
IP:                     10.0.0.153
Port:                   <unnamed>       27017/TCP
NodePort:               <unnamed>       30092/TCP
Endpoints:              172.17.0.2:27017,172.17.0.3:27017,172.17.0.4:27017 + 1 m
ore...
Session Affinity:       None
No events.
```

Figure 7-46. *Describing the Service mongo after Scaling*

Deleting the Service and Replication Controller

The mongo service and the mongo replication controller may be deleted with the following commands.

```
kubectl delete service mongo
kubectl delete rc mongo
```

The "mongo" service and the "mongo" replication controller get deleted as shown in Figure 7-47. Deleting one does not delete the other; the decoupling of the replication controller from the service is a feature suitable to evolve one without having to modify the other.

```
ubuntu@ip-172-30-1-39:~$ kubectl delete service mongo
services/mongo
ubuntu@ip-172-30-1-39:~$ kubectl delete rc mongo
replicationcontrollers/mongo
ubuntu@ip-172-30-1-39:~$ ▌
```

Figure 7-47. *Deleting the Service and the Replication Controller*

Summary

In this chapter we used the Kubernetes cluster manager to create and orchestrate a MongoDB cluster. We created a replication controller and a service both imperatively and declaratively. We also demonstrated scaling a cluster. We introduced two other features of Kubernetes replication controllers: volumes and host port. This chapter is about using Kubernetes with MongoDB and the emphasis is less on MongoDB; but if MongoDB is to be explored in more detail, refer to the Apress book *Pro MongoDB Development* (`http://www.apress.com/9781484215999?gtmf=s`). In the next chapter we shall discuss another NoSQL database, Apache Cassandra.

CHAPTER 8

Using Apache Cassandra Database

Apache Cassandra is an open source wide column data store. Cassandra is a scalable, reliable, fault-tolerant, and highly available NoSQL database. Cassandra is based on a flexible schema data model in which data is stored in rows in a table (also called column family) with a primary key identifying a row. The primary key could be a single column or multiple column (compound) row key. A relational database also stores data in table rows, but what makes Cassandra different is that the table rows do not have to follow a fixed schema. Each row in a table could have different columns or some of the columns could be the same as other rows. Each row does not have to include all the columns or any column data at all. In this regard Cassandra provides a dynamic column specification. A keyspace is a namespace container for the data stored in Cassandra. In this chapter we shall discuss using Kubernetes cluster manager with Apache Cassandra. This chapter has the following sections.

Setting the Environment

Creating a Cassandra Cluster Declaratively

Creating a Cassandra Cluster Imperatively

Setting the Environment

The following software is required for this chapter.

-Docker Engine (latest version)

-Kubernetes (version 1.01)

-Kubectl (version 1.01)

-Docker image for Apache Cassandra (latest version)

Install the software on an Amazon EC2 instance created from Ubuntu Server 14.04 LTS (HVM), SSD Volume Type - ami-d05e75b8 AMI as explained in chapter 1. SSH Login to the Ubuntu instance using the Public IP Address of the Amazon EC2 instance.

```
ssh -i "docker.pem" ubuntu@52.23.160.7
```

Start the Docker engine and verify its status.

```
sudo service docker start
sudo service docker status
```


D. Vohra, *Kubernetes Microservices with Docker*, DOI 10.1007/978-1-4842-1907-2_8

The Docker engine should be running as shown in Figure 8-1.

```
ubuntu@ip-172-30-1-13:~$ sudo service docker start
start: Job is already running: docker
ubuntu@ip-172-30-1-13:~$ sudo service docker status
docker start/running, process 823
ubuntu@ip-172-30-1-13:~$
```

Figure 8-1. *Starting Docker*

List the services.

```
kubectl get services
```

The "kubernetes" service should be listed as shown in Figure 8-2.

```
ubuntu@ip-172-30-1-13:~$ kubectl get services
NAME         LABELS                                    SELECTOR   IP(S)      POR
T(S)
kubernetes   component=apiserver,provider=kubernetes   <none>     10.0.0.1   443
/TCP
ubuntu@ip-172-30-1-13:~$
```

Figure 8-2. *Listing the "kubernetes" Service*

List the Pods and the nodes with the following commands.

```
kubectl get pods
kubectl get nodes
```

Initially the only pod running is the Kubernetes pod as shown in Figure 8-3.

```
ubuntu@ip-172-30-1-13:~$ kubectl get pods
NAME                    READY     STATUS    RESTARTS   AGE
k8s-master-127.0.0.1    3/3       Running   3          12m
ubuntu@ip-172-30-1-13:~$ kubectl get nodes
NAME        LABELS                               STATUS
127.0.0.1   kubernetes.io/hostname=127.0.0.1     Ready
ubuntu@ip-172-30-1-13:~$
```

Figure 8-3. *Listing the Pod and Node for Kubernetes*

A Cassandra cluster may be created and managed both declaratively and imperatively, and we shall discuss both the options.

Creating a Cassandra Cluster Declaratively

In the following subsections we have discussed creating a Cassandra cluster using definition files based on the YAML format. First, create a service to represent a Cassandra cluster. A service is the external interface for a cluster of Pods, Apache Cassandra pods in the context of this chapter.

Creating a Service

Create a service definition file called `cassandra-service.yaml`. Add the fields discussed in Table 8-1.

Table 8-1. *Fields in the Service Definition File*

Field	Description	Value
apiVersion	API Version.	v1
kind	Kind of the definition file.	Service
metadata	Metadata of the service.	
metadata - > name	Service name. Required field.	cassandra
metadata - > labels	Service labels. A label could be any key- > value pair. A service label is set as app:cassandra.	app:cassandra
spec	The service specification.	
spec - > labels	The spec labels. A label could be any key- > value pair. The service label is set as app:Cassandra.	app:cassandra
spec - > selector	Service selector. Used to select Pods to manage. Pods with a label the same as the selector expression are selected or managed by the service. The selector expression could be any key:value pair. Or, multiple requirements or expressions could be specified using a ','. The app:cassandra setting translates to service selector app = cassandra.	app:cassandra
spec - > ports	The service ports. The ports field is required.	
spec - > ports - > port	A single service port at which the service is exposed for access by external clients.	9042
spec - > type	The service type.	LoadBalancer

The `cassandra-service.yaml` is listed below. Use the YAML Lint (`http://www.yamllint.com/`) to validate the syntax.

```
apiVersion: v1
kind: Service
metadata:
  name: cassandra
  labels:
    app: cassandra
```

```
spec:
  labels:
    app: cassandra
  selector:
    app: cassandra
  ports:
    -
      port: 9042
  type: LoadBalancer
```

The `cassandra-service.yaml` file may be created in a vi editor and saved using the :wq command as shown in Figure 8-4.

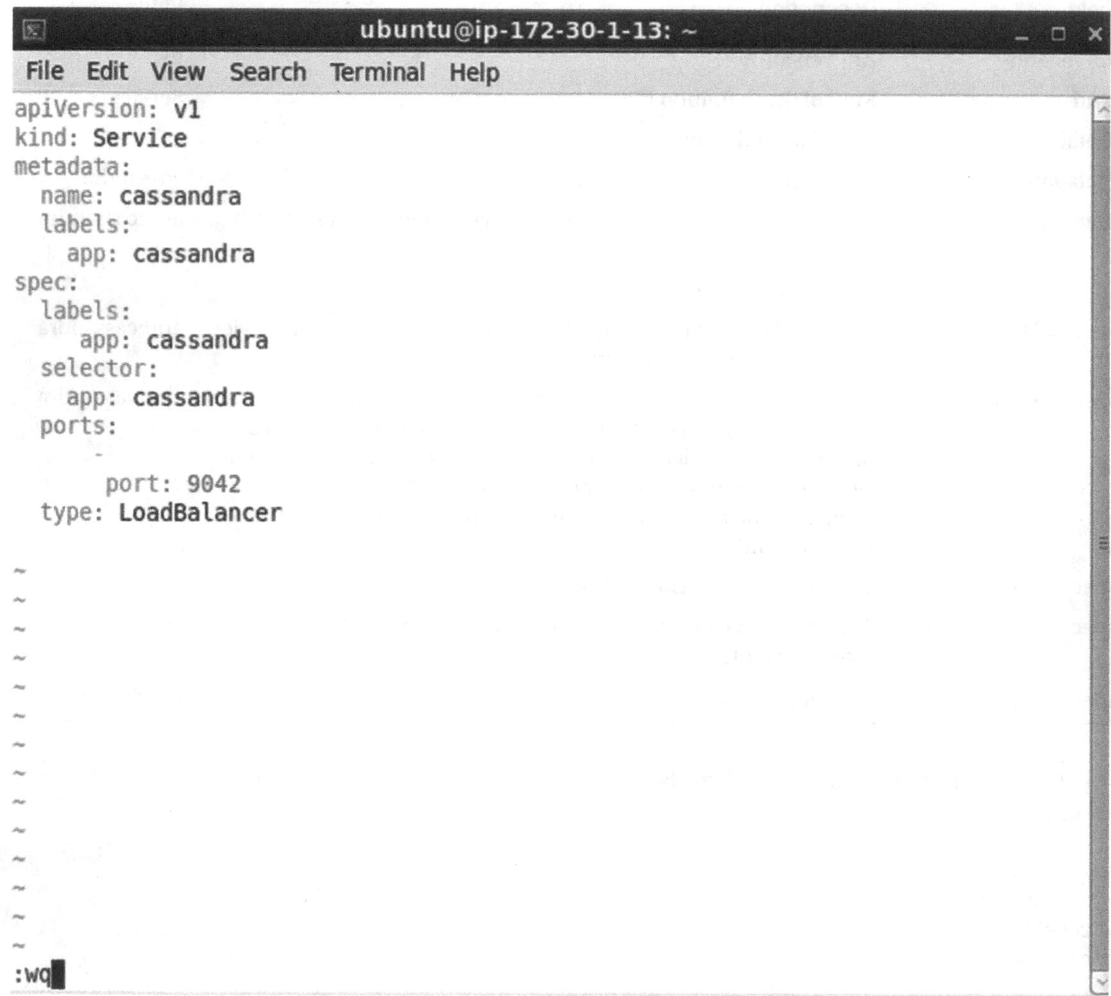

```
apiVersion: v1
kind: Service
metadata:
  name: cassandra
  labels:
    app: cassandra
spec:
  labels:
     app: cassandra
  selector:
    app: cassandra
  ports:
    -
      port: 9042
  type: LoadBalancer

~
~
~
~
~
~
~
~
~
~
~
~
~
~
:wq
```

Figure 8-4. *Service Definition File in vi Editor*

To create a service run the following command.

```
kubectl create -f cassandra-service.yaml
```

Subsequently list the services.

```
kubectl get services
```

The cassandra service gets listed as shown in Figure 8-5.

```
ubuntu@ip-172-30-1-13:~$ kubectl create -f cassandra-service.yaml
services/cassandra
ubuntu@ip-172-30-1-13:~$ kubectl get services
NAME         LABELS                                    SELECTOR        IP(S)
   PORT(S)
cassandra    app=cassandra                             app=cassandra   10.0.0.24
5   9042/TCP
kubernetes   component=apiserver,provider=kubernetes   <none>          10.0.0.1
   443/TCP
ubuntu@ip-172-30-1-13:~$
```

Figure 8-5. *Creating and listing a Service for Apache Cassandra*

Describe the cassandra service with the following command.

```
kubectl describe svc cassandra
```

The service name, namespace, labels, selector, type, IP, Port, NodePort and endpoints get listed as shown in Figure 8-6. No service endpoint is listed initially because a Pod has not been created yet.

```
ubuntu@ip-172-30-1-13:~$ kubectl describe svc cassandra
Name:                   cassandra
Namespace:              default
Labels:                 app=cassandra
Selector:               app=cassandra
Type:                   LoadBalancer
IP:                     10.0.0.245
Port:                   <unnamed>       9042/TCP
NodePort:               <unnamed>       32434/TCP
Endpoints:              <none>
Session Affinity:       None
No events.

ubuntu@ip-172-30-1-13:~$
```

Figure 8-6. *Describing the Service for Apache Cassandra*

Creating a Replication Controller

Next, we shall create a replication controller for Cassandra. A replication controller defines the configuration for the containers and their respective Docker images in the Pod. Create a definition file `cassandra-rc.yaml` and add the following (Table 8-2) fields.

Table 8-2. *Fields in the Replication Controller Definition File*

Field	Description	Value
apiVersion	The API Version.	v1
kind	Kind of definition file.	ReplicationController
metadata	Replication controller metadata.	
metadata -> labels	Replication controller labels. The key:value pair app:cassandra is set as a label on the replication controller.	app:cassandra
spec	The replication controller specification.	
spec -> replicas	The number of replicas.	1
spec-> selector	The selector expression for the replication controller. Must be the same as one of the labels in the spec -> template -> metadata -> labels field. Required field but not required to be set explicitly and defaults to the labels in spec -> template -> metadata -> labels field. If multiple requirements are set in the selector multiple labels in the Pod template labels must match. For example if the `selector` is `app=cassandra,name=cassandra` the Pod template labels spec -> template -> metadata -> labels must include both of these labels.	
spec -> template	The Pod template. Required field.	
spec -> template -> metadata	Template metadata.	
spec -> template -> metadata -> labels	Template labels. The key:value pair app:cassandra is set as a label on the Pod. A label must be set on the template. The label setting translates to Pod label app=cassandra.	app:cassandra
spec -> template -> spec	The container specification.	
spec -> template -> spec -> containers	The containers in the Pod.	
spec -> template -> spec -> containers -> image	The Docker image for a container.	cassandra
spec -> template -> spec -> containers -> name	The container name.	cassandra
spec -> template -> spec -> containers -> ports	The container ports.	

(*continued*)

Table 8-2. *(continued)*

Field	Description	Value
spec -> template -> spec -> containers -> ports -> containerPort	The container port for CQL command shell.	9042
spec -> template -> spec -> containers -> ports -> name	The port name.	cql
spec -> template -> spec -> containers -> ports -> containerPort	The container port for thrift clients.	9160
spec -> template -> spec -> containers -> ports -> name	The port name.	thrift

The `cassandra-rc.yaml` is listed.

```
apiVersion: v1
kind: ReplicationController
metadata:
  name: cassandra-rc
  labels:
    app: cassandra
spec:
  replicas: 1
  template:
    metadata:
      labels:
        app: cassandra
    spec:
      containers:
        -
        image: cassandra
        name: cassandra
        ports:
          -
            containerPort: 9042
            name: cql
          -
            containerPort: 9160
            name: thrift
```

The `cassandra-rc.yaml` field may be created in a vi editor and saved with the :wq command as shown in Figure 8-7.

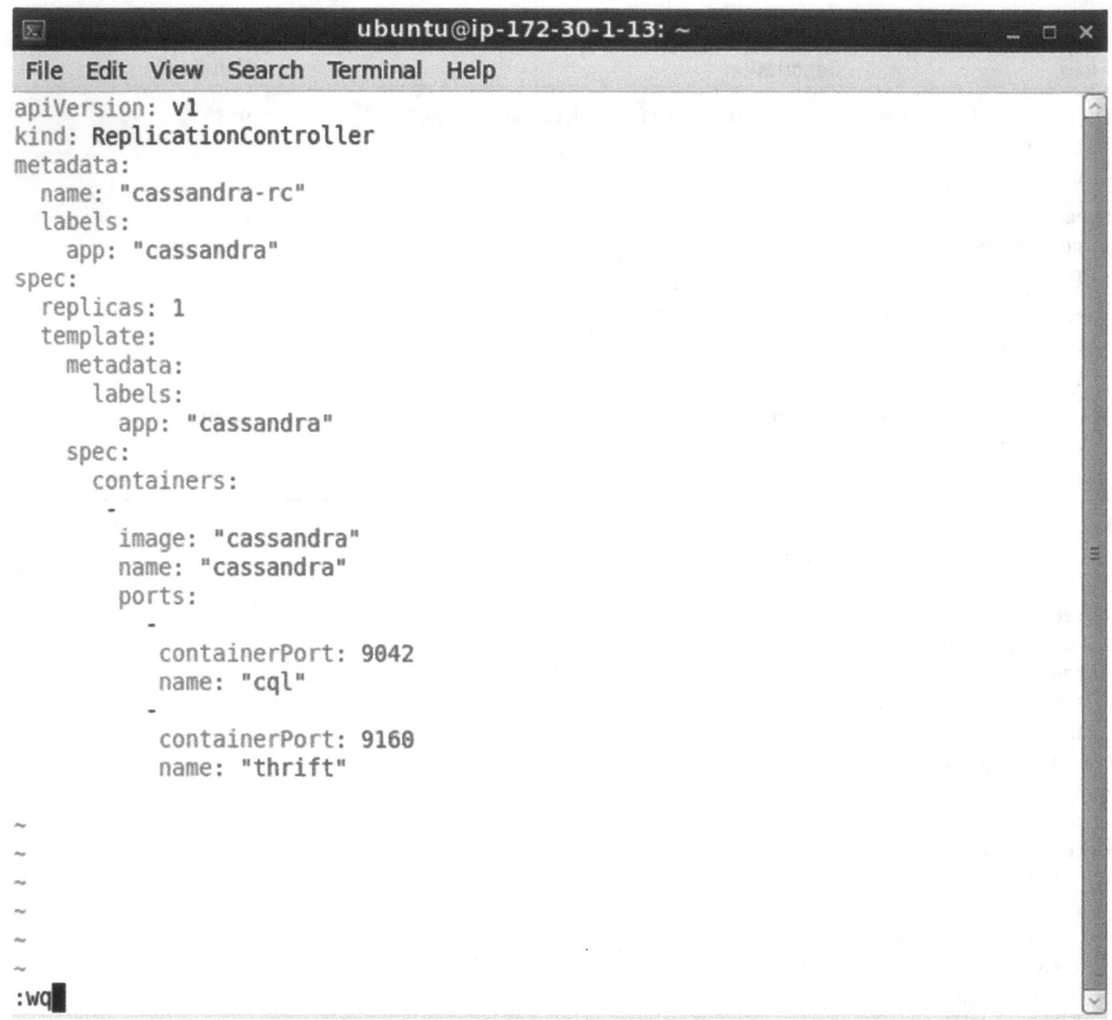
```
apiVersion: v1
kind: ReplicationController
metadata:
  name: "cassandra-rc"
  labels:
    app: "cassandra"
spec:
  replicas: 1
  template:
    metadata:
      labels:
        app: "cassandra"
    spec:
      containers:
        -
          image: "cassandra"
          name: "cassandra"
          ports:
            -
              containerPort: 9042
              name: "cql"
            -
              containerPort: 9160
              name: "thrift"
```

Figure 8-7. Replication Controller Definition File in vi Editor

Create a replication controller with the following command.

```
kubectl create -f cassandra-rc.yaml
```

Subsequently list the replication controllers.

```
kubectl get rc
```

The `cassandra-rc` replication controller gets created and listed as shown in Figure 8-8.

```
ubuntu@ip-172-30-1-13:~$ kubectl create -f cassandra-rc.yaml
replicationcontrollers/cassandra-rc
ubuntu@ip-172-30-1-13:~$ kubectl get rc
CONTROLLER     CONTAINER(S)   IMAGE(S)    SELECTOR        REPLICAS
cassandra-rc   cassandra      cassandra   app=cassandra   1
ubuntu@ip-172-30-1-13:~$
```

Figure 8-8. *Creating a Replication Controller from Definition File*

List the Pods created by the replication controller.

```
kubectl get pods
```

As the number of replicas is set to 1 in the replication controller definition file, one Pod gets created and is listed in Figure 8-9. The preceding command may have to be run multiple times to list the Pod as running and ready. Alternatively run the command for the first time after a few seconds of having created the replication controller; by a minute all Pods should have started.

```
ubuntu@ip-172-30-1-13:~$ kubectl get pods
NAME                   READY     STATUS    RESTARTS   AGE
cassandra-rc-tou4u     1/1       Running   0          24s
k8s-master-127.0.0.1   3/3       Running   3          53m
ubuntu@ip-172-30-1-13:~$
```

Figure 8-9. *Listing Pod/s for Apache Cassandra*

Describe the Cassandra service.

```
kubectl describe svc cassandra
```

An endpoint gets listed for the Pod as shown in Figure 8-10. When the service description was listed before creating a replication controller, no endpoint got listed.

```
ubuntu@ip-172-30-1-13:~$ kubectl describe svc cassandra
Name:                   cassandra
Namespace:              default
Labels:                 app=cassandra
Selector:               app=cassandra
Type:                   LoadBalancer
IP:                     10.0.0.245
Port:                   <unnamed>       9042/TCP
NodePort:               <unnamed>       32434/TCP
Endpoints:              172.17.0.2:9042
Session Affinity:       None
No events.

ubuntu@ip-172-30-1-13:~$
```

Figure 8-10. *Describing the Service after creating the Replication Controller*

In the preceding example we created a replication controller with the number of replicas set as 1. The replication controller does not have to create a replica to start with. To demonstrate we shall create the replication controller again, but with a different replicas setting. Delete the replication controller previously created.

```
kubectl delete rc cassandra-rc
```

Modify the `cassandra-rc.yaml` to set replicas field to 0 as shown in Figure 8-11.

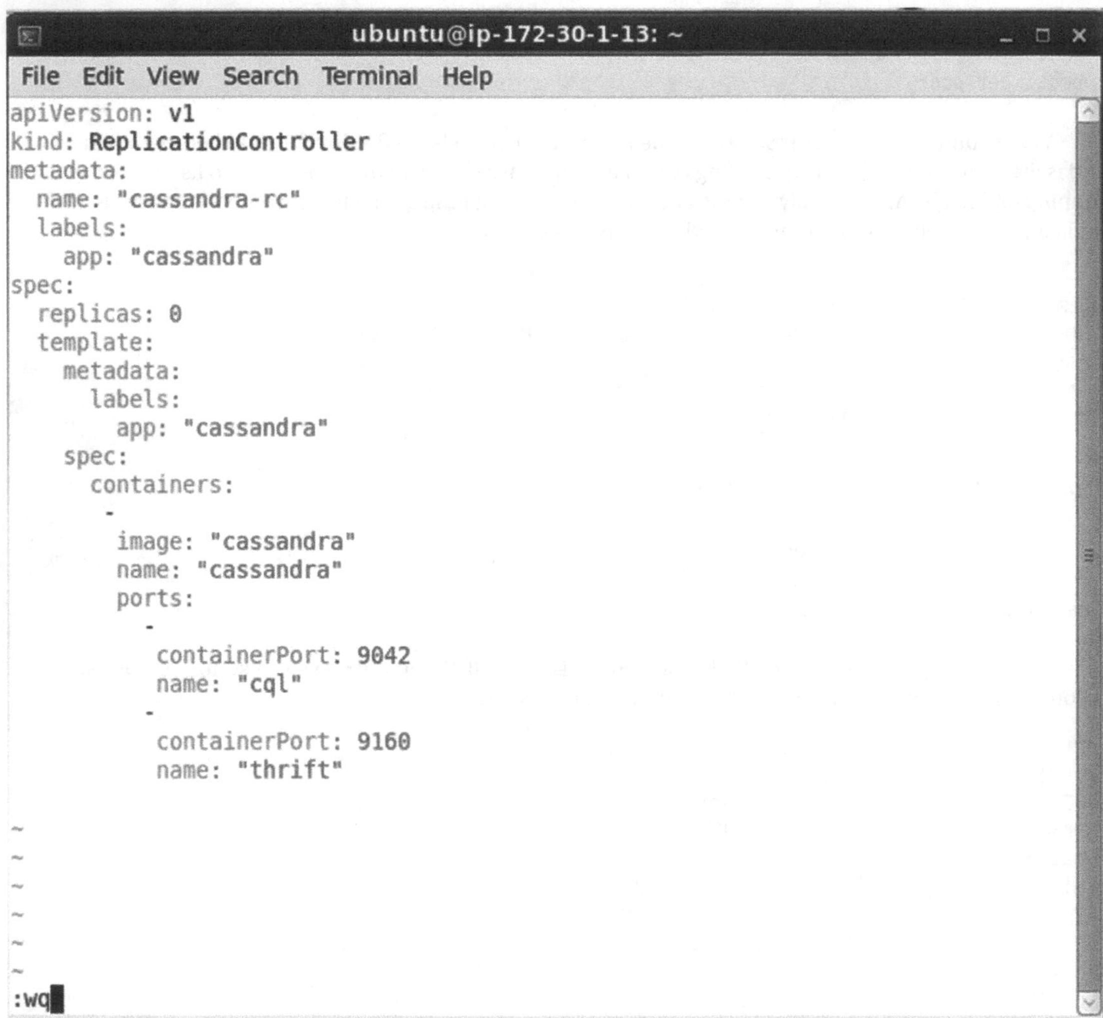

Figure 8-11. *Setting Replicas to 0*

Create the replication controller again with the modified definition file.

```
kubectl create -f cassandra-rc.yaml
```

Subsequently list the replicas.

```
kubectl get rc
```

The cassandra-rc replication controller gets created and gets listed as shown in Figure 8-12.

```
ubuntu@ip-172-30-1-13:~$ kubectl create -f  cassandra-rc.yaml
replicationcontrollers/cassandra-rc
ubuntu@ip-172-30-1-13:~$ kubectl get rc
CONTROLLER     CONTAINER(S)   IMAGE(S)    SELECTOR        REPLICAS
cassandra-rc   cassandra      cassandra   app=cassandra   0
ubuntu@ip-172-30-1-13:~$
```

Figure 8-12. *Creating the Replication Controller with Modified Definition File*

List the Pods.

```
kubectl get pods
```

Because the replicas field is set to 0 the REPLICAS get listed as 0 as shown in Figure 8-13.

```
ubuntu@ip-172-30-1-13:~$ kubectl create -f  cassandra-rc.yaml
replicationcontrollers/cassandra-rc
ubuntu@ip-172-30-1-13:~$ kubectl get rc
CONTROLLER     CONTAINER(S)   IMAGE(S)    SELECTOR        REPLICAS
cassandra-rc   cassandra      cassandra   app=cassandra   0
ubuntu@ip-172-30-1-13:~$ kubectl get pods
NAME                     READY     STATUS    RESTARTS   AGE
k8s-master-127.0.0.1     3/3       Running   3          1h
```

Figure 8-13. *With Replicas as 0 no Pod gets created*

Scaling the Database

Starting with the replication controller with 0 replicas created we shall scale up the cluster to a single replica. Run the following command to scale the Pod cluster to 1 replica.

```
kubectl scale rc cassandra-rc --replicas=1
```

Subsequently list the Pods.

```
kubectl get pods
```

The output from the preceding commands is shown in Figure 8-14. A "scaled" output indicates that the cluster has been scaled. The single Pod could take a while (a few seconds) to get started and become ready.

```
ubuntu@ip-172-30-1-13:~$ kubectl scale rc cassandra-rc --replicas=1
scaled
ubuntu@ip-172-30-1-13:~$ kubectl get pods
NAME                   READY     STATUS    RESTARTS   AGE
cassandra-rc-9p7gc     0/1       Running   0          11s
k8s-master-127.0.0.1   3/3       Running   3          1h
ubuntu@ip-172-30-1-13:~$ kubectl get pods
NAME                   READY     STATUS    RESTARTS   AGE
cassandra-rc-9p7gc     0/1       Running   0          15s
k8s-master-127.0.0.1   3/3       Running   3          1h
ubuntu@ip-172-30-1-13:~$ kubectl get pods
NAME                   READY     STATUS    RESTARTS   AGE
cassandra-rc-9p7gc     1/1       Running   0          29s
k8s-master-127.0.0.1   3/3       Running   3          1h
ubuntu@ip-172-30-1-13:~$
```

Figure 8-14. *Scaling the Replication Controller to 1 Pod*

Describe the cassandra service again.

```
kubectl describe svc cassandra
```

A single endpoint should get listed for the Pod added as shown in Figure 8-15.

```
ubuntu@ip-172-30-1-13:~$ kubectl describe svc cassandra
Name:                   cassandra
Namespace:              default
Labels:                 app=cassandra
Selector:               app=cassandra
Type:                   LoadBalancer
IP:                     10.0.0.245
Port:                   <unnamed>       9042/TCP
NodePort:               <unnamed>       32434/TCP
Endpoints:              172.17.0.2:9042
Session Affinity:       None
No events.

ubuntu@ip-172-30-1-13:~$
```

Figure 8-15. *Describing the Service after Scaling the Cluster*

Describing the Pod

To describe the Pod run the following command.

```
kubectl describe pod cassandra-rc-tou4u
```

Detailed information about the Pod such as name, namespace, image, node, labels, status, IP address, and events gets output as shown in Figure 8-16. The Pod label is app=cassandra as specified in the replication controller definition file.

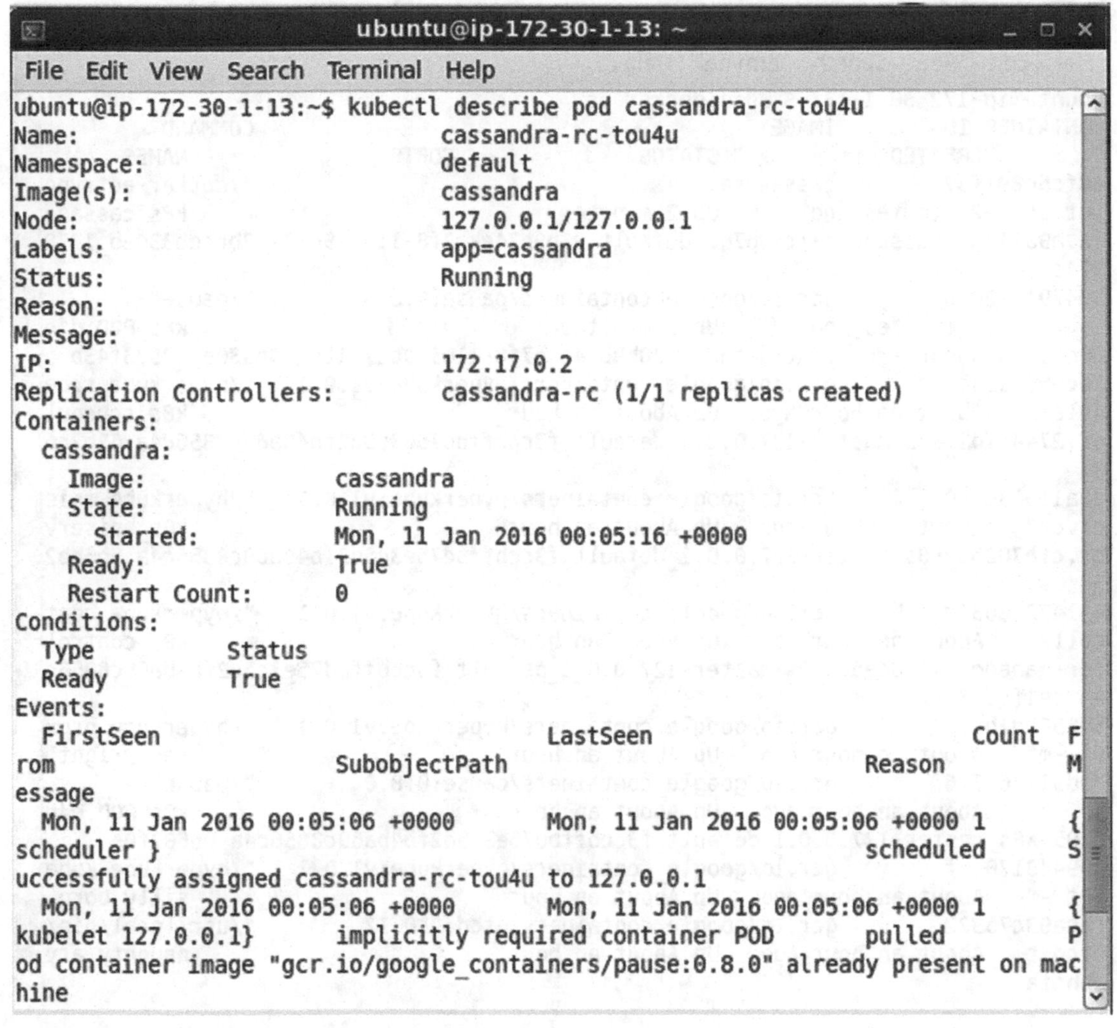

```
ubuntu@ip-172-30-1-13:~$ kubectl describe pod cassandra-rc-tou4u
Name:                           cassandra-rc-tou4u
Namespace:                      default
Image(s):                       cassandra
Node:                           127.0.0.1/127.0.0.1
Labels:                         app=cassandra
Status:                         Running
Reason:
Message:
IP:                             172.17.0.2
Replication Controllers:        cassandra-rc (1/1 replicas created)
Containers:
  cassandra:
    Image:              cassandra
    State:              Running
      Started:          Mon, 11 Jan 2016 00:05:16 +0000
    Ready:              True
    Restart Count:      0
Conditions:
  Type          Status
  Ready         True
Events:
  FirstSeen                             LastSeen                                Count   F
rom                             SubobjectPath                           Reason          M
essage
  Mon, 11 Jan 2016 00:05:06 +0000       Mon, 11 Jan 2016 00:05:06 +0000 1       {
scheduler }                                                             scheduled       S
uccessfully assigned cassandra-rc-tou4u to 127.0.0.1
  Mon, 11 Jan 2016 00:05:06 +0000       Mon, 11 Jan 2016 00:05:06 +0000 1       {
kubelet 127.0.0.1}              implicitly required container POD       pulled          P
od container image "gcr.io/google_containers/pause:0.8.0" already present on mac
hine
```

Figure 8-16. *Describing the single Pod*

Starting an Interactive Shell

As the "cassandra" Docker image inherits from the "debian" Docker image an interactive bash shell may be used to access a Docker container based on the cassandra image. To start an interactive bash shell to access the Cassandra server running in a Docker container, we need to obtain the container id. List the running containers.

```
sudo docker ps
```

All the running containers get listed as shown in Figure 8-17. Copy the container id for the container for the `cassandra` image.

```
ubuntu@ip-172-30-1-13: ~
File  Edit  View  Search  Terminal  Help
ubuntu@ip-172-30-1-13:~$ sudo docker ps
CONTAINER ID        IMAGE                                          COMMAND
          CREATED             STATUS                   PORTS               NAMES
e8fc5e8dff57        cassandra                                      "/docker-entrypo
int.s"   2 minutes ago       Up 2 minutes                                 k8s_cassand
ra.a9a314d7_cassandra-rc-9p7gc_default_28b9b74e-b7f8-11e5-9c17-12bccdb330eb_1778
374c
50479f2e20a6        gcr.io/google_containers/pause:0.8.0           "/pause"
          2 minutes ago       Up 2 minutes                                 k8s_POD.dfb
60ee1_cassandra-rc-9p7gc_default_28b9b74e-b7f8-11e5-9c17-12bccdb330eb_2573f43b
8ec906d124e2        gcr.io/google_containers/hyperkube:v1.0.1      "/hyperkube sche
duler"   About an hour ago   Up About an hour                             k8s_schedul
er.2744e742_k8s-master-127.0.0.1_default_f3ccbffbd75e3c5d2fb4ba69c8856c4a_62b2c6
87
dda11503ceb0        gcr.io/google_containers/hyperkube:v1.0.1      "/hyperkube apis
erver"   About an hour ago   Up About an hour                             k8s_apiserv
er.cfb70250_k8s-master-127.0.0.1_default_f3ccbffbd75e3c5d2fb4ba69c8856c4a_5b6bb2
54
441472c8631d        gcr.io/google_containers/hyperkube:v1.0.1      "/hyperkube cont
rolle"   About an hour ago   Up About an hour                             k8s_control
ler-manager.1598ee5c_k8s-master-127.0.0.1_default_f3ccbffbd75e3c5d2fb4ba69c8856c
4a_ce1fc688
3d858bd1b5ca        gcr.io/google_containers/hyperkube:v1.0.1      "/hyperkube prox
y --m"   About an hour ago   Up About an hour                             sad_wright
dad911766776        gcr.io/google_containers/pause:0.8.0           "/pause"
          About an hour ago   Up About an hour                             k8s_POD.e4c
c795_k8s-master-127.0.0.1_default_f3ccbffbd75e3c5d2fb4ba69c8856c4a_06602f0e
369443170caf        gcr.io/google_containers/hyperkube:v1.0.1      "/hyperkube kube
let -"   About an hour ago   Up About an hour                             silly_borg
fbca93c75322        gcr.io/google_containers/etcd:2.0.12           "/usr/local/bin/
etcd "   About an hour ago   Up About an hour                             naughty_ary
abhata
```

Figure 8-17. *Listing the Docker Containers*

Using the container id start an interactive bash shell.

```
sudo docker exec -it e8fc5e8ddff57 bash
```

An interactive shell gets started as shown in Figure 8-18.

```
ubuntu@ip-172-30-1-13:~$ sudo docker exec -it e8fc5e8dff57 bash
root@cassandra-rc-9p7gc:/#
```

Figure 8-18. *Starting the Interactive Shell*

Starting the CQL Shell

Cassandra Query Language (CQL) is the query language for Apache Cassandra. In the following sections we shall run CQL commands to create a keyspace and a table. Start the CQL Shell with the following command.

```
cqlsh
```

CQL Shell 5.0.1 gets started as shown in Figure 8-19.

```
root@cassandra-rc-9p7gc:/# cqlsh
Connected to Test Cluster at 127.0.0.1:9042.
[cqlsh 5.0.1 | Cassandra 3.1.1 | CQL spec 3.3.1 | Native protocol v4]
Use HELP for help.
cqlsh>
```

Figure 8-19. Starting the cqlsh Shell

Creating a Keyspace

Next, create a keyspace called CatalogKeyspace using the replication class as SimpleStrategy and replication factor as 3.

```
CREATE KEYSPACE CatalogKeyspace
            WITH replication = {'class': 'SimpleStrategy', 'replication_factor' : 3};
```

A keyspace gets created as shown in Figure 8-20.

```
cqlsh> CREATE KEYSPACE CatalogKeyspace
<ication = {'class': 'SimpleStrategy', 'replication_factor' : 3};
cqlsh>
```

Figure 8-20. Creating a Keyspace

Altering a Keyspace

A keyspace may be altered with the ALTER KEYSPACE command. Run the following command to alter the keyspace setting replication factor to 1.

```
ALTER KEYSPACE CatalogKeyspace
          WITH replication = {'class': 'SimpleStrategy', 'replication_factor' : 1};
```

Keyspace gets altered as shown in Figure 8-21.

```
cqlsh> ALTER KEYSPACE CatalogKeyspace
<cation = {'class': 'SimpleStrategy', 'replication_factor' : 1};
cqlsh>
```

Figure 8-21. Altering a Keyspace

Using a Keyspace

To use the CatalogKeyspace keyspace run the following command.

```
use CatalogKeyspace;
```

Keyspace CatalogKeyspace gets set as shown in Figure 8-22.

```
cqlsh> use CatalogKeyspace;
cqlsh:catalogkeyspace>
```

Figure 8-22. *Setting a Keyspace to be used*

Creating a Table

A table is also called a column family. Both CREATE TABLE and CREATE COLUMN FAMILY clauses may be used to create a table (column family). Create a table called catalog using the following CQL statement.

```
CREATE TABLE catalog(catalog_id text,journal text,publisher text,edition text,title
text,author text,PRIMARY KEY (catalog_id)) WITH compaction = { 'class' :
'LeveledCompactionStrategy' };
```

Add two rows of data to the table using the following CQL statements.

```
INSERT INTO catalog (catalog_id, journal, publisher, edition,title,author) VALUES
('catalog1','Oracle Magazine', 'Oracle Publishing', 'November-December 2013', 'Engineering
as a Service','David A. Kelly') IF NOT EXISTS;
INSERT INTO catalog (catalog_id, journal, publisher, edition,title,author) VALUES
('catalog2','Oracle Magazine', 'Oracle Publishing', 'November-December 2013',
'Quintessential and Collaborative','Tom Haunert') IF NOT EXISTS;
```

Output from the preceding commands is shown in Figure 8-23. A Cassandra table gets created and two rows of data get added.

```
<ompaction = { 'class' : 'LeveledCompactionStrategy' };
<'Engineering as a Service','David A.  Kelly') IF NOT EXISTS;

 [applied]
-----------
      True

cqlsh:catalogkeyspace>
<'Quintessential and Collaborative','Tom Haunert') IF NOT EXISTS;

 [applied]
-----------
      True

cqlsh:catalogkeyspace>
```

Figure 8-23. *Creating an Apache Cassandra Table*

Run the following CQL query statement to select data from the catalog table.

```
SELECT * FROM catalog;
```

The two rows of data added gets listed as shown in Figure 8-24.

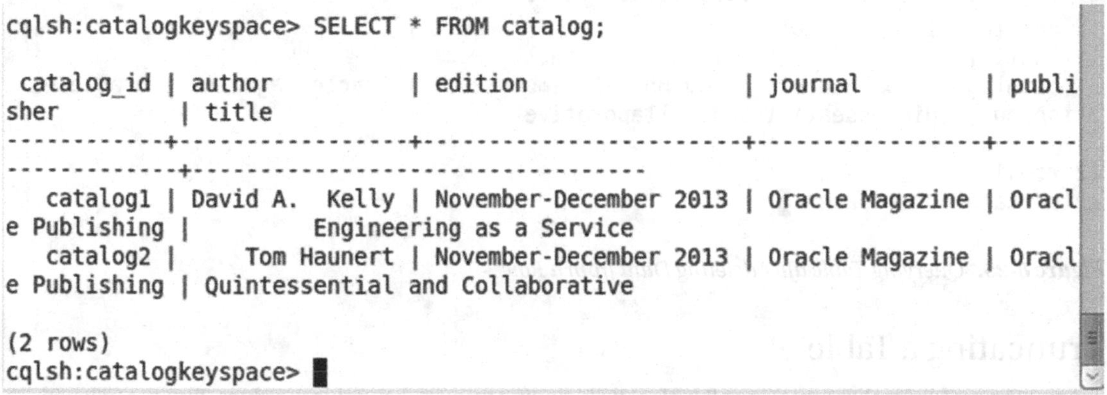

```
cqlsh:catalogkeyspace> SELECT * FROM catalog;

 catalog_id | author          | edition                  | journal          | publi
sher             | title
------------+-----------------+--------------------------+------------------+------
-------------+-------------------------------------
   catalog1 | David A.  Kelly | November-December 2013 | Oracle Magazine | Oracl
e Publishing |         Engineering as a Service
   catalog2 |      Tom Haunert | November-December 2013 | Oracle Magazine | Oracl
e Publishing | Quintessential and Collaborative

(2 rows)
cqlsh:catalogkeyspace>
```

Figure 8-24. *Querying an Apache Cassandra Table*

Deleting from a Table

To delete row/s of data run a DELETE CQL statement. The primary key column value cannot be deleted with DELETE. Delete the other column values for the row with catalog_id as 'catalog' with the following CQL statement.

```
DELETE journal, publisher, edition, title, author from catalog WHERE catalog_id='catalog1';
```

Subsequently run the following CQL query to select data from the catalog table.

```
SELECT * FROM catalog;
```

As shown in Figure 8-25 only one complete row of data gets output. The other row lists only the catalog_id column value, and all the other column values are null.

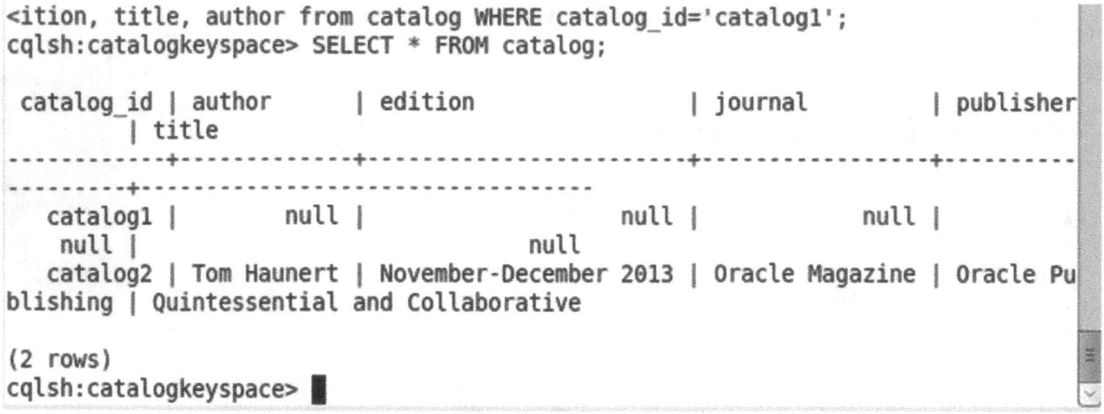

```
<ition, title, author from catalog WHERE catalog_id='catalog1';
cqlsh:catalogkeyspace> SELECT * FROM catalog;

 catalog_id | author      | edition                 | journal          | publisher
         | title
------------+-------------+-------------------------+------------------+----------
---------+----------------------------------
   catalog1 |        null |                    null |             null |
    null |                         null
   catalog2 | Tom Haunert | November-December 2013 | Oracle Magazine | Oracle Pu
blishing | Quintessential and Collaborative

(2 rows)
cqlsh:catalogkeyspace>
```

Figure 8-25. Querying Table after deleting Data from a Row

Truncating a Table

Truncating a table implies removing all table data including primary key column values. Run the following TRUNCATE CQL statement to remove all rows.

```
TRUNCATE catalog;
```

Subsequently run the CQL query statement again.

```
SELECT * from catalog;
```

No rows get listed as shown in Figure 8-26; not even null values are listed after running a TRUNCATE statement.

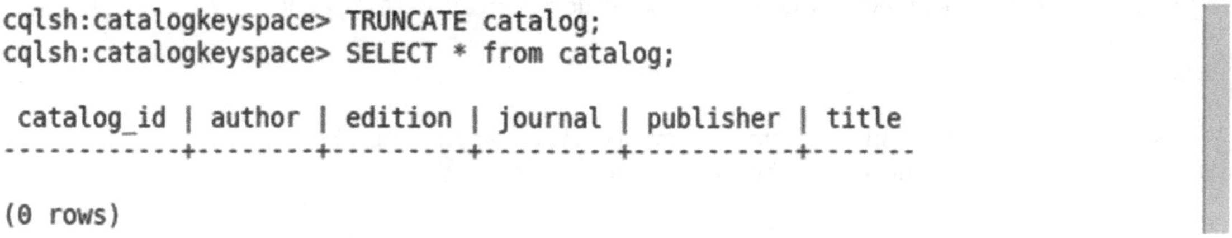

```
cqlsh:catalogkeyspace> TRUNCATE catalog;
cqlsh:catalogkeyspace> SELECT * from catalog;

 catalog_id | author | edition | journal | publisher | title
------------+--------+---------+---------+-----------+-------

(0 rows)
```

Figure 8-26. Querying a Table after Truncating a Table

Dropping a Table and Keyspace

To drop a table run the CQL statement with the DROP TABLE clause. The IF EXISTS clause drops the table if it exists but does not return an error if the table does not exist.

```
DROP TABLE IF EXISTS catalog;
```

Drop the CatalogKeyspace keyspace using the DROP KEYSPACE clause statement. The IF EXISTS clause drops the keyspace if it exists but does not return an error if the keyspace does not exist.

```
DROP KEYSPACE IF EXISTS CatalogKeyspace;
```

To verify that the keyspace CatalogKeyspace has been removed, run the following statement.

```
use CatalogKeyspace;
```

As the CatalogKeyspace keyspace does not exist an error gets generated as shown in Figure 8-27.

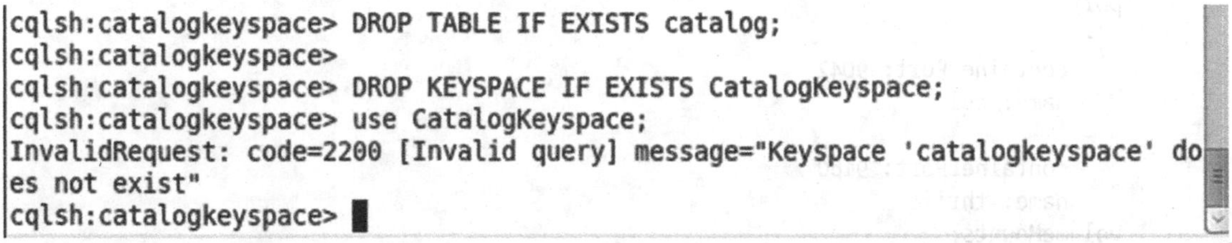

```
cqlsh:catalogkeyspace> DROP TABLE IF EXISTS catalog;
cqlsh:catalogkeyspace>
cqlsh:catalogkeyspace> DROP KEYSPACE IF EXISTS CatalogKeyspace;
cqlsh:catalogkeyspace> use CatalogKeyspace;
InvalidRequest: code=2200 [Invalid query] message="Keyspace 'catalogkeyspace' do
es not exist"
cqlsh:catalogkeyspace>
```

Figure 8-27. *Dropping a Table*

Creating a Volume

In chapter 7 we introduced volumes, how they are mounted into a Pod using volume mounts, and how they are accessed within a container. We introduced various types of volumes and demonstrated the emptyDir type of volume. In this section we shall use another type of volume, the hostPath volume. The hostPath volume mounts a directory from the host into the Pod. All containers in the Pod and all Pods based on a Pod template using a hostPath type of volume may access the directory on the host. As a modification of the replication controller used earlier, we shall add a volume of type hostPath to the cassandra-rc.yaml file. For example, if the host directory /cassandra/data is to be mounted in a Pod add the following volume in the spec->template field.

```
volumes:
  -
    hostPath:
      path: /cassandra/data
    name: cassandra-storage
```

The volume is mounted in the Pod using the same fields as a emptyDir volume. The modified cassandra-rc.yaml is listed.

```
apiVersion: v1
kind: ReplicationController
metadata:
  name: cassandra-rc
  labels:
    app: cassandra
```

```
spec:
  replicas: 1
  template:
    metadata:
      labels:
        app: cassandra
    spec:
      containers:
        -
        image: cassandra
        name: cassandra
        ports:
          -
            containerPort: 9042
            name: cql
          -
            containerPort: 9160
            name: thrift
        volumeMounts:
          -
            mountPath: /cassandra/data
            name: cassandra-storage
      volumes:
        -
          hostPath:
            path: /cassandra/data
          name: cassandra-storage
```

The `cassandra-rc.yaml` definition file may be edited in vi editor and saved with the :wq command as shown in Figure 8-28. It is recommended to add quotes in field values.

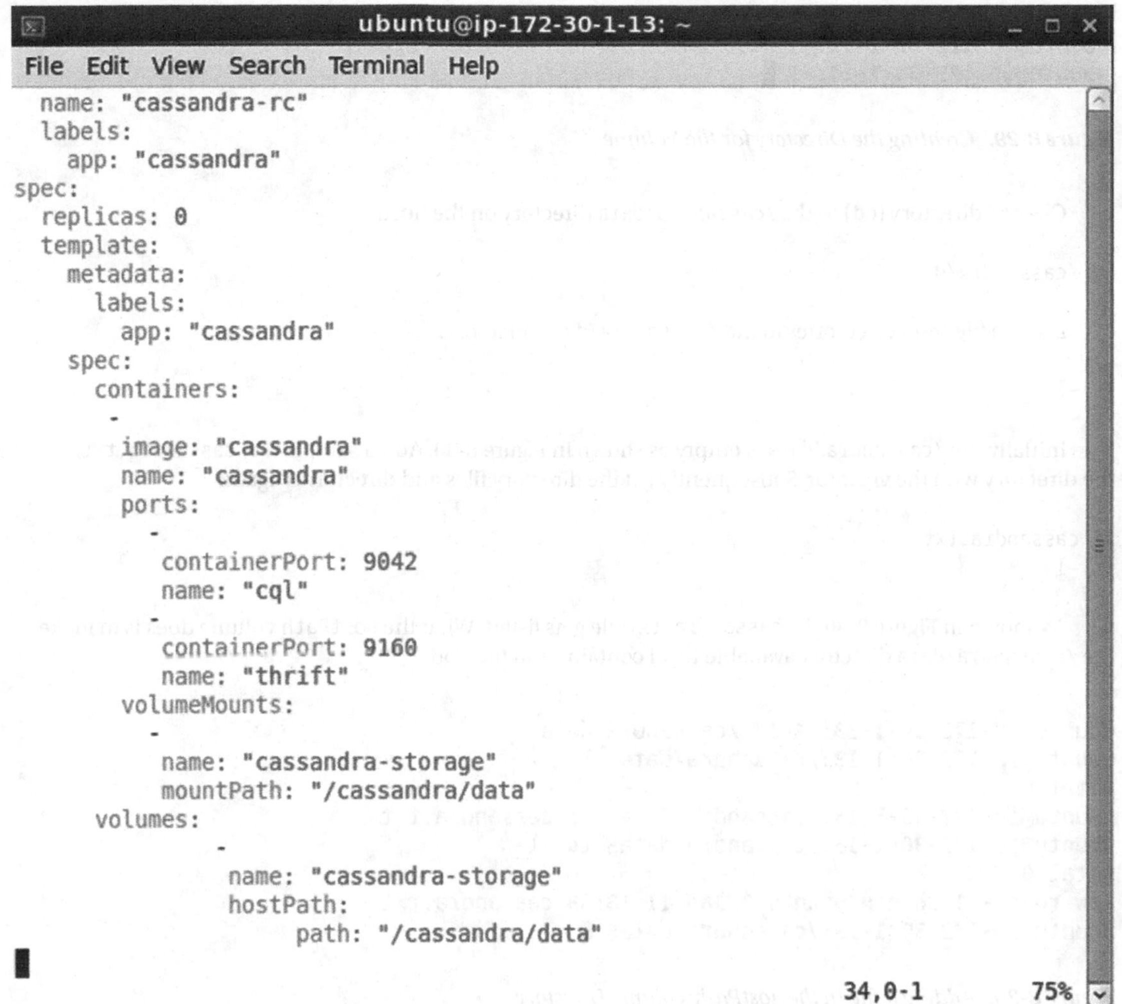
ubuntu@ip-172-30-1-13: ~
File Edit View Search Terminal Help
name: "cassandra-rc"
labels:
app: "cassandra"
spec:
replicas: 0
template:
metadata:
labels:
app: "cassandra"
spec:
containers:
-
image: "cassandra"
name: "cassandra"
ports:
-
containerPort: 9042
name: "cql"
-
containerPort: 9160
name: "thrift"
volumeMounts:
-
name: "cassandra-storage"
mountPath: "/cassandra/data"
volumes:
-
name: "cassandra-storage"
hostPath:
path: "/cassandra/data"
34,0-1 75%

Figure 8-28. *Replication Controller Definition File with a Volume of type hostPath*

The host directory that is mounted into a Pod has to pre-exist. Create the /cassandra/data directory and set its permissions to global (777).

```
sudo mkdir -p /cassandra/data
sudo chmod -R 777 /cassandra/data
```

The output from the preceding commands is shown in Figure 8-29. The /cassandra/data directory gets created.

```
ubuntu@ip-172-30-1-13:~$ sudo mkdir -p /cassandra/data
ubuntu@ip-172-30-1-13:~$ sudo chmod -R 777 /cassandra/data
ubuntu@ip-172-30-1-13:~$ ▌
```

***Figure 8-29.** Creating the Directory for the Volume*

Change directory (cd) to the /cassandra/data directory on the host.

```
cd /cassandra/data
```

List the files and directories in the /cassandra/data directory.

```
ls -l
```

Initially the /cassandra/data is empty as shown in Figure 8-30. Add a sample file, cassandra.txt, to the directory with the vi editor. Subsequently list the directory files and directories again.

```
vi cassandra.txt
ls -l
```

As shown in Figure 8-30 the cassandra.txt file gets listed. What the hostPath volume does is to make the /cassandra/data directory available to all containers in the Pod.

```
ubuntu@ip-172-30-1-13:~$ cd /cassandra/data
ubuntu@ip-172-30-1-13:/cassandra/data$ ls -l
total 0
ubuntu@ip-172-30-1-13:/cassandra/data$ vi cassandra.txt
ubuntu@ip-172-30-1-13:/cassandra/data$ ls -l
total 0
-rw-rw-r-- 1 ubuntu ubuntu 0 Jan 11 18:39 cassandra.txt
ubuntu@ip-172-30-1-13:/cassandra/data$ ▌
```

***Figure 8-30.** Adding a file in the hostPath Volume Directory*

Create a replication controller as discussed for the definition file used previously. One Pod should get created. List the Docker containers.

```
sudo docker ps
```

Copy the container id for the Docker container for image "cassandra" as shown in Figure 8-31.

```
ubuntu@ip-172-30-1-13: ~
File Edit View Search Terminal Help
ubuntu@ip-172-30-1-13:~$ sudo docker ps
CONTAINER ID        IMAGE                                           COMMAND
      CREATED             STATUS              PORTS               NAMES
11a4b26d9a09        cassandra                                       "/docker-entrypo
int.s"   2 minutes ago       Up 2 minutes                            k8s_cassand
ra.69193449_cassandra-rc-tounc_default_f810d16d-b892-11e5-a7b1-12bccdb330eb_bf52
fe8c
1ac2b8fef2ca        gcr.io/google_containers/pause:0.8.0            "/pause"
      2 minutes ago       Up 2 minutes                            k8s_POD.dfb
60ee1_cassandra-rc-tounc_default_f810d16d-b892-11e5-a7b1-12bccdb330eb_887bfd97
849f86603d91        gcr.io/google_containers/hyperkube:v1.0.1       "/hyperkube prox
y --m"   7 minutes ago       Up 7 minutes                            hopeful_sah
a
aaec2d3d6ff6        gcr.io/google_containers/hyperkube:v1.0.1       "/hyperkube sche
duler"   7 minutes ago       Up 7 minutes                            k8s_schedul
er.2744e742_k8s-master-127.0.0.1_default_f3ccbffbd75e3c5d2fb4ba69c8856c4a_5ae720
1c
246eda75a335        gcr.io/google_containers/hyperkube:v1.0.1       "/hyperkube apis
erver"   7 minutes ago       Up 7 minutes                            k8s_apiserv
er.cfb70250_k8s-master-127.0.0.1_default_f3ccbffbd75e3c5d2fb4ba69c8856c4a_f937d0
22
76bffee1493b        gcr.io/google_containers/hyperkube:v1.0.1       "/hyperkube cont
rolle"   7 minutes ago       Up 7 minutes                            k8s_control
ler-manager.1598ee5c_k8s-master-127.0.0.1_default_f3ccbffbd75e3c5d2fb4ba69c8856c
4a_2184a674
bdae0b9de6de        gcr.io/google_containers/pause:0.8.0            "/pause"
      7 minutes ago       Up 7 minutes                            k8s_POD.e4c
c795_k8s-master-127.0.0.1_default_f3ccbffbd75e3c5d2fb4ba69c8856c4a_956c4456
8295574a1ceb        gcr.io/google_containers/hyperkube:v1.0.1       "/hyperkube kube
let -"   7 minutes ago       Up 7 minutes                            compassiona
te_khorana
ea8d9ec5177f        gcr.io/google_containers/etcd:2.0.12            "/usr/local/bin/
```

Figure 8-31. *Listing the Docker Containers*

Using the container id start an interactive shell.

```
sudo docker exec -it 11a4b26d9a09 bash
```

The interactive shell gets started as shown in Figure 8-32.

```
ubuntu@ip-172-30-1-13:~$ sudo docker exec -it 11a4b26d9a09  bash
root@cassandra-rc-tounc:/#
```

Figure 8-32. *Starting an Interactive Shell*

Change directory (cd) to the /cassandra/data directory and list the files in the directory.

```
cd /cassandra/data
ls -l
```

As shown in Figure 8-33 the cassandra.txt file gets listed. The /cassandra/data directory exists on the host but is accessible from a container.

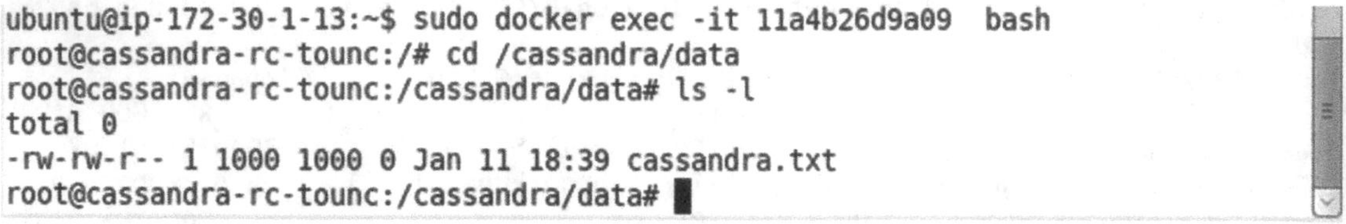

```
ubuntu@ip-172-30-1-13:~$ sudo docker exec -it 11a4b26d9a09  bash
root@cassandra-rc-tounc:/# cd /cassandra/data
root@cassandra-rc-tounc:/cassandra/data# ls -l
total 0
-rw-rw-r-- 1 1000 1000 0 Jan 11 18:39 cassandra.txt
root@cassandra-rc-tounc:/cassandra/data# 
```

Figure 8-33. *Accessing the Volume in a Docker Container*

Similarly volumes of other types could be created. Following is the volumeMounts and volumes fields settings for a AWS Volume. The volumeID field has the format aws://zone/volume id.

```
    volumeMounts:
      -
        mountPath: /aws-ebs
        name: aws-volume
  volumes:
    -
      name: aws-volume
      awsElasticBlockStore:
          volumeID: aws://us-east-ib/vol-428ba3ae
          fsType: ext4
```

A more complete cassandra-rc.yaml file is shown in Figure 8-34.

```
ubuntu@ip-172-30-1-13: ~
File Edit View Search Terminal Help
  labels:
    app: "cassandra"
spec:
  replicas: 2
  template:
    metadata:
      labels:
        app: "cassandra"
    spec:
      containers:
        -
          image: "cassandra"
          name: "cassandra"
          ports:
            -
              containerPort: 9042
              name: "cql"
            -
              containerPort: 9160
              name: "thrift"
          volumeMounts:
                        -
                          mountPath: "/aws-ebs"
                          name: "aws-volume"
      volumes:
              -
                name: "aws-volume"
                awsElasticBlockStore:
                     volumeID: "aws://us-east-ib/vol-428ba3ae"
                     fsType: "ext4"

:wq
```

Figure 8-34. *Volume of type awsElasticBlockStore in a Replication Controller Definition File*

Creating a Cassandra Cluster Imperatively

If the default settings for most of the fields are to be used, creating a replication controller imperatively is the better option.

Creating a Replication Controller

To create a replication controller on the command line use the `kubectl run` command. For a replication controller based on the Docker image "cassandra" run the following command in which replication controller name is "cassandra" and port is 9042. The replicas is set to 1, also the default value.

```
kubectl run cassandra --image=cassandra --replicas=1 --port=9042
```

Subsequently list the replication controllers.

```
kubectl get rc
```

The "cassandra" replication controller gets created and get listed as shown in Figure 8-35.

```
ubuntu@ip-172-30-1-13:~$ kubectl  run cassandra --image=cassandra --replicas=1 -
-port=9042
CONTROLLER   CONTAINER(S)   IMAGE(S)    SELECTOR        REPLICAS
cassandra    cassandra      cassandra   run=cassandra   1
ubuntu@ip-172-30-1-13:~$ kubectl get rc
CONTROLLER   CONTAINER(S)   IMAGE(S)    SELECTOR        REPLICAS
cassandra    cassandra      cassandra   run=cassandra   1
```

Figure 8-35. *Creating a Replication Controller Imperatively*

To list the Pods run the following command.

```
kubectl get pods
```

The single Pod created gets listed as shown in Figure 8-36.

```
ubuntu@ip-172-30-1-13:~$ kubectl get pods
NAME                   READY     STATUS    RESTARTS   AGE
cassandra-zv7ei        1/1       Running   0          7m
k8s-master-127.0.0.1   3/3       Running   3          1h
ubuntu@ip-172-30-1-13:~$ █
```

Figure 8-36. *Listing the single Pod*

To describe the replication controller run the following command.

```
kubectl describe rc cassandra
```

The replication controller's name, namespace, image, selector, labels, replicas, pod status, and events get listed as shown in Figure 8-37. The selector defaults to "run=cassandra" for the `cassandra` replication controller.

```
ubuntu@ip-172-30-1-13:~$ kubectl describe rc cassandra
Name:           cassandra
Namespace:      default
Image(s):       cassandra
Selector:       run=cassandra
Labels:         run=cassandra
Replicas:       1 current / 1 desired
Pods Status:    1 Running / 0 Waiting / 0 Succeeded / 0 Failed
Events:
  FirstSeen                             LastSeen                        Count F
rom                             SubobjectPath   Reason                  Message
  Mon, 11 Jan 2016 00:28:27 +0000       Mon, 11 Jan 2016 00:28:27 +0000 1       {
replication-controller }                        successfulCreate        Created
pod: cassandra-zv7ei
```

Figure 8-37. *Describing the Replication Controller*

Creating a Service

To expose the replication controller cassandra as a service, run the kubectl expose command. The port is required to be specified and is set to 9042 for the service.

```
kubectl expose rc cassandra --port=9042 --type=LoadBalancer
```

The cassandra service gets created as shown in Figure 8-38.

```
ubuntu@ip-172-30-1-13:~$ kubectl expose rc cassandra --port=9042 --type=LoadBala
ncer
NAME        LABELS          SELECTOR        IP(S)     PORT(S)
cassandra   run=cassandra   run=cassandra             9042/TCP
ubuntu@ip-172-30-1-13:~$ kubectl get services
NAME         LABELS                                      SELECTOR        IP(S)
    PORT(S)
cassandra    run=cassandra                               run=cassandra   10.0.0.21
0   9042/TCP
kubernetes   component=apiserver,provider=kubernetes     <none>          10.0.0.1
    443/TCP
ubuntu@ip-172-30-1-13:~$
```

Figure 8-38. *Creating a Service for Apache Cassandra Imperatively*

Describe the service with the following command.

```
kubectl describe service cassandra
```

As shown in Figure 8-39 the service name, namespace, labels, selector, type, IP, Port, NodePort, and Endpoint get listed. The service selector run=cassandra must be the same as the label on the Pod to manage.

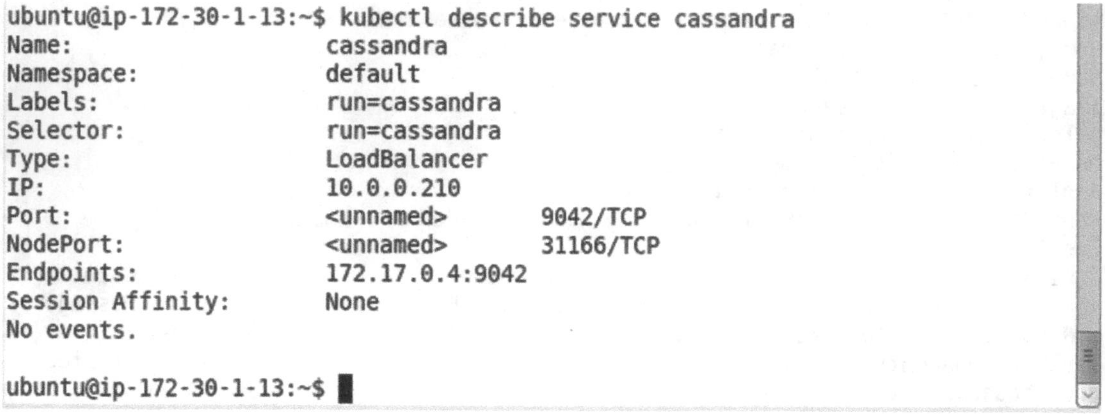

```
ubuntu@ip-172-30-1-13:~$ kubectl describe service cassandra
Name:                   cassandra
Namespace:              default
Labels:                 run=cassandra
Selector:               run=cassandra
Type:                   LoadBalancer
IP:                     10.0.0.210
Port:                   <unnamed>       9042/TCP
NodePort:               <unnamed>       31166/TCP
Endpoints:              172.17.0.4:9042
Session Affinity:       None
No events.

ubuntu@ip-172-30-1-13:~$ █
```

Figure 8-39. *Describing the Service*

Scaling the Database

To scale the cluster, run the `kubectl scale` command. An important reason, to scale the Cassandra replication controller is to run more Cassandra nodes and have them join the cluster, and we demonstrated scaling up a cluster. But it is not always necessary to scale up a cluster. A cluster may also be scaled down. To scale down the cluster to 0 replicas run the following command.

```
kubectl scale rc cassandra --replicas=0
```

A output of "scaled" in Figure 8-40 indicates that the cluster has been scaled down.

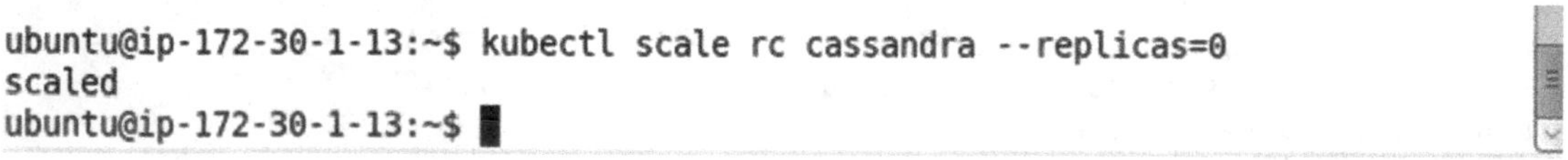

```
ubuntu@ip-172-30-1-13:~$ kubectl scale rc cassandra --replicas=0
scaled
ubuntu@ip-172-30-1-13:~$ █
```

Figure 8-40. *Scaling Down the Database Cluster to 0 Replicas*

List the Pods.

```
kubectl get pods
```

No pod gets listed as shown in Figure 8-41.

```
ubuntu@ip-172-30-1-13:~$ kubectl get pods
NAME                   READY     STATUS    RESTARTS   AGE
k8s-master-127.0.0.1   3/3       Running   3          1h
ubuntu@ip-172-30-1-13:~$ █
```

Figure 8-41. *Listing the Pods after Scaling Down*

List the services with the following command.

```
kubectl get services
```

Scaling the cluster to 0 replicas would leave no Pod for the service to manage but the service is still running as shown in Figure 8-42.

```
ubuntu@ip-172-30-1-13:~$ kubectl scale rc cassandra --replicas=0
scaled
ubuntu@ip-172-30-1-13:~$ kubectl get services
NAME         LABELS                                     SELECTOR        IP(S)
    PORT(S)
cassandra    run=cassandra                              run=cassandra   10.0.0.21
0   9042/TCP
kubernetes   component=apiserver,provider=kubernetes    <none>          10.0.0.1
    443/TCP
ubuntu@ip-172-30-1-13:~$
```

Figure 8-42. *Listing the Services after Scaling Down*

But the service does not have any endpoint associated with it as shown with the `kubectl describe` command in Figure 8-43.

```
ubuntu@ip-172-30-1-13:~$ kubectl describe service cassandra
Name:                   cassandra
Namespace:              default
Labels:                 run=cassandra
Selector:               run=cassandra
Type:                   LoadBalancer
IP:                     10.0.0.210
Port:                   <unnamed>       9042/TCP
NodePort:               <unnamed>       31166/TCP
Endpoints:              <none>
Session Affinity:       None
No events.

ubuntu@ip-172-30-1-13:~$
```

Figure 8-43. *Describing the Service after Scaling Down*

Deleting the Replication Controller and Service

To delete the replication controller "cassandra" run the following command.

```
kubectl delete rc cassandra
```

Subsequently list the replication controllers.

```
kubectl get rc
```

To delete the service "cassandra" run the following command.

```
kubectl delete service cassandra
```

Subsequently list the services.

```
kubectl get services
```

The output from the preceding commands is shown in Figure 8-44. The replication controller and service get deleted and do not get listed.

```
ubuntu@ip-172-30-1-13:~$ kubectl delete rc cassandra
replicationcontrollers/cassandra
ubuntu@ip-172-30-1-13:~$ kubectl delete service cassandra
services/cassandra
ubuntu@ip-172-30-1-13:~$ kubectl get rc
CONTROLLER   CONTAINER(S)   IMAGE(S)   SELECTOR   REPLICAS
ubuntu@ip-172-30-1-13:~$ kubectl get services
NAME         LABELS                                    SELECTOR   IP(S)      POR
T(S)
kubernetes   component=apiserver,provider=kubernetes   <none>     10.0.0.1   443
/TCP
ubuntu@ip-172-30-1-13:~$
```

Figure 8-44. *Deleting the Replication Controller and the Service*

Summary

In this chapter we used Kubernetes to create an Apache Cassandra cluster. We used both the declarative and imperative approaches. We introduced the volumes in the previous chapter and in this chapter we discussed using two other types of volumes: hostPath and AWS Volume. We scaled the cluster not only up but also down. We demonstrated that a replication controller does not require a Pod to be running and could specify 0 replicas. In the next chapter we shall discuss using Kubernetes cluster manager with another NoSQL database, Couchbase.

CHAPTER 9

Using Couchbase

Couchbase is a distributed NoSQL database based on the JSON data model. Couchbase is faster than MongoDB and Apache Cassandra. Couchbase offers some features not available in MongoDB and Cassandra such as a Graphical User Interface (GUI), the Couchbase Web Console. Couchbase also provides command-line tools such as `couchbase-cli`, `cbbackup`, `cbrestore`, and `cbtransfer`. Couchbase, being a distributed database, could benefit from the cluster management provided by Kubernetes cluster manager, which is what we shall discuss in this chapter. This chapter has the following sections.

Setting the Environment

Creating a Couchbase Cluster Declaratively

Creating a Couchbase Cluster Imperatively

Setting the Environment

We have used an Ubuntu instance on Amazon EC2 created using the same AMI as used in the other chapters, the Ubuntu Server 14.04 LTS (HVM), SSD Volume Type - ami-d05e75b8. If an instance created from the AMI already exists the same may be used. The following software is required for this chapter.

-Docker Engine (latest version)

-Kubernetes (version 1.01)

-Kubectl (version 1.01)

-Docker image for Couchbase (latest version)

First, we need to log in to the Ubuntu instance. Obtain the Public IP Address of the Ubuntu instance from the Amazon EC2 instance console as shown in Figure 9-1.

D. Vohra, *Kubernetes Microservices with Docker*, DOI 10.1007/978-1-4842-1907-2_9

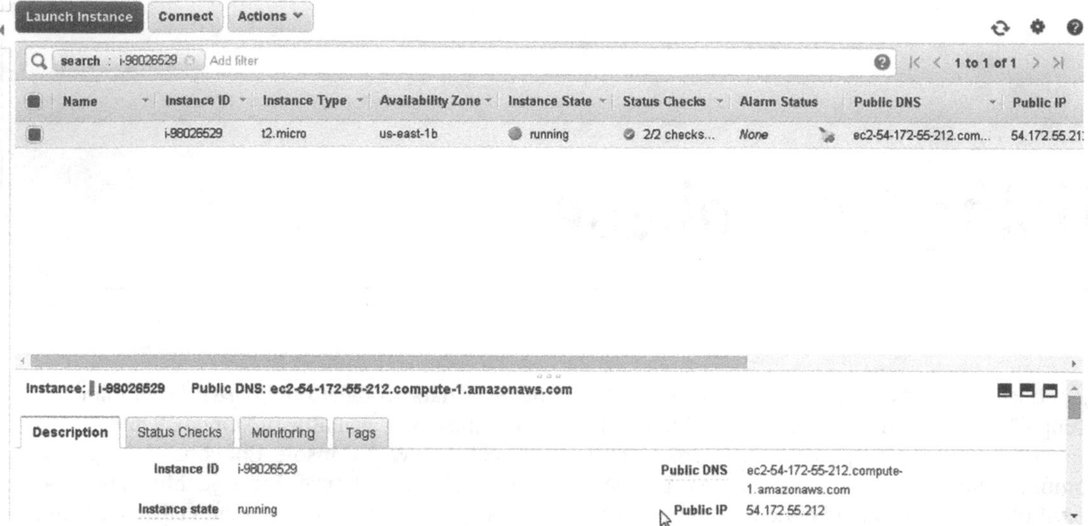

***Figure 9-1.** Getting Public IP Address*

Use the Public IP Address log in to the Ubuntu instance.

```
ssh -i "docker.pem" ubuntu@54.172.55.212
```

The Ubuntu instance gets logged into as shown in Figure 9-2.

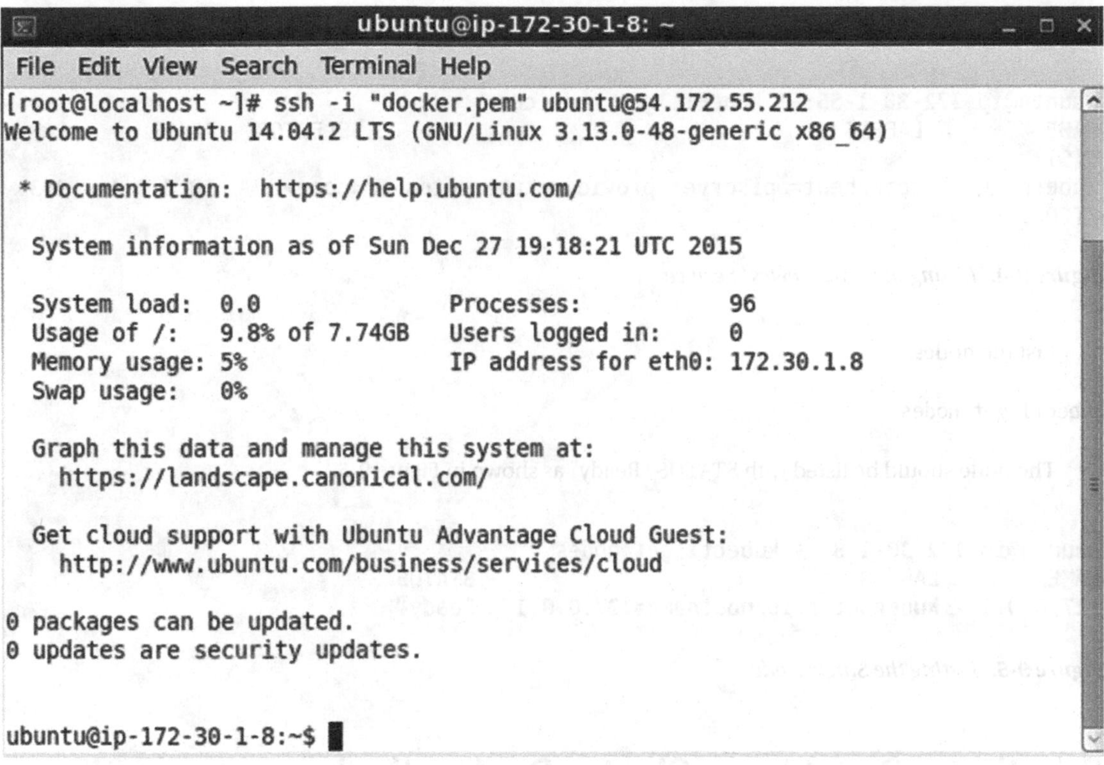
ubuntu@ip-172-30-1-8: ~
File Edit View Search Terminal Help
[root@localhost ~]# ssh -i "docker.pem" ubuntu@54.172.55.212
Welcome to Ubuntu 14.04.2 LTS (GNU/Linux 3.13.0-48-generic x86_64)
* Documentation: https://help.ubuntu.com/
System information as of Sun Dec 27 19:18:21 UTC 2015
System load: 0.0 Processes: 96
Usage of /: 9.8% of 7.74GB Users logged in: 0
Memory usage: 5% IP address for eth0: 172.30.1.8
Swap usage: 0%
Graph this data and manage this system at:
https://landscape.canonical.com/
Get cloud support with Ubuntu Advantage Cloud Guest:
http://www.ubuntu.com/business/services/cloud
0 packages can be updated.
0 updates are security updates.
ubuntu@ip-172-30-1-8:~$

Figure 9-2. *Logging into Ubuntu Instance on Amazon EC2*

Start the Docker Engine and verify its status.

```
sudo service docker start
sudo service docker status
```

Docker engine should be listed as running as shown in Figure 9-3.

```
ubuntu@ip-172-30-1-8:~$ sudo service docker start
start: Job is already running: docker
ubuntu@ip-172-30-1-8:~$ sudo service docker status
docker start/running, process 2697
ubuntu@ip-172-30-1-8:~$
```

Figure 9-3. *Starting Docker Engine*

List the running services.

```
kubectl get services
```

The kubernetes service should be listed as running as shown in Figure 9-4.

```
ubuntu@ip-172-30-1-55:~$ kubectl get services
NAME         LABELS                                    SELECTOR    IP(S)       POR
T(S)
kubernetes   component=apiserver,provider=kubernetes   <none>      10.0.0.1    443
/TCP
```

Figure 9-4. *Listing the "kubernetes" Service*

List the nodes.

```
kubectl get nodes
```

The node should be listed with STATUS "Ready" as shown in Figure 9-5.

```
ubuntu@ip-172-30-1-8:~$ kubectl get nodes
NAME        LABELS                               STATUS
127.0.0.1   kubernetes.io/hostname=127.0.0.1    Ready
```

Figure 9-5. *Listing the Single Node*

Creating a Couchbase Cluster Declaratively

In the following subsections we shall create a Couchbase Pod, a replication controller, and a service all using definition files.

Creating a Pod

A Pod definition file is used to create a single Pod. A Pod could have 0 or more container configurations. Create a definition file `couchbase.yaml`. Add the following (Table 9-1) fields to the definition file.

Table 9-1. Pod Definition File Fields

Field	Description	Value
apiVersion		v1
kind	The kind of definition file.	Pod
metadata	The Pod metadata.	
metadata ->labels	The Pod labels. A service selector makes use of the labels to select the Pods to manage.	app: couchbaseApp
metadata ->name	The Pod name.	couchbase
spec	The Pod specification.	
spec ->containers	The containers in the Pod.	
spec ->containers ->image	A container image. For Couchbase server the image is "couchbase."	couchbase
spec ->containers ->name	The container name.	couchbase
spec ->containers ->ports	The container ports.	
spec ->containers ->ports ->containerPort	A container port for Couchbase server.	8091

The `couchbase.yaml` definition file is listed.

```
apiVersion: v1
kind: Pod
metadata:
  labels:
    app: couchbaseApp
  name: couchbase
spec:
  containers:
    -
      image: couchbase
      name: couchbase
      ports:
        -
          containerPort: 8091
```

The couchbase.yaml file could be created in the vi editor and saved with the :wq command as shown in Figure 9-6.

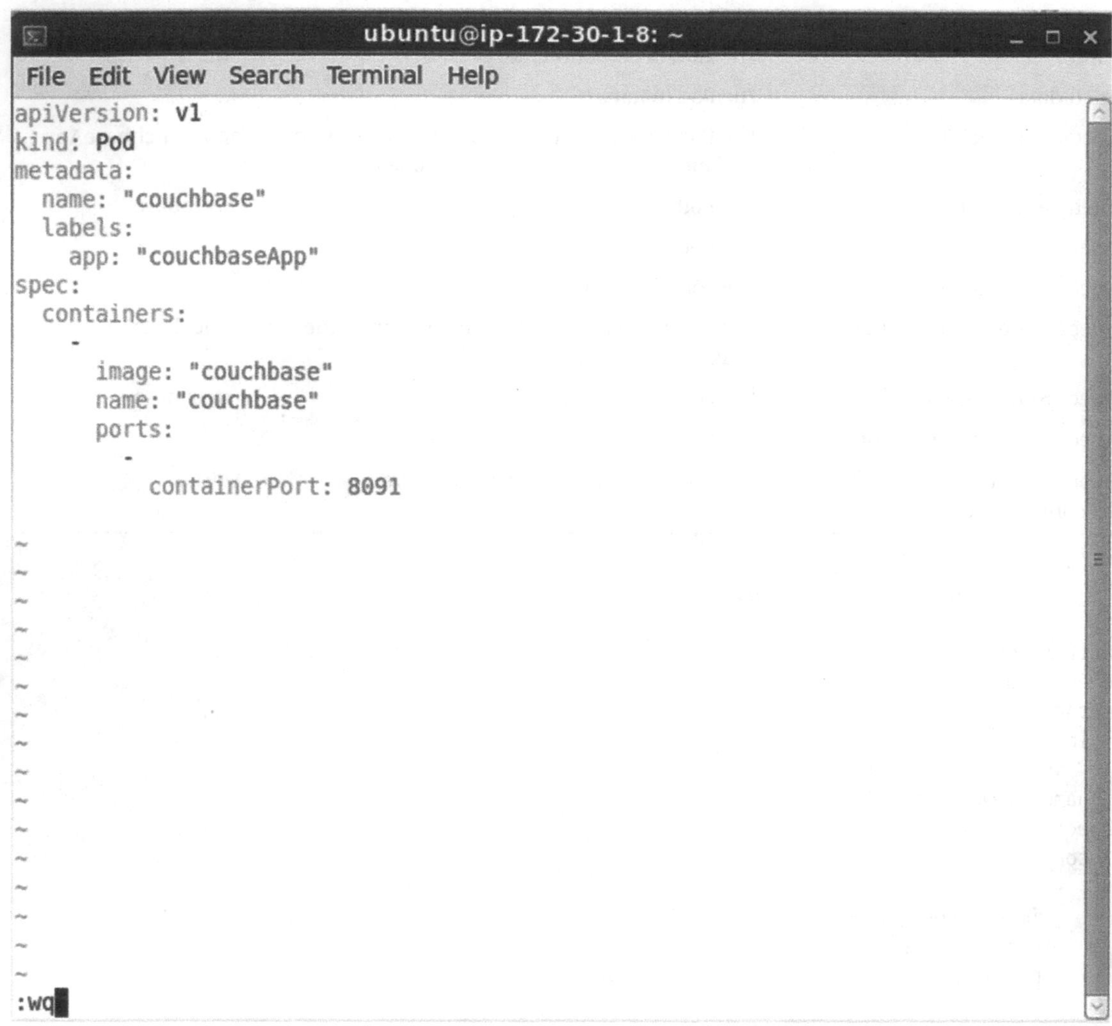

Figure 9-6. *Pod Definition file couchbase.yaml in vi Editor*

Run the following command to create a Pod from the definition file.

```
kubectl create -f couchbase.yaml
```

A Pod gets created as indicated by the "pods/couchbase" output in Figure 9-7.

```
ubuntu@ip-172-30-1-8:~$ kubectl create -f couchbase.yaml
pods/couchbase
ubuntu@ip-172-30-1-8:~$ kubectl get pods
NAME                     READY     STATUS                                      RES
TARTS   AGE
couchbase                0/1       Image: couchbase is not ready on the node   0
        18s
k8s-master-127.0.0.1     3/3       Running                                     0
        9m
```

Figure 9-7. *Creating a Pod from the Definition File*

Subsequently list the Pods.

```
kubectl get pods
```

A Pod called "couchbase" gets listed as shown in Figure 9-7. Initially the STATUS could be different from "Running" and the READY column could be not ready; 1/1 is ready state and 0/1 is not ready.

Run the following command again after a few more seconds.

```
kubectl get pods
```

The couchbase Pod is listed as "Running" and READY-> 1/1 as shown in Figure 9-8.

```
ubuntu@ip-172-30-1-8:~$ kubectl get pods
NAME                     READY     STATUS     RESTARTS   AGE
couchbase                1/1       Running    0          1m
k8s-master-127.0.0.1     3/3       Running    0          9m
ubuntu@ip-172-30-1-8:~$
```

Figure 9-8. *Listing the couchbase Pod*

Creating a Service

In this section we shall create a service using a service definition file. Create a `couchbase-service.yaml` file and add the following (Table 9-2) fields to the file.

Table 9-2. Service Definition File couchbase-service.yaml

Field	Description	Value
apiVersion		v1
kind	The kind of definition file.	Service
metadata	The service metadata.	
metadata ->labels	The service labels.	app: couchbaseApp
metadata ->name	The service name.	couchbase
spec	The service specification.	
spec ->ports	The ports exposed by the service.	
spec ->ports ->port	A port exposed by the service.	8091
spec ->ports ->targetPort	The target port for the service, which could be a port number or the name of a port on the backend. The target port setting adds flexibility as the port number could be modified while the port name is kept fixed.	8091
spec ->selector	The Pod selector, which could be one or more label key:value expressions/labels. All of the key:value expressions in a selector must match with a Pod's labels for the Pod to be selected by the service. A Pod could have additional labels but must include labels in the selector to be selected by the service. Service routes traffic to the Pods with label/s matching the selector expression/s. Only a single selector expression is used in the example service definition file. If the selector is empty all Pods are selected. The app: couchbaseApp setting defaults to selector app = couchbaseApp.	app: couchbaseApp
spec ->selector ->type	The service type.	LoadBalancer

The `couchbase-service.yaml` is listed.

```
apiVersion: v1
kind: Service
metadata:
  labels:
    app: couchbaseApp
  name: couchbase
spec:
  ports:
    -
      port: 8091
      targetPort: 8091
  selector:
    app: couchbaseApp
  type: LoadBalancer
```

Create a service from the definition file with the following command.

```
kubectl create -f couchbase-service.yaml
```

Subsequently list the running services.

```
kubectl get services
```

An output of "services/couchbase" as shown in Figure 9-9 indicates that the couchbase service has been created. The "couchbase" service gets listed, also shown in Figure 9-9.

```
ubuntu@ip-172-30-1-8:~$ kubectl create -f couchbase-service.yaml
services/couchbase
ubuntu@ip-172-30-1-8:~$ kubectl get services
NAME         LABELS                                    SELECTOR            IP(S)
    PORT(S)
couchbase    app=couchbaseApp                          app=couchbaseApp    10.0.0
.212   8091/TCP
kubernetes   component=apiserver,provider=kubernetes   <none>              10.0.0
.1     443/TCP
```

Figure 9-9. Listing the couchbase Service

List the service endpoints with the following command.

```
kubectl get endpoints
```

The service endpoint for the couchbase service gets listed as shown in Figure 9-10.

```
ubuntu@ip-172-30-1-8:~$ kubectl get endpoints
NAME         ENDPOINTS
couchbase    172.17.0.2:8091
kubernetes   172.30.1.8:6443
ubuntu@ip-172-30-1-8:~$ █
```

Figure 9-10. Listing the Endpoints

Creating a Replication Controller

In this section we shall create a replication controller using a definition file. Create a couchbase-rc.yaml file and add the following (Table 9-3) fields to the file.

Table 9-3. Definition File for Replication Controller

Field	Description	Value	Required Field (includes default settings)
apiVersion		v1	yes
kind	The kind of definition file.	ReplicationController	yes
metadata	The replication controller metadata.		yes
metadata - > labels	The replication controller labels.	app: couchbaseApp	no
metadata - > name	The replication controller name.	couchbase	yes
spec	The replication controller specification.		yes
spec - > replicas	The number of Pod replicas. Defaults to 1 replica.	2	yes
spec - > selector	One or more key:value expressions for selecting the Pods to manage. Pods that include label/s with the same expression/s as the selector expression/s are managed by the replication controller. A Pod could include additional labels but must include the ones in the selector to be managed by the replication controller. The selector defaults to the spec - > template - > metadata - > labels key:value expression/s if not specified. A setting of app: couchbaseApp translates to selector app = couchbaseApp.	app: couchbaseApp	yes
spec - > template	The Pod template.		yes
spec - > template - > metadata	The Pod template metadata.		yes
spec - > template - > metadata - > labels	The Pod template labels.	app: couchbaseApp	yes
spec - > template - > spec	The Pod template specification.		yes
spec - > template - > spec - > containers	The containers configuration for the Pod template.		yes
spec - > template - > spec - > containers - > image	The Docker image.	couchbase	yes
spec - > template - > spec - > containers - > name	The container name.	couchbase	yes
spec - > template - > spec - > containers - > ports	The container ports.		no
spec - > template - > spec - > containers - > ports - > containerPort	A container port.	8091	no

The couchbase-rc.yaml is listed.

```
apiVersion: v1
kind: ReplicationController
metadata:
  labels:
    app: couchbaseApp
  name: couchbase
spec:
  replicas: 2
  selector:
    app: couchbaseApp
  template:
    metadata:
      labels:
        app: couchbaseApp
    spec:
      containers:
        -
          image: couchbase
          name: couchbase
          ports:
          -
            containerPort: 8091
```

The couchbase-rc.yaml may be created in vi editor as shown in Figure 9-11.

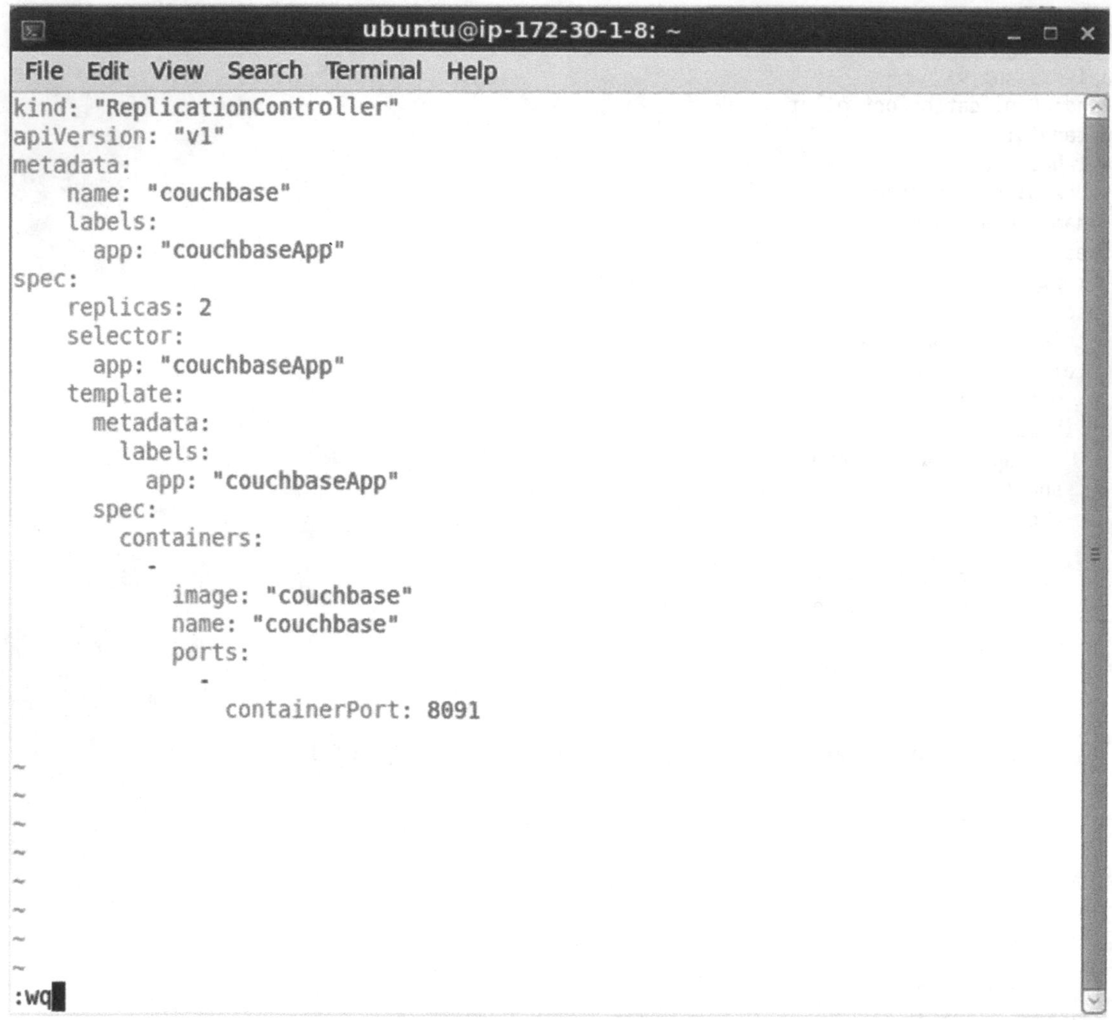

Figure 9-11. *Replication Controller Definition File couchbase-rc.yaml in vi Editor*

Create the replication controller with the following command.

```
kubectl create -f couchbase-rc.yaml
```

Subsequently, list the replication controllers.

```
kubectl get rc
```

An output of "replicationcontrollers/couchbase" as shown in Figure 9-12 indicates that the "couchbase" replication controller has been created. The "couchbase" replication controller gets listed with the second command. The REPLICAS is listed as 2, but it does not imply that the replication controller created two new replicas. The replication controller manages Pods based on selector expression matching a Pod label. If some other Pod with the matching label is already running it is counted toward the replicas setting.

```
ubuntu@ip-172-30-1-8:~$ kubectl create -f couchbase-rc.yaml
replicationcontrollers/couchbase
ubuntu@ip-172-30-1-8:~$ kubectl get rc
CONTROLLER   CONTAINER(S)   IMAGE(S)    SELECTOR           REPLICAS
couchbase    couchbase      couchbase   app=couchbaseApp   2
ubuntu@ip-172-30-1-8:~$ ▌
```

Figure 9-12. *Creating and listing a Replication Controller from the Definition File*

Listing the Pods

To list the Pods run the following command.

```
kubectl get pods
```

Two Pods get listed as shown in Figure 9-13, and one of the Pods is the Pod created earlier using a Pod definition file. The label in the Pod definition file was app: "couchbaseApp," which is also the selector expression for the replication controller. The expression app: "couchbaseApp" translates to app= couchbaseApp. As a result only one new Pod gets created when the replication controller with replicas set to 2 is created.

```
ubuntu@ip-172-30-1-8:~$ kubectl get pods
NAME                    READY     STATUS    RESTARTS   AGE
couchbase               1/1       Running   0          3m
couchbase-0hglx         1/1       Running   0          40s
k8s-master-127.0.0.1    3/3       Running   0          12m
ubuntu@ip-172-30-1-8:~$ ▌
```

Figure 9-13. *Listing the Pods for Couchbase Server*

Listing the Logs

To list the logs for a Pod run the `kubectl logs` command. The pod name may be copied from the preceding listing of Pods.

```
kubectl logs couchbase-0hglx
```

The output is shown in Figure 9-14. The output indicates that the WEB UI is available at `http://<ip>:8091`.

```
ubuntu@ip-172-30-1-8:~$ kubectl logs couchbase-0hglx
Starting Couchbase Server -- Web UI available at http://<ip>:8091
ubuntu@ip-172-30-1-8:~$ ▌
```

Figure 9-14. *Listing Pod Logs*

Describing the Service

To describe the couchbase service run the following command.

```
kubectl describe svc couchbase
```

The service name, namespace, labels, selector, type, IP, Port, NodePort, and endpoints get listed as shown in Figure 9-15. The `selector` is listed as app=couchbaseApp.

```
ubuntu@ip-172-30-1-8:~$ kubectl describe svc couchbase
Name:                   couchbase
Namespace:              default
Labels:                 app=couchbaseApp
Selector:               app=couchbaseApp
Type:                   LoadBalancer
IP:                     10.0.0.212
Port:                   <unnamed>       8091/TCP
NodePort:               <unnamed>       32123/TCP
Endpoints:              172.17.0.2:8091,172.17.0.3:8091
Session Affinity:       None
No events.

ubuntu@ip-172-30-1-8:~$
```

Figure 9-15. *Describing the Service for Couchbase*

Listing the Endpoints

List the endpoints again.

```
kubectl get endpoints
```

When the endpoints were listed earlier only one endpoint was listed because only one Pod was running. With two Pods running two endpoints get listed as shown in Figure 9-16.

```
ubuntu@ip-172-30-1-8:~$ kubectl get endpoints
NAME          ENDPOINTS
couchbase     172.17.0.2:8091,172.17.0.3:8091
kubernetes    172.30.1.8:6443
ubuntu@ip-172-30-1-8:~$
```

Figure 9-16. *Listing the Endpoints for Couchbase*

Setting Port Forwarding

When we listed the logs for a Couchbase Pod the URL to invoke the web console was listed as `http://<ip>:8091`. The `< ip >` is the service endpoint of the Pod. The previous section listed two service endpoints. Invoking either of these on a host browser, for example, `http://172.17.0.2:8091` would open the web console. An Amazon EC2 Ubuntu instance does not install a web browser by default. Alternatively, we shall set port forwarding to a local machine and open the web console from a browser on a local machine, which is required to have a browser available. To set port forwarding we need to know the Public DNS of the Amazon EC2 instance running Kubernetes. The Public DNS may be obtained from the Amazon EC2 console as shown in Figure 9-17.

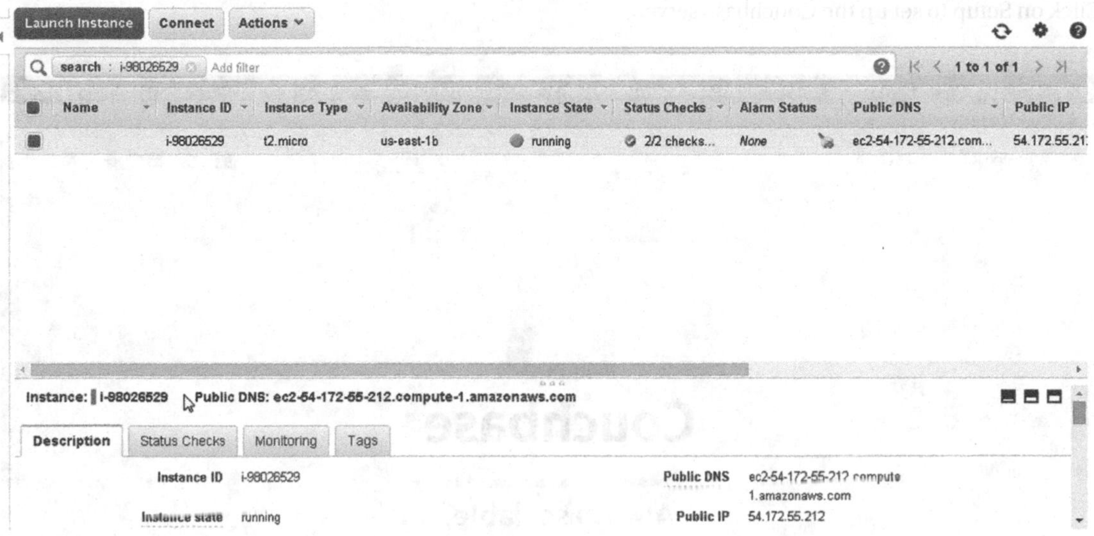

Figure 9-17. *Obtaining the Public DNS*

The ports to forward to on the local machine must be open and not already bound. As an example, bind one of the endpoints to port 8093 on `localhost` and the other to port 8094 on the `localhost` with the following commands.

```
ssh -i "docker.pem" -f -nNT -L 8093:172.17.0.3:8091 ubuntu@ec2-54-172-55-212.compute-1.
amazonaws.com
ssh -i "docker.pem" -f -nNT -L 8094:172.17.0.2:8091 ubuntu@ec2-54-172-55-212.compute-1.
amazonaws.com
```

The port forwarding from the service endpoints to `localhost` ports gets set as shown in Figure 9-18.

```
[root@localhost ~]# ssh -i "docker.pem" -f -nNT -L  8093:172.17.0.3:8091 ubuntu@
ec2-54-172-55-212.compute-1.amazonaws.com
[root@localhost ~]# ssh -i "docker.pem" -f -nNT -L  8094:172.17.0.2:8091 ubuntu@
ec2-54-172-55-212.compute-1.amazonaws.com
[root@localhost ~]# 
```

Figure 9-18. *Setting Port Forwarding to localhost:8093 and localhost:8094*

Logging into Couchbase Web Console

Two ports are available on the local machine to open the Couchbase web console, 8093 and 8094. Either or both of these could be used to open a Couchbase web console. For example, open the URL `http://localhost:8093` in a web browser. The Couchbase Console gets opened as shown in Figure 9-19. Click on Setup to set up the Couchbase server.

Figure 9-19. *Setting Up Couchbase Server*

Configuring Couchbase Server

In this section we shall configure the Couchbase server, which is not directly related to using Kubernetes but is discussed for completeness. When the Setup button is clicked the CONFIGURE SERVER window gets displayed as shown in Figure 9-20.

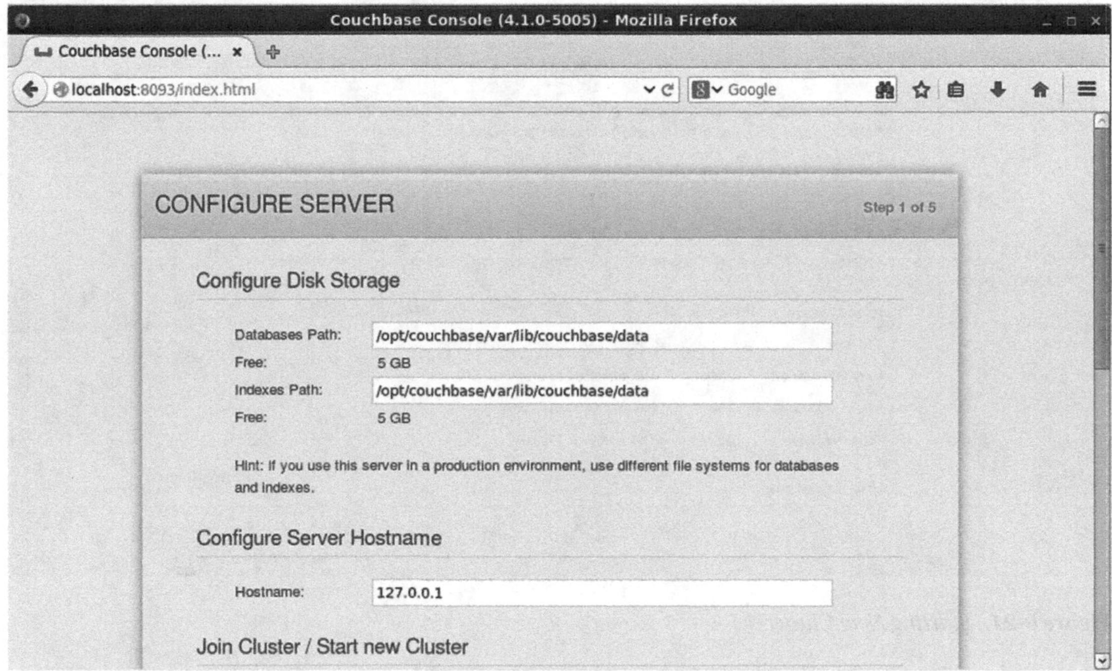

Figure 9-20. *Configuring Server Disk Storage, Hostname*

Keep the default settings and scroll down to select Start a new cluster. The RAM settings may have to be reduced if sufficient RAM is not available. Click on Next as shown in Figure 9-21.

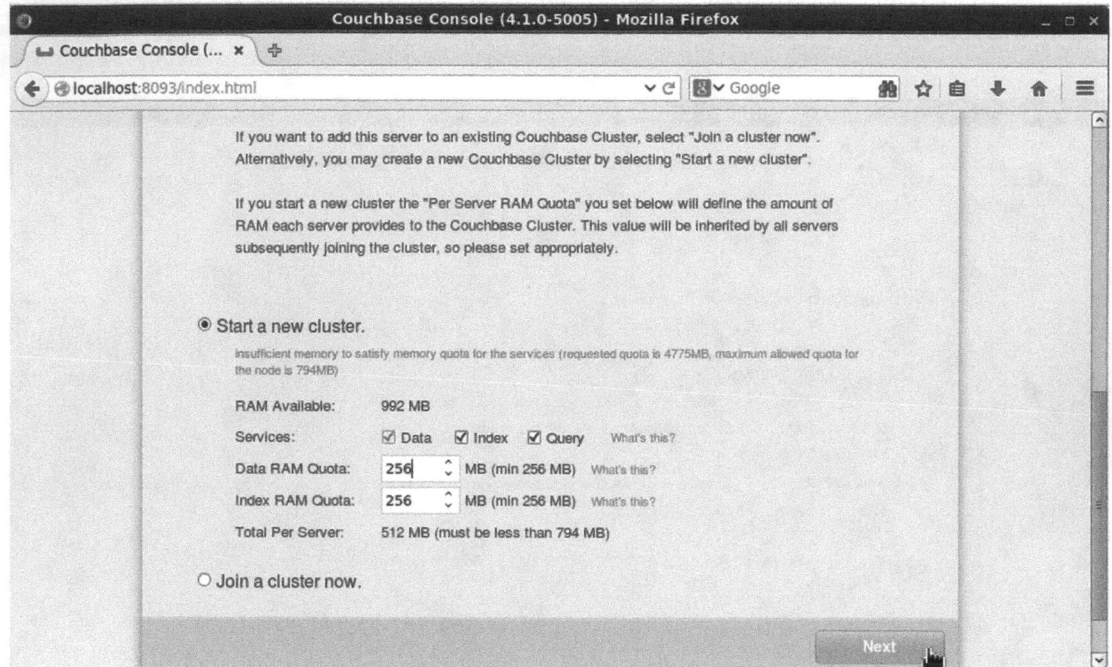

Figure 9-21. *Starting New Cluster*

Some sample buckets get listed but a sample bucket is not required to be selected. Click on Next as shown in Figure 9-22.

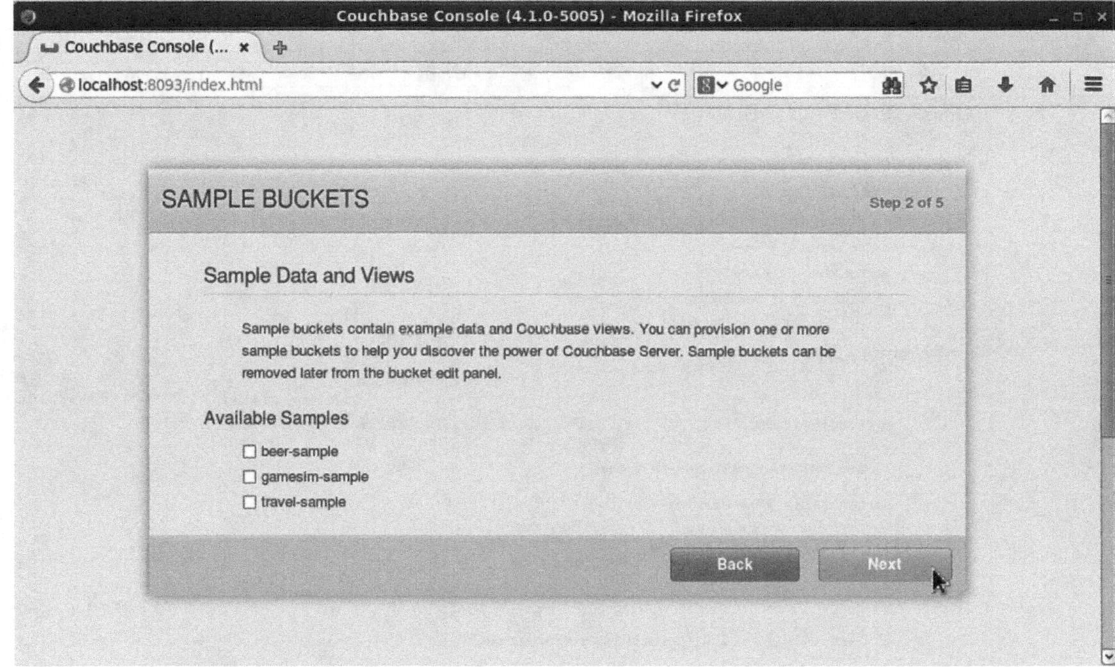

Figure 9-22. *Sample Buckets are not required to be selected*

The Create Default Bucket settings include the Bucket Type, which should be Couchbase as shown in Figure 9-23. Replicas should be enabled with the "Enable" check box.

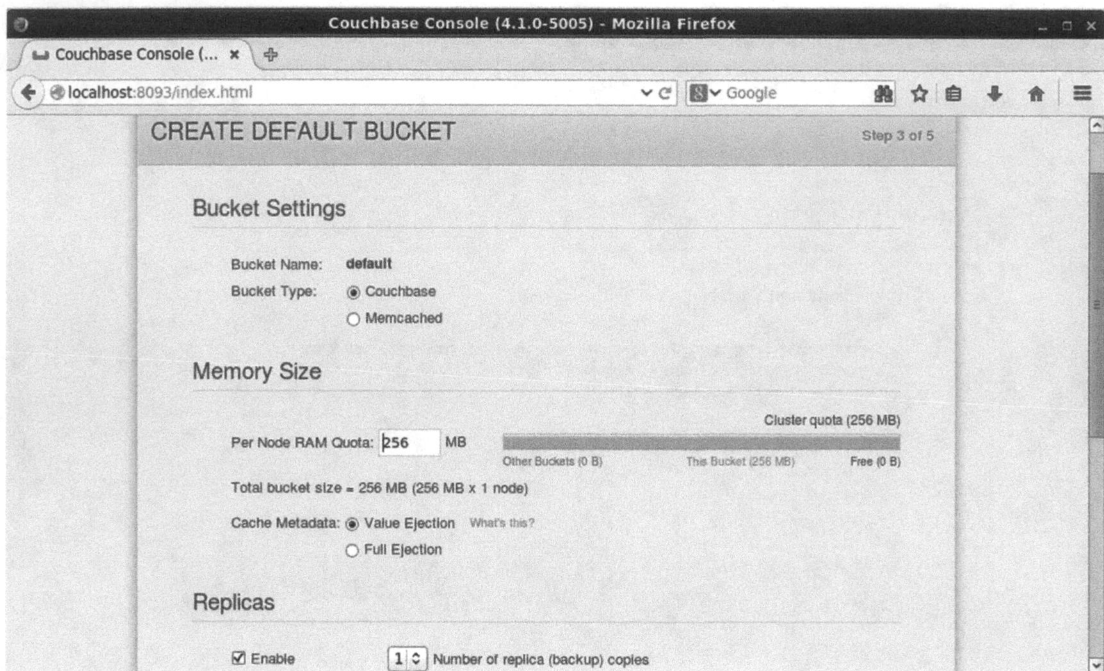

Figure 9-23. *Configuring Default Bucket*

Scroll down to enable the Flush mode with the "Enable" check box. Click on Next as shown in Figure 9-24.

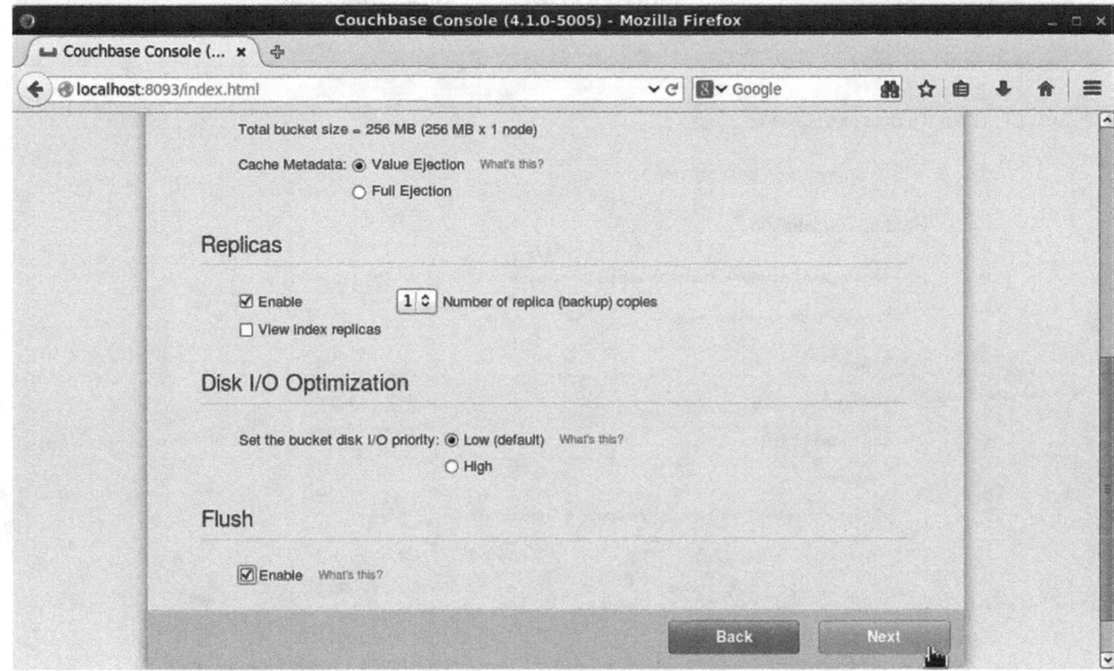

Figure 9-24. *Enabling Flush Mode and completing Server Configuration*

Next, accept the terms and conditions as shown in Figure 9-25 and click on Next.

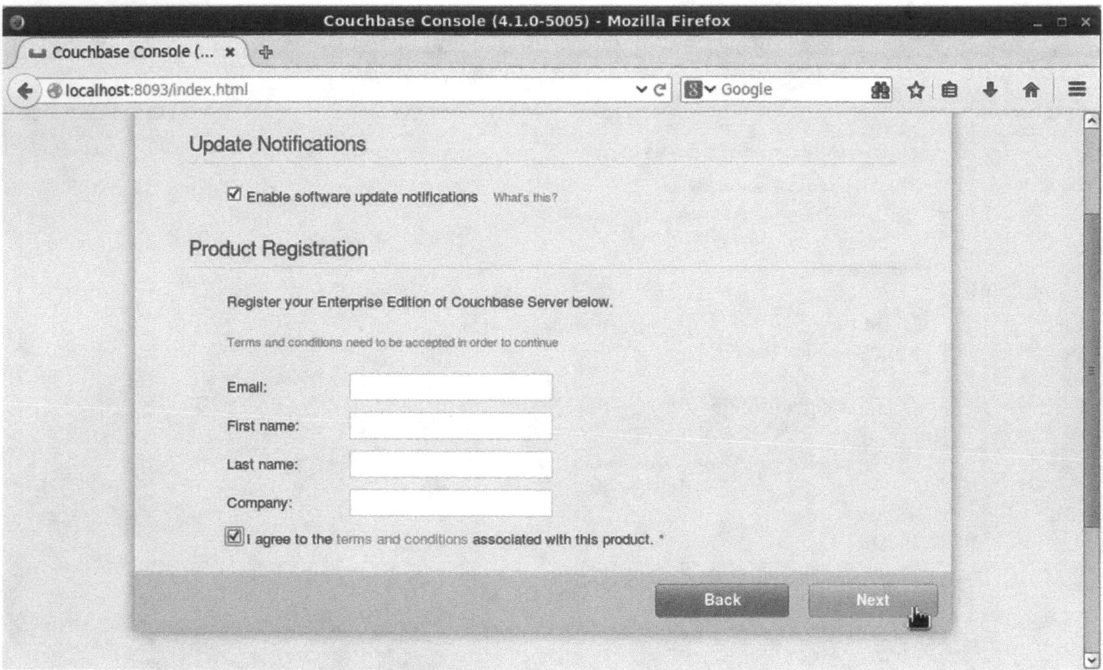

Figure 9-25. *Accepting Terms and Conditions*

To secure the server specify a Password and specify the same password in the Verify Password field as shown in Figure 9-26.

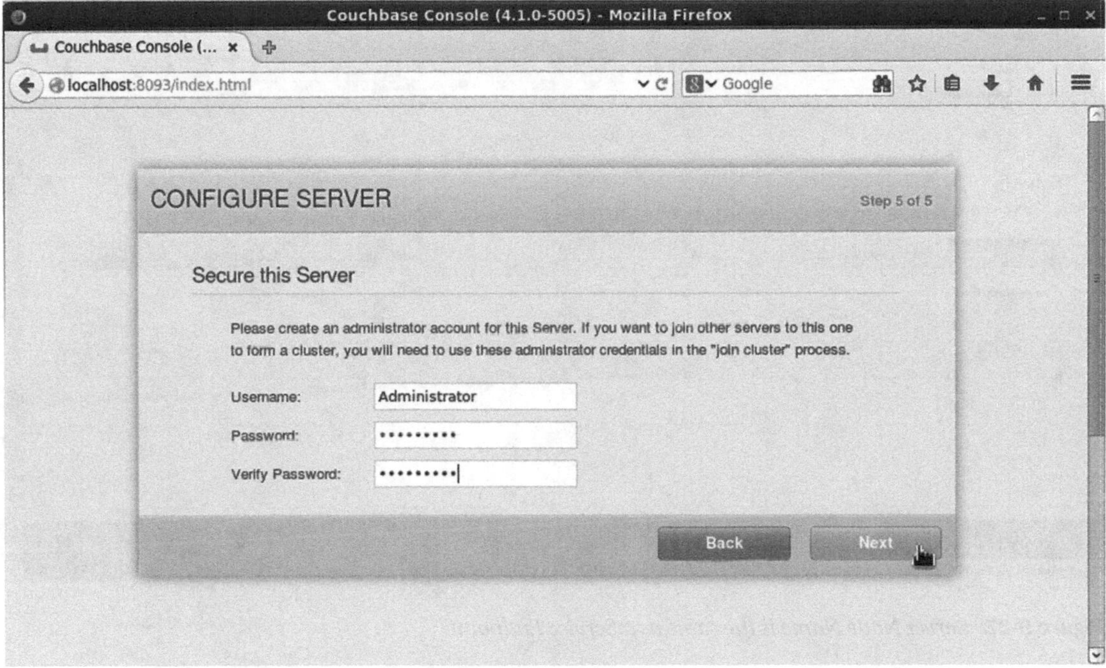

Figure 9-26. *Securing the Server with Username and Password*

The Couchbase server gets configured. Select the Server Nodes tab and the Server Node Name is listed as shown in Figure 9-27. The Server Node Name is one of the service endpoints.

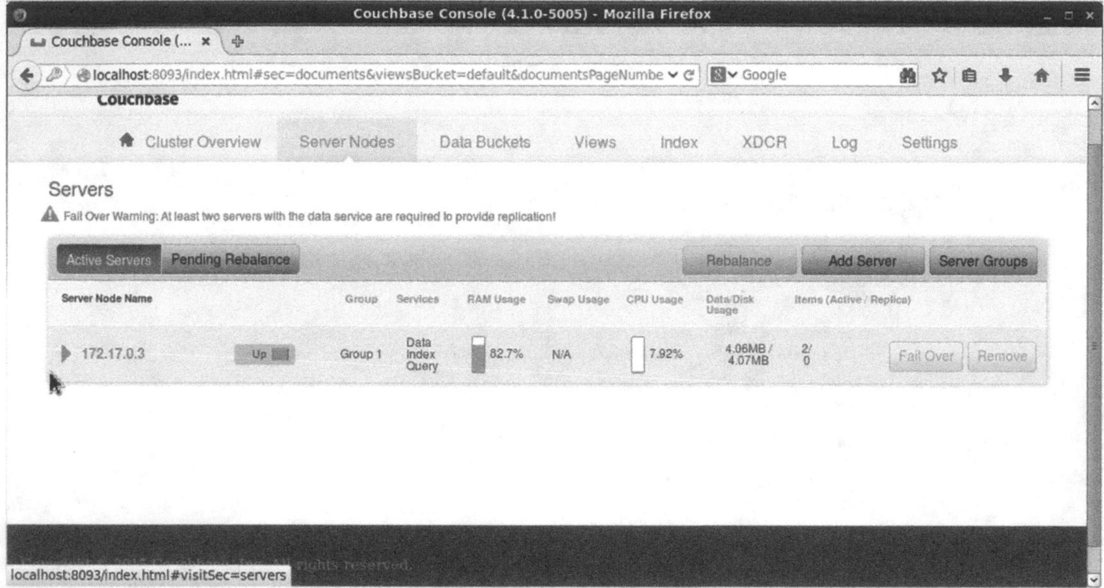

Figure 9-27. Server Node Name is the same as a Service Endpoint

Adding Documents

Next, we shall add some documents to the Couchbase server. Select the Data Buckets tab as shown in Figure 9-28.

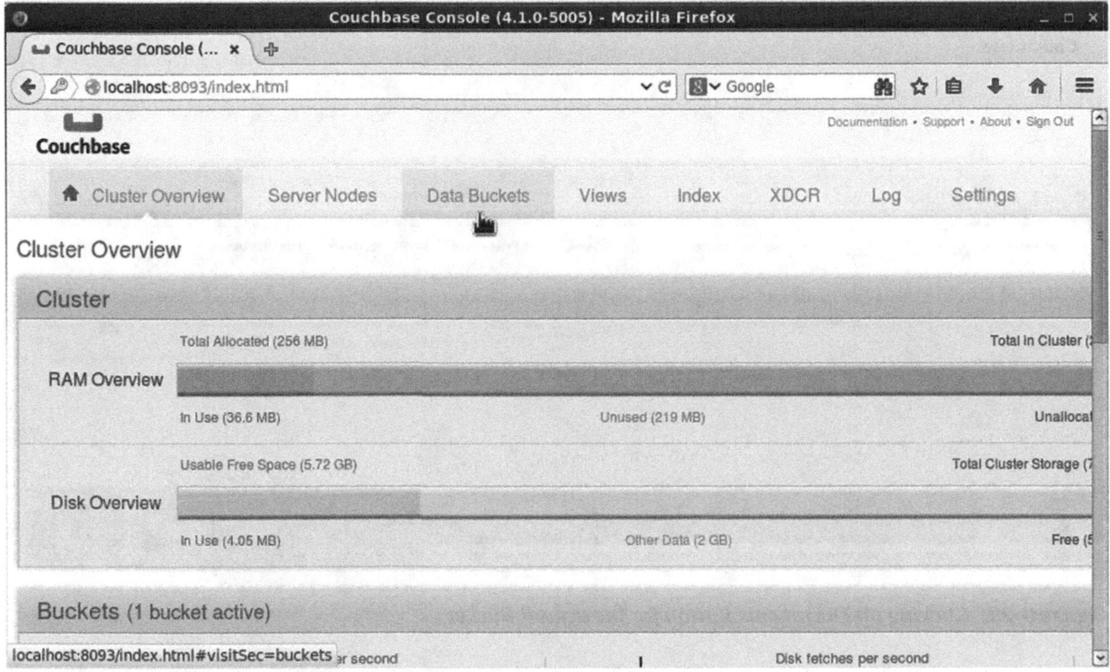

Figure 9-28. *Selecting Data Buckets Tab*

The default bucket gets listed as shown in Figure 9-29. Click on Documents.

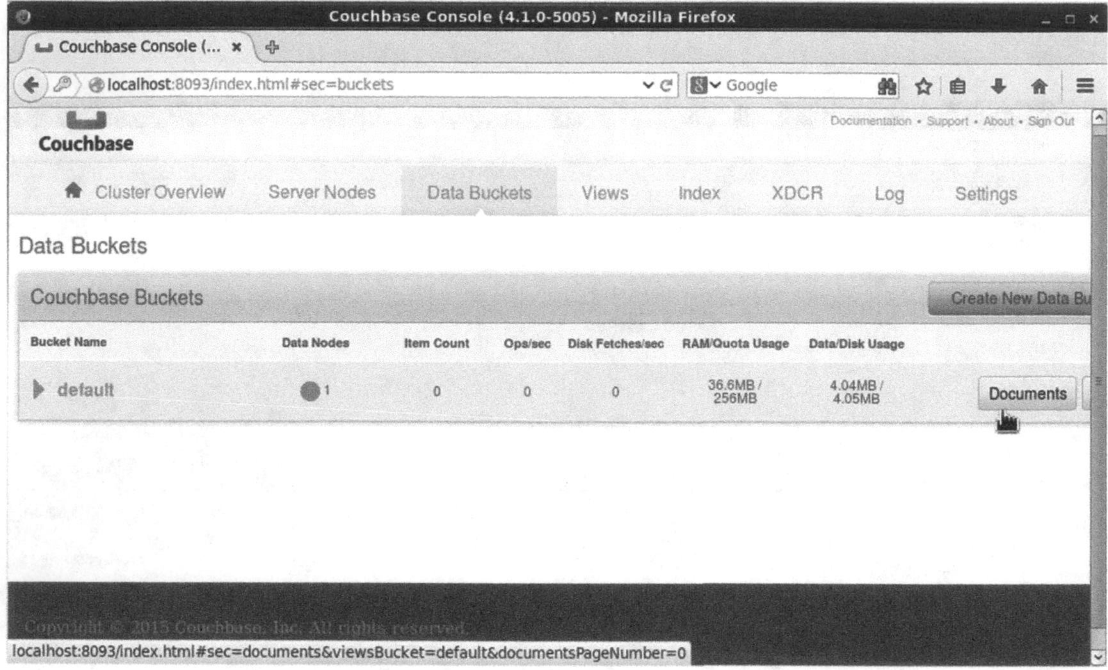

***Figure 9-29.** Clicking on Documents Button for the default Bucket*

Initially the "default" bucket is empty as shown in Figure 9-30.

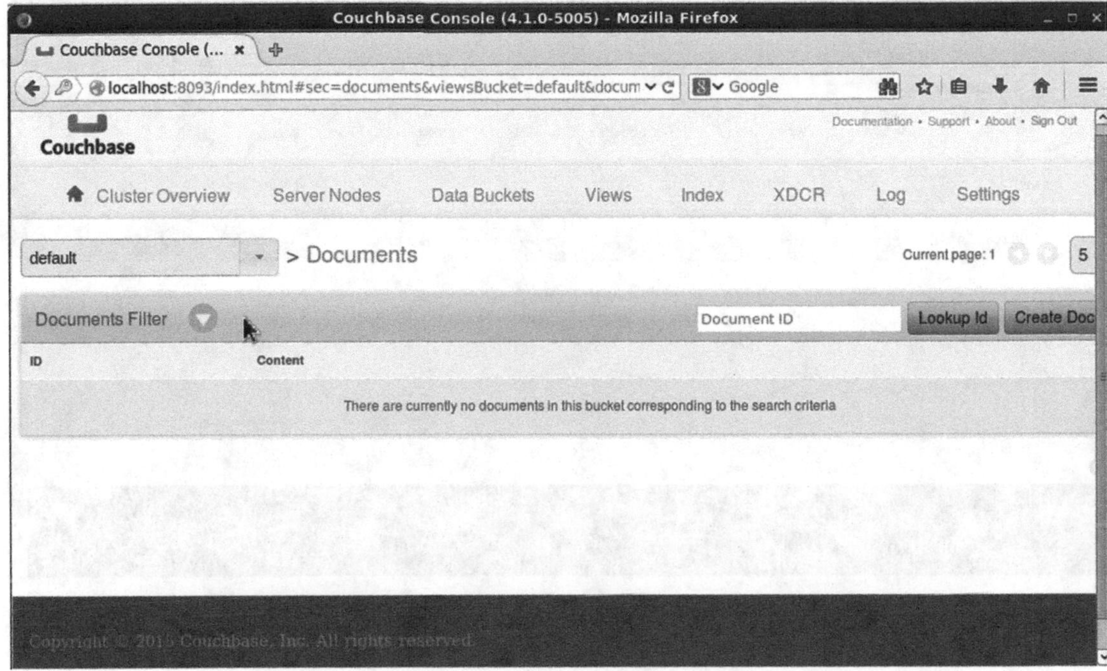

Figure 9-30. *Initially no Documents are present in the default Data Bucket*

Click on Create Document to add a document as shown in Figure 9-31.

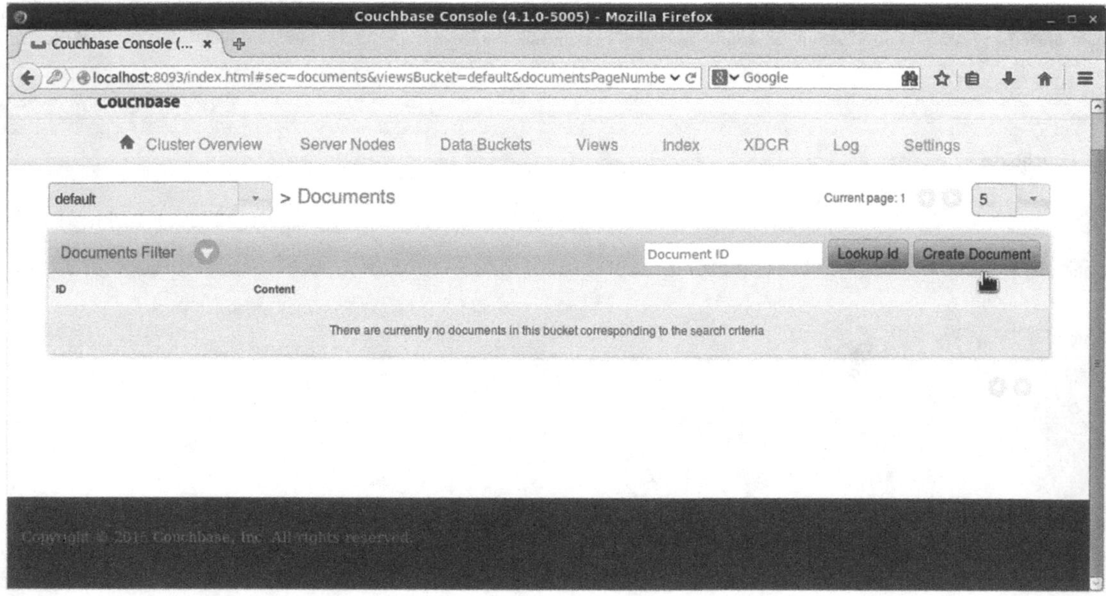

Figure 9-31. Clicking on Create Document

In the Create Document dialog specify a Document Id and click on Create as shown in Figure 9-32.

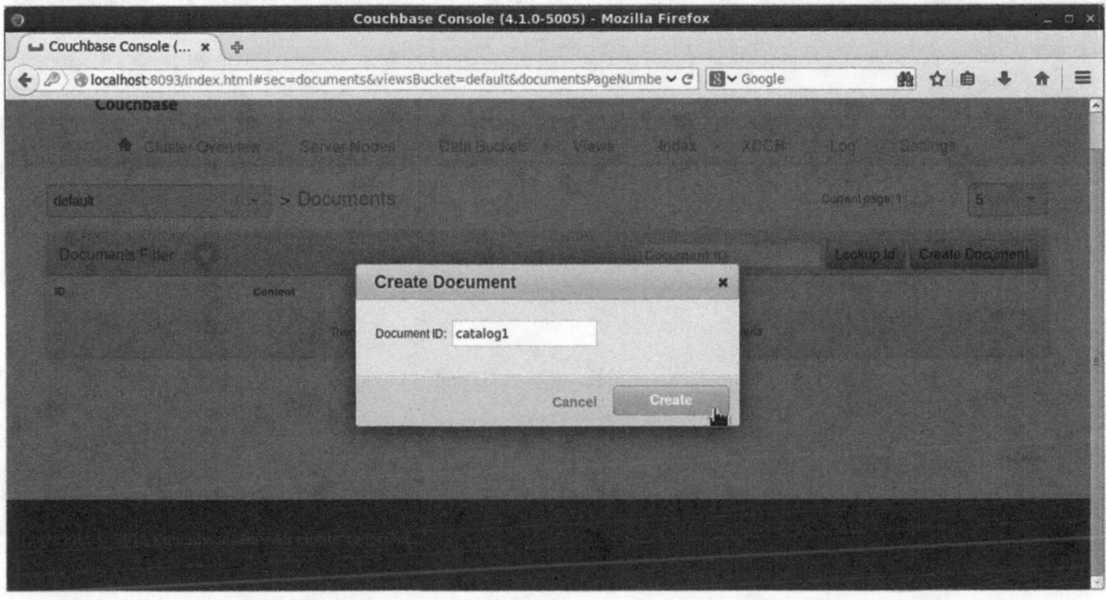

Figure 9-32. *Specifying Document ID*

A new JSON document with default fields gets added as shown in Figure 9-33.

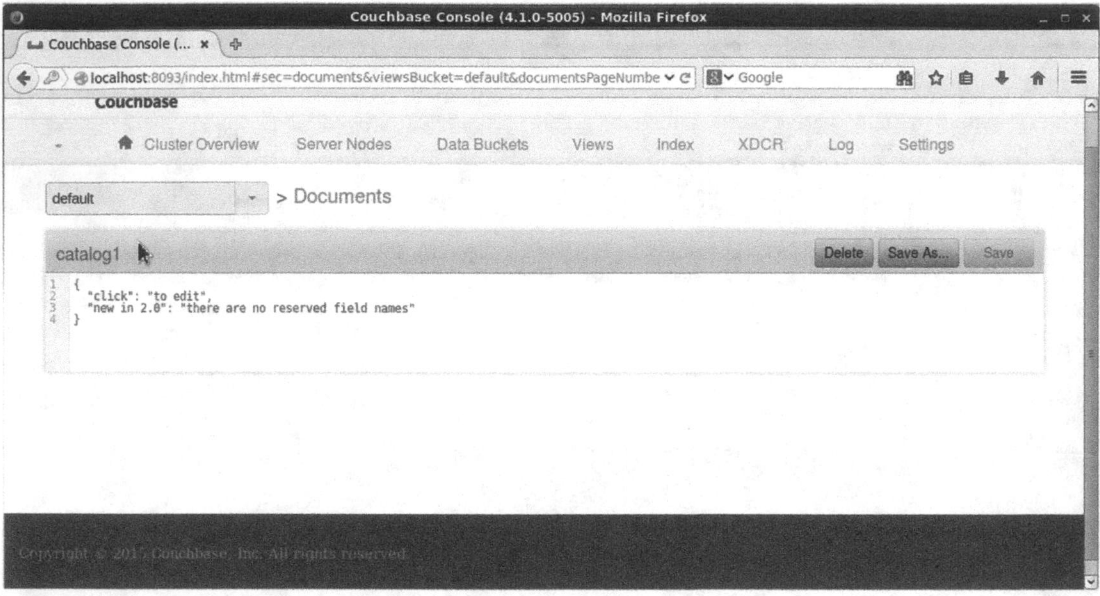

Figure 9-33. *The catalog1 Document gets created with Default Fields*

Copy and paste the following JSON document into the `catalog1` document.

```
{
  "journal": "Oracle Magazine",
  "publisher": "Oracle Publishing",
  "edition": "November-December 2013",
  "title": "Quintessential and Collaborative",
  "author": "Tom Haunert"
}
```

Click on Save to update the `catalog1` document as shown in Figure 9-34.

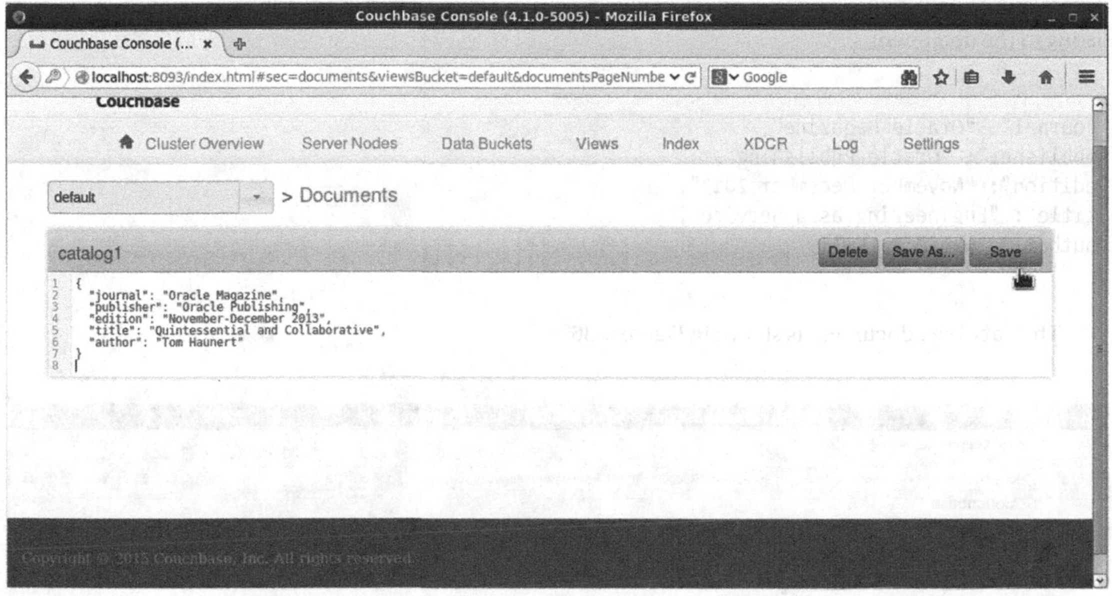

Figure 9-34. *Saving a JSON Document*

The `catalog1` document gets saved and gets listed when the Documents link for the "default" bucket is selected as shown in Figure 9-35.

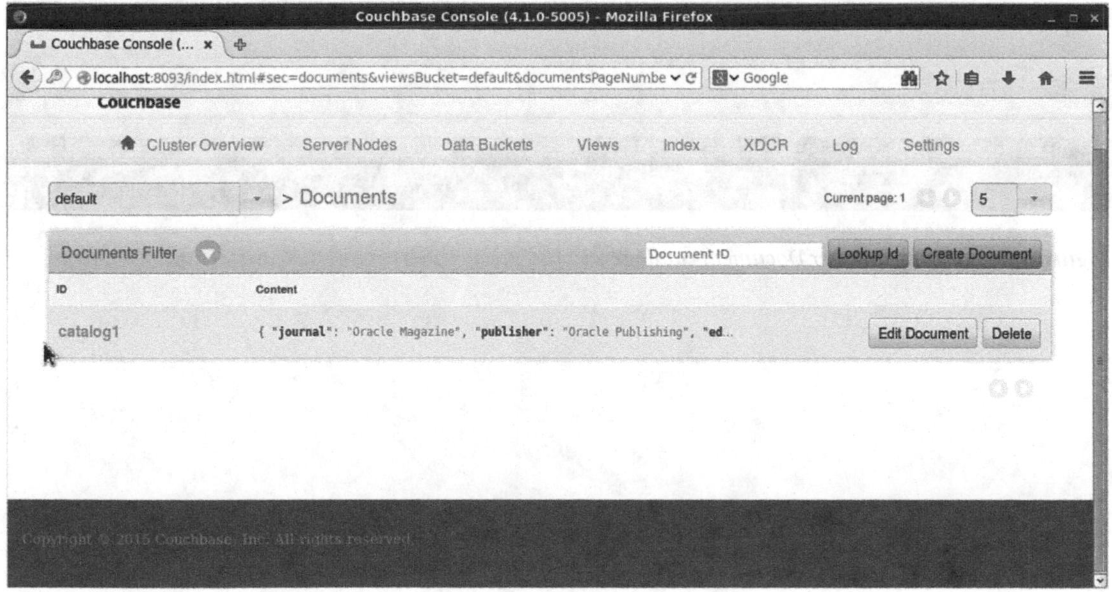

Figure 9-35. *The catalog1 Document in default Bucket*

Similarly add another document with Document ID as catalog2 and copy and paste the following listing to the document.

```
{
"journal": "Oracle Magazine",
"publisher": "Oracle Publishing",
"edition": "November December 2013",
"title": "Engineering as a Service",
"author": "David A. Kelly",
}
```

The catalog2 document is shown in Figure 9-36.

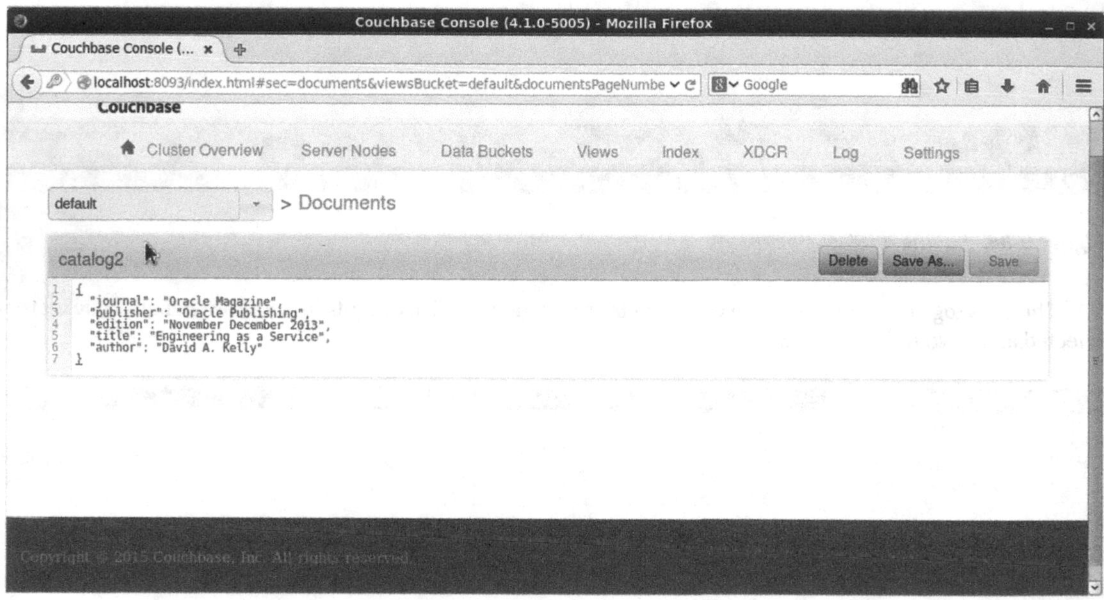

***Figure 9-36.** Adding another Document catalog2*

The Documents link for the "default" bucket links the two documents added as shown in Figure 9-37.

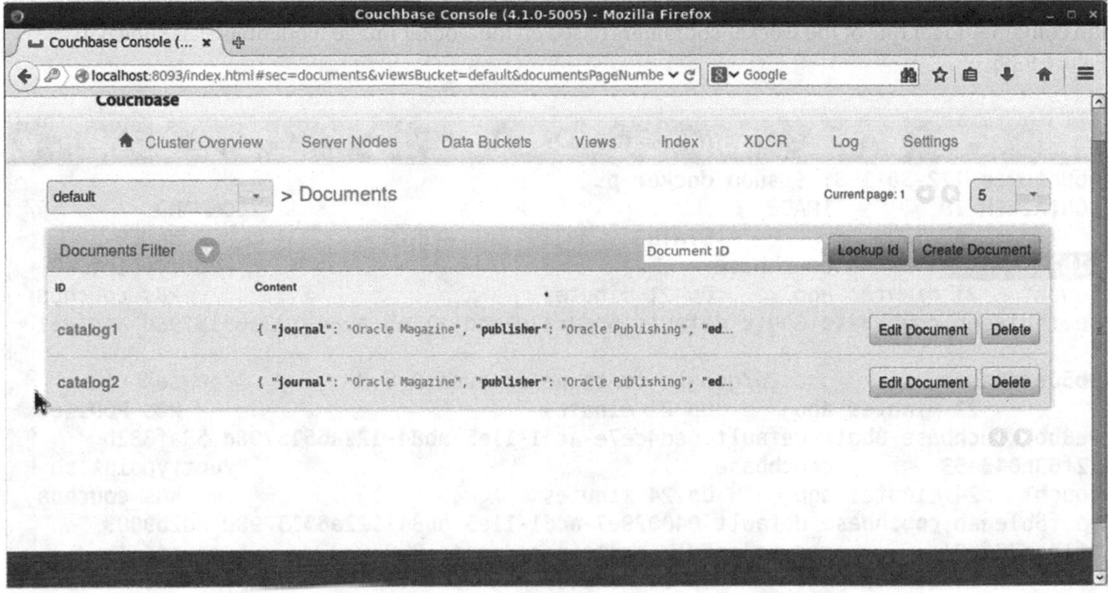

Figure 9-37. *Listing the two Documents in the default Bucket*

Starting an Interactive Shell

Next, we shall start and interactive bash shell to access Couchbase server from the command line. Obtain the container id for one of the Docker containers based on the Docker image "couchbase" as shown in Figure 9-38.

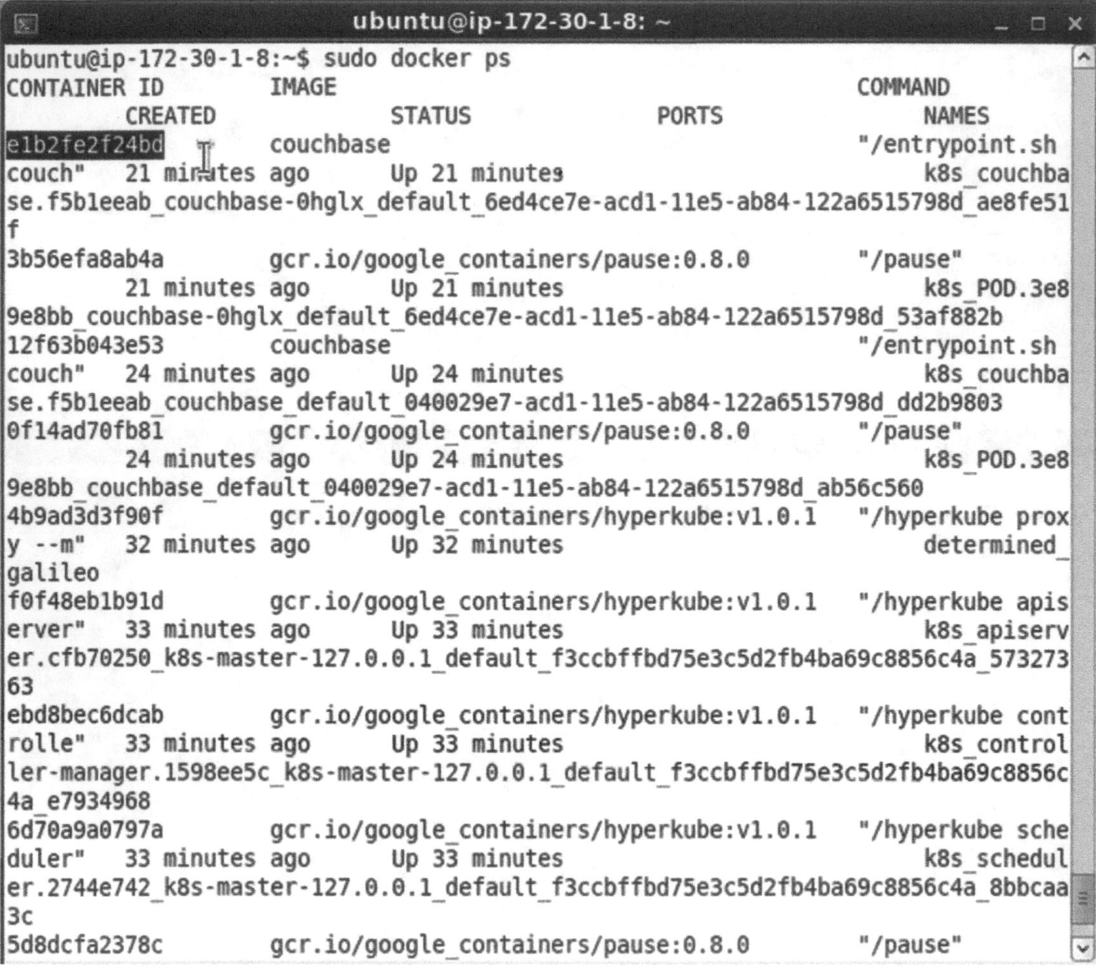

Figure 9-38. *Obtaining the Container Id*

Using the container id, start an interactive shell.

```
sudo docker exec -it e1b2fe2f24bd bash
```

An interactive shell gets started as shown in Figure 9-39.

```
ubuntu@ip-172-30-1-8:~$ sudo docker exec -it e1b2fe2f24bd bash
root@couchbase-0hglx:/#
```

Figure 9-39. *Starting an Interactive Shell*

Using the cbtransfer Tool

From the interactive shell command-line tools may be run to access the Couchbase server. As an example run the `cbtransfer` tool, which is used to transfer data between clusters and to/from files, to output the documents in the default bucket at server `http://172.17.0.3:8091` to `stdout`.

```
cbtransfer http://172.17.0.3:8091/ stdout:
```

The two documents added from the web console get output as shown in Figure 9-40.

```
root@couchbase-0hglx:/# cbtransfer http://172.17.0.3:8091/ stdout:
set catalog2 0 0 157
{"journal":"Oracle Magazine","publisher":"Oracle Publishing","edition":"November
 December 2013","title":"Engineering as a Service","author":"David A. Kelly"}
set catalog1 0 0 162
{"journal":"Oracle Magazine","publisher":"Oracle Publishing","edition":"November
-December 2013","title":"Quintessential and Collaborative","author":"Tom Haunert
"}
  [####################] 100.0% (2/estimated 2 msgs)
bucket: default, msgs transferred...
       :                total |       last |     per sec
 byte  :                  319 |        319 |       449.0
done
root@couchbase-0hglx:/#
```

Figure 9-40. *Using the cbtransfer Tool*

In the next section we shall create a Couchbase cluster imperatively using Kubernetes on the command line. As we shall be using the same replication controller name and service name, delete the replication controller "couchbase" and also delete the service called "couchbase."

```
kubectl delete rc couchbase
kubectl delete svc couchbase
```

Creating a Couchbase Cluster Imperatively

In the following subsections we shall create a Couchbase cluster on the command line.

Creating a Replication Controller

Create a replication controller called "couchbase" using the Docker image "couchbase" with two replicas and container port as 8091 with the following command.

```
kubectl run couchbase --image=couchbase --replicas=2 --port=8091
```

The replication controller gets created as shown in Figure 9-41. The default selector is "run=couchbase," which implies that pods with the label "run=couchbase" shall be managed by the replication controller. The Pod labels get set to "run=couchbase".

```
ubuntu@ip-172-30-1-55:~$ kubectl  run couchbase --image=couchbase --replicas=2 -
-port=8091
CONTROLLER   CONTAINER(S)   IMAGE(S)    SELECTOR        REPLICAS
couchbase    couchbase      couchbase   run=couchbase   2
ubuntu@ip-172-30-1-55:~$ 
```

Figure 9-41. *Creating a Replication Controller Imperatively*

List the replication controllers with the following command.

```
kubectl get rc
```

The couchbase replication controller gets listed as shown in Figure 9-42.

```
ubuntu@ip-172-30-1-55:~$ kubectl get rc
CONTROLLER   CONTAINER(S)   IMAGE(S)    SELECTOR        REPLICAS
couchbase    couchbase      couchbase   run=couchbase   2
```

Figure 9-42. *Listing the Replication Controllers*

Listing the Pods

To list the Pods run the following command.

```
kubectl get pods
```

The two pods get listed as shown in Figure 9-43.

```
ubuntu@ip-172-30-1-55:~$ kubectl get pods
NAME                   READY   STATUS    RESTARTS   AGE
couchbase-rd44o        1/1     Running   0          31s
couchbase-x4cyu        1/1     Running   0          31s
k8s-master-127.0.0.1   3/3     Running   0          1m
```

Figure 9-43. *Listing the Pods*

To describe any particular Pod run the `kubectl describe` pod command, for example, the Pod `couchbase-rd44o` is described with the following command.

```
kubectl describe pod couchbase-rd44o
```

The Pod detail gets output as shown in Figure 9-44. The Pod label is listed as `run=couchbase`.

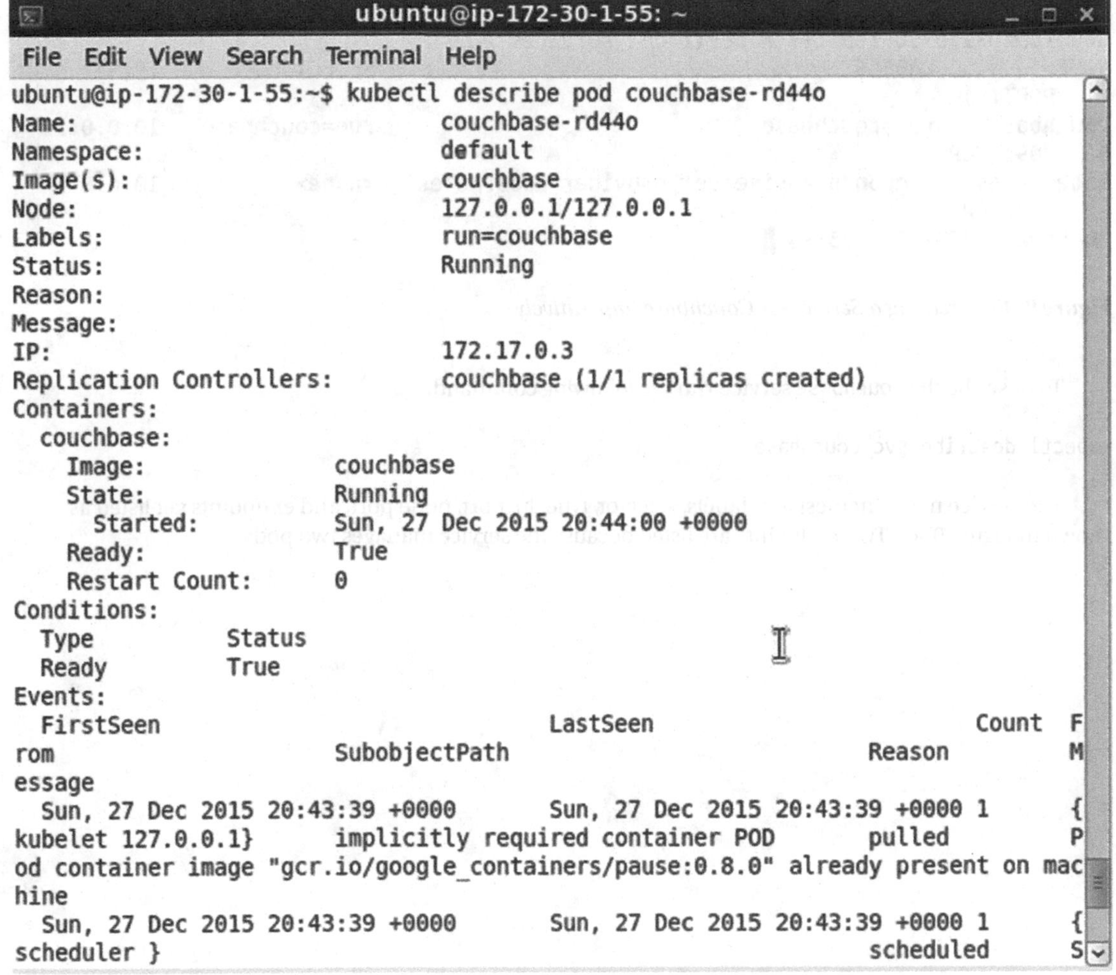

ubuntu@ip-172-30-1-55: ~
File Edit View Search Terminal Help
ubuntu@ip-172-30-1-55:~$ kubectl describe pod couchbase-rd44o
Name: couchbase-rd44o
Namespace: default
Image(s): couchbase
Node: 127.0.0.1/127.0.0.1
Labels: run=couchbase
Status: Running
Reason:
Message:
IP: 172.17.0.3
Replication Controllers: couchbase (1/1 replicas created)
Containers:
couchbase:
Image: couchbase
State: Running
Started: Sun, 27 Dec 2015 20:44:00 +0000
Ready: True
Restart Count: 0
Conditions:
Type Status
Ready True
Events:
FirstSeen LastSeen Count F
rom SubobjectPath Reason M
essage
Sun, 27 Dec 2015 20:43:39 +0000 Sun, 27 Dec 2015 20:43:39 +0000 1 {
kubelet 127.0.0.1} implicitly required container POD pulled P
od container image "gcr.io/google_containers/pause:0.8.0" already present on mac
hine
Sun, 27 Dec 2015 20:43:39 +0000 Sun, 27 Dec 2015 20:43:39 +0000 1 {
scheduler } scheduled S

Figure 9-44. *Describing a Pod*

Creating a Service

To create a service from the replication controller exposed at port 8091, run the following command, which also specified the service type.

```
kubectl expose rc couchbase --port=8091 --type=LoadBalancer
```

Subsequently list the services.

```
kubectl get services
```

The couchbase service gets created and listed as shown in Figure 9-45.

```
ubuntu@ip-172-30-1-55:~$ kubectl expose rc couchbase --port=8091 --type=LoadBala
ncer
NAME         LABELS           SELECTOR         IP(S)     PORT(S)
couchbase    run=couchbase    run=couchbase              8091/TCP
ubuntu@ip-172-30-1-55:~$ kubectl get services
NAME          LABELS                                    SELECTOR         IP(S)
    PORT(S)
couchbase     run=couchbase                             run=couchbase    10.0.0.23
8   8091/TCP
kubernetes    component=apiserver,provider=kubernetes   <none>           10.0.0.1
    443/TCP
ubuntu@ip-172-30-1-55:~$
```

Figure 9-45. *Creating a Service for Couchbase Imperatively*

To describe the couchbase service run the following command.

```
kubectl describe svc couchbase
```

The service name, namespace, labels, selector, type, Ip, port, node port, and endpoints get listed as shown in Figure 9-46. Two endpoints are listed because the service manages two pods.

```
ubuntu@ip-172-30-1-55:~$ kubectl describe svc couchbase
Name:                   couchbase
Namespace:              default
Labels:                 run=couchbase
Selector:               run=couchbase
Type:                   LoadBalancer
IP:                     10.0.0.238
Port:                   <unnamed>       8091/TCP
NodePort:               <unnamed>       32218/TCP
Endpoints:              172.17.0.2:8091,172.17.0.3:8091
Session Affinity:       None
No events.

ubuntu@ip-172-30-1-55:~$
```

Figure 9-46. *Describing a Service*

Scaling the Cluster

A Couchbase cluster may be scaled up or down using the Kubernetes cluster manager. For example, to scale down the replication controller called "couchbase" to 1 replica, run the following `kubectl scale` command.

```
kubectl scale rc couchbase --replicas=1
```

An output of "scaled" indicates that the rc has been scaled. But the "scaled" output does not always imply that the scaled number of replicas are running and ready. Run the following command to list the Pods.

```
kubectl get pods
```

A single Couchbase Pod gets listed as shown in Figure 9-47.

```
ubuntu@ip-172-30-1-55:~$ kubectl scale rc couchbase --replicas=1
scaled
ubuntu@ip-172-30-1-55:~$ kubectl get pods
NAME                     READY     STATUS    RESTARTS   AGE
couchbase-rd44o          1/1       Running   0          1m
k8s-master-127.0.0.1     3/3       Running   0          2m
```

Figure 9-47. *Scaling Down the Couchbase Cluster to a Single Pod*

Run the following command to list the replication controllers and the `couchbase` rc is listed with replicas as 1 as shown in Figure 9-48.

```
kubectl get rc
```

To scale the rc back to 2 Pods run the following command.

```
kubectl scale rc couchbase --replicas=2
```

Subsequently list the Pods.

```
kubectl get pods
```

Initially the new Pod to be added could be not running or not ready but after a few seconds two Pods get listed as running and ready as shown in Figure 9-48.

```
ubuntu@ip-172-30-1-55:~$ kubectl get rc
CONTROLLER   CONTAINER(S)   IMAGE(S)    SELECTOR        REPLICAS
couchbase    couchbase      couchbase   run=couchbase   1
ubuntu@ip-172-30-1-55:~$ kubectl scale rc couchbase --replicas=2
scaled
ubuntu@ip-172-30-1-55:~$ kubectl get pods
NAME                    READY     STATUS
    RESTARTS   AGE
couchbase-h1xm3         0/1       Image: couchbase is ready, container is creatin
g   0          10s
couchbase-rd44o         1/1       Running
    0          3m
k8s-master-127.0.0.1    3/3       Running
    0          4m
ubuntu@ip-172-30-1-55:~$ kubectl get pods
NAME                    READY     STATUS    RESTARTS   AGE
couchbase-h1xm3         1/1       Running   0          22s
couchbase-rd44o         1/1       Running   0          3m
k8s-master-127.0.0.1    3/3       Running   0          4m
ubuntu@ip-172-30-1-55:~$ █
```

Figure 9-48. *Scaling Up the Couchbase Cluster*

Keeping the Replication Level

The main purpose of a replication controller is to keep the number of replicas to the configured level. With 2 replicas configured in the couchbase rc the number of Pods is maintained at 2. As an example, delete one of the Pods.

```
kubectl delete pod couchbase-4z3hx
```

One pod gets deleted, but it takes the total number of pods to 1, which is below the number of configured replicas. As a result the replication controller starts a new replica. Subsequently list the pods.

```
kubectl get pods
```

Initially the new Pod could be not running and/or not ready but after a few seconds two pods are running and ready as shown in Figure 9-49.

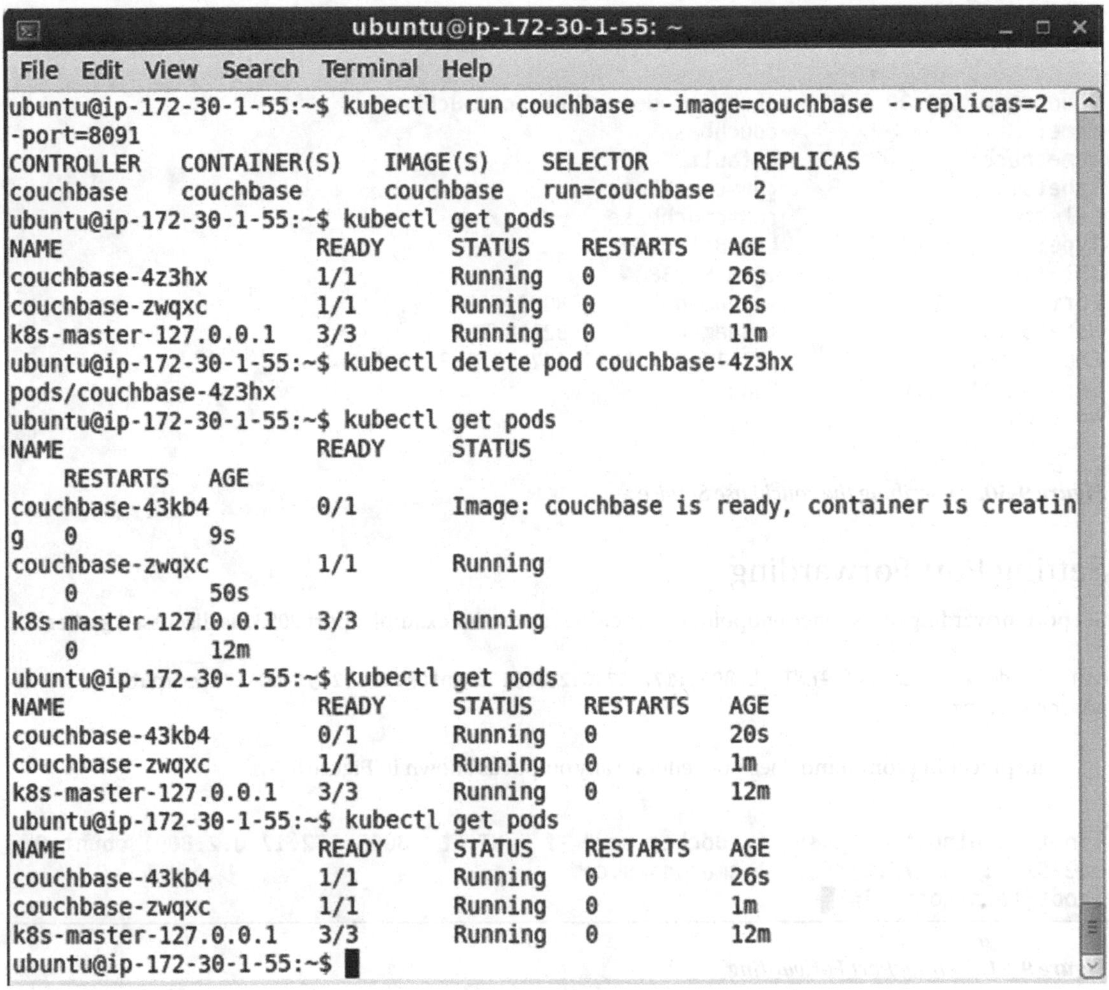

```
ubuntu@ip-172-30-1-55: ~
File  Edit  View  Search  Terminal  Help
ubuntu@ip-172-30-1-55:~$ kubectl  run couchbase --image=couchbase --replicas=2 -
-port=8091
CONTROLLER   CONTAINER(S)   IMAGE(S)    SELECTOR         REPLICAS
couchbase    couchbase      couchbase   run=couchbase    2
ubuntu@ip-172-30-1-55:~$ kubectl get pods
NAME                     READY      STATUS     RESTARTS   AGE
couchbase-4z3hx          1/1        Running    0          26s
couchbase-zwqxc          1/1        Running    0          26s
k8s-master-127.0.0.1     3/3        Running    0          11m
ubuntu@ip-172-30-1-55:~$ kubectl delete pod couchbase-4z3hx
pods/couchbase-4z3hx
ubuntu@ip-172-30-1-55:~$ kubectl get pods
NAME                     READY      STATUS
     RESTARTS   AGE
couchbase-43kb4          0/1        Image: couchbase is ready, container is creatin
g   0          9s
couchbase-zwqxc          1/1        Running
    0          50s
k8s-master-127.0.0.1     3/3        Running
    0          12m
ubuntu@ip-172-30-1-55:~$ kubectl get pods
NAME                     READY      STATUS     RESTARTS   AGE
couchbase-43kb4          0/1        Running    0          20s
couchbase-zwqxc          1/1        Running    0          1m
k8s-master-127.0.0.1     3/3        Running    0          12m
ubuntu@ip-172-30-1-55:~$ kubectl get pods
NAME                     READY      STATUS     RESTARTS   AGE
couchbase-43kb4          1/1        Running    0          26s
couchbase-zwqxc          1/1        Running    0          1m
k8s-master-127.0.0.1     3/3        Running    0          12m
ubuntu@ip-172-30-1-55:~$
```

Figure 9-49. *Running the kubectl get pods Command Multiple Times until all Pods are Running and Ready*

Describe the couchbase service.

```
kubectl describe svc couchbase
```

Two endpoints get listed as shown in Figure 9-50.

```
ubuntu@ip-172-30-1-55:~$ kubectl describe svc couchbase
Name:                   couchbase
Namespace:              default
Labels:                 run=couchbase
Selector:               run=couchbase
Type:                   LoadBalancer
IP:                     10.0.0.238
Port:                   <unnamed>       8091/TCP
NodePort:               <unnamed>       32218/TCP
Endpoints:              172.17.0.2:8091,172.17.0.3:8091
Session Affinity:       None
No events.
```

Figure 9-50. *Describing the couchbase Service*

Setting Port Forwarding

Set port forwarding of a service endpoint to a `localhost` port, for example, port 8095, as discussed earlier.

```
ssh -i "docker.pem" -f -nNT -L 8095:172.17.0.2:8091 ubuntu@ec2-52-91-80-177.compute-1.
amazonaws.com
```

The preceding command does not generate any output as shown in Figure 9-51.

```
[root@localhost ~]# ssh -i "docker.pem" -f -nNT -L  8095:172.17.0.2:8091 ubuntu@
ec2-52-91-80-177.compute-1.amazonaws.com
[root@localhost ~]# 
```

Figure 9-51. *Setting Port Forwarding*

Logging in to Couchbase Admin Console

Login to the Couchbase Web Console using the forwarded port on `localhost`.

```
http://localhost:8095/index.html
```

The Couchbase Web Console gets displayed as shown in Figure 9-52.

Figure 9-52. *Displaying the Couchbase Console*

Summary

In this chapter we used Kubernetes cluster manager to create a Couchbase cluster. We discussed both the declarative and imperative approaches. The declarative approach makes use of definition files and the imperative approach makes use of command-line configuration parameters. We demonstrated accessing the Couchbase Web Console from a localhost browser using port forwarding. We also used the cbtransfer tool in an interactive shell for a Docker container running Couchbase server. Docker image "couchbase" is used to create a Couchbase server. In the next chapter we shall discuss using Kubernetes cluster manager for an Apache Hadoop cluster.

PART IV

Apache Hadoop Ecosystem

CHAPTER 10

Using Apache Hadoop Ecosystem

Apache Hadoop has evolved to be the de facto framework for processing large quantities of data. Apache Hadoop ecosystem consists of a several projects including Apache Hive and Apache HBase. The Docker image "svds/cdh" is based on the latest CDH release and includes all the main frameworks in the Apache Hadoop ecosystem. All the frameworks such as Apache Hadoop, Apache Hive, and Apache HBase are installed in the same Docker image as a result facilitating development of applications that make use of multiple frameworks from the Apache Hadoop ecosystem. In this chapter we shall discuss using Kubernetes cluster manager to manage a cluster of Pods based on the svds/cdh image.

Setting the Environment

Creating an Apache Hadoop Cluster Declaratively

Creating an Apache Hadoop Cluster Imperatively

Setting the Environment

The following software is required to be installed for this chapter, which is the same as the software used in other chapters except for the Docker image.

-Docker Engine (latest version)

-Kubernetes Cluster Manager (version 1.01)

-Kubectl (version 1.01)

-Docker image svds/cdh (latest version)

Install the software as discussed in chapter 1 on an Ubuntu instance on Amazon EC2. SSH Login to the Ubuntu instance.

```
ssh -i "docker.pem" ubuntu@54.86.45.173
```

Start the Docker engine with the following command.

```
sudo service docker start
```

Subsequently run the following command to verify the status of Docker.

```
sudo service docker status
```


D. Vohra, *Kubernetes Microservices with Docker*, DOI 10.1007/978-1-4842-1907-2_10

As shown in Figure 10-1, Docker should be listed as "running."

```
ubuntu@ip-172-30-1-45:~$ sudo service docker status
docker start/running, process 3296
ubuntu@ip-172-30-1-45:~$
```

Figure 10-1. *Starting Docker*

List the services with the following command.

```
kubectl get services
```

The `kubernetes` service should be listed as running as shown in Figure 10-2.

```
ubuntu@ip-172-30-1-45:~$ kubectl get services
NAME          LABELS                                      SELECTOR    IP(S)       POR
T(S)
kubernetes    component=apiserver,provider=kubernetes     <none>      10.0.0.1    443
/TCP
ubuntu@ip-172-30-1-45:~$
```

Figure 10-2. *Listing the "kubernetes" Service*

List the Pods with the following command.

```
kubectl get pods
```

List the nodes with the following command.

```
kubectl get nodes
```

The only Pod that gets listed is for Kubernetes as shown in Figure 10-3. The node 127.0.0.1 also gets listed.

```
ubuntu@ip-172-30-1-45:~$ kubectl get pods
NAME                     READY     STATUS     RESTARTS    AGE
k8s-master-127.0.0.1     3/3       Running    0           19m
ubuntu@ip-172-30-1-45:~$ kubectl get nodes
NAME         LABELS                                STATUS
127.0.0.1    kubernetes.io/hostname=127.0.0.1      Ready
ubuntu@ip-172-30-1-45:~$
```

Figure 10-3. *Listing the Pod and Node for Kubernetes*

Creating an Apache Hadoop Cluster Declaratively

In the following subsections we shall create a Kubernetes service and a Kubernetes replication controller declaratively using definition files. A service is the external interface for Pods and routes client requests to one of the Pods. A replication controller manages the replication level of the Pods and maintains the number of replicas to the specified value in the definition file. The replication controller is also used to scale the cluster of Pods.

Creating a Service

To run a service for the CDH Pods create a service definition file `cdh-service.yaml` and add the following (Table 10-1) fields to the definition file.

Table 10-1. *Service Definition File Fields*

Field	Description	Value	Required Field (including defaults)
apiVersion		v1	yes
kind	The kind of definition file.	Service	yes
metadata	The service metadata.		yes
metadata -> labels	The service labels.	app: cdh	no
metadata -> name	The service name.	cdh	yes
spec	The service specification.		yes
spec -> ports	The ports exposed by the service.		yes
spec -> ports -> port	A port exposed by the service. The 50010 port is for the DataNode.	50010	
spec -> ports -> port	Another port exposed by the service. The 8020 port is for the NameNode.	8020	
spec -> selector	The Pod selector. Service routes traffic to the Pods with a label matching the selector expression.	app: cdh	yes
spec -> selector -> type	The service type.	LoadBalancer	no

The service definition file `cdh-service.yaml` is listed:

```
apiVersion: v1
kind: Service
metadata:
  labels:
    app: cdh
  name: cdh
spec:
  ports:
    -
      port: 50010
    -
      port: 8020
  selector:
    app: cdh
  type: LoadBalancer
```

The service definition file may be created and saved in the vi editor as shown in Figure 10-4.

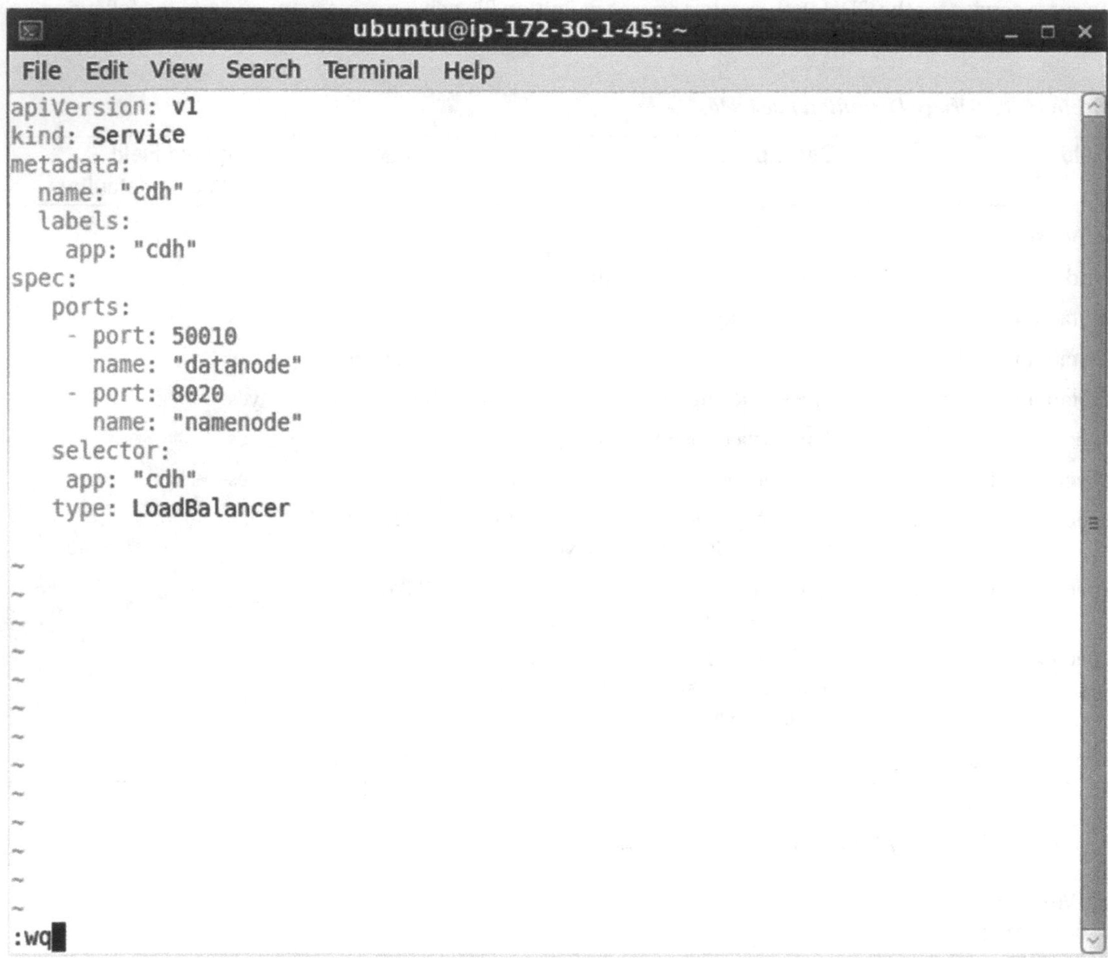

Figure 10-4. *Service Definition File in vi Editor*

Create a service from the definition file with the following command.

```
kubectl create -f cdh-service.yaml
```

Subsequently list the services.

```
kubectl get services
```

An output of "services/cdh" from the first command indicates that the service has been created as shown in Figure 10-5. The second command lists the service called "cdh." The service selector is listed as app=cdh in the SELECTOR column.

```
ubuntu@ip-172-30-1-45:~$ kubectl create -f cdh-service.yaml
services/cdh
ubuntu@ip-172-30-1-45:~$ kubectl get services
NAME          LABELS                                    SELECTOR    IP(S)        P
ORT(S)
cdh           app=cdh                                   app=cdh     10.0.0.109   5
0010/TCP
                                                                                 8
020/TCP
kubernetes    component=apiserver,provider=kubernetes   <none>      10.0.0.1     4
43/TCP
```

Figure 10-5. *Creating a Service from a Definition File*

Creating a Replication Controller

In this section we shall create a replication controller using a definition file. Create a cdh-rc.yaml file and add the following (Table 10-2) fields to the file.

Table 10-2. *Replication Controller Definition File Fields*

Field	Description	Value
apiVersion		v1
kind	The kind of definition file.	ReplicationController
metadata	The replication controller metadata.	
metadata - > labels	The replication controller labels.	app: cdh
metadata - > name	The replication controller name.	cdh-rc
spec	The replication controller specification.	
spec - > replicas	The number of Pod replicas.	2
spec - > selector	Selector key:value expression/s for selecting the Pods to manage. Pods with label/s the same as the selector expression/s are managed by the replication controller. For a single selector expression the selector expression must be the same as a spec - > template - > metadata - > labels label. The selector defaults to the spec - > template - > metadata - > labels if not specified.	Not set. Defaults to the same value as the key:value pairs in spec - > template - > metadata - > labels.
spec - > template	The Pod template.	
spec - > template- > metadata	The Pod template metadata.	
spec - > template- > metadata- > labels	The Pod template labels.	app: cdh name: cdh
spec - > template - > spec	The Pod template specification	

(*continued*)

Table 10-2. (*continuted*)

Field	Description	Value
spec -> template ->spec->containers	The containers configuration for the Pod template	
spec -> template ->spec->containers -> image	The Docker image	svds/cdh
spec -> template -> spec -> containers -> name	The container name	cdh

The definition file for the replication controller, cdh-rc.yaml, is listed.

```
apiVersion: v1
kind: ReplicationController
metadata:
  labels:
    app: cdh
  name: cdh-rc
spec:
  replicas: 2
  template:
    metadata:
      labels:
      app: cdh
      name: cdh
    spec:
      containers:
      image: svds/cdh
      name: cdh
```

Run the following command to create a replication controller from the definition file.

```
kubectl create -f cdh-rc.yaml
```

List the replication controllers.

```
kubectl get rc
```

The first command outputs "replicationcontrollers/cdh," which implies that an rc has been created successfully. The second command lists the replication controllers. The replication controller "cdh" gets listed as shown in Figure 10-6. The SELECTOR was not specified in the replication controller file and is listed as the same two key:value pairs, app=cdh,name=cdh, as the template labels. A Pod managed by the replication controller must include both of these labels, and may include additional labels. The number of replicas is set to 2.

```
ubuntu@ip-172-30-1-45:~$ kubectl create -f  cdh-rc.yaml
replicationcontrollers/cdh
ubuntu@ip-172-30-1-45:~$ kubectl get rc
CONTROLLER   CONTAINER(S)   IMAGE(S)    SELECTOR              REPLICAS
cdh          cdh            svds/cdh    app=cdh,name=cdh      2
ubuntu@ip-172-30-1-45:~$
```

***Figure 10-6.** Creating a Replication Controller from a Definition File*

Listing the Pods

To list the Pods run the following command.

```
kubectl get pods
```

Two Pods get listed as shown in Figure 10-7. Initially the Pods could be listed as not running or/and not ready. A not ready pod is indicated by the 0/1 value in the READY column, which implies that 0 of 1 containers in the Pod are rready.

```
ubuntu@ip-172-30-1-45:~$ kubectl get pods
NAME                    READY     STATUS                                   REST
ARTS    AGE
cdh-6l2pr               0/1       Image: svds/cdh is not ready on the node   0
        38s
cdh-xka62               0/1       Image: svds/cdh is not ready on the node   0
        38s
k8s-master-127.0.0.1    3/3       Running                                    0
        26m
ubuntu@ip-172-30-1-45:~$ kubectl get pods
NAME                    READY     STATUS                                   REST
ARTS    AGE
cdh-6l2pr               0/1       Image: svds/cdh is not ready on the node   0
        42s
cdh-xka62               0/1       Image: svds/cdh is not ready on the node   0
        42s
```

***Figure 10-7.** Listing the Pods for CDH, created but not Ready*

Run the same command again to list the Pods.

```
kubectl get pods
```

The two Pods should get listed as STATUS->Running and READY->1/1 as shown in Figure 10-8.

```
ubuntu@ip-172-30-1-45:~$ kubectl get pods
NAME                    READY     STATUS    RESTARTS   AGE
cdh-6l2pr               1/1       Running   0          2m
cdh-xka62               1/1       Running   0          2m
k8s-master-127.0.0.1    3/3       Running   0          27m
ubuntu@ip-172-30-1-45:~$
```

Figure 10-8. *Listing the Pods as Ready*

Listing Logs

To list the logs for a particular Pod, for example, the cdh-612pr Pod, run the following command.

```
kubectl logs cdh-612pr
```

The output from the command lists the logs, which indicate that the Hadoop datanode, namenode, secondarynamenode, resourcemanager, and nodemanager have been started as shown in Figure 10-9.

```
ubuntu@ip-172-30-1-45: ~
File Edit View Search Terminal Help
ubuntu@ip-172-30-1-45:~$ kubectl logs cdh-6l2pr
Start HDFS
starting datanode, logging to /var/log/hadoop-hdfs/hadoop-hdfs-datanode-cdh-6l2p
r.out
 * Started Hadoop datanode (hadoop-hdfs-datanode):
starting namenode, logging to /var/log/hadoop-hdfs/hadoop-hdfs-namenode-cdh-6l2p
r.out
 * Started Hadoop namenode:
starting secondarynamenode, logging to /var/log/hadoop-hdfs/hadoop-hdfs-secondar
ynamenode-cdh-6l2pr.out
 * Started Hadoop secondarynamenode:
Start Yarn
starting resourcemanager, logging to /var/log/hadoop-yarn/yarn-yarn-resourcemana
ger-cdh-6l2pr.out
 * Started Hadoop resourcemanager:
starting nodemanager, logging to /var/log/hadoop-yarn/yarn-yarn-nodemanager-cdh-
6l2pr.out
 * Started Hadoop nodemanager:
chown: changing ownership of '/var/log/hadoop-mapreduce': Operation not permitte
d
starting historyserver, logging to /var/log/hadoop-mapreduce/mapred-mapred-histo
ryserver-cdh-6l2pr.out
15/12/21 16:20:36 INFO hs.JobHistoryServer: STARTUP_MSG:
/************************************************************
STARTUP_MSG: Starting JobHistoryServer
STARTUP_MSG:   host = cdh-6l2pr/172.17.0.3
STARTUP_MSG:   args = []
STARTUP_MSG:   version = 2.6.0-cdh5.4.7
STARTUP_MSG:   classpath = /etc/hadoop/conf:/usr/lib/hadoop/lib/aws-java-sdk-1.7
.14.jar:/usr/lib/hadoop/lib/jets3t-0.9.0.jar:/usr/lib/hadoop/lib/guava-11.0.2.ja
```

Figure 10-9. *Listing Pod Logs*

Other components such as HBase are also started.

Scaling a Cluster

Initially the CDH cluster has 2 replicas. To scale the replicas to 4 run the following command.

```
kubectl scale rc cdh --replicas=4
```

Subsequently list the Pods in the cluster.

```
kubectl get pods
```

After scaling up the cluster 4 Pods get listed instead of the 2 listed initially. Some of the Pods could be listed as not running or not ready. Run the preceding command after a few seconds periodically, and all the pods should get started as shown in Figure 10-10.

```
ubuntu@ip-172-30-1-45: ~
File  Edit  View  Search  Terminal  Help
exit
ubuntu@ip-172-30-1-45:~$ kubectl scale rc cdh --replicas=4
scaled
ubuntu@ip-172-30-1-45:~$ kubectl get pods
NAME                   READY   STATUS    RESTARTS   AGE
cdh-4q74m              0/1     Running   0          11s
cdh-6l2pr              1/1     Running   0          54m
cdh-itpi0              1/1     Running   0          11s
cdh-xka62              1/1     Running   0          54m
k8s-master-127.0.0.1   3/3     Running   0          1h
ubuntu@ip-172-30-1-45:~$ kubectl get pods
NAME                   READY   STATUS    RESTARTS   AGE
cdh-4q74m              0/1     Running   0          15s
cdh-6l2pr              1/1     Running   0          54m
cdh-itpi0              1/1     Running   0          15s
cdh-xka62              1/1     Running   0          54m
k8s-master-127.0.0.1   3/3     Running   0          1h
ubuntu@ip-172-30-1-45:~$ kubectl get pods
NAME                   READY   STATUS    RESTARTS   AGE
cdh-4q74m              1/1     Running   0          26s
cdh-6l2pr              1/1     Running   0          54m
cdh-itpi0              1/1     Running   0          26s
cdh-xka62              1/1     Running   0          54m
k8s-master-127.0.0.1   3/3     Running   0          1h
ubuntu@ip-172-30-1-45:~$
```

Figure 10-10. *Scaling the Pod Cluster*

Starting an Interactive Shell

As the "svds/cdh" Docker image is based on the Linux "ubuntu" Docker image an interactive bash shell may be started to access Docker containers based on the svds/cdh Docker image. To start an interactive bash shell for the cdh software we need to obtain the container id for a Docker container running the "cdh" image as shown in Figure 10-11.

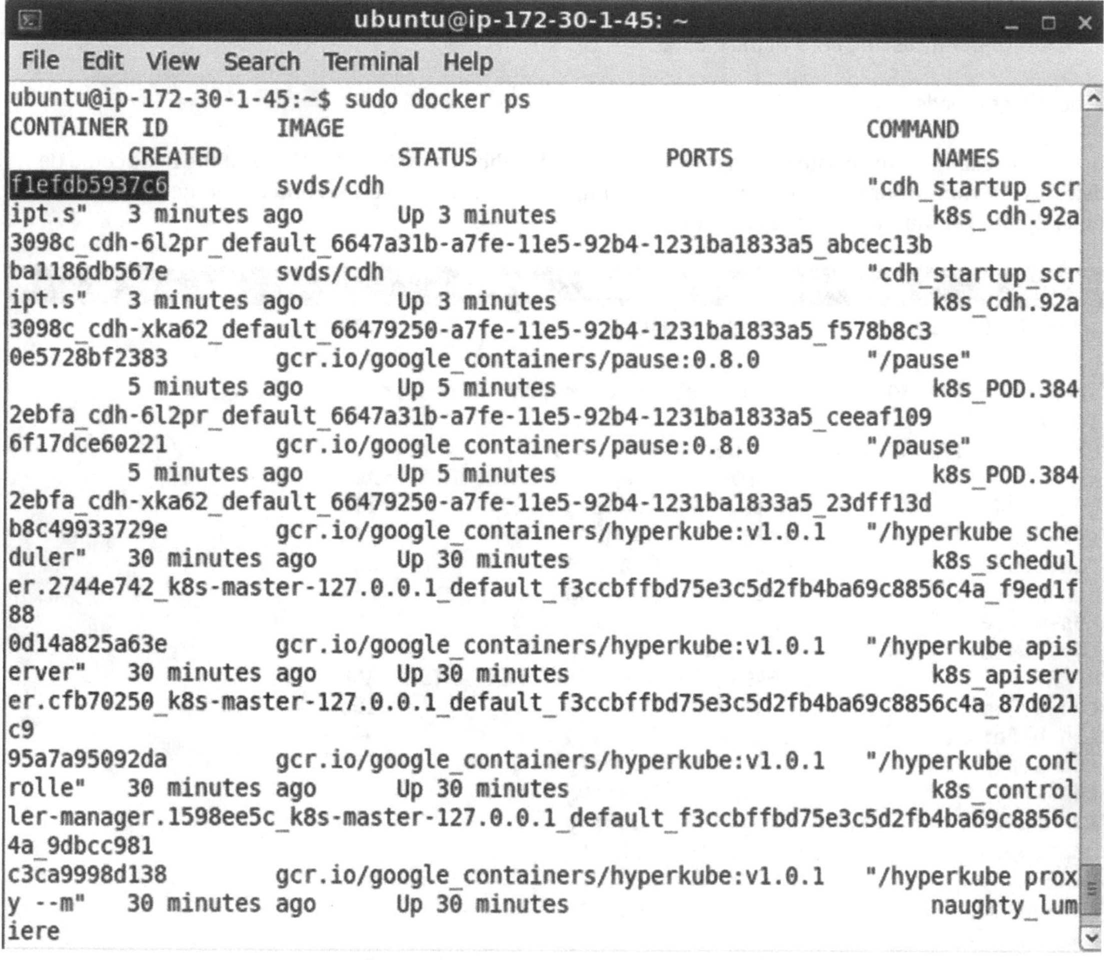

Figure 10-11. *Copying the Docker Container Id*

Subsequently start the interactive shell using the container id.

```
sudo docker exec -it f1efdb5937c6 bash
```

The interactive shell gets started as shown in Figure 10-12.

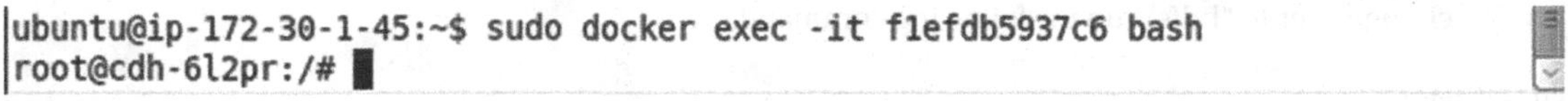

```
ubuntu@ip-172-30-1-45:~$ sudo docker exec -it f1efdb5937c6 bash
root@cdh-6l2pr:/# 
```

Figure 10-12. *Starting an Interactive Shell*

Running a MapReduce Application

In this section we shall run an example MapReduce application in the interactive shell. The `hdfs` command is used to run a MapReduce application. Invoke the `hdfs` command in the interactive shell.

```
hdfs
```

The command usage should get displayed as shown in Figure 10-13.

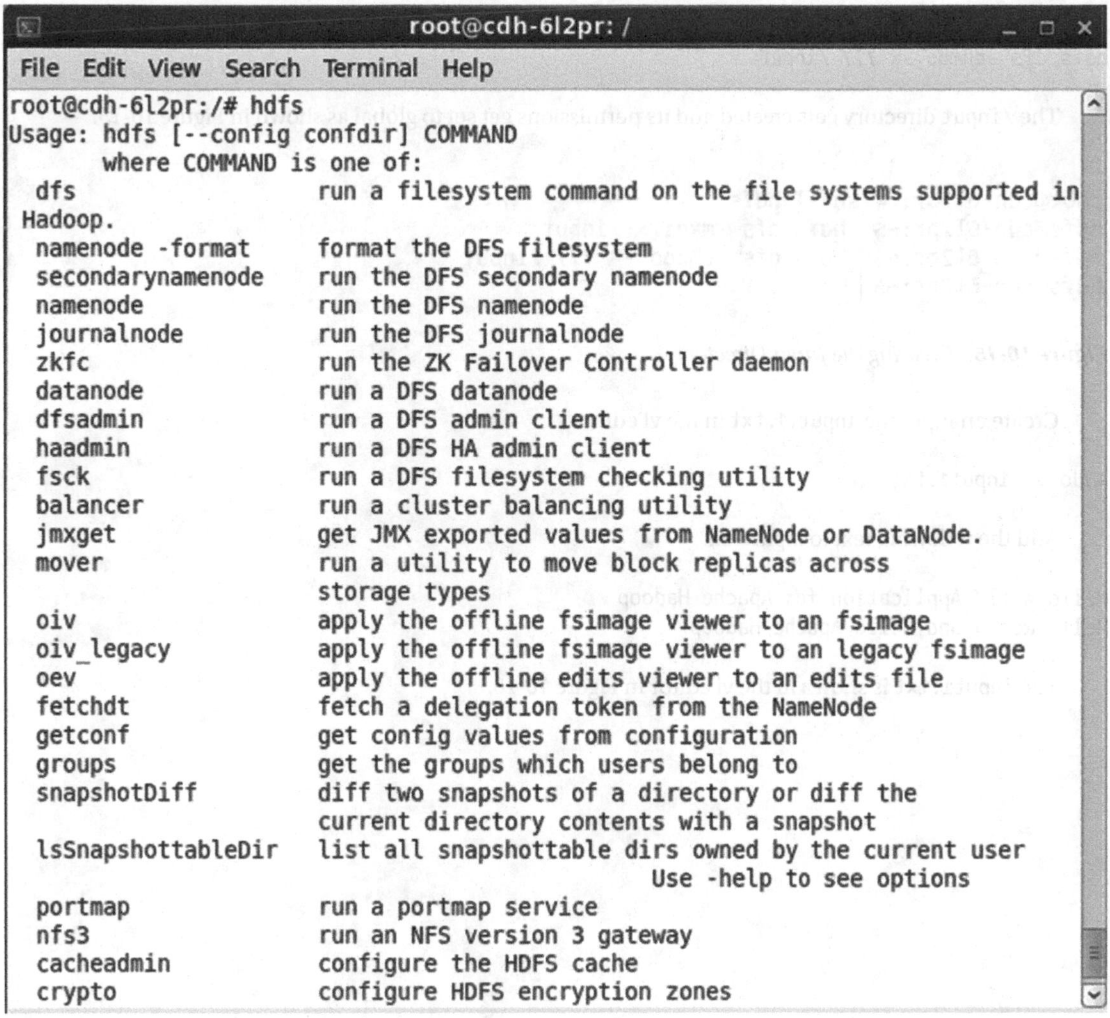

```
root@cdh-6l2pr: /
File  Edit  View  Search  Terminal  Help
root@cdh-6l2pr:/# hdfs
Usage: hdfs [--config confdir] COMMAND
       where COMMAND is one of:
  dfs                  run a filesystem command on the file systems supported in
 Hadoop.
  namenode -format     format the DFS filesystem
  secondarynamenode    run the DFS secondary namenode
  namenode             run the DFS namenode
  journalnode          run the DFS journalnode
  zkfc                 run the ZK Failover Controller daemon
  datanode             run a DFS datanode
  dfsadmin             run a DFS admin client
  haadmin              run a DFS HA admin client
  fsck                 run a DFS filesystem checking utility
  balancer             run a cluster balancing utility
  jmxget               get JMX exported values from NameNode or DataNode.
  mover                run a utility to move block replicas across
                       storage types
  oiv                  apply the offline fsimage viewer to an fsimage
  oiv_legacy           apply the offline fsimage viewer to an legacy fsimage
  oev                  apply the offline edits viewer to an edits file
  fetchdt              fetch a delegation token from the NameNode
  getconf              get config values from configuration
  groups               get the groups which users belong to
  snapshotDiff         diff two snapshots of a directory or diff the
                       current directory contents with a snapshot
  lsSnapshottableDir   list all snapshottable dirs owned by the current user
                                                Use -help to see options
  portmap              run a portmap service
  nfs3                 run an NFS version 3 gateway
  cacheadmin           configure the HDFS cache
  crypto               configure HDFS encryption zones
```

Figure 10-13. *Command Usage for hdfs Command*

To change user to "hdfs" run the following command.

```
su -l hdfs
```

The user becomes "hdfs" as shown in Figure 10-14.

```
root@cdh-6l2pr:/# su -l hdfs
hdfs@cdh-6l2pr:~$
```

Figure 10-14. *Setting User as hdfs*

Next, we shall run a `wordcount` application. We shall get input from the `/input` directory files and output in the `/output` directory. Create the `/input` directory and set its permissions to global (777).

```
hdfs dfs -mkdir /input
hdfs dfs -chmod -R 777 /input
```

The `/input` directory gets created and its permissions get set to global as shown in Figure 10-15.

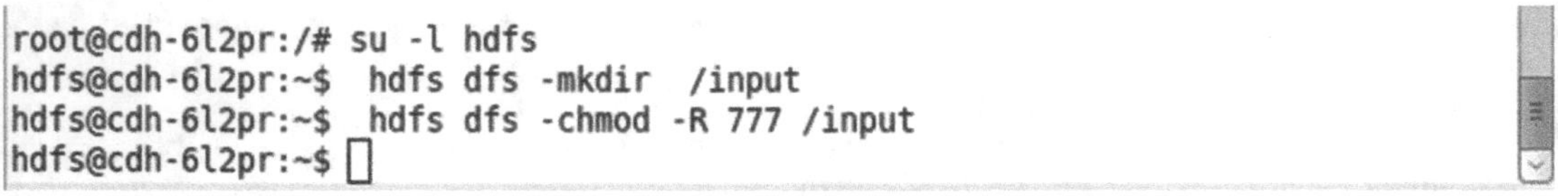

```
root@cdh-6l2pr:/# su -l hdfs
hdfs@cdh-6l2pr:~$  hdfs dfs -mkdir  /input
hdfs@cdh-6l2pr:~$  hdfs dfs -chmod -R 777 /input
hdfs@cdh-6l2pr:~$
```

Figure 10-15. *Creating the Input Directory*

Create an input file `input.1.txt` in the vi editor.

```
sudo vi input1.txt
```

Add the following text to input1.txt.

```
Hello World Application for Apache Hadoop
Hello World and Hello Apache Hadoop
```

The `input1.txt` is shown in the vi editor in Figure 10-16.

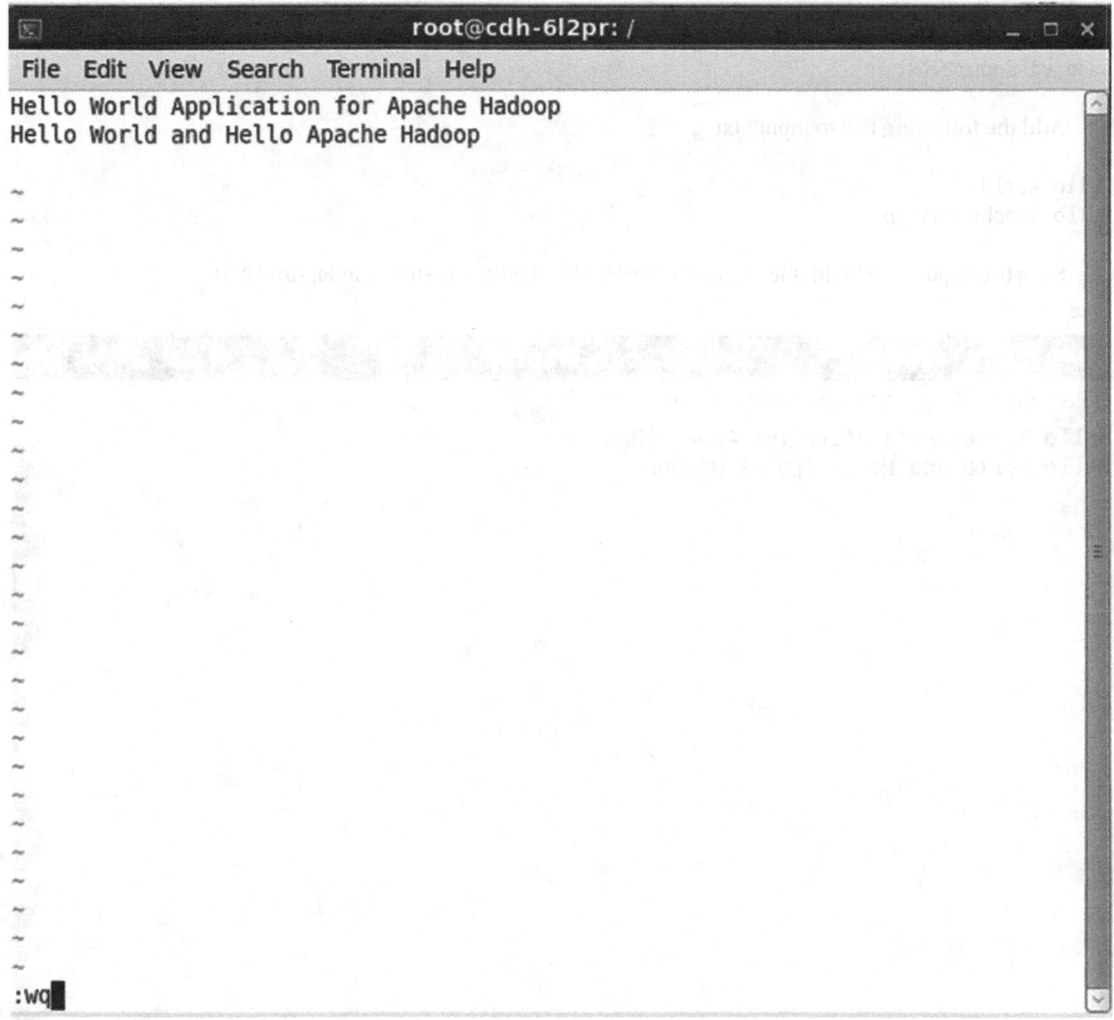

Figure 10-16. *Creating an Input Text File*

Put the `input1.txt` in the HDFS directory `/input` with the following command, which should be run with `sudo -u hdfs` if run as `root` user. If the user is already set to "hdfs" omit the "sudo -u hdfs" from the command.

```
sudo -u hdfs hdfs dfs -put input1.txt /input
```

The `input1.txt` file gets added to the `/input` directory and no output is generated from the command as shown in Figure 10-17.

```
root@cdh-6l2pr:/# sudo  vi input1.txt
root@cdh-6l2pr:/# sudo -u hdfs hdfs dfs -put input1.txt /input
root@cdh-6l2pr:/# 
```

Figure 10-17. *Putting the Input Text File in HDFS*

Similarly create another file input2.txt.

```
sudo vi input2.txt
```

Add the following text to input2.txt.

```
Hello World
Hello Apache Hadoop
```

Save the `input2.txt` with the :wq command in the vi editor as shown in Figure 10-18.

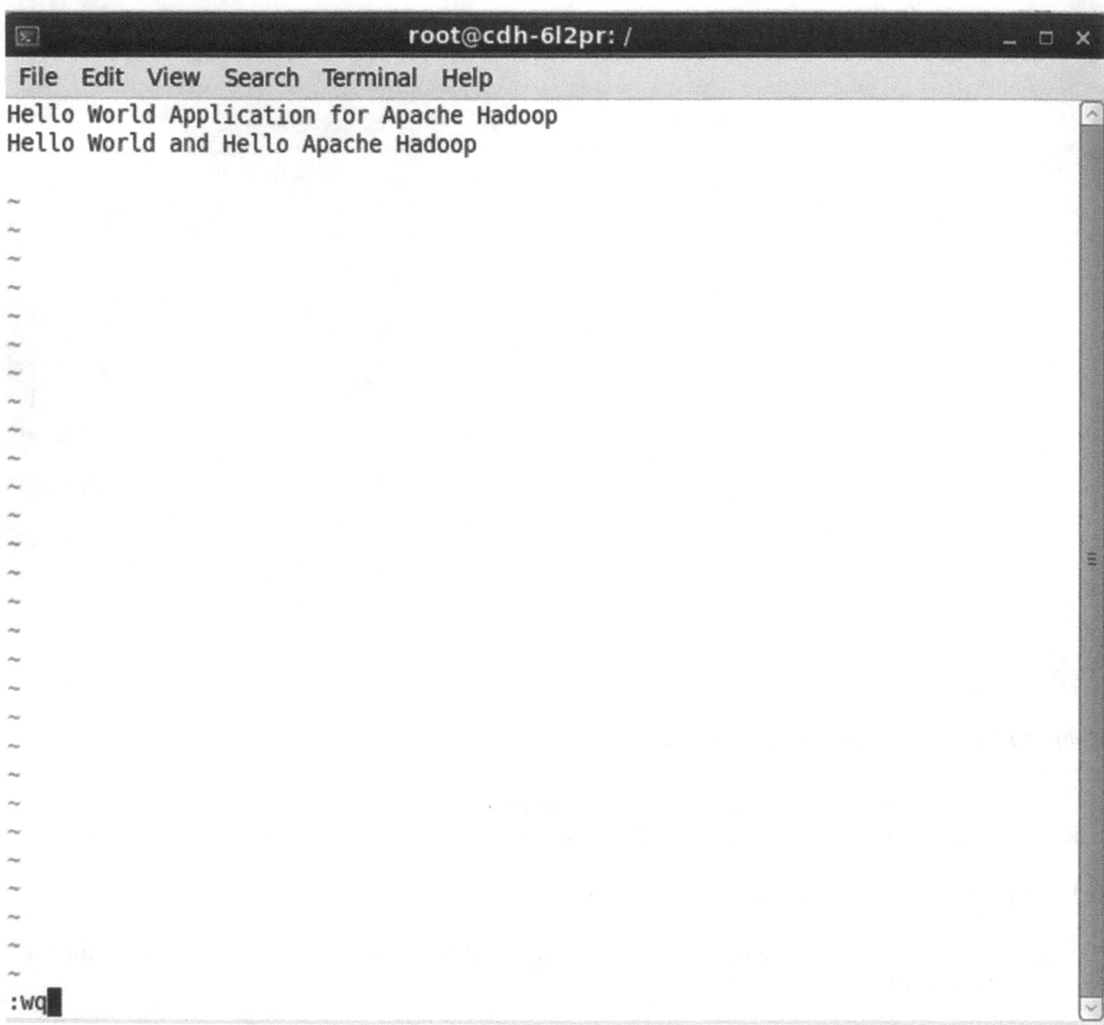

Figure 10-18. *Creating another Text File input2.txt*

Put the `input2.txt` into the `/input` directory.

```
sudo -u hdfs hdfs dfs -put input2.txt /input
```

The `input2.txt` also gets added to the `/input` directory as shown in Figure 10-19.

```
root@cdh-6l2pr:/# sudo  vi input1.txt
root@cdh-6l2pr:/# sudo -u hdfs hdfs dfs -put input1.txt /input
root@cdh-6l2pr:/# sudo vi input2.txt
root@cdh-6l2pr:/# sudo -u hdfs hdfs dfs -put input2.txt /input
```

Figure 10-19. *Putting the input2.txt File into HDFS*

The files in the `/input` directory in the HDFS may be listed with the following command.

```
hdfs dfs -ls /input
```

The two files added `input1.txt` and `input2.txt` get listed as shown in Figure 10-20.

```
root@cdh-6l2pr:/# hdfs dfs -ls /input
Found 2 items
-rw-r--r--   1 hdfs supergroup          79 2015-12-21 16:35 /input/input1.txt
-rw-r--r--   1 hdfs supergroup          32 2015-12-21 16:36 /input/input2.txt
```

Figure 10-20. *Listing the Files in HDFS*

Next, run the `wordcount` example application with the following command in which the jar file containing the example application is specified with the jar parameter and the `/input` and `/output` directories are set as the last two command parameters for the input directory and the output directory respectively.

```
sudo -u hdfs hadoop jar /usr/lib/hadoop-mapreduce/hadoop-mapreduce-examples-2.6.0-
cdh5.4.7.jar wordcount /input /output
```

A MapReduce job gets started as shown in Figure 10-21.

```
root@cdh-6l2pr:/# sudo -u hdfs hadoop jar /usr/lib/hadoop-mapreduce/hadoop-mapre
duce-examples-2.6.0-cdh5.4.7.jar wordcount  /input /output
15/12/21 16:39:52 INFO client.RMProxy: Connecting to ResourceManager at /0.0.0.0
:8032
15/12/21 16:39:53 INFO input.FileInputFormat: Total input paths to process : 2
15/12/21 16:39:53 INFO mapreduce.JobSubmitter: number of splits:2
15/12/21 16:39:53 INFO mapreduce.JobSubmitter: Submitting tokens for job: job_14
50714825612_0002
15/12/21 16:39:53 INFO impl.YarnClientImpl: Submitted application application_14
50714825612_0002
15/12/21 16:39:53 INFO mapreduce.Job: The url to track the job: http://cdh-6l2pr
:8088/proxy/application_1450714825612_0002/
15/12/21 16:39:53 INFO mapreduce.Job: Running job: job_1450714825612_0002
15/12/21 16:39:59 INFO mapreduce.Job: Job job_1450714825612_0002 running in uber
 mode : false
15/12/21 16:39:59 INFO mapreduce.Job:  map 0% reduce 0%
```

Figure 10-21. *Starting a YARN Application for Word Count Example*

The MapReduce job completes to run the `wordcount` application. The output from the `wordcount` MapReduce job, not the word count result, is shown in Figure 10-22.

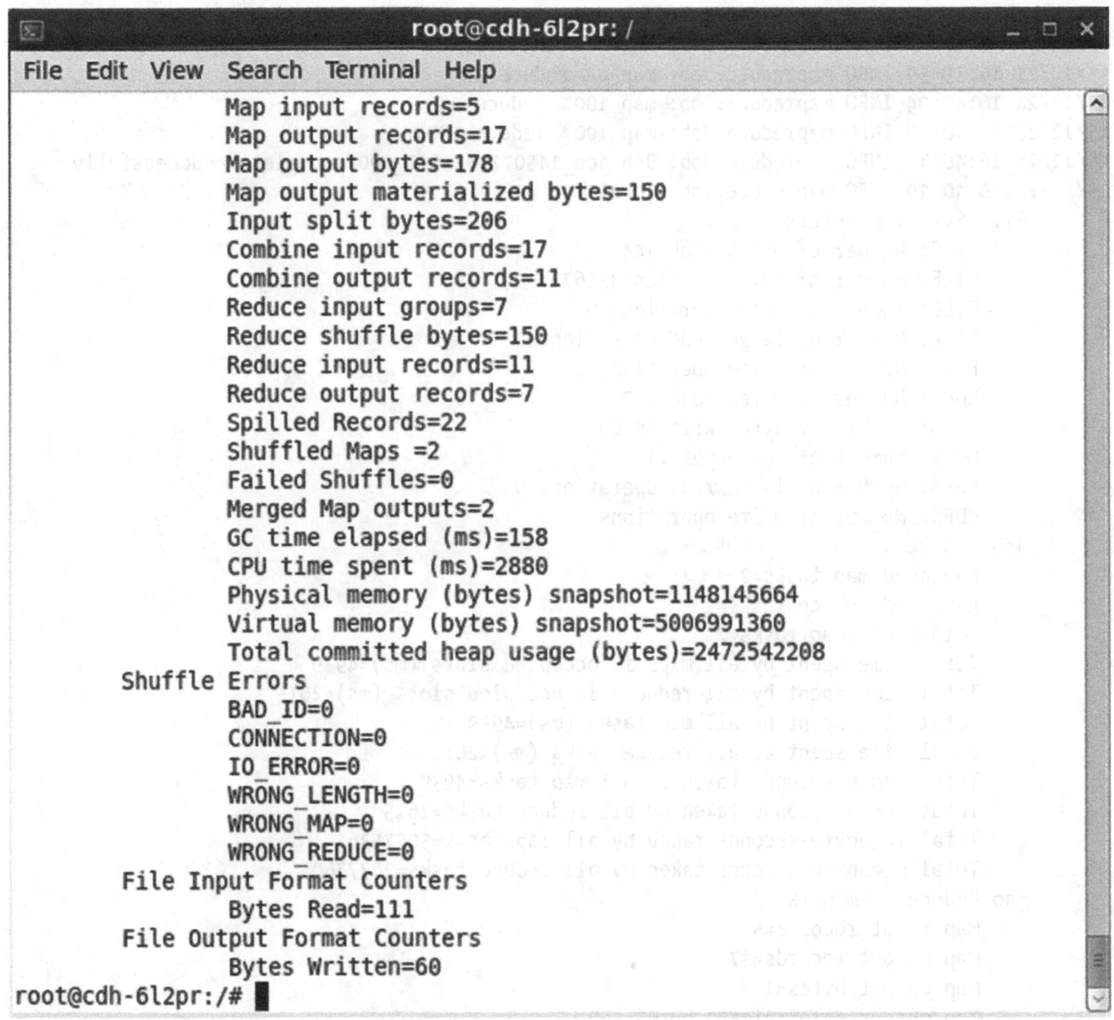

Figure 10-22. *Output from the MapReduce Job*

A more detailed output from the MapReduce application is listed:

```
root@cdh-6l2pr:/# sudo -u hdfs hadoop jar /usr/lib/hadoop-mapreduce/hadoop-mapreduce-
examples-2.6.0-cdh5.4.7.jar wordcount /input /output
15/12/21 16:39:52 INFO client.RMProxy: Connecting to ResourceManager at /0.0.0.0:8032
15/12/21 16:39:53 INFO input.FileInputFormat: Total input paths to process : 2
15/12/21 16:39:53 INFO mapreduce.JobSubmitter: number of splits:2
15/12/21 16:39:53 INFO mapreduce.JobSubmitter: Submitting tokens for job:
job_1450714825612_0002
15/12/21 16:39:53 INFO impl.YarnClientImpl: Submitted application
application_1450714825612_0002
15/12/21 16:39:53 INFO mapreduce.Job: The url to track the job: http://cdh-6l2pr:8088/proxy/
application_1450714825612_0002/
15/12/21 16:39:53 INFO mapreduce.Job: Running job: job_1450714825612_0002
```

```
15/12/21 16:39:59 INFO mapreduce.Job: Job job_1450714825612_0002 running in uber mode :
false
15/12/21 16:39:59 INFO mapreduce.Job:  map 0% reduce 0%
15/12/21 16:40:04 INFO mapreduce.Job:  map 100% reduce 0%
15/12/21 16:40:10 INFO mapreduce.Job:  map 100% reduce 100%
15/12/21 16:40:10 INFO mapreduce.Job: Job job_1450714825612_0002 completed successfully
15/12/21 16:40:10 INFO mapreduce.Job: Counters: 49
        File System Counters
            FILE: Number of bytes read=144
            FILE: Number of bytes written=332672
            FILE: Number of read operations=0
            FILE: Number of large read operations=0
            FILE: Number of write operations=0
            HDFS: Number of bytes read=317
            HDFS: Number of bytes written=60
            HDFS: Number of read operations=9
            HDFS: Number of large read operations=0
            HDFS: Number of write operations=2
        Job Counters
            Launched map tasks=2
            Launched reduce tasks=1
            Data-local map tasks=2
            Total time spent by all maps in occupied slots (ms)=4939
            Total time spent by all reduces in occupied slots (ms)=2615
            Total time spent by all map tasks (ms)=4939
            Total time spent by all reduce tasks (ms)=2615
            Total vcore-seconds taken by all map tasks=4939
            Total vcore-seconds taken by all reduce tasks=2615
            Total megabyte-seconds taken by all map tasks=5057536
            Total megabyte-seconds taken by all reduce tasks=2677760
        Map-Reduce Framework
            Map input records=5
            Map output records=17
            Map output bytes=178
            Map output materialized bytes=150
            Input split bytes=206
            Combine input records=17
            Combine output records=11
            Reduce input groups=7
            Reduce shuffle bytes=150
            Reduce input records=11
            Reduce output records=7
            Spilled Records=22
            Shuffled Maps =2
            Failed Shuffles=0
            Merged Map outputs=2
            GC time elapsed (ms)=158
            CPU time spent (ms)=2880
            Physical memory (bytes) snapshot=1148145664
            Virtual memory (bytes) snapshot=5006991360
            Total committed heap usage (bytes)=2472542208
```

```
        Shuffle Errors
                BAD_ID=0
                CONNECTION=0
                IO_ERROR=0
                WRONG_LENGTH=0
                WRONG_MAP=0
                WRONG_REDUCE=0
        File Input Format Counters
                Bytes Read=111
        File Output Format Counters
                Bytes Written=60
root@cdh-6l2pr:/#
```

Subsequently, list the files in the /output directory.

```
bin/hdfs dfs -ls /output
```

Two files get listed: _SUCCESS and part-r-00000 as shown in Figure 10-23. The _SUCCESS file is to indicate that the MapReduce command completed successfully and the part-r-00000 command contains the result of the word count.

```
root@cdh-6l2pr:/# hdfs dfs -ls  /output
Found 2 items
-rw-r--r--   1 hdfs supergroup          0 2015-12-21 16:40 /output/_SUCCESS
-rw-r--r--   1 hdfs supergroup         60 2015-12-21 16:40 /output/part-r-00000
root@cdh-6l2pr:/#
```

Figure 10-23. *Listing the Files generated by the MapReduce Job*

To list the result of the wordcount application run the following command.

```
hdfs dfs -cat /output/part-r-00000
```

The word count for each of the words in the input gets listed as shown in Figure 10-24.

```
root@cdh-6l2pr:/# sudo -u hdfs hdfs dfs -cat /output/part-r-00000
Apache  3
Application     1
Hadoop  3
Hello   5
World   3
and     1
for     1
root@cdh-6l2pr:/#
```

Figure 10-24. *The Word Count for the Input Files*

Running Hive

Apache Hive is a data warehouse framework for storing, managing, and querying large data sets in HDFS. As mentioned before all/most of the components of CDH get installed when the `svds/cdh` image is run. In this section we shall test the Apache Hive framework. The Hive configuration directory is in the Hive `conf` directory, in the `/etc/hive` directory. Change directory (cd) to the `/etc/hive` directory.

```
cd /etc/hive
```

The `conf` directory gets listed as shown in Figure 10-25.

```
root@cdh-6l2pr:/# cd /etc/hive
root@cdh-6l2pr:/etc/hive# ls -l
total 4
lrwxrwxrwx 1 root root   27 Oct 23 15:46 conf -> /etc/alternatives/hive-conf
drwxr-xr-x 2 root root 4096 Oct 23 15:46 conf.dist
```

Figure 10-25. *Listing the Files and Directories in the Hive Root Directory*

The Hive metastore is kept in the `/var/lib/hive` directory. Cd to the `/var/lib/hive` directory.

```
cd /var/lib/hive
```

The `metastore` directory gets listed as shown in Figure 10-26.

```
root@cdh-6l2pr:/# cd /var/lib/hive
root@cdh-6l2pr:/var/lib/hive# ls -l
total 4
drwxrwxrwt 3 hive hive 4096 Dec 21 16:20 metastore
root@cdh-6l2pr:/var/lib/hive#
```

Figure 10-26. *Listing the Hive Metastore Directory*

The Hive home directory is `/usr/lib/hive`. Cd to the `/usr/lib/hive` directory. Subsequently list the files and directories.

```
cd /usr/lib/hive
ls -l
```

The `bin`, `conf`, and `lib` directories for Apache Hive get listed as shown in Figure 10-27. The `bin` directory contains the executables, the `conf` directory the configuration files, and the `lib` directory the jar files.

```
root@cdh-6l2pr:/var/lib/hive# cd /usr/lib/hive
root@cdh-6l2pr:/usr/lib/hive# ls -l
total 56
-rw-r--r-- 1 root root 23169 Sep 17 09:00 LICENSE
-rw-r--r-- 1 root root   397 Sep 17 09:00 NOTICE
drwxr-xr-x 3 root root  4096 Oct 23 15:46 bin
drwxr-xr-x 2 root root  4096 Oct 23 15:46 cloudera
lrwxrwxrwx 1 root root    14 Sep 17 09:19 conf -> /etc/hive/conf
drwxr-xr-x 4 root root 12288 Oct 23 15:46 lib
drwxr-xr-x 3 root root  4096 Oct 23 15:46 scripts
drwxr-xr-x 3 root root  4096 Oct 23 15:46 sentry
root@cdh-6l2pr:/usr/lib/hive# 
```

Figure 10-27. *The Hive Home Directory*

All the environment variables are preconfigured. Run the following command to start the Beeline CLI.

```
beeline
```

Beeline version 1.1.0-cdh5.4.7 gets started as shown in Figure 10-28.

```
root@cdh-6l2pr:/# beeline
Beeline version 1.1.0-cdh5.4.7 by Apache Hive
beeline> 
```

Figure 10-28. *Starting Beeline CLI*

Initially no connection to the Apache Hive server is available. To demonstrate, run the following commands to set the database as default and show the tables.

```
use default;
show tables;
```

The message "No current connection" is displayed as shown in Figure 10-29.

```
root@cdh-6l2pr:/# beeline
Beeline version 1.1.0-cdh5.4.7 by Apache Hive
beeline> use default;
No current connection
beeline> show tables;
No current connection
beeline> 
```

Figure 10-29. *No Current Connection*

Connect with Hive2 server using the default settings for the driver, username, and password as indicated by the three empty "".

```
!connect jdbc:hive2://localhost:10000/default "" "" ""
```

Apache Hive2 server gets connected to using the Apache Hive JDBC driver as shown in Figure 10-30.

```
beeline> !connect jdbc:hive2://localhost:10000/default "" "" ""
scan complete in 3ms
Connecting to jdbc:hive2://localhost:10000/default
Connected to: Apache Hive (version 1.1.0-cdh5.4.7)
Driver: Hive JDBC (version 1.1.0-cdh5.4.7)
Transaction isolation: TRANSACTION_REPEATABLE_READ
0: jdbc:hive2://localhost:10000/default>
```

Figure 10-30. *Connecting with Hive Server*

Run the commands to set the database to default and show the tables.

```
use default;
show tables;
```

The database connected to is already default, and the first command essentially is redundant but what is to be noted is the error generated earlier is not generated. The second command lists the table and because initially the default database does not have any tables, none get listed. The output from the preceding commands is shown in Figure 10-31.

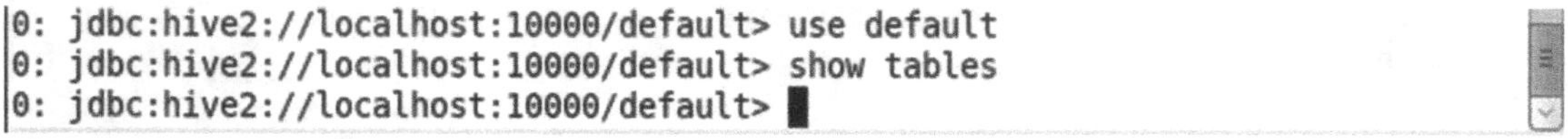

```
0: jdbc:hive2://localhost:10000/default> use default
0: jdbc:hive2://localhost:10000/default> show tables
0: jdbc:hive2://localhost:10000/default>
```

Figure 10-31. *Setting the database to Use and the listing to the Hive Tables*

Before creating a Hive table we need to set the permissions for the `/user/hive/warehouse` directory to global (777).

```
sudo -u hdfs hdfs dfs -chmod -R 777 /user/hive/warehouse
```

Permissions for the Hive warehouse directory get set as shown in Figure 10-32.

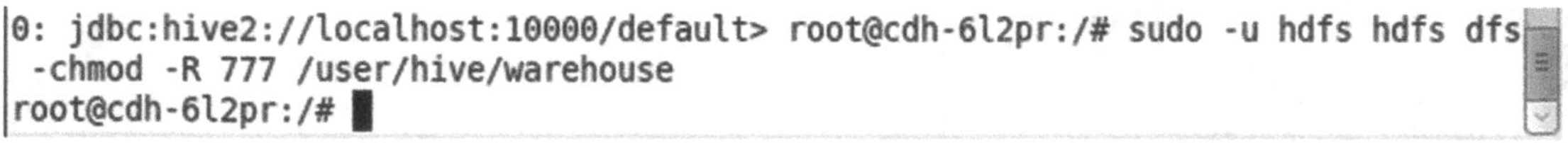

```
0: jdbc:hive2://localhost:10000/default> root@cdh-6l2pr:/# sudo -u hdfs hdfs dfs
 -chmod -R 777 /user/hive/warehouse
root@cdh-6l2pr:/#
```

Figure 10-32. *Setting Permissions on the Hive Warehouse Directory*

Create a table called `wlslog` with the following HiveQL command.

```
CREATE TABLE wlslog(time_stamp STRING,category STRING,type STRING,servername STRING,code
STRING,msg STRING) ROW FORMAT DELIMITED FIELDS TERMINATED BY ',' LINES TERMINATED BY '\n';
```

The `wlslog` table gets created in the default database as shown in Figure 10-33.

```
0: jdbc:hive2://localhost:10000/default> CREATE TABLE wlslog(time_stamp STRING,c
ategory STRING,type STRING,servername STRING,code STRING,msg STRING)ROW FORMAT D
ELIMITED FIELDS TERMINATED BY ',' LINES TERMINATED BY '\n';
No rows affected (0.301 seconds)
```

Figure 10-33. *Creating a Hive Table called wlslog*

Describe the wlslog table with the following command.

```
desc wlslog;
```

The table columns (name and data type) get listed as shown in Figure 10-34.

```
0: jdbc:hive2://localhost:10000/default> desc wlslog;
+-------------+------------+----------+--+
|  col_name   | data_type  | comment  |
+-------------+------------+----------+--+
| time_stamp  | string     |          |
| category    | string     |          |
| type        | string     |          |
| servername  | string     |          |
| code        | string     |          |
| msg         | string     |          |
+-------------+------------+----------+--+
6 rows selected (0.473 seconds)
0: jdbc:hive2://localhost:10000/default>
```

Figure 10-34. *Describing the Hive Table wlslog*

Add 7 rows of data to the `wlslog` table.

```
INSERT INTO TABLE wlslog VALUES ('Apr-8-2014-7:06:16-PM-PDT','Notice','WebLogicServer',
'AdminServer,BEA-000365','Server state changed to STANDBY');
INSERT INTO TABLE wlslog VALUES ('Apr-8-2014-7:06:17-PM-PDT','Notice','WebLogicServer',
'AdminServer','BEA-000365','Server state changed to STARTING');
INSERT INTO TABLE wlslog VALUES ('Apr-8-2014-7:06:18-PM-PDT','Notice','WebLogicServer',
'AdminServer','BEA-000365','Server state changed to ADMIN');
INSERT INTO TABLE wlslog VALUES ('Apr-8-2014-7:06:19-PM-PDT','Notice','WebLogicServer',
'AdminServer','BEA-000365','Server state changed to RESUMING');
INSERT INTO TABLE wlslog VALUES ('Apr-8-2014-7:06:20-PM-PDT','Notice','WebLogicServer',
'AdminServer','BEA-000331','Started WebLogic AdminServer');
INSERT INTO TABLE wlslog VALUES ('Apr-8-2014-7:06:21-PM-PDT','Notice','WebLogicServer',
'AdminServer','BEA-000365','Server state changed to RUNNING');
INSERT INTO TABLE wlslog VALUES ('Apr-8-2014-7:06:22-PM-PDT','Notice','WebLogicServer',
'AdminServer','BEA-000360','Server started in RUNNING mode');
```

A MapReduce job runs for each `INSERT` statement to add the data to Hive table `wlslog` as shown in Figure 10-35.

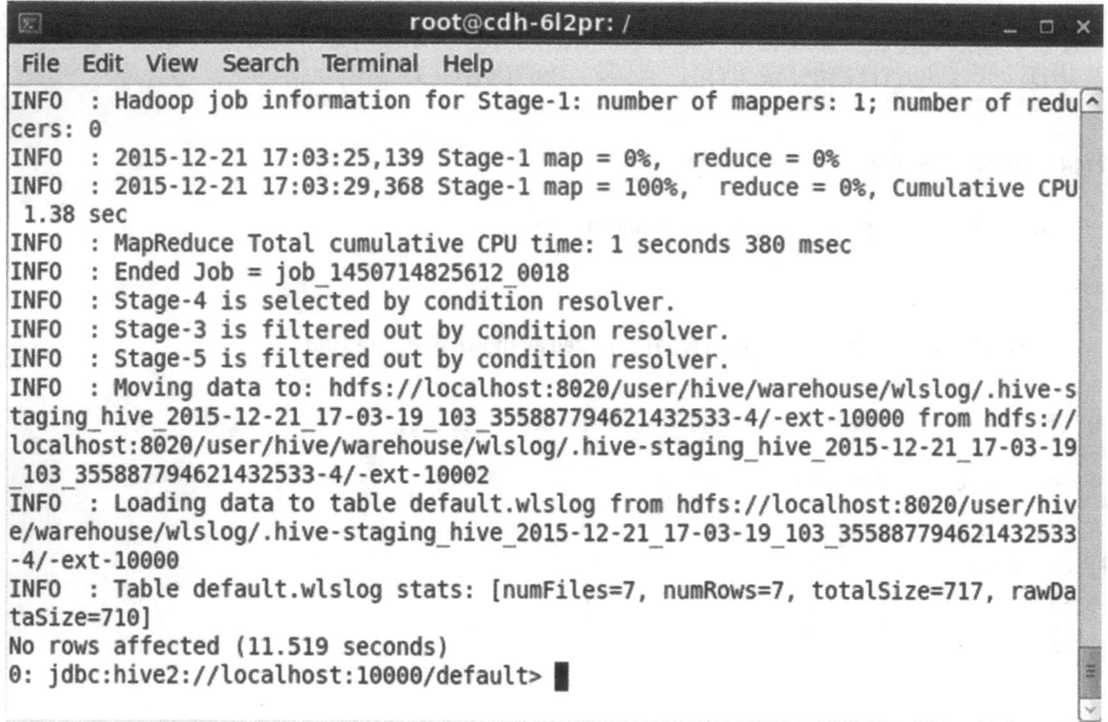

Figure 10-35. *Adding Data to Hive Table wlslog*

Subsequently query the `wlslog` table.

```
select * from wlslog;
```

The 7 rows of data added get listed as shown in Figure 10-36.

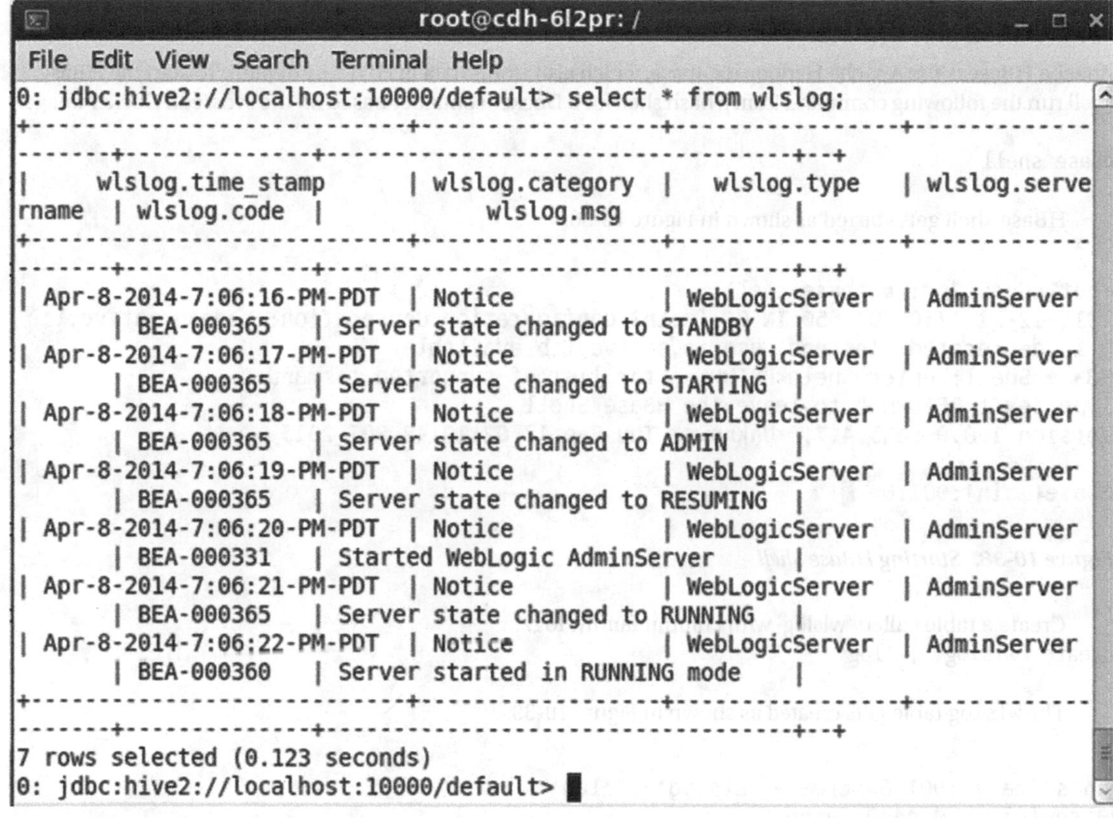
root@cdh-6l2pr: /
File Edit View Search Terminal Help
0: jdbc:hive2://localhost:10000/default> select * from wlslog;
wlslog.time_stamp	wlslog.category	wlslog.type	wlslog.servername	wlslog.code	wlslog.msg
Apr-8-2014-7:06:16-PM-PDT	Notice	WebLogicServer	AdminServer	BEA-000365	Server state changed to STANDBY
Apr-8-2014-7:06:17-PM-PDT	Notice	WebLogicServer	AdminServer	BEA-000365	Server state changed to STARTING
Apr-8-2014-7:06:18-PM-PDT	Notice	WebLogicServer	AdminServer	BEA-000365	Server state changed to ADMIN
Apr-8-2014-7:06:19-PM-PDT	Notice	WebLogicServer	AdminServer	BEA-000365	Server state changed to RESUMING
Apr-8-2014-7:06:20-PM-PDT	Notice	WebLogicServer	AdminServer	BEA-000331	Started WebLogic AdminServer
Apr-8-2014-7:06:21-PM-PDT	Notice	WebLogicServer	AdminServer	BEA-000365	Server state changed to RUNNING
Apr-8-2014-7:06:22-PM-PDT	Notice	WebLogicServer	AdminServer	BEA-000360	Server started in RUNNING mode
7 rows selected (0.123 seconds)
0: jdbc:hive2://localhost:10000/default>

Figure 10-36. *Querying the Hive Table*

To quit the Beeline CLI run the following command.

```
!q
```

As shown in Figure 10-37 the Hive Beeline CLI gets exited. The interactive shell command prompt gets displayed.

```
0: jdbc:hive2://localhost:10000/default> !q
Closing: 0: jdbc:hive2://localhost:10000/default
root@cdh-6l2pr:/#
```

Figure 10-37. *Exiting the Beeline CLI*

From the interactive shell any of the frameworks in CDH may be run. Next, we shall run Apache HBase.

Running HBase

Apache HBase is the Apache Hadoop database, which also stores data in HDFS by default. To start the HBase shell run the following command from a bash shell for a Docker container based on the svds/cdh Docker image.

```
hbase shell
```

HBase shell gets started as shown in Figure 10-38.

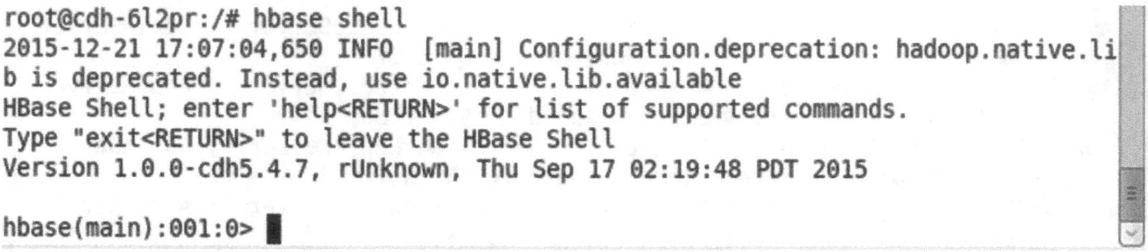

```
root@cdh-6l2pr:/# hbase shell
2015-12-21 17:07:04,650 INFO  [main] Configuration.deprecation: hadoop.native.li
b is deprecated. Instead, use io.native.lib.available
HBase Shell; enter 'help<RETURN>' for list of supported commands.
Type "exit<RETURN>" to leave the HBase Shell
Version 1.0.0-cdh5.4.7, rUnknown, Thu Sep 17 02:19:48 PDT 2015

hbase(main):001:0>
```

Figure 10-38. *Starting HBase Shell*

Create a table called 'wlslog' with column family 'log'.

```
create 'wlslog' , 'log'
```

The `wlslog` table gets created as shown in Figure 10-39.

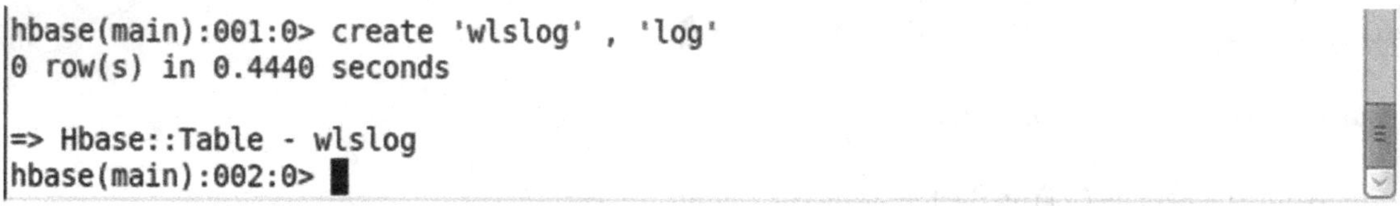

```
hbase(main):001:0> create 'wlslog' , 'log'
0 row(s) in 0.4440 seconds

=> Hbase::Table - wlslog
hbase(main):002:0>
```

Figure 10-39. *Creating a HBase Table*

Put 7 rows of data into the `wlslog` table.

```
put 'wlslog', 'log1', 'log:time_stamp', 'Apr-8-2014-7:06:16-PM-PDT'
put 'wlslog', 'log1', 'log:category', 'Notice'
put 'wlslog', 'log1', 'log:type', 'WeblogicServer'
put 'wlslog', 'log1', 'log:servername', 'AdminServer'
put 'wlslog', 'log1', 'log:code', 'BEA-000365'
put 'wlslog', 'log1', 'log:msg', 'Server state changed to STANDBY'

put 'wlslog', 'log2', 'log:time_stamp', 'Apr-8-2014-7:06:17-PM-PDT'
put 'wlslog', 'log2', 'log:category', 'Notice'
put 'wlslog', 'log2', 'log:type', 'WeblogicServer'
put 'wlslog', 'log2', 'log:servername', 'AdminServer'
put 'wlslog', 'log2', 'log:code', 'BEA-000365'
put 'wlslog', 'log2', 'log:msg', 'Server state changed to STARTING'
put 'wlslog', 'log3', 'log:time_stamp', 'Apr-8-2014-7:06:18-PM-PDT'
put 'wlslog', 'log3', 'log:category', 'Notice'
```

```
put 'wlslog', 'log3', 'log:type', 'WeblogicServer'
put 'wlslog', 'log3', 'log:servername', 'AdminServer'
put 'wlslog', 'log3', 'log:code', 'BEA-000365'
put 'wlslog', 'log3', 'log:msg', 'Server state changed to ADMIN'
put 'wlslog', 'log4', 'log:time_stamp', 'Apr-8-2014-7:06:19-PM-PDT'
put 'wlslog', 'log4', 'log:category', 'Notice'
put 'wlslog', 'log4', 'log:type', 'WeblogicServer'
put 'wlslog', 'log4', 'log:servername', 'AdminServer'
put 'wlslog', 'log4', 'log:code', 'BEA-000365'
put 'wlslog', 'log4', 'log:msg', 'Server state changed to RESUMING'
put 'wlslog', 'log5', 'log:time_stamp', 'Apr-8-2014-7:06:20-PM-PDT'
put 'wlslog', 'log5', 'log:category', 'Notice'
put 'wlslog', 'log5', 'log:type', 'WeblogicServer'
put 'wlslog', 'log5', 'log:servername', 'AdminServer'
put 'wlslog', 'log5', 'log:code', 'BEA-000331'
put 'wlslog', 'log5', 'log:msg', 'Started Weblogic AdminServer'
put 'wlslog', 'log6', 'log:time_stamp', 'Apr-8-2014-7:06:21-PM-PDT'
put 'wlslog', 'log6', 'log:category', 'Notice'
put 'wlslog', 'log6', 'log:type', 'WeblogicServer'
put 'wlslog', 'log6', 'log:servername', 'AdminServer'
put 'wlslog', 'log6', 'log:code', 'BEA-000365'
put 'wlslog', 'log6', 'log:msg', 'Server state changed to RUNNING'
put 'wlslog', 'log7', 'log:time_stamp', 'Apr-8-2014-7:06:22-PM-PDT'
put 'wlslog', 'log7', 'log:category', 'Notice'
put 'wlslog', 'log7', 'log:type', 'WeblogicServer'
put 'wlslog', 'log7', 'log:servername', 'AdminServer'
put 'wlslog', 'log7', 'log:code', 'BEA-000360'
put 'wlslog', 'log7', 'log:msg', 'Server started in RUNNING mode'
```

The output from the put commands is shown in Figure 10-40.

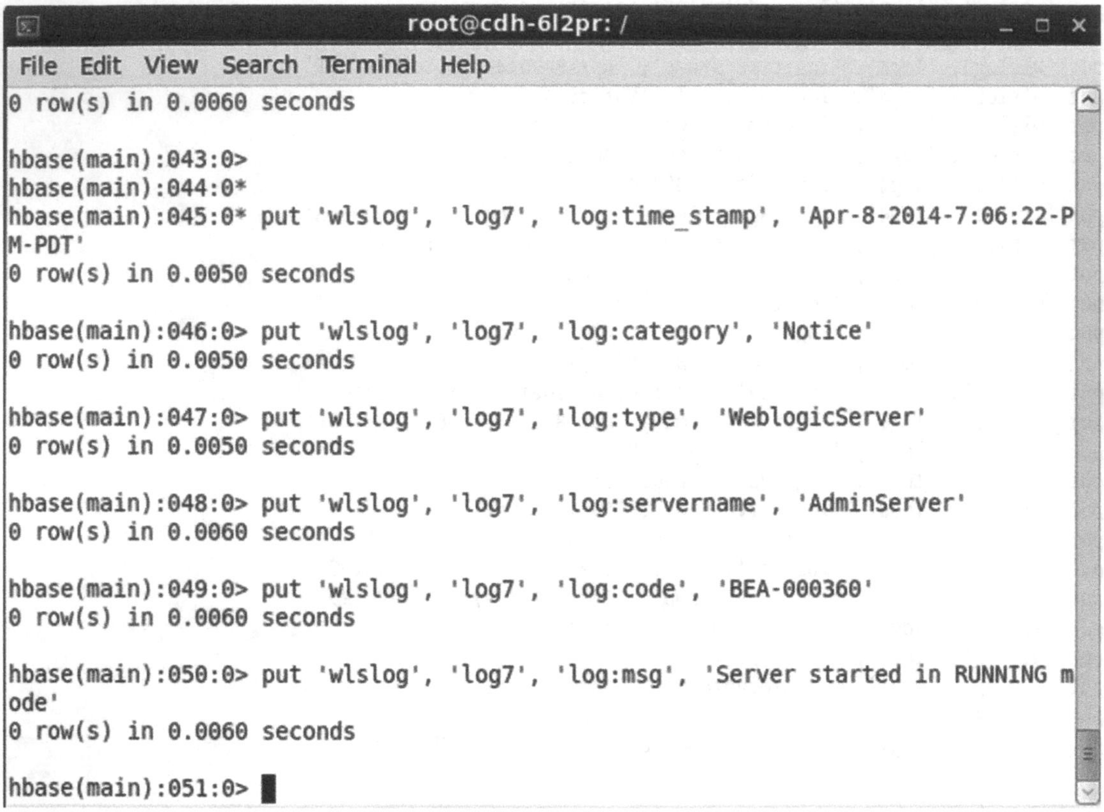

```
root@cdh-6l2pr: /
File Edit View Search Terminal Help
0 row(s) in 0.0060 seconds

hbase(main):043:0>
hbase(main):044:0*
hbase(main):045:0* put 'wlslog', 'log7', 'log:time_stamp', 'Apr-8-2014-7:06:22-P
M-PDT'
0 row(s) in 0.0050 seconds

hbase(main):046:0> put 'wlslog', 'log7', 'log:category', 'Notice'
0 row(s) in 0.0050 seconds

hbase(main):047:0> put 'wlslog', 'log7', 'log:type', 'WeblogicServer'
0 row(s) in 0.0050 seconds

hbase(main):048:0> put 'wlslog', 'log7', 'log:servername', 'AdminServer'
0 row(s) in 0.0060 seconds

hbase(main):049:0> put 'wlslog', 'log7', 'log:code', 'BEA-000360'
0 row(s) in 0.0060 seconds

hbase(main):050:0> put 'wlslog', 'log7', 'log:msg', 'Server started in RUNNING m
ode'
0 row(s) in 0.0060 seconds

hbase(main):051:0>
```

Figure 10-40. *Putting Data into HBase Table*

To list the tables run the following command.

```
list
```

The `wlslog` table gets listed as shown in Figure 10-41.

```
hbase(main):051:0> list
TABLE
wlslog
1 row(s) in 0.0370 seconds

=> ["wlslog"]
hbase(main):052:0>
```

Figure 10-41. *Listing HBase Tables*

To get the data in row with row key 'log1' run the following command.

```
get 'wlslog', 'log1'
```

A single row of data gets listed as shown in Figure 10-42.

```
hbase(main):052:0> get 'wlslog', 'log1'
COLUMN                CELL
 log:category         timestamp=1450717691754, value=Notice
 log:code             timestamp=1450717691891, value=BEA-000365
 log:msg              timestamp=1450717691927, value=Server state changed to STA
                      NDBY
 log:servername       timestamp=1450717691853, value=AdminServer
 log:time_stamp       timestamp=1450717691690, value=Apr-8-2014-7:06:16-PM-PDT
 log:type             timestamp=1450717691803, value=WeblogicServer
6 row(s) in 0.0330 seconds

hbase(main):053:0>
```

Figure 10-42. Getting a Single Row of Data

Get the data in a single column, the `log.msg` column from row with row key `log7`. A column is specified with column family:column format.

```
get 'wlslog', 'log7', {COLUMNS=>['log:msg']}
```

The single column data gets output as shown in Figure 10-43.

```
hbase(main):053:0> get  'wlslog', 'log7', {COLUMNS=>['log:msg']}
COLUMN                CELL
 log:msg              timestamp=1450717746343, value=Server started in RUNNING m
                      ode
1 row(s) in 0.0170 seconds

hbase(main):054:0>
```

Figure 10-43. Getting a Single Column Value in a Row

Scan the `wlslog` table with the scan command.

```
scan 'wlslog'
```

The scan command is shown in Figure 10-44.

```
root@cdh-6l2pr: /
File  Edit  View  Search  Terminal  Help
hbase(main):054:0> scan 'wlslog'
ROW                     COLUMN+CELL
 log1                   column=log:category, timestamp=1450717691754, value=Notice
 log1                   column=log:code, timestamp=1450717691891, value=BEA-000365
 log1                   column=log:msg, timestamp=1450717691927, value=Server stat
                        e changed to STANDBY
 log1                   column=log:servername, timestamp=1450717691853, value=Admi
                        nServer
 log1                   column=log:time_stamp, timestamp=1450717691690, value=Apr-
                        8-2014-7:06:16-PM-PDT
 log1                   column=log:type, timestamp=1450717691803, value=WeblogicSe
                        rver
 log2                   column=log:category, timestamp=1450717692009, value=Notice
 log2                   column=log:code, timestamp=1450717692118, value=BEA-000365
 log2                   column=log:msg, timestamp=1450717692162, value=Server stat
                        e changed to STARTING
 log2                   column=log:servername, timestamp=1450717692080, value=Admi
                        nServer
 log2                   column=log:time_stamp, timestamp=1450717691978, value=Apr-
                        8-2014-7:06:17-PM-PDT
 log2                   column=log:type, timestamp=1450717692043, value=WeblogicSe
                        rver
 log3                   column=log:category, timestamp=1450717718336, value=Notice
 log3                   column=log:code, timestamp=1450717718455, value=BEA-000365
 log3                   column=log:msg, timestamp=1450717718488, value=Server stat
```

Figure 10-44. *Scanning a HBase Table*

All the data from the `wlslog` table gets listed as shown in Figure 10-45.

```
root@cdh-6l2pr: /
File  Edit  View  Search  Terminal  Help
 log5                  column=log:type, timestamp=1450717718827, value=WeblogicSe
                       rver
 log6                  column=log:category, timestamp=1450717746009, value=Notice
 log6                  column=log:code, timestamp=1450717746104, value=BEA-000365
 log6                  column=log:msg, timestamp=1450717746137, value=Server stat
                       e changed to RUNNING
 log6                  column=log:servername, timestamp=1450717746073, value=Admi
                       nServer
 log6                  column=log:time_stamp, timestamp=1450717745967, value=Apr-
                       8-2014-7:06:21-PM-PDT
 log6                  column=log:type, timestamp=1450717746043, value=WeblogicSe
                       rver
 log7                  column=log:category, timestamp=1450717746216, value=Notice
 log7                  column=log:code, timestamp=1450717746305, value=BEA-000360
 log7                  column=log:msg, timestamp=1450717746343, value=Server star
                       ted in RUNNING mode
 log7                  column=log:servername, timestamp=1450717746274, value=Admi
                       nServer
 log7                  column=log:time_stamp, timestamp=1450717746189, value=Apr-
                       8-2014-7:06:22-PM-PDT
 log7                  column=log:type, timestamp=1450717746246, value=WeblogicSe
                       rver
7 row(s) in 0.0870 seconds

hbase(main):055:0>
```

Figure 10-45. *The scan Command outputs 7 Rows of Data*

Deleting the Replication Controller and Service

In the next section we shall create a cluster for the svds/cdh image imperatively on the command line. Delete the replication controller and the service created declaratively.

```
kubectl delete rc cdh
kubectl delete service cdh
```

Creating an Apache Hadoop Cluster Imperatively

In the following subsections we shall create a CDH cluster from the svds/cdh Docker image on the command line. First, we shall create a replication controller.

Creating a Replication Controller

Run the following command to create a replication controller called cdh with 2 replicas.

```
kubectl run cdh --image=svds/cdh --replicas=2
```

The cdh controller gets created as shown in Figure 10-46. The selector is set to run=cdh by default.

```
ubuntu@ip-172-30-1-45:~$ kubectl  run cdh --image=svds/cdh --replicas=2
CONTROLLER   CONTAINER(S)   IMAGE(S)    SELECTOR    REPLICAS
cdh          cdh            svds/cdh    run=cdh     2
```

Figure 10-46. *Creating a Replication Controller Imperatively*

List the replication controllers.

```
kubectl get rc
```

The cdh replication controller gets listed as shown in Figure 10-47.

```
ubuntu@ip-172-30-1-45:~$ kubectl get rc
CONTROLLER   CONTAINER(S)   IMAGE(S)    SELECTOR    REPLICAS
cdh          cdh            svds/cdh    run=cdh     2
```

Figure 10-47. *Getting the Replication Controller*

Listing the Pods

To list the Pods in the cluster run the following command.

```
kubectl get pods
```

The two Pods get listed. Initially some or all of the Pods could be not "Running" or not in the READY state 1/1 as shown in Figure 10-48.

```
ubuntu@ip-172-30-1-45:~$ kubectl get pods
NAME                    READY     STATUS    RESTARTS   AGE
cdh-5hhqg               0/1       Running   0          13s
cdh-fi83b               1/1       Running   0          13s
```

Figure 10-48. *Listing the Pods with some Pod/s not READY yet*

Run the preceding command again after a few seconds.

```
kubectl get pods
```

All the pods should be listed with STATUS "Running" and READY state 1/1 as shown in Figure 10-49.

```
ubuntu@ip-172-30-1-45:~$ kubectl get pods
NAME                    READY     STATUS    RESTARTS   AGE
cdh-5hhqg               1/1       Running   0          27s
cdh-fi83b               1/1       Running   0          27s
k8s-master-127.0.0.1    3/3       Running   0          1h
ubuntu@ip-172-30-1-45:~$ █
```

Figure 10-49. *Listing all Pods as Running and Ready*

Scaling a Cluster

To scale the cluster to 4 replicas run the following command.

```
kubectl scale rc cdh --replicas=4
```

Subsequently list the Pods.

```
kubectl get pods
```

An output of "scaled" from the first command indicates that the cluster got scaled. The second command lists 4 Pods instead of the 2 created initially as shown in Figure 10-50. The second command may have to be run multiple times to list all Pods with STATUS "Running" and READY state 1/1.

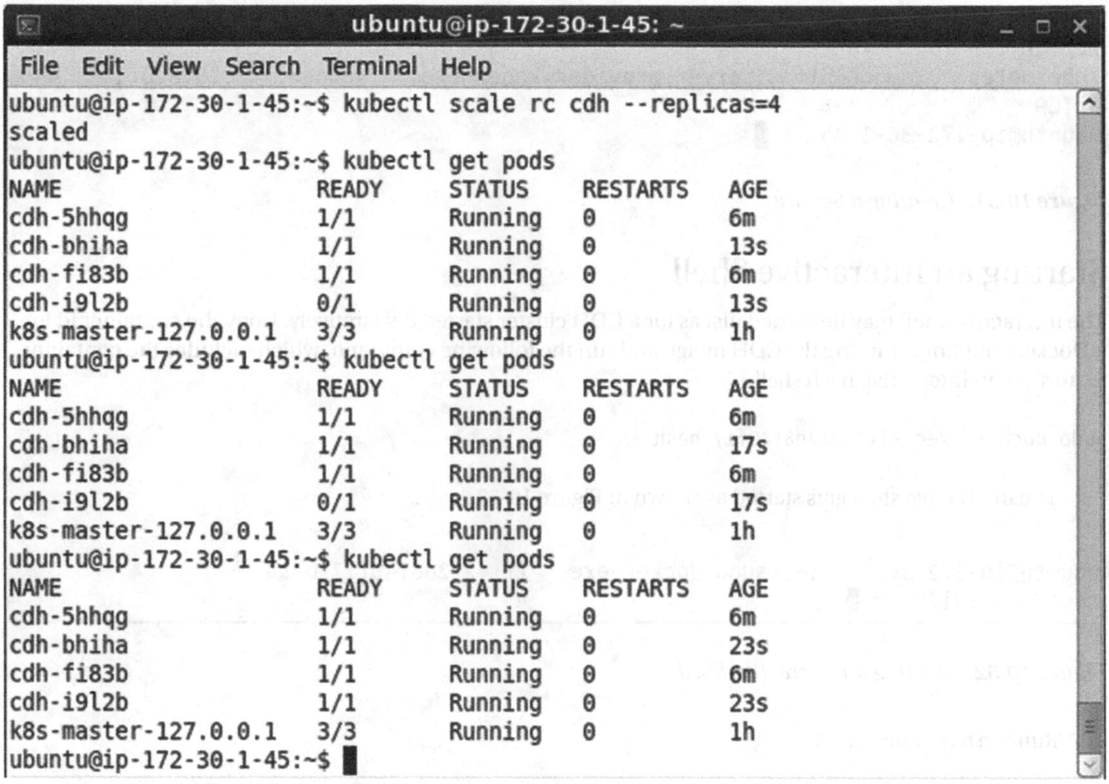
ubuntu@ip-172-30-1-45: ~
File Edit View Search Terminal Help
ubuntu@ip-172-30-1-45:~$ kubectl scale rc cdh --replicas=4
scaled
ubuntu@ip-172-30-1-45:~$ kubectl get pods
NAME READY STATUS RESTARTS AGE
cdh-5hhqg 1/1 Running 0 6m
cdh-bhiha 1/1 Running 0 13s
cdh-fi83b 1/1 Running 0 6m
cdh-i9l2b 0/1 Running 0 13s
k8s-master-127.0.0.1 3/3 Running 0 1h
ubuntu@ip-172-30-1-45:~$ kubectl get pods
NAME READY STATUS RESTARTS AGE
cdh-5hhqg 1/1 Running 0 6m
cdh-bhiha 1/1 Running 0 17s
cdh-fi83b 1/1 Running 0 6m
cdh-i9l2b 0/1 Running 0 17s
k8s-master-127.0.0.1 3/3 Running 0 1h
ubuntu@ip-172-30-1-45:~$ kubectl get pods
NAME READY STATUS RESTARTS AGE
cdh-5hhqg 1/1 Running 0 6m
cdh-bhiha 1/1 Running 0 23s
cdh-fi83b 1/1 Running 0 6m
cdh-i9l2b 1/1 Running 0 23s
k8s-master-127.0.0.1 3/3 Running 0 1h
ubuntu@ip-172-30-1-45:~$

Figure 10-50. *Scaling the CDH Cluster*

Creating a Service

A service exposes the Pods managed by the replication controller at service endpoints, which are just host:port settings at which external clients may invoke the application. Run the following command to create a service.

```
kubectl expose rc cdh --type=LoadBalancer
```

Subsequently list the services.

```
kubectl get services
```

The "cdh" service gets listed with default settings for SELECTOR and PORT as shown in Figure 10-51. The default service selector is `run=cdh`, which has the default format run=<servicename>. The default port is 8020.

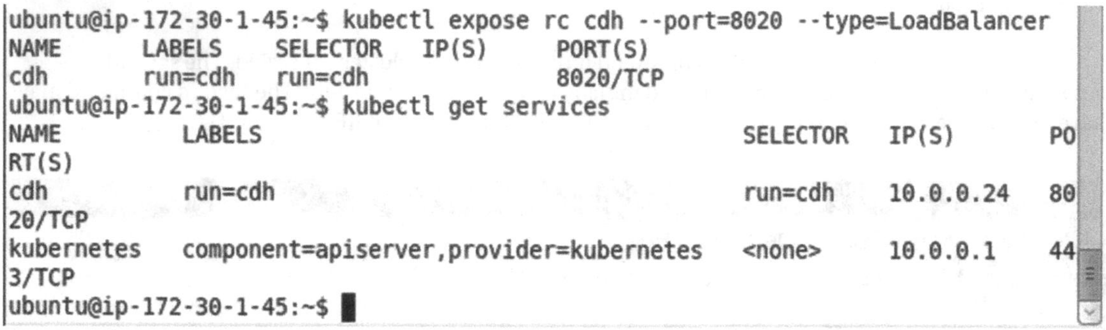

```
ubuntu@ip-172-30-1-45:~$ kubectl expose rc cdh --port=8020 --type=LoadBalancer
NAME      LABELS    SELECTOR   IP(S)     PORT(S)
cdh       run=cdh   run=cdh              8020/TCP
ubuntu@ip-172-30-1-45:~$ kubectl get services
NAME         LABELS                                     SELECTOR   IP(S)       PO
RT(S)
cdh          run=cdh                                    run=cdh    10.0.0.24   80
20/TCP
kubernetes   component=apiserver,provider=kubernetes    <none>     10.0.0.1    44
3/TCP
ubuntu@ip-172-30-1-45:~$ ▌
```

Figure 10-51. *Creating a Service*

Starting an Interactive Shell

The interactive shell may be started just as for a CDH cluster started declaratively. Copy the container id for a Docker container running the CDH image and run the following command, which includes the container id, to start an interactive bash shell.

```
sudo docker exec -it 42f2d8f40f17 bash
```

The interactive shell gets started as shown in Figure 10-52.

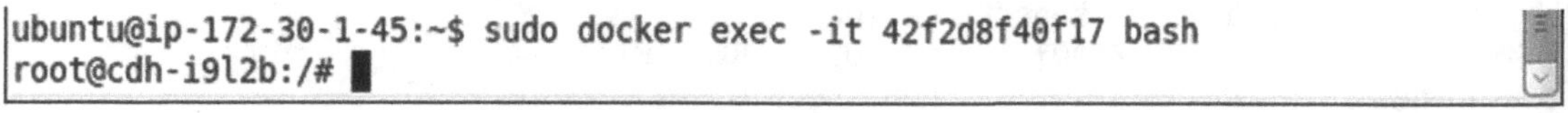

```
ubuntu@ip-172-30-1-45:~$ sudo docker exec -it 42f2d8f40f17 bash
root@cdh-i9l2b:/# ▌
```

Figure 10-52. *Starting an Interactive Shell*

Run the `hdfs` command.

```
hdfs
```

The `hdfs` command usage gets output as shown in Figure 10-53.

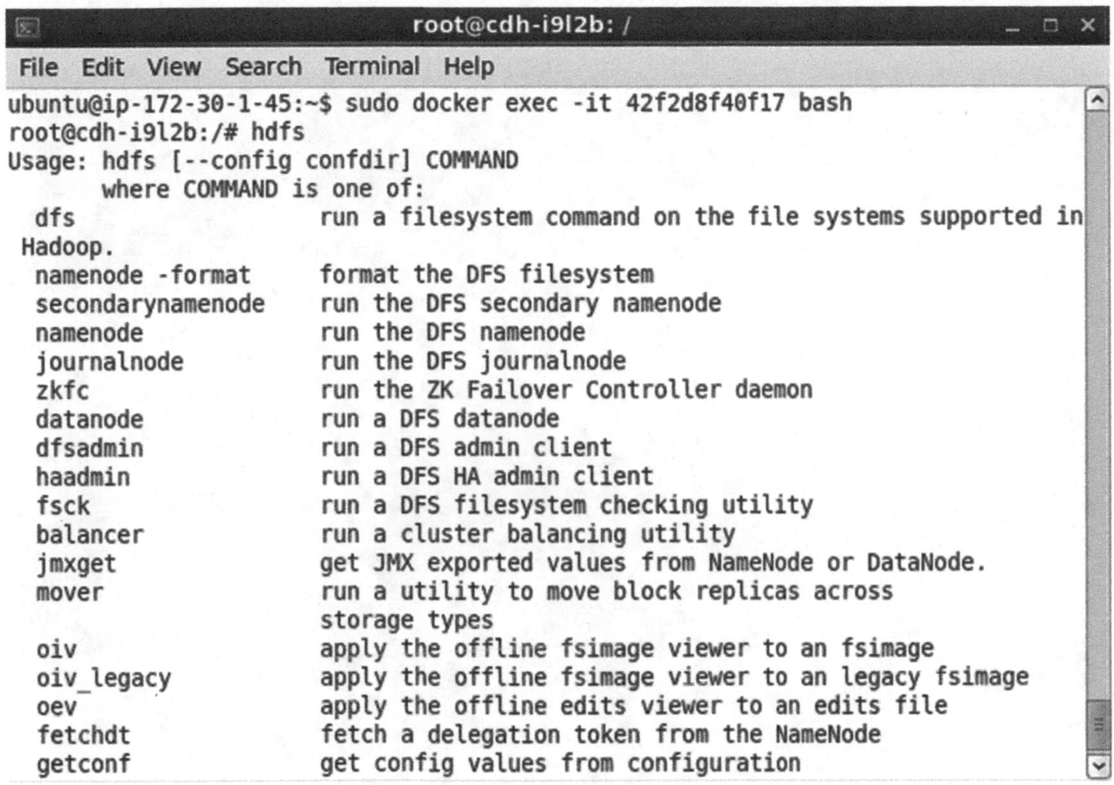

Figure 10-53. *Command Usage for hdfs Command*

Summary

In this chapter we used the Kubernetes cluster manager to create a cluster of Pods based on the Docker image `svds/cdh`. We used both the declarative and imperative approaches to create the cluster. We scaled the cluster using the kubectl scale command. We also demonstrated using some of the Apache Hadoop frameworks packaged in the `cdh` image. We ran a MapReduce `wordcount` example application. We also ran the Apache Hive and Apache HBase tools. In the next chapter we shall discuss using Kubernetes with the indexing and storage framework Apache Solr.

CHAPTER 11

Using Apache Solr

Apache Solr is an Apache Lucene-based enterprise search platform providing features such as full-text search, near real-time indexing, and database integration. Apache Solr runs as a full-text search server within a servlet container, the default being Jetty, which is included with the Solr installation. In this chapter we shall discuss using Kubernetes cluster manager with Apache Solr. We shall be using only the declarative approach, which makes use of definition files, for creating and managing a Solr cluster. This chapter has the following sections.

- Setting the Environment
- Creating a Service
- Listing Service Endpoints
- Describing the Service
- Creating a Replication Controller
- Listing the Pods
- Describing a Pod
- Listing the Logs
- Starting an Interactive Shell
- Creating a Solr Core
- Adding Documents
- Accessing Solr on Command Line with a REST Client
- Setting Port Forwarding
- Accessing Solr in Admin Console
- Scaling the Cluster

D. Vohra, *Kubernetes Microservices with Docker*, DOI 10.1007/978-1-4842-1907-2_11

Setting the Environment

The following software is required for this chapter.

-Docker Engine (latest version)

-Kubernetes (version 1.01)

-Kubectl (version 1.01)

-Docker image for Apache Solr (latest version)

We have used the same Amazon EC2 instance AMI as in the other chapters. SSH login to the Ubuntu instance from a local machine.

```
ssh -i "docker.pem" ubuntu@54.152.82.142
```

Install the required software as discussed in chapter 1. Start Docker and verify its status.

```
sudo service docker start
sudo service docker status
```

As shown in Figure 11-1 Docker should be running.

```
ubuntu@ip-172-30-1-163:~$ sudo service docker start
start: Job is already running: docker
ubuntu@ip-172-30-1-163:~$ sudo service docker status
docker start/running, process 2697
ubuntu@ip-172-30-1-163:~$
```

***Figure 11-1.** Starting Docker and Verifying Status*

List the services.

```
kubectl get services
```

As shown in Figure 11-2 Kubernetes service should be running.

```
ubuntu@ip-172-30-1-163:~$ kubectl get services
NAME          LABELS                                      SELECTOR    IP(S)       POR
T(S)
kubernetes    component=apiserver,provider=kubernetes     <none>      10.0.0.1    443
/TCP
ubuntu@ip-172-30-1-163:~$
```

***Figure 11-2.** Listing the "kubernetes" Service*

To list the nodes run the following command.

```
kubectl get nodes
```

The 127.0.0.1 node gets listed as shown in Figure 11-3.

```
ubuntu@ip-172-30-1-163:~$ kubectl get nodes
NAME        LABELS                              STATUS
127.0.0.1   kubernetes.io/hostname=127.0.0.1   Ready
ubuntu@ip-172-30-1-163:~$ █
```

Figure 11-3. Listing a Single Node

List the endpoints with the following command.

```
kubectl get endpoints
```

Initially only the endpoint for kubernetes is listed as shown in Figure 11-4.

```
ubuntu@ip-172-30-1-34:~$ kubectl get endpoints
NAME         ENDPOINTS
kubernetes   172.30.1.34:6443
ubuntu@ip-172-30-1-34:~$ █
```

Figure 11-4. Listing "kubernetes" Endpoint

Creating a Service

Create a definition file `solr-service.yaml` and add the following (Table 11-1) fields to the definition file.

Table 11-1. Service Definition File for Apache Solr

Field	Description	Value
apiVersion		v1
kind	The kind of definition file.	Service
metadata	The service metadata.	
metadata -> labels	The service labels. Not required.	app: solrApp
metadata -> name	The service name. Required.	solr-service
spec	The service specification.	
spec -> ports	The ports exposed by the service.	
spec -> ports-> port	A port exposed by the service.	8983
spec -> ports-> targetPort	The target port.	8983
spec -> selector	The Pod selector. Service routes traffic to the Pods with a label matching the selector expression.	app: solrApp

The solr-service.yaml is listed.

```
apiVersion: v1
kind: Service
metadata:
  labels:
    app: solrApp
  name: solr-service
spec:
  ports:
    -
      port: 8983
      targetPort: 8983
  selector:
    app: solrApp
```

The solr-service.yaml may be edited in the vi editor and saved with :wq as shown in Figure 11-5.

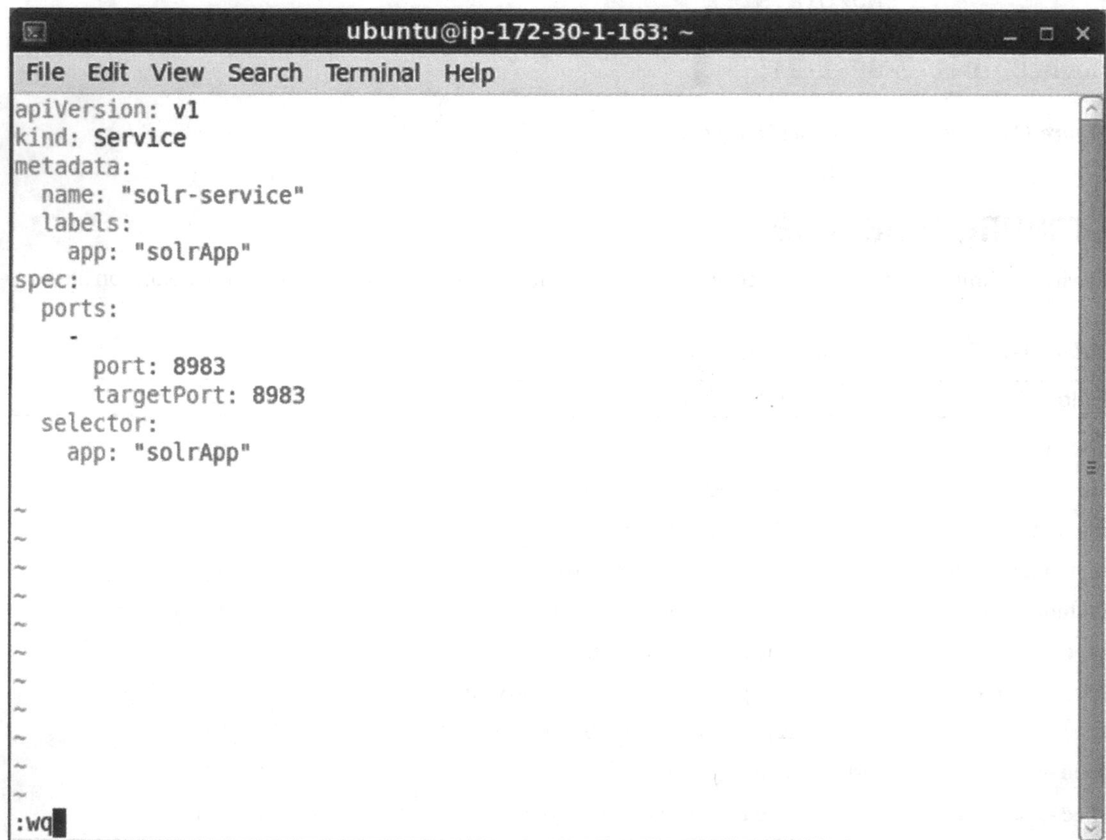

Figure 11-5. *Service Definition File in vi Editor*

Create a service from the definition file with the following command.

```
kubectl create -f solr-service.yaml
```

Subsequently list the services.

```
kubectl get services
```

An output of "services/solr-service" as shown in Figure 11-6 indicates that the service has been created. Subsequently the `solr-service` gets listed. The service has label `app=solrApp` and selector `app=solrApp`.

```
ubuntu@ip-172-30-1-163:~$ kubectl create -f  solr-service.yaml
services/solr-service
ubuntu@ip-172-30-1-163:~$ kubectl get services
NAME           LABELS                                      SELECTOR      IP(S)
   PORT(S)
kubernetes     component=apiserver,provider=kubernetes     <none>        10.0.0.1
   443/TCP
solr-service   app=solrApp                                 app=solrApp   10.0.0.24
3   8983/TCP
```

Figure 11-6. *Creating a Service from Definition File*

Listing Service Endpoints

To list the endpoints run the following command.

```
kubectl get endpoints
```

As the `solr-service` is not managing any Pods initially, no endpoint gets listed as shown in Figure 11-7.

```
ubuntu@ip-172-30-1-163:~$ kubectl get endpoints
NAME           ENDPOINTS
kubernetes     172.30.1.163:6443
solr-service   <none>
```

Figure 11-7. *Listing the Endpoint for the Solr Service*

Describing the Service

To describe the `solr-service` run the following command.

```
kubectl describe service solr-service
```

The service name, namespace, labels, selector, type, IP, Port, endpoints, and events get listed as shown in Figure 11-8.

```
ubuntu@ip-172-30-1-163:~$ kubectl describe service solr-service
Name:                   solr-service
Namespace:              default
Labels:                 app=solrApp
Selector:               app=solrApp
Type:                   ClusterIP
IP:                     10.0.0.243
Port:                   <unnamed>       8983/TCP
Endpoints:              <none>
Session Affinity:       None
No events.

ubuntu@ip-172-30-1-163:~$ ▌
```

Figure 11-8. *Describing the Apache Solr Service*

Creating a Replication Controller

Create a definition file `solr-rc.yaml` for the replication controller and add the following (Table 11-2) fields to the definition file.

Table 11-2. *Replication Controller Definition File Fields*

Field	Description	Value
apiVersion		v1
kind	The kind of definition file.	Replication Controller
metadata	The replication controller metadata.	
metadata -> labels	The replication controller labels.	app: solrApp
metadata -> name	The replication controller name.	solr-rc
spec	The replication controller specification.	
spec -> replicas	The number of Pod replicas.	2
spec -> selector	A key: value expression for selecting the Pods to manage. Pods with a label the same as the selector expression are managed by the replication controller. For a single label/ selector expression Pod/Replication Controller combination the selector expression must be the same as the spec- > template- > metadata- > labels expression. The selector defaults to the spec- > template- > metadata- > labels not specified. The app: solrApp setting translates to app=solrApp.	app: solrApp
spec -> template	The Pod template.	
spec -> template -> metadata	The Pod template metadata.	

(*continued*)

Table 11-2. (*continued*)

Field	Description	Value
spec -> template-> metadata-> labels	The Pod template labels.	app: solrApp
spec -> template -> spec	The Pod template specification.	
spec -> template -> spec -> containers	The containers configuration for the Pod template.	
spec -> template -> spec -> containers -> image	The Docker image.	solr
spec -> template -> spec -> containers -> name	The container name.	solr
spec -> template -> spec -> containers -> ports	Container ports.	
spec -> template -> spec -> containers -> ports -> containerPort	Container port for Solr server.	8983
spec -> template -> spec -> containers -> ports -> name	Solr port name.	solrApp

The `solr-rc.yaml` is listed.

```
apiVersion: v1
kind: ReplicationController
metadata:
  labels:
    app: solrApp
  name: solr-rc
spec:
  replicas: 2
  selector:
    app: solrApp
  template:
    metadata:
      labels:
        app: solrApp
    spec:
      containers:
        -
          image: solr
          name: solr
          ports:
            -
              containerPort: 8983
              name: solrApp
```

The `solr-rc.yaml` definition file may be created and saved in vi editor as shown in Figure 11-9.

```
ubuntu@ip-172-30-1-163: ~
File Edit View Search Terminal Help
kind: ReplicationController
apiVersion: v1
metadata:
    name: "solr-rc"
    labels:
      app: "solrApp"
spec:
    replicas: 2
    selector:
      app: "solrApp"
    template:
      metadata:
        labels:
          app: "solrApp"
      spec:
        containers:
          -
            image: "solr"
            name: "solr"
            ports:
              -
                containerPort: 8983
                name: "solrApp"

~
:wq
```

Figure 11-9. Replication Controller Definition File in vi Editor

Run the following command to create a replication controller from the definition file.

```
kubectl create -f solr-rc.yaml
```

The solr-rc replication controller gets created as shown in Figure 11-10. Subsequently list the replication controllers.

```
kubectl get rc
```

The solr-rc replication controller gets listed as shown in Figure 11-10.

```
ubuntu@ip-172-30-1-163:~$ kubectl create -f  solr-rc.yaml
replicationcontrollers/solr-rc
ubuntu@ip-172-30-1-163:~$ kubectl get rc
CONTROLLER   CONTAINER(S)   IMAGE(S)   SELECTOR      REPLICAS
solr-rc      solr           solr       app=solrApp   2
ubuntu@ip-172-30-1-163:~$
```

Figure 11-10. Creating a Replication Controller from Definition File

Listing the Pods

List the Pods with the following command.

```
kubectl get pods
```

The two Pods created by the replication controller get listed as shown in Figure 11-11. Initially some of the Pods could be not running and not ready.

```
ubuntu@ip-172-30-1-163:~$ kubectl get pods
NAME                    READY     STATUS                                 RESTARTS
   AGE
k8s-master-127.0.0.1    3/3       Running                                0
   11m
solr-rc-s82ip           0/1       Image: solr is not ready on the node   0
   38s
solr-rc-ui66u           0/1       Image: solr is not ready on the node   0
   38s
```

Figure 11-11. *Listing the Pods, all of them not yet Ready*

Run the same command again after a few seconds to list the Pods again.

```
kubectl get pods
```

The Pods should get listed with STATUS "Running" and READY state 1/1 as shown in Figure 11-12.

```
ubuntu@ip-172-30-1-163:~$ kubectl get pods
NAME                    READY     STATUS    RESTARTS   AGE
k8s-master-127.0.0.1    3/3       Running   0          11m
solr-rc-s82ip           1/1       Running   0          46s
solr-rc-ui66u           1/1       Running   0          46s
ubuntu@ip-172-30-1-163:~$
```

Figure 11-12. *Listing the Pods as Ready*

To describe the `solr-service` run the following command.

```
kubectl describe svc solr-service
```

The service description gets listed as shown in Figure 11-13. The service endpoints for the two Pods are also listed. A service is accessed at its endpoints. When described previously, before creating the replication controller, no service endpoints got listed as shown in Figure 11-8.

```
ubuntu@ip-172-30-1-163:/var/lib$ kubectl describe svc solr-service
Name:                   solr-service
Namespace:              default
Labels:                 app=solrApp
Selector:               app=solrApp
Type:                   ClusterIP
IP:                     10.0.0.243
Port:                   <unnamed>       8983/TCP
Endpoints:              172.17.0.2:8983,172.17.0.3:8983
Session Affinity:       None
No events.
```

Figure 11-13. *Describing the Solr Service including the Service Endpoints*

The endpoints may also be listed separately.

```
kubectl get endpoints
```

The endpoints get listed as shown in Figure 11-14.

```
ubuntu@ip-172-30-1-34:~$ kubectl get endpoints
NAME            ENDPOINTS
kubernetes      172.30.1.34:6443
solr-service    172.17.0.2:8983,172.17.0.3:8983
ubuntu@ip-172-30-1-34:~$
```

Figure 11-14. *Listing the Endpoints for Solr Service*

Describing a Replication Controller

To describe the replication controller `solr-rc` run the following command.

```
kubectl describe rc solr-rc
```

The replication controller description gets listed as shown in Figure 11-15.

```
ubuntu@ip-172-30-1-163:~$ kubectl describe rc solr-rc
Name:           solr-rc
Namespace:      default
Image(s):       solr
Selector:       app=solrApp
Labels:         app=solrApp
Replicas:       2 current / 2 desired
Pods Status:    2 Running / 0 Waiting / 0 Succeeded / 0 Failed
Events:
  FirstSeen                       LastSeen                        Count  F
rom                             SubobjectPath   Reason                 Message
  Thu, 31 Dec 2015 18:50:41 +0000     Thu, 31 Dec 2015 18:50:41 +0000 1      {
replication-controller }                          successfulCreate       Created
pod: solr-rc-ui66u
  Thu, 31 Dec 2015 18:50:41 +0000     Thu, 31 Dec 2015 18:50:41 +0000 1      {
replication-controller }                          successfulCreate       Created
pod: solr-rc-s82ip

ubuntu@ip-172-30-1-163:~$
```

Figure 11-15. *Describing the Replication Controller*

Listing the Logs

To list the logs for a particular command run the `kubectl logs` command. For example, logs for the `solr-rc-s82ip` Pod are listed with the following command.

```
kubectl logs solr-rc-s82ip
```

In the log output the Solr server is starting as shown in Figure 11-16.

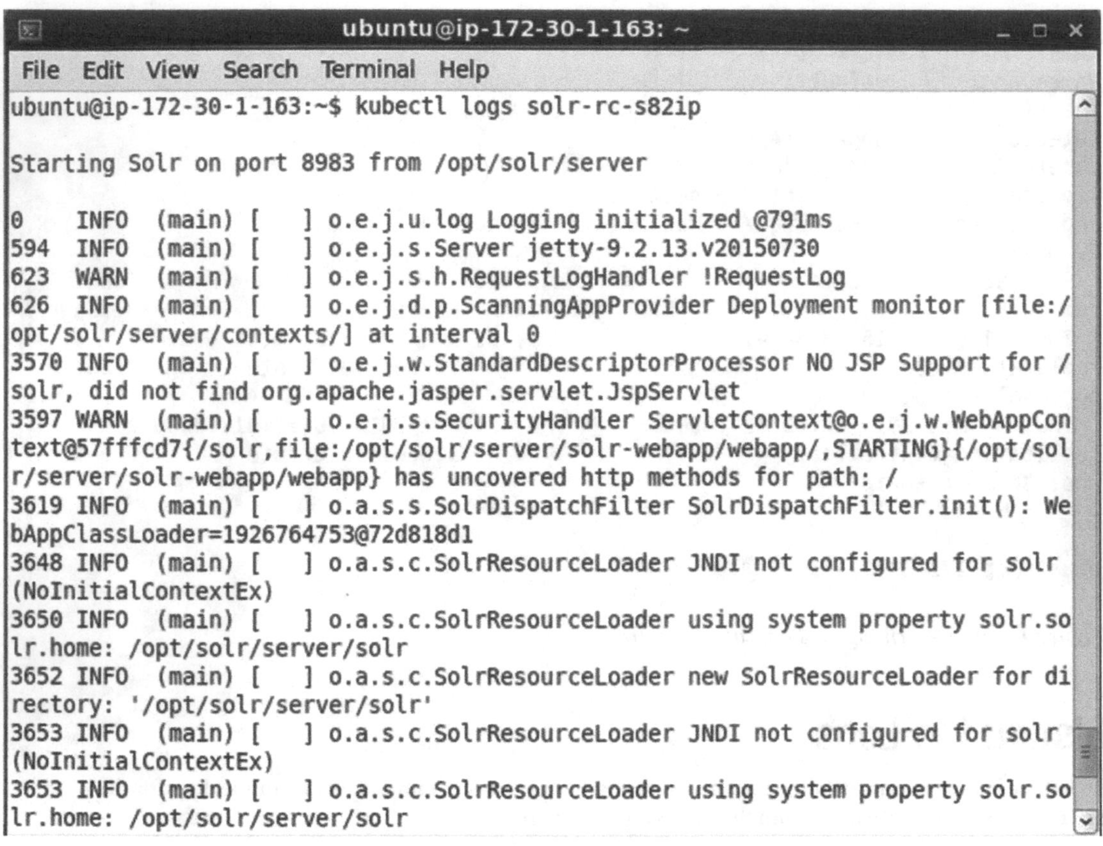

Figure 11-16. *Listing Logs for the Pod*

After the server has started the output "Server Started" gets output as shown in Figure 11-17.

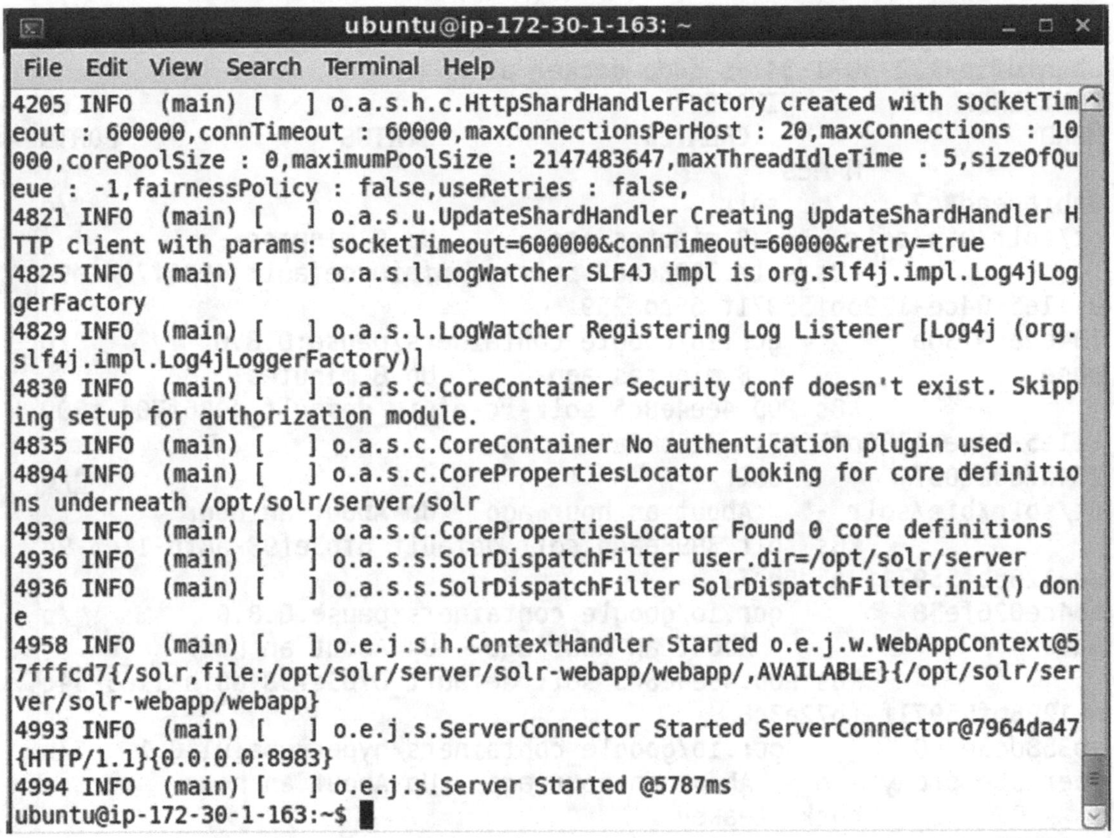

```
ubuntu@ip-172-30-1-163: ~
File Edit View Search Terminal Help
4205 INFO  (main) [   ] o.a.s.h.c.HttpShardHandlerFactory created with socketTim
eout : 600000,connTimeout : 60000,maxConnectionsPerHost : 20,maxConnections : 10
000,corePoolSize : 0,maximumPoolSize : 2147483647,maxThreadIdleTime : 5,sizeOfQu
eue : -1,fairnessPolicy : false,useRetries : false,
4821 INFO  (main) [   ] o.a.s.u.UpdateShardHandler Creating UpdateShardHandler H
TTP client with params: socketTimeout=600000&connTimeout=60000&retry=true
4825 INFO  (main) [   ] o.a.s.l.LogWatcher SLF4J impl is org.slf4j.impl.Log4jLog
gerFactory
4829 INFO  (main) [   ] o.a.s.l.LogWatcher Registering Log Listener [Log4j (org.
slf4j.impl.Log4jLoggerFactory)]
4830 INFO  (main) [   ] o.a.s.c.CoreContainer Security conf doesn't exist. Skipp
ing setup for authorization module.
4835 INFO  (main) [   ] o.a.s.c.CoreContainer No authentication plugin used.
4894 INFO  (main) [   ] o.a.s.c.CorePropertiesLocator Looking for core definitio
ns underneath /opt/solr/server/solr
4930 INFO  (main) [   ] o.a.s.c.CorePropertiesLocator Found 0 core definitions
4936 INFO  (main) [   ] o.a.s.s.SolrDispatchFilter user.dir=/opt/solr/server
4936 INFO  (main) [   ] o.a.s.s.SolrDispatchFilter SolrDispatchFilter.init() don
e
4958 INFO  (main) [   ] o.e.j.s.h.ContextHandler Started o.e.j.w.WebAppContext@5
7fffcd7{/solr,file:/opt/solr/server/solr-webapp/webapp/,AVAILABLE}{/opt/solr/ser
ver/solr-webapp/webapp}
4993 INFO  (main) [   ] o.e.j.s.ServerConnector Started ServerConnector@7964da47
{HTTP/1.1}{0.0.0.0:8983}
4994 INFO  (main) [   ] o.e.j.s.Server Started @5787ms
ubuntu@ip-172-30-1-163:~$
```

Figure 11-17. *Listing the Solr Server as started*

Starting an Interactive Shell

As the "solr" Docker image inherits from the "java:openjdk-8-jre" Docker image, which further inherits from the "buildpack-deps:jessie-curl" image, which inherits from Docker image "debian" for Linux an interactive bash shell may be started to access a Docker container based on the "solr" Docker image. To access the Solr software we need to start an interactive bash shell for a Docker container running Solr. Obtain the container if for a Docker container running Solr with the following command.

```
sudo docker ps
```

The Docker containers get listed as shown in Figure 11-18.

```
File  Edit  View  Search  Terminal  Help
ubuntu@ip-172-30-1-34:~$ sudo docker ps
CONTAINER ID          IMAGE                                              COM
MAND                    CREATED                   STATUS               PORTS
               NAMES
8abfbdead3c7          solr                                               "/o
pt/solr/bin/solr -"    8 minutes ago         Up 8 minutes
               k8s_solr.3998eadb_solr-rc-pfpiu_default_4986f704-a90
9-11e5-94ce-1296bf55971f_65cde259
134edae973ba          gcr.io/google_containers/pause:0.8.0               "/p
ause"                   8 minutes ago         Up 8 minutes
               k8s_POD.4ee4e8c5_solr-rc-pfpiu_default_4986f704-a909
-11e5-94ce-1296bf55971f_325b86a5
2d4d7d02c05f          solr                                               "/o
pt/solr/bin/solr -"    About an hour ago   Up About an hour
               k8s_solr.3998eadb_solr_default_6fb3ef93-a8fb-11e5-94
ce-1296bf55971f_a5d6bc71
a64ce026fe58          gcr.io/google_containers/pause:0.8.0               "/p
ause"                   About an hour ago   Up About an hour
               k8s_POD.4ee4e8c5_solr_default_6fb3ef93-a8fb-11e5-94c
e-1296bf55971f_fb72a3c8
eb358dc3e2b0          gcr.io/google_containers/hyperkube:v1.0.1   "/h
yperkube proxy --m"    About an hour ago   Up About an hour
               cocky_leakey
ab27389cdf62          gcr.io/google_containers/hyperkube:v1.0.1   "/h
yperkube scheduler"    About an hour ago   Up About an hour
               k8s_scheduler.2744e742_k8s-master-127.0.0.1_default_
f3ccbffbd75e3c5d2fb4ba69c8856c4a_b9fd94ee
f26b84120226          gcr.io/google_containers/hyperkube:v1.0.1   "/h
yperkube apiserver"    About an hour ago   Up About an hour
               k8s_apiserver.cfb70250_k8s-master-127.0.0.1_default_
f3ccbffbd75e3c5d2fb4ba69c8856c4a_da559699
18aa70eee943          gcr.io/google_containers/hyperkube:v1.0.1   "/h
```

Figure 11-18. *Listing the Docker Container for Apache Solr*

Copy the container if and start an interactive shell.

```
sudo docker exec -it 2d4d7d02c05f bash
```

The interactive shell gets started as shown in Figure 11-19. To list the status of the Solr server run the following command.

```
bin/solr status
```

One Solr node is found as shown in Figure 11-19.

```
ubuntu@ip-172-30-1-34:~$ sudo docker exec -it 2d4d7d02c05f bash
solr@solr:/opt/solr$ bin/solr status

Found 1 Solr nodes:

Solr process 1 running on port 8983
{
  "solr_home":"/opt/solr/server/solr",
  "version":"5.4.0 1718046 - upayavira - 2015-12-04 23:16:46",
  "startTime":"2015-12-22T22:30:04.132Z",
  "uptime":"0 days, 1 hours, 48 minutes, 59 seconds",
  "memory":"42.4 MB (%8.6) of 490.7 MB"}
```

Figure 11-19. *Listing the Solr Status in an Interactive Shell for the Docker Container*

Solr 5.x introduce *configsets*. The configsets directory consists of example configurations that may be used as a base to create new Solr cores or collections. The configsets replace the `collection1` example core configuration in Solr 4.x. Cd (change directory) to the `configsets` directory.

```
cd /opt/solr/server/solr/configsets
```

List the files and directories in the `configsets` directory.

```
ls -l
```

Three example configurations get listed as shown in Figure 11-20.

```
solr@solr:/opt/solr/server/solr/configsets$ ls -l
total 12
drwxr-xr-x 3 solr solr 4096 Dec  3 09:03 basic_configs
drwxr-xr-x 3 solr solr 4096 Dec  3 09:03 data_driven_schema_configs
drwxr-xr-x 3 solr solr 4096 Dec  3 09:03 sample_techproducts_config
s
solr@solr:/opt/solr/server/solr/configsets$
```

Figure 11-20. *Listing the Example Configurations*

When we create a Solr core later in the chapter we shall be using the basic_configs configuration. List the files in the `//configsets/ basic_configs/conf` directory.

```
cd conf
ls -l
```

The configuration files for `basic_configs` example get listed and include the `schema.xml` and solrconfig.xml as shown in Figure 11-21.

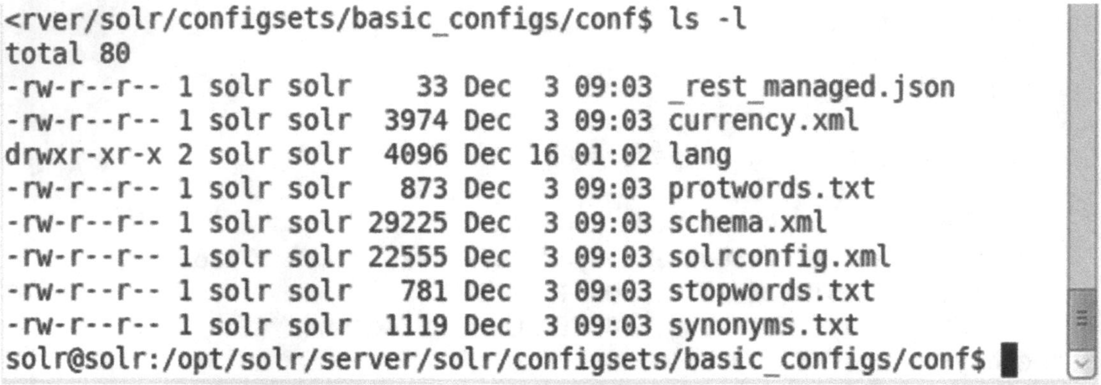

```
<rver/solr/configsets/basic_configs/conf$ ls -l
total 80
-rw-r--r-- 1 solr solr    33 Dec  3 09:03 _rest_managed.json
-rw-r--r-- 1 solr solr  3974 Dec  3 09:03 currency.xml
drwxr-xr-x 2 solr solr  4096 Dec 16 01:02 lang
-rw-r--r-- 1 solr solr   873 Dec  3 09:03 protwords.txt
-rw-r--r-- 1 solr solr 29225 Dec  3 09:03 schema.xml
-rw-r--r-- 1 solr solr 22555 Dec  3 09:03 solrconfig.xml
-rw-r--r-- 1 solr solr   781 Dec  3 09:03 stopwords.txt
-rw-r--r-- 1 solr solr  1119 Dec  3 09:03 synonyms.txt
solr@solr:/opt/solr/server/solr/configsets/basic_configs/conf$
```

***Figure 11-21.** Listing the Configuration Files in the basic_configs Example Configuration*

Creating a Solr Core

A new Solr core may also be created from the command line. The `solr create` command is used to create a new core or a collection. As an example, create a core called `wlslog` with the `solr create_core` command. Use the configset `basic_configs` with the `-d` option. The default config set used if none is specified (with the `-d` option) is `data_driven_schema_configs`. Cd to the `/opt/solr` directory and run the following command.

```
bin/solr create_core -c wlslog -d /opt/solr/server/solr/configsets/basic_configs
```

A Solr core called `wlslog` gets created as shown in Figure 11-22.

```
ubuntu@ip-172-30-1-163:~$ sudo docker exec -it 23f48c21cf91 bash
<  wlslog -d  /opt/solr/server/solr/configsets/basic_configs

Copying configuration to new core instance directory:
/opt/solr/server/solr/wlslog

Creating new core 'wlslog' using command:
http://localhost:8983/solr/admin/cores?action=CREATE&name=wlslog&instanceDir=wls
log

{
  "responseHeader":{
    "status":0,
    "QTime":1216},
  "core":"wlslog"}


solr@solr-rc-s82ip:/opt/solr$
```

***Figure 11-22.** Creating a Solr Core called wlslog*

Indexing Documents

Apache Solr provides the post tool for indexing documents from the command line. The post tool supports different input file formats such as XML, CSV and JSON. We shall index an XML format document Save the following XML document to the wlslog.xml file.

```
<add>
<doc>
<field name="id">wlslog1</field>
  <field name="time_stamp_s">Apr-8-2014-7:06:16-PM-PDT</field>
  <field name="category_s">Notice</field>
  <field name="type_s">WebLogicServer</field>
  <field name="servername_s">AdminServer</field>
  <field name="code_s">BEA-000365</field>
  <field name="msg_s">Server state changed to STANDBY</field>

</doc>

<doc>
<field name="id">wlslog2</field>

  <field name="time_stamp_s">Apr-8-2014-7:06:17-PM-PDT</field>
  <field name="category_s">Notice</field>
  <field name="type_s">WebLogicServer</field>

  <field name="servername_s">AdminServer</field>
  <field name="code">BEA-000365</field>
  <field name="msg_s">Server state changed to STARTING</field>

</doc>

<doc>
<field name="id">wlslog3</field>

  <field name="time_stamp_s">Apr-8-2014-7:06:18-PM-PDT</field>
  <field name="category_s">Notice</field>
  <field name="type_s">WebLogicServer</field>

  <field name="servername_s">AdminServer</field>
  <field name="code">BEA-000365</field>
  <field name="msg_s">Server state changed to ADMIN</field>
</doc>
<doc>
<field name="id">wlslog4</field>
  <field name="time_stamp_s">Apr-8-2014-7:06:19-PM-PDT</field>
  <field name="category_s">Notice</field>
  <field name="type_s">WebLogicServer</field>
```

```
  <field name="servername_s">AdminServer</field>
  <field name="code">BEA-000365</field>
  <field name="msg_s">Server state changed to RESUMING</field>

</doc>

<doc>
<field name="id">wlslog5</field>

  <field name="time_stamp_s">Apr-8-2014-7:06:20-PM-PDT</field>
  <field name="category_s">Notice</field>
  <field name="type_s">WebLogicServer</field>
  <field name="servername_s">AdminServer</field>
  <field name="code">BEA-000331</field>
  <field name="msg_s">Started WebLogic AdminServer</field>
</doc>
<doc>
<field name="id">wlslog6</field>

  <field name="time_stamp_s">Apr-8-2014-7:06:21-PM-PDT</field>
  <field name="category_s">Notice</field>
  <field name="type_s">WebLogicServer</field>
  <field name="servername_s">AdminServer</field>
  <field name="code">BEA-000365</field>
  <field name="msg_s">Server state changed to RUNNING</field>
</doc>
<doc>
<field name="id">wlslog7</field>
  <field name="time_stamp_s">Apr-8-2014-7:06:22-PM-PDT</field>
  <field name="category_s">Notice</field>
  <field name="type_s">WebLogicServer</field>
  <field name="servername_s">AdminServer</field>
  <field name="code">BEA-000360</field>
  <field name="msg_s">Server started in RUNNING mode</field>
</doc>
</add>
```

The `wlslog.xml` file may be created in the vi editor and saved with the :wq command as shown in Figure 11-23.

```
ubuntu@ip-172-30-1-34: ~
File  Edit  View  Search  Terminal  Help
  <field name="type_s">WebLogicServer</field>

  <field name="servername_s">AdminServer</field>
  <field name="code_s">BEA-000331</field>
  <field name="msg_s">Started WebLogic AdminServer</field>

</doc>

<doc>
<field name="id">wlslog6</field>

  <field name="time_stamp_s">Apr-8-2014-7:06:21-PM-PDT</field>
  <field name="category_s">Notice</field>
  <field name="type_s">WebLogicServer</field>

  <field name="servername_s">AdminServer</field>
  <field name="code_s">BEA-000365</field>
  <field name="msg_s">Server state changed to RUNNING</field>

</doc>

<doc>
<field name="id">wlslog7</field>

  <field name="time_stamp_s">Apr-8-2014-7:06:22-PM-PDT</field>
  <field name="category_s">Notice</field>
  <field name="type_s">WebLogicServer</field>

  <field name="servername_s">AdminServer</field>
  <field name="code_s">BEA-000360</field>
  <field name="msg_s">Server started in RUNNING mode</field>
:wq
```

Figure 11-23. *The wlslog.xml File*

Cd to the `/opt/solr` directory and run the post tool to add the documents in the `wlslog.xml` file to Solr server.

```
bin/post -c wlslog ./wlslog.xml
```

One file gets indexed as shown in Figure 11-24.

```
solr@solr:/opt/solr$ bin/post -c wlslog ./wlslog.xml
java -classpath /opt/solr/dist/solr-core-5.4.0.jar -Dauto=yes -Dc=w
lslog -Ddata=files org.apache.solr.util.SimplePostTool ./wlslog.xml
SimplePostTool version 5.0.0
Posting files to [base] url http://localhost:8983/solr/wlslog/updat
e...
Entering auto mode. File endings considered are xml,json,csv,pdf,do
c,docx,ppt,pptx,xls,xlsx,odt,odp,ods,ott,otp,ots,rtf,htm,html,txt,l
og
POSTing file wlslog.xml (application/xml) to [base]
1 files indexed.
COMMITting Solr index changes to http://localhost:8983/solr/wlslog/
update...
Time spent: 0:00:00.104
solr@solr:/opt/solr$ 
```

Figure 11-24. *Posting the wlslog.xml File to the Solr Index*

Accessing Solr on Command Line with a REST Client

Solr request handler commands such as /update, /select may be run using a REST client such as curl and wget. In this section we shall use the curl tool to run some of the /select request handler commands. For example, query all documents using the following curl command.

```
curl http://localhost:8983/solr/wlslog/select?q=*%3A*&wt=json&indent=true
```

The curl command is shown in Figure 11-25.

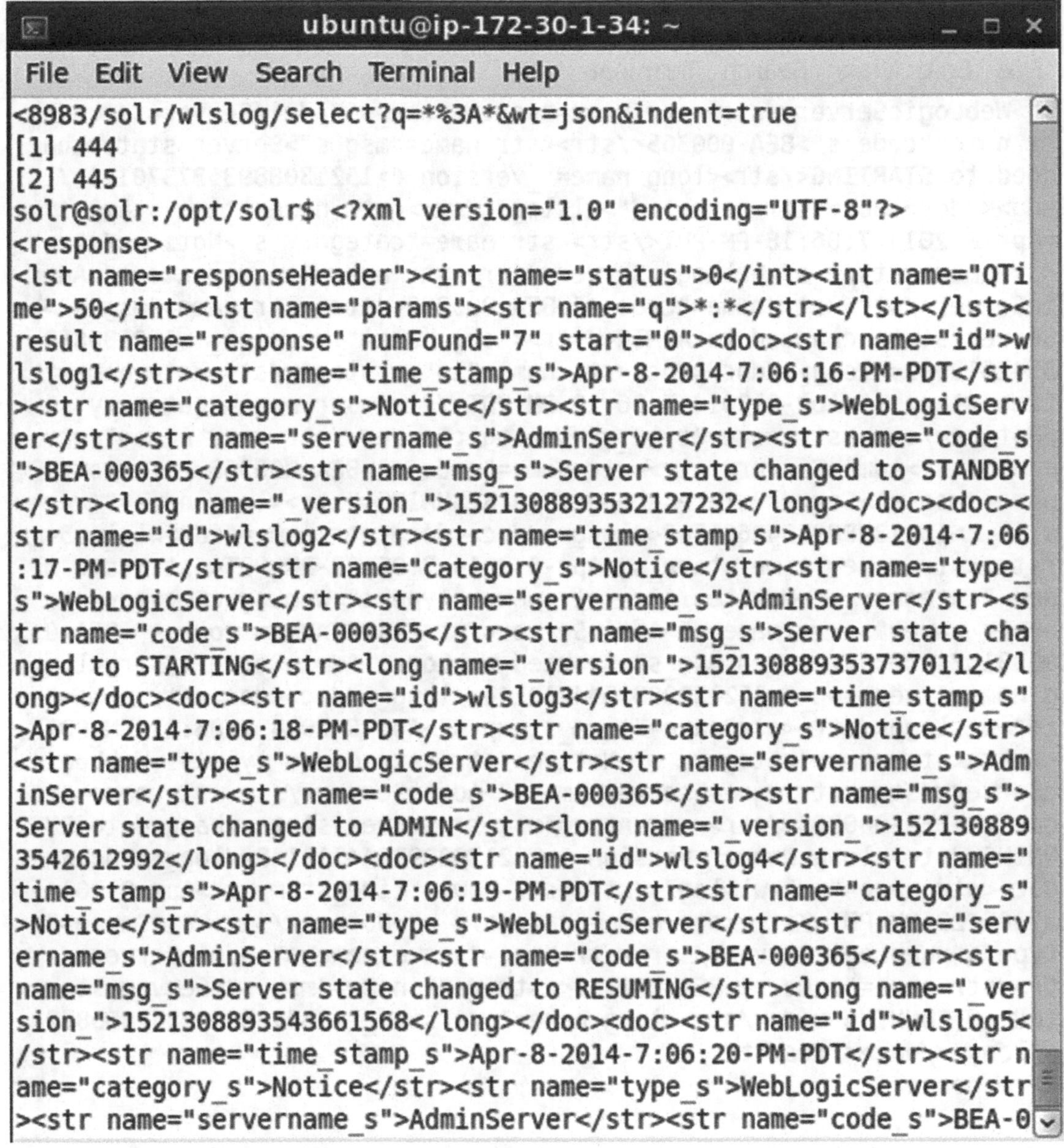
ubuntu@ip-172-30-1-34: ~
File Edit View Search Terminal Help
<8983/solr/wlslog/select?q=*%3A*&wt=json&indent=true
[1] 444
[2] 445
solr@solr:/opt/solr$ <?xml version="1.0" encoding="UTF-8"?>
<response>
<lst name="responseHeader"><int name="status">0</int><int name="QTi
me">50</int><lst name="params"><str name="q">*:*</str></lst></lst><
result name="response" numFound="7" start="0"><doc><str name="id">w
lslog1</str><str name="time_stamp_s">Apr-8-2014-7:06:16-PM-PDT</str
><str name="category_s">Notice</str><str name="type_s">WebLogicServ
er</str><str name="servername_s">AdminServer</str><str name="code_s
">BEA-000365</str><str name="msg_s">Server state changed to STANDBY
</str><long name="_version_">1521308893532127232</long></doc><doc><
str name="id">wlslog2</str><str name="time_stamp_s">Apr-8-2014-7:06
:17-PM-PDT</str><str name="category_s">Notice</str><str name="type_
s">WebLogicServer</str><str name="servername_s">AdminServer</str><s
tr name="code_s">BEA-000365</str><str name="msg_s">Server state cha
nged to STARTING</str><long name="_version_">1521308893537370112</l
ong></doc><doc><str name="id">wlslog3</str><str name="time_stamp_s"
>Apr-8-2014-7:06:18-PM-PDT</str><str name="category_s">Notice</str>
<str name="type_s">WebLogicServer</str><str name="servername_s">Adm
inServer</str><str name="code_s">BEA-000365</str><str name="msg_s">
Server state changed to ADMIN</str><long name="_version_">152130889
3542612992</long></doc><doc><str name="id">wlslog4</str><str name="
time_stamp_s">Apr-8-2014-7:06:19-PM-PDT</str><str name="category_s"
>Notice</str><str name="type_s">WebLogicServer</str><str name="serv
ername_s">AdminServer</str><str name="code_s">BEA-000365</str><str
name="msg_s">Server state changed to RESUMING</str><long name="_ver
sion_">1521308893543661568</long></doc><doc><str name="id">wlslog5<
/str><str name="time_stamp_s">Apr-8-2014-7:06:20-PM-PDT</str><str n
ame="category_s">Notice</str><str name="type_s">WebLogicServer</str
><str name="servername_s">AdminServer</str><str name="code_s">BEA-0

Figure 11-25. *Using curl to send a Request to Solr Server with Request Handler /select*

The 7 documents added get listed as shown in Figure 11-26.

ubuntu@ip-172-30-1-34: ~

File Edit View Search Terminal Help


```
s">WebLogicServer</str><str name="servername_s">AdminServer</str><s
tr name="code_s">BEA-000365</str><str name="msg_s">Server state cha
nged to STARTING</str><long name="_version_">1521308893537370112</l
ong></doc><doc><str name="id">wlslog3</str><str name="time_stamp_s"
>Apr-8-2014-7:06:18-PM-PDT</str><str name="category_s">Notice</str>
<str name="type_s">WebLogicServer</str><str name="servername_s">Adm
inServer</str><str name="code_s">BEA-000365</str><str name="msg_s">
Server state changed to ADMIN</str><long name="_version_">152130889
3542612992</long></doc><doc><str name="id">wlslog4</str><str name="
time_stamp_s">Apr-8-2014-7:06:19-PM-PDT</str><str name="category_s"
>Notice</str><str name="type_s">WebLogicServer</str><str name="serv
ername_s">AdminServer</str><str name="code_s">BEA-000365</str><str
name="msg_s">Server state changed to RESUMING</str><long name="_ver
sion_">1521308893543661568</long></doc><doc><str name="id">wlslog5<
/str><str name="time_stamp_s">Apr-8-2014-7:06:20-PM-PDT</str><str n
ame="category_s">Notice</str><str name="type_s">WebLogicServer</str
><str name="servername_s">AdminServer</str><str name="code_s">BEA-0
00331</str><str name="msg_s">Started WebLogic AdminServer</str><lon
g name="_version_">1521308893544710144</long></doc><doc><str name="
id">wlslog6</str><str name="time_stamp_s">Apr-8-2014-7:06:21-PM-PDT
</str><str name="category_s">Notice</str><str name="type_s">WebLogi
cServer</str><str name="servername_s">AdminServer</str><str name="c
ode_s">BEA-000365</str><str name="msg_s">Server state changed to RU
NNING</str><long name="_version_">1521308893544710145</long></doc><
doc><str name="id">wlslog7</str><str name="time_stamp_s">Apr-8-2014
-7:06:22-PM-PDT</str><str name="category_s">Notice</str><str name="
type_s">WebLogicServer</str><str name="servername_s">AdminServer</s
tr><str name="code_s">BEA-000360</str><str name="msg_s">Server star
ted in RUNNING mode</str><long name="_version_">1521308893547855872
</long></doc></result>
</response>
```


***Figure 11-26.** Listing the Documents returned by the /select Request Handler*

As another example run the `/select` request handler to query for the document with id `wlslog7`.

```
curl http://localhost:8983/solr/wlslog/select?q=id:wlslog7&wt=json&indent=true
```

The document for id `wlslog7` gets listed as shown in Figure 11-27.

```
<8983/solr/wlslog/select?q=id:wlslog7&wt=json&indent=true
[1] 456
[2] 457
solr@solr:/opt/solr$ <?xml version="1.0" encoding="UTF-8"?>
<response>
<lst name="responseHeader"><int name="status">0</int><int name="QTi
me">1</int><lst name="params"><str name="q">id:wlslog7</str></lst><
/lst><result name="response" numFound="1" start="0"><doc><str name=
"id">wlslog7</str><str name="time_stamp_s">Apr-8-2014-7:06:22-PM-PD
T</str><str name="category_s">Notice</str><str name="type_s">WebLog
icServer</str><str name="servername_s">AdminServer</str><str name="
code_s">BEA-000360</str><str name="msg_s">Server started in RUNNING
 mode</str><long name="_version_">1521308893547855872</long></doc><
/result>
</response>
```

Figure 11-27. *Querying for a Single Document with id wlslog7 using /select Request Handler and curl*

Documents may be deleted with the post tool. For example, delete a document with id `wlslog1` using the following command.

```
bin/post -c wlslog -d "<delete><id>wlslog1</id></delete>"
```

The document with id `wlslog1` gets deleted as shown in Figure 11-28.

```
<in/post -c wlslog -d "<delete><id>wlslog1</id></delete>"
java -classpath /opt/solr/dist/solr-core-5.4.0.jar -Dauto=yes -Dc=w
lslog -Ddata=args org.apache.solr.util.SimplePostTool <delete><id>w
lslog1</id></delete>
SimplePostTool version 5.0.0
POSTing args to http://localhost:8983/solr/wlslog/update...
COMMITting Solr index changes to http://localhost:8983/solr/wlslog/
update...
Time spent: 0:00:00.050
solr@solr:/opt/solr$
```

Figure 11-28. *Deleting a Document using post Tool*

Subsequently run the following curl command to list the documents in the `wlslog` index.

```
curl http://localhost:8983/solr/wlslog/select?q=*%3A*&wt=json&indent=true
```

The document with id `wlslog1` does not get listed as shown in Figure 11-29.

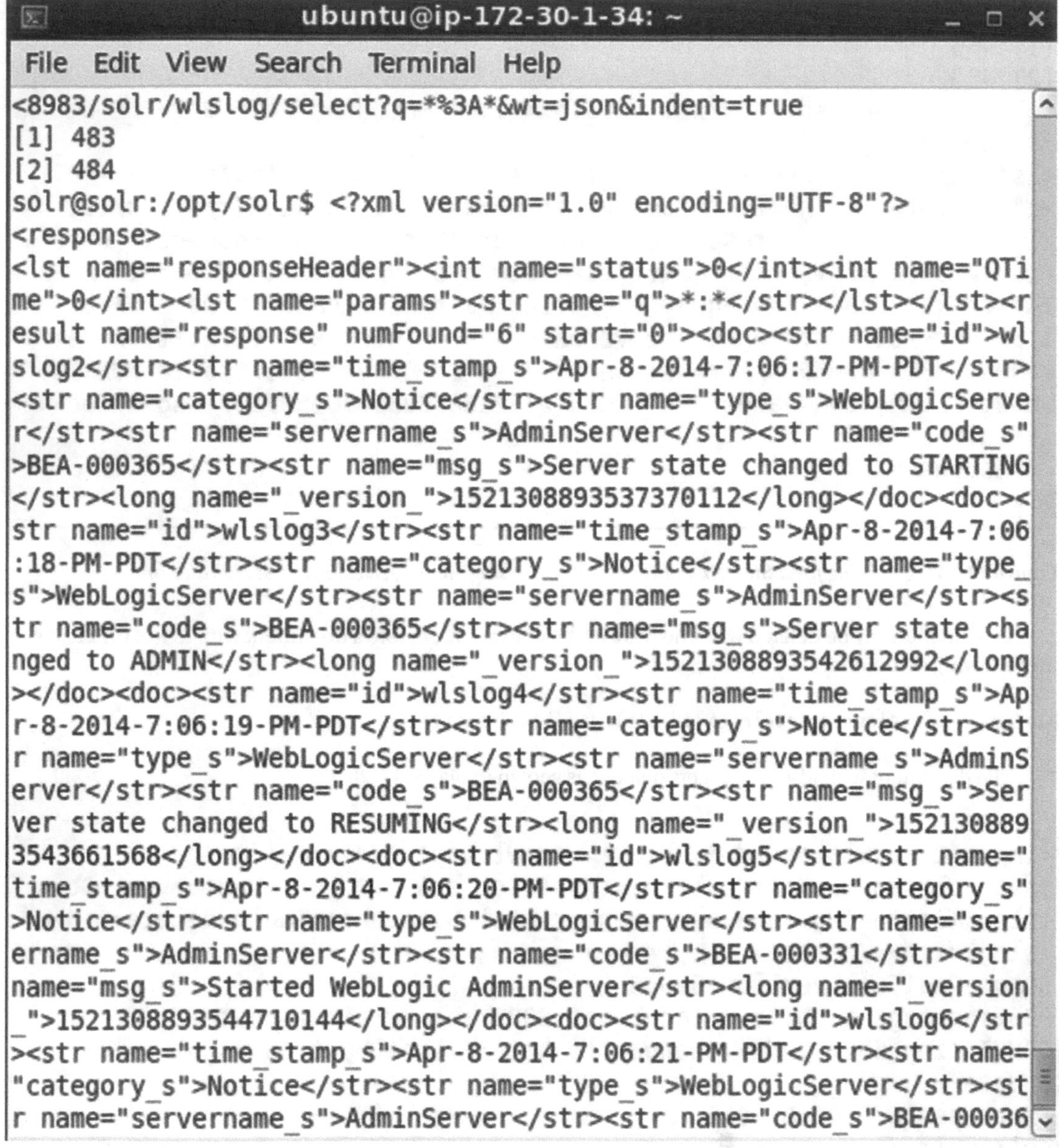
ubuntu@ip-172-30-1-34: ~
File Edit View Search Terminal Help
<8983/solr/wlslog/select?q=*%3A*&wt=json&indent=true
[1] 483
[2] 484
solr@solr:/opt/solr$ <?xml version="1.0" encoding="UTF-8"?>
<response>
<lst name="responseHeader"><int name="status">0</int><int name="QTi
me">0</int><lst name="params"><str name="q">*:*</str></lst></lst><r
esult name="response" numFound="6" start="0"><doc><str name="id">wl
slog2</str><str name="time_stamp_s">Apr-8-2014-7:06:17-PM-PDT</str>
<str name="category_s">Notice</str><str name="type_s">WebLogicServe
r</str><str name="servername_s">AdminServer</str><str name="code_s"
>BEA-000365</str><str name="msg_s">Server state changed to STARTING
</str><long name="_version_">1521308893537370112</long></doc><doc><
str name="id">wlslog3</str><str name="time_stamp_s">Apr-8-2014-7:06
:18-PM-PDT</str><str name="category_s">Notice</str><str name="type_
s">WebLogicServer</str><str name="servername_s">AdminServer</str><s
tr name="code_s">BEA-000365</str><str name="msg_s">Server state cha
nged to ADMIN</str><long name="_version_">1521308893542612992</long
></doc><doc><str name="id">wlslog4</str><str name="time_stamp_s">Ap
r-8-2014-7:06:19-PM-PDT</str><str name="category_s">Notice</str><st
r name="type_s">WebLogicServer</str><str name="servername_s">AdminS
erver</str><str name="code_s">BEA-000365</str><str name="msg_s">Ser
ver state changed to RESUMING</str><long name="_version_">152130889
3543661568</long></doc><doc><str name="id">wlslog5</str><str name="
time_stamp_s">Apr-8-2014-7:06:20-PM-PDT</str><str name="category_s"
>Notice</str><str name="type_s">WebLogicServer</str><str name="serv
ername_s">AdminServer</str><str name="code_s">BEA-000331</str><str
name="msg_s">Started WebLogic AdminServer</str><long name="_version
_">1521308893544710144</long></doc><doc><str name="id">wlslog6</str
><str name="time_stamp_s">Apr-8-2014-7:06:21-PM-PDT</str><str name=
"category_s">Notice</str><str name="type_s">WebLogicServer</str><st
r name="servername_s">AdminServer</str><str name="code_s">BEA-00036

Figure 11-29. *Querying after Deleting a Document*

The /update request handler may be used to delete documents as in the following curl command, which deletes all documents in the wlslog core.

```
curl http://localhost:8983/solr/wlslog/update --data '<delete><query>*:*</query></delete>'
-H 'Content-type:text/xml; charset=utf-8'
```

If auto commit has not been configured the following curl command must be run to commit the changes.

```
curl http://localhost:8983/solr/wlslog/update --data '<commit/>' -H 'Content-type:text/xml;
charset=utf-8'
```

Subsequently run the curl command to invoke the `/select` request handler.

```
curl http://localhost:8983/solr/wlslog/select?q=*%3A*&wt=json&indent=true
```

No document gets listed as all have been deleted as shown in Figure 11-30.

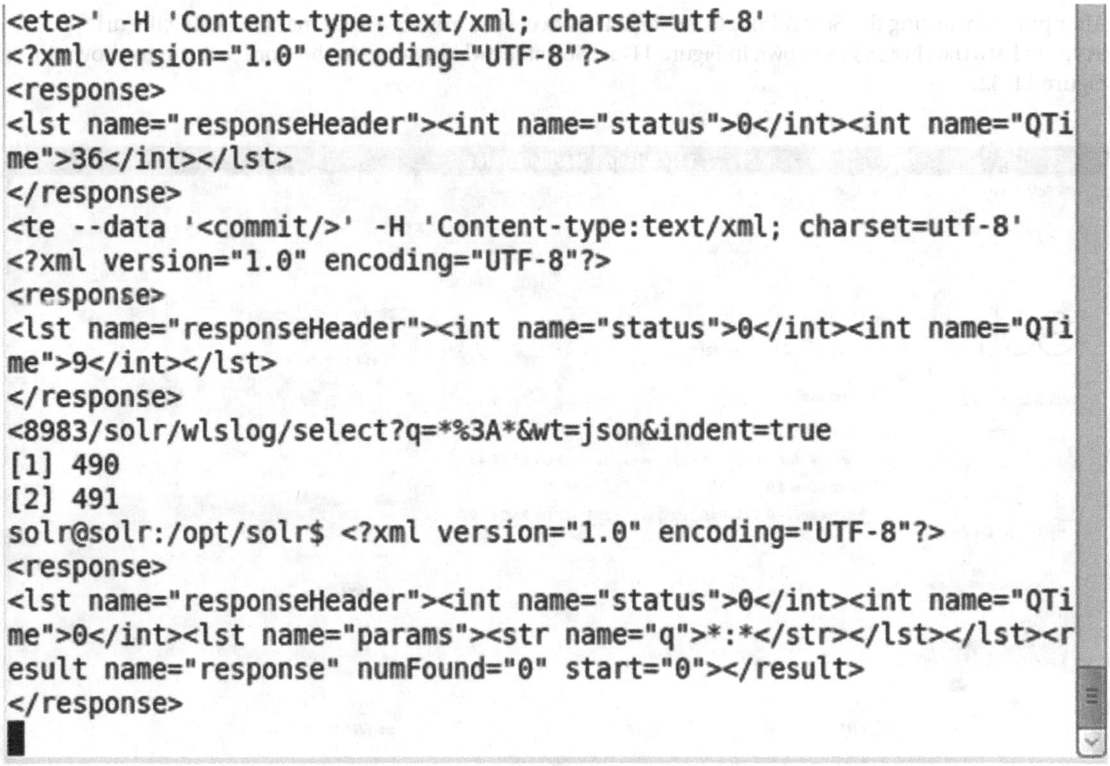

```
<ete>' -H 'Content-type:text/xml; charset=utf-8'
<?xml version="1.0" encoding="UTF-8"?>
<response>
<lst name="responseHeader"><int name="status">0</int><int name="QTi
me">36</int></lst>
</response>
<te --data '<commit/>' -H 'Content-type:text/xml; charset=utf-8'
<?xml version="1.0" encoding="UTF-8"?>
<response>
<lst name="responseHeader"><int name="status">0</int><int name="QTi
me">9</int></lst>
</response>
<8983/solr/wlslog/select?q=*%3A*&wt=json&indent=true
[1] 490
[2] 491
solr@solr:/opt/solr$ <?xml version="1.0" encoding="UTF-8"?>
<response>
<lst name="responseHeader"><int name="status">0</int><int name="QTi
me">0</int><lst name="params"><str name="q">*:*</str></lst></lst><r
esult name="response" numFound="0" start="0"></result>
</response>
```

Figure 11-30. *Deleting all Documents in Solr Index with /update*

Setting Port Forwarding

If we were running Kubernetes on a local machine we could have opened the Solr Admin Console with url `http://localhost:8983` but because we are using Amazon EC2 instance we need to set port forwarding on a local machine with a web browser from localhost:8983 to 172.17.0.2:8983. Set port forwarding from `localhost` port 8983 with the following command run from a local machine.

```
ssh -i key-pair-file -f -nNT -L 8983:172.17.0.2:8983 ubuntu@ec2-54-152-82-142.compute-1.
amazonaws.com
```

The preceding command forwards the localhost:8983 URL to endpoint 172.17.0.2:8983 as shown in Figure 11-31.

```
[root@localhost ~]# ssh -i docker.pem -f -nNT -L  8983:172.17.0.2:8983 ubuntu@ec2-54-152-82-142.compute-1.amazonaws.com
[root@localhost ~]# 
```

Figure 11-31. *Setting Port Forwarding to localhost*

Accessing Solr in Admin Console

After port forwarding the Solr Admin Console may be accessed from the local machine using the url `http://localhost:8983` as shown in Figure 11-32. Select the `wlslog` core in the Core Selector as shown in Figure 11-32.

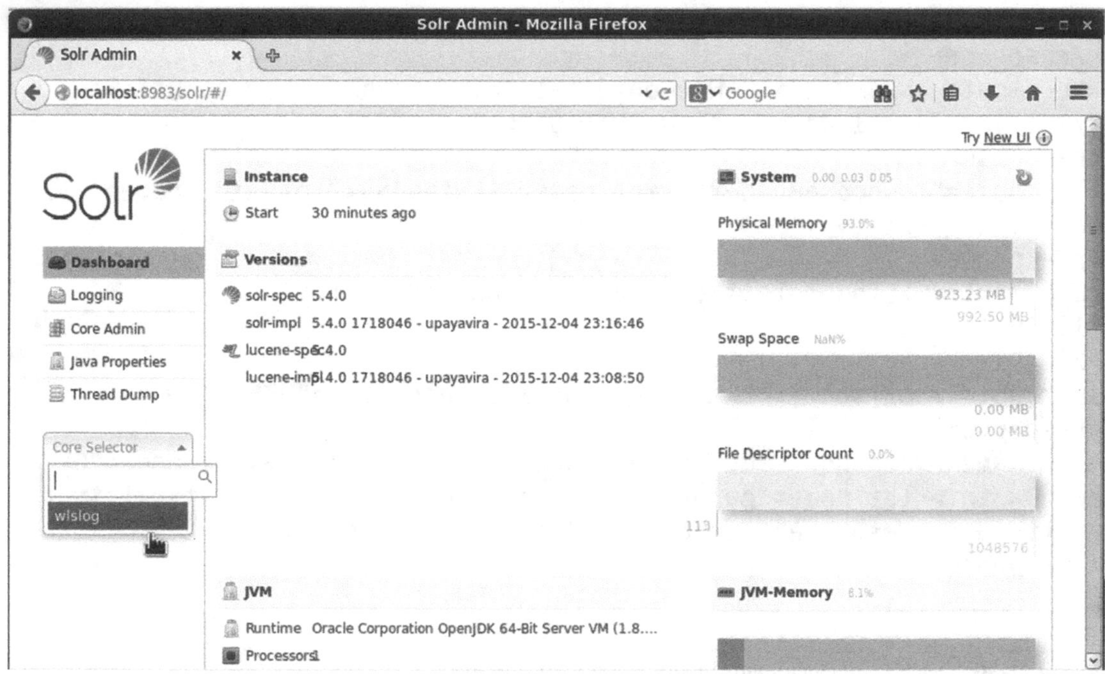

Figure 11-32. *Displaying the Solr Admin Console*

Select the Documents tab and set Document Type as XML for the `/update` Request handler as shown in Figure 11-33. Copy and paste the XML document wlslog.xml listed earlier in the Document (s) field and click on Submit Document.

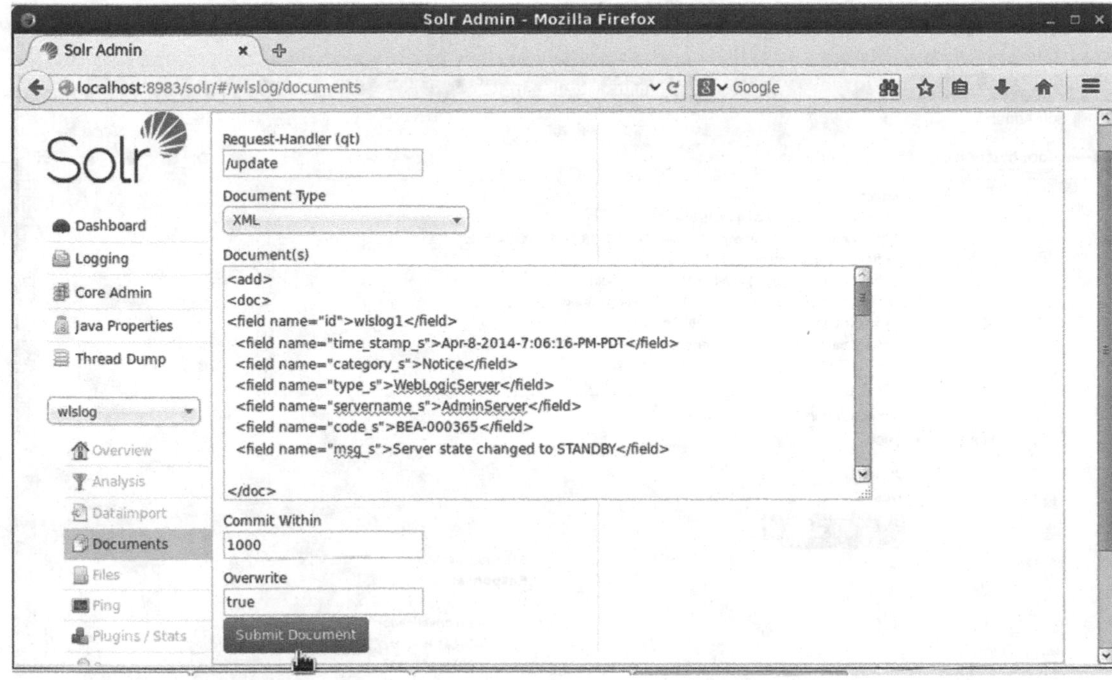

***Figure 11-33.** Adding Document to the wlslog Core*

An output of "success" as shown in Figure 11-34 indicates that the documents got indexed.

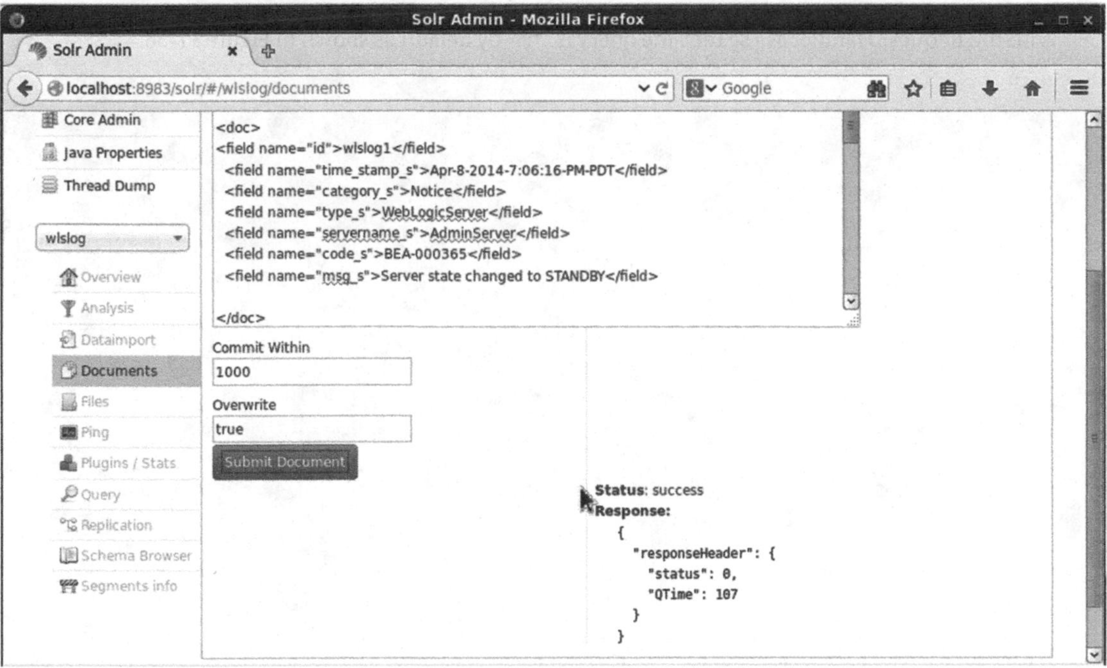

***Figure 11-34.** Response from adding Documents*

Next, we shall query the wlslog index. Select the Query tab as shown in Figure 11-35.

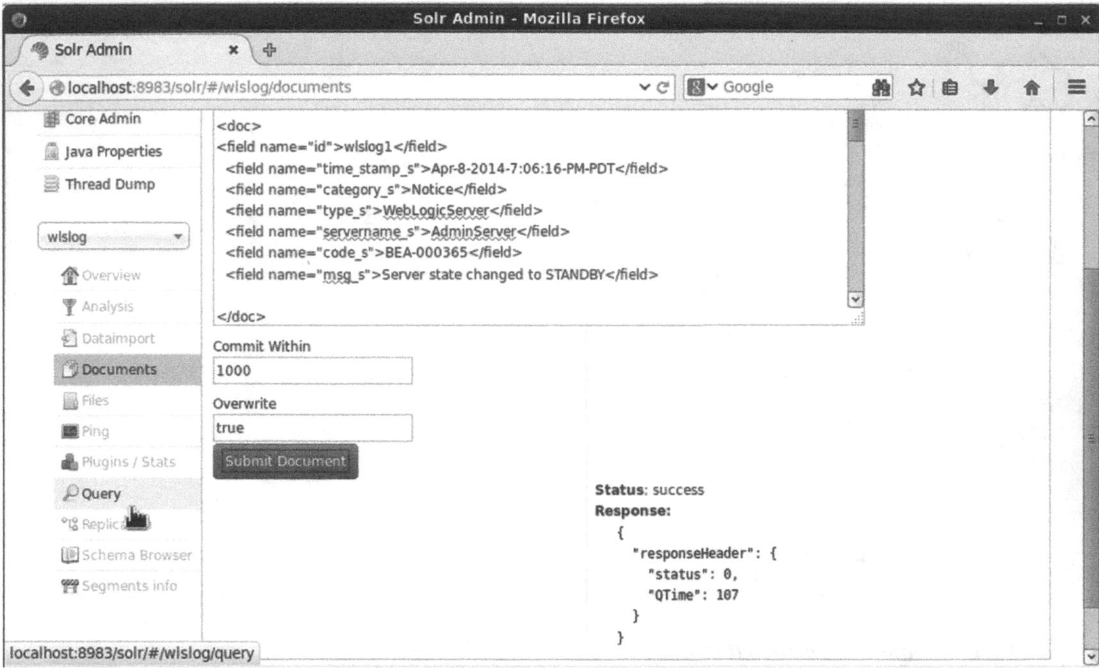

Figure 11-35. *Selecting the Query Tab*

With the Request Handler as /select the query is "*:*" by default as shown in Figure 11-36.

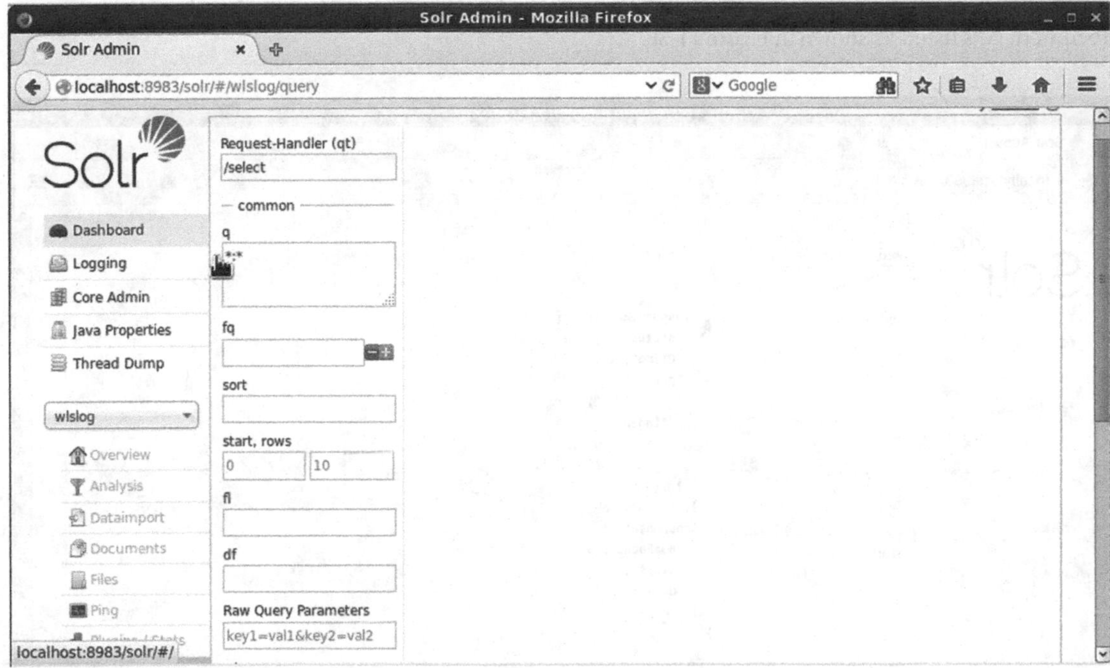

Figure 11-36. *Using the Request Handler /select to Query Solr index wlslog*

Click on Execute Query as shown in Figure 11-37.

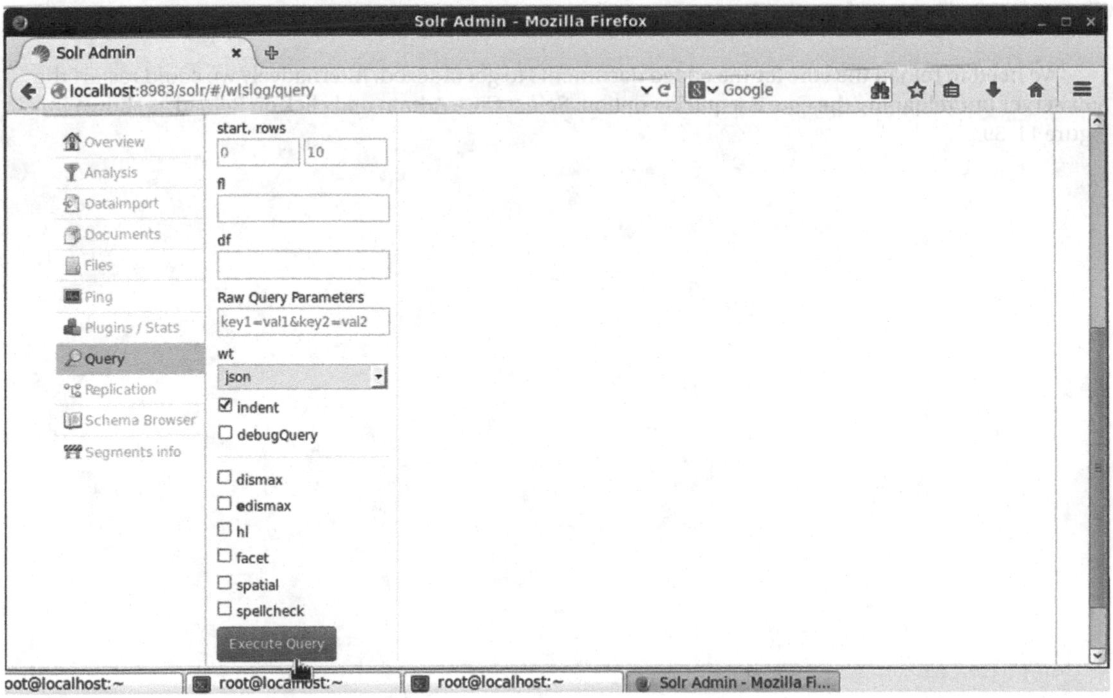

Figure 11-37. *Submitting a Query to select all Documents in the wlslog Index*

Because we have not set auto commit the documents added have not yet been indexed. As a result no document gets listed as shown in Figure 11-38.

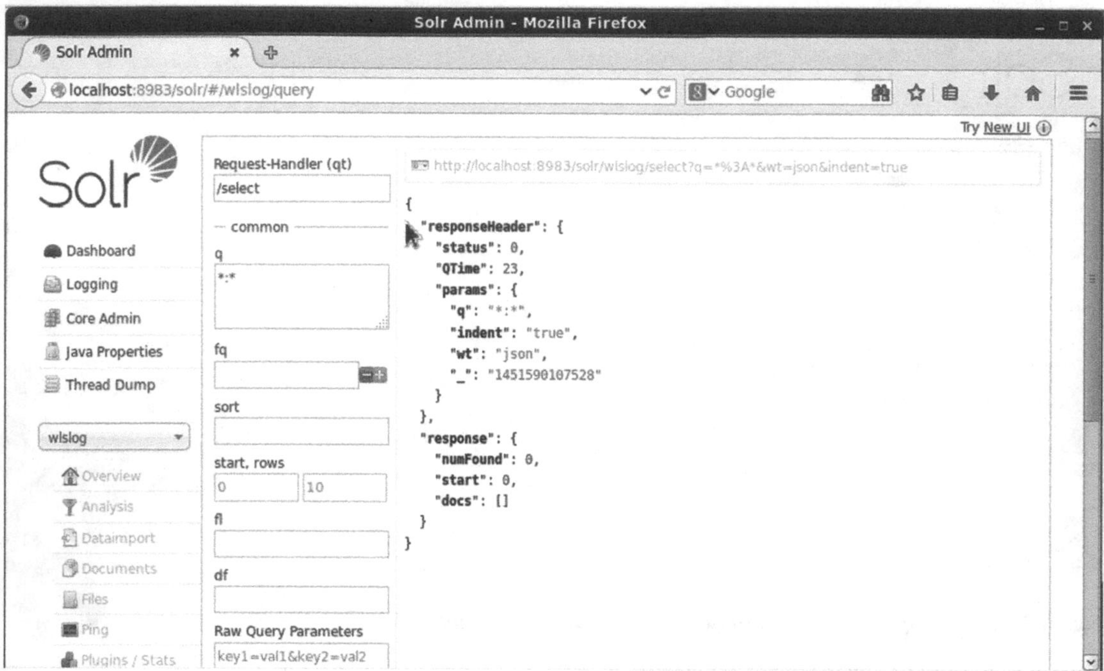

Figure 11-38. *Response from the Query*

We need to reload the core for the added documents to get indexed. Alternatively we could restart the Solr server but reloading the core is a quicker option. Select Core Admin and click on Reload as shown in Figure 11-39.

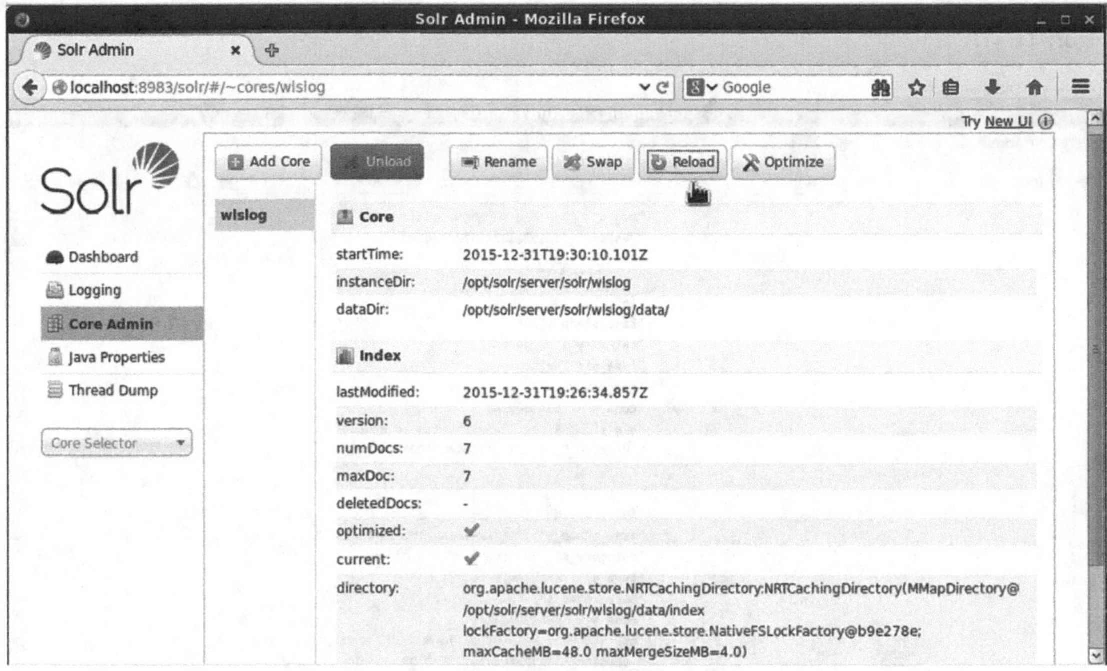

Figure 11-39. *Reloading the Core*

Run the query again and as shown in Figure 11-40 the 7 documents added get listed.

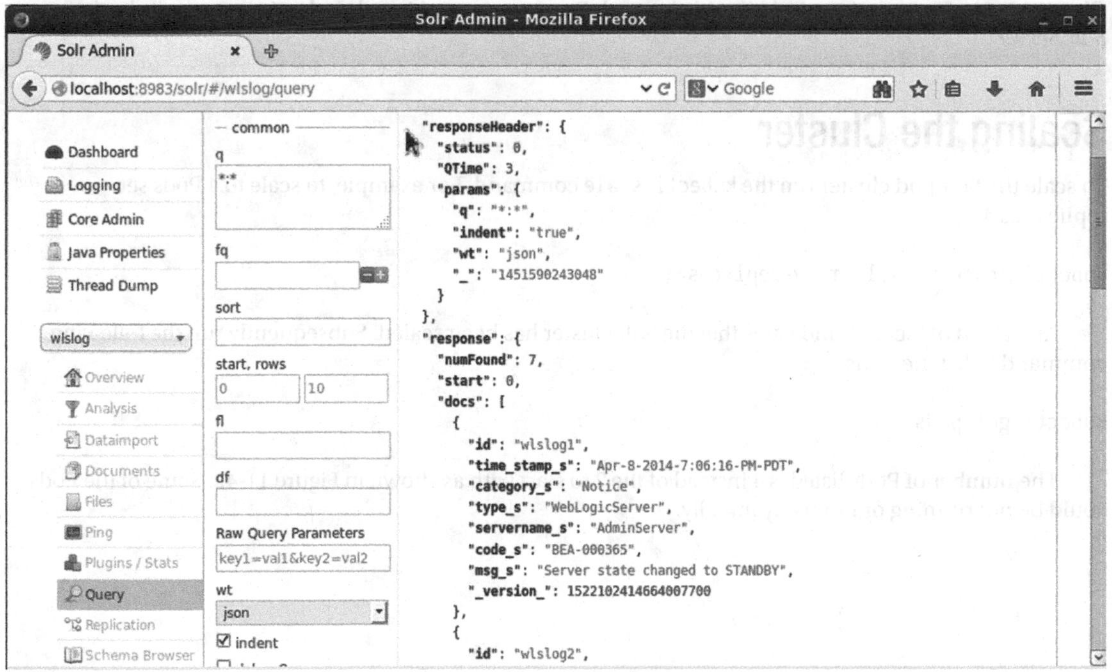

Figure 11-40. *Query Response with 7 Documents*

The `_version_` field has been added to each document automatically by the Solr server as shown in Figure 11-41.

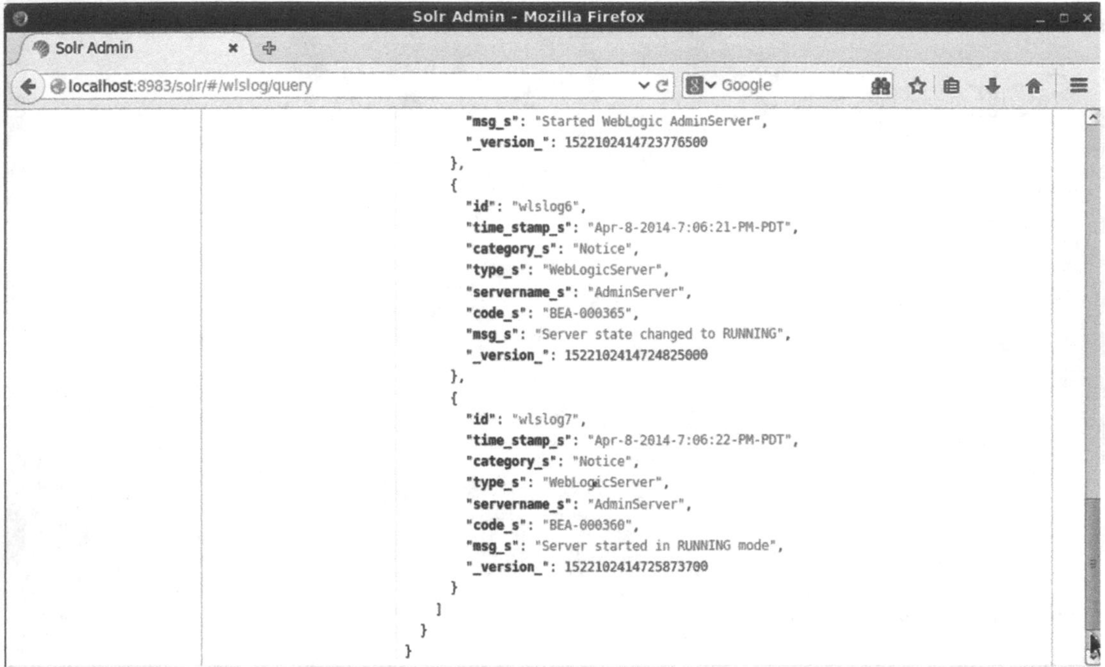

Figure 11-41. *The _version_ Field is added to each Document stored in Solr Index Automatically by the Solr Server*

Scaling the Cluster

To scale the Solr pod cluster run the `kubectl scale` command. For example, to scale to 4 Pods set replicas as 4.

```
kubectl scale rc solr-rc --replicas=4
```

An output of "scaled" indicates that the Solr cluster has been scaled. Subsequently run the following command to list the Pods.

```
kubectl get pods
```

The number of Pods listed is 4 instead of the 2 to start with as shown in Figure 11-42. Some of the Pods could be not running or not ready initially.

```
ubuntu@ip-172-30-1-34:~$ kubectl scale rc solr-rc --replicas=4
scaled
ubuntu@ip-172-30-1-34:~$ kubectl get pods
NAME                    READY     STATUS    RESTARTS   AGE
k8s-master-127.0.0.1    3/3       Running   0          3h
solr                    1/1       Running   0          2h
solr-rc-pfpiu           1/1       Running   0          1h
solr-rc-rwquj           0/1       Running   0          11s
solr-rc-voe3o           1/1       Running   0          11s
```

Figure 11-42. *Scaling the Apache Solr Cluster to 4 Pods*

Summary

Apache Solr is an indexing and search engine that makes use of the local filesystem to store data. In this chapter we used Docker image "solr" with Kubernetes cluster manage to create and manage a cluster of Solr instances. We demonstrated accessing a Solr instance from an interactive shell for a Docker container and also using the Admin Console. In the next chapter we shall use Kubernetes with Apache Kafka.

CHAPTER 12

Using Apache Kafka

Apache Kafka is publish-subscribe, high throughput, distributed messaging system. A single broker in Kafka could handle 100s MB (Terabytes)/sec of reads & writes from multiple clients. Messages are replicated across the cluster and persisted to disk. Kafka could be used for stream processing, web site activity tracking, metrics collection, and monitoring and log aggregation.

The main components of Kafka architecture are Producer, Broker, Topic, and Consumer. Kafka keeps feeds of messages in topics. Producers send (or write) messages to topics and Consumers consume (or read) messages from topics. Messages are byte arrays of data and could be in any format with String, JSON, and Avro being the most common. Messages are retained for a specified amount of time. A Zookeeper coordinates the Kafka cluster. In a single producer-consumer architecture, a single Producer sends messages to a Topic and a single Consumer consumes messages from the topic.

Kafka is similar to Flume in that it streams messages, but Kafka is designed for a different purpose. While Flume is designed to stream messages to a sink such as HDFS or HBase, Kafka is designed for messages to be consumed by multiple applications.

In this chapter we shall discuss using Kubernetes cluster manager with Apache Kafka.

- Setting the Environment
- Modifying the Docker Image
- Creating a Service
- Creating a Replication Controller
- Listing the Pods
- Describing a Pod
- Starting an Interactive Shell
- Starting the Kafka Server
- Creating a Topic
- Starting a Kafka Producer
- Starting a Kafka Consumer
- Producing and Consuming Messages
- Scaling the Cluster
- Deleting Replication Controller and Service

D. Vohra, *Kubernetes Microservices with Docker*, DOI 10.1007/978-1-4842-1907-2_12

Setting the Environment

We have used an Amazon EC2 instance created from AMI Ubuntu Server 14.04 LTS (HVM), SSD Volume Type - ami-d05e75b8. The following software is required for this chapter.

-Docker Engine (latest version)

-Kubernetes Cluster Manager (version 1.01)

-Kubectl (version 1.01)

-Docker image dockerkafka/kafka (latest version)

We have used the Docker image `dockerkafka/kafka` in this chapter. The default settings of the `dockerkafka/kafka` image Dockerfile are not suitable for orchestration with Kubernetes. In the next section we have modified and rebuilt the default Docker image. First, connect with the Ubuntu instance using the Public IP Address for the Amazon EC2 instance.

```
ssh -i "docker.pem" ubuntu@54.146.140.160
```

The Ubuntu instance gets connected to as shown in Figure 12-1.

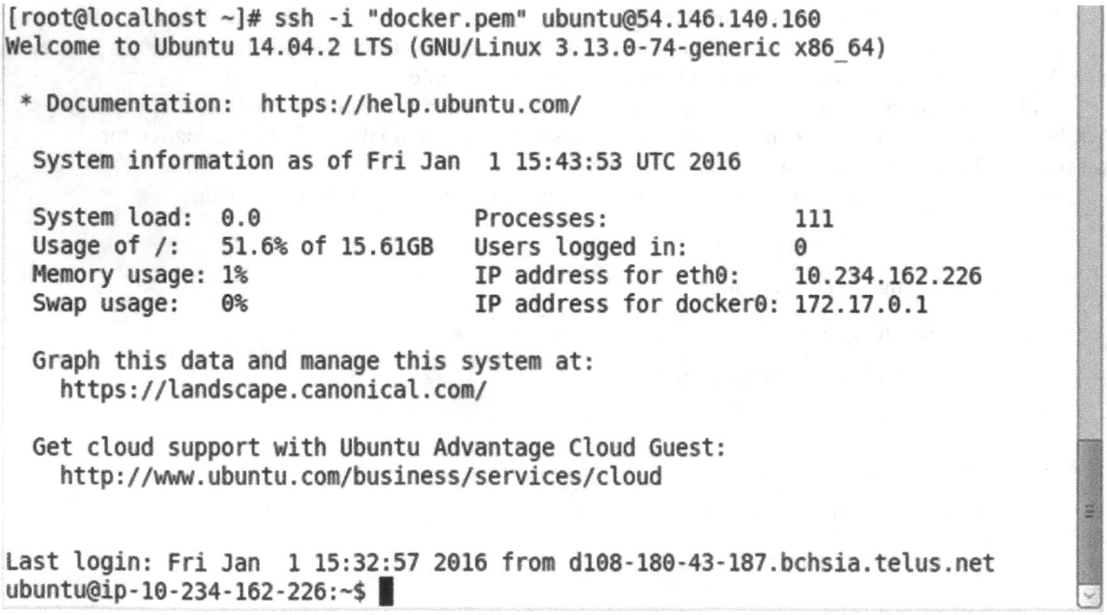

```
[root@localhost ~]# ssh -i "docker.pem" ubuntu@54.146.140.160
Welcome to Ubuntu 14.04.2 LTS (GNU/Linux 3.13.0-74-generic x86_64)

 * Documentation:  https://help.ubuntu.com/

  System information as of Fri Jan  1 15:43:53 UTC 2016

  System load:  0.0               Processes:              111
  Usage of /:   51.6% of 15.61GB  Users logged in:        0
  Memory usage: 1%                IP address for eth0:    10.234.162.226
  Swap usage:   0%                IP address for docker0: 172.17.0.1

  Graph this data and manage this system at:
    https://landscape.canonical.com/

  Get cloud support with Ubuntu Advantage Cloud Guest:
    http://www.ubuntu.com/business/services/cloud


Last login: Fri Jan  1 15:32:57 2016 from d108-180-43-187.bchsia.telus.net
ubuntu@ip-10-234-162-226:~$
```

Figure 12-1. *Connecting to an Ubuntu Instance on Amazon EC2*

Install the required software as discussed in chapter 1. Start the Docker service and find its status.

```
sudo service docker start
sudo service docker status
```

Docker should be listed as running as shown in Figure 12-2.

```
ubuntu@ip-10-234-162-226:~$ sudo service docker start
start: Job is already running: docker
ubuntu@ip-10-234-162-226:~$ sudo service docker status
docker start/running, process 861
ubuntu@ip-10-234-162-226:~$ ▌
```

Figure 12-2. *Starting Docker*

List the Kubernetes services.

```
kubectl get services
```

The "kubernetes" service should be listed as shown in Figure 12-3.

```
ubuntu@ip-10-234-162-226:~$ kubectl get services
NAME          LABELS                                    SELECTOR   IP(S)      POR
T(S)
kubernetes    component=apiserver,provider=kubernetes   <none>     10.0.0.1   443
/TCP
ubuntu@ip-10-234-162-226:~$ ▌
```

Figure 12-3. *Listing the "kubernetes" Service*

Modifying the Docker Image

The procedure to start Apache Kafka involves the following sequence.

1. Start Zookeeper Server
2. Start Apache Kafka Server

The Apache Kafka Server has a dependency on Zookeeper server and as a result requires the Zookeeper server to be running before the Kafka server may be started. The Kafka server makes use of the `server.properties` configuration file when started. The default settings in the `server.properties` file are not suitable for the Kafka server to start based on a Zookeeper server running at `localhost:2181`. We need to modify the connect url for Zookeeper in the `server.properties` file.

In this section we shall download the `dockerkafka/kafka` image, modify the `server.properties` and rebuild the Docker image. Download the source code for the `dockerkafka/kafka` image with the following command.

```
git clone https://github.com/DockerKafka/kafka-docker.git
```

The source code for the `dockerkafka/kafka` image gets downloaded as shown in Figure 12-4.

```
ubuntu@ip-10-234-162-226:~$ git clone https://github.com/DockerKafka/kafka-docke
r.git
Cloning into 'kafka-docker'...
remote: Counting objects: 318, done.
remote: Total 318 (delta 0), reused 0 (delta 0), pack-reused 318
Receiving objects: 100% (318/318), 98.02 KiB | 0 bytes/s, done.
Resolving deltas: 100% (139/139), done.
Checking connectivity... done.
```

Figure 12-4. *Downloading the kafka-docker Docker Image Source Code*

Change directory (cd) to the kafka-docker directory and list the files/directories.

```
cd kafka-docker
ls -l
```

The files/directories in the Docker image get listed as shown in Figure 12-5.

```
ubuntu@ip-10-234-162-226:~/kafka-docker$ ls -l
total 32
-rw-rw-r-- 1 ubuntu ubuntu   261 Jan  1 15:34 docker-compose.yml
-rwxrwxr-x 1 ubuntu ubuntu   229 Jan  1 15:34 docker-entrypoint.sh
-rw-rw-r-- 1 ubuntu ubuntu   462 Jan  1 15:34 Dockerfile
drwxrwxr-x 3 ubuntu ubuntu  4096 Jan  1 15:34 image
-rw-rw-r-- 1 ubuntu ubuntu 11325 Jan  1 15:34 LICENSE
-rw-rw-r-- 1 ubuntu ubuntu  2022 Jan  1 15:34 README.md
ubuntu@ip-10-234-162-226:~/kafka-docker$
```

Figure 12-5. *Listing the Dockerfile and Image Directory for the kafka-source Docker Image*

We need to modify the settings in the server.properties file, which is in the image/conf directory. Cd to the image/conf directory and list the directory's file/directories.

```
cd image/conf
ls -l
```

The server.properties file gets listed as shown in Figure 12-6.

```
ubuntu@ip-10-234-162-226:~/kafka-docker/image/conf$ ls -l
total 32
-rw-rw-r-- 1 ubuntu ubuntu 1199 Jan  1 15:34 consumer.properties
-rw-rw-r-- 1 ubuntu ubuntu 3846 Jan  1 15:34 log4j.properties
-rw-rw-r-- 1 ubuntu ubuntu 2228 Jan  1 15:34 producer.properties
-rw-rw-r-- 1 ubuntu ubuntu 5559 Jan  1 15:34 server.properties
-rw-rw-r-- 1 ubuntu ubuntu 3325 Jan  1 15:34 test-log4j.properties
-rw-rw-r-- 1 ubuntu ubuntu  993 Jan  1 15:34 tools-log4j.properties
-rw-rw-r-- 1 ubuntu ubuntu 1023 Jan  1 15:34 zookeeper.properties
ubuntu@ip-10-234-162-226:~/kafka-docker/image/conf$
```

Figure 12-6. *Listing the Configuration Files for the Docker Image*

Open the server.properties file in a vi editor.

```
sudo vi server.properties
```

The server.properties file is shown in Figure 12-7. Uncomment the line with the host.name=localhost setting.

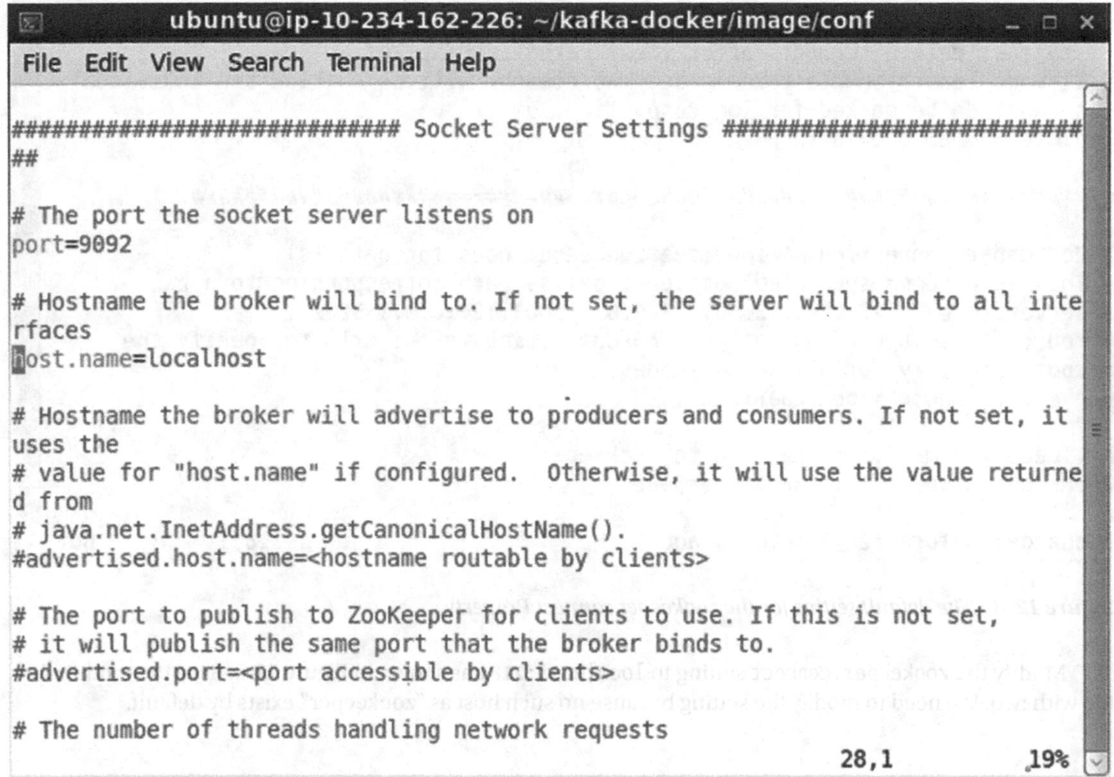

Figure 12-7. *Uncommenting the host.name Property*

As shown in Figure 12-8 the default setting for the zookeeper.connect is zookeeper:2181.

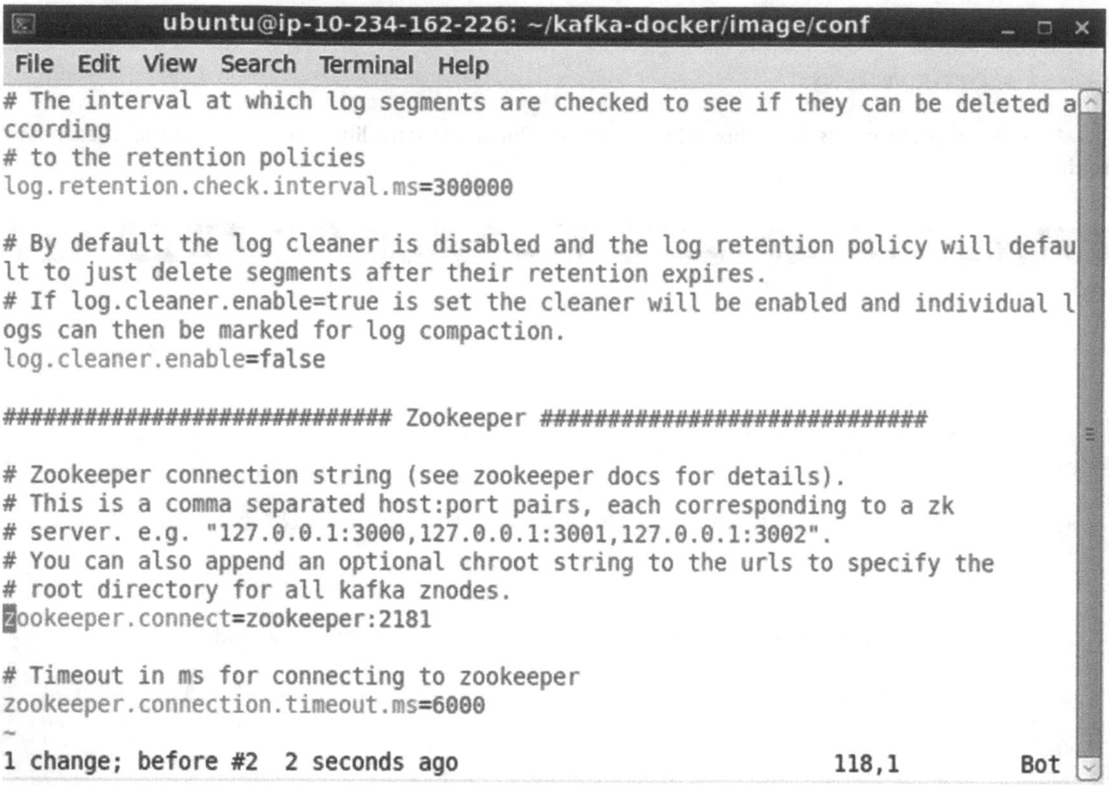

```
ubuntu@ip-10-234-162-226: ~/kafka-docker/image/conf
File Edit View Search Terminal Help
# The interval at which log segments are checked to see if they can be deleted a
ccording
# to the retention policies
log.retention.check.interval.ms=300000

# By default the log cleaner is disabled and the log retention policy will defau
lt to just delete segments after their retention expires.
# If log.cleaner.enable=true is set the cleaner will be enabled and individual l
ogs can then be marked for log compaction.
log.cleaner.enable=false

############################# Zookeeper #############################

# Zookeeper connection string (see zookeeper docs for details).
# This is a comma separated host:port pairs, each corresponding to a zk
# server. e.g. "127.0.0.1:3000,127.0.0.1:3001,127.0.0.1:3002".
# You can also append an optional chroot string to the urls to specify the
# root directory for all kafka znodes.
zookeeper.connect=zookeeper:2181

# Timeout in ms for connecting to zookeeper
zookeeper.connection.timeout.ms=6000
~
1 change; before #2  2 seconds ago                          118,1         Bot
```

Figure 12-8. *The default setting for the zookeeper.connect Property*

Modify the `zookeeper.connect` setting to `localhost:2181` as shown in Figure 12-9. Save the modified file with :wq. We need to modify the setting because no such host as "zookeeper" exists by default.

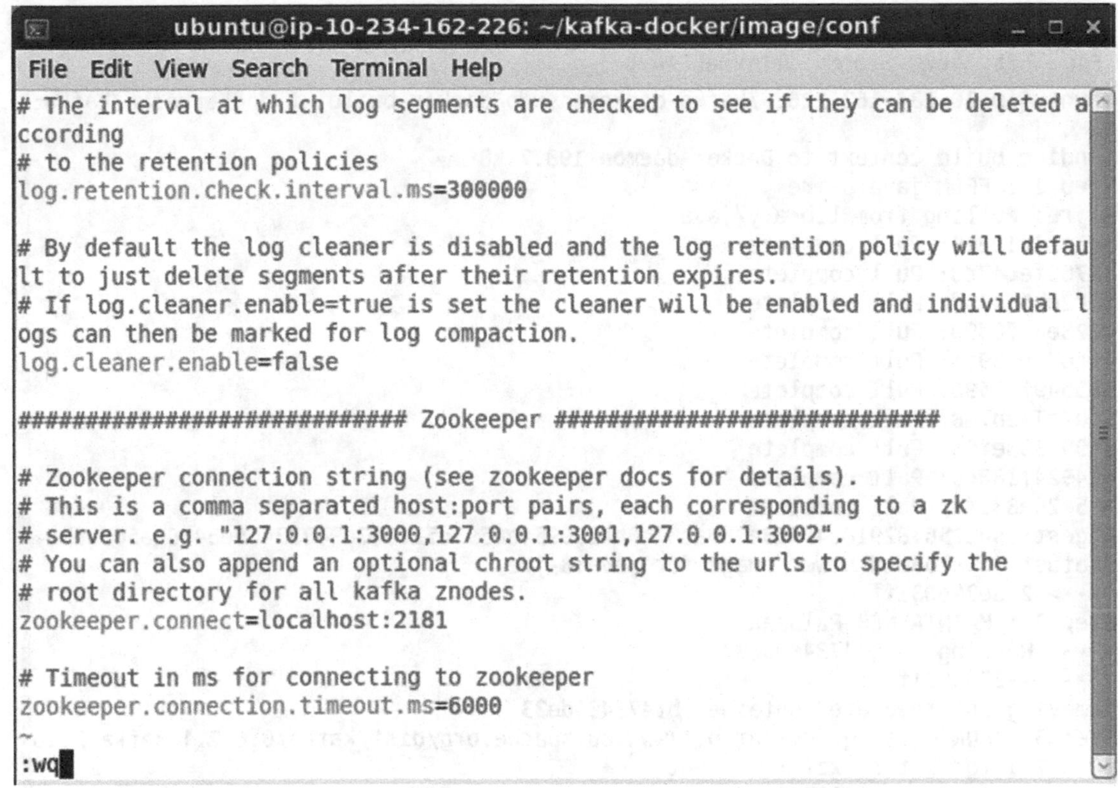

Figure 12-9. *Setting zookeeper.connect to localhost: 2181*

Subsequently cd back to the root directory for the Docker image, the `kafka-docker` directory, and run the following command to rebuild the Docker image.

```
sudo docker build -t dockerkafka/kafka:v2.
```

The output from the command is shown in Figure 12-10.

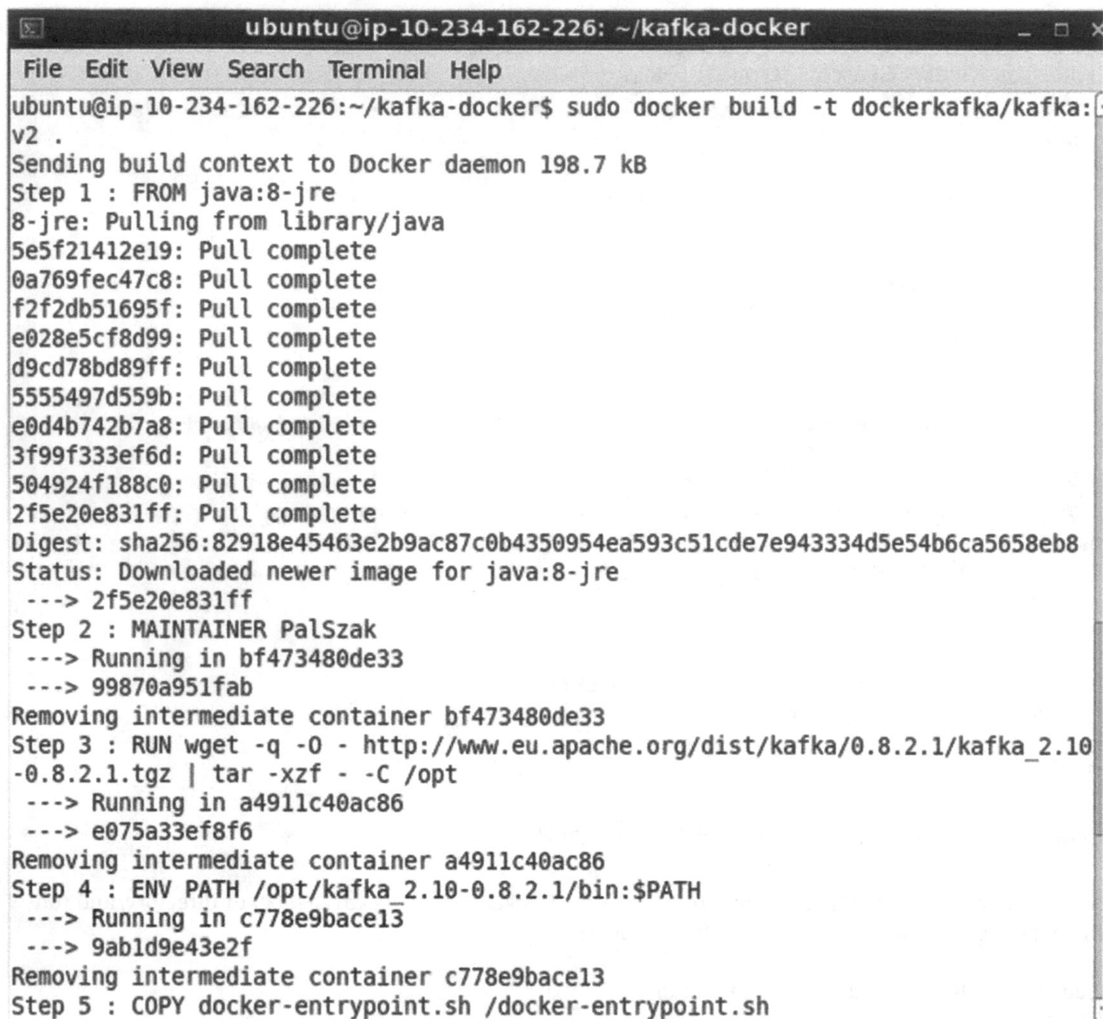

```
ubuntu@ip-10-234-162-226:~/kafka-docker$ sudo docker build -t dockerkafka/kafka:
v2 .
Sending build context to Docker daemon 198.7 kB
Step 1 : FROM java:8-jre
8-jre: Pulling from library/java
5e5f21412e19: Pull complete
0a769fec47c8: Pull complete
f2f2db51695f: Pull complete
e028e5cf8d99: Pull complete
d9cd78bd89ff: Pull complete
5555497d559b: Pull complete
e0d4b742b7a8: Pull complete
3f99f333ef6d: Pull complete
504924f188c0: Pull complete
2f5e20e831ff: Pull complete
Digest: sha256:82918e45463e2b9ac87c0b4350954ea593c51cde7e943334d5e54b6ca5658eb8
Status: Downloaded newer image for java:8-jre
 ---> 2f5e20e831ff
Step 2 : MAINTAINER PalSzak
 ---> Running in bf473480de33
 ---> 99870a951fab
Removing intermediate container bf473480de33
Step 3 : RUN wget -q -O - http://www.eu.apache.org/dist/kafka/0.8.2.1/kafka_2.10
-0.8.2.1.tgz | tar -xzf - -C /opt
 ---> Running in a4911c40ac86
 ---> e075a33ef8f6
Removing intermediate container a4911c40ac86
Step 4 : ENV PATH /opt/kafka_2.10-0.8.2.1/bin:$PATH
 ---> Running in c778e9bace13
 ---> 9ab1d9e43e2f
Removing intermediate container c778e9bace13
Step 5 : COPY docker-entrypoint.sh /docker-entrypoint.sh
```

Figure 12-10. *Rebuilding the Docker Image for Kafka*

Docker image gets rebuilt as shown in Figure 12-11.

***Figure 12-11.** Completing the Rebuild of the Docker Image*

The Docker image we shall use subsequently is not `dockerkafka/kafka` but is `dockerkafka/kafka:v2`.

Creating a Service

Create a service definition file called `kafka-service.yaml` and add the following (Table 12-1) fields to the file.

Table 12-1. *The Fields in the Service Definition File*

Field	Description	Value
apiVersion		v1
kind	The kind of definition file.	Service
metadata	The service metadata.	
metadata ->labels	The service labels. Not required.	app: kafkaApp
metadata ->name	The service name. Required.	kafka
spec	The service specification.	
spec ->ports	The ports exposed by the service.	
spec ->ports->port	A port exposed by the service. The 9092 port is used for the Kafka server.	port: 9092 targetPort: 9092
spec ->ports->port	Another port exposed by the service. The 2181 port is for the Zookeeper.	port: 2181 targetPort: 2181
spec ->selector	The Pod selector. Service routes traffic to the Pods with label matching the selector expression.	app: kafkaApp
spec ->selector->type	The service type.	LoadBalancer

The `kafka-service.yaml` is listed.

```
apiVersion: v1
kind: Service
metadata:
  labels:
    app: kafkaApp
  name: kafka
spec:
  ports:
    -
      port: 9092
      targetPort: 9092
    -
      port: 2181
      targetPort: 2181
  selector:
    app: kafkaApp
  type: LoadBalancer
```

The `kafka-service.yaml` may be created in vi editor and saved with :wq as shown in Figure 12-12.

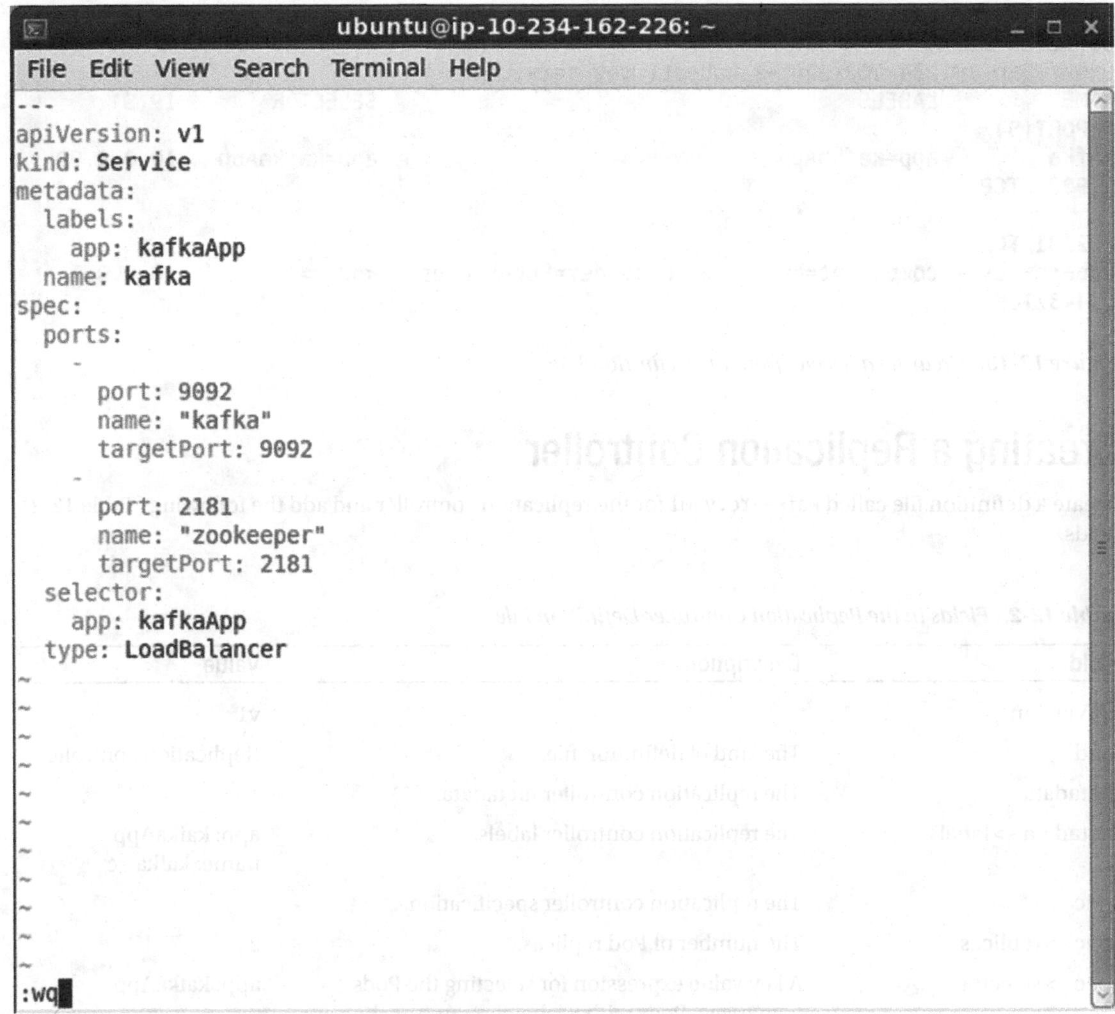

Figure 12-12. *Service Definition File in vi Editor*

Create the service from the definition file.

```
kubectl create -f kafka-service.yaml
```

Subsequently list the services.

```
kubectl get services
```

The "kafka" service gets listed as shown in Figure 12-13. The service selector is app=kafkaApp.

```
ubuntu@ip-10-234-162-226:~$ kubectl create -f  kafka-service.yaml
services/kafka
ubuntu@ip-10-234-162-226:~$ kubectl get services
NAME          LABELS                                      SELECTOR       IP(S)
  PORT(S)
kafka         app=kafkaApp                                app=kafkaApp   10.0.0.90
  9092/TCP

  2181/TCP
kubernetes    component=apiserver,provider=kubernetes     <none>         10.0.0.1
  443/TCP
```

Figure 12-13. *Creating a Service from the Definition File*

Creating a Replication Controller

Create a definition file called `kafka-rc.yaml` for the replication controller and add the following (Table 12-2) fields.

Table 12-2. *Fields in the Replication Controller Definition File*

Field	Description	Value
apiVersion		v1
kind	The kind of definition file.	ReplicationController
metadata	The replication controller metadata.	
metadata -> labels	The replication controller labels.	app: kafkaApp name: kafka-rc
spec	The replication controller specification.	
spec -> replicas	The number of Pod replicas.	2
spec -> selector	A key:value expression for selecting the Pods to manage. Pods with a label the same as the selector expression are managed by the replication controller. The selector expression must be the same as the spec-> template-> metadata-> labels expression. The selector defaults to the spec-> template-> metadata-> labels key:value expression if not specified.	app: kafkaApp
spec -> template	The Pod template.	
spec -> template-> metadata	The Pod template metadata.	
spec -> template -> metadata -> labels	The Pod template labels.	app: kafkaApp
spec -> template -> spec	The Pod template specification.	
spec -> template -> spec -> containers	The containers configuration for the Pod template.	

(*continued*)

Table 12-2. (*continued*)

Field	Description	Value
spec -> template -> spec -> containers -> command	The command/s to run for the Docker image. The default command in the Dockerfile is CMD ["kafka-server-start.sh", "/opt/kafka_2.10-0.8.2.1/config/server.properties"]. The default command starts the Kakfa server, but we want the Zookeeper server before the Kafka server as the Kafka server won't start unless the Zookeeper server is running. The modified command starts only the Zookeeper server. We shall start the Kafka server separately.	- zookeeper-server-start.sh - /opt/kafka_2.10-0.8.2.1/config/zookeeper.properties
spec -> template -> spec -> containers -> image	The Docker image.	dockerkafka/kafka:v2
spec -> template -> spec -> containers -> name	The container name.	zookeeper
ports	Specifies the container port/s.	containerPort: 2181

The `kafka-rc.yaml` is listed.

```
---
apiVersion: v1
kind: ReplicationController
metadata:
  labels:
    app: kafkaApp
  name: kafka-rc
spec:
  replicas: 1
  selector:
    app: kafkaApp
  template:
    metadata:
      labels:
        app: kafkaApp
    spec:
      containers:
        -
          command:
            - zookeeper-server-start.sh
            - /opt/kafka_2.10-0.8.2.1/config/zookeeper.properties
          image: "dockerkafka/kafka:v2"
          name: zookeeper
          ports:
            -
              containerPort: 2181
```

The kafka-rc.yaml file may be created and saved in the vi editor as shown in Figure 12-14.

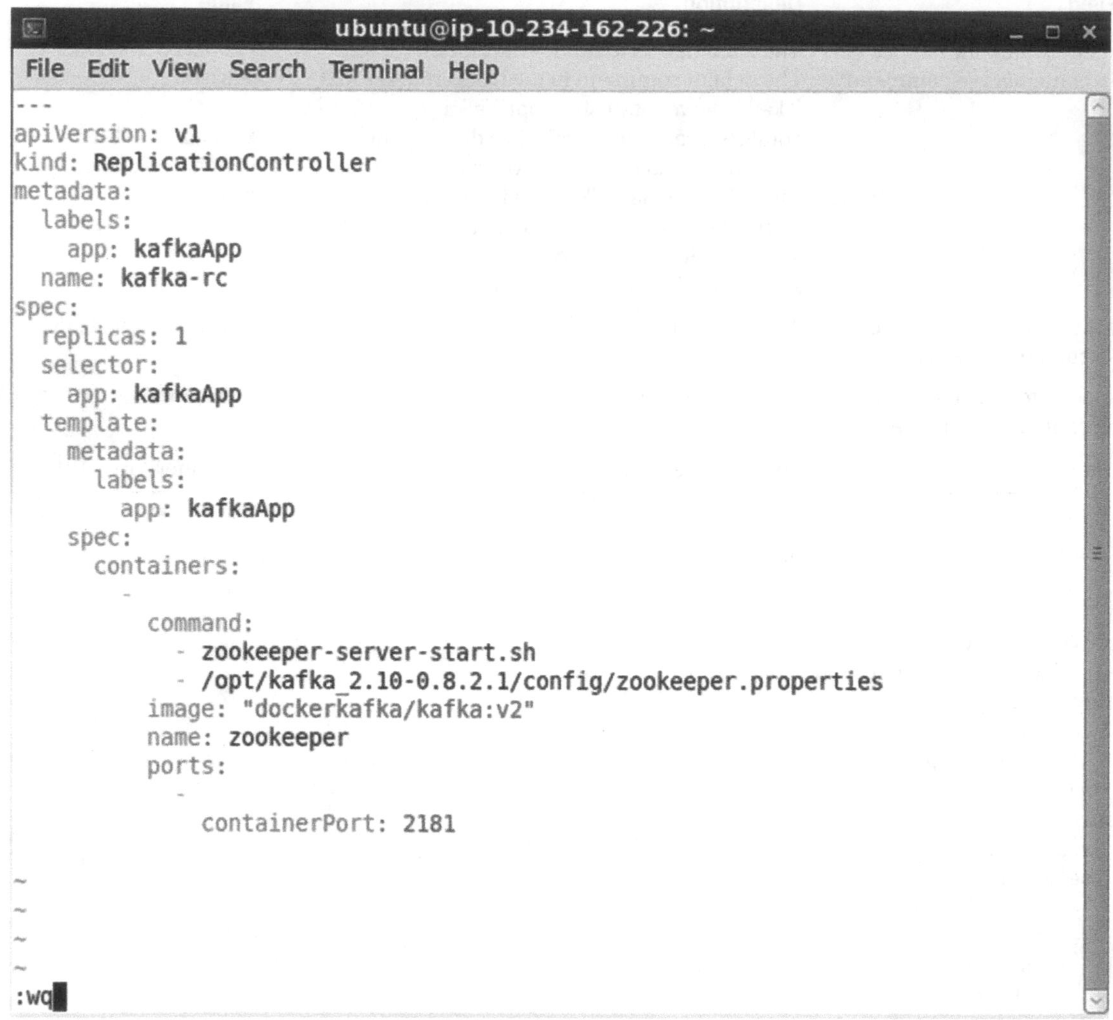

Figure 12-14. *Replication Controller Definition File in vi Editor*

Create the replication controller from the definition file.

```
kubectl create -f kafka-rc.yaml
```

Subsequently list the replication controllers.

```
kubectl get rc
```

The replication controller gets created and listed as shown in Figure 12-15.

```
ubuntu@ip-10-234-162-226:~$ kubectl create -f  kafka-rc.yaml
replicationcontrollers/kafka-rc
ubuntu@ip-10-234-162-226:~$ kubectl get rc
CONTROLLER   CONTAINER(S)   IMAGE(S)               SELECTOR        REPLICAS
kafka-rc     zookeeper      dockerkafka/kafka:v2   app=kafkaApp    1
```

Figure 12-15. Creating the Replication Controller from the Definition File

To describe the kafka-rc run the following command.

```
kubectl describe rc kafka-rc
```

The replication controller description gets listed as shown in Figure 12-16.

```
ubuntu@ip-10-234-162-226:~$ kubectl describe rc kafka-rc
Name:           kafka-rc
Namespace:      default
Image(s):       dockerkafka/kafka:v2
Selector:       app=kafkaApp
Labels:         app=kafkaApp
Replicas:       1 current / 1 desired
Pods Status:    1 Running / 0 Waiting / 0 Succeeded / 0 Failed
Events:
  FirstSeen                             LastSeen                        Count  F
rom                             SubobjectPath   Reason                  Message
  Fri, 01 Jan 2016 16:08:04 +0000       Fri, 01 Jan 2016 16:08:04 +0000 1      {
replication-controller }                        successfulCreate        Created
pod: kafka-rc-k8as1


ubuntu@ip-10-234-162-226:~$
```

Figure 12-16. Describing the Replication Controller

Listing the Pods

To list the Pods run the following command.

```
kubectl get pods
```

The Pods get listed as shown in Figure 12-17.

```
ubuntu@ip-10-234-162-226:~$ kubectl get pods
NAME                    READY     STATUS    RESTARTS   AGE
k8s-master-127.0.0.1    3/3       Running   3          23m
kafka-rc-k8as1          1/1       Running   0          1m
ubuntu@ip-10-234-162-226:~$
```

Figure 12-17. Listing the pods for Kafka

Describing a Pod

Only a single Pod is created because the “replicas” setting in the definition file `kafka-rc.yaml` is 1. To describe the Pod run the following command.

```
kubectl describe pod kafka-rc-k8as1
```

The pod description gets listed as shown in Figure 12-18. The Pod label app=kafkaApp is the same as the service selector and the replication controller selector which makes the Pod manageable by the service and the replication controller.

```
ubuntu@ip-10-234-162-226:~$ kubectl describe pod kafka-rc-k8asl
Name:                           kafka-rc-k8asl
Namespace:                      default
Image(s):                       dockerkafka/kafka:v2
Node:                           127.0.0.1/127.0.0.1
Labels:                         app=kafkaApp
Status:                         Running
Reason:
Message:
IP:                             172.17.0.2
Replication Controllers:        kafka-rc (1/1 replicas created)
Containers:
  zookeeper:
    Image:              dockerkafka/kafka:v2
    State:              Running
      Started:          Fri, 01 Jan 2016 16:08:14 +0000
    Ready:              True
    Restart Count:      0
Conditions:
  Type          Status
  Ready         True
Events:
  FirstSeen                             LastSeen                                Count  F
rom                     SubobjectPath                                   Reason          M
essage
  Fri, 01 Jan 2016 16:08:04 +0000       Fri, 01 Jan 2016 16:08:04 +0000 1       {
scheduler }                                                             scheduled       S
uccessfully assigned kafka-rc-k8asl to 127.0.0.1
```

Figure 12-18. *Describing a pod for Kafka*

When the Pod is created and started, the Zookeeper server gets started as the command for the modified Docker image is to start the Zookeeper server. Next we shall start the Kafka server from an interactive shell for the Docker container for the modified Docker image.

Starting an Interactive Shell

To be able to start an interactive bash shell to access the Kafka software installed we need to know the container id for the Docker container running the modified Docker image. List the Docker containers with the following command.

```
sudo docker ps
```

The Docker containers get listed as shown in Figure 12-19.

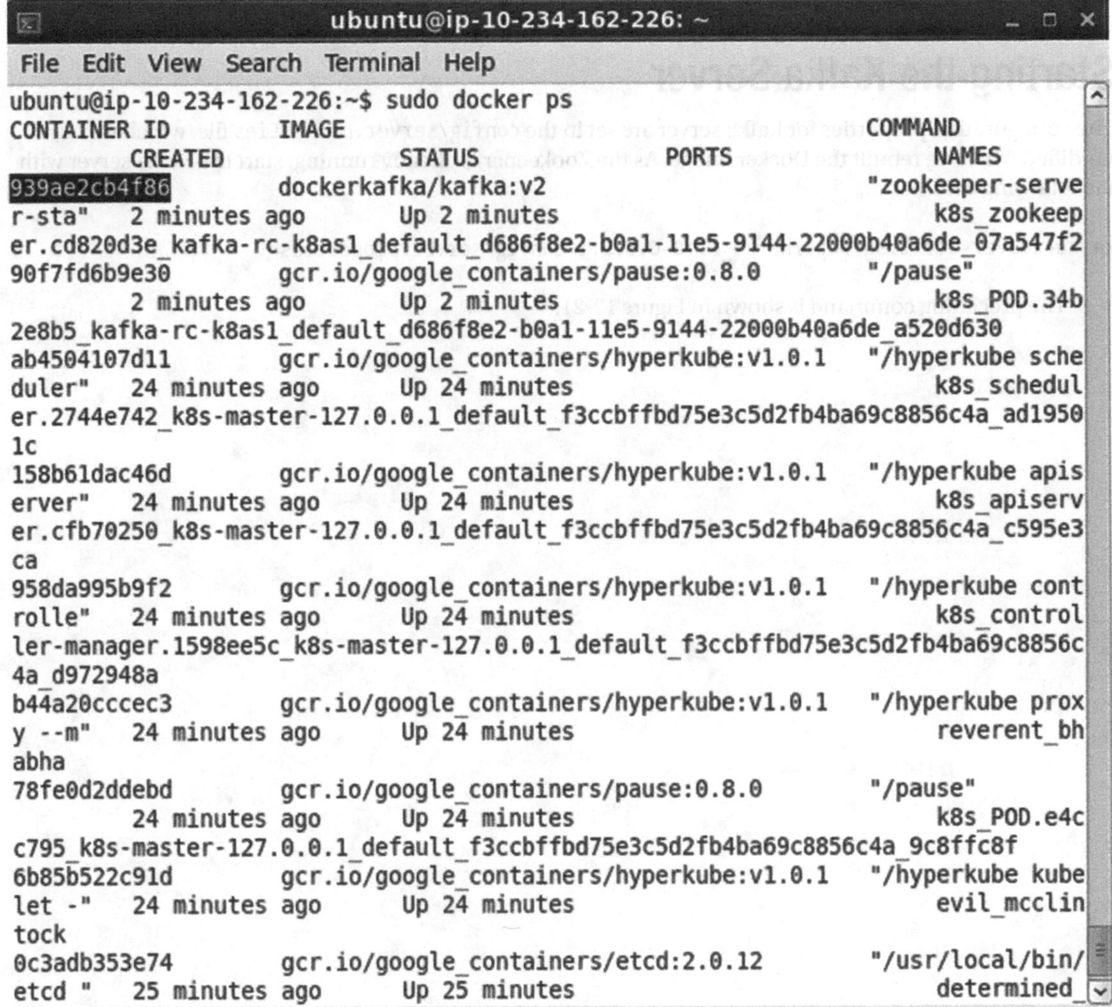

Figure 12-19. *Obtaining the Docker Container Id*

Copy the container id and start the interactive bash shell.

```
sudo docker exec -it 939ae2cb4f86 bash
```

The interactive shell gets started as shown in Figure 12-20.

```
ubuntu@ip-10-234-162-226:~$ sudo docker exec -it 939ae2cb4f86 bash
root@kafka-rc-k8as1:/#
```

Figure 12-20. *Starting the Interactive TTY for the Docker Container*

Starting the Kafka Server

The configuration properties for Kafka server are set in the `config/server.properties` file, which we modified when we rebuilt the Docker image. As the Zookeeper is already running, start the Kafka server with the following command.

```
kafka-server-start.sh /opt/kafka_2.10-0.8.2.1/config/server.properties
```

The preceding command is shown in Figure 12-21.

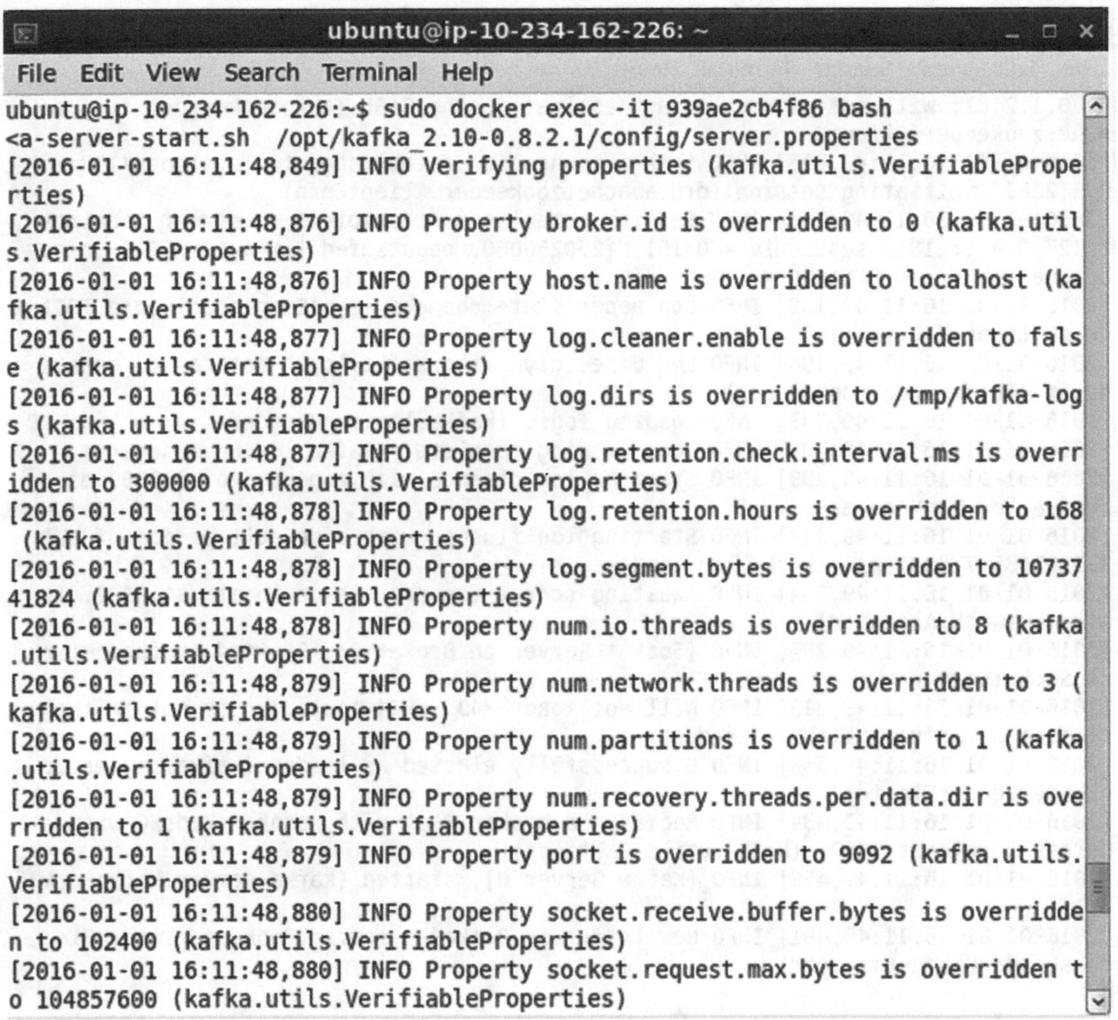

Figure 12-21. *Starting the Kafka Server*

Kafka server gets started as shown in Figure 12-22.

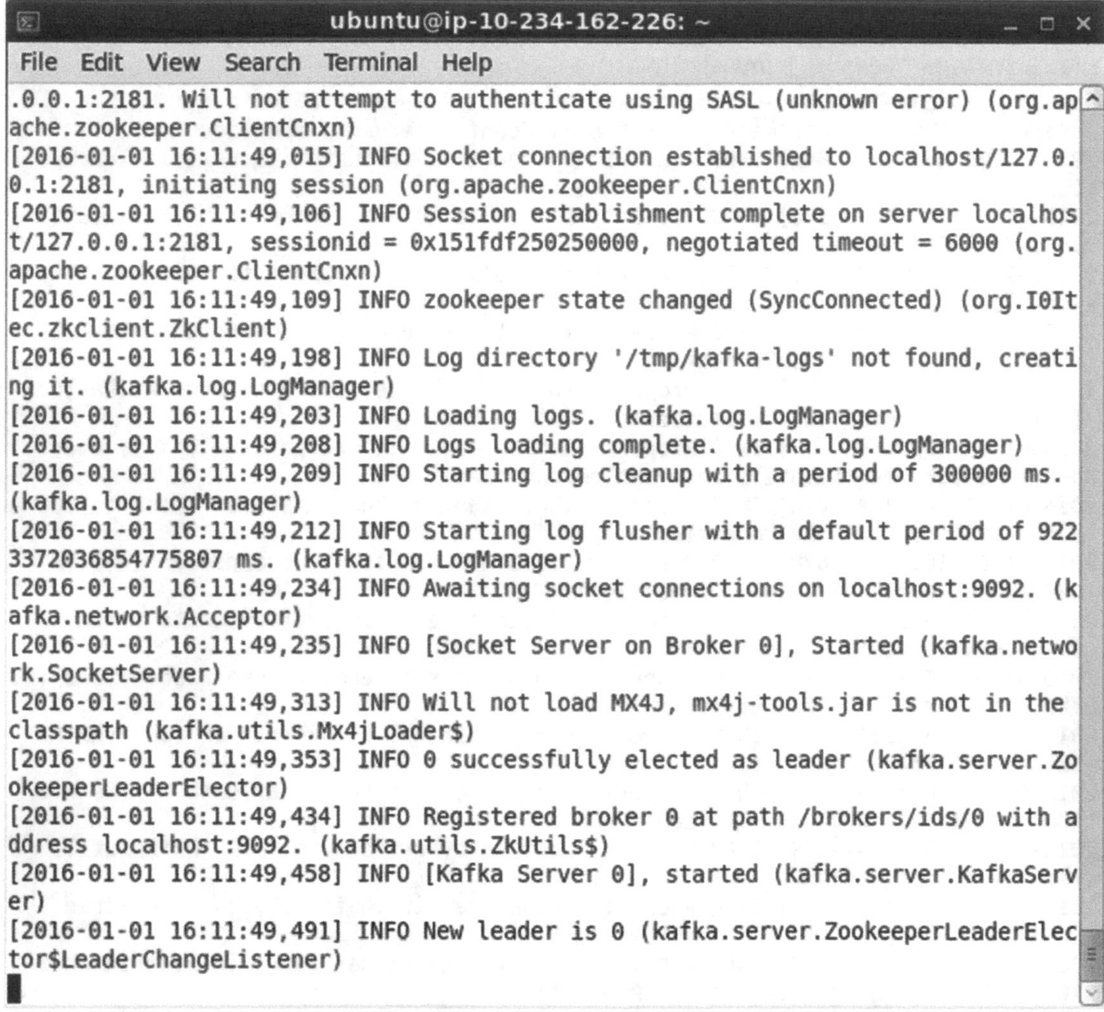

Figure 12-22. *Kafka Server started at localhost:9092*

Creating a Topic

Next, create a topic called 'kafka-on-kubernetes' with the following command. Set the number of partitions to 1 and replication factor to 1. The Zookeeper is set to `localhost:2181`.

```
kafka-topics.sh --create --topic kafka-on-kubernetes --zookeeper localhost:2181
--replication-factor 1 --partitions 1
```

As shown in Figure 12-23 the `kafka-on-kubernetes` topic gets created.

```
<zookeeper localhost:2181 --replication-factor 1  --partitions 1
Created topic "kafka-on-kubernetes".
root@kafka-rc-k8as1:/#
```

Figure 12-23. *Creating a Kafka Topic*

Starting a Kafka Producer

A Kafka producer is used to produce messages. After starting the ZooKeeper and the Kafka server, start the Kafka producer. Specify the topic with the `-topic` option as 'kafka-on-kubernetes'. The `--broker-list` specifies the Kafka server as `localhost:9092`, which are the settings configured in `server.properties` file.

```
kafka-console-producer.sh --topic kafka-on-kubernetes --broker-list localhost:9092
```

As shown in Figure 12-24 the Kafka producer gets started.

```
<pic kafka-on-kubernetes --broker-list localhost:9092
[2016-01-01 16:28:13,680] WARN Property topic is not valid (kafka.utils.Verifiab
leProperties)
```

Figure 12-24. *Starting a Kafka Producer*

Starting a Kafka Consumer

A Kafka consumer consumes messages. Start the Kafka consumer with the following command. Specify the topic with the `-topic` option as 'kafka-on-kubernetes'. The `--zookeeper` specifies the Zookeeper server as `localhost:2181`, which are the settings configured in `server.properties` file. The `--from-beginning` option specifies that messages from the beginning are to be consumed, not just the messages consumed after the consumer was started.

```
kafka-console-consumer.sh --topic kafka-on-kubernetes --from-beginning --zookeeper
localhost:2181
```

As shown in Figure 12-25 the Kafka producer gets started.

```
<pic kafka-on-kubernetes --from-beginning --zookeeper localhost:2181
```

Figure 12-25. *Starting a Kafka Consumer*

Producing and Consuming Messages

Having started the Producer and the Consumer, we shall produce message/s at the Producer and consume message/s at the Consumer. At the Producer add a message, for example, "Message from Kafka Producer" as shown in Figure 12-26 and click on Enter button. The message gets sent.

```
<pic kafka-on-kubernetes --broker-list localhost:9092
[2016-01-01 16:28:13,680] WARN Property topic is not valid (kafka.utils.Verifiab
leProperties)
Message from Kafka Producer
```

Figure 12-26. Producing a Message at the Kafka Producer

At the Consumer the message gets consumed as shown in Figure 12-27.

```
<pic kafka-on-kubernetes --from-beginning --zookeeper localhost:2181
Message from Kafka Producer
```

Figure 12-27. Consuming a Message at the Kafka Consumer

Send more messages at the Producer as shown in Figure 12-28.

```
<pic kafka-on-kubernetes --broker-list localhost:9092
[2016-01-01 16:28:13,680] WARN Property topic is not valid (kafka.utils.Verifiab
leProperties)
Message from Kafka Producer
message FROM kafka PRODUCER
MESSAGE FROM KAFKA PRODUCER
message from kafka producer
mESSAGE fROM kAFKA pRODUCER
```

Figure 12-28. Producing More Messages at the Kafka Producer

And the messages get consumed at the Consumer as shown in Figure 12-29.

```
<pic kafka-on-kubernetes --from-beginning --zookeeper localhost:2181
Message from Kafka Producer
message FROM kafka PRODUCER
MESSAGE FROM KAFKA PRODUCER
message from kafka producer
mESSAGE fROM kAFKA pRODUCER
```

Figure 12-29. Consuming More Messages at the Kafka Consumer

Scaling the Cluster

To scale the cluster to 4 Pods from 1 Pod run the following command.

```
kubectl scale rc kafka-rc --replicas=4
```

Subsequently list the Pods.

```
kubectl get pods
```

An output of "scaled" indicates that the cluster has been scaled as shown in Figure 12-30. Subsequently the Pods get listed, also shown in Figure 12-30.

```
ubuntu@ip-10-234-162-226:~$ kubectl scale rc kafka-rc  --replicas=4
scaled
ubuntu@ip-10-234-162-226:~$ kubectl get pods
NAME                     READY     STATUS    RESTARTS   AGE
k8s-master-127.0.0.1     3/3       Running   3          33m
kafka-rc-38bji           0/1       Running   0          16s
kafka-rc-idffn           1/1       Running   0          16s
kafka-rc-k8as1           1/1       Running   0          11m
kafka-rc-w1083           1/1       Running   0          16s
ubuntu@ip-10-234-162-226:~$ kubectl get pods
NAME                     READY     STATUS    RESTARTS   AGE
k8s-master-127.0.0.1     3/3       Running   3          33m
kafka-rc-38bji           1/1       Running   0          29s
kafka-rc-idffn           1/1       Running   0          29s
kafka-rc-k8as1           1/1       Running   0          11m
kafka-rc-w1083           1/1       Running   0          29s
ubuntu@ip-10-234-162-226:~$ 
```

Figure 12-30. *Scaling the Kafka Cluster*

When the number of Pods are increased to 4, the service endpoints also increase to 4. Describe the service `kafka`.

```
kubectl describe svc kafka
```

As shown in Figure 12-31, 4 endpoints are listed for each of the two services, one for Zookeeper server and the other for the Kafka server.

```
ubuntu@ip-10-234-162-226:~$ kubectl describe svc kafka
Name:                   kafka
Namespace:              default
Labels:                 app=kafkaApp
Selector:               app=kafkaApp
Type:                   LoadBalancer
IP:                     10.0.0.90
Port:                   kafka   9092/TCP
NodePort:               kafka   31927/TCP
Endpoints:              172.17.0.2:9092,172.17.0.3:9092,172.17.0.4:9092 + 1 more
...
Port:                   zookeeper       2181/TCP
NodePort:               zookeeper       32576/TCP
Endpoints:              172.17.0.2:2181,172.17.0.3:2181,172.17.0.4:2181 + 1 more
...
Session Affinity:       None
No events.

ubuntu@ip-10-234-162-226:~$
```

Figure 12-31. *Describing the Kafka Service with 4 Endpoints*

Deleting Replication Controller and Service

To delete the replication controller and service run the following commands.

```
kubectl delete rc kafka-rc
kubectl delete service kafka
```

As shown in Figure 12-32 the replication controller and service get deleted.

```
ubuntu@ip-10-234-162-226:~$ kubectl get rc
CONTROLLER   CONTAINER(S)   IMAGE(S)                 SELECTOR       REPLICAS
kafka-rc     zookeeper      dockerkafka/kafka:v2     app=kafkaApp   4
ubuntu@ip-10-234-162-226:~$ kubectl delete rc kafka-rc
replicationcontrollers/kafka-rc
ubuntu@ip-10-234-162-226:~$ kubectl delete service kafka
services/kafka
ubuntu@ip-10-234-162-226:~$
```

Figure 12-32. *Deleting the Kafka Replication Controller and Service*

Summary

Apache Kafka is a producer–consumer-based messaging system. In this chapter we discussed managing a Kafka cluster with Kubernetes. Managing the Kafka is different from some of the other applications as two servers have to be started: the Zookeeper server and the Kafka server. And the Kafka server has a dependency on the Zookeeper server, which implies that the Zookeeper must be started before the Kafka server. We needed to modify the default image `dockerkafka/kafka` for the zookeeper connect url. In the replication controller definition file we used a custom command to run the modified Docker image to start the Zookeeper server, the default settings in the Docker image being to start the Kafka server. All the applications we have run as yet were based on a single container Pod. In the next chapter we shall develop a multi-container Pod.

PART V

Multi Containers and Nodes

CHAPTER 13

Creating a Multi-Container Pod

A Pod is the atomic unit of an application managed by Kubernetes. A Pod has a single filesystem and IP Address; the containers in the Pod share the filesystem and networking IP. A Pod could consist of one or more containers. A Pod is defined in a definition file for a Pod or a replication controller using the specification for a Pod (`http://kubernetes.io/v1.1/docs/api-reference/v1/definitions.html#_v1_podspec`). A single container within a Pod is specified using the container specification (`http://kubernetes.io/v1.1/docs/api-reference/v1/definitions.html#_v1_container`). In all of the applications discussed as yet, in preceding chapters, a single container Pod was used. In this chapter we shall develop a multi-container Pod. We have used the `tutum/hello-world` and `postgres` Docker images for the multi-container Pod. Each of these images have been used in a single container Pods in preceding chapters. This chapter will cover the following topics.

How to Find Number of Containers in a Pod?

Type of applications Using a Multi-Container Pod

Setting the Environment

Creating a Service

Describing a Service

Creating a Replication Container

Listing the Pods

Listing the Docker Containers

Describing the Service after Creating Replication Controller

Invoking the Hello World Application on Command Line

Starting the Interactive Shell

Starting PostgreSQL Shell

Setting Port Forwarding

Opening the Hello World Application in a Browser

Scaling the Cluster

Describing the Service after Scaling

Describing a Pod

Setting Port Forwarding

D. Vohra, *Kubernetes Microservices with Docker*, DOI 10.1007/978-1-4842-1907-2_13

How to find Number of Containers in a Pod?

As discussed previously the Pods may be listed with the following command.

```
kubectl get pods
```

The Kubernetes Pod `k8s-master-127.0.0.1` Pod has 3/3 in the READY column as shown in Figure 13-1. The 3/3 indicates that the Pod has 3 containers and all three containers are ready. The n/n in the READY column for any Pod indicates the number of containers ready out of the total number of containers. All the containers are running on a single node as indicated by the subsequent listing of nodes.

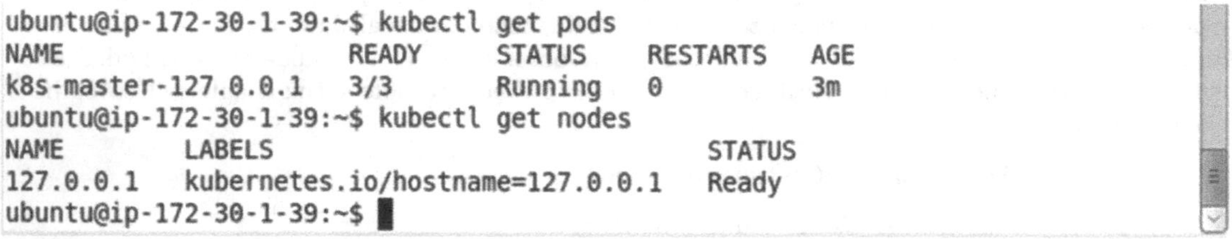

```
ubuntu@ip-172-30-1-39:~$ kubectl get pods
NAME                   READY     STATUS    RESTARTS   AGE
k8s-master-127.0.0.1   3/3       Running   0          3m
ubuntu@ip-172-30-1-39:~$ kubectl get nodes
NAME        LABELS                             STATUS
127.0.0.1   kubernetes.io/hostname=127.0.0.1   Ready
ubuntu@ip-172-30-1-39:~$
```

Figure 13-1. *Listing the Pods and the Number of Containers in the Pods*

Types of Applications Using a Multi-Container Pod

Various types of applications could make use of a multi-container Pod. Some of the examples are as follows:

-An Apache Sqoop application makes use of a CDH Docker image-based container and a MySQL database Docker image-based container for bulk transferring data from MySQL database into HDFS.

-An Apache Flume application makes use of a CDH Docker image-based container and a Kafka-based container for streaming data from a Kafka source into HDFS.

-An Apache Solr application makes use of a Oracle Database-based container and the Solr container for data import from Oracle Database into Solr.

-An Apache Hive application makes use a CDH container and a MongoDB container to create a Hive table using the MongoDB storage handler.

-An Apache Solr container and a CDH container are required to store Solr data in HDFS instead of the local filesystem.

Setting the Environment

We have used an Amazon EC2 instance created from AMI Ubuntu Server 14.04 LTS (HVM), SSD Volume Type - ami-d05e75b8 to install the following required software.

-Docker Engine (latest version)

-Kubernetes (version 1.01)

-Kubectl (version 1.01)

-Docker image tutum/hello-world (latest version)

-Docker image postgres (latest version)

Install Docker, Kubernetes, and Kubectl as discussed in chapter 1. To log in to the Ubuntu instance the Public IP Adress may be obtained from the Amazon EC2 console as shown in Figure 13-2.

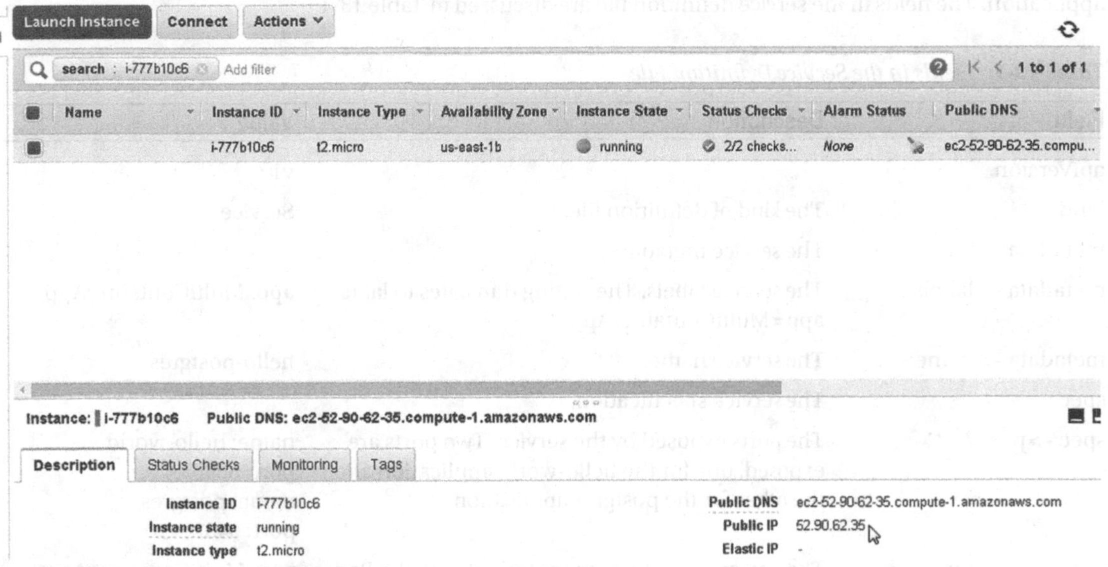

Figure 13-2. *Obtaining the Public IP Address*

SSH Login to the Ubuntu instance.

```
ssh -i "docker.pem" ubuntu@52.90.62.35
```

After having installed Docker start Docker and verify its status.

```
sudo service docker start
sudo service docker status
```

Docker should be listed as being "running" as shown in Figure 13-3.

```
ubuntu@ip-172-30-1-237:~$ sudo service docker start
start: Job is already running: docker
ubuntu@ip-172-30-1-237:~$ sudo service docker status
docker start/running, process 2697
ubuntu@ip-172-30-1-237:~$
```

Figure 13-3. *Starting Docker*

Creating a Service

Create a service definition file `hello-postgres-service.yaml` to configure the service ports. We shall be configuring two service ports, one for the `hello-world` application and the other for the `postgres` application. The fields in the service definition file are discussed in Table 13-1.

Table 13-1. *Fields in the Service Definition File*

Field	Description	Value
apiVersion		v1
kind	The kind of definition file.	Service
metadata	The service metadata.	
metadata ->labels	The service labels. The setting translates to label app=MultiContainerApp	app: MultiContainerApp
metadata ->name	The service name.	hello-postgres
spec	The service specification.	
spec ->ports	The ports exposed by the service. Two ports are exposed, one for the hello-world application and the other for the postgres application.	name: hello-world port: 8080 name: postgres port: 5432
spec ->selector	The Pod selector. Service routes traffic to the Pods with label matching the selector expression. The setting translates to selector app=MultiContainerApp	app: MultiContainerApp
spec ->selector ->type	The service type.	LoadBalancer

The `hello-postgres-service.yaml` is listed:

```
apiVersion: v1
kind: Service
metadata:
  labels:
    app: MultiContainerApp
  name: hello-postgres
```

```
spec:
  ports:
    -
      name: hello-world
      port: 8080
    -
      name: postgres
      port: 5432
  selector:
    app: MultiContainerApp
  type: LoadBalancer
```

Create a service from the definition file.

```
kubectl create -f hello-postgres-service.yaml
```

Subsequently list the services.

```
kubectl get services
```

The hello-postgres service gets created and listed as shown in Figure 13-4.

```
ubuntu@ip-172-30-1-237:~$ kubectl create -f hello-postgres-service.yaml
services/hello-postgres
ubuntu@ip-172-30-1-237:~$ kubectl get services
NAME             LABELS                                        SELECTOR
   IP(S)         PORT(S)
hello-postgres   app=MultiContainerApp                         app=MultiContainerApp
   10.0.0.186    5432/TCP

                 8020/TCP
kubernetes       component=apiserver,provider=kubernetes       <none>
   10.0.0.1      443/TCP
```

Figure 13-4. *Creating a Service from the Definition File*

Describing a Service

The hello-postgres service may be described with the following command.

```
kubectl describe service hello-postgres
```

The service description includes the name, namespace, labels, selector, type, IP, ports, and endpoints as shown in Figure 13-5. Initially the service is not managing any pods and as a result no endpoints are listed.

```
ubuntu@ip-172-30-1-237:~$ kubectl describe svc hello-postgres
Name:                   hello-postgres
Namespace:              default
Labels:                 app=MultiContainerApp
Selector:               app=MultiContainerApp
Type:                   LoadBalancer
IP:                     10.0.0.186
Port:                   postgres        5432/TCP
NodePort:               postgres        32065/TCP
Endpoints:              <none>
Port:                   hello-world     8020/TCP
NodePort:               hello-world     32540/TCP
Endpoints:              <none>
Session Affinity:       None
No events.

ubuntu@ip-172-30-1-237:~$
```

Figure 13-5. *Describing the Service*

Creating a Replication Container

Create a definition file `hello-postgres-rc.yaml` for a replication controller. Add the following (Table 13-2) fields to the definition file.

Table 13-2. *Fields in the Replication Controller Definition File*

Field	Description	Value
apiVersion		v1
kind	The kind of definition file.	ReplicationController
metadata	The replication controller metadata.	
metadata -> labels	The replication controller labels.	app: "MultiContainerApp"
metadata -> name	The replication controller name.	"hello-postgres"
spec	The replication controller specification.	
spec -> replicas	The number of Pod replicas.	1
spec -> selector	A key:value expression for selecting the Pods to manage. Pods with a label the same as the selector expression is managed by the replication controller. The selector expression must be the same as the spec -> template -> metadata -> labels expression. The selector defaults to the spec -> template -> metadata -> labels key: value expression if not specified.	app: "MultiContainerApp"

(*continued*)

Table 13-2. (*continued*)

Field	Description	Value
spec - > template	The Pod template.	
spec - > template- > metadata	The Pod template metadata.	
spec - > template - > metadata - > labels	The Pod template labels. The selector if not specified defaults to this setting. The service selector must be the same as one of the Pod template labels for the service to represent the Pod. The service selector does not default to the same value as the label and we already set the service selector to app: MultiContainerApp.	app: "MultiContainerApp"
spec - > template - > spec	The Pod template specification.	
spec - > template - > spec - > containers	The containers configuration for the Pod template.	
spec - > template - > spec - > containers - > image	The Docker image for the hello-world container.	tutum/hello-world
spec - > template - > spec - > containers - > name	The container name for the hello-world container.	hello-world
ports	Specifies the container port for the hello-world container.	containerPort: 8080
spec - > template - > spec - > containers - > image	The Docker image for the postgres container.	postgres
spec - > template - > spec - > containers - > name	The container name for the postgres container.	postgres
ports	Container port for postgres container.	containerPort: 5432

The `hello-postgres-rc.yaml` is listed:

```
apiVersion: v1
kind: ReplicationController
metadata:
  labels:
    app: "MultiContainerApp"
  name: "hello-postgres"
spec:
  replicas: 1
  selector:
    app: "MultiContainerApp"
  template:
    metadata:
      labels:
        app: "MultiContainerApp"
```

```
spec:
  containers:
    -
      image: "tutum/hello-world"
      name: "hello-world"
      ports:
        -
          containerPort: 8080
    -
      image: "postgres"
      name: "postgres"
      ports:
        -
          containerPort: 5432
```

Create a replication controller from the definition file.

```
kubectl create -f hello-postgres-rc.yaml
```

Subsequently list the replication controllers.

```
kubectl get rc
```

As shown in Figure 13-6 the hello-postgres replication controller gets created and listed.

```
ubuntu@ip-172-30-1-237:~$ kubectl create -f hello-postgres-rc.yaml
replicationcontrollers/hello-postgres
ubuntu@ip-172-30-1-237:~$ kubectl get rc
CONTROLLER       CONTAINER(S)   IMAGE(S)             SELECTOR                REPL
ICAS
hello-postgres   postgres       postgres             app=MultiContainerApp   1
                 hello-world    tutum/hello-world
```

Figure 13-6. *Creating a Replication Controller from the Definition File*

Listing the Pods

To list the Pods run the following command.

```
kubectl get pods
```

As replicas field is set to 1 in the replication controller only one Pod gets created as shown in Figure 13-7. The READY column lists 0/2, which indicates that 0 or none of the two containers in the pod are ready. Initially the container could be listed as not running and creating. Run the preceding command after a few seconds and the Pod STATUS should be "Running" and the READY state should be 2/2, implying that 2 of 2 containers are running.

```
ubuntu@ip-172-30-1-237:~$ kubectl get pods
NAME                    READY     STATUS
          RESTARTS   AGE
hello-postgres-29ypb    0/2       Image: tutum/hello-world is ready, container is
 creating   0        18s
k8s-master-127.0.0.1    3/3       Running
          0          44m
ubuntu@ip-172-30-1-237:~$ kubectl get pods
NAME                    READY     STATUS    RESTARTS   AGE
hello-postgres-29ypb    2/2       Running   0          32s
k8s-master-127.0.0.1    3/3       Running   0          44m
ubuntu@ip-172-30-1-237:~$
```

Figure 13-7. *Listing the Pods*

Listing the Docker Containers

To list the Docker containers started, run the following command.

```
sudo docker ps
```

Two of the listed containers, the container based on the `postgres` image and the container based on the `tutum/hello-world` image, as shown in Figure 13-8, are started with the replication controller `hello-postgres`.

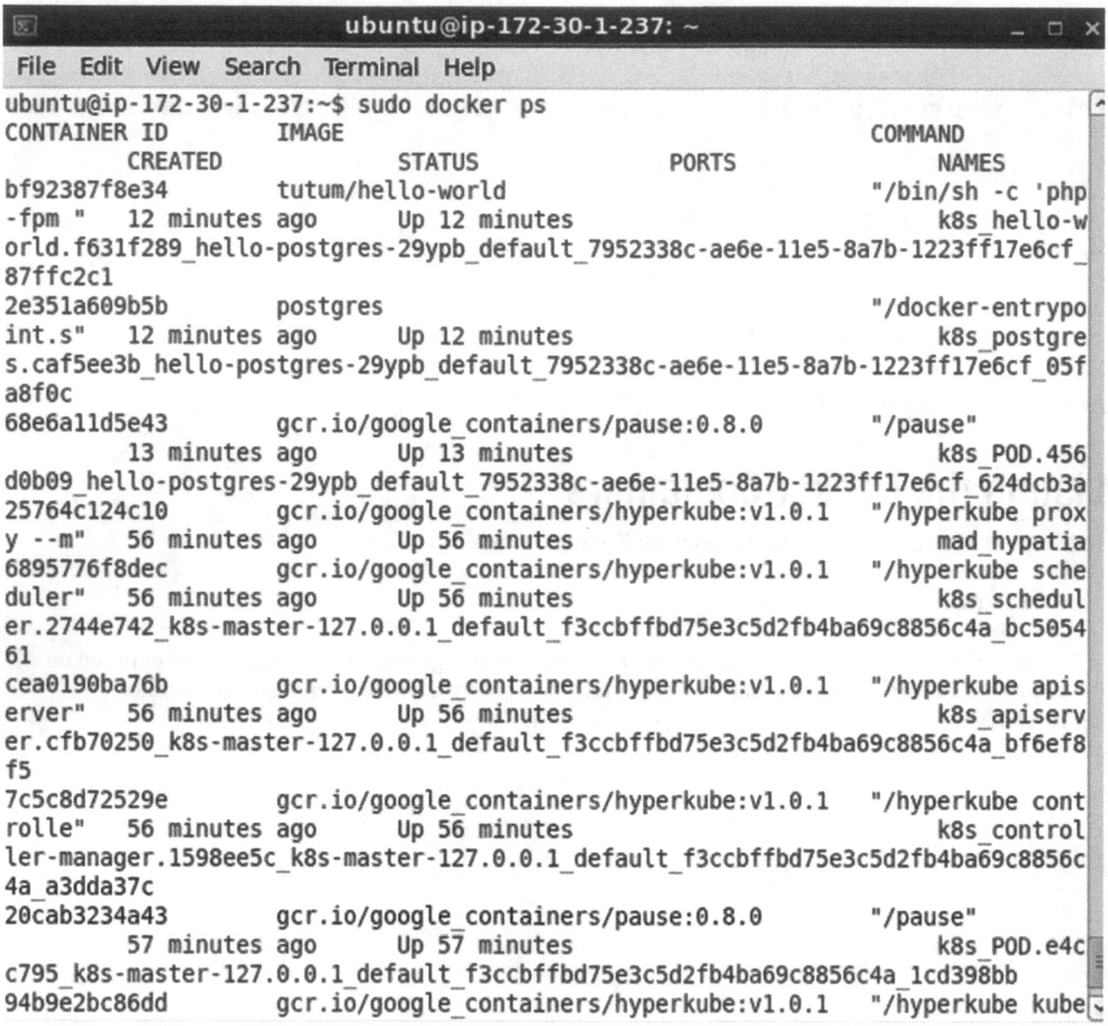

```
ubuntu@ip-172-30-1-237: ~
File  Edit  View  Search  Terminal  Help
ubuntu@ip-172-30-1-237:~$ sudo docker ps
CONTAINER ID        IMAGE                                        COMMAND
         CREATED             STATUS              PORTS               NAMES
bf92387f8e34        tutum/hello-world                            "/bin/sh -c 'php
-fpm "   12 minutes ago      Up 12 minutes                           k8s_hello-w
orld.f631f289_hello-postgres-29ypb_default_7952338c-ae6e-11e5-8a7b-1223ff17e6cf_
87ffc2c1
2e351a609b5b        postgres                                     "/docker-entrypo
int.s"   12 minutes ago      Up 12 minutes                           k8s_postgre
s.caf5ee3b_hello-postgres-29ypb_default_7952338c-ae6e-11e5-8a7b-1223ff17e6cf_05f
a8f0c
68e6a11d5e43        gcr.io/google_containers/pause:0.8.0         "/pause"
         13 minutes ago      Up 13 minutes                           k8s_POD.456
d0b09_hello-postgres-29ypb_default_7952338c-ae6e-11e5-8a7b-1223ff17e6cf_624dcb3a
25764c124c10        gcr.io/google_containers/hyperkube:v1.0.1    "/hyperkube prox
y --m"   56 minutes ago      Up 56 minutes                           mad_hypatia
6895776f8dec        gcr.io/google_containers/hyperkube:v1.0.1    "/hyperkube sche
duler"   56 minutes ago      Up 56 minutes                           k8s_schedul
er.2744e742_k8s-master-127.0.0.1_default_f3ccbffbd75e3c5d2fb4ba69c8856c4a_bc5054
61
cea0190ba76b        gcr.io/google_containers/hyperkube:v1.0.1    "/hyperkube apis
erver"   56 minutes ago      Up 56 minutes                           k8s_apiserv
er.cfb70250_k8s-master-127.0.0.1_default_f3ccbffbd75e3c5d2fb4ba69c8856c4a_bf6ef8
f5
7c5c8d72529e        gcr.io/google_containers/hyperkube:v1.0.1    "/hyperkube cont
rolle"   56 minutes ago      Up 56 minutes                           k8s_control
ler-manager.1598ee5c_k8s-master-127.0.0.1_default_f3ccbffbd75e3c5d2fb4ba69c8856c
4a_a3dda37c
20cab3234a43        gcr.io/google_containers/pause:0.8.0         "/pause"
         57 minutes ago      Up 57 minutes                           k8s_POD.e4c
c795_k8s-master-127.0.0.1_default_f3ccbffbd75e3c5d2fb4ba69c8856c4a_1cd398bb
94b9e2bc86dd        gcr.io/google_containers/hyperkube:v1.0.1    "/hyperkube kube
```

Figure 13-8. *Listing the Docker Containers*

Describing the Service after Creating Replication Controller

Before we had created the replication controller the service `hello-postgres` was not associated with any endpoints. After creating the replication controller and the Pod/s, run the following command again to describe the service again.

```
kubectl describe service hello-postgres
```

An endpoint is listed for each of the ports exposed by the service as shown in Figure 13-9.

```
ubuntu@ip-172-30-1-237:~$ kubectl describe service hello-postgres
Name:                   hello-postgres
Namespace:              default
Labels:                 app=MultiContainerApp
Selector:               app=MultiContainerApp
Type:                   LoadBalancer
IP:                     10.0.0.186
Port:                   postgres        5432/TCP
NodePort:               postgres        32065/TCP
Endpoints:              172.17.0.2:5432
Port:                   hello-world     8020/TCP
NodePort:               hello-world     32540/TCP
Endpoints:              172.17.0.2:8020
Session Affinity:       None
No events.
```

Figure 13-9. *Describing the Service*

Invoking the Hello World Application on Command Line

Invoke the service endpoint `172.17.0.2` using curl as follows.

```
curl 172.17.0.2
```

The HTML generated by the application gets output as shown in Figure 13-10.

```
ubuntu@ip-172-30-1-237: ~
File Edit View Search Terminal Help
ubuntu@ip-172-30-1-237:~$ curl 172.17.0.2
<html>
<head>
        <title>Hello world!</title>
        <link href='http://fonts.googleapis.com/css?family=Open+Sans:400,700' re
l='stylesheet' type='text/css'>
        <style>
        body {
                background-color: white;
                text-align: center;
                padding: 50px;
                font-family: "Open Sans","Helvetica Neue",Helvetica,Arial,sans-s
erif;
        }

        #logo {
                margin-bottom: 40px;
        }
        </style>
</head>
<body>
        <img id="logo" src="logo.png" />
        <h1>Hello world!</h1>
        <h3>My hostname is hello-postgres-29ypb</h3>                    <h3>Link
s found</h3>
                                        <b>HELLO_POSTGRES</b> listening in 8020
available at tcp://10.0.0.186:8020<br />
                                                <b>HELLO_POSTGRES</b> listening
in 5432 available at tcp://10.0.0.186:5432<br />
                                                <b>KUBERNETES</b> listening in 4
43 available at tcp://10.0.0.1:443<br />
                                </body>
```

Figure 13-10. *Invoking an Endpoint for the Service*

Starting the Interactive Shell

To start an interactive shell for the software installed, either of the Docker containers, listed previously in Figure 13-8, for the multi-container Pod may be used. Both the containers access the same filesystem and IP. Use the following command to start an interactive shell.

```
sudo docker exec -it 2e351a609b5b bash
```

An interactive shell gets started as shown in Figure 13-11.

```
ubuntu@ip-172-30-1-237:~$ sudo docker exec -it 2e351a609b5b bash
root@hello-postgres-29ypb:/#
```

Figure 13-11. *Starting an Interactive Shell*

Starting PostgreSQL Shell

To start the PostgreSQL command shell called `psql` run the following command in the interactive shell.

```
psql postgres
```

The `psql` gets started and the `postgres` command prompt gets displayed as shown in Figure 13-12.

```
ubuntu@ip-172-30-1-237:~$ sudo docker exec -it 2e351a609b5b bash
root@hello-postgres-29ypb:/# su -l postgres
No directory, logging in with HOME=/
$ psql postgres
psql (9.4.5)
Type "help" for help.

postgres=#
```

Figure 13-12. *Starting psql Shell*

PostgreSQL with Kubernetes is discussed in chapter 5.

Setting Port Forwarding

We had earlier invoked the service endpoint to output the HTML generated using curl on the command line, but HTML is best displayed in a browser. As an Amazon EC2 instance does not provide a browser by default, we need to set port forwarding to a local machine to be able to access the service endpoint in a browser. Set the port forwarding for `172.17.0.2:80` to `localhost:80` with the following command.

```
ssh -i "docker.pem" -f -nNT -L 80:172.17.0.2:80 ubuntu@ec2-52-90-62-35.compute-1.amazonaws.com
```

The port forwarding to `localhost` gets set as shown in Figure 13-13.

```
[root@localhost ~]# ssh -i "docker.pem" -f -nNT -L 80:172.17.0.2:80 ubuntu@ec2-5
2-90-62-35.compute-1.amazonaws.com
[root@localhost ~]#
```

Figure 13-13. *Setting Port Forwarding*

The Public DNS for the Amazon EC2 instance may be obtained from the Amazon EC2 console as shown in Figure 13-14.

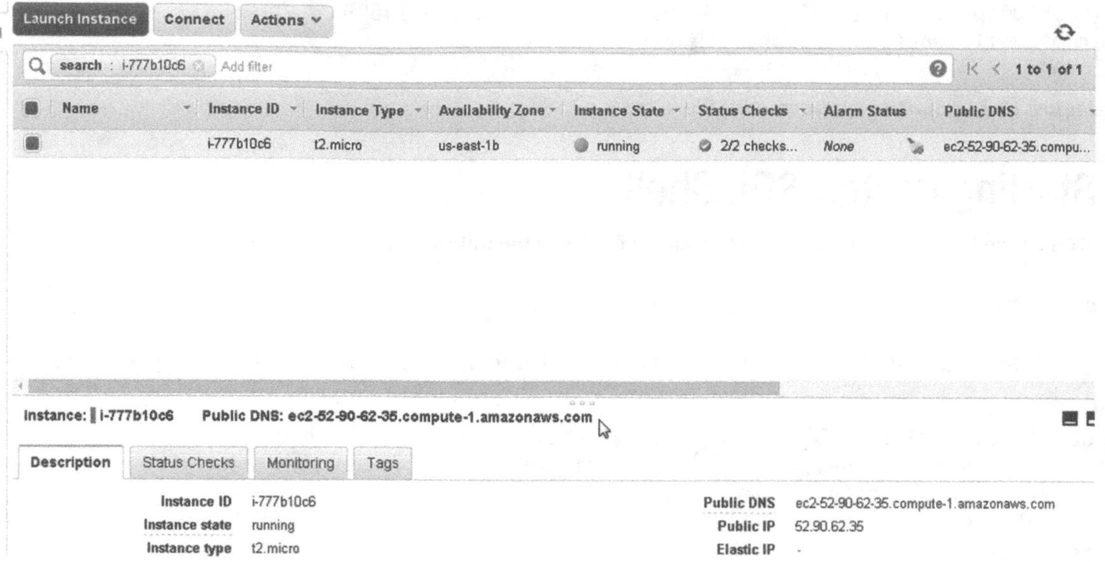

Figure 13-14. *Obtaining Public DNS*

Opening the Hello World Application in a Browser

Having set port forwarding the application may be opened in a browser on a local machine with url `http://localhost` as shown in Figure 13-15. In addition to the hostname the two ports at which the `HELLO_POSTGRES` is listening at get listed.

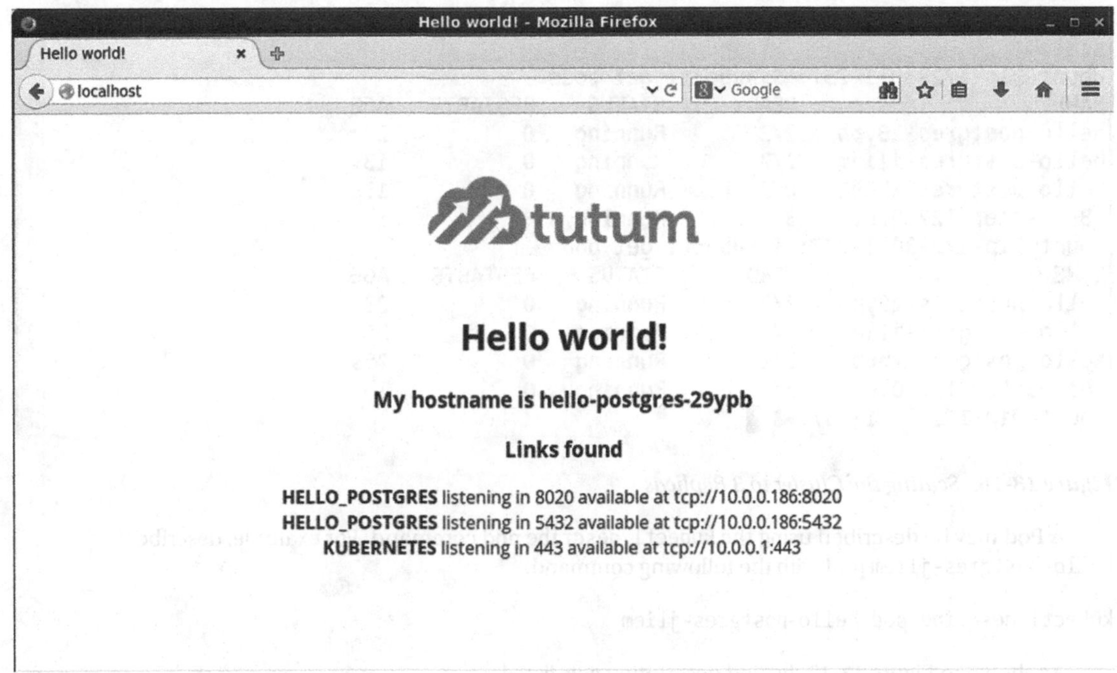

Figure 13-15. *Invoking the Service Endpoint in a Browser*

Scaling the Cluster

To scale the cluster to 3 replicas or Pods run the following command.

```
kubectl scale rc hello-postgres --replicas=3
```

Subsequently list the Pods.

```
kubectl get pods
```

Three Pods get listed as shown in Figure 13-16. Some of the Pods could be not running or not ready initially. Run the preceding command again after a few seconds to list all the Pods with STATUS as "Running" and READY state as 2/2.

```
ubuntu@ip-172-30-1-237:~$ kubectl scale rc hello-postgres --replicas=3
scaled
ubuntu@ip-172-30-1-237:~$ kubectl get pods
NAME                     READY     STATUS    RESTARTS   AGE
hello-postgres-29ypb     2/2       Running   0          23m
hello-postgres-jliem     2/2       Running   0          13s
hello-postgres-xb6b8     0/2       Running   0          13s
k8s-master-127.0.0.1     3/3       Running   0          1h
ubuntu@ip-172-30-1-237:~$ kubectl get pods
NAME                     READY     STATUS    RESTARTS   AGE
hello-postgres-29ypb     2/2       Running   0          23m
hello-postgres-jliem     2/2       Running   0          25s
hello-postgres-xb6b8     2/2       Running   0          25s
k8s-master-127.0.0.1     3/3       Running   0          1h
ubuntu@ip-172-30-1-237:~$
```

Figure 13-16. *Scaling the Cluster to 3 Replicas*

A Pod may be described using the `kubectl describe` pod command. For example, describe the `hello-postgres-jliem` pod with the following command.

```
kubectl describe pod hello-postgres-jliem
```

As shown in Figure 13-17 the Pod description gets listed.

```
ubuntu@ip-172-30-1-237:~$ kubectl describe pod hello-postgres-jliem
Name:                           hello-postgres-jliem
Namespace:                      default
Image(s):                       postgres,tutum/hello-world
Node:                           127.0.0.1/127.0.0.1
Labels:                         app=MultiContainerApp
Status:                         Running
Reason:
Message:
IP:                             172.17.0.3
Replication Controllers:        hello-postgres (3/3 replicas created)
Containers:
  postgres:
    Image:              postgres
    State:              Running
      Started:          Tue, 29 Dec 2015 21:18:27 +0000
    Ready:              True
    Restart Count:      0
  hello-world:
    Image:              tutum/hello-world
    State:              Running
      Started:          Tue, 29 Dec 2015 21:18:27 +0000
    Ready:              True
    Restart Count:      0
Conditions:
  Type          Status
```

Figure 13-17. *Describing a Pod*

Listing the Docker Containers

As each Pod consists of two containers, scaling up the cluster to 3 Pods or replicas starts four new containers, 2 containers for each of the two new Pods. After scaling up the cluster run the following command to list the running Docker containers again using the default output format.

```
sudo docker ps
```

A total of 3 containers based on the `postgres` image and 3 containers based on the `tutum/hello-world` image get listed as shown in Figure 13-18.

```
ubuntu@ip-172-30-1-237: ~
File Edit View Search Terminal Help
ubuntu@ip-172-30-1-237:~$ sudo docker ps
CONTAINER ID        IMAGE                                          COMMAND
       CREATED             STATUS              PORTS               NAMES
72f610466562        tutum/hello-world                              "/bin/sh -c 'php
-fpm "   6 minutes ago       Up 6 minutes                            k8s_hello-w
orld.f631f289_hello-postgres-xb6b8_default_b32d7de6-ae71-11e5-8a7b-1223ff17e6cf_
df833892
02b68f8532bf        postgres                                       "/docker-entrypo
int.s"   6 minutes ago       Up 6 minutes                            k8s_postgre
s.caf5ee3b_hello-postgres-xb6b8_default_b32d7de6-ae71-11e5-8a7b-1223ff17e6cf_0a9
d2642
fd4a423f73ee        tutum/hello-world                              "/bin/sh -c 'php
-fpm "   6 minutes ago       Up 6 minutes                            k8s_hello-w
orld.f631f289_hello-postgres-j1iem_default_b32d6287-ae71-11e5-8a7b-1223ff17e6cf_
0337b3e0
94ddb3160cdb        postgres                                       "/docker-entrypo
int.s"   6 minutes ago       Up 6 minutes                            k8s_postgre
s.caf5ee3b_hello-postgres-j1iem_default_b32d6287-ae71-11e5-8a7b-1223ff17e6cf_124
91b18
4d74dfdff121        gcr.io/google_containers/pause:0.8.0           "/pause"
       6 minutes ago       Up 6 minutes                            k8s_POD.456
d0b09_hello-postgres-xb6b8_default_b32d7de6-ae71-11e5-8a7b-1223ff17e6cf_fa4fd993
485aeef65df7        gcr.io/google_containers/pause:0.8.0           "/pause"
       6 minutes ago       Up 6 minutes                            k8s_POD.456
d0b09_hello-postgres-j1iem_default_b32d6287-ae71-11e5-8a7b-1223ff17e6cf_4f3b4c27
bf92387f8e34        tutum/hello-world                              "/bin/sh -c 'php
-fpm "   29 minutes ago      Up 28 minutes                           k8s_hello-w
orld.f631f289_hello-postgres-29ypb_default_7952338c-ae6e-11e5-8a7b-1223ff17e6cf_
87ffc2c1
2e351a609b5b        postgres                                       "/docker-entrypo
int.s"   29 minutes ago      Up 28 minutes                           k8s_postgre
s.caf5ee3b_hello-postgres-29ypb_default_7952338c-ae6e-11e5-8a7b-1223ff17e6cf_05f
```

Figure 13-18. *Listing the Docker Containers*

Describing the Service after Scaling

Describe the service again after scaling up the cluster.

```
kubectl describe service hello-postgres
```

Each of the ports exposed by the service is associated with three endpoints because 3 Pods are running as shown in Figure 13-19.

```
ubuntu@ip-172-30-1-237:~$ kubectl describe service hello-postgres
Name:                   hello-postgres
Namespace:              default
Labels:                 app=MultiContainerApp
Selector:               app=MultiContainerApp
Type:                   LoadBalancer
IP:                     10.0.0.186
Port:                   postgres        5432/TCP
NodePort:               postgres        32065/TCP
Endpoints:              172.17.0.2:5432,172.17.0.3:5432,172.17.0.4:5432
Port:                   hello-world     8020/TCP
NodePort:               hello-world     32540/TCP
Endpoints:              172.17.0.2:8020,172.17.0.3:8020,172.17.0.4:8020
Session Affinity:       None
No events.

ubuntu@ip-172-30-1-237:~$
```

Figure 13-19. *Describing the Service including the Service Endpoints*

Setting Port Forwarding

To be able to open the application in a browser we need to set port forwarding to locahost. Set the port forwarding to ports not previously bound. The `localhost:80` beind address is already sued up in the port forwarding of the single Pod created earlier. To set port forwarding for the two new Pods use ports 81 and 82 on localhost.

```
ssh -i "docker.pem" -f -nNT -L 81:172.17.0.3:80 ubuntu@ec2-52-90-62-35.compute-1.amazonaws.com
ssh -i "docker.pem" -f -nNT -L 82:172.17.0.4:80 ubuntu@ec2-52-90-62-35.compute-1.amazonaws.com
```

The preceding commands do not generate any output but the ports get forwarded to the `localhost` as shown in Figure 13-20.

```
[root@localhost ~]# ssh -i "docker.pem" -f -nNT -L 81:172.17.0.3:80 ubuntu@ec2-5
2-90-62-35.compute-1.amazonaws.com
[root@localhost ~]# ssh -i "docker.pem" -f -nNT -L 82:172.17.0.4:80 ubuntu@ec2-5
2-90-62-35.compute-1.amazonaws.com
[root@localhost ~]#
```

Figure 13-20. *Setting Port Forwarding*

Opening the Hello World Application in a Browser

The application may be opened in a browser at each of the forwarded ports; for example, open a browser at `http://localhost:81`. The application HTML gets displayed as shown in Figure 13-21. The `HELLO_POSTGRES` service is listening at two ports 8020 and 5432.

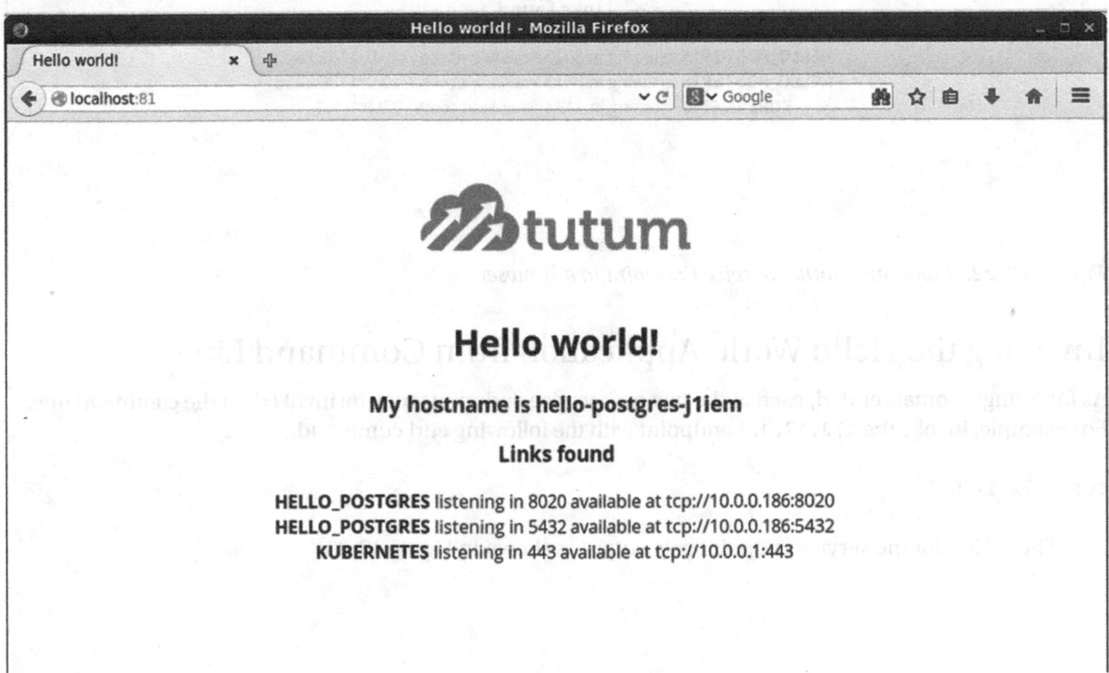

Figure 13-21. *Invoking a Service Endpoint in a Browser*

Similarly open the other service endpoint in a browser with url `http://localhost:82`. Different hostnames listening on the same port are forwarded to different ports on the `localhost`. The service endpoint HTML gets output as shown in Figure 13-22.

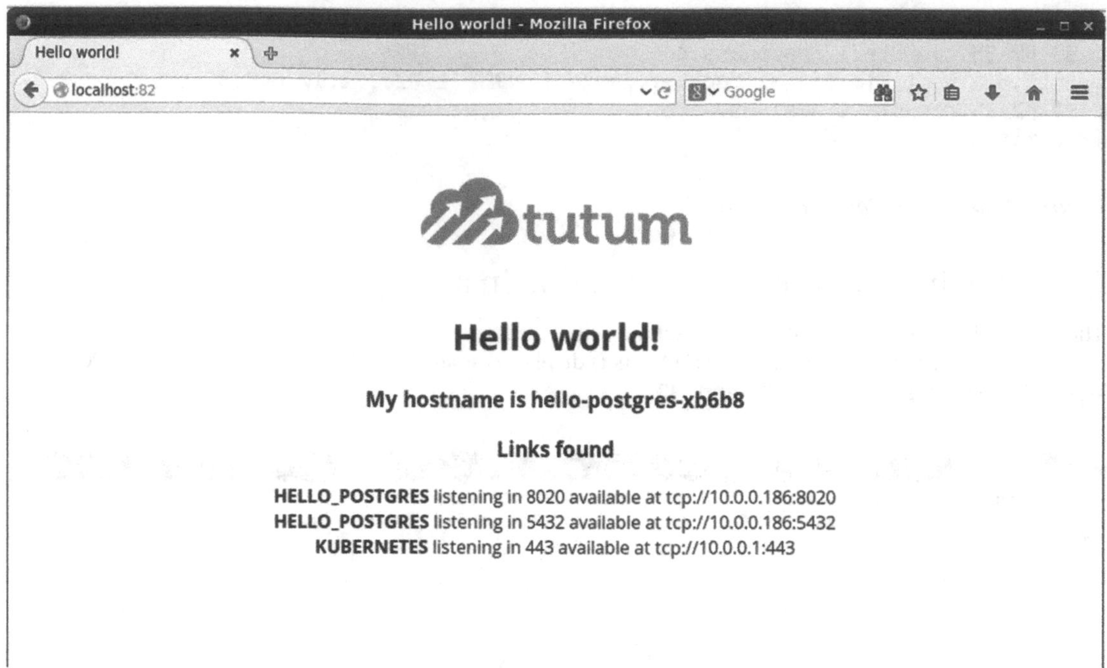

Figure 13-22. *Invoking another Service Endpoint in a Browser*

Invoking the Hello World Application from Command Line

As for a single container Pod, each of the two new service endpoints may be invoked on the command line. For example, invoke the `172.17.0.3` endpoint with the following curl command.

```
curl 172.17.0.3
```

The HTML for the service endpoint gets output as shown in Figure 13-23.

```
ubuntu@ip-172-30-1-237:~$ curl 172.17.0.3
<html>
<head>
        <title>Hello world!</title>
        <link href='http://fonts.googleapis.com/css?family=Open+Sans:400,700' re
l='stylesheet' type='text/css'>
        <style>
        body {
                background-color: white;
                text-align: center;
                padding: 50px;
                font-family: "Open Sans","Helvetica Neue",Helvetica,Arial,sans-s
erif;
        }

        #logo {
                margin-bottom: 40px;
        }
        </style>
</head>
<body>
        <img id="logo" src="logo.png" />
        <h1>Hello world!</h1>
        <h3>My hostname is hello-postgres-j1iem</h3>                    <h3>Link
s found</h3>
                                        <b>HELLO_POSTGRES</b> listening in 8020
available at tcp://10.0.0.186:8020<br />
                                                <b>HELLO_POSTGRES</b> listening
in 5432 available at tcp://10.0.0.186:5432<br />
                                                <b>KUBERNETES</b> listening in 4
43 available at tcp://10.0.0.1:443<br />
                                        </body>
```

Figure 13-23. *Invoking a Service Endpoint with curl*

Invoke the `172.17.0.4` endpoint with the following curl command.

```
curl 172.17.0.4
```

The HTML for the service endpoint gets output as shown in Figure 13-24.

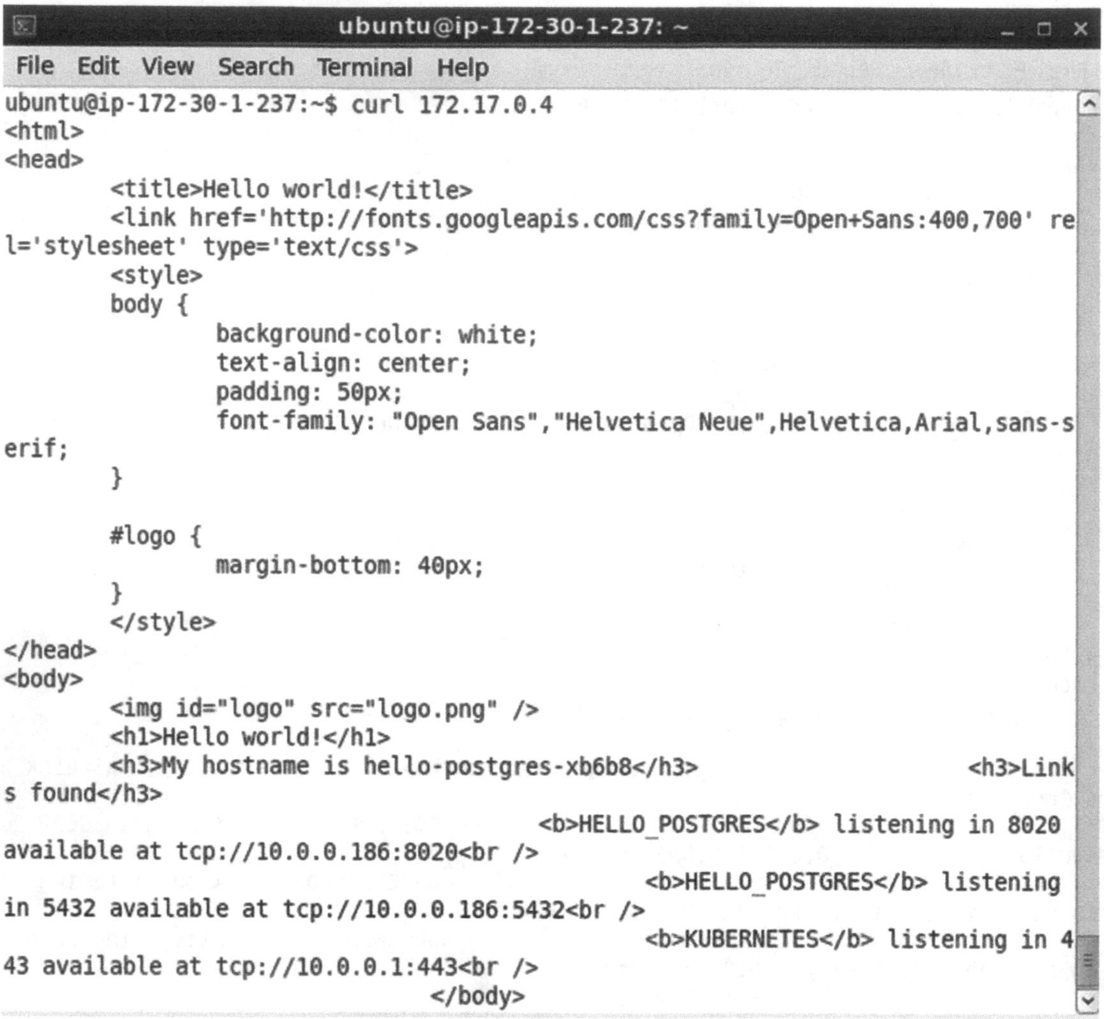

```
ubuntu@ip-172-30-1-237:~$ curl 172.17.0.4
<html>
<head>
        <title>Hello world!</title>
        <link href='http://fonts.googleapis.com/css?family=Open+Sans:400,700' re
l='stylesheet' type='text/css'>
        <style>
        body {
                background-color: white;
                text-align: center;
                padding: 50px;
                font-family: "Open Sans","Helvetica Neue",Helvetica,Arial,sans-s
erif;
        }

        #logo {
                margin-bottom: 40px;
        }
        </style>
</head>
<body>
        <img id="logo" src="logo.png" />
        <h1>Hello world!</h1>
        <h3>My hostname is hello-postgres-xb6b8</h3>                    <h3>Link
s found</h3>
                                        <b>HELLO_POSTGRES</b> listening in 8020
available at tcp://10.0.0.186:8020<br />
                                                <b>HELLO_POSTGRES</b> listening
in 5432 available at tcp://10.0.0.186:5432<br />
                                                <b>KUBERNETES</b> listening in 4
43 available at tcp://10.0.0.1:443<br />
                                </body>
```

Figure 13-24. Invoking another Service Endpoint with curl

Deleting the Replication Controller

To delete the hello-postgres replication controller run the following command.

```
kubectl delete rc hello-postgres
```

Subsequently list the Pods with the following command.

```
kubectl get pods
```

The Pods for the hello-postgres replication controller are not listed as shown in Figure 13-25.

```
ubuntu@ip-172-30-1-237:~$ kubectl delete rc hello-postgres
replicationcontrollers/hello-postgres
ubuntu@ip-172-30-1-237:~$ kubectl get pods
NAME                   READY     STATUS    RESTARTS   AGE
k8s-master-127.0.0.1   3/3       Running   0          1h
ubuntu@ip-172-30-1-237:~$ █
```

Figure 13-25. *Deleting the Replication Controller*

Deleting the Service

To delete the service `hello-postgres` run the following command.

```
kubectl delete service hello-postgres
```

Subsequently run the following command to list the services.

```
kubectl get services
```

The `hello-postgres` service is not listed as shown in Figure 13-26.

```
ubuntu@ip-172-30-1-237:~$ kubectl delete service hello-postgres
services/hello-postgres
ubuntu@ip-172-30-1-237:~$ kubectl get services
NAME         LABELS                                    SELECTOR   IP(S)      POR
T(S)
kubernetes   component=apiserver,provider=kubernetes   <none>     10.0.0.1   443
/TCP
ubuntu@ip-172-30-1-237:~$ █
```

Figure 13-26. *Deleting the Service*

Summary

In this chapter we discussed using multiple containers in a Pod. We discussed the use case for a multi-container Pod and used the `tutum/hello-world` and `postgres` Docker images to create a multi-container Pod. A multi-container pod starts multiple Docker containers for each Pod even though the Pod is the atomic unit. The multiple containers in a Pod share the same IP address and filesystem. When a multi-container Pod is scaled, multiple containers are started for each of the new Pods. In the next chapter we shall discuss installing Kubernetes on a multi-node cluster.

CHAPTER 14

Installing Kubernetes on a Multi-Node Cluster

In all of the preceding chapters in the book we have used a single-node cluster. For most small scale applications a single-node cluster should suffice. But, for relatively large scale, distributed applications a multi-node cluster is a more suitable option. In this chapter we shall install Kubernetes on a multi-node (2 nodes) cluster. This chapter has the following sections.

- Components of a Multi-Node Cluster
- Setting the Environment
- Installing the Master Node
- Setting Up Flanneld and etcd
- Starting the Kubernetes on Master Node
- Running the Service Proxy
- Testing the Master Node
- Adding a Worker Node
- Exporting the Master IP
- Setting Up Flanneld and etcd
- Starting Up Kubernetes on Worker Node
- Running the Service Proxy
- Testing the Kubernetes Cluster
- Running an Application on the Cluster
- Exposing the Application as a Service
- Testing the Application in a Browser
- Scaling the Application

D. Vohra, *Kubernetes Microservices with Docker*, DOI 10.1007/978-1-4842-1907-2_14

Components of a Multi-Node Cluster

A multi-node cluster consists of the following main and ancillary components.

-Kubernetes Master Node

-Kubernetes Worker Node/s

-Etcd

-Flannel

-Service Proxy

-Kubectl

etcd, kubernetes master, and service proxy were discussed in chapter 1. etcd as introduced in chapter 1 is a distributed, key-value store used by the Kubernetes cluster manager. We have installed etcd on the same node as the Kubernetes master but in a production environment etcd would typically be installed as separate cluster installed on nodes different than the Kubernetes master node. A commit to an etcd cluster is based on replication to a majority (quorum) of available nodes with provision for failure of one or more nodes. While the majority of a 1-node cluster is 1, the majority of a 3-node cluster is 2, majority of a 4-node cluster is 3, majority of a 5-node cluster is 3. A etcd cluster would typically have an odd number (>2) of nodes with tolerance for failure. For example, a 5-node etcd cluster could loose up to 2 nodes resulting in a 3-node cluster in which the majority is still determinable. A 3-node cluster has a failure tolerance for one more node. A 2-node etcd cluster does not have any failure tolerance and the majority of a 2-node cluster is considered as 2. The recommended etcd cluster size in production is 3,5, or 7.

Flannel is a network fabric for containers. Flannel provides a subnet to each host that is used by containers at runtime. Actually, Flannel runs an agent called flanneld on each host that allocates subnets. Flannel sets up and manages the network that interconnects all the Docker containers created by Kubernetes. Flannel is etcd backed and uses etcd to store the network configuration, allocated subnets, and auxiliary data such as the IP Address of the host.

Setting the Environment

We have used Amazon EC2 instances created from Ubuntu Server 14-04 LTS (HVM), SSD Volume Type - ami-d05e75b8 AMI for this chapter. The following software is required to be installed for this chapter.

-Docker Engine (latest version)

-Kubernetes on Master Node (version 1.01)

-Kubernetes on Worker Node (version 1.01)

-Kubectl (version 1.01)

Because we are creating a multi-node cluster we need to create multiple Amazon EC2 instances. For a two-node cluster create two Amazon EC2 instances - KubernetesMaster and KubernetesWorker - as shown in Figure 14-1.

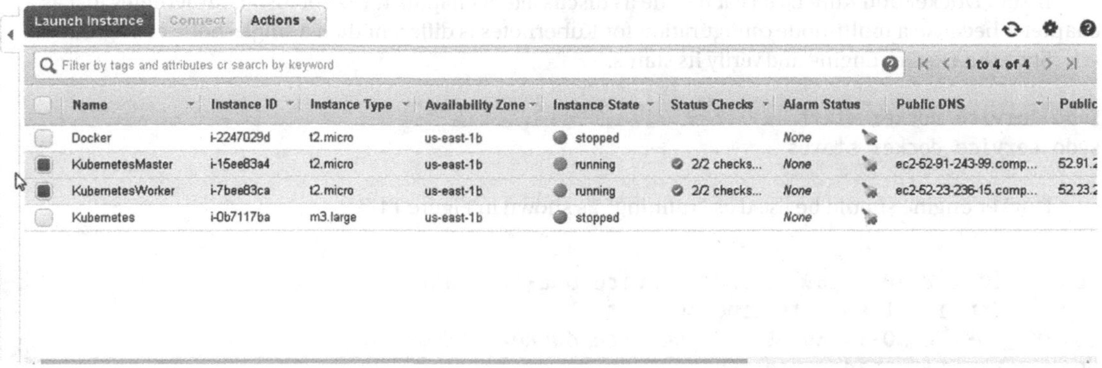

Figure 14-1. Creating two Ubuntu Instances for Kubernetes Master and Worker Nodes

SSH Login to each node separately. The Public IP Address for the Master Node may be obtained from the Amazon EC2 console as shown in Figure 14-2.

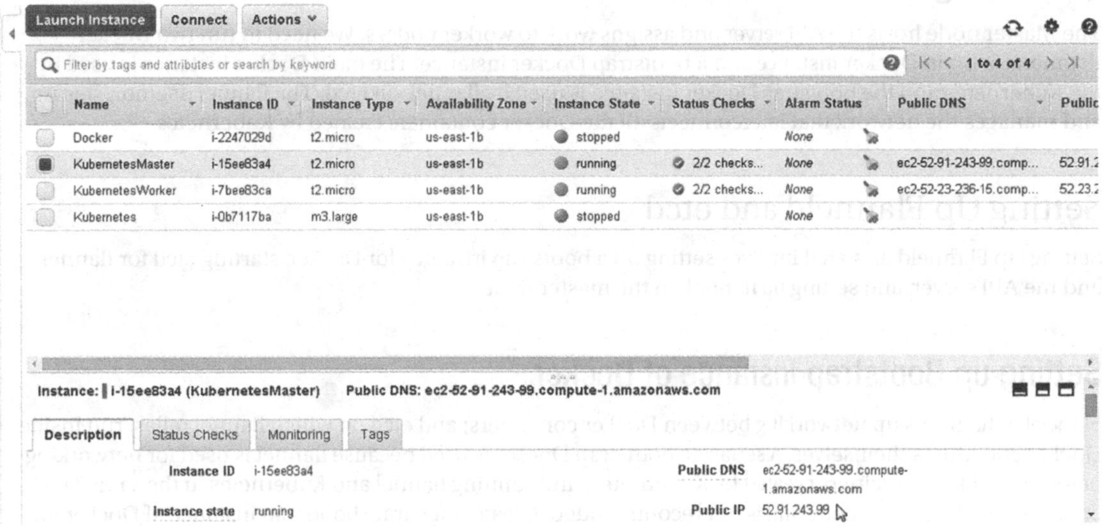

Figure 14-2. Obtaining the Public IP Address for a Ubuntu Instance

Log in to the Ubuntu instance for the Master node.

```
ssh -i "docker.pem" ubuntu@52.91.243.99
```

Similarly, obtain the Public IP Address for the Ubuntu instance for the Worker node and log in to the Ubuntu instance for the Worker node.

```
ssh -i "docker.pem" ubuntu@52.23.236.15
```

Install Docker and Kubectl on each node as discussed in chapter 1. Do not install Kubernetes just as chapter 1 because a multi-node configuration for Kubernetes is different than a single-node configuration.

Start the Docker Engine and verify its status.

```
sudo service docker start
sudo service docker status
```

Docker engine should be listed as "running" as shown in Figure 14-3.

```
ubuntu@ip-172-30-1-189:~$ sudo service docker start
start: Job is already running: docker
ubuntu@ip-172-30-1-189:~$ sudo service docker status
docker start/running, process 2701
ubuntu@ip-172-30-1-189:~$
```

Figure 14-3. *Starting Docker*

Installing the Master Node

The Master node hosts the API server and assigns work to worker node/s. We need to run two Docker daemons, a main Docker instance and a bootstrap Docker instance. The main Docker instance is used by the Kubernetes and the bootstrap Docker instance is used by flannel, an etcd. The flannel daemon sets up and manages the network that interconnects all the Docker containers created by Kubernetes.

Setting Up Flanneld and etcd

Setting Up Flanneld and etcd involves setting up a bootstrap instance for Docker, starting etcd for flannel and the API server, and setting up flannel on the master node.

Setting up Bootstrap Instance of Docker

Flannel, which sets up networking between Docker containers; and etcd on which flannel relies, run inside Docker containers themselves. A separate bootstrap Docker is used because flannel is used for networking between Docker containers created by Kubernetes; and running flannel and Kubernetes in the same Docker engine could be problematic and is not recommended. Create a separate bootstrap instance of Docker for flannel and etcd.

```
sudo sh -c 'docker daemon -H unix:///var/run/docker-bootstrap.sock -p /var/run/docker-
bootstrap.pid --iptables=false --ip-masq=false --bridge=none --graph=/var/lib/docker-
bootstrap 2> /var/log/docker-bootstrap.log 1> /dev/null &'
```

The bootstrap Docker daemon gets started and the output from the preceding command is shown in Figure 14-4.

```
root@ip-172-30-1-62:~# sudo sh -c 'docker daemon -H unix:///var/run/docker-boots
trap.sock -p /var/run/docker-bootstrap.pid --iptables=false --ip-masq=false --br
idge=none --graph=/var/lib/docker-bootstrap 2> /var/log/docker-bootstrap.log 1>
/dev/null &'
```

Figure 14-4. *Starting the Bootstrap Daemon on the Master Node*

The '–d' option is completely removed in Docker 1.10 and replaced with 'daemon'. If using the Docker version prior to Docker 1.10, for example Docker 1.9.1, replace 'daemon' with '-d' in the preceding command to run the command as follows:

```
sudo sh -c 'docker -d -H unix:///var/run/docker-bootstrap.sock -p /var/run/docker-bootstrap.
pid --iptables=false --ip-masq=false --bridge=none --graph=/var/lib/docker-bootstrap 2> /
var/log/docker-bootstrap.log 1> /dev/null &'
```

Setting Up etcd

Set up etcd for the flannel and the API server with the following command.

```
sudo docker -H unix:///var/run/docker-bootstrap.sock run --net=host -d gcr.io/google_
containers/etcd:2.0.12 /usr/local/bin/etcd --addr=127.0.0.1:4001 --bind-addr=0.0.0.0:4001
--data-dir=/var/etcd/data
```

The container for etcd gets downloaded and etcd gets installed as shown in Figure 14-5.

```
ubuntu@ip-172-30-1-189:~$ sudo docker -H unix:///var/run/docker-bootstrap.sock r
un --net=host -d gcr.io/google_containers/etcd:2.0.12 /usr/local/bin/etcd --addr
=127.0.0.1:4001 --bind-addr=0.0.0.0:4001 --data-dir=/var/etcd/data
Unable to find image 'gcr.io/google_containers/etcd:2.0.12' locally
Pulling repository gcr.io/google_containers/etcd
fafe47352699: Download complete
cf2616975b4a: Download complete
6ce2e90b0bc7: Download complete
8c2e06607696: Download complete
25b7f6392583: Download complete
b4b56c254ad5: Download complete
Status: Downloaded newer image for gcr.io/google_containers/etcd:2.0.12
gcr.io/google_containers/etcd: this image was pulled from a legacy registry.  Im
portant: This registry version will not be supported in future versions of docke
r.
32dd85f0479ab974c907e1be84b9517dfe4563a389e1714bd01b539bdaf9b17a
ubuntu@ip-172-30-1-189:~$ 
```

Figure 14-5. *Setting up etcd on the Master Node*

Set up a Classless Inter-Domain Routing (CIDR), which is an IP Addressing scheme that reduces the size of routing tables and makes more addresses available, range for flannel.

```
sudo docker -H unix:///var/run/docker-bootstrap.sock run --net=host gcr.io/google_
containers/etcd:2.0.12 etcdctl set /coreos.com/network/config '{ "Network": "10.1.0.0/16" }'
```

The preceding command does not generate any output as shown in Figure 14-6.

```
ubuntu@ip-172-30-1-189:~$ sudo docker -H unix:///var/run/docker-bootstrap.sock r
un --net=host gcr.io/google_containers/etcd:2.0.12 etcdctl set /coreos.com/netwo
rk/config '{ "Network": "10.1.0.0/16" }'
{ "Network": "10.1.0.0/16" }
ubuntu@ip-172-30-1-189:~$
```

Figure 14-6. *Setting Up CIDR on the Master Node*

Setting Up Flannel

By default Docker does provide a networking between containers and Pods but the networking provided by Flannel is much more simplified. We shall be using Flannel for networking. First, we need to stop Docker.

```
sudo service docker stop
```

Docker gets stopped as shown in Figure 14-7.

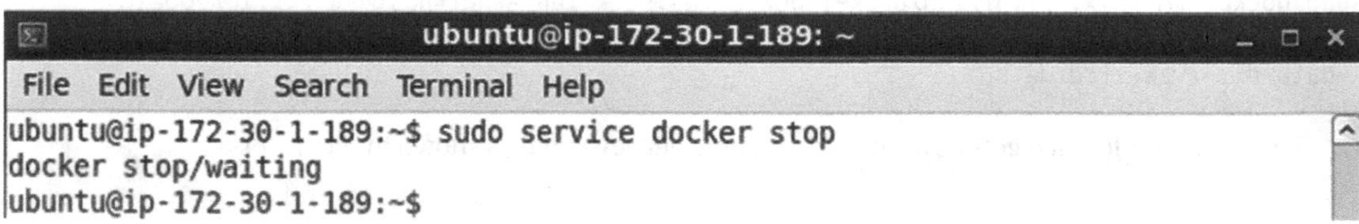
ubuntu@ip-172-30-1-189: ~
File Edit View Search Terminal Help
ubuntu@ip-172-30-1-189:~$ sudo service docker stop
docker stop/waiting
ubuntu@ip-172-30-1-189:~$

Figure 14-7. *Stopping Docker Temporarily*

Run flannel with the following command.

```
sudo docker -H unix:///var/run/docker-bootstrap.sock run -d --net=host --privileged -v /dev/
net:/dev/net quay.io/coreos/flannel:0.5.0
```

Flannel gets installed as shown in Figure 14-8.

```
ubuntu@ip-172-30-1-189:~$ sudo docker -H unix:///var/run/docker-bootstrap.sock r
un -d --net=host --privileged -v /dev/net:/dev/net quay.io/coreos/flannel:0.5.0
Unable to find image 'quay.io/coreos/flannel:0.5.0' locally
0.5.0: Pulling from coreos/flannel
9bed7aeb7782: Pull complete
52ad3964bb99: Pull complete
a1559bfac5ad: Pull complete
68044461bbdb: Pull complete
c447f3b3ac87: Pull complete
Digest: sha256:315ed9675123aa9368eed2fcbc5f48494fc1b8874e433e6de8e3ad16460a0dc0
Status: Downloaded newer image for quay.io/coreos/flannel:0.5.0
56610d2aa8077865d6c1b426fadbb07ee481363e94d260439162e509cea7a948
ubuntu@ip-172-30-1-189:~$
```

Figure 14-8. *Installing Flannel*

Flannel generates a hash as shown in Figure 14-9. Copy the Hash.

```
ubuntu@ip-172-30-1-189:~$ sudo docker -H unix:///var/run/docker-bootstrap.sock r
un -d --net=host --privileged -v /dev/net:/dev/net quay.io/coreos/flannel:0.5.0
Unable to find image 'quay.io/coreos/flannel:0.5.0' locally
0.5.0: Pulling from coreos/flannel
9bed7aeb7782: Pull complete
52ad3964bb99: Pull complete
a1559bfac5ad: Pull complete
68044461bbdb: Pull complete
c447f3b3ac87: Pull complete
Digest: sha256:315ed9675123aa9368eed2fcbc5f48494fc1b8874e433e6de8e3ad16460a0dc0
Status: Downloaded newer image for quay.io/coreos/flannel:0.5.0
56610d2aa8077865d6c1b426fadbb07ee481363e94d260439162e509cea7a948
```

Figure 14-9. *Obtaining the Hash Generated by Flannel*

Copy and paste the hash into the following command, and run the command to obtain the subnet settings.

```
sudo docker -H unix:///var/run/docker-bootstrap.sock exec <really-long-hash-from-above-here>
cat /run/flannel/subnet.env
```

The subnet settings get listed as shown in Figure 14-10.

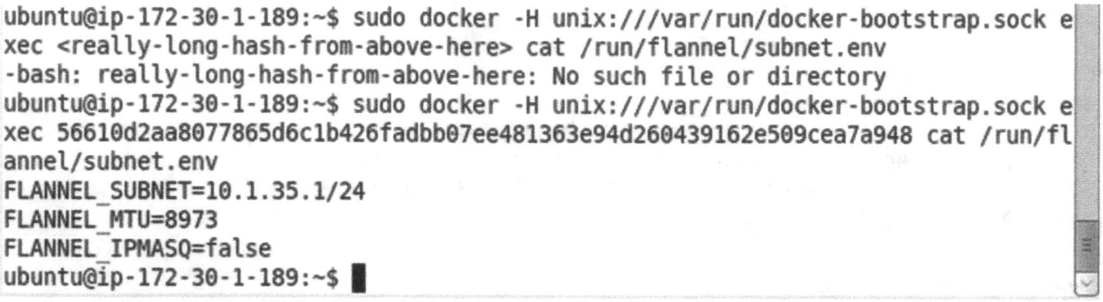

```
ubuntu@ip-172-30-1-189:~$ sudo docker -H unix:///var/run/docker-bootstrap.sock e
xec <really-long-hash-from-above-here> cat /run/flannel/subnet.env
-bash: really-long-hash-from-above-here: No such file or directory
ubuntu@ip-172-30-1-189:~$ sudo docker -H unix:///var/run/docker-bootstrap.sock e
xec 56610d2aa8077865d6c1b426fadbb07ee481363e94d260439162e509cea7a948 cat /run/fl
annel/subnet.env
FLANNEL_SUBNET=10.1.35.1/24
FLANNEL_MTU=8973
FLANNEL_IPMASQ=false
ubuntu@ip-172-30-1-189:~$
```

Figure 14-10. *Listing the Subnet Settings*

Make a note of the `FLANNEL_SUBNET` and `FLANNEL_MTU` values as we shall need these to edit the Docker configuration. Open the Docker configuration file in a vi editor.

```
sudo vi /etc/default/docker
```

The default settings in the docker configuration file are shown in Figure 14-11.

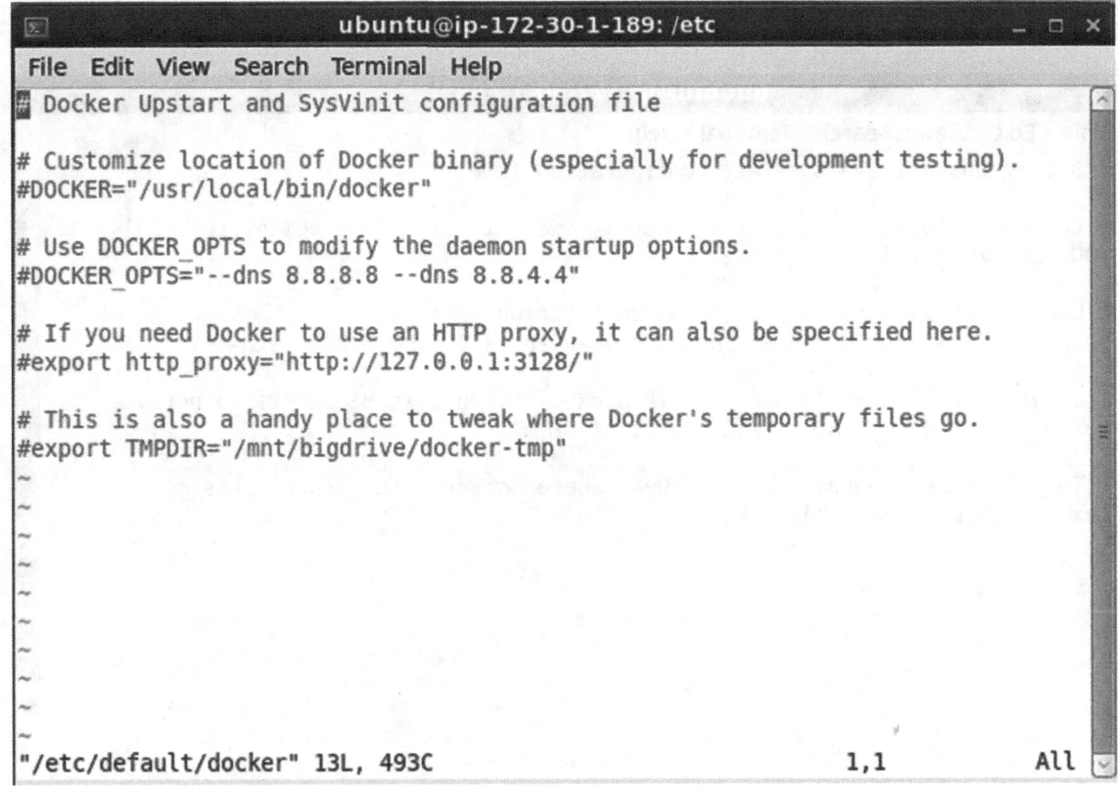

Figure 14-11. *Docker Configuration File Default Settings*

To the DOCKER_OPTS setting append the following parameters whose values are obtained from the output in Figure 14-10.

```
--bip=${FLANNEL_SUBNET} --mtu=${FLANNEL_MTU}
```

The modified docker configuration file is shown in Figure 14-12.

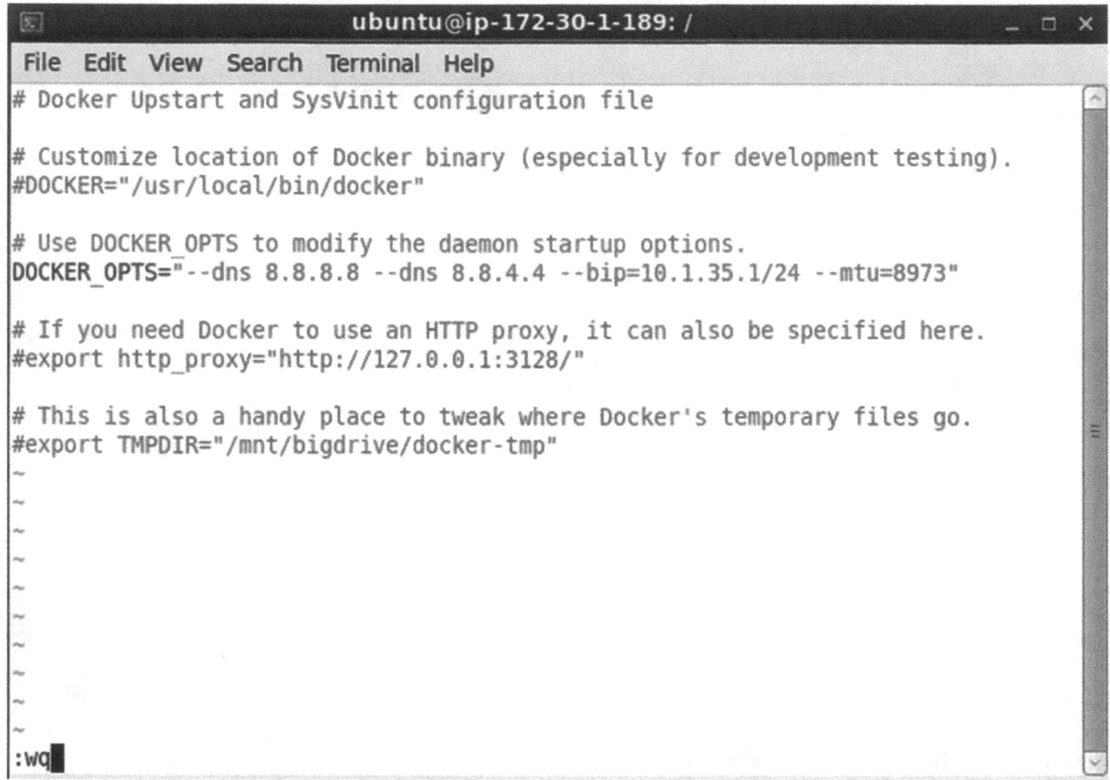

Figure 14-12. *Modified Docker Configuration File*

As mentioned before Docker provides its own networking with a Docker bridge called `docker0`. As we won't be using the default Docker bridge remove the default Docker bridge. For the brctl binaries first install the bridge-utils package.

```
sudo /sbin/ifconfig docker0 down
sudo apt-get install bridge-utils
sudo brctl delbr docker0
```

The output from installing the bridge-utils package and removing the docker0 bridge is shown in Figure 14-13.

```
ubuntu@ip-172-30-1-189:/$ sudo apt-get install bridge-utils
Reading package lists... Done
Building dependency tree
Reading state information... Done
The following NEW packages will be installed:
  bridge-utils
0 upgraded, 1 newly installed, 0 to remove and 139 not upgraded.
Need to get 29.2 kB of archives.
After this operation, 146 kB of additional disk space will be used.
Get:1 http://us-east-1.ec2.archive.ubuntu.com/ubuntu/ trusty/main bridge-utils a
md64 1.5-6ubuntu2 [29.2 kB]
Fetched 29.2 kB in 0s (0 B/s)
Selecting previously unselected package bridge-utils.
(Reading database ... 57916 files and directories currently installed.)
Preparing to unpack .../bridge-utils_1.5-6ubuntu2_amd64.deb ...
Unpacking bridge-utils (1.5-6ubuntu2) ...
Processing triggers for man-db (2.6.7.1-1ubuntu1) ...
Setting up bridge-utils (1.5-6ubuntu2) ...
ubuntu@ip-172-30-1-189:/$ sudo brctl delbr docker0
ubuntu@ip-172-30-1-189:/$
```

Figure 14-13. *Removing docker0 bridge*

Restart Docker.

```
sudo service docker start
```

Docker gets restarted as shown in Figure 14-14.

```
ubuntu@ip-172-30-1-189:/$ sudo service docker start
docker start/running, process 5461
ubuntu@ip-172-30-1-189:/$
```

Figure 14-14. *Restarting Docker*

Starting the Kubernetes Master

Setting up flannel networking is the main difference between setting up a single-node cluster and a multi-node cluster. Start the Kubernetes master with the same command as used for a single-node cluster.

```
sudo docker run \
  --volume=/:/rootfs:ro \
  --volume=/sys:/sys:ro \
  --volume=/dev:/dev \
  --volume=/var/lib/docker/:/var/lib/docker:rw \
  --volume=/var/lib/kubelet/:/var/lib/kubelet:rw \
```

```
  --volume=/var/run:/var/run:rw \
  --net=host \
  --privileged=true \
  --pid=host \
  -d \
  gcr.io/google_containers/hyperkube:v1.0.1 /hyperkube kubelet --api-servers=
http://localhost:8080 --v=2 --address=0.0.0.0 --enable-server --hostname-override=127.0.0.1 --config=/
etc/kubernetes/manifests-multi --cluster-dns=10.0.0.10 --cluster-domain=cluster.local
```

The preceding command is run from the Master Node as shown in Figure 14-15.

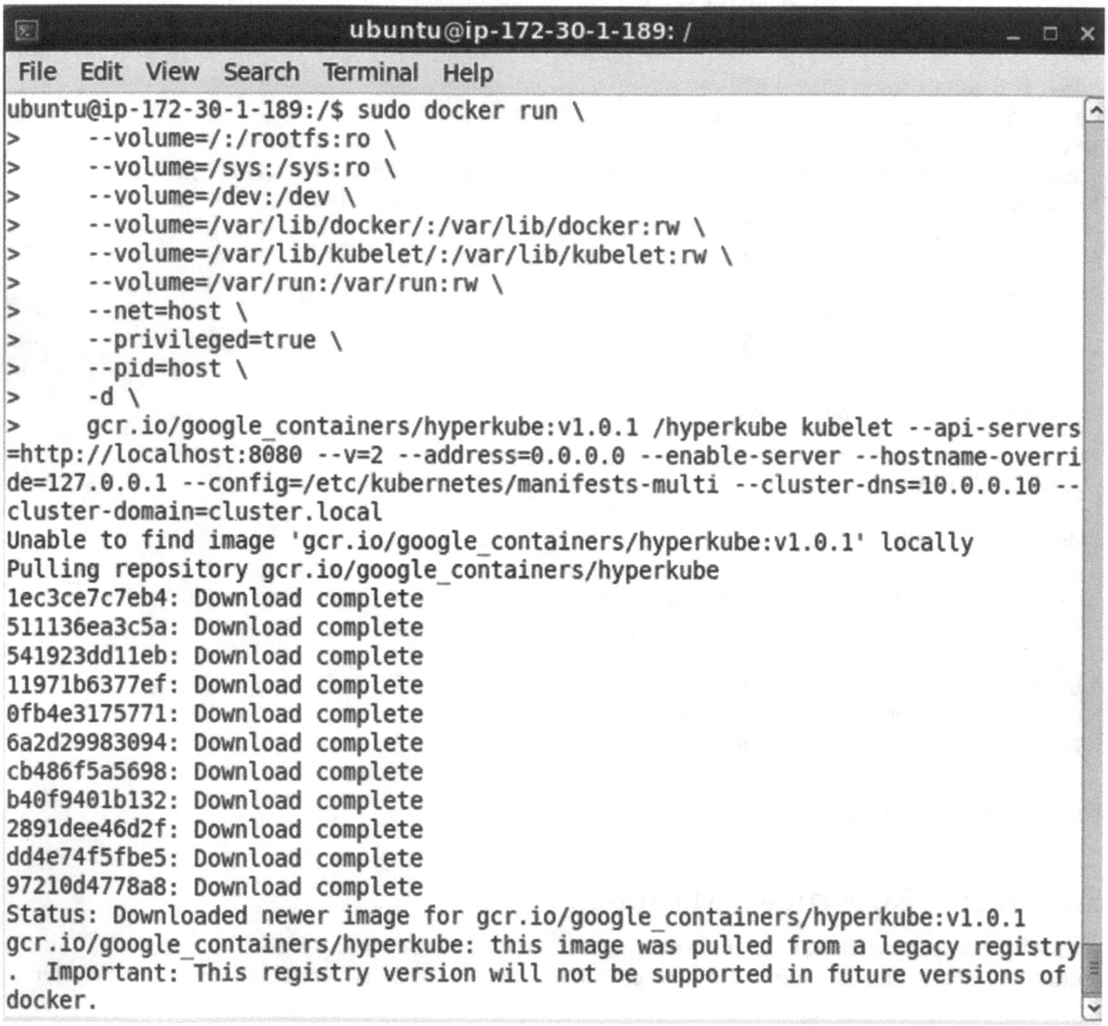

```
ubuntu@ip-172-30-1-189: /
File Edit View Search Terminal Help
ubuntu@ip-172-30-1-189:/$ sudo docker run \
>     --volume=/:/rootfs:ro \
>     --volume=/sys:/sys:ro \
>     --volume=/dev:/dev \
>     --volume=/var/lib/docker/:/var/lib/docker:rw \
>     --volume=/var/lib/kubelet/:/var/lib/kubelet:rw \
>     --volume=/var/run:/var/run:rw \
>     --net=host \
>     --privileged=true \
>     --pid=host \
>     -d \
>     gcr.io/google_containers/hyperkube:v1.0.1 /hyperkube kubelet --api-servers
=http://localhost:8080 --v=2 --address=0.0.0.0 --enable-server --hostname-overri
de=127.0.0.1 --config=/etc/kubernetes/manifests-multi --cluster-dns=10.0.0.10 --
cluster-domain=cluster.local
Unable to find image 'gcr.io/google_containers/hyperkube:v1.0.1' locally
Pulling repository gcr.io/google_containers/hyperkube
1ec3ce7c7eb4: Download complete
511136ea3c5a: Download complete
541923dd11eb: Download complete
11971b6377ef: Download complete
0fb4e3175771: Download complete
6a2d29983094: Download complete
cb486f5a5698: Download complete
b40f9401b132: Download complete
2891dee46d2f: Download complete
dd4e74f5fbe5: Download complete
97210d4778a8: Download complete
Status: Downloaded newer image for gcr.io/google_containers/hyperkube:v1.0.1
gcr.io/google_containers/hyperkube: this image was pulled from a legacy registry
. Important: This registry version will not be supported in future versions of
docker.
```

Figure 14-15. *Starting Kubernetes on the Master Node*

Kubernetes gets installed on the master node as shown in Figure 14-16.

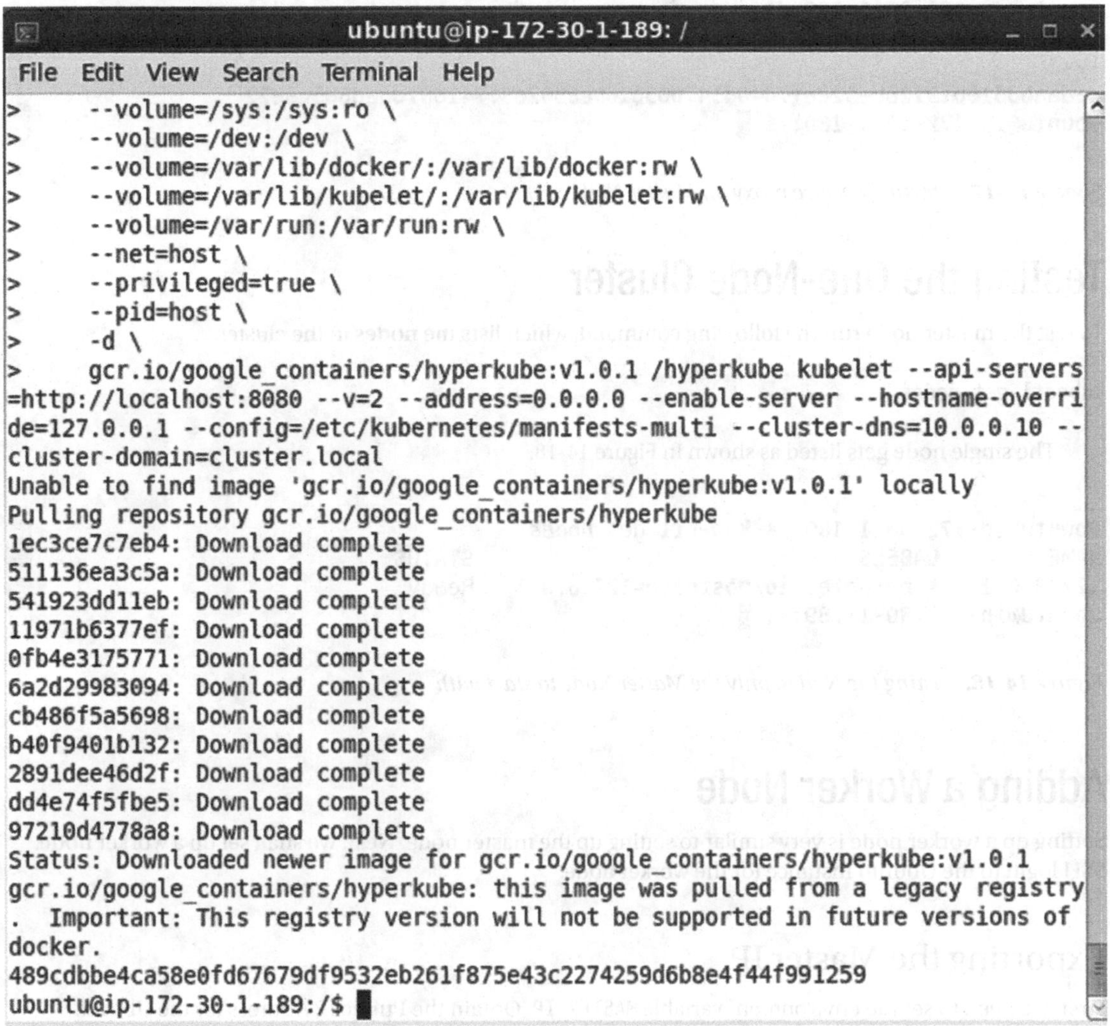

```
ubuntu@ip-172-30-1-189: /
File Edit View Search Terminal Help
>     --volume=/sys:/sys:ro \
>     --volume=/dev:/dev \
>     --volume=/var/lib/docker/:/var/lib/docker:rw \
>     --volume=/var/lib/kubelet/:/var/lib/kubelet:rw \
>     --volume=/var/run:/var/run:rw \
>     --net=host \
>     --privileged=true \
>     --pid=host \
>     -d \
>     gcr.io/google_containers/hyperkube:v1.0.1 /hyperkube kubelet --api-servers
=http://localhost:8080 --v=2 --address=0.0.0.0 --enable-server --hostname-overri
de=127.0.0.1 --config=/etc/kubernetes/manifests-multi --cluster-dns=10.0.0.10 --
cluster-domain=cluster.local
Unable to find image 'gcr.io/google_containers/hyperkube:v1.0.1' locally
Pulling repository gcr.io/google_containers/hyperkube
1ec3ce7c7eb4: Download complete
511136ea3c5a: Download complete
541923dd11eb: Download complete
11971b6377ef: Download complete
0fb4e3175771: Download complete
6a2d29983094: Download complete
cb486f5a5698: Download complete
b40f9401b132: Download complete
2891dee46d2f: Download complete
dd4e74f5fbe5: Download complete
97210d4778a8: Download complete
Status: Downloaded newer image for gcr.io/google_containers/hyperkube:v1.0.1
gcr.io/google_containers/hyperkube: this image was pulled from a legacy registry
.  Important: This registry version will not be supported in future versions of
docker.
489cdbbe4ca58e0fd67679df9532eb261f875e43c2274259d6b8e4f44f991259
ubuntu@ip-172-30-1-189:/$
```

Figure 14-16. *Kubernetes Started on Master Node*

Running the Service Proxy

Run the service proxy also using the same command as used for a single-node cluster.

```
sudo docker run -d --net=host --privileged gcr.io/google_containers/hyperkube:v1.0.1 /
hyperkube proxy --master=http://127.0.0.1:8080 --v=2
```

Service proxy gets installed as shown in Figure 14-17.

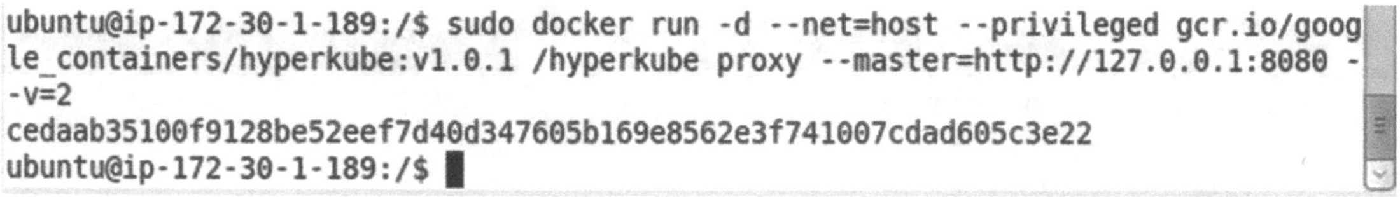

```
ubuntu@ip-172-30-1-189:/$ sudo docker run -d --net=host --privileged gcr.io/goog
le_containers/hyperkube:v1.0.1 /hyperkube proxy --master=http://127.0.0.1:8080 -
-v=2
cedaab35100f9128be52eef7d40d347605b169e8562e3f741007cdad605c3e22
ubuntu@ip-172-30-1-189:/$ ▌
```

Figure 14-17. *Starting Service proxy on Master Node*

Testing the One-Node Cluster

To test the master node run the following command, which lists the nodes in the cluster.

```
kubectl get nodes
```

The single node gets listed as shown in Figure 14-18.

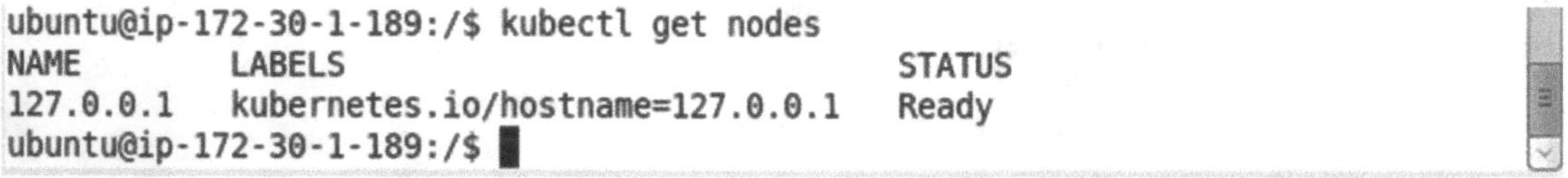

```
ubuntu@ip-172-30-1-189:/$ kubectl get nodes
NAME        LABELS                               STATUS
127.0.0.1   kubernetes.io/hostname=127.0.0.1     Ready
ubuntu@ip-172-30-1-189:/$ ▌
```

Figure 14-18. *Listing the Nodes, only the Master Node to start with*

Adding a Worker Node

Setting up a worker node is very similar to setting up the master node. Next, we shall set up a worker node. SSH login to the Ubuntu instance for the worker node.

Exporting the Master IP

First, we need to set the environment variable `MASTER_IP`. Obtain the Public IP Address for the Ubuntu instance running the master node as shown in Figure 14-19.

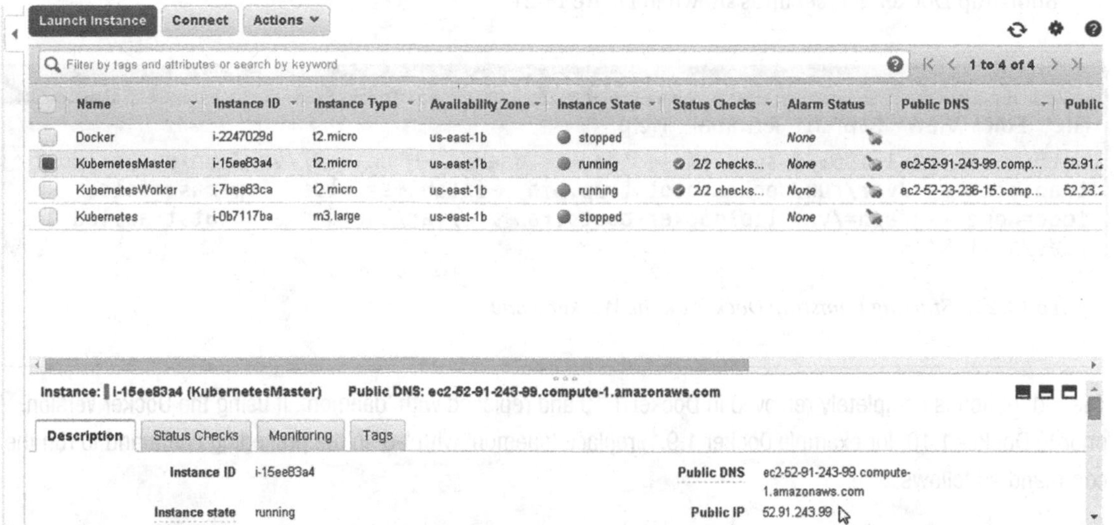

***Figure 14-19.** Obtaining the Master Node's IP Address*

Export the environment variable `MASTER_IP` using the Public IP Address.

```
export MASTER_IP=52.91.243.99
```

Echo the `MASTER_IP` environment variable.

```
echo $MASTER_IP
```

The output from the preceding command is shown in Figure 14-20.

```
ubuntu@ip-172-30-1-66:~$ export MASTER_IP=52.91.243.99
ubuntu@ip-172-30-1-66:~$ echo $MASTER_IP
52.91.243.99
ubuntu@ip-172-30-1-66:~$ 
```

***Figure 14-20.** Exporting the MASTER_IP Environment Variable on a Worker Node*

Setting Up Flanneld

Start a bootstrap Docker daemon just for the flannel networking.

```
sudo sh -c 'docker daemon -H unix:///var/run/docker-bootstrap.sock -p /var/run/docker-
bootstrap.pid --iptables=false --ip-masq=false --bridge=none --graph=/var/lib/docker-
bootstrap 2> /var/log/docker-bootstrap.log 1> /dev/null &'
```

Bootstrap Docker gets set up as shown in Figure 14-21.

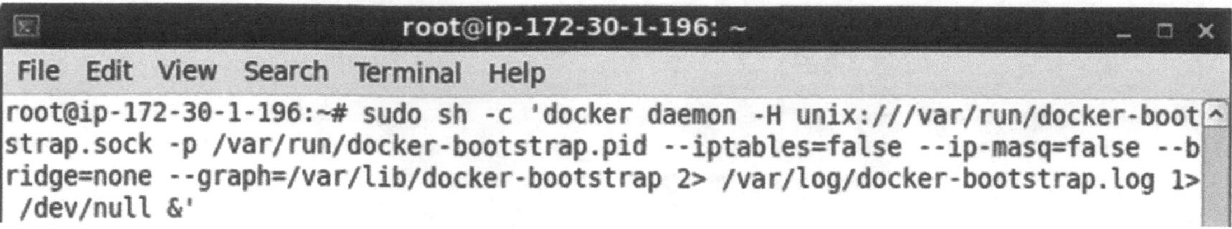

Figure 14-21. *Starting Bootstrap Docker on the Worker Node*

The '–d' option is completely removed in Docker 1.10 and replaced with 'daemon'. If using the Docker version prior to Docker 1.10, for example Docker 1.9.1, replace 'daemon' with '-d' in the preceding command to run the command as follows:

```
sudo sh -c 'docker -d -H unix:///var/run/docker-bootstrap.sock -p /var/run/docker-bootstrap.
pid --iptables=false --ip-masq=false --bridge=none --graph=/var/lib/docker-bootstrap 2> /
var/log/docker-bootstrap.log 1> /dev/null &'
```

To install Flannel, first we need to stop the Docker engine.

```
sudo service docker stop
```

Docker engine gets stopped as shown in Figure 14-22.

```
ubuntu@ip-172-30-1-66:~$ sudo service docker stop
docker stop/waiting
ubuntu@ip-172-30-1-66:~$ sudo service docker status
docker stop/waiting
ubuntu@ip-172-30-1-66:~$
```

Figure 14-22. *Stopping Docker Temporarily on the Worker Node*

Next, install flannel on the worker node. The same etcd that is running on the master is used for the flanneld on the worker node. The etcd instance includes the Master's Ip using the `MASTER_IP` environment variable.

```
sudo docker -H unix:///var/run/docker-bootstrap.sock run -d --net=host --privileged
-v /dev/net:/dev/net quay.io/coreos/flannel:0.5.0 /opt/bin/flanneld --etcd-
endpoints=http://${MASTER_IP}:4001
```

Flannel gets set up on the worker node as shown in Figure 14-23.

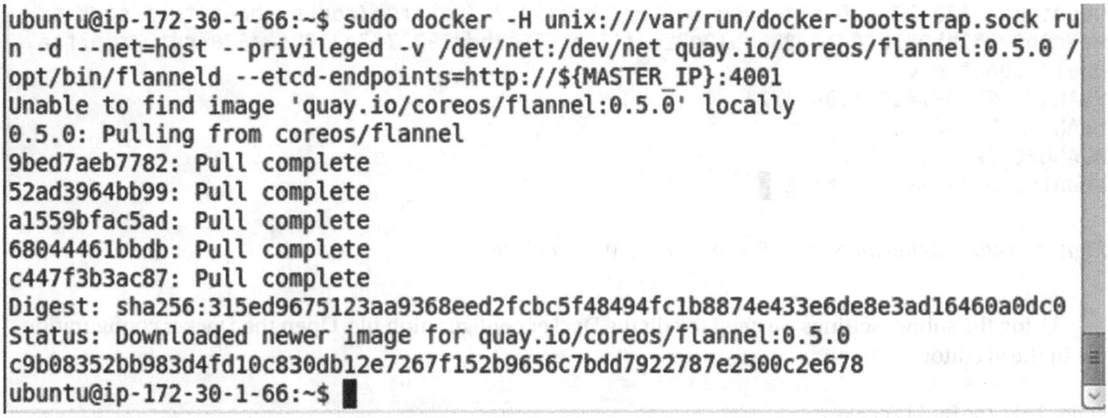

```
ubuntu@ip-172-30-1-66:~$ sudo docker -H unix:///var/run/docker-bootstrap.sock ru
n -d --net=host --privileged -v /dev/net:/dev/net quay.io/coreos/flannel:0.5.0 /
opt/bin/flanneld --etcd-endpoints=http://${MASTER_IP}:4001
Unable to find image 'quay.io/coreos/flannel:0.5.0' locally
0.5.0: Pulling from coreos/flannel
9bed7aeb7782: Pull complete
52ad3964bb99: Pull complete
a1559bfac5ad: Pull complete
68044461bbdb: Pull complete
c447f3b3ac87: Pull complete
Digest: sha256:315ed9675123aa9368eed2fcbc5f48494fc1b8874e433e6de8e3ad16460a0dc0
Status: Downloaded newer image for quay.io/coreos/flannel:0.5.0
c9b08352bb983d4fd10c830db12e7267f152b9656c7bdd7922787e2500c2e678
ubuntu@ip-172-30-1-66:~$
```

Figure 14-23. *Installing Flannel on the Worker Node*

Copy the hash generated by the preceding command as shown in Figure 14-24.

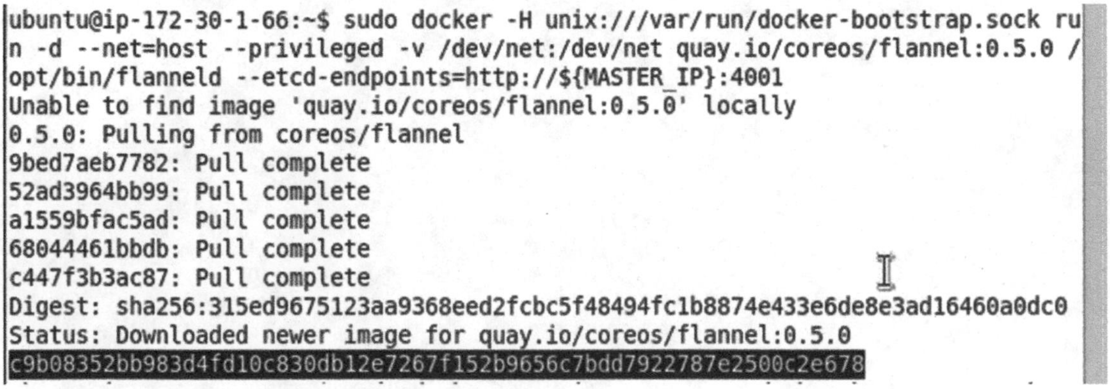

```
ubuntu@ip-172-30-1-66:~$ sudo docker -H unix:///var/run/docker-bootstrap.sock ru
n -d --net=host --privileged -v /dev/net:/dev/net quay.io/coreos/flannel:0.5.0 /
opt/bin/flanneld --etcd-endpoints=http://${MASTER_IP}:4001
Unable to find image 'quay.io/coreos/flannel:0.5.0' locally
0.5.0: Pulling from coreos/flannel
9bed7aeb7782: Pull complete
52ad3964bb99: Pull complete
a1559bfac5ad: Pull complete
68044461bbdb: Pull complete
c447f3b3ac87: Pull complete
Digest: sha256:315ed9675123aa9368eed2fcbc5f48494fc1b8874e433e6de8e3ad16460a0dc0
Status: Downloaded newer image for quay.io/coreos/flannel:0.5.0
c9b08352bb983d4fd10c830db12e7267f152b9656c7bdd7922787e2500c2e678
```

Figure 14-24. *Obtaining the Hash geenrated by Flannel*

Using the hash value in the following command obtain the subnet settings from flannel.

```
sudo docker -H unix:///var/run/docker-bootstrap.sock exec <really-long-hash-from-above-here>
cat /run/flannel/subnet.env
```

The subnet settings get output as shown in Figure 14-25.

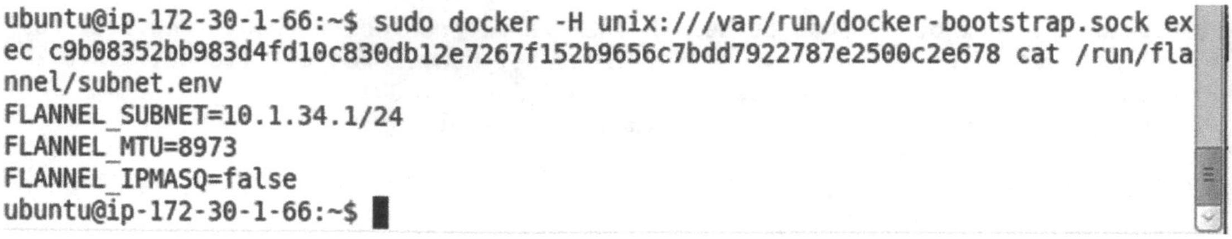

```
ubuntu@ip-172-30-1-66:~$ sudo docker -H unix:///var/run/docker-bootstrap.sock ex
ec c9b08352bb983d4fd10c830db12e7267f152b9656c7bdd7922787e2500c2e678 cat /run/fla
nnel/subnet.env
FLANNEL_SUBNET=10.1.34.1/24
FLANNEL_MTU=8973
FLANNEL_IPMASQ=false
ubuntu@ip-172-30-1-66:~$
```

Figure 14-25. *Listing the Subnet Settings on the Worker Node*

Using the subnet settings we need to edit the Docker configuration file. Open the Docker configuration file in the vi editor.

```
sudo /etc/default/docker
```

Append the following parameters to the `DOCKER_OPTS` setting. Substitute the values for `FLANNEL_SUBNET` and `FLANNEL_MTU` as obtained from Figure 14-25.

```
--bip=${FLANNEL_SUBNET} --mtu=${FLANNEL_MTU}
```

The modified Docker configuration file is shown in Figure 14-26.

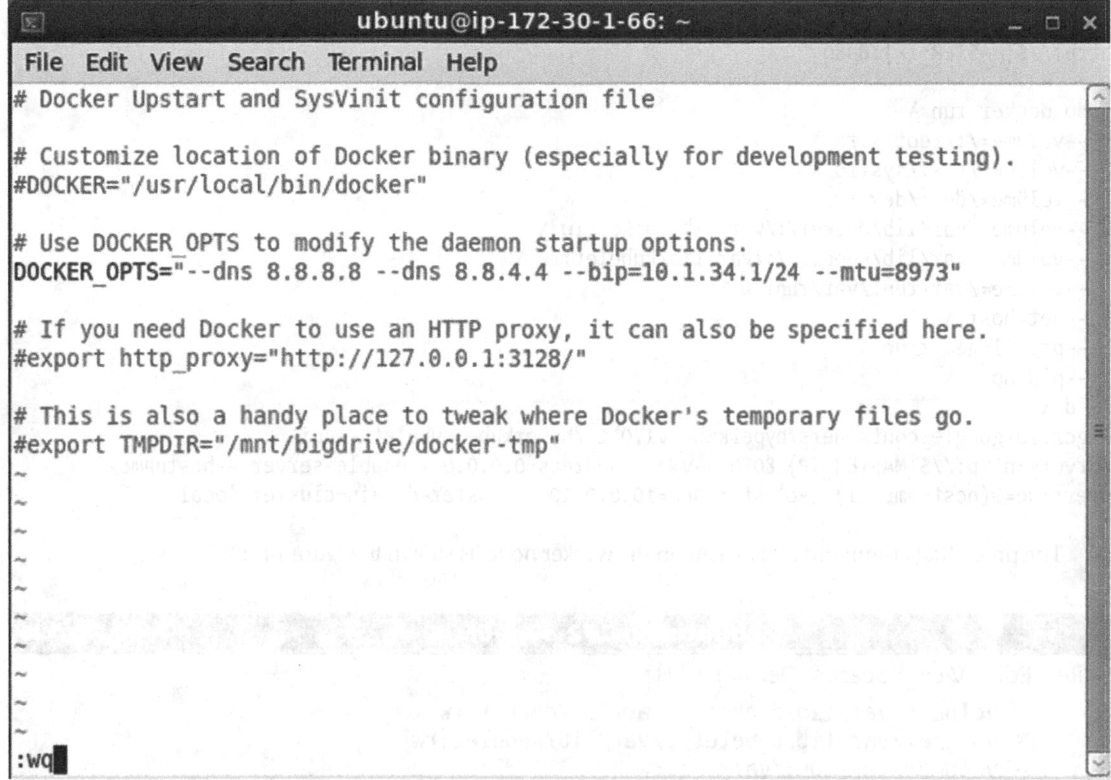

Figure 14-26. *Modified Docker Configuration File*

Shut down and remove the existing Docker bridge docker0, which is used by default by Docker for networking between containers and Pods. The bridge-utils package is needed to be installed as it is not available by default on an Ubuntu instance on Amazon EC2.

```
sudo /sbin/ifconfig docker0 down
sudo apt-get install bridge-utils
sudo brctl delbr docker0
```

Restart Docker.

```
sudo service docker start
```

The Docker engine gets started as shown in Figure 14-27.

```
ubuntu@ip-172-30-1-66:~$ sudo service  docker start
docker start/running, process 3731
ubuntu@ip-172-30-1-66:~$
```

Figure 14-27. *Restarting Docker*

Starting Up Kubernetes on Worker Node

Start up Kubernetes on the worker node with the same command as used in the Master node with the difference that instead of setting the `--api-servers` to `http://localhost:8080` set the --api-servers to the `http://${MASTER_IP}:8080`.

```
sudo docker run \
  --volume=/:/rootfs:ro \
  --volume=/sys:/sys:ro \
  --volume=/dev:/dev \
  --volume=/var/lib/docker/:/var/lib/docker:rw \
  --volume=/var/lib/kubelet/:/var/lib/kubelet:rw \
  --volume=/var/run:/var/run:rw \
  --net=host \
  --privileged=true \
  --pid=host \
  -d \
  gcr.io/google_containers/hyperkube:v1.0.1 /hyperkube kubelet --api-
servers=http://${MASTER_IP}:8080 --v=2 --address=0.0.0.0 --enable-server --hostname-
override=$(hostname -i) --cluster-dns=10.0.0.10 --cluster-domain=cluster.local
```

The preceding command is to be run on the worker node as shown in Figure 14-28.

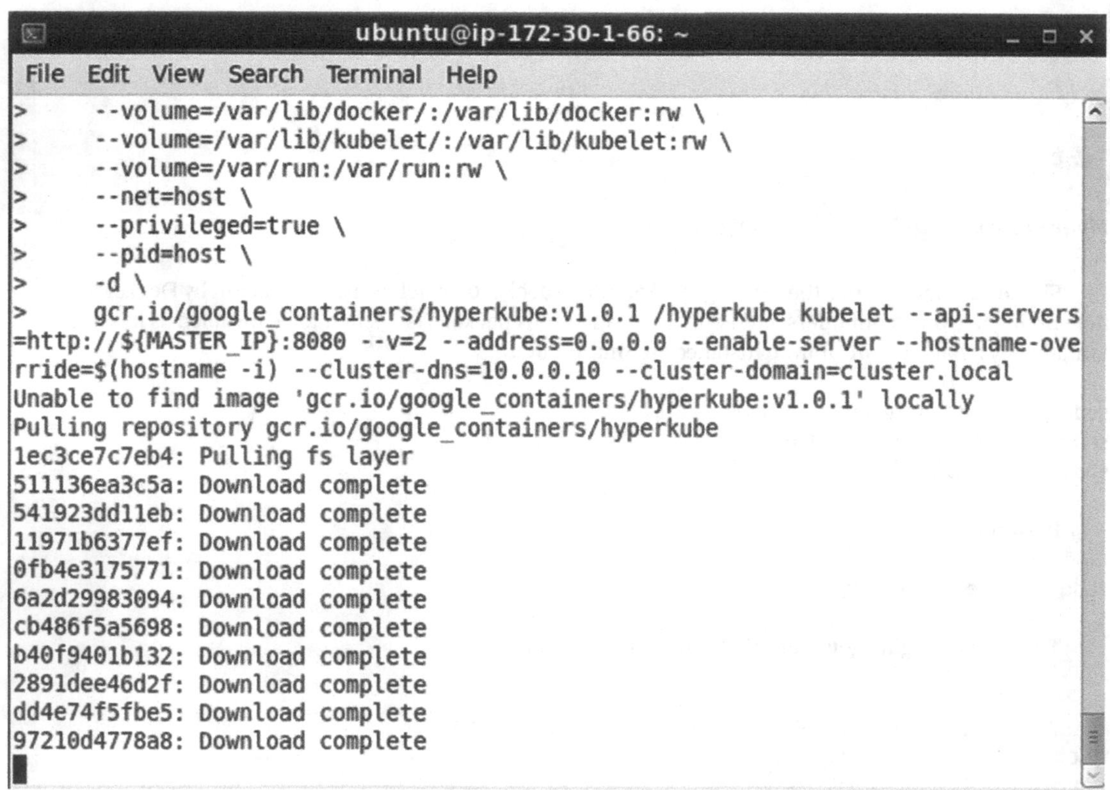

Figure 14-28. *Starting Kubernetes on the Worker Node*

Running the Service Proxy

The service proxy on the worker node is also run with the same command as for the master node except that the Master's Ip parameter `-- master=http://127.0.0.1:8080` should be replaced with `--master=http://${MASTER_IP}:8080`.

```
sudo docker run -d --net=host --privileged gcr.io/google_containers/hyperkube:v1.0.1 /
hyperkube proxy --master=http://${MASTER_IP}:8080 --v=2
```

The service proxy gets started as shown in Figure 14-29.

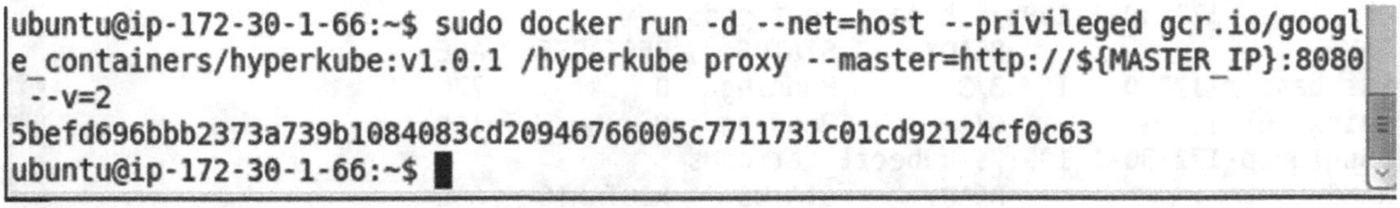

```
ubuntu@ip-172-30-1-66:~$ sudo docker run -d --net=host --privileged gcr.io/googl
e_containers/hyperkube:v1.0.1 /hyperkube proxy --master=http://${MASTER_IP}:8080
 --v=2
5befd696bbb2373a739b1084083cd20946766005c7711731c01cd92124cf0c63
ubuntu@ip-172-30-1-66:~$
```

Figure 14-29. *Starting Service Proxy on the Worker Node*

Testing the Kubernetes Cluster

From the Master node, not the worker node that was being configured in the preceding commands, list the nodes in the cluster.

```
kubectl get nodes
```

Two nodes get listed as shown in Figure 14-30: the master node and the worker node.

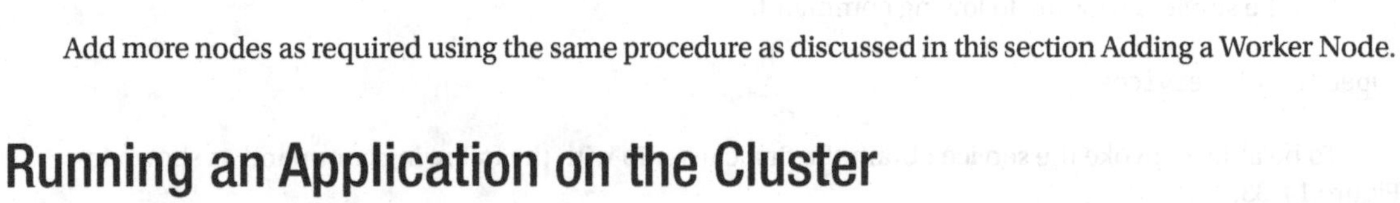

```
ubuntu@ip-172-30-1-189:/$ kubectl get nodes
NAME           LABELS                                STATUS
127.0.0.1      kubernetes.io/hostname=127.0.0.1      Ready
172.30.1.66    kubernetes.io/hostname=172.30.1.66    Ready
ubuntu@ip-172-30-1-189:/$
```

Figure 14-30. *Listing a Two-Node Cluster*

Add more nodes as required using the same procedure as discussed in this section Adding a Worker Node.

Running an Application on the Cluster

To test the cluster run an application on the command line using kubectl. As an example, run the Docker image "nginx" with the following command.

```
kubectl -s http://localhost:8080 run nginx --image=nginx --port=80
```

Subsequently list the Pods.

```
kubectl get pods
```

The nginx application container is created and the nginx replication controller is created with default of 1 replicas as shown in Figure 14-31. One pod gets listed, also shown in Figure 14-31. Initially the Pod could be listed as Pending status. Run the preceding command after a few seconds to list the Pod as running and ready. To find on which instance/s (node/s) in the cluster the Pod/s is/are running on, run the command.

```
kubectl get pods -o wide.
```

```
ubuntu@ip-172-30-1-189:/$ kubectl -s http://localhost:8080 run nginx --image=ngi
nx --port=80
CONTROLLER   CONTAINER(S)   IMAGE(S)   SELECTOR    REPLICAS
nginx        nginx          nginx      run=nginx   1
ubuntu@ip-172-30-1-189:/$ kubectl get pods
NAME                    READY     STATUS    RESTARTS   AGE
k8s-master-127.0.0.1    3/3       Running   0          27m
nginx-2hl9z             0/1       Pending   0          11s
ubuntu@ip-172-30-1-189:/$ kubectl get pods
NAME                    READY     STATUS    RESTARTS   AGE
k8s-master-127.0.0.1    3/3       Running   0          27m
nginx-2hl9z             1/1       Running   0          22s
ubuntu@ip-172-30-1-189:/$
```

Figure 14-31. *Installing an Application on the Cluster*

Exposing the Application as a Service

To expose the replication controller nginx as a service run the following command.

```
kubectl expose rc nginx --port=80
```

The nginx service gets created as shown in Figure 14-32.

```
ubuntu@ip-172-30-1-189:/$ kubectl expose rc nginx --port=80
NAME      LABELS      SELECTOR    IP(S)     PORT(S)
nginx     run=nginx   run=nginx             80/TCP
```

Figure 14-32. *Creating a Service*

List the services with the following command.

```
kubectl get services
```

To be able to invoke the service obtain the first cluster Ip with the following command as shown in Figure 14-33.

```
kubectl get svc nginx --template={{.spec.clusterIP}}
```

Invoke the web server using the cluster Ip returned, 10.0.0.99.

```
curl 10.0.0.99
```

```
ubuntu@ip-172-30-1-189:/$ kubectl get svc nginx --template={{.spec.clusterIP}}
10.0.0.99ubuntu@ip-172-30-1-189:/$ curl 10.0.0.99
<!DOCTYPE html>
<html>
<head>
<title>Welcome to nginx!</title>
<style>
    body {
        width: 35em;
        margin: 0 auto;
        font-family: Tahoma, Verdana, Arial, sans-serif;
    }
</style>
</head>
<body>
<h1>Welcome to nginx!</h1>
<p>If you see this page, the nginx web server is successfully installed and
```

Figure 14-33. *Invoking a Web Server with Curl*

The HTML returned from the nginx application is output as shown in Figure 14-34.

```
10.0.0.99ubuntu@ip-172-30-1-189:/$ curl 10.0.0.99
<!DOCTYPE html>
<html>
<head>
<title>Welcome to nginx!</title>
<style>
    body {
        width: 35em;
        margin: 0 auto;
        font-family: Tahoma, Verdana, Arial, sans-serif;
    }
</style>
</head>
<body>
<h1>Welcome to nginx!</h1>
<p>If you see this page, the nginx web server is successfully installed and
working. Further configuration is required.</p>

<p>For online documentation and support please refer to
<a href="http://nginx.org/">nginx.org</a>.<br/>
Commercial support is available at
<a href="http://nginx.com/">nginx.com</a>.</p>

<p><em>Thank you for using nginx.</em></p>
</body>
</html>
ubuntu@ip-172-30-1-189:/$
```

Figure 14-34. *The HTML generated by the Application*

Testing the Application in a Browser

To invoke the service endpoint in a browser, set port forwarding from `10.0.0.99:80` endpoint to `localhost:80`.

```
ssh -i docker.pem -f -nNT -L 80:10.0.0.99:80 ubuntu@ec2-52-91-243-99.compute-1.amazonaws.com
```

Port forwarding gets set as shown in Figure 14-35.

```
[root@localhost ~]# ssh -i docker.pem -f -nNT -L 80:10.0.0.99:80 ubuntu@ec2-52-9
1-243-99.compute-1.amazonaws.com
The authenticity of host 'ec2-52-91-243-99.compute-1.amazonaws.com (52.91.243.99
)' can't be established.
RSA key fingerprint is d4:81:3b:fe:9b:49:dd:0a:ff:df:ac:7c:93:dd:e3:ee.
Are you sure you want to continue connecting (yes/no)? yes
Warning: Permanently added 'ec2-52-91-243-99.compute-1.amazonaws.com' (RSA) to t
he list of known hosts.
[root@localhost ~]#
```

Figure 14-35. *Setting Port Forwarding*

Invoke the nginx application in a local browser with url `http://localhost` as shown in Figure 14-36.

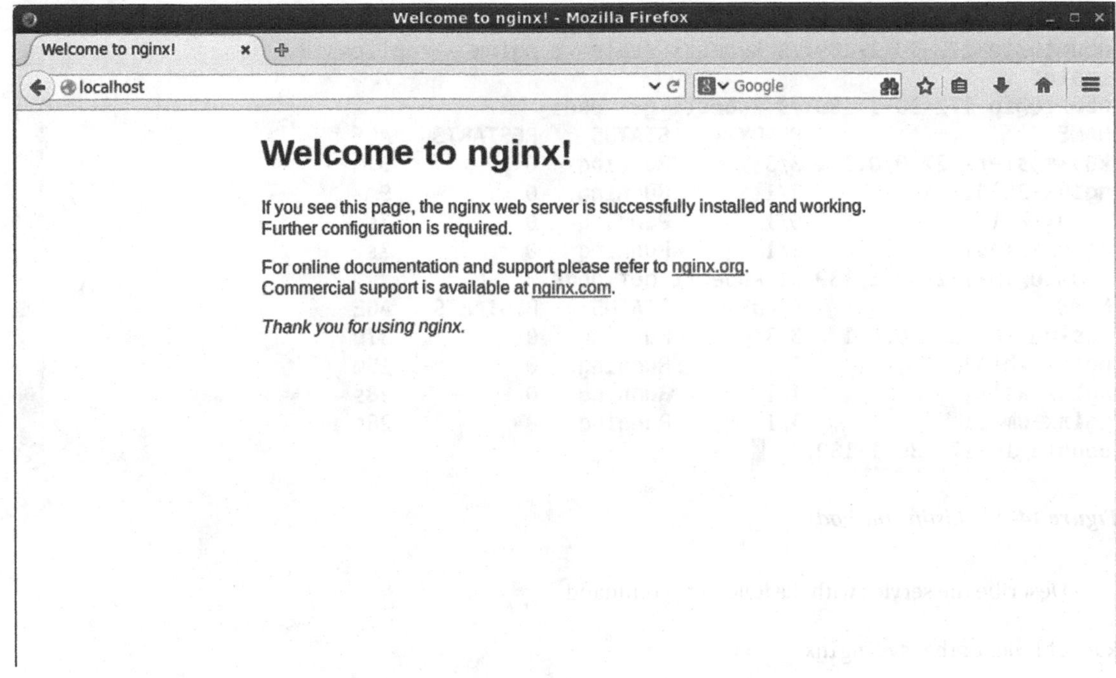

Figure 14-36. *Invoking a Service Endpoint in a Browser*

Scaling the Application

Scaling is a common usage pattern of Replication Controller. The nginx replication controller may be scaled with the `kubectl scale` command. As an example, scale to 3 replicas.

```
kubectl scale rc nginx --replicas=3
```

Subsequently list the Pods.

```
kubectl get pods
```

An output of "scaled" indicates that the replication controller has been scaled. Three Pods get listed as shown in Figure 14-37.

```
ubuntu@ip-172-30-1-189:/$ kubectl scale rc nginx --replicas=3
scaled
ubuntu@ip-172-30-1-189:/$ kubectl get pods
NAME                    READY     STATUS     RESTARTS   AGE
k8s-master-127.0.0.1    3/3       Running    0          37m
nginx-2hl9z             1/1       Running    0          9m
nginx-kslkj             0/1       Pending    0          7s
nginx-qmesi             0/1       Running    0          7s
ubuntu@ip-172-30-1-189:/$ kubectl get pods
NAME                    READY     STATUS     RESTARTS   AGE
k8s-master-127.0.0.1    3/3       Running    0          37m
nginx-2hl9z             1/1       Running    0          10m
nginx-kslkj             1/1       Running    0          28s
nginx-qmesi             1/1       Running    0          28s
ubuntu@ip-172-30-1-189:/$ 
```

Figure 14-37. *Listing the Pods*

Describe the service with the following command.

```
kubectl describe svc nginx
```

Three service endpoints get listed as shown in Figure 14-38.

```
ubuntu@ip-172-30-1-189:/$ kubectl describe svc nginx
Name:                   nginx
Namespace:              default
Labels:                 run=nginx
Selector:               run=nginx
Type:                   ClusterIP
IP:                     10.0.0.99
Port:                   <unnamed>       80/TCP
Endpoints:              10.1.34.2:80,10.1.35.2:80,10.1.35.3:80
Session Affinity:       None
No events.

ubuntu@ip-172-30-1-189:/$ 
```

Figure 14-38. *Describing the Service*

To be able to invoke each of the service endpoints in a browser on a local machine, set the port forwarding.

```
ssh -i docker.pem -f -nNT -L 8081:10.1.34.2:80 ubuntu@ec2-52-91-243-99.compute-1.amazonaws.com
ssh -i docker.pem -f -nNT -L 8082:10.1.35.2:80 ubuntu@ec2-52-91-243-99.compute-1.amazonaws.com
ssh -i docker.pem -f -nNT -L 8083:10.1.35.3:80 ubuntu@ec2-52-91-243-99.compute-1.amazonaws.com
```

Port forwarding gets set as shown in Figure 14-39.

```
[root@localhost ~]# ssh -i docker.pem -f -nNT -L 8081:10.1.34.2:80 ubuntu@ec2-52
-91-243-99.compute-1.amazonaws.com
[root@localhost ~]#
[root@localhost ~]# ssh -i docker.pem -f -nNT -L 8082:10.1.35.2:80 ubuntu@ec2-52
-91-243-99.compute-1.amazonaws.com
[root@localhost ~]#
[root@localhost ~]# ssh -i docker.pem -f -nNT -L 8083:10.1.35.3:80 ubuntu@ec2-52
-91-243-99.compute-1.amazonaws.com
[root@localhost ~]#
```

Figure 14-39. *Setting port Forwarding for the additional Service Endpoints*

The service endpoints may be invoked in a local browser. For example the url `http://localhost:8081` invokes one of the service endpoints as shown in Figure 14-40.

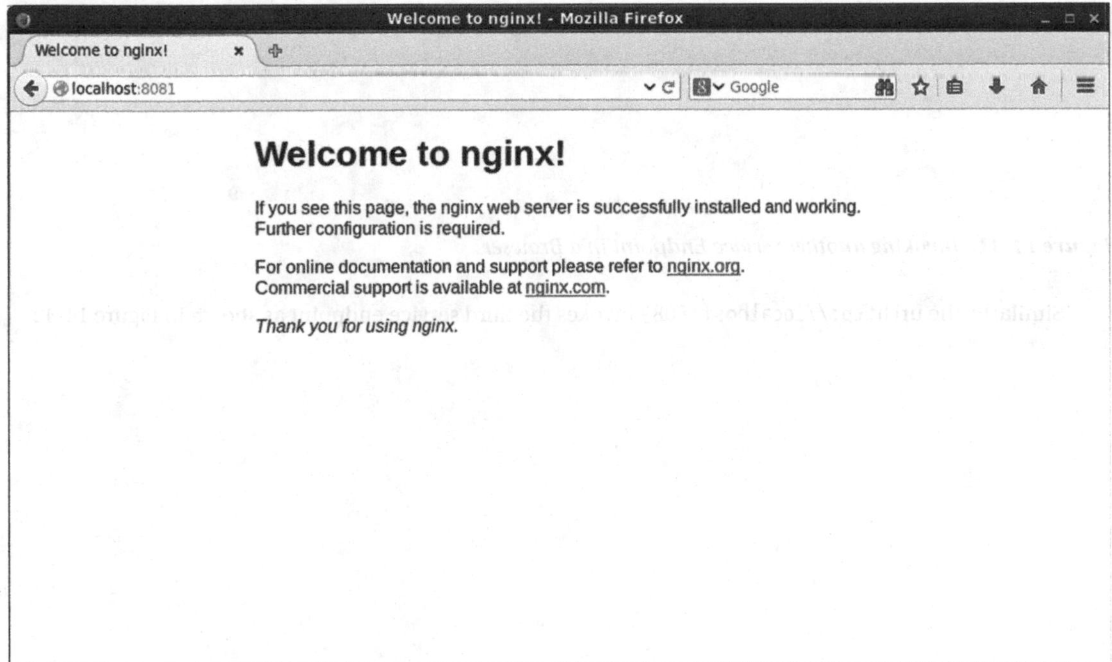

Figure 14-40. *Invoking a Service Endpoint in a Browser*

Similarly, the url `http://localhost:8082` invokes another service endpoint as shown in Figure 14-41.

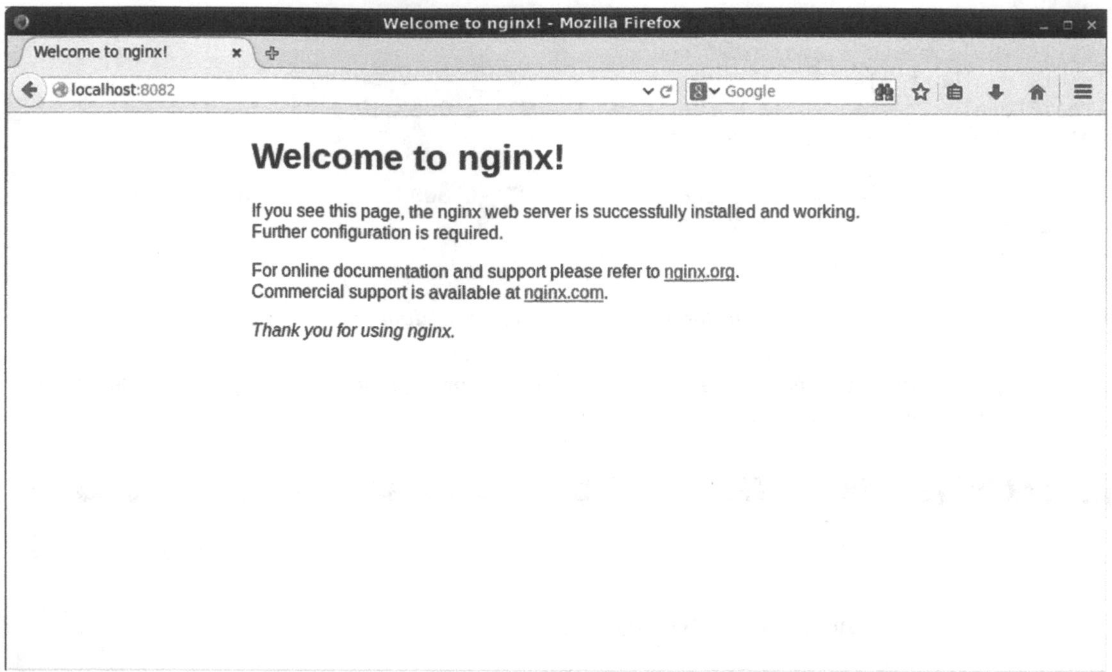

Figure 14-41. *Invoking another Service Endpoint in a Browser*

Similarly, the url `http://localhost:8083` invokes the third service endpoint as shown in Figure 14-42.

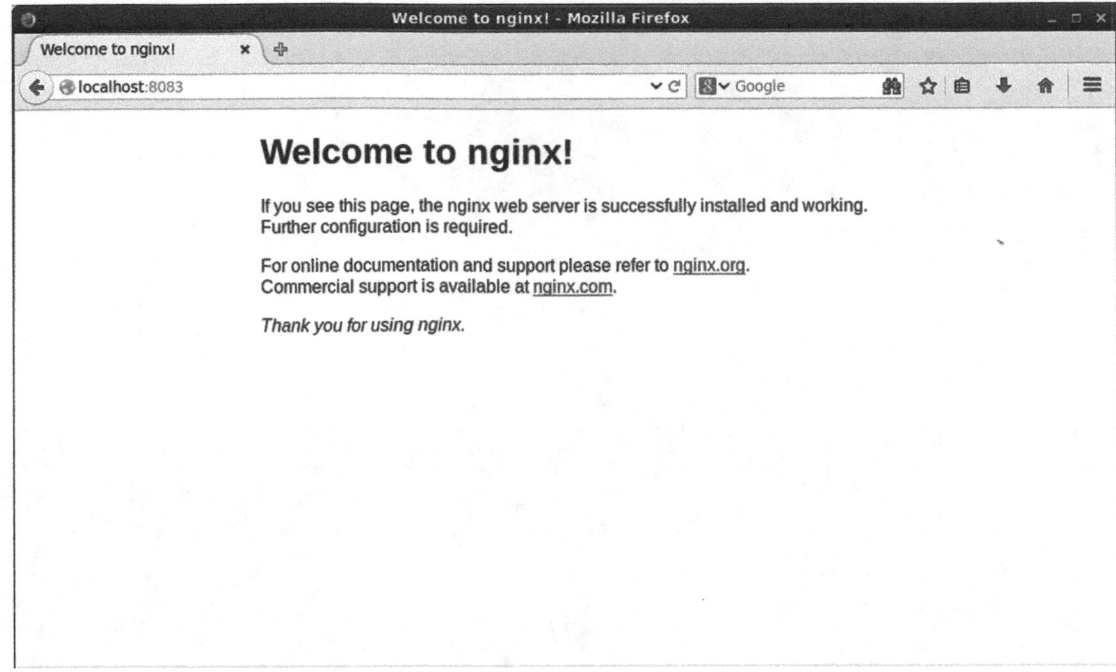

Figure 14-42. *Invoking a Third Service Endpoint in a Browser*

Summary

In this chapter we installed Kubernetes on a multi-node cluster. The multi-node configuration makes use of flannel for networking instead of the default networking provided by Docker. First, we installed Kubernetes on the master node. Using the Master's Ip Address we installed Kubernetes on a worker node, as a result creating a two-node cluster. As many worker nodes as required may be added using the same procedure. We created an application using the nginx Docker image and invoked the application on the command line using curl, and in a local browser using port forwarding. We also scaled the application. In a single-node cluster an application runs on the master node itself. In a multi-node cluster an application runs on both the worker nodes and the master node. This chapter concludes the book on Kubernetes Microservices with Docker.

Index

A, B

D. Vohra, *Kubernetes Microservices with Docker*, DOI 10.1007/978-1-4842-1907-2

C, D

E, F, G, H, I, J

K, L

M, N

O

P, Q, R

S, T, U

V

W, X, Y

Z

Apress®
THE EXPERT'S VOICE™

Printed in the United States
By Bookmasters

Printed in the United States
By Bookmasters